HIDDEN
Southwest

HIDDEN
Southwest

THIRD EDITION

Ulysses Press
BERKELEY, CALIFORNIA

Published by:
ULYSSES PRESS
3286 Adeline Street, Suite 1
Berkeley, CA 94703

Library of Congress Catalog Card Number 96-60079
ISBN 1-56975-052-1

Printed in the United States of America
by R.R. Donnelley & Sons

10 9 8 7 6 5 4

AUTHORS: Richard Harris, Laura Daily, Madeleine
Osberger, Carolyn Scarborough, Mary Ann Reese,
Ron Butler and Steve Cohen
EDITORIAL DIRECTOR: Leslie Henriques
MANAGING EDITOR: Claire Chun
PROJECT DIRECTOR: Jennifer Wilkoff
COPY EDITOR: David Sweet
EDITORIAL ASSOCIATES: Lee Micheaux, Deema Khorsheed,
Joy Clark, Toby Bielawski, Mark Rosen, Jennifer Knight
COVER DESIGN: Sarah Levin
INDEXER: Sayre Van Young
COVER PHOTOGRAPHY: Kerrick James (front cover and back
middle cover), Jan Butchofsky (front cover circle
and back cover bottom)
ILLUSTRATOR: Glenn Kim

Distributed in the United States by Publishers
Group West, in Canada by Raincoast Books,
and in Great Britain and Europe by World
Leisure Marketing

What's Hidden?

At different points throughout this book, you'll find special listings marked with a hidden symbol:

◀ *HIDDEN*

This means that you have come upon a place off-the-beaten tourist-track, a spot that will carry you a step closer to the local people and natural environment of the Southwest.

The goal of this guide is to lead you beyond the realm of everyday tourist facilities. While we include traditional sightseeing listings and popular attractions, we also offer alternative sights and adventure activities. Instead of filling this guide with reviews of standard hotels and chain restaurants, we concentrate on one-of-a-kind places and locally owned establishments.

Our authors seek out locales that are popular with residents but usually overlooked by visitors. Some are more hidden than others (and are marked accordingly), but all the listings in this book are intended to help you discover the true nature of the Southwest and put you on the path of adventure.

Write to us!

If in your travels you discover a spot that captures the spirit of the Southwest, or if you live in the region and have a favorite place to share, or if you just feel like expressing your views, write to us and we'll pass your note along to the author.

We can't guarantee that the author will add your personal find to the next edition, but if the writer does use the suggestion, we'll acknowledge you in the credits and send you a free autographed copy of the new edition.

ULYSSES PRESS
3286 Adeline Street, Suite 1
Berkeley, CA 94703
E-mail: ulypress@aol.com

Contents

Maps

Special Features

OUTDOOR ADVENTURE SYMBOLS

The following symbols accompany national, state and regional park listings, as well as beach descriptions throughout the text.

Camping

Hiking

Biking

Horseback Riding

Downhill Skiing

Cross-country Skiing

Swimming

Snorkeling or Scuba Diving

Surfing

Waterskiing

Windsurfing

Canoeing or Kayaking

Boating

Boat Ramps

Fishing

ONE

The Southwest

The Southwest is a land unlike any other. It is sheer sandstone cliffs and slickrock mesas, secluded beaches on bright blue lakes, vast deserts alive with giant cacti and unusual animals, high mountain peaks that guard some of the largest wilderness areas in America. Strange landscapes conceal Indian ruins as old and haunting as Europe's medieval castles. And unlike in other parts of the United States, the people who lived in the Southwest when the first white men arrived still live here today. Although it was the first part of the United States where European colonists settled permanently, today it remains, on the whole, one of the least-populated parts of the country.

The Southwest attracts vacationers from around the world at all times of year. It is warm in the winter (some places), cool in the summer (other places) and sunnier than Florida. People come for the climate, the great outdoors, the unique cultural mix and the scenic beauty. Most of all, people come to explore, for the best places in the Southwest are not necessarily marked by big green-and-white signs or entrance gates. In this land of astonishing diversity, you'll find something new around every curve in the road.

Land of contrasts, proudly provincial, the Southwest lives up to its romantic reputation. Lost cities and hidden treasures await your discovery. If curiosity is in your nature, the Southwest is one of the best places on earth to unleash it.

Hidden Southwest is designed to help you explore Arizona, New Mexico, southern Utah and southwestern Colorado. It covers popular, "must-see" places, offering advice on how best to enjoy them. It also tells you about many off-the-beaten-path spots, the kind you would find by talking with folks at the local café or with someone who has lived in the area all his or her life. It describes the region's history, its natural areas and its residents, both human and animal. It suggests places to eat, to lodge, to play, to camp. Taking into account varying interests, budgets and tastes, it provides the information you need whether your vacation style involves backpacking, golf, museum browsing, shopping or all of the above.

This book covers the Southwest in three sections. Arizona, the most recently settled and fastest-growing part, claims among its virtues warm winter weather, famous sunsets and the largest Indian reservation in the country. New Mexico offers antiquity and a unique tricultural heritage that set it apart from anyplace else in America. The land north of the Grand Canyon and Navajo Indian Reservation extending into Utah and Colorado, still largely unpopulated, is best known for its wild canyons and rugged mountains, portions of which are made accessible to the public in no less than six national parks.

The traveling part of the book begins in Chapter Two on the rim of the Grand Canyon. Chapter Three wanders through Indian Country in northeastern Arizona to help you experience the world of the Navajo and Hopi people. Sedona, Jerome, Flagstaff and Prescott are all covered in Chapter Four. Chapter Five travels down the state's western edge from Kingman to Lake Havasu City and the London Bridge. The greater Phoenix area, including nearby Scottsdale, Tempe and Mesa, is revealed in Chapter Six. Chapter Seven ventures east into the mountains and scenic areas from Globe to Pinetop–Lakeside and the Coronado Trail. Chapter Eight moves farther south to Tucson, Tombstone and the Mexican border.

Chapter Nine covers Santa Fe, as well as the Las Vegas and the Los Alamos areas. Chapter Ten focuses on the treasures of Taos and the Enchanted Circle. Chapter Twelve takes a good look at Albuquerque, from the top of a mountain as well as from the city's historic center, then investigates an array of central New Mexico side trips to lakes and volcanic badlands, ruins of abandoned pueblos and Spanish missions. Chapter Thirteen ranges across southern New Mexico from Carlsbad Caverns through Billy the Kid country to the remote canyons of the Gila Wilderness.

The terrain and culture of the Southwest do not stop at the arbitrarily squared-off state lines of Arizona and New Mexico but sprawl untidily over the Four Corners area into neighboring parts of Utah and Colorado. Chapter Fourteen takes you through the geological wonderland of southwestern Utah, including Bryce Canyon, Zion and Capitol Reef national parks. Chapter Fifteen continues into southeastern Utah with visits to Arches and Canyonlands national parks and all the information you need to rent a boat and cruise Lake Powell. Finally, Chapter Sixteen is your guide to the southwestern corner of Colorado, where the top attractions are Mesa Verde National Park and the Durango–Silverton Narrow Gauge Railroad.

What you choose to see and do is up to you. The old cliché that "there is something for everyone" pretty well rings true in the Southwest. In this book, you'll find free campgrounds with hiking trails and fantastic views as well as several playgrounds for the wealthy and well-known. And you can take some of the most spectacular scenic drives anywhere as well as hikes into wild areas that can't be reached by car. Or check into a bed and breakfast that has delightful little galleries and boutiques within walking distance.

There's so much to experience in the Southwest that even most lifelong residents can count on making new discoveries once in a while. First-time vacation visitors are hard pressed just to make brief stops at the region's best-known highlights, while seasoned travelers often prefer to explore a more limited area in depth and then return on later trips to different spots, perhaps in different seasons. Either way, people generally come back, and often to stay. For the Southwest has so many unique ways—food, landscapes, customs, climate, art, architecture, languages—to create lingering memories.

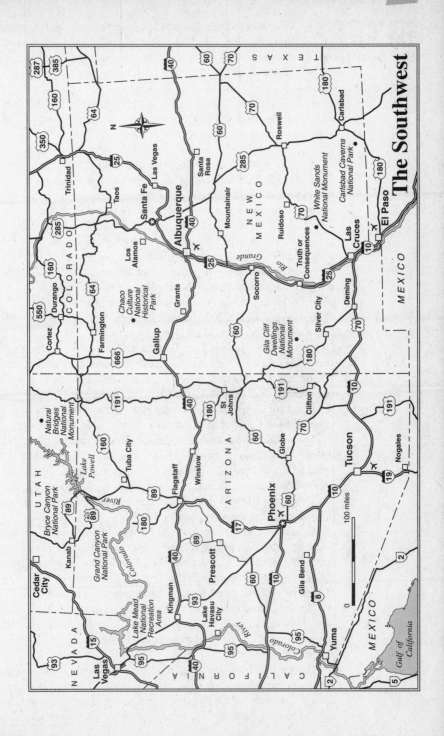

The Southwest

▼▼▼▼▼▼▼▼▼▼
**The Story of
the Southwest**

GEOLOGY

The walls of the Grand Canyon reveal one billion years in stone. Over countless centuries, geological shifting raised the plateau up to slowly higher elevations as the Colorado River sliced it in half. The dark rocks at river level, which contain no fossils, are some of the oldest matter on the face of the earth. The different layers of color and texture in the layered cliffs attest to times when the area was sea floor, forest and swamp. Tiny fossilized sea creatures from the Paleozoic era, long before dinosaurs, trace the development of some of the first life on the planet up through strata of shale, limestone and sandstone.

The geological features of the Southwest are so varied and spectacular that it is certainly possible to appreciate the landscapes for their beauty without knowing how they formed. But travelers who take a little time to learn about the region's geology in natural history museums or park visitors centers along the way develop a different perspective. They come to see how the many different colors and kinds of surface rock connect in a wonderfully complex formation hundreds of miles across. They learn to explore the panorama in three dimensions, not just two.

For example, Kaibab limestone, the 250,000,000-year-old, 300-foot-thick, grayish-white layer along the top rim of the Grand Canyon, is also visible at Lee's Ferry, a half-day's drive to the east, and at Capitol Reef National Park, a similar distance to the north. The orange Wingate sandstone layer is seen in Capitol Reef as well as in Arches National Park, the Island in the Sky and Newspaper Rock units of Canyonlands National Park, and at Dead Horse Point State Park—all part of the same rock.

The delight of Southwestern geology lies not only in its grand overviews but also in its myriad unique details. Dinosaur tracks. Petrified wood. Pure white gypsum sand dunes. Huge underground caverns. Salt domes, arches, natural bridges, hoodoos and goblins fancifully shaped by water and weather. Huge volcanic boulders pushed great distances by glaciers.

Volcanoes created some of the most dramatic scenery in the Southwest. In some places, like New Mexico's Valley of Fires Recreation Area and El Malpais National Monument, lava has paved the desert floor for many miles into tortured, twisted, surfaces that cannot be crossed, laced with ice caves where water stays frozen even on the hottest summer days. Elsewhere, as in the volcano fields northeast of Flagstaff, Arizona, fields of pumice gravel prevent vegetation from growing but make hiking easy at the foot of picture-perfect volcanic cones.

The Jemez Mountains in northern New Mexico formed from the crumbled remnant of what many scientists believe may have been the world's tallest volcano nearly two million years ago. In the canyons of Bandelier National Monument on the slope of the

Jemez stand tent rocks, strange spires left behind when steam vents hardened volcanic ash in the distant past. Farther north, near Taos, the massive lava flow from the Jemez volcano forms the walls of deep gorges along the Rio Grande. There are no active volcanoes in the Southwest today, but that could change at any time. Volcanoes have been erupting in the Southwest for millions of years, and the most recent ones exploded less than a thousand years ago. As geologists reckon time, a thousand years is just yesterday.

NATIVE PEOPLE Spear points found near Clovis, New Mexico, prove that human beings lived in the Southwest at least 10,000 years ago. The Clovis points are some of the oldest Indian artifacts found anywhere, dating back to the last Ice Age. At that time, the region that is now the American Southwest was rich, green countryside where mastodons and giant bison grazed just beyond the reach of glaciers. The hunting and gathering tribes who followed the animals' tracks may have been some of the first people to walk on North American soil. They stayed. Across millenniums, their descendants walked softly through the Southwest leaving few traces—only small bone and obsidian tools and mysterious paintings of magical beings on the red walls of canyons in southern Utah.

HISTORY

Less than 2000 years ago, the people of the Southwest learned how to grow corn, beans and watermelons. This new technology allowed them to establish permanent homes. By about 1000 A.D., individual pit houses gave way to cliff dwellings like the ones at Mesa Verde in Colorado and large multifamily stone pueblos like the ones at Chaco Canyon in New Mexico. Besides agriculture and architecture, Pueblo people of the Anasazi, Mimbres and Sinagua civilizations were known for pottery making, cotton weaving and sophisticated astronomical observations and spiritual practices.

One thousand years ago, American Indians of the Southwest had extensive trade contacts, including the Toltecs of central Mexico.

The saga of the pre-Columbian Southwest is one of migration and change. The great Anasazi pueblos of the Four Corners region, then the largest cities in what is now the United States, were occupied for a century or two and suddenly abandoned. Archaeologists disagree about the reasons. The Mesa Verde people may have moved to Acoma, the Mimbres of the Gila canyons to Zuni Pueblo or perhaps Casas Grandes in Old Mexico, the Chacoans to sites along the Rio Grande such as the pueblos at Bandelier National Monument. The Hopi people stayed on their remote desert mesa tops, where some structures standing today have been used by the same families for 900 years.

During the century just before Columbus's ships reached American shores, a new group of people arrived in the Southwest. They were Athabascans, nomads from the far north who had gradually wandered down the front range of the Rocky Mountains in small groups. They would become the Apache and Navajo nations—but only after another kind of stranger had come to change the character of the Southwest forever.

SPANISH CONQUEST   In the year 1540, a Spanish expedition under the command of *conquistador* Francisco Vasquez de Coronado set out from Mexico City and headed north across the parched, forbidding Chihuahuan Desert in search of the fabled Seven Cities of Cibola. Instead of the gold-paved cities of legend, he found pueblos such as Zuni, occupied by subsistence farmers who drew magical lines of cornmeal in unsuccessful attempts to fend off the Spaniards with their armor, horses and steel swords. Coronado and his followers were the first Europeans to visit the Hopi Mesas, the Rio Grande pueblos or the Grand Canyon. For two years they explored the Southwest, but finding no gold they returned to Mexico City with disappointing reports. After that, exploration of the territory Coronado had visited, which came to be called Nuevo Mexico, was left to Franciscan missionaries for the rest of the 16th century.

In 1598, a wealthy mine owner from Zacatecas, Mexico, named Don Juan de Oñate mounted an expedition at his own expense to colonize Nuevo Mexico under a grant from the Spanish government. The group consisted of 400 soldiers and settlers, 83 wagons and 7000 head of livestock. Oñate founded the first permanent Spanish settlement near modern-day Española, New Mexico, but the cost of his expeditions bankrupted him and he resigned his position as governor. The new governor, Don Pedro de Peralta, moved the capital to Santa Fe in 1610.

The Spanish colonists grew in number and established villages, farms and ranches up and down the Rio Grande over several generations, but slavery practices and erratic religious policies toward

BIRTH OF THE NAVAJO NATION

The Pueblo Revolt created the Navajo nation. To persuade their Athabascan neighbors to help chase away the Spanish, Pueblo leaders agreed that the Athabascans could keep the livestock driven off from ranches they attacked. In that way, the tribe came to own sheep and horses, which would profoundly change their culture. When the Spanish colonists returned, many Pueblo people who had participated in the revolt fled to avoid retaliation and went to live with the nomads, bringing with them such advanced technologies as weaving cloth and growing corn. The Athabascan descendants who herded sheep and farmed became known as the Navajo people, while those who held to the old way of life came to be called Apache.

the Indians inspired the Pueblo Revolt of 1680. The people of the Rio Grande pueblos, aided by fierce Athabascan nomads, attacked the Spanish towns and ranches, killing hundreds of settlers and driving the survivors downriver all the way to the site of present-day El Paso, Texas, where they camped for 11 years before soldiers arrived from Mexico City to help them regain Nuevo Mexico.

After the Pueblo Revolt, Nuevo Mexico endured as an outpost of the Spanish empire for another 130 years. During all of that time, the conquerors and colonists were never able to settle the surrounding areas of the Southwest or even establish roads between Nuevo Mexico and other Spanish colonies in California and central Texas. The lands to the north and east were controlled by warrior horsemen of the Comanche tribe, whose raids forced abandonment of Spanish missions such as those at Pecos and Gran Quivira. To the south and west, the Apache and Navajo people used fear to keep Europeans out of the land that is now Arizona.

Nor did the Spanish settlers have any contact with English-speaking American colonists. Near the end of the colonial era, explorers from the United States, such as early U.S. Army explorer Captain Zebulon Pike, who accidentally strayed into Nuevo Mexico were arrested.

TERRITORIAL PERIOD   Beginning in 1821, distant events changed the lives of the Spanish inhabitants of the Southwest. Mexico won its independence from Spain, and government policies changed. The border was opened, and trade was established along the Santa Fe Trail, which linked Nuevo Mexico to United States territory. At the same time, all Franciscan monks were exiled from Mexican territory, leaving Nuevo Mexico without spiritual leadership. They were replaced by a lay brotherhood of *penitentes* whose spiritual guidance did much to create a uniquely New Mexican culture and tradition that survives to this day in remote mountain villages around Santa Fe and Taos.

When the Texas republic won its independence from Mexico in 1836, many Texans contended that Nuevo Mexico should be part of their new nation—a sentiment that the people of Nuevo Mexico did not share. Texas troops occupied Nuevo Mexico in 1841, but their authority was not acknowledged. Five years later, when Texas had joined the United States and the Mexican War was underway, federal soldiers took possession of New Mexico. When the war ended in 1848, the peace treaty with Mexico ceded the territories of California and Nuevo Mexico (which included the modern-day states of New Mexico and Arizona) to the United States. To confuse the local people further, 13 years after they had become Americans, the Civil War broke out and Confederate troops from Texas fought numerous battles in New Mexico, briefly capturing Albuquerque, Santa Fe and Mesilla. Before the war ended, New Mexico and its people had been part of five different nations in about 40 years.

The first English-speaking settlers in the Southwest were Mormons, who chose to live free from persecution in the empty desert. Beginning in the 1840s, they established settlements throughout southern Utah and northern Arizona, often in places that are still remote today.

The United States government in the late 19th century was far less tolerant of Indians than the Spanish and Mexicans rulers had been. After the Civil War, the Army set out to make the lands ruled by the Comanches, Apaches, Navajos and Utes safe for homesteaders. The Comanches were annihilated. The Utes, who had roamed from the eastern slope of the Colorado Rockies to the canyonlands of southern Utah, were confined to a narrow reservation south of present-day Durango, Colorado. Kit Carson rounded up the entire Navajo tribe and marched them from their homeland to a reservation in eastern New Mexico, but after explorations revealed nothing of value on the Navajo land, and after thousands of Navajo people had died, he marched the survivors back home to the land where they live today. The longest and most violent army campaign against the Indians was the Apache Wars. Though never numerous, the Apaches were so fierce and elusive that the wars lasted for 19 bloody years, ending in 1884 with the surrender of the rebel leader Geronimo. Only then could settlers from the United States establish the first towns in Arizona.

Law enforcement was unreliable in the territorial era, giving rise to timeless legends of the Wild West. In New Mexico, Billy the Kid and his gang fought against an army of gunmen hired by a ruthless cattle baron in the Lincoln County War. In Utah, Butch Cassidy robbed trains and plundered banks and always eluded capture. In Arizona, Ike Clanton and his boys shot it out with lawman Wyatt Earp and gunman Doc Holliday at Tombstone's O.K. Corral. Out of all the turmoil and gunfire emerged a new multicultural society. In 1910, Arizona and New Mexico became the 47th and 48th states in the union—the last to be admitted until Alaska 50 years later.

MODERN TIMES   The traditional Spanish and Indian cultures of the Southwest remain strong even as waves of visitors and newcomers have swept across the land during the 20th century. Beginning shortly before World War I, artists and writers fleeing Paris's West Bank began to congregate around Taos, New Mexico. Since the 1940s, the Institute of American Indian Arts, the only federal Indian school dedicated to teaching traditional and contemporary art, has established Santa Fe, New Mexico, as the world's leading Indian art market. Exotic locations and reliable sunshine have drawn film production companies to the Southwest ever since 1898 and continue to do so. Today, visual and performing arts form one of the most important industries in many parts of the Southwest.

In World War II, the Southwest became America's center for nuclear research. The nation's best physicists were sent to a top secret base at Los Alamos, New Mexico, deep in a labyrinth of volcanic canyons, to develop the world's first atomic bomb. They tested it in 1945 in the desert near White Sands, New Mexico. After the war ended, nuclear weapons research continued at Los Alamos, as did development of peacetime uses for nuclear energy, bringing a stampede of prospectors and mining companies to the uranium-rich badlands of the Four Corners area. Today, Los Alamos National Laboratory and other federal laboratories in the region also study nuclear fusion, geothermal and solar energy research and genetic studies. The technologies developed at the laboratories have brought private high-tech companies to the major cities of the Southwest. Meanwhile, the nuclear industry has reached the top of the list of environmental controversies that stir heated debate in the region.

Although population growth since World War II has been phenomenal in the Phoenix, Tucson and Albuquerque areas, most of the Southwest remains sparsely inhabited. Water is the limiting factor. Although a series of huge manmade reservoirs—Lake Powell, Lake Mead, Lake Havasu and others—along the Colorado River runs through the heart of the desert Southwest, the water and electricity from them is used far away in southern California, while the land along the banks of the river remains almost entirely undeveloped.

Well over half of the land in the region covered by this book is owned by the public. Large expanses of grasslands and canyonlands are administered by the federal Bureau of Land Management and leased to ranchers for cattle grazing. Other stretches are military reservations. The region includes 15 national forests, 12 national wildlife refuges and 54 national parks, monuments and recreation areas—more than any other part of the United States.

Tourism is key among the forces that have shaped the modern Southwest. With a relatively small population, few manufacturing industries and limited agriculture, the economy relies heavily on travelers, who support hotels, restaurants and other service businesses. In general, Southwesterners display a friendly, positive attitude toward tourists. Beauty is one of the region's most important natural resources, and there is plenty to share. Besides, as locals like to point out, who would want to live in a place strangers didn't want to visit?

FLORA

Drivers crossing the Southwest at high speed on interstate highways can easily form the mistaken impression that this region is mostly open ranchland so arid that it takes 50 acres to graze a single cow. This is because main highways follow the flattest, most featureless routes. All one has to do is take a detour into the mountains and canyons where the main highways don't go in order to discover that the dry climate and extreme elevation changes create a surprising variety of ecosystems, each with its own unique beauty.

At low altitudes where winter temperatures rarely dip to freezing, cacti and other succulents thrive. Ocatillo, century plants, yuccas and prickly pear, barrel and cholla cacti, as well as mesquite and creosote bushes, are found throughout both the Chihuahuan Desert of southern New Mexico and the Sonoran Desert of southern Arizona. The Sonoran Desert is best known for its magnificent forests of giant saguaro and organ pipe cacti. When spring rains come, which may be once in five years or more, the deserts burst forth for a few weeks in a fantastic display of wildflowers.

Miniature evergreen forests of piñon, juniper and cedar cover the desert hills at higher elevations where winter temperatures fall below freezing. Cactus and yucca stay small in the high desert.

Mountain forests change with elevation, forming three distinct bands. On the lower slopes of the mountains, ponderosa pine stand 50 feet tall and more. At middle elevations, shimmering stands of aspen trees fill the mountainsides and paint them bright yellow in early October. Douglas fir dominates the higher reaches of the mountains. In some parts of the forest, accessible only by hiking trail and out of reach of timber cutters, fir trees 100 feet tall and bigger around than a man's reach stand spirelike in ancient forests dripping with moss and silence. The San Juan Mountains near Durango, Colorado, contain peaks reaching above timberline, where temperatures always fall below freezing at night and trees will not grow. There is only the alpine tundra, a world of grassy meadows rooted in permafrost where tiny flowers appear for brief moments in midsummer.

Of all the various ecosystems that characterize the Southwest, the real gems are the riparian woodlands. Since almost all of the Southwestern landscape is dry and can only support the hardiest of plants, plant life flourishes around even the least trickle of year-round running water. Creek and river banks support thick forests of cottonwood trees and tamarisks, along with isolated stands of hardwood trees such as maple and hickory.

FAUNA

The last grizzly bear sighted in the Southwest was in the San Juan Mountains near Silverton, Colorado, in the mid-1970s. Packs of Mexican wolves in Albuquerque's Rio Grande Zoo and the Desert Museum in Carlsbad, New Mexico, are the last of their species, preserved from extinction by a federal captive-breeding program.

But other animals of Western legend still roam free in the forests and canyons of the Southwestern back country. Mountain lions, rarely seen because they inhabit remote areas and hunt in the dark, sometimes flash past late-night drivers' headlight beams. Many black bears live deep in the mountains, and in drought summers when food is short they may stray into Albuquerque, Flagstaff or other towns to raid trash cans. Coyotes, the most commonly seen Southwestern predators, abound in all rural areas and frequently surround campgrounds with their high-pitched yipping and howling.

> Once every seven years in the fall, piñon trees produce pine nuts, which many consider a delicacy.

Open rangelands throughout the Southwest support sizable herds of pronghorn antelope alongside grazing cattle. Most visitors to national parks and other protected areas will spot mule deer, and in some parks such as Mesa Verde as well as in the remote canyonlands of southern Utah, wild horses still roam. The elk population in the Southwestern mountains is the largest it has been in this century. Because elk prefer high mountain meadows, only serious hikers are likely to spot one. Herds of mountain sheep live above timberline on the highest mountains of the San Juan and Sangre de Cristo ranges, while their solitary relatives, desert bighorn sheep, live in most desert areas.

One of the most distinctive regional birds is the magpie, an exotic-looking, long-tailed, iridescent, black-and-white cousin of Asian myna birds. Another is the roadrunner, which is often seen hunting lizards alongside the highway. Large birds often seen by motorists or hikers include turkey vultures, ravens and many different kinds of hawks. Both golden and bald eagles live throughout the Southwest and are occasionally spotted soaring in the distance. Eagles and vultures are about the same size, and the easiest way to tell them apart is to remember that eagles glide with their wings horizontal, while vultures' wings sweep upward in a V-shape.

A thought that preoccupies many visitors to the Southwest is of living hazards like rattlesnakes, gila monsters, scorpions and tarantulas. Poisonous animals live in most parts of the region except for the high mountains. Yet even local residents who spend most weekends hiking say that they rarely encounter one. When outdoors in desert country, walk loudly and never put your hand or foot where you can't see it.

Where to Go

The Southwest is no more one entity than is Europe. Don't try to "see it all" in a single trip or you may find yourself focused so much on covering large distances that you sacrifice quiet opportunities to appreciate the natural beauty you came to see. Deciding what to see and where to go is a tough choice. The good news is, you'll just have to keep coming back and exploring at different times of year to get to know the "real" Southwest.

To help you with your decisions, we'll entice you with a brief description of each area covered in this book. To get the whole story, read the introduction to each chapter, then the more detailed material on the regions that appeal to you.

The **Grand Canyon**, the largest single geological feature in the Southwest, splits northwestern Arizona between north and south. The "village" on the South Rim of the Grand Canyon, just an hour's drive from interstate Route 40, is developed on a grand scale, complete with an airport. Hikers discover that only a tiny part of either rim of the Grand Canyon is accessible by vehicle, and that a moderate walk can provide total solitude. The North Rim, farther by road from major cities and main routes, is more relaxed and secluded, though still busy enough to make advance lodging or camping reservations essential. Closed during the winter, the North Rim combines perfectly with visits to Lake Powell and the national parks of southwestern Utah, as well as Las Vegas, Nevada.

Northeastern Arizona, also known as Indian Country, includes the vast, sprawling Navajo Indian Reservation, larger than some East Coast states, as well as the remote, ancient mesatop pueblos of the Hopi Indian Reservation, fiercely traditional and indepen-dent although completely surrounded by Navajo land. The center of the Navajo world according to legend, Canyon de Chelly is still inhabited by people who herd sheep and live without electricity. Visitors can view their hogans and pastures from high above on the canyon rim but can only enter the labyrinth accompanied by a Navajo guide. Another national park service unit operated by the tribe, Navajo National Monument protects some of the best Anasazi ruins in the area. The monument's biggest Indian ruin is only accessible on horseback. The third major park on the reser-vation is Monument Valley Tribal Park, a landscape so familiar from the many films, television shows and advertisements filmed here that visitors may feel like they're driving through a movie as they travel the backcountry road around the valley and visit the hogans of the people who live in this, one of the most remote places in the United States. A tour of Hubbell Trading Post National Historic Site and perhaps a stop at a still-operating trading post will round out your Indian Country experience.

Route 40 through **North Central Arizona** will bring you to Flagstaff, a winter ski resort and college town, sitting on the edge of the dramatic San Francisco Peaks at 7000 feet and blanketed with ponderosa pine trees. Drive south through spectacular Oak Creek Canyon to Sedona, an upscale artist community with a New Age bent and an abundance of shopping. This is also the heart of scenic Red Rock Country, where red sandstone has eroded into dramatic formations of incomparable beauty. Jerome, scenically perched in the Mingus Mountains, is a former mining town that's now home to a small community of artists. Just down the road is Prescott, the original territorial capital of Arizona, which draws visitors with its numerous museums and low-key charm.

Never mind that **Western Arizona** is surrounded by parched desert. The 340-mile-long stretch of the Colorado River that establishes the state's "west coast" border has created an aquatic playground spilling over with unparalleled scenic and recreational opportunities. Kingman is the northern gateway to a succession of lakes, resorts and riverfront coves, as well as to the historic gold and silver mining ghost towns of Oatman and Chloride. The Lake Mead National Recreation Area extends to include Lake Mohave, where you'll find Bullhead City, Arizona's fastest growing city. Farther south is Lake Havasu City, home to the authentic London Bridge, which was brought over from England and reassembled here. Continue down Route 95 and you'll come to Quartzsite, which attracts more than half a million visitors every January and February for its annual rock and mineral extravaganzas.

Phoenix, the state capital and the largest city in the Southwest, is the focus of **South Central Arizona**. At first, this rectilinear sprawl of suburbs and shopping malls, giant retirement communities, towering office buildings, industrial parks and farmlands full of year-round citrus and cotton crops may seem to offer few charms for the vacationer. But those who take time to explore Phoenix and beyond will soon discover that this city where it is often better to spend daytime hours indoors has more than its share of fine museums. Winter is the time for outdoor adventuring in the Phoenix area, and hiking, horseback riding, boating and fishing opportunities abound. Nearby Scottsdale blends the architecture of the Old West with exclusive shops, galleries, restaurants and night clubs, while other towns within easy day-trip distance

RIDERS OF THE PURPLE SAGE

The allure of Arizona has not gone unnoticed by the publishing and film industry. Zane Grey based many of his western novels on north central Arizona, and his books include *Riders of the Purple Sage* and *West of the Pecos*. Tony Hillerman's contemporary murder mysteries are often set in the Navajo Indian Reservation and Four Corners area and include *Thief of Time*, *The Blessing Way* and *Listening Woman*. *Laughing Boy* by Oliver LaFarge is a Pulitzer Prize–winning novel that describes Navajo life. There have also been many movies filmed in Arizona at Old Tucson Studios, including John Wayne's *Rio Lobo*, *Rio Bravo* and *El Dorado*; Paul Newman's *The Life and Times of Judge Roy Bean*; Clint Eastwood's *The Outlaw Josey Wales*; and *Gunfight at the O.K. Corral* with Kirk Douglas.

of Phoenix, such as Wickenburg, recall grittier and more authentic memories of the rough-and-rowdy mining boomtown era of turn-of-the-century Arizona.

Towering mountain peaks, sparkling streams and lakes, and dense pine forests surprise many travelers to the high country of **Eastern Arizona**. This forest primeval encompasses the mountain hamlets of Show Low, Pinetop and Lakeside, summer resorts famous for their hiking and fishing, and popular with those trying to escape the scorching temperatures on the desert floor. During winter, skiers flock to the downhill runs and cross-country trails at nearby Sunrise ski resort on the White Mountain Apache Indian Reservation. The forests deepen as you travel east to Alpine, a mountain village just a few miles from the New Mexico border. At the heart of the "Arizona Alps," Alpine is a mecca for nature buffs, who love the profusion of outdoor activities—hiking, camping, hunting and fishing. Alpine is also a northern guidepost along the Coronado Trail, which snakes south through some of the most spectacular scenery in the Southwest to the historic mining town of Clifton. Built along the banks of the San Francisco River, Clifton and its historic Chase Creek Street give a glimpse of what Arizona was like at the turn of the century. Traveling south from Clifton, juniper foothills give way to rolling grasslands and the fertile Gila River Valley, where cotton is king and the town of Safford marks Arizona's eastern anchor of the Old West Highway. This strip of Arizona, stretching 203 miles from Apache Junction to the New Mexico state line, is rich in the frontier history of the Old West. Tracing a course first charted by Coronado, Geronimo, the Dutchman, Billy the Kid, Johnny Ringo and pioneers looking for a place to call their own, you'll pass through cactus-studded valleys, pine-topped mountains, rugged and craggy canyons, lost treasure and historic copper mines. Along the way you can sample the area's history in Globe's plantation-style mansions and antique shops and its pre-history at the Besh-Ba-Gowah archaeological site.

Southern Arizona in the springtime, when the desert flowers bloom, is as close as most of us will find to paradise on earth. The secret is well-kept because during the summer tourist season, when most visitors come to the Southwest, Tucson is considerably hotter than paradise—or just about anyplace else. Those who visit at any time other than summer will discover the pleasure of wandering through the forests of giant saguaro cactus that cover the foothills at the edge of town, perhaps learning more at the wonderful Arizona-Sonora Desert Museum and seeing the 18th-century Spanish Mission San Xavier del Bac. For more desert beauty, drive west through the cactus forest of the Tohono O'Odham (Papago) Indian Reservation to Organ Pipe Cactus National Monument on

The cholla cactus prefers to grow in areas that were once stripped of vegetation, such as old Indian ruins.

the Mexican border. Many people consider the monument to be the most beautiful part of the Southwestern desert. Another great side trip from the Tucson area is Cochise County to the east. National monuments in the rugged, empty mountains preserve the strongholds of Apache warlords and the cavalrymen who fought to subdue them. Old Bisbee, until recently the headquarters for one of the nation's largest open-pit copper mining operations, has been reincarnated as a picturesque, far-from-everything tourist town. Tombstone, meanwhile, milks the tourist appeal of a famous gunfight that occurred more than a century ago to sustain one of the most authentically preserved historic towns of the Old West.

Visitors to the **Santa Fe Area** find themselves in a magical place where art openings and operas complement rodeos, horse races and wilderness adventures. The sky-high state capital, situated at 7000 feet elevation and backdropped by the spectacular Sangre de Cristo Mountains, is also the oldest colonial city in the United States. Strict guidelines mandate the now well-known Santa Fe–style look of territorial and Spanish Colonial architecture. Thanks to city codes, no high-rises block the mountain views or the ever-changing colors at dawn and dusk.

Northwest of Santa Fe is the city of Los Alamos, birthplace to the atomic bomb. Modern in its technology and scientific findings, Los Alamos' laboratories coexist within a stone's throw of ancient ruins and Indian pueblos—in other words, caveman meets the Jetsons. Those who head southeast of Santa Fe will come across the country's original Las Vegas, a charismatic town that may look familiar at first—and second—glance. That's probably because Las Vegas, New Mexico, has been featured in countless silent movies. Perhaps what's most intriguing about the region, however, is the unique population mix, which includes the world's foremost nuclear scientists and major communities of visual artists, performers and writers, plus a colorful and varied cultural melting pot of Anglo, American Indian and Spanish peoples.

Driving north from New Mexico's capital city, you'll pass vast forests and mountain villages centuries old on your way to **Taos and the Enchanted Circle Area**. Taos is a legendary artists' community, a step down in the frenetic category from the hustle-bustle of Santa Fe. It is a casually sophisticated town where galleries and working artists flourish. Surrounding the city are the raging Rio Grande, the Sangre de Cristo Mountains and the Carson National Forest, making recreational pursuits easily accessible for the many sports-minded people who are drawn to Taos' world-class ski slopes. Also in the area is the nation's largest scouting camp and dormant Capulin Volcano.

Northwestern New Mexico is also known for its rich tapestry of experiences. The areas around Grants and Gallup are close enough that they could be glimpsed as day trips out of Albuquerque, but you might consider them as a vacation destination on their own. Here visitors can explore the Indian pueblos of Acoma and Zuni, where American Indians have lived continuously since long before Christopher Columbus sighted land. Grants is situated at the center of an intriguing array of places—the most ancient continuously inhabited pueblos in New Mexico, a vast and forbidding lava bed with ice caves, a landmark where centuries of explorers left their marks and solitary, massive Mt. Taylor, a sacred mountain in Navajo tradition. Gallup, which bills itself as the "Gateway to Indian Country," presents a cultural contrast as striking as any to be found along the Mexican border, as the interstate brings the outside world to the doorstep of the largest Indian nation in the country. Pawn shops, bars and a row of neon motels lend a hard edge to the local ambience, but the annual Inter-Tribal Ceremonial and large concentration of American Indians make it a prime place to view native crafts. In the Four Corners area, you can step out of New Mexico into one of three other states or use every limb to simultaneously be in each of the four—New Mexico, Arizona, Colorado and Utah. It's the only spot in the United States where four states come together. Three rivers also meet at this unique junction, feeding a carpet of desert flora in an area that is often perceived as arid.

Billy the Kid once roamed the area that now encompasses **Albuquerque and Central New Mexico.** Now you can, too. The vast ranchland plains east of the Rocky Mountains haven't changed much since the Kid rode into legend more than a century ago. But Albuquerque is another story. Just another small town on the banks of the Rio Grande downriver from Santa Fe in the heyday of the Wild West, it has been transformed into a bustling metropolis boasting a unique mosaic of lifestyles and cultures. Places, such as the Indian Pueblo Cultural Center, showcase the city's multicultural heritage. But perhaps the best way to gain an understanding of Albuquerque is to walk around the Old Town Plaza, a historic district that preserves the architectural grace of Albuquerque's

WEATHER FOR THE HOT AND COLD BLOODED

In the Southwest, where the high, rugged Rocky Mountains collide with the subtropical Chihuahuan and Sonoran deserts, small changes in elevation can mean big variations in climate. As a rule, climbing 1000 feet in elevation alters the temperature as much as going 300 miles north. For instance, the bottom of the Grand Canyon is always about 20 degrees warmer than the top rim. In Tucson during the winter, some people bask by swimming pools while others ski on the slopes of nearby Mount Lemmon.

Spanish Colonial era. Sandia Crest, the massive mountain that flanks the city's Northeast Heights, offers skiing, wilderness hiking, a thrilling tramway ride and cool forests. With a gnarled old forest of cottonwoods along its banks, the Rio Grande has great secluded trails for urban hiking, jogging, bicycling and horseback riding. Traveling east from Albuquerque takes you into the high plains, where the major tourist spots are all lakes. Driving south takes you to Bosque del Apache, where huge flocks of cranes spend the winter months, or to Salinas Missions, a group of national monument units preserving the ruins of Indian pueblos and old Spanish missions. This is the Central New Mexico that beckons the traveler: a mixture of the wild and sublime, the small town and the big city, the past and the present.

Travelers who continue into **Southern New Mexico** face a choice among three different areas, each with its own character. In the east, the premier attraction is Carlsbad Caverns National Park, which draws millions of visitors annually to this remote corner of the state. A visit to Carlsbad Caverns combines easily with a side trip to Ruidoso, a bustling mountain resort town that caters primarily to Texans with its Indian-owned ski slopes and some of the richest horse racing in the country. Nearby, the historic town of Lincoln still remembers the days of Billy the Kid, when it was one of the most lawless places in the Wild West. In south central New Mexico, a series of unique sightseeing highlights—lava fields, Indian petroglyphs, wilderness hiking trails and the vast dunes of White Sands National Monument—invites vacation travelers to leave the interstate and loop through the Tularosa Valley. The dominant feature in the southwestern sector of New Mexico is the Gila Wilderness, the largest roadless area in the 48 contiguous United States. Gila Cliff Dwellings National Monument is the starting point for hikers entering the wilderness, whether for an afternoon or a month. Visitors with plenty of time to explore the area can drive around the wilderness boundary to see the well-preserved ghost town of Mogollon or walk up a sheer-sided canyon on a series of narrow footbridges known as The Catwalk.

Few people actually live in the wild landscape of hoodoos and slickrock canyons that comprise **Southwestern Utah** and **Southeastern Utah**, but millions of visitors come each year to visit the remarkable string of five national parks, each within a few hours' drive of the next. Each of the five is strikingly different from the others. Arches, Bryce Canyon and Zion national parks all present distinctively shaped stone landscapes, erosion as an art form, en route to the North Rim of the Grand Canyon. Canyonlands, the most challenging to explore thoroughly, is reached by any of three dead-end roads into the park that start a hundred miles apart and do not connect. In Capitol Reef, the least known of Utah's national parks, the remains of an old pioneer community provide a hub for a network of dirt roads and trails through side canyons and among strange rock formations. Canyonlands and the Moab area are favored by backpackers, mountain bikers and river rafters. Besides the national parks, another major destination in southern Utah is Lake Powell, the largest reservoir on the Colorado River. Most of its shoreline is far from any road and only accessible by boat. You can rent anything from a speedboat to a houseboat at one of the marinas and cruise for days, exploring side canyons and isolated desert shorelines.

Southwestern Colorado's top visitor attraction is Mesa Verde National Park, the site of the largest, most impressive and mysterious cliff dwellings in North America. While crowd control to protect archaeological sites means that backcountry hiking opportunities are limited at Mesa Verde, the park roads are ideal for bicycles. Those who prefer to visit Indian ruins in solitude can see less-known ruins at Hovenweep National Monument and sites around nearby Dolores, Colorado. Durango, the area's principal town, has a quaint Old West–Victorian ambience in the central historic district, which is the departure point for the Durango & Silverton Narrow Gauge Railroad. The popular passenger train follows an old rail route to an old mining town in the heart of the San Juan Mountains. Drivers, too, can explore the San Juans and find alpine hiking trails, old mining towns and great campgrounds along the San Juan Skyway, one of the most spectacular scenic routes anywhere.

▼▼▼▼▼▼▼▼▼▼
When to Go

SEASONS

Many people imagine the Southwest to be a scorching hot place. Part of it—Tucson, Phoenix, southern and western Arizona—lives up to expectations with daytime high temperatures averaging well above the 100-degree mark through the summer. Even in January, thermometers in this area generally reach the high 60s in the afternoon and rarely fall to freezing at night. The clement winter weather and practically perpetual sunshine have made the Arizona desert a haven for retired persons and migratory human "snowbirds."

Yet less than 200 miles away, the North Rim of the Grand Canyon is closed in the winter because heavy snows make the road impassable. Northern Arizona, northern New Mexico and southern Utah and Colorado experience cold, dry winters with temperatures usually rising above freezing during the day but often dropping close to zero at night. The high mountains remain snowcapped all winter and boast several popular ski areas. At lower elevations, lighter snowfalls and plenty of sunshine keep roads clear most of the time.

Springtime in the Southwest is a mixed blessing. Flooding rivers, chilly winds and sandstorms sometimes await visitors in March and early April, but those who take a chance are more likely to experience mild weather and spectacular displays of desert wildflowers. Leaves do not appear on the trees until late April at moderate elevations, late May in the higher mountains.

Throughout the region, June is the hottest month. Even in cool areas such as northern New Mexico, the thermometer frequently hits the 100-degree mark. In July and August the thunderstorms of what locals refer to as the "monsoon season" usually cool things down quickly on hot afternoons. The majority of the moisture for the entire year falls during these two months, so try to plan outdoor activities in the morning hours. Although New Mexico and Arizona are pretty much safe from natural disasters like earthquakes, tornadoes and hurricanes, meteorologists have discovered from satellite data that the region has more lightning strikes than anywhere else in the United States.

Autumn is the nicest time of year throughout the Southwest. Locals used to keep this fact to themselves, and until recently tourists in October were about as rare as snowflakes in Phoenix. Nowadays the secret is out, and record numbers of people are visiting during the fall "shoulder season" to experience fall colors and bright Indian summer days.

CALENDAR OF EVENTS

Besides all-American-style annual community celebrations with parades, arts-and-crafts shows, concerts—and, in the Southwest, rodeos—the region has other, less familiar kinds of festivals. Most towns that trace their heritage back to Spanish colonialism observe annual fiestas, normally on the feast day of the town's patron saint. Fiestas tend to mix sacred and secular, with solemn religious processions and dancing in the streets. Indian pueblos mark their patron saints' feast days differently, with elaborately costumed ceremonial dances that include a pueblo's entire population, from toddlers to elders. Besides ceremonials, all Indian nations host annual powwows—gatherings of people from many tribes around the country who compete for money in colorful contest dances.

JANUARY

Northeastern Arizona Relive a tradition of the frontier West on the **Hashknife Sheriff Posse's Pony Express Ride** from Holbrook to Scottsdale.

Western Arizona The **Dixieland Jazz Festival**, held in Lake Havasu City, includes a parade, live music aboard a riverboat, dancing and a banjorama.

South Central Arizona Crowds gather in Scottsdale to watch some of the PGA Tour's best golfers at the **Phoenix Open**, one of Arizona's largest spectator events. The **Barrett-Jackson Auction** is a huge classic and collectible car auction in Scottsdale, with some 900 vehicles ranging in price from several thousand to millions of dollars.

Throughout New Mexico New Year's Day is celebrated with dances at Picuris, Santa Clara and Taos pueblos. Dance ceremonies are also held at San Felipe, Santa Ana and Santo Domingo pueblos. Most pueblos also celebrate **Kings Day** in early January.

Santa Fe Area San Ildefonso Pueblo's **Fiesta de San Ildefonso** features all-day animal dances including an awe-inspiring dawn performance.

Albuquerque and Central New Mexico New Year's Day is observed at Cochiti Pueblo with a corn dance.

FEBRUARY

North Central Arizona Gold Rush Days in Wickenburg features a parade, rodeo, arts-and-crafts show, melodrama, gold mucking and drilling competitions and a beard-growing contest.

Western Arizona Quartzsite attracts several hundred thousand rock hounds and gem collectors from around the world for its **Gemborees** held in early February.

South Central Arizona Casa Grande is the site of O'Odham Tash Casa–Grande Indian Days, including Indian rituals, a rodeo and arts and crafts.

Southern Arizona The **Tucson Gem and Mineral Show** draws jewelers and collectors worldwide. The **Tohono O'Odham Nation** at Sells, west of Tucson on the reservation, features outstanding pottery, rug and jewelry exhibits as well as a rodeo.

Throughout New Mexico: **Candeleria** (Candlemas) is observed with ceremonial dances at Santo Domingo and San Felipe pueblos.

Santa Fe Area At the Picuris Pueblo, **Candeleria** is observed with ceremonial dances. Participants "ski" the snow slopes with . . . shovels at the annual **Shovel Races** in Angel Fire.

MARCH

South Central Arizona The **Scottsdale Arts Festival** features dance and music performances and crafts exhibitions.

Eastern Arizona Lost Dutchman Days in Apache Junction near Phoenix is another community celebration full of traditional small-town events—like a Fourth of July in February.

Southern Arizona The high point of **Tombstone Territorial Days** is a reenactment of the events leading up to the gunfight at the O.K. Corral. In Tucson, the **Waik Powwow** is a weekend intertribal event featuring dancing, food, crafts and a fiddlers' contest.

Northwestern New Mexico Laguna Pueblo observes the **St. Joseph Feast Day** with harvest and social dances.

Southern New Mexico Each March 9, Columbus holds a military-style **Columbus Raid Commemoration** to remember the victims of Mexican revolutionist Pancho Villa's 1916 raid.

APRIL

Southern Arizona Tucson is home to the **International Mariachi Conference**, a week-long celebration of mariachi music with concerts, workshops, an art exhibit and a golf tournament.

Taos and the Enchanted Circle Area The Taos Spring Arts Celebration, continuing over several weekends, features artists' studio tours, performing arts and live entertainment.

Northwestern New Mexico Swing your partner at the Square Dance Festival at the Red Rock State Park near Gallup.

Albuquerque and Central New Mexico At the Gathering of Nations Powwow in Albuquerque, more than 5000 costumed dancers from all over the country compete for prize money in one of the biggest Indian events staged anywhere.

Southwestern Utah The St. George Art Festival fills Main Street and the art center with juried art exhibits and continuous musical performances.

North Central Arizona Bill Williams Rendezvous Days, held on Memorial Day weekend in Williams, re-creates the days of the mountain men with barn dances, black-powder shoots and evening "whooplas."

MAY

Southern Arizona Tombstone's Wyatt Earp Days celebration fills the Memorial Day weekend with Old West costumes and staged shootouts in the streets and arts and crafts.

Santa Fe Area The Crafts Fair in Los Alamos displays work by over 100 artisans.

Albuquerque and Central New Mexico The Fiesta de San Felipe is observed at the San Felipe Pueblo with a large, spectacular corn dance involving more than 500 dancers.

Southern New Mexico Mayfair, held on Memorial Day weekend, is the big community festival in Cloudcroft.

North Central Arizona The Festival of Native American Arts opens at the Coconino Center for the Arts with extensive exhibits and craft demonstrations continuing through early August.

JUNE

Santa Fe Area San Juan Pueblo observes the Fiesta de San Juan with buffalo and Comanche dances. The Spring Festival at El Rancho de las Golondrinas near Santa Fe presents Spanish Colonial craft demonstrations and re-creates 17th-century hacienda life.

Albuquerque and Central New Mexico Madrid Summer Festival enlivens the old mining town on the Turquoise Trail with an old-fashioned country fair, live music and art studio tours. Old Fort Days in Fort Sumner feature a rodeo, staged bank robbery, melodrama and barbecue. The New Mexico Arts and Crafts Fair, held at Albuquerque's State Fairgrounds, is the state's largest. The Piñata Festival, Tucumcari's annual celebration, features sporting events, a beauty pageant, parade, rodeo and chili cook-off.

Southwestern Utah The Utah Shakespearean Festival, from mid-July to September in Cedar City, features three plays performed on an outdoor stage along with related seminars and entertainment events.

Southwestern Colorado The Telluride Bluegrass Festival packs this little mountain town to overflowing with musicians and fans.

JULY **North Central Arizona** The Hopi Craftsman Exhibit is presented at the Museum of Northern Arizona in Flagstaff in early July in connection with the Festival of Native American Arts. The Navajo Craftsman Exhibition opens there later in the month.

South Central Arizona The Phoenix Parks Department Summer Show is one of the Southwest's largest arts-and-crafts fairs.

Santa Fe Area The Rodeo de Santa Fe comes to the state capital with a parade and pancake breakfast on the plaza. About a week later, the Santa Fe Opera season opens and the city's lodging accommodations fill to capacity through August. The Eight Northern Pueblos Arts and Crafts Fair, held each year at a different Indian pueblo north of Santa Fe, hosts hundreds of Indian exhibitors. The Jicarilla Apache tribe sponsors the Little Beaver Roundup, a three-day celebration in Dulce with dances, an Indian rodeo and an arts-and-crafts show. In Española, Las Fiestas del Valle de Española, commemorating the founding of the first Spanish settlement in New Mexico, includes a costumed procession and climaxes in a rowdy all-night street dance.

Taos and the Enchanted Circle Area The Taos School of Music Summer Chamber Music Festival combines concerts by top classical musicians with educational seminars. Later in the month, the Taos Fiesta fills the streets with a parade and music.

Southern New Mexico The Ruidoso Arts Festival is a major juried arts-and-crafts fair with continuous live entertainment.

Southwestern Colorado Durango's five-day Durango Fiesta Day offers rodeo events, horse racing and square dancing.

AUGUST **North Central Arizona** Enjoy the evergreens of northern Arizona during the Flagstaff Festival in the Pines, which features more than 250 artisans, live entertainment and children's activities.

South Central Arizona Payson hosts the 112th Annual Oldest Continuous Rodeo, which draws cowboys from all over the Southwest.

Santa Fe Area The Santa Fe Indian Market, the largest American Indian arts show and sale anywhere, draws collectors from around the world. The Santa Clara Pueblo observes Fiesta de Santa Clara with ceremonial dancing.

Albuquerque and Central New Mexico Santo Domingo Pueblo's observance of the Fiesta de Santo Domingo with a huge corn dance in the streets and narrow plazas of this ancient village is one of the most spectacular Indian ceremonials in the Southwest. At the Inter-Tribal Indian Ceremonial held in Red Rock State Park near Gallup, American Indians from more than 50 tribes participate in ritual and contest dances, an arts-and-crafts show, a rodeo and other events. **Old Lincoln Days** features costumed re-enactments of scenes from the Lincoln County War, including one portraying Billy the Kid's last jailbreak. The **Zuni Tribal Fair** includes an arts-and-crafts show, food booths and competition dancing.

Southern New Mexico Deming hosts the **Great Deming Duck Race**, where waterfowl race for money and compete in such events as a Best-Dressed Duck Contest and a Duck Queen pageant.

Southeastern Utah **Navajo Mountain Pioneer Days** in Blanding focuses on the area's American Indian heritage with horse and foot races, Indian food booths and live entertainment.

Southwestern Colorado Telluride hosts its annual two-weekend **Chamber Music Festival** featuring outstanding classical music performers. Later in the month, the **Telluride Jazz Festival** is one of the biggest in the country.

Northeastern Arizona The **Navajo Nation Fair** in Window Rock has carnival rides, a rodeo, horse races, dance competitions, a pretty-baby contest, the Miss Navajo pageant and a wonderful arts-and-crafts pavilion.

SEPTEMBER

South Central Arizona Payson hosts the **Old-Time Fiddlers Contest and Festival** at the rodeo grounds.

Southern Arizona **Rendezvous of Gunfighters**, one of several practically identical town festivals held in Tombstone throughout the year, features a parade and a costume party. Nogales joins its twin city across the border in celebrating **Mexican Independence Day** with food, live music and street dancing.

Santa Fe Area The **Santa Fe Fiesta** starts with the ritual burning in effigy of a 35-foot-tall "Old Man Gloom" and continues through a weekend of parades, processions and wild celebration.

Taos and the Enchanted Circle Area The **Taos Arts Festival** presents art exhibits, lectures and an arts-and-crafts fair, coinciding with the **Fiesta de San Geronimo** ceremonial dances at the nearby pueblo.

Northwestern New Mexico **Go-jii-ya** the Jicarilla Apache tribe's annual celebration in Dulce, includes a rodeo and powwow.

Albuquerque and Central New Mexico In Albuquerque, the **New Mexico State Fair**, has horse racing, top country performers, a rodeo and livestock.

Southern New Mexico The **16th of September Fiesta** in Mesilla celebrates Mexico's independence with two days of folk dancing, mariachi music and food.

North Central Arizona The **Sedona Arts Festival** draws artisans from all over the West to participate in one of the region's major arts-and-crafts fairs.

OCTOBER

Western Arizona In Lake Havasu City, **London Bridge Days** commemorates the relocation of the bridge to this improbable site with a parade, live entertainment, costume contests and lots of Olde English fun.

South Central Arizona The **Arizona State Fair,** held in Phoenix, runs until early November.

Southern Arizona Tombstone celebrates **Heldorado Days** with music, arts and crafts and gunfight re-enactments.

Santa Fe Area Costumed volunteers re-create the Spanish Colonial era at **Harvest Festival** at the Rancho de las Golondrinas, a historic hacienda located near Santa Fe. The Nambe Pueblo observes the feast day of **Saint Francis of Assisi** with tribal dances. The artists of secluded Dixon, open their homes and workplaces to the public in the **Dixon Studio Tour;** the even more off-the-beaten-path artists' community of El Rito also sponsors a studio tour this month.

Albuquerque and Central New Mexico The **Albuquerque Balloon Fiesta** lasts for a week and a half with races, mass ascensions and other events featuring hundreds of hot-air balloons—the world's largest such event.

Southern New Mexico Ruidoso celebrates fall foliage with a boisterous **Oktoberfest,** coinciding with Cloudcroft's **Aspencade.** Alamogordo's once-a-year **Trinity Site Tour** is your only chance to see where the first atomic bomb was tested. In Las Cruces, the **Whole Enchilada Festival** features a parade, live entertainment, races (including a grocery cart race) and the "World's Largest Enchilada." **Columbus Day** is observed in Columbus with a parade, all-day live music and a street dance.

NOVEMBER **South Central Arizona** The **Four Corner States Bluegrass Festival** in Wickenburg presents three days of music as bands compete for thousands of dollars in prize money.

Southern Arizona The largest perimeter bicycling event in the United States, **El Tour de Tucson** is a colorful spectator sport and a charity fundraiser.

Santa Fe Area Tesuque Pueblo celebrates the **Fiesta de San Diego** with dances. Jemez Pueblo observes the day with dances and a trade fair.

Albuquerque and Central New Mexico The **Southwest Arts Festival,** an invitational show focusing on visual arts, presents the works of over 150 artists at the State Fairgrounds in Albuquerque.

Southern New Mexico Nearly 100 exhibitors participate in the **Renaissance Craftfaire,** a juried art show in Las Cruces.

DECEMBER **Western Arizona** Christmas lights sparkle during Lake Mead Marina's **Harbor Parade of Lights.**

South Central Arizona   The **Fiesta Bowl Parade** in Phoenix has marching bands, equestrian units and floats. Tempe's **New Year's Eve Block Party** welcomes the two Fiesta Bowl teams with food, rides, music and fireworks.

Throughout New Mexico   Christmas is celebrated with ceremonial dances at all Indian pueblos.

Santa Fe Area   The **Fiesta of Our Lady of Guadalupe** is observed with dances and ceremonies at Pojoaque Pueblo. The Christmas holidays hold particular charm in Santa Fe and Taos, where instead of colored lights, building exteriors glow with thousands of small candles called *farolitos*.

Albuquerque and Central New Mexico   **Luminarias** (altar candles) light up the skyline of Albuquerque's Old Town. Between Albuquerque and Santa Fe, the **Turquoise Trail Artisans' Open House** lets visitors see the studios of regional artists.

Southern New Mexico   Las Cruces celebrates the fiesta with a **torchlight ascent** of a nearby mountain, musical concerts and other festivities.

For free visitor information packets including maps and current details on special events, lodging and camping, contact a visitors center or tourism board. As well as large cities, most small towns have chambers of commerce or visitor information centers. Many of them are listed in *Hidden Southwest* under the appropriate regions. Tourist information centers are usually not open on weekends.

Before You Go

VISITORS CENTERS

Travel information on Arizona is available from the **Arizona Office of Tourism.** ~ 2702 North 3rd Street, Phoenix, AZ 85003; 602-248-1480.

For New Mexico, contact the **New Mexico Department of Tourism.** ~ 491 Old Santa Fe Trail, Santa Fe, NM 87503; 800-545-2070.

In Utah, you can write or call the **Utah Travel Council.** ~ Council Hall/Capitol Hill, Salt Lake City, UT 84114; 801-538-1030, 800-200-1160.

The **Colorado Travel and Tourism Authority** provides information on Colorado. ~ 23202 South Trenton Way, Denver, CO 80216; 800-433-2656.

PACKING

The old adage that you should take along twice as much money and half as much stuff as you think you'll need is sound advice as far as it goes, but bear in mind that in many parts of the Southwest you are unlikely to find a store selling anything more substantial than curios and beef jerky.

Southwesterners are casual in their dress and expect the same of visitors. Restaurants with dress codes are few and far between.

Text continued on page 28.

People of the Southwest

The population of the Southwest is often called "tricultural"—Indian, Spanish and Anglo. Each of the three cultures has been an enemy to the others in centuries past, yet all live in harmony as neighbors today. Through centuries of life in close proximity, and despite persistent attempts by both Spanish and Anglos to assimilate the Indian people, each group proudly maintains its cultural identity while respecting the others. The resulting tricultural balance is truly unique to the region.

All three cultural groups share freely in each other's ways. For example, Southwestern cooking blends traditional Anasazi/Pueblo foods—blue corn, beans and squash—with green chile and cooking techniques imported by early Spanish colonists from the Aztecs of central Mexico, and the result is a staple in Anglo kitchens. The distinctive architecture of the desert uses adobe bricks, of Moorish origin and brought to the New World by the Spanish, while the architectural style derives from Anasazi pueblos and incorporates refinements Anglos brought west by railroad.

An Anglo, in local parlance, is anyone who comes from English-speaking America. Anglos first came to the Southwest less than 150 years ago, after the end of the Mexican War, and are still a minority group in many parts today. Newcomers are often surprised to learn that Americans of Jewish, Japanese and African ancestry, among others, are referred to as Anglos. Many Anglos in the more remote parts of the Southwest, from traditional Mormons in rural Utah to residents of old-fashioned hippie communes and artists' colonies in the mountains of New Mexico, hold to ways of life that are a far cry from modern mainstream America.

The Spanish residents of New Mexico trace their ancestry back to the pioneer era around the year 1600—the time of Don Quixote, of the Spanish Inquisition, of the conquest of the New World by the Spanish Armada. Today, the Spanish remain the dominant political and cultural force in many parts of New Mexico, and travelers can still find isolated mountain villages where many aspects of everyday life remain unchanged since the 17th century. Mexican immigration in the 20th century has created a separate Hispanic subculture in southern New Mexico and Arizona.

Visitors today have little opportunity to experience the uniqueness of such tribes as the Apache, Ute, Paiute and other nomadic tribes for whom confinement to reservations has meant adopting conventional ways of rural life. But among groups such as the Pueblo and Navajo people, who still occupy their traditional homelands, the old ways are still very much alive.

The Pueblo people who live along the Rio Grande in Isleta, Santo Domingo, Cochiti, Tesuque, San Ildefonso, Santa Clara, Taos and other Indian communities are descendants of the Anasazi, or "Ancient Ones," who built the impressive castlelike compounds at literally thousands of sites such as those we know as Chaco Canyon, Bandelier, Pecos and Salinas. Although they have lived in close contact with Spanish and Anglo neighbors for centuries, the Rio Grande Pueblo people have carefully guarded their own cultural identity. They often have Spanish names and attend services at mission churches, yet they observe Catholic feast days with sacred dances and kiva ceremonies that reach back to pre-Columbian antiquity. While most Pueblo Indians speak English, they converse among themselves in the dialect of their particular pueblo—Tewa, Tiwa, Towa or Keresan.

The more isolated pueblos of western New Mexico and northeastern Arizona retain their own distinctive cultures. The Acoma people, thought to be descendants of the Mesa Verde Anasazi, practice secret rites that are closed to outsiders. The people of Zuni, who speak a language unrelated to any other Indian group and may be the heirs of the Mimbres who lived in southern New Mexico, follow the ancient kachina religion, becoming embodiments of nature's forces in strange, colorful blessing ceremonies. The Hopi people, whose Sinagua ancestors once lived throughout central Arizona from the Grand Canyon to the Verde Valley, have banned non-Indian visitors from many of their religious ceremonies because of their objections to the publication of various books sensationalizing their snake and eagle dances and their ancient tradition of prophecies.

Nowhere is the blending of cultures more evident than among the Navajo, the largest Indian tribe in the United States. The roots of their religious traditions stretch far into the past, and their hogan dwellings originated in the frozen northlands from which they came. Since arriving in the Southwest in the 1400s, they have borrowed from their neighbors to create their own unique culture. They learned to grow corn and weave textiles from the Pueblo people, and to herd sheep and ride horses from the Spanish. Early Anglo traders helped them develop their "traditional" art forms, rugs and silver jewelry. Even the more modern aspects of Navajo life—pickup trucks, satellite dishes, blue jeans—are not so much signs of assimilation into the white man's world as of the continuing evolution of a uniquely Navajo way of life.

Even if you attend a fancy $100-a-plate fundraiser or go out for a night at the opera, you'll find that a coat and tie or evening gown and heels instantly brand you as a tourist. Chic apparel in these parts is more likely to mean a western-cut suit, ostrich hide boots and a bolo tie with a flashy turquoise-and-silver slide, or for women, a fiesta dress with a concho belt, long-fringed moccasins and a squash blossom necklace—all fairly expensive items that you may never have an occasion to wear back home. Relax. Sporty, comfortable clothing will pass practically anywhere in the Southwest.

When packing clothes, plan to dress in layers. Temperatures can turn hot or cold in a flash at any time of year. During the course of a single vacation day, you can expect to start wearing a heavy jacket, a sweater or flannel shirt and a pair of slacks or jeans, peeling down to a T-shirt and shorts as the day warms up, then putting the extra layers back on soon after the sun goes down.

Other essentials to pack or buy along the way include a good sunscreen and high-quality sunglasses. If you are planning to camp in the mountains during the summer months, you'll be glad you brought mosquito repellent. Umbrellas are considered an oddity in the Southwest. When it rains, as it sometimes does though rarely for long, the approved means of keeping cold water from running down the back of your neck is a cowboy hat.

For outdoor activities, tough-soled hiking boots are more comfortable than running shoes on rocky terrain. Even RV travelers and those who prefer to spend most nights in motels may want to take along a backpacking tent and sleeping bag for irresistible urges to stay out under star-spangled Southwestern skies. A canteen, first-aid kit, flashlight and other routine camping gear are also likely to come in handy. Cycling enthusiasts should bring their own bikes. Especially when it comes to mountain biking, there are a lot more great places to ride than there are towns where you can find bicycles for rent. The same goes for boating, golf and other activities that call for special equipment.

If you're the kind of person who likes to pick up souvenirs for free in the form of unusual stones, pine cones and the like, take along some plastic bags for hauling treasures. A camera, of course, is essential for capturing your travel experience; of equal importance is a good pair of binoculars, which let you explore distant landscapes from scenic overlooks. And don't, for heaven's sake, forget your copy of *Hidden Southwest*.

LODGING

Lodgings in the Southwest run the gamut from tiny one-room mountain cabins to luxurious hotels that blend Indian pueblo architecture with contemporary elegance. Bed and breakfasts can be found not only in chic destinations like Santa Fe and Sedona but also in such unlikely locales as former ghost towns and the outskirts of Indian reservations. They come in all types, sizes and price ranges. Typical of the genre are lovingly restored old mansions comfortably furnished with period decor, usually with under a dozen rooms. Some bed and breakfasts, however, are guest cottages or rooms in nice suburban homes, while others are larger establishments, approaching hotel size, of the type sometimes referred to as country inns.

The abundance of motels in towns along all major highway routes presents a range of choices, from name-brand motor inns to traditional mom-and-pop establishments that have endured for half a century since motels were invented. Older motels along main truck routes, especially interstate Route 40, offer some of the lowest room rates to be found anywhere in the United States today.

At the other end of the price spectrum, the height of self-indulgent vacationing is to be found at upscale resorts in some destinations such as Tucson, Sedona, Ruidoso and Santa Fe. These resorts offer riding stables, golf courses, tennis courts, fine dining, live entertainment and exclusive shops on the premises so that guests can spend their entire holidays without leaving the grounds—a boon for celebrities seeking a few days' rest and relaxation away from the public eye, but a very expensive way to miss out on experiencing the real Southwest.

Other lodgings throughout the region offer a different kind of personality. Many towns—preserved historic districts like Tombstone and Lincoln as well as larger communities like Durango and Flagstaff—have historic hotels dating back before the turn of the century. Some of them have been lavishly restored to far surpass their original Victorian elegance. Others may lack the polished antique decor and sophisticated ambience but make up for it in their authentic feel. These places give visitors a chance to spice up their vacation experience by spending the night where lawman Wyatt Earp or novelist Zane Grey once slept and awakening to look out their window onto a Main Street that has changed surprisingly little since the days of the Old West.

LODGING IN THE NATIONAL PARKS

Both rims of the Grand Canyon, as well as Bryce Canyon and Zion, have classic, rustic-elegant lodges built during the early years of the 20th century. Though considerably more expensive than budget motel rooms, the national park lodges are moderate in price and well worth it in terms of ambience and location. Reservations should be made far in advance.

Whatever your preference and budget, you can probably find something to suit your taste with the help of the regional chapters in this book. Remember, rooms can be scarce and prices may rise during the peak season, which is summer throughout most of the region and winter in low-lying desert communities such as Phoenix, Scottsdale and Tucson. Travelers planning to visit a place in peak season should either make advance reservations or arrive early in the day, before the "No Vacancy" signs start lighting up. Those who plan to stay in Santa Fe, Sedona, Grand Canyon National Park or Mesa Verde National Park at any time of year are wise to make lodging reservations well ahead of time.

A growing number of Arizona restaurants offer "New Southwestern" menus that feature offbeat dishes using local ingredients—green-chile tempura, snow-crab enchiladas.

Accommodations in this book are organized by region and classified according to price. Rates referred to are high-season rates, so if you are looking for off-season bargains, it's good to inquire. *Budget* lodgings generally run less than $50 per night for two people and are satisfactory and clean but modest. *Moderate* hotels range from $50 to $90; what they have to offer in the way of luxury will depend on where they are located, but they generally offer larger rooms and more attractive surroundings. At *deluxe*-priced accommodations, you can expect to spend between $90 and $130 for a homey bed and breakfast or a double in a hotel or resort. In hotels of this price you'll generally find spacious rooms, a fashionable lobby, a restaurant and often a group of shops. *Ultra-deluxe* facilities, priced above $130, are a region's finest, offering all the amenities of a deluxe hotel plus plenty of extras.

Room rates vary as much with locale as with quality. Some of the trendier destinations have no rooms at all in the budget price range. In other communities—especially those along interstate highways where rates are set with truck drivers in mind—every motel falls into the budget category, even though accommodations may range from $19.95 at run-down, spartan places to $45 or so at the classiest motor inn in town. The price categories listed in this book are relative, designed to show you where to get the most out of your travel budget, however large or small it may be.

DINING   Restaurants seem to be one of the main industries in some parts of the Southwest. Santa Fe, New Mexico, for example, has approximately 200 restaurants in a city of just 62,000 people. While the specialty cuisine throughout most of the Southwest consists of variations on Mexican and Indian food, you'll find many restaurants catering to customers whose tastes don't include hot chile peppers.

Within a particular chapter, restaurants are categorized by region, with each restaurant entry describing the establishment according to price. Dinner entrées at *budget* restaurants usually cost

$8 or less. The ambience is informal, service usually speedy and the crowd often a local one. *Moderately* priced restaurants range between $8 and $16 at dinner; surroundings are casual but pleasant, the menu offers more variety and the pace is usually slower. *Deluxe* establishments tab their entrées from $16 to $24; cuisines may be simple or sophisticated, depending on the location, but the decor is plusher and the service more personalized. *Ultra-deluxe* dining rooms, where entrées begin at $24, are often the gourmet places; here cooking has become a fine art and the service should be impeccable.

Some restaurants change hands often and are occasionally closed in low seasons. Efforts have been made in this book to include places with established reputations for good eating. Breakfast and lunch menus vary less in price from restaurant to restaurant than evening dinners.

DRIVING NOTES

The mountains and deserts of the Southwest are clearly the major sightseeing attractions for many visitors. This is a rugged area and there are some important things to remember when driving on the side roads throughout the region. First and foremost, believe it if you see a sign indicating four-wheel drive only. These roads can be very dangerous in a car without high ground clearance and the extra traction afforded by four-wheel drive—and there may be no safe place to turn around if you get stuck. During rainy periods dirt roads may become impassable muck. And in winter, heavy snows necessitate the use of snow tires or chains on main roads, while side roads may or may not be maintained at all.

Some side roads will take you far from civilization so be sure to have a full radiator and tank of gas. Carry spare fuel, water and food. In winter, it is always wise to travel with a shovel and blankets in your car. Should you become stuck, local people are usually quite helpful about offering assistance to stranded vehicles, but in case no one else is around, for extended backcountry driving, a CB radio or a car phone would not be a bad idea.

TRAVELING WITH CHILDREN

Any place that has cowboys and Indians, rocks to climb and limitless room to run is bound to be a hit with youngsters. Plenty of family adventures are available in the Southwest, from manmade attractions to experiences in the wild. A few guidelines will help make travel with children a pleasure.

Book reservations in advance, making sure that the places you stay accept children. Many bed and breakfasts do not. If you need a crib or extra cot, arrange for it ahead of time. A travel agent can be of help here, as well as with most other travel plans.

If you are traveling by air, try to reserve bulkhead seats where there is plenty of room. Take along extras you may need, such as diapers, changes of clothing, snacks and toys or small games. When traveling by car, be sure to take along the extras, too. Make sure you have plenty of water and juices to drink; dehydration can be a subtle but serious problem. Most towns, as well as some national parks, have stores that carry diapers, baby food, snacks and other essentials, though they usually close early. Larger towns often have all-night grocery or convenience stores.

A first-aid kit is a must for any trip. Along with adhesive bandages, antiseptic cream and something to stop itching, include any medicines your pediatrician might recommend to treat allergies, colds, diarrhea or any chronic problems your child may have. Southwestern sunshine is intense. Take extra care for the first few days. Children's skin is usually more tender than adult skin and severe sunburn can happen before you realize it. A hat is a good idea, along with a reliable sunblock.

Many national parks and monuments offer special activities designed just for children. Visitors center film presentations and rangers' campfire slide shows can help inform children about the natural history of the Southwest and head off some questions. However, kids tend to find a lot more things to wonder about than adults have answers for. To be as prepared as possible, seize every opportunity to learn more—particularly about Indians, a constant curiosity for young minds.

GAY & LESBIAN TRAVELERS

The unique beauty of the Southwest is appealing to many: the wide open spaces stretching for miles and miles invite people who are looking to get away from it all. It's a region that gives people a lot of space, literally, and encourages you to do your own thing, which allows gay or lesbian travelers to feel comfortable here. Whether you're interested in exploring the area's magnificent scenery, sightseeing in the cosmopolitan cities, or just relaxing by the pool, the Southwest has much to offer.

You'll find gay and lesbian communities in a few of the bigger cities such as Santa Fe and Albuquerque, New Mexico. The region also boasts the gay and lesbian hot spot of Phoenix, Arizona, to which this book has dedicated a special "gay-specific" section. Phoenix is home to a large gay and lesbian community and there's a growing number of gay-friendly bars, nightclubs and restaurants.

Gay and lesbian publications providing entertainment listings and happenings are available in some of the larger gay enclaves. *Echo Magazine* is a free bi-weekly that is distributed in cafés, bookstores and bars. In it you'll find news and entertainment offerings in Phoenix. ~ 602-266-0550. In New Mexico, you can pick up the free monthly *Out Magazine* (not to be confused with the national magazine called *Out*) at bookstores throughout the state. ~ 505-243-2540. *Weekly Alibi*, a free, alternative newspaper offers entertainment listings specifically for the Albuquerque area. ~ 505-268-8111.

For information on virtually anything from lodging to HIV/AIDS resources in Phoenix, call **The Valley of the Sun Gay and Lesbian Community Center** between 10 a.m. and 10 p.m. seven days a week. ~ 602-234-2752.

SENIOR TRAVELERS

The Southwest is a hospitable place for older vacationers, many of whom turn into part-time or full-time residents thanks to the dry, pleasant climate and the friendly senior citizen communities that have developed in southern Arizona and, on a smaller scale, in other parts of the region. The large number of national parks and monuments in the Southwest means that persons age 62 and older can save considerable money with a Golden Age Passport, which allows free admission. Apply for one in person at any national park unit that charges an entrance fee. Many private sightseeing attractions also offer significant discounts for seniors.

The **American Association of Retired Persons** (AARP) offers membership to anyone over 50. AARP's benefits include travel discounts with a number of firms. ~ 3200 East Carson Street, Lakewood, CA 90712; 310-496-2277.

Elderhostel offers educational courses that are all-inclusive packages at colleges and universities. In the Southwest, Elderhostel courses are available in numerous locations including: in Arizona—Flagstaff, Nogales, Phoenix, Prescott and Tucson; and in New Mexico—Albuquerque, Las Cruces, Santa Fe, Silver City and Taos. Courses are also offered in Durango, Colorado, and Cedar City, Utah. ~ 75 Federal Street, Boston, MA 02110; 617-426-7788.

Be extra careful about health matters. In the changeable climate of the Southwest, seniors are more at risk of suffering hypothermia. High altitudes may present a risk to persons with heart or respiratory conditions; ask your physician for advice when planning your trip. Many tourist destinations in the region are a long way from any hospital or other health care facility.

In addition to the medications you ordinarily use, it's a good idea to bring along the prescriptions for obtaining more. Consider carrying a medical record with you, including your history and current medical status as well as your doctor's name, phone number and address. Make sure that your insurance covers you while you are away from home.

DISABLED TRAVELERS

All of the Southwestern states are striving to make public areas fully accessible to persons with disabilities. Parking spaces and restroom facilities for the handicapped are provided according to both state law and national park regulations. National parks and monuments also post signs that tell which trails are wheelchair-accessible.

There are many organizations offering information for travelers with disabilities, including the **Society for the Advancement of Travel for the Handicapped** at 347 5th Avenue, Suite 610, New York, NY 10016 (212-447-7284), the **Travel Information Service** (215-329-5715) and **Mobility International USA** at P.O. Box 10767, Eugene, OR 97440 (503-343-1284).

For general travel advice, contact **Travelin' Talk**, a networking organization. ~ P.O. Box 3534, Clarksville, TN 37043; 615-552-6670.

FOREIGN TRAVELERS

Passports and Visas   Most foreign visitors need a passport and tourist visa to enter the United States. Contact your nearest U.S. Embassy or Consulate well in advance to obtain a visa and to check on any other entry requirements.

Customs Requirements   Foreign travelers are allowed to carry in the following: 200 cigarettes (1 carton), 50 cigars, or 2 kilograms (4.4 pounds) of smoking tobacco; one liter of alcohol for personal use only (you must be 21 years of age to bring in alcohol); and US$100 worth of duty-free gifts that can include an additional quantity of 100 cigars. You may bring in any amount of currency, but must fill out a form if you bring in over US$10,000. Carry any prescription drugs in clearly marked containers. (You may have to produce a written prescription or doctor's statement for the custom's officer.) Meat or meat products, seeds, plants, fruits and narcotics are not allowed to be brought into the United States. Contact the **United States Customs Service** for further information. ~ 1301 Constitution Avenue NW, Washington, DC 20229; 202-927-6724.

Driving   If you plan to rent a car, an international driver's license should be obtained before arriving in the United States. Some car rental agencies require both a foreign license and an international driver's license. Many also require a lessee to be at least 25 years of age; all require a major credit card.

Currency   United States money is based on the dollar. Bills generally come in denominations of $1, $5, $10, $20, $50 and $100. Every dollar is divided into 100 cents. Coins are the penny (1 cent), nickel (5 cents), dime (10 cents) and quarter (25 cents). Half-dollar and dollar coins are rarely used. You may not use foreign currency to purchase goods and services in the United States. Consider buying traveler's checks in dollar amounts. You may also use credit cards affiliated with an American company such as Interbank, Barclay Card, VISA and American Express.

Electricity   Electric outlets use currents of 110 volts, 60 cycles. For appliances made for other electrical systems, you need a transformer or other adapter.

Weights and Measures   The United States uses the English system of weights and measures. American units and their metric equivalents are: 1 inch = 2.5 centimeters; 1 foot (12 inches) = 0.3 meter;

1 yard (3 feet) = 0.9 meter; 1 mile (5280 feet) = 1.6 kilometers; 1 ounce = 28 grams; 1 pound (16 ounces) = 0.45 kilogram; 1 quart (liquid) = 0.9 liter.

▼▼▼▼▼▼▼▼▼▼▼▼▼▼

Outdoor Adventures

CAMPING

RV or tent camping is a great way to tour the Southwest. Besides saving substantial sums of money, campers enjoy the freedom to watch sunsets from beautiful places, spend nights under spectacularly starry skies and wake up to find themselves in lovely surroundings that few hotels can match.

Most towns have commercial RV parks of some sort, and long-term mobile-home parks often rent spaces to RVers by the night. But unless you absolutely need cable television, none of these places can compete with the wide array of public campgrounds available in national and state parks, monuments and forests. Federal campground sites are typically less developed; only the biggest ones have electrical hookups. National forest campgrounds don't have hookups, while state park campgrounds just about always do. The largest public campgrounds offer tent camping loops separate from RV loops and backcountry camping areas offer the option of spending the night in the primeval Southwest.

With the exception of both rims of the Grand Canyon, where campsite reservations are booked up to 56 days in advance through DESTINET (800-365-2267, credit cards only), you won't find much in the way of sophisticated reservation systems in the Southwest. The general rule in public campgrounds is still first-come, first-served, even though they fill up practically every night in peak season. For campers, this means traveling in the morning and reaching your intended campground by early afternoon. In many areas, campers may find it more convenient to keep a single location for as much as a week and explore surrounding areas on day trips.

For listings of state parks in Arizona with camping facilities and reservation information, contact **Arizona State Parks.** ~ 1300 West Washington Street, Phoenix, AZ 85007; 602-542-4174.

The New Mexico State Park and Recreation Division has information on state parks in New Mexico open for camping. ~ 408 Galisteo Street, Santa Fe, NM 87504; 505-827-7465.

Fees and regulations for camping in Utah are available from the **Utah Division of Parks and Recreation.** ~ 1636 West North Temple, Salt Lake City, UT 84116; 801-538-7221.

To obtain information on camping in Colorado, contact **Colorado Parks and Outdoor Recreation.** ~ 1313 Sherman Street, Denver, CO 80203; 303-866-3437, 800-678-2267.

Information on camping in the national forests in New Mexico and Arizona is available from **National Forest Service–Southwestern Region.** ~ Public Affairs Office, 517 Gold Avenue Southwest, Albuquerque, NM 87102; 505-842-3292. For national forests in

Utah, contact **National Forest Service–Intermountain Region.** ~ 324 25th Street, Ogden, UT 84401; 801-625-5347. For those in Colorado, contact **National Forest Service–Rocky Mountain Region.** ~ 740 Simms Street, Lakewood, CO 80225; 303-275-5350, 800-280-2267. Camping and reservation information for parks and monuments is available from the parks and monuments listed in this book or from **National Park Service–Southwest System Support Office.** ~ 1100 Old Santa Fe Trail, Santa Fe, NM 87501; 505-988-6100.

Many Indian lands have public campgrounds, which usually don't appear in campground directories. For information, contact: **Navajo Parks and Recreation.** ~ P.O. Box 9000, Window Rock, AZ 86515; 520-871-6647. **Hopi Tribal Headquarters.** ~ P.O. Box 123, Kykotsmovi, AZ 86039; 520-734-2441. **Havasupai Tourist Enterprise.** ~ Supai, AZ 86435; 520-448-2121. The **White Mountain Apache Game and Fish Department.** ~ P.O. Box 220, Whiteriver, AZ 85941; 520-338-4385. The **Mescalero Apache Tribe.** ~ P.O. Box 176, Mescalero, NM 88340; 505-671-4494. **Zuni Pueblo.** ~ P.O. Box 339, Zuni, NM 87327; 505-782-4481.

Also see the "Parks" sections in each chapter to discover where camping is available.

PERMITS Tent camping is allowed in the backcountry of all national forests here except in a few areas where signs are posted prohibiting it. You may need a permit to hike or camp in national forest wilderness areas, so contact specific forests for more information. Ranger stations provide trail maps and advice on current conditions and fire regulations. In dry seasons, emergency rules may prohibit campfires and sometimes ban cigarette smoking, with stiff enforcement penalties.

For backcountry hiking in national parks and monuments, you must first obtain a permit from the ranger at the front desk in the visitors center. The permit procedure is simple and free. It helps park administrators measure the impact on sensitive ecosystems and distribute use evenly among major trails to prevent overcrowding.

BOATING Most of the large desert lakes along the Colorado, Rio Grande and other major rivers are administered as National Recreation Areas and supervised by the U.S. Army Corps of Engineers. Federal boating safety regulations that apply to these lakes may vary slightly from state regulations. Indian reservations have separate rules for boating on tribal lakes. More significant than any differences between federal, state and tribal regulations are the local rules in force for any particular lake. Ask for applicable boating regulations at a local marina or fishing supply store or use the addresses

The Cactus League

Each year, eight major league baseball teams migrate to the sunny Arizona desert during the months of February and March for their Cactus League spring training schedule. And where there's baseball, the fans aren't far behind.

It's become an increasingly popular way to spend a vacation as more and more fans take the opportunity to enjoy a little welcome sunshine, root for their favorite teams, and get a close-up look at some of professional baseball's super stars, all at the same time. If you can't wait for the first ball of the regular season to be thrown out in April, catch the preseason action at Arizona's Cactus League.

National League fans root for the following teams at their practice fields: **San Francisco Giants** (Scottsdale Stadium, 7408 East Osborn Road, Scottsdale; 602-990-7972); **Chicago Cubs** (Hohokam Park, 1238 Center Street, Mesa; 602-964-4467); **Colorado Rockies** (Hi Corbett Field in Reid Park, 22nd Street and Randolph Way, Tucson; 520-327-9467); and the **San Diego Padres** (Peoria Municipal Stadium, 10601 North 83rd Drive, Peoria; 602-486-7000).

If the American League teams are your favorites, take a seat in the bleachers to watch the **Milwaukee Brewers** (Compadre Stadium, 1425 West Ocotillo Road, Chandler; 602-895-1200); **Oakland A's** (Phoenix Municipal Stadium, 5999 East Van Buren Boulevard, Phoenix; 602-392-0074); **Seattle Mariners** (Peoria Municipal Stadium, 10601 North 83rd Drive, Peoria; 602-412-4210); and the **California Angels** (Diablo Stadium, 2200 West Alameda Street, Tempe; 602-350-5205).

Adding to the excitement is the intimacy and informality of the small-town ballparks, where stadium bleachers are much closer to the action, and ticket prices are substantially less than regular season prices, although tickets to some games—like the Chicago Cubs'—can be surprisingly hard to come by.

To save on the cost of the tickets, look into package deals offered by many local hotels and tour companies. **Hands-On Sports Marketing and Management** has several packages if you plan on seeing the San Francisco Giants in action. ~ P.O. Box 120009-27, Scottsdale, AZ 85267. For hotel reservations and tickets to Chicago Cubs games, call the **Mesa Convention and Visitors Bureau**. ~ 120 North Center Street; 800-283-6372. Contact your local travel agency for information on hotel and ticket prices for other teams.

and phone numbers listed in "Parks" or other sections of each chapter in this book to contact the headquarters for lakes you plan to visit.

Boats, from small power boats to houseboats, can be rented for 24 hours or longer at marinas on several of the larger lakes. At most marinas, you can get a boat on short notice if you come on a weekday, since much of their business comes from local weekend recreation. The exception is Lake Powell, where houseboats and other craft are booked far in advance. Take a look at Chapter Fifteen (Southeastern Utah) for details on how to arrange for a Lake Powell boat trip.

River rafting is a very popular sport in several parts of the Southwest, notably on the Chama River and Rio Grande in northern New Mexico, the Green River in southern Utah and the Animas River near Durango, Colorado. The ultimate whitewater rafting experience, of course, is a trip through the Grand Canyon. Independent rafters are welcome, but because of the bulky equipment and specialized knowledge of river hazards involved, most adventurous souls stick with group trips offered by any of the many rafting companies located in Page, Flagstaff, Taos, Santa Fe, Moab and Durango. Rafters, as well as people using canoes, kayaks, windsurfers or inner tubes, are required by state and federal regulations to wear life jackets.

FISHING

In a land as arid as the Southwest, many residents have an irresistible fascination with water. During the warm months, lake shores and readily accessible portions of streams are often packed with anglers, especially on weekends. Vacationers can beat the crowds to some extent by planning their fishing days during the week.

Fish hatcheries in all four states keep busy stocking streams with trout, particularly rainbows, the most popular game fish throughout the West. Catch-and-release fly fishing is the rule in some popular areas such as the upper Pecos River near Santa Fe, allowing more anglers a chance at bigger fish. Be sure to inquire locally about eating the fish you catch, since some seemingly remote streams and rivers have contamination problems from old mines and mills.

The larger reservoirs offer an assortment of sport fish, including crappie, carp, white bass, smallmouth bass, largemouth bass and walleye pike. Striped bass, an ocean import, can run as large as 40 pounds, while catfish in the depths of dammed desert canyons sometimes attain mammoth proportions.

For copies of state fishing regulations, inquire at a local fishing supply store or marina. Information for Arizona is available from the **Arizona Game and Fish Department**. ~ 2222 Greenway Road, Phoenix, AZ 85023; 602-942-3000. The **New Mexico Depart-**

ment of Game and Fish can give regulations for New Mexico. ~ Villagra Building, Santa Fe, NM 87503; 505-827-7911, 800-275-3474. For rules in Utah, contact the **Utah Division of Wildlife Resources.** ~ 1596 West North Temple, Salt Lake City, UT 84116; 801-596-8660. Colorado's fishing regulation are available from the **Colorado Division of Wildlife.** ~ 6060 Broadway, Denver, CO 80216; 303-291-7533.

State fishing licenses are required for fishing in national parks and national recreation areas, but not on Indian reservations, where daily permits are sold by the tribal governments. For more information about fishing on Indian lands, contact the tribal agencies listed in "Camping" above.

TWO

The Grand Canyon

Awesome. Magnificent. Breathtaking. It's easy to slip into hyperbole when trying to describe the Grand Canyon, but it's understandable. No matter how many spectacular landscapes you've seen in your lifetime, none can compare with this mighty chasm stretching across the northwest corner of Arizona.

The Grand Canyon comes as a surprise. Whether you approach the South Rim or the North Rim, the landscape gives no hint that the canyon is there until suddenly you find yourself on the rim looking into the chasm ten miles wide from rim to rim and a mile down to the Colorado River, winding silver through the canyon's inner depths. From anywhere along the rim, you can feel the vast, silent emptiness of the canyon and wonder at the sheer mass of the walls, striated into layer upon colorful layer of sandstone, limestone and shale.

More than five million years ago, the Colorado River began carving out this canyon that offers a panoramic look at the geologic history of the Southwest. Sweeping away sandstones and sediments, limestones and fossils, the river cut its way through Paleozoic and Precambrian formations. By the time mankind arrived, the canyon extended nearly all the way down to schist, a basement formation.

The Grand Canyon is aptly named—being, perhaps, the grandest geological marvel of them all. It is as long as any mountain range in the Rockies and as deep as the highest of the Rocky Mountains are tall. For centuries, it posed the most formidable of all natural barriers to travel in the West, and to this day no road has ever penetrated the wilderness below the rim. No matter how many photographs you take, paintings you make or postcards you buy, the view from anywhere along the Grand Canyon rim can never be truly captured in two dimensions. Nor can the mind fully comprehend it; no matter how many times you have visited the Grand Canyon before, the view will always inspire the same awe as it did the first time you stood and gazed in wonder at the canyon's immensity and the silent grandeur of its massive cliffs.

The Grand Canyon extends east to west for some 277 miles, from the western boundary of the Navajo Indian Reservation to the vicinity of Lake Mead and the Nevada border. Only the highest section of each rim of the Grand Canyon is accessible by motor vehicle. Most of Grand Canyon National Park, both above and below the rim, is a designated wilderness area that can only be explored on foot or by river raft.

The South Rim and the North Rim are essentially separate destinations, more than 200 miles apart by road. This chapter covers the developed national park areas on both rims. For the adventuresome, we've also included hiking possibilities in the canyon, as well as two lesser-known areas of the Grand Canyon that are challenging to reach—Toroweap Point in the Arizona Strip on the North Rim and the scenic area below the Indian village of Supai on the South Rim.

With more than five million visitors a year, the Grand Canyon is one of the most popular national parks in the United States. While many come to enjoy the panoramic vistas, others come to tackle the most challenging hiking trails in the country or to explore the narrow canyons and gorges by pack mule. Whatever reason you choose to visit the Grand Canyon, it will be worth it.

▼▼▼▼▼▼▼▼▼▼
The South Rim

The South Rim is the most accessible area of the Grand Canyon. It's no wonder that you'll find most of the facilities here. The many trailheads leading into the canyon and along the rim make this a good place to start your Grand Canyon tour.

SIGHTS

The **South Rim** (day-use fee, $10 per vehicle) is the busy part of the park. From **Grand Canyon Village**, the large concession complex where the hotels, restaurants and stores are located on the rim near the south entrance, two paved rim drives run in opposite directions. The **East Rim Drive** goes 25 miles east to the national park's east entrance, which is the entrance you will use if you are driving in from the North Rim, Lake Powell or the Navajo Indian Reservation. The first point of interest you come to after entering the park on East Rim Drive is the **Desert View Watchtower**, built in the 1930s as a replica of an ancient Hopi watchtower. It offers the first panoramic view of the Grand Canyon. As you proceed along East Rim Drive toward Grand Canyon Village, other overlooks—**Lipan Point, Zuni Point, Grandview Point, Moran Point, Yaki Point**—will beckon, each with a different perspective on the canyon's immensity.

The **Tusayan Museum**, three miles west of the park's east entrance, has exhibits on the Hopi people and their Anasazi ancestors who used to live along the rim of the Grand Canyon. In the Hopi belief system, the canyon is said to be the *sipapu*, the hole through which the earth's first people climbed from the mountaintop of their previous world into our present one. ~ East Rim Drive; 520-638-2305.

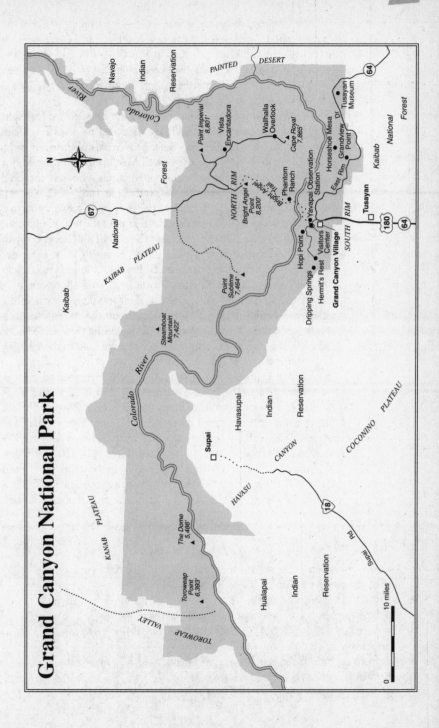

Grand Canyon National Park

The **Yavapai Observation Station**, about half a mile east of the visitors center, offers spectacular views of the Grand Canyon; from here you can see Phantom Ranch, the Colorado River and the black bridge on the Kaibab Trail used by hikers to cross the river. There are several daily interpretive programs including ranger-led rim walks and geology talks. ~ 520-638-7888.

The **West Rim Drive**, which follows the canyon rim for eight miles west of Grand Canyon Village, is closed to private vehicles in the summer months. Visitors see it by free park shuttle bus or by bicycle. The drive runs past the **Powell Memorial**, honoring Major John Wesley Powell, the one-armed adventurer who first surveyed the Grand Canyon for the U.S. government in 1869—in a wooden boat. The road clings to the rim of the canyon as it takes you to a series of overlooks, each more spectacular than the last. **Pima Point**, in particular, offers what is probably the best of all Grand Canyon views. The drive ends at a place called **Hermit's Rest**, a former tourist camp where there are a snack bar and a hikers' trailhead.

The **Grand Canyon Visitors Center** is located about one mile east of Grand Canyon Village. We suggest leaving your car in the village and walking to the visitors center on the paved, magnificently scenic Rim Trail (or, if you're not spending the night at park lodgings, parking at the visitors center and walking to the village). The most interesting exhibit in the visitors center is the display in the outdoor central plaza of boats that have been used to explore the Grand Canyon by river. A burned fragment is all that remains of one of the original wooden boats used by Major Powell in 1869. Other wooden boats are of more recent vintage. There is also one of the original inflatable river rafts used by the woman who in 1955 invented whitewater rafting as we know it today. ~ 520-638-7888.

You can take a romantic trip into yesteryear on the **Grand Canyon Railway**. A turn-of-the-century steam train leaves Williams in the morning for a two-and-a-half-hour trip through Kaibab

✔ **CHECK THESE OUT—UNIQUE EXPERIENCES**

- Get nostalgic when you chug through the Kaibab National Forest on the turn-of-the-century **Grand Canyon Railway**. *page 44*
- Retreat at the **Phantom Ranch**, which sits at the bottom of the canyon and is reached by foot, mule and river raft only. *page 46*
- Reserve a table at the **Grand Canyon Lodge Dining Room** and feast on the stunning views of the canyon. *page 52*
- Trek from the rim to the bottom of the canyon and back, one of the most memorable hikes in the park. *page 54*

National Forest, tracing the route that brought early tourists to the national park, arriving around noon at the historic 1908 Santa Fe Railroad depot in Grand Canyon Village. The return trip departs for Williams in the late afternoon. Trains run daily throughout the year. ~ Route 40, Williams; 800-843-8724.

Just outside the park's south entrance, the town of Tusayan has an **IMAX Theatre** that show films about the Grand Canyon on a seven-story, 82-foot-wide wraparound screen with six-track Dolby sound. ~ 520-638-2203. The **Over the Edge Theatre** also features Grand Canyon films. ~ 520-638-2229. Why one should wish to watch a movie when the real thing is just a few minutes away is not immediately apparent, but in fact the theaters add an extra dimension to the Grand Canyon experience by presenting river-rafting footage, aerial photography and close-up looks at places in the canyon that are hard to get to.

For the adventuresome, an intriguing Grand Canyon experience that is only accessible by foot is found far downriver near the west end of the canyon. The **Havasu Canyon Trail** (16 miles), entirely within the Havasupai Indian Reservation, is reached by leaving the interstate at Seligman (westbound) or Kingman (eastbound) and driving to the Supai turnoff near Peach Springs. From there, the Supai Road goes for 65 miles before the pavement ends. In another 11 miles, the road dead-ends and a foot trail descends 2000 feet in eight miles to the Indian village of **Supai** where about 500 people live. All hikers must check in at tribal headquarters. From there, the main trail continues for about four more miles into Havasu Canyon, a side canyon from the Grand Canyon, which includes a series of three high waterfalls—75-foot **Navajo Falls**, 100-foot **Havasu Falls** and 200-foot **Mooney Falls**—with large pools that are ideal for swimming. There is a campground near Mooney Falls, and from there the trail continues down to the Colorado River in the bottom of the Grand Canyon, while another trail forks over to Beaver Canyon, where there is another waterfall. Whether you plan to stay in the campground or the modern lodge at Supai, advance reservations are essential. For camping, write Havasupai Tourist Enterprise, Supai, AZ 86435 or call 520-448-2141. For accommodations, see "Lodging" below.

◄ HIDDEN

The South Rim offers many lodging choices. For information about South Rim accommodations, call 520-638-2631. Reservations at any of them can be made up to 23 months in advance by writing to the **Grand Canyon National Park Lodges.** ~ 14001 East Iliff Avenue, Suite 600, Aurora, CO 80014; 303-297-2757, fax 303-297-3175.

LODGING

Top of the line is the **El Tovar Hotel**. Designed after European hunting lodges, El Tovar was built by the Fred Harvey Company in 1905 and some staff members still wear the traditional black-and-white uniforms of the famous "Harvey Girls" of that era. The lobby retains its original backwoods elegance, with a big fireplace, massive wood ceiling beams and dark-stained pine decor throughout. The rooms were renovated in the 1990s. All have full baths, color television and telephones. ~ DELUXE.

More affordable historic lodging is available nearby at **Bright Angel Lodge**. The main log and stone lodge was built in 1935 on the site of Bright Angel Camp, the first tourist facility in the park. Its lobby features Indian motifs and a huge fireplace. Rooms are clean and modest. Most have televisions and phones; some have shared baths. Besides rooms in the main building, the lodge also rents several historic cabins, a few with fireplaces. Budget to moderate for rooms in the main lodge and historic cabins. Moderate to deluxe for rooms on the canyon rim. ~ BUDGET TO DELUXE.

Also in Grand Canyon Village, on the rim between El Tovar and Bright Angel Lodge, are the modern twin stone lodges, **Thunderbird Lodge** and **Kachina Lodge**. Located on the rim trail, these caravansaries are within easy walking distance of the restaurants at the older lodges. All have televisions and phones. ~ DELUXE.

The largest lodging facility in the park, **Yavapai Lodge** is situated in a wooded setting about one mile from the canyon rim, near the general store, across the road from the visitors center and about one mile from Grand Canyon Village. The contemporary rooms are equivalent in quality to what you would expect for the same price at a national chain motor inn. Closed December to March. ~ MODERATE.

Maswik Lodge is set away from the canyon rim at the southwest end of Grand Canyon Village. It presents a variety of motel-style rooms as well as cabins. All the rooms have TVs and phones. The cabins are available June through August only. ~ BUDGET.

An elegant modern-rustic building with the look of a ski lodge and a lobby with multistory picture windows, **Moqui Lodge** is managed as part of the national park lodge system although it is located in Kaibab National Forest just outside the park's Southgate entrance. Closed December and January. ~ 520-638-2424. MODERATE.

HIDDEN ►

No survey of lodgings at the Grand Canyon would be complete without mentioning **Phantom Ranch**. Located at the bottom of the canyon, this 1922 lodge and cabins is at the lower end of the North Kaibab Trail from the North Rim and the Bright Angel and South Kaibab trails from the South Rim. It can only be reached by foot, mule or river raft. Cabins are normally reserved for guests on overnight mule trips, but hikers with plenty of advance notice can also arrange lodging. Prices, including overnight mule trips, are in the moderate range. Bunk beds are available by reservation only in four budget-rate ten-person dormitories for hikers. There is no television at the ranch, and only one pay phone. There is outgoing mail service, however, and mail sent from Phantom Ranch bears the postmark, "Mailed by Mule from the Bottom of the Canyon." Meals are served in a central dining hall which becomes a beer hall after dinner. Do not arrive at Phantom Ranch without reservations! You can reserve space up to a year in advance by calling 520-638-2401 or writing Grand Canyon National Park Lodges at the address above. ~ BUDGET TO MODERATE.

Located in a remote red rock canyon on the Supai Indian Reservation, the 24 motel-style units at **Havasupai Lodge** is a truly hidden destination. There's a café next door, swimming in the nearby creek and a convenient barbecue pit. Just two miles away are Navajo, Havasu and Mooney falls. You can also enjoy American Indian–led horseback and hiking tours of this scenic region. ~ Supai; 520-448-2111. MODERATE.

◄ HIDDEN

Just outside the South Rim entrance gate, the community of Tusayan has several motels and motor inns that are not affiliated with the national park. If you cannot get reservations at one of the national park lodges, try one of the typical deluxe-priced chain motels, such as the **Red Feather Lodge**. ~ 520-638-2414, 800-538-2345, fax 520-638-9216. The **Best Western Grand Canyon Squire Inn** is another such establishment. ~ 520-638-2681, 800-622-6966, fax 520-638-0162. Or try the **Quality Inn Grand Canyon**. ~ 520-638-2673, 800-221-2222, fax 520-638-9537. DELUXE.

The phone number for all South Rim Grand Canyon restaurants is 520-638-2631 and reservations are not required.

DINING

The most elegant South Rim restaurant is **El Tovar Dining Room**. Entrées such as filet mignon with crab legs béarnaise are served on fine china by candlelight. Prices are high, the ambience is classy, but casual dress is perfectly acceptable. ~ DELUXE.

More informal surroundings and lower prices are to be found at the **Bright Angel Restaurant** in the Bright Angel Lodge. Menu selections include chicken piccata, grilled rainbow trout and fajitas. Cocktails and wine are available. Adjoining the Bright Angel Lodge, the **Arizona Steakhouse** specializes in steaks and seafood. The open kitchen lets you watch the chefs cook while you eat. The Arizona Steakhouse is closed during winter. ~ MODERATE.

In the Yavapai Lodge, located across the highway from the visitors center, the **Yavapai Cafeteria** serves fast food—burgers and fries, pizza and fried chicken—for breakfast, lunch and dinner. Nearby in the general store, **Babbitt's Delicatessen** features sandwiches, salads and fried-chicken box lunches to go or eat on the premises. ~ BUDGET.

There are two other cafeterias in the park—the **Maswik Cafeteria** at Maswik Lodge, at the west end of Grand Canyon Village, and the **Desert View Snack Shop**. Both serve a changing selection of hot meals. ~ Located 23 miles east of the village along the East Rim Drive. BUDGET.

Ice cream, hot dogs and soft drinks are available at the **Hermit's Rest Snack Bar** at the end of the West Rim Drive as well as at the **Bright Angel Fountain,** which is open only during summer, near the trailhead for the Bright Angel Trail. BUDGET.

Outside the park entrance, the town of Tusayan has nearly a dozen eating establishments ranging from McDonald's to the beautiful **Moqui Lodge Dining Room,** which specializes in Mexican food. ~ Tusayan; 520-638-2424. MODERATE.

SHOPPING Of several national park concession tourist stores on the South Rim, the best are **Hopi House,** the large Indian pueblo replica across from El Tovar Hotel, and the adjacent **Verkamp's Curios.** Both have been in continuous operation for almost a century and specialize in authentic American Indian handicrafts, with high standards of quality and some genuinely old pieces.

Other Grand Canyon shops, at least as interesting for their historic architecture as their wares, include the old **Kolb Studio,** originally a 1904 photographic studio and now a bookstore, and the **Lookout Studio,** which has rock specimens and conventional curios. Both are in Grand Canyon Village. Another souvenir shop is the **Hermit's Rest Gift Shop** ~ End of West Rim Drive. With more of the same is the **Desert View Watchtower** ~ East Rim Drive.

NIGHTLIFE **Bright Angel Lodge** offers live weekly entertainment—usually a folk guitarist—and **El Tovar Lounge** has a piano bar. In general, though, Grand Canyon National Park does not have much in the way of hot nightlife. We suggest taking in one of the ranger-produced slide shows presented in the amphitheaters on both the North Rim and the South Rim or simply sitting in the dark along the canyon rim and listening to the vast, deep silence.

▼▼▼▼▼▼▼▼▼▼
The North Rim The North Rim of the Grand Canyon receives only about one-tenth of the number of visitors the South Rim gets. Snowbound during the winter because it is 1200 feet higher in elevation, the North Rim is only open from mid-May through October, while the South Rim is open year-round. The South Rim is much more convenient for more travelers since it is much closer to a major interstate highway route and to the large population centers of southern Arizona and California. But if your tour of the Southwest includes destinations such as the Navajo Indian Reservation, Lake Powell, Bryce Canyon and Zion national parks—or even Las Vegas, then your route will take you closer to the North Rim, giving you an opportunity to explore the cooler, quieter side of the canyon.

The **North Rim** (day-use fee, $10 per vehicle) does not have the long, heavily traveled scenic drives that the South Rim has. The main road into the park dead-ends at the lodge and other tourist facilities at one of the park's most popular overlooks, **Bright Angel Point**. The only other paved road is **Cape Royal Scenic Drive**, a 15-mile trip through stately ponderosa pine forest that takes you to several of the national park's most beautiful viewpoints—**Point Imperial, Vista Encantadora, Walhalla Overlook** and **Cape Royal**. Another road, unpaved and only passable in a high-clearance vehicle, runs 17 miles to **Point Sublime**. Other viewpoints on the North Rim are reached by foot trails. (For more information on these trails, see the "Hiking" section at the end of the chapter.)

Extremely adventuresome motorists can visit a separate area along the North Rim of the Grand Canyon, Toroweap Point, by leaving Route 89A at Fredonia, about 75 miles north of the North Rim entrance. Don't forget to fill up the gas tank in Fredonia, because you won't see another gas station for nearly 200 miles. Next, proceed west from Fredonia for 14 miles on Route 389 to **Pipe Spring National Monument**. Take time to see the monument. The remote, fortresslike old Mormon ranching outpost, which had the only telegraph station in the Arizona Territory north of the Grand Canyon, was home to the Winsor family and their employees, thus its historical nickname, Winsor Castle. The ranch buildings and equipment are well preserved, and the duck pond provides a cool oasis. Park rangers costumed in period dress re-create the pioneer lifestyle during the summer months. Admission. ~ Route 389; 520-643-7105.

The layers of rock exposed by erosion on the walls of the Grand Canyon range from 250 million to more than two billion years in age, the oldest exposed rock on earth.

Backtracking, nine miles from the Fredonia turnoff and six miles before you reach Pipe Springs, an unpaved road turns off to the south. It goes 67 miles to the most remote point that can be reached by motor vehicle on the Grand Canyon rim. The road is wide and well maintained, easily passable by passenger car, but very isolated. You will not find a telephone or any other sign of habitation anywhere along the way. You may not see another car all day. Several other dirt roads branch off along the way, but if you keep to the road that goes straight ahead and looks well used, following the "Toroweap" and "Grand Canyon National Monument" signs whenever you see them, it's hard to get lost. Have fun experiencing this wide-open countryside as empty as all of Arizona used to be long ago.

◄ HIDDEN

There is a small, primitive campground at **Toroweap Point** but no water. As likely as not, you may find that you have the place all to yourself. The elevation is 2000 feet lower than at the main North Rim visitor area, so instead of pine forest the vegetation

Text continued on page 52.

Touring the Grand Canyon

It seems like there are more ways to explore the Grand Canyon than there are routes down its walls. Hikers, mule riders, aviators and even white-water enthusiasts have all discovered its sporting opportunities.

Of course the most rigorous way to tour the famous chasm is by *hiking*. If you have the time, making your way by foot down to the bottom is an amazing experience. Be forewarned—it is impossible to complete the journey in a day; people are often airlifted out for trying. Rest stops with shade and refreshing cold water are scattered intermittently along the trails. Plan ahead and camp or stay at the Phantom Ranch. (Do not arrive at the Phantom Ranch without reservations!)

For a taste of the Old West, mules are a classic mode of transport. *Mule trips* range from one-day excursions that venture as far as Plateau Point to two- and three-day trips to the bottom of the canyon. The cost is several hundred dollars per person, including meals and accommodations at the Phantom Ranch. Mule trips depart from both the North and South rims. Reservations must be made well ahead of time—as much as a year in advance for weekends, holidays and the summer months. For South Rim departures, contact **Grand Canyon National Park Lodges**. ~ 14001 East Iliff Avenue, Suite 600, Aurora, CO 80014; 303-297-2757, fax 303-297-3175. For North Rim departures, call **Grand Canyon Trail Rides**. ~ P.O. Box 128, Tropic, UT 84776; 801-679-8665.

Many *"flightseeing"* tours offer spectacular eagle-eye views of the Grand Canyon. **Grand Canyon Airlines'** fully narrated tour circles the canyon starting at the South Rim and offers views of the Painted Desert and the confluence of the Colorado and Little Colorado rivers. ~ P.O. Box 3038, Grand Canyon, AZ 86023; 520-638-2407. With **Air Grand Canyon** you can choose from four different trips ranging from a 30-minute tour of the Eastern Gorge and the confluence of the Colorado and Little Colorado rivers to a 100-minute flight that visits all the major canyon sights. ~ P.O. Box 3399, Grand Canyon, AZ 86023; 520-638-2686. **Windrock Aviation** also offers four tours ranging from 30 to 100 minutes. ~ P.O. Box 3125, Grand Canyon, AZ 86023; 520-638-

9591. All of these companies operate from Grand Canyon Airport near Tusayan.

Even more thrilling—and more expensive—are *helicopter tours*. Helicopters can fly considerably lower than airplanes, affording an even closer look at the magnificent canyon. Neither helicopters nor planes are allowed to fly beneath the rim, however, keeping the canyon peaceful for hikers and riders. The 45-minute Imperial Flight offered by **Papillon Grand Canyon Helicopters** affords views of the Painted Desert, Marble Canyon and Dragon's Corridor. The shorter North Canyon flight explores the Central Corridor. ~ P.O. Box 455, Grand Canyon, AZ 86023; 520-638-2419. **Kenai Helicopters'** 30-minute and 50-minute tours start at the West Rim and cross the canyon to visit the major sights. ~ P.O. Box 1429, Grand Canyon, AZ 86023; 520-638-2412. With **AirStar Helicopters** you can choose the 30-minute Central Corridor tour, the 45-minute Eastern Canyon tour or a 60-minute tour combining the two. ~ P.O. Box 3379, Grand Canyon, AZ 86023; 520-638-2622.

If simply looking at the bottom of the canyon isn't enough, water adventurers might consider a *rafting trip* down the Colorado River. Raft trips operate from April through October. Most start at Lee's Ferry, northeast of the national park boundary near Page, Arizona, and just below Glen Canyon Dam. The rafts are motorized, with pontoons, and provide seating for about 14 people.

More exciting are the smaller oar-operated dories that ride closer to the water and occasionally tip over in the rough rapids. Rafting the full length of the canyon, 280 miles from Lee's Ferry to Lake Mead, takes a leisurely eight days, providing plenty of time to hike and explore remote parts of the canyon inaccessible by other means. Many rafting companies also offer shorter trips that involve being picked up or dropped off by helicopter part way through the canyon.

One of the leading raft tour companies is **Grand Canyon Expeditions**. ~ P.O. Box O, Kanab, UT 84741; 801-644-2691. Another good organization is **Arizona River Runners**. ~ P.O. Box 47788, Phoenix, AZ 85068; 520-867-4866. A complete list of river trip outfitters is available from the South Rim visitors center. ~ 520-638-7888. Private parties can take the river route through the Grand Canyon. Contact the South Rim visitors center for information.

around Toroweap Point is desert scrub. Being closer to the river, still some 3000 feet below, you can watch the parade of river rafts drifting past and even eavesdrop on passengers' conversations.

LODGING   On the North Rim, the only lodging within the park is the **Grand Canyon Lodge,** which consists of a beautiful 1930s-vintage main lodge building overlooking the canyon and a number of cabins— some rustic, others modern, a few with canyon views. Clean and homelike, both rooms and cabins have an old-fashioned feel, though they can be a little noisy. North Rim accommodations are in very high demand, so reservations should be made far ahead. They are accepted up to 23 months in advance. Reservations for the lodge are booked through TW Recreational Services Inc., which also handles reservations for the lodges at Bryce Canyon and Zion national parks. The lodge is closed during winter and early spring. ~ Lodge: 520-638-2611, fax 520-638-2554. Reservations: 14001 East Iliff Avenue, Suite 600, Aurora, CO 80014; 303-297-2757, fax 303-297-3175. MODERATE.

Aside from the national park lodge, the closest accommodations to the North Rim are 44 miles away at **Jacob Lake Inn.** This small, rustic resort complex surrounded by national forest offers both motel rooms and cabins, including some two-bedroom units. Again, reservations should be made well in advance. ~ 520-643-7232. MODERATE.

DINING   The **Grand Canyon Lodge Dining Room** offers breakfast, lunch and dinner at moderate prices. The food is good, conventional meat-and-potatoes fare and the atmosphere—a spacious, rustic log-beamed dining room with huge picture windows overlooking the canyon—is simply incomparable. Reservations are required for dinner. The lodge also operates a budget-priced snack shop serving breakfast, lunch and dinner in plain, simple surroundings, as well as a saloon offering pizza and sandwiches. Nearby, the camper store sells pizza sandwiches. ~ 520-638-2611. BUDGET TO MODERATE.

PARKS   **KAIBAB NATIONAL FOREST**   This 1,500,000-acre expanse of pine, fir, spruce and aspen forest includes both sides of the Grand Canyon outside the park boundaries. Most recreational facilities are located near the North Rim, where they supplement the park's limited camping facilities. There are restrictions for boating so call ahead. Wildlife in the forest includes mule deer, wild turkeys, several other bird species and even a few bison. Picnic areas, restrooms and a visitors center; day-use fee, $10. The facilities in the forest close from about October to April. ~ The national forest visitors center is at Jacob Lake, the intersection of Routes 89A and 67. Jacob Lake Campground is at the same location, while Demotte Campground is 30 miles south on Route 67, about five miles from the national park entrance; 520-635-4061.

▲ Demotte Campground has 22 sites, $10 per night, and Jacob Lake Campground has 53 sites, $10 per night; information, 520-643-7395. RV hookups are available at the privately owned Jacob Lake RV Park, $16 to $18 a night per vehicle with two persons. ~ 520-643-7804.

LEE'S FERRY, GLEN CANYON NATIONAL RECREATION AREA 🚶 ⛵

Halfway along the most direct route between the North Rim and South Rim of the Grand Canyon, this beach area on the river below Glen Canyon Dam makes a good picnic or camping spot. It is situated at the confluence of the Colorado and Paria rivers, which often have distinctly different colors, giving the water a strange two-toned appearance. Historically, Lee's Ferry was the first crossing point on the Colorado River, established by John D. Lee in 1871. Lee, a Mormon, was a fugitive at the time, wanted by federal authorities for organizing the massacre of a non-Mormon wagon train from Arkansas. He lived here with one of his 17 wives for several years before federal marshals found and killed him. Today, Lee's Ferry is the departure point for raft trips into the Grand Canyon. Shaded picnic tables and restrooms; groceries are 65 miles away in Page. ~ Located in Marble Canyon about five miles off Route 89A, 85 miles from the North Rim entrance to Grand Canyon National Park and 104 miles from the east entrance to the South Rim; 520-645-2471. To reach Lee's Ferry Campground, take Lee's Ferry Road north about three miles from Marble Canyon. Wahweep Campground and Wahweep RV Park are located off Route 89, one mile north of Page. Page Lake Powell Campground is located half a mile outside of Page on Route 98.

▲ Within Glen Canyon National Recreation Area, **Lee's Ferry Campground** has 52 tent/RV sites (no hookups); $10 per night. **Wahweep Campground** with 708 sites, $10 per night, and **Wahweep RV Park** with 123 sites, $22 per night, are privately owned. ~ 520-645-2433. Another privately owned campground is **Page Lake Powell Campground** with 105 sites; $15 per night for tents and $17 to $20 per night for hookups. ~ 520-645-3374.

▼▼▼▼▼▼▼▼▼▼▼▼▼▼
Outdoor Adventures

RIDING STABLES

At the Grand Canyon, the **Moqui Lodge stable** in Tusayan, near the park's south entrance, offers a selection of guided rides to various points along the South Rim. Most popular is the four-hour East Rim ride, which winds through Long Jim Canyon to a viewpoint overlooking the Grand Canyon. One- and two-hour rides are also available. Horseback rides do not go below the canyon rim. ~ 520-638-2891.

For information on mule trips into the canyon, see "Touring the Grand Canyon" in this chapter.

BIKING   Although trails within the national park are closed to bicycles, Kaibab National Forest surrounding the park on both the North and South Rims offers a wealth of mountain biking possibilities. The forest areas adjoining Grand Canyon National Park are laced with old logging roads and the relatively flat terrain makes for low-stress riding.

SOUTH RIM   Located at the South Rim of the Grand Canyon, the **West Rim Drive** is closed to private motor vehicles during the summer months but open to bicycles. This fairly level route, 16 miles round-trip, makes for a spectacular cycling tour. One ride the National Forest Service recommends in the vicinity of the South Rim is the **Coconino Rim Trail** (9.2 miles), a loop trail, which starts near Grandview Point and travels southeast through ponderosa forests.

For other suggestions, stop in at the Tusayan Ranger Station just outside the South Rim entrance or the National Forest Information Booth at Jacob Lake or contact Kaibab National Forest Headquarters. ~ 800 South 6th Street, Williams, AZ 86046; 520-635-2681.

NORTH RIM   Toward the west end of the Grand Canyon on its North Rim, visitors to **Toroweap Point** will find endless mountain biking opportunities along the hundreds of miles of remote, unpaved roads in the Arizona Strip.

HIKING   The ultimate hiking experience in Grand Canyon National Park— and perhaps in the entire Southwest—is an expedition from either rim to the bottom of the canyon and back. With an elevation change of 4800 feet from the South Rim to the river, or 5800 feet from the North Rim, the hike is as ambitious as an ascent of a major Rocky Mountain peak, except that the greatest effort is required in the last miles of the climb out, when leg muscles may already be sore from the long downhill trek. Strenuous as it may be, hiking the Grand Canyon is an experience sure to stay vivid for a lifetime.

Though some people claim to have done it, hiking round-trip from the rim to river level and back in a single day is a monumental feat that takes from 16 to 18 hours. Most hikers who plan to go the whole way will want to plan at least two, preferably three, days for the trip. A wilderness permit, required for any overnight trip into the park back country, can be obtained free of charge at the backcountry office on either rim.

SOUTH RIM   The **Bright Angel Trail** (7.8 miles to the river or 9.3 miles to Phantom Ranch), the most popular trail in the canyon, starts at Grand Canyon Village on the South Rim, near the mule corral. It has the most developed facilities, including resthouses with emergency phones along the upper part of the trail and a ranger station, water and a campground midway down at Indian Garden where the Havasupai people used to grow crops. The one-day round-trip hike will take you along a ridgeline to Plateau Point, overlooking the Colorado River from 1300 feet above, just before the final steep descent. Allow about five hours to hike from the rim down to the river and about ten hours to climb back up. It is therefore advisable to camp and make the return trip the following day. Remember, a permit is required for overnight trips. A lot of hikers use this trail, as do daily mule riders—not the route to take if you seek solitude.

Accommodations in the Grand Canyon are in great demand, so if you're planning to stay, be sure to make reservations way in advance.

Another major trail from the South Rim is the **South Kaibab Trail** (7 miles to Phantom Ranch), which starts from the trailhead on East Rim Drive, four-and-a-half miles from Grand Canyon Village. The shortest of the main trails into the canyon, it is also the steepest, and due to lack of water and shade along the route, it is not recommended during the summer months.

Several less-used trails also descend from the South Rim. All of them intersect the **Tonto Trail** (95 miles), which runs along the edge of the inner gorge about 1300 feet above river level. The **Grandview Trail** (3 miles), an old mine access route that starts at Grandview Point on East Rim Drive, goes down to Horseshoe Mesa where it joins a loop of the Tonto Trail that circles the mesa, passing ruins of an old copper mine. There is a primitive campground on the mesa.

The **Hermit Trail** (8.5 miles) begins at Hermit's Rest at the end of West Rim Drive and descends to join the Tonto Trail. Branching off from the Dripping Springs Trail, which also starts at Hermit's Rest, the **Boucher Trail** (11 miles) also goes down to join the Tonto Trail and is considered one of the more difficult hiking trails in the park. Ask for details at the rangers' counter in the South Rim visitor center.

The paved, handicapped-accessible **Rim Trail** (1.5 miles) goes between the Kolb Studio at the west side of Grand Canyon Village and the Yavapai Observation Station. A one-third-mile spur links the Rim Trail with the visitor center. At each end of the designated Rim Trail, the pavement ends but unofficial trails continue for several more miles, ending at Hopi Point near the Powell Memorial on West Rim Drive and at Yaki Point, the trailhead for the South Kaibab Trail, on East Rim Drive.

NORTH RIM The main trail into the canyon from the North Rim is the **North Kaibab Trail** (14.2 miles). The trail starts from the trailhead two miles north of Grand Canyon Lodge and descends abruptly down Roaring Springs Canyon for almost five miles to

Bright Angel Creek. This is the steepest part of the trip. Where the trail reaches the creek, there are several swimming holes, a good destination for a one-day round trip. The trail then follows the creek all the way to Phantom Ranch at the bottom of the canyon. Park rangers recommend that hikers allow a full day to hike from the rim to the ranch and two days to climb back to the rim, stopping overnight at Cottonwood Camp, the midway point. Because of heavy snows on the rim, the trail is only open from mid-May through mid-October.

Without descending below the canyon rim, hikers can choose from a variety of trails ranging from short scenic walks to all-day hikes. The easy, paved, handicapped-accessible **Transept Trail** (2 miles) runs between the campground and the lodge, then continues gradually downward to Bright Angel Point, which affords the best view of the Bright Angel Trail down into the canyon.

The **Uncle Jim Trail** (2.5 miles) starts at the same trailhead as the Roaring Springs Canyon fork of the Bright Angel Trail, two miles north of the lodge. It circles through the ponderosa woods to an overlook, Uncle Jim Point.

The **Ken Patrick Trail** (10 miles) forks off the Uncle Jim Trail, continuing straight as the shorter trail turns south, and eventually reaches a remote point on the rim where it descends to follow Bright Angel Creek and eventually joins the Bright Angel Trail. It is possible to make a strenuous, all-day 15-mile loop trip of the Ken Patrick Trail and the upper portion of the Bright Angel Trail.

A quiet North Rim trail that leads through the forest to a remote canyon viewpoint is the **Widforss Trail** (5 miles), named after artist Gunnar Widforss, who painted landscapes in the national parks during the 1920s. The trail winds along the lip of the plateau through scrubby oak, piñon pines, ponderosa pines and juniper. The viewpoint overlooks a side canyon known as Haunted Canyon.

HIDDEN ►

Visitors to remote Toroweap Point may wish to try the **Lava Falls Trail** (2 miles), which begins as a jeep road midway between the old ranger station and the point. Although this trail is not long, it is rocky, edgy and very steep, descending 2500 feet to the Colorado River and the "falls"—actually a furious stretch of white water formed when lava spilled into the river. Allow all day for the round-trip hike and do not attempt it during the hot months.

▼▼▼▼▼▼▼▼▼▼
Transportation

CAR

The Grand Canyon's North Rim is at the end of **Route 67**, which forks off of **Route 89A** at the resort village of Jacob Lake. It is more than 150 miles from the nearest interstate highway—**Route 15**, taking Exit 15 north of St. George, Utah—but is within an easy morning's drive of either Zion National Park or Bryce Canyon National Park (see Chapter Fourteen) or Lake Powell (see Chapter Fifteen).

Although only 12 miles of straight-line distance separate them, the shortest driving distance between the North Rim and South Rim visitors areas of the Grand Canyon is 216 miles around the eastern end of the canyon via Route 67, Route 89A, **Route 89** and **Route 64**, crossing the Colorado River at Navajo Bridge. The only other alternative for driving from rim to rim is to go by way of Las Vegas, Nevada—a trip of more than 500 miles.

From Route 40, eastbound motorists can reach Grand Canyon Village on the South Rim by exiting at Williams and driving 57 miles north on Route 64 and **Route 180**. Westbound travelers, leaving the interstate at Flagstaff, have a choice between the more direct way to Grand Canyon Village, 79 miles via Route 180, or the longer way, 105 miles via Route 89 and Route 64, which parallels the canyon rim for 25 miles. These routes combine perfectly into a spectacular loop trip from Flagstaff.

AIR

Flights can be booked from most major cities to **Grand Canyon Airport**, which is located near Tusayan just outside the south entrance to the national park. Airlines that fly there include Air Nevada, Air Vegas, Alpha Air, Argosy Airlines, Arizona Pacific, Eagle Canyon and Scenic Airlines. A shuttle service runs hourly between the airport and Grand Canyon Village.

BUS

Nava-Hopi Xpress provides bus service to the Grand Canyon South Rim, as well as Flagstaff, Williams and Phoenix. ~ 114 West Santa Fe Avenue, Flagstaff; 520-774-5003. **Trans Canyon Shuttle** operates a daily shuttle bus service between the two rims of Grand Canyon National Park. ~ Tusayan; 520-638-2820.

CAR RENTALS

The only car-rental agency at the Grand Canyon Airport is **Budget Rent A Car**. ~ 800-527-0700.

THREE

Northeastern Arizona

East of the Grand Canyon stretches a land of sandstone monuments and steep-walled canyons that turns vermilion by dawn or dusk, a land of foreign languages and ancient traditions, of sculptured mesas and broad rocky plateaus, of pine forests and high deserts. This is the heart of the Southwest's Indian Country. It is home to the Navajos, the biggest American Indian tribe, and the Hopis, one of the most traditional. To them belongs the top northeastern third of Arizona, 150 miles in length and 200 miles across the state. In addition to this impressive expanse, Navajoland spills into New Mexico, Utah and Colorado.

Here, by horseback or jeep, on foot or in cars, visitors can explore the stark beauty of the land, delve into its uninterrupted centuries of history, then dine on mutton stew and crispy blue-corn piki bread. You can watch dances little changed in centuries or shop for a stunning array of crafts in American Indian homes, galleries and trading posts dating back to the end of the Civil War. And here, in the pit houses, pueblos and cliff dwellings of people who have occupied this land for 12,000 years, are more remnants of prehistoric American Indian life than anywhere else in the United States.

Five generations of archaeologists have sifted through ruins left by the region's dominant prehistoric culture, the Anasazi—Navajo for "ancient ones." None are more beautiful or haunting than Betatakin and Keet Seel at Navajo National Monument, 45 miles due north of today's Hopi mesas.

Hopi traditions today offer insights about life in those older cities. Traditional and independent, most villages are run by their religious chiefs. Each maintains an ancient, complex, year-long dance cycle tied to the renewal and fertility of the land they regard with reverence. As one Hopi leader put it, the land is "the Hopi's social security." Their multistoried architecture, much of it set within the protection of caves, has influenced many 20th-century architects.

Surrounding the Hopis is Navajoland, the largest Indian reservation in the United States. At 26,000 square miles, it is twice the size of Israel. Unlike the village-dwelling Hopis, most of the 200,000 Navajos still live in far-flung family compounds—a house, a hogan, a trailer or two, near their corrals and fields. (Some clans still follow their livestock to suitable grazing lands as seasons change.)

This is both an arid, sun-baked desert and verdant forested land, all of it situated on the southeastern quarter of the Colorado Plateau. At elevations of 4500 to 8000 feet above sea level, summer temperatures average in the 80s. July through September is monsoon season, when clear skies suddenly fill with clouds that turn a thunderous lightning-streaked black. These localized, brief, intense summer rains bearing wondrous smells have been courted by Hopi rituals for centuries and are crucial to the survival of their farms.

For the modern adventurer, September and October can be the most alluring months to visit—uncrowded, less expensive, sunny, crisp, with splashes of fall color.

The Colorado Plateau is famous for its rainbow-colored canyons and monuments that have been cut by rivers and eroded by weather. Erosion's jewels here are Monument Valley on the Arizona-Utah border, a stunning pocket of towering red spires, bluffs and sand dunes, and Canyon de Chelly, a trio of red-rock canyons that form the heart of Navajo country.

At Navajoland's southernmost boundary, the world's densest, most colorful petrified logs dot Petrified Forest National Park. They're located amid bare hills that look like they were spray painted by a giant artist and aptly named the Painted Desert.

This mesmerizing geography serves as a backdrop to the region's riveting history. Navajos probably began arriving from the north a century or two before the Spaniards rode in from the south in the 1540s. The conquistadors brought horses, sheep, peaches, melons, guns and silversmithing—all of which would dramatically change the lives of the indigenous Indians. The Navajos had arrived in small groups, nomadic hunters, primitive compared to their Pueblo neighbors.

Cultural anthropologists now believe the turning point in Navajo history followed the Pueblo Indian Revolt of 1680 when all the village-dwelling Indians of the Southwest united to push the hated Spanish out of what is now New Mexico. When the Spaniards returned a dozen years later, heavily armed and promising slavery for unyielding villagers, many Pueblo people from the Rio Grande fled west to the canyons of Navajo country, intermarrying and living as neighbors for three-quarters of a century.

During that time the Navajos grew in wealth due to their legendary raiding parties—helping themselves to Indian- or Anglo-owned sheep, horses and slaves. By the late 1700s, a much-changed race of part Athabascan and part Pueblo blood—the Dineh, Navajo for "the people"—had emerged. Powerful horsemen, wealthy sheepherders and farmers, they had developed a complex mythology and had surpassed their Pueblo teachers at the craft of weaving.

Navajo "shopping spree" raids continued along the Spanish, Mexican and Anglo frontiers. The United States army built Fort Defiance, near present-day Window Rock, and dispatched Colonel Kit Carson to end the incursions. Carson's tactic was to starve the Navajos out of Canyon de Chelly and neighboring areas

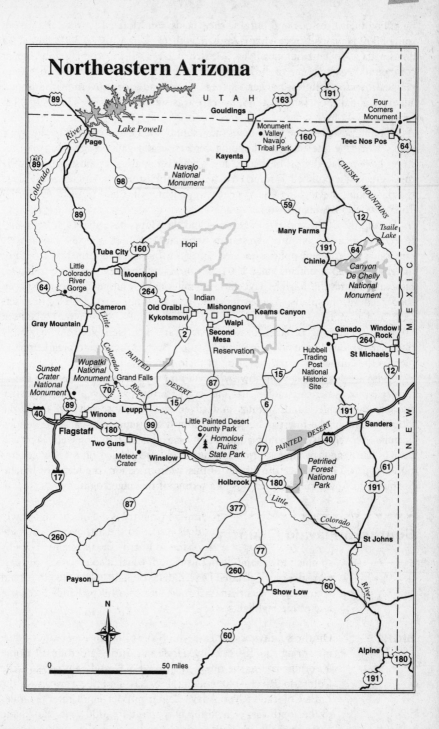

Northeastern Arizona

by killing their livestock and burning their fields. On March 14, 1864, the first of some 8000 Navajos began what is known as their "long walk"—300 miles at 15 miles a day—to Fort Sumner, New Mexico. Here a 40-square-mile government compound became home to the Navajo for four of their bitterest years. They were plagued by crop failures, hunger, sickness, death and gross government mismanagement. Finally, on June 1, 1868, a treaty was signed, and some 7000 survivors moved back home.

Trading posts became the Indians' new supply source and conduit to the white man's world. While modern shopping centers, crafts galleries and convenience stores have replaced most of them, a few originals remain. The most famous is the rural, creek-side Hubbell Trading Post, a National Historic Site at Ganado. Others worth seeking out include Oljeto near Monument Valley and posts at Cameron, Tuba City and Keams Canyon.

During the 20th century the Navajos and the Hopis have moved from a subsistence to a cash economy. The Indian Reorganization Act of 1934 ended overt repressive government policies toward American Indians and launched an era of increased self-government. Since 1961, when oil and coal reserves were found on reservation lands, both tribes have parlayed millions of resulting dollars into paved roads, schools, hospitals, civic centers, low-cost housing, expanded electrical services and running water for more homes. Three mines, three power plants, a 60,000-acre farming project, forest industries and scattered electronic assembly plants are gradually providing jobs for Navajos. But the most widespread employment is the cottage industry—creation of their own arts and crafts.

Today in every village and town you will find the rich and wonderfully evolving legacy of American Indian arts and crafts. From the Navajo—weavings respected worldwide, sandpaintings and silver and turquoise jewelry. From the Hopis—some of the finest pottery in the Southwest, superb carvings of wooden kachinas, woven basketry and plaques and masterful incised silver jewelry. You will hear Indian languages and see rich spiritual traditions carried on by new generations. You will experience the history of this Western region, the blend of Indian, Spanish and Anglo cultures. All this in a setting of striking geography.

▼▼▼▼▼▼▼▼▼▼▼▼▼▼▼▼▼▼▼

Southern Navajo Country

Indian Country is a concept that barely does justice to the astonishing diversity of the southern Navajo realm. There is so much to see and do in this region, which also embraces the pastel realm of the Painted Desert, that you may be tempted to extend your stay. Ancient Anasazi ruins and colorful badlands are just a few of the highlights.

SIGHTS
On the southwest corner of the Navajo Indian Reservation, during spring runoff—usually March and April—a detour off Route 40 brings you to the thundering, muddy **Grand Falls** of the Little Colorado River—plummeting 185 feet into the canyon of the Little Colorado River. A lava flow from Merriam Crater ten miles to the southwest created the falls about 100,000 years ago. Some years the falls are only a trickle, and even during the best years

they dry up by May, resuming again briefly during abundant summer monsoons. It is wise to inquire in Winslow or Flagstaff about the level of the Little Colorado River before making the trip. To get there, turn off Route 40 either at Winona, 17 miles northeast of Flagstaff to Route 15, or at the Leupp Junction (Route 99), ten miles west of Winslow to Route 15. Either way, ask at the turnoff for exact directions. The Winona route is the shortest from the highway—about 20 miles, the last eight unpaved.

Many locals contend the most colorful and dramatic concentration of Painted Desert hills in central Arizona is at **Little Painted Desert County Park**, 15 miles north of Winslow. A two-mile scenic rim drive, a hiking trail and picnic tables overlook this vast basin where clay and silt deposited by ancient rivers have eroded into gray, red, purple, ochre and white striped badlands—300 feet to 400 feet tall. Colors are most vivid at dawn and dusk. ~ Route 87; 520-524-4250.

◄ HIDDEN

The scattered broken pottery, rock drawings and crumbling walls speak with quiet eloquence of an ancient past at **Homolovi Ruins State Park** three miles east of Winslow. The park contains four major 14th-century pueblos of 40 to 2000 rooms, with over 300 identified archaeological sites, a visitors center and museum where interpretive programs are presented. Nine miles of paved roads and a mile of hiking trails lead to the two largest village ruins, inhabited between 1150 and 1450 A.D. The park also includes petroglyphs and a pithouse village dating from 600 to 900 A.D. Hopis believe this was home to their ancestors just before they migrated north to today's mesas. They still consider the ruins—located on both sides of the Little Colorado River—sacred and leave *pahos* (prayer feathers) for the spirits. Admission. ~ Route 87; 520-289-4106.

Winslow, the hub of Northeastern Arizona, is a railroad town and was an early trade center. Its current history goes back to Mormon pioneers who arrived in 1876 and built a small rock fort known as Brigham City, as well as a few other small settlements. The town grew, and soon a water system, stores and an opera house appeared, along with a school, saloons and, that harbinger of all frontier civilizations, sidewalks. The Aztec Land and Cattle Company purchased a million acres of land from the railroad in the late 1800s and thousands of head of cattle were brought in to be handled by local cowboys. The town was incorporated in 1900. For information contact **Winslow Chamber of Commerce**. ~ 300 West North Road; 520-289-2434.

The **Old Trail Museum** houses changing exhibits related to Winslow's history, including American Indian and pioneering artifacts, and a collection of railroad and Route 66 memorabilia. Closed Sunday and Monday. ~ 212 Kinsley Avenue, Winslow; 520-289-5861.

To the east of Winslow on Route 40 you'll come to **Holbrook**. Headquarters for the Sitgreaves National Forest, Holbrook was named for H. R. Holbrook, first engineer of the Atlantic and Pacific Railroad, forerunner of the Santa Fe Line. It was once a tough cowboy town—the Aztec Land and Cattle Company drove cattle here, a rough-and-tough bunch that shot up everything and earned the name the Hashknife Posse. There are probably more people still wearing ten-gallon hats and cowboy boots here than in any other small town in the West.

The **Courthouse Museum** is located in the historic Navajo County Courthouse, which flourished from 1898 until 1976. It's now a museum focusing on Holbrook's past, including the town's original one-piece iron jail. It also houses the Holbrook Tourism Information Center. Closed Saturday and Sunday. ~ 100 East Arizona Street, Holbrook; 520-524-6558.

The signs advertising sale of "gems" and "petrified wood" on every other block in Holbrook offers a good clue that **Petrified Forest National Park** can't be far away. Entrances at the northern and southern gateways to this park are located 26 miles east of Holbrook—the northern entrance on Route 40, the southern one on Route 180. Either one launches you on the park's 28-mile scenic drive. Frequent pullouts let you walk amid two stunning marvels of nature. The park lies within the colorful, heavily eroded mudstone and siltstone known as the Painted Desert. The southern third is also home to the world's densest concentration of petrified forest—ancient logs that crystallized 200 million years ago now lie strewn along the surface; others yet unseen lie buried in 300 feet of rock. Admission. ~ 520-524-6228.

Continue on the scenic drive from the Route 40 (north) entrance to the **Painted Desert Visitors Center**. Here you'll see a 17-minute film on the mysteries of the making of the forest—silica crystals replacing wood cells in the cone-bearing trees—aricarioxylon pine.

✔ **CHECK THESE OUT—UNIQUE SIGHTS**

- Marvel at the Hopi murals and the hand-carved wood furnishings inside the **Painted Desert Inn Museum,** a 1930s pueblo-style building that was once a Fred Harvey Hotel. *page 65*
- Give the locals a small tip and you will be escorted to the impressions left by a 20-foot-long Dilophasaurus at **Dinosaur Tracks**. *page 70*
- Appreciate how Window Rock got its name when you see **Tseghahodzani,** "the rock with a hole in it." *page 81*
- Cruise by the natural roadside attraction, **Elephant Feet,** a sandstone formation resembling the legs and feet of elephants. *page 89*

The center also offers cafeteria and gift-shop amenities. ~ Route 40; 520-524-6228.

North of Route 40, eight overlooks highlight different Painted Desert panoramas. Here you'll see bands of red, white and pink—the effect of the sun reflecting on mudstone and siltstone stained by iron, magnesium and other minerals. Colors are the most intense nearest sunrise, sunset or on cloudy days.

The **Painted Desert Inn Museum** is a 1930s pueblo-style building, once a Fred Harvey inn. Detailed hand-carved wood and tin furnishings were made by the CCC. Murals painted by the late Hopi artist Fred Kabotie depict scenes of Hopi life: a January buffalo dance to ensure return of buffalo each spring, the journey of two Hopis to Zuni lands to gather salt. ~ Three miles north of the visitors center at Kachina Point on the scenic drive; 520-524-2550.

South of Route 40 on the scenic drive, the park's midsection contains prehistoric sites of ancient American Indian cultures dating from 300 A.D. to 1400 A.D. Scientists have discovered petroglyphs here used as solar calendars. A trail at Puerco Indian Ruins, the first pullout south of Route 40, leads through pueblo ruins occupied until about 1400 A.D. A few excavated rooms are partially restored, and an overlook gives views of Newspaper Rock, a sandstone block covered with petroglyphs.

The first petrified wood occurs at Blue Mesa, where a trail leads through dramatic towering hills. The southern third of the park holds the greatest concentration of petrified logs. At **Jasper Forest Overlook** you'll see a petrified log jam, some logs complete with root systems indicating they had grown nearby. A trail at Crystal Forest leads you close to dense pockets of logs, many over 100 feet long and a foot or two in diameter. In 1886, on a $10 bet, a daring cowboy rode his steed across a treacherous divide spanned by petrified Long Log, now shored up with cement.

At **Rainbow Forest Museum**, photographs, drawings and samples tell the story of the area's geologic and human history. Outside, the half-mile-long Giant Logs trail leads past enormous rainbow-hued trees. The scenic drive ends two miles farther south at Route 180. ~ Two miles in from Route 180, near the park's southern entrance; 520-524-6822.

Check in at **Petrified Forest Gift Shop** to pick up sample minerals, geodes (cut on the premises) and petrified wood. Popular with commercial petrified-wood and gem buffs, some 200,000 pounds are collected here annually. ~ Route 180, 19 miles southeast of Holbrook; 520-524-3470.

◄ HIDDEN

LODGING

The top two hotels in Winslow are both Best Westerns. The two-story **Adobe Inn** has 72 rooms, each decorated in typical motel fashion. You'll find a café and an indoor pool on the premises. ~

1701 North Park Drive, Winslow; 520-289-4638, 800-528-1234, fax 520-289-5514. MODERATE.

On the western edge of town, the **Town House Lodge** has 68 rooms with modern furnishings all on the first floor. Amenities include a laundry, an outdoor pool and a restaurant. ~ 1914 West 3rd Street, Winslow; 602-289-4611, 800-528-1234. MODERATE.

Fifteen dazzling white stucco wigwams, the sort of kitsch old Route 66 was famous for, are found in Holbrook. They make up one of the world's most novel motels, and affordable yet! **Wigwam Motel and Curios** "is the funnest place I've ever slept," insisted our three-year-old neighbor. We couldn't argue. Built in 1950 by Chester Lewis (six other cities had wigwam motels of similar design; only one other survives), the wigwams were restored by his children and grandchildren who still operate them. Inside each, matching red-plaid curtains and bedspreads adorn original handmade hickory furniture. Scenes from Tony Hillerman's *Dark Wind* were filmed here in 1990. There's no extra charge for lulling vibrations as trains rumble by in the night. ~ 811 West Hopi Drive, Holbrook; 520-524-3048. BUDGET.

For a more traditional resting spot there's the **Adobe Inn**, a two-story, 54-room Best Western that has typical motel furnishings and a pool. ~ 615 West Hopi Drive, Holbrook; 520-524-3948, 800-528-1234, fax 520-524-3612. BUDGET TO MODERATE.

Another Best Western motel is the **Arizonian Inn** with 70 guest rooms, contemporary furnishings and a pool. ~ 2508 East Navajo Boulevard, Holbrook; 520-524-2611, 800-528-1234, fax 520-524-2611. BUDGET TO MODERATE.

DINING

Dining out in the Southern Navajo Indian Reservation area is not a very exciting experience. You can take a counter seat on one of the swivel stools or settle into a booth at **Falcon Restaurant** where the menu includes steaks, chicken, roast turkey and seafood. This brown stucco establishment also features the only Greek mural we found in Navajo country. ~ 1113 East 3rd Street, Winslow; 520-289-2342. BUDGET TO MODERATE.

Celebrated in newspapers ranging from New York to San Francisco, the **Casa Blanca Café** is known for its tacos, chimichangas, cheese crisps and burgers. Choose between booth and table seating at this ceramic-tiled establishment where cactus baskets grace the walls. The dining room is cooled by Casablanca fans but, alas, there's no trace of Bogie. ~ 1201 East 2nd Street, Winslow; 520-289-4191. BUDGET.

At **Gabrielle's Pancake and Steak House**, Navajo sandpaintings line the wall, adding a decorative touch. Inside this shake-shingle coffee shop you can enjoy burgundy booth or counter seating and dine on steaks, Chinese food, seafood and homemade pies. Closed

Sunday and Monday for dinner. ~ 918 East 2nd Street, Winslow; 520-289-2508. BUDGET.

In Holbrook, **Aguilera's Restaurant** serves authentic Mexican cuisine in a casual, café-style room with pictures of comical love stories from Mexico. ~ 200 Navajo Boulevard, Holbrook; 520-524-3806. BUDGET TO MODERATE.

Rock walls add an earthy note to **The Plainsman**. For casual dining try the coffee shop where there's booth seating. Enjoy meals such as liver and onions, veal cutlet and turkey sandwiches. The dining room is a favorite of the local Chamber of Commerce which meets here monthly. Popular items include châteaubriand, prime rib, frogs' legs and grilled trout. ~ 1001 West Hopi Drive, Holbrook; 520-524-3345. MODERATE.

The **Roadrunner Café** offers everything from grilled-cheese sandwiches to pot roast and steaks. The carpeted dining room has table and booth seating. Plants and wildflower photos bring the Southwest indoors. ~ 1501 East Navajo Boulevard, Holbrook; 520-524-2787. BUDGET.

SHOPPING

Founded in 1903, **Bruchman's Gallery** features American Indian art and crafts—fetishes, Hopi kachina dolls, Navajo jewelry, drums, wallhangings, saddle blankets, baskets and rare pottery. ~ 113 West 2nd Street, Winslow; 520-289-3831.

Linda's Indian Arts and Crafts is a small shop but offers a good selection of American Indian jewelry and crafts. ~ 405 Navajo Boulevard, Holbrook; 520-524-2500.

For the biggest selection of top-of-the-line American Indian arts and crafts, **McGee's Beyond Native Tradition** sells everything from Hopi jewelry to Navajo blankets and drums. ~ 2114 East Navajo Boulevard, Holbrook; 520-524-1977.

Navajo ceramics are simple, unadorned brown pieces glazed with hot pitch. The pieces look wonderful when made by a master.

Nakai Indian Cultural Trade Center, in business for over 27 years, also features top-quality American Indian products as well as jewelry made on the premises. ~ 357 Navajo Boulevard, Holbrook; 520-524-2329.

More American Indian jewelry, kachinas, baskets and crafts can be found at **Tribal Treasures**. ~ 104 Crestview Drive, Holbrook; 520-524-2847.

Painted Desert Visitors Center Gift Shop sells polished and natural petrified wood, from tiny stones to great slabs, plus other gems as well as Southwestern Indian crafts and curios. ~ Route 40 entrance to the Petrified Forest National Park; 520-524-3756.

At **R. B. Burnham & Co. Trading Post** is a room lined with naturally dyed yarns. Behind that room is a shrine to Hopi and Navajo crafts. Assembled with much care, and for sale, are gallery-quality Navajo rugs, carved furniture upholstered in Navajo weavings, plus the whole array of American Indian arts and crafts. It's worth a stop just to look! ~ Route 191, at Route 40 in Sanders; 520-688-2777.

NIGHTLIFE   It's pretty quiet out this way. For nightlife the choices are limited.

The **Tumbleweed Lounge** is one of the hottest nightspots in Winslow, drawing the biggest crowds, with guitars and country-and-western poetry put to music—Who's going to mend my broken heart? There is live music every Friday and Saturday. ~ 1500 East 3rd Street; 520-289-5213.

All the action happens at **Young's Corral Bar** where weekends are filled with the sounds of live country-and-western music. ~ 865 East Navajo Boulevard, Holbrook; 520-524-1875.

PARKS   **LITTLE PAINTED DESERT COUNTY PARK** 🏃 One of the nicest, most colorful chunks of the 40-mile-long Painted Desert is concentrated in this 900-acre park, at 5500-foot elevation near the southern boundary of the Navajo Indian Reservation north of Winslow. Large 300- to 400-foot-tall fragile mounds of mud slate in grays, reds, purples and yellows tend to change in color intensity throughout the day. Colors are most vivid at dawn and dusk. There's an overlook, two picnic ramadas and restrooms. ~ Located 15 miles north of Winslow on Route 87; 520-524-4250.

MCHOOD PARK CLEAR CREEK RESERVOIR 🏊 🚤 🎣 Once an important water source for Winslow, the deep canyon five miles from town is now a favorite boating, swimming and picnic area. Fishing is good for trout, bass and catfish. Picnic area, restrooms, showers. ~ Take Route 87 south to Route 99, and turn left; 520-289-5714.

▲ There are 11 sites (3 with RV hookups); $6 per night, $7 for hookups.

CHOLLA LAKE COUNTY PARK 🏊 🚤 🎣 One of the larger bodies of water in northeastern Arizona, the park is adjacent to a power station. This manmade lake offers swimming, boating, fishing (for bass, catfish, bluegill and carp) and picnicking. Picnic tables, restrooms, showers; groceries and restaurants are two miles away in Joseph City; day-use fee, $2. ~ Take Route 40 east from Winslow for about 20 miles to Exit 277, then follow the power plant road to the park; 520-288-3717.

▲ There are 20 sites (8 with RV hookups); $7 per night for standard sites, $10 for hookups.

PETRIFIED FOREST NATIONAL PARK 🏃 🚵 Straddling Route 40 and abutting the southern boundary of the Navajo Indian Reservation, this 28-mile-long (north to south) park features rolling badlands of the Painted Desert—mainly red-hued hills—north of

Route 40. South of Route 40 lies the densest concentration of petrified prehistoric forests in the world. Each section has a wilderness area. At each entrance is a visitors center with restaurant, restrooms and museum. A 28-mile road leads visitors past nine
Painted Desert vistas and 13 Petrified Forest stops; day-use fee, $3.
~ Both park entrances are 18 miles east of Holbrook: the northernmost on Route 40, the southern one on Route 180;
520-524-6228.

▲ Back country only; get permit at visitors center.

The Western Navajo Indian Reservation,
bordering such wonders as the Grand
Canyon National Park and Lake Powell

▼▼▼▼▼▼▼▼▼▼▼▼▼▼▼▼▼
Western Navajo Country

National Recreation Area, is a land of great beauty and ancient
sights. President William McKinley signed an order January 8,
1900, deeding these one-and-a-half-million acres of land to the
Navajos who had migrated westward 32 years earlier after out-
growing their original reserve.

Where Routes 89 and 64 meet, the Navajos operate **Cameron Visi-**
tors Center, offering advice and brochures on tribal attractions. ~
520-679-2303.

SIGHTS

Follow Route 64 west ten miles to an unpaved spur road and
walk a few hundred feet to a dramatic overlook. At the bottom of
hundreds of feet of sheer canyon walls is a muddy ribbon of the
Little Colorado River. Upper limestone cliffs, layered like flapjack
stacks, contrast with massive sandstone slabs below, evidence of a
shallow sea 250 million years ago. This **Grand Canyon of the Little**
Colorado Gorge Tribal Park is owned by the Navajos. From
Memorial Day through Labor Day a festive air reigns as Indians set
up their flag and banner-bedecked crafts booths in the parking area.

A mile north of the visitors center is **Cameron Trading Post,**
Motel and Restaurant, a stone pueblo-style complex built in 1916
by Hopis and Navajos, and recently restored. Long known as an
oasis of hospitality, it's located by Tanner's Crossing, the last place
wagons could cross the Little Colorado before the river enters
gorges too deep to navigate. Quicksand pockets made this one especially treacherous. ~ Route 89; 520-679-2231.

Today this mini-city is a great place to people watch: old
Navajo women in traditional velvet blouses, men in tall, black
reservation hats and turquoise jewelry accompanied by youngsters
in mod T-shirts and tennies. Inside the post, packed with curios
and quality crafts, you'll often see a weaver at work. Next door,
don't miss **Cameron Collector's Gallery** offering antique Indian
crafts and outstanding works of contemporary American Indian
art—rare chief's blankets, pottery, dolls, weaponry and ceremonial

◀ HIDDEN

garb. Behind the gallery, **Mrs. Richardson's Terraced Garden**, recently revived, is a garden spot of vegetables and flowers.

North of Cameron, continuing on Route 89 to The Gap, lies the northernmost extension of the **Painted Desert**, a multihued ancient land of silt and volcanic ash hills barren of vegetation. Red sphynx shapes astride crumbling pyramids of eroded solidified sand, these badlands are red and white along some miles; gray and white along others. They're part of the Chinle Formation beloved by geologists for its dinosaur-era fossils.

At **Dinosaur Tracks**, jewelry shacks mark the spot where scientists believe a 20-foot-long carnivorous Dilophosaurus left tracks. For a small tip locals escort you to the several impressions—three-toed footprints twice as big as adult hands. (Look for the reconstructed skeleton of this dinosaur in Window Rock at the Navajo Tribal Museum.) ~ The turnoff is seven miles west of Tuba City on Route 160, then north one-eighth mile along a dirt road.

Worth a stop in Tuba City, named for a 19th-century Hopi leader, is the hogan-shaped, two-story native stone **Tuba Trading Post**. Built in 1905 during a tourism boom, its door faces east to the rising sun; crafts, groceries and sundries are for sale. Next door, you can enter a built-for-tourists hogan replica. Now administrative and trade center for western Navajos, Tuba City was founded by Mormons in 1877. ~ Main Street and Moenave Avenue; 520-283-5441.

LODGING

Lodging in Navajo and Hopi country can be summed up in one word: scarce. In an area about the size of Massachusetts, barely 720 rooms are available, so it's no wonder reservation motels claim 100 percent occupancy most nights from Memorial Day through Labor Day. If you get stuck, reservation border towns (Holbrook, Winslow and Flagstaff) usually have vacancies, though they too can sell out, especially on weekends of special events.

✔ CHECK THESE OUT—UNIQUE LODGING

- Re-live '50s kitsch at **Wigwam Motel and Curios**, where the wigwams are decorated with red-plaid curtains and handmade hickory furniture. *page 66*
- Immerse yourself in the daily activities of Indian Country when you stay over at the **Cameron Trading Post and Motel.** *page 71*
- Experience rural Navajo life by sleeping in an authentic dirt-floor hogan and using the old-fashioned outhouses at the **Coyote Pass Hospitality: Hogan Bed and Breakfast.** *page 84*
- Check into **Gouldings Lodge** for front-row views of Monument Valley's red and orange sandstone buttes. *page 89*

Budget: under $50 Moderate: $50–$90 Deluxe: $90–$120 Ultra-deluxe: over $120

Padded headboards and brown Santa Fe–style bedspreads and drapes cozy up 112 simple, cementblock rooms in the **Anasazi Inn,** located 42 miles north of Flagstaff. It boasts the Western Navajo Indian Reservation's only swimming pool. ~ Route 89, Gray Mountain; 520-679-2214, 800-678-2214, fax 520-679-2234. MODERATE.

Cameron Trading Post and Motel, 40 miles east of the Grand Canyon's east entrance, and 54 miles north of Flagstaff, is a favorite overnight stop in Indian Country. This tiny, self-contained, 112-acre, privately owned outpost sits on a bluff overlooking the eastern prelude to the Grand Canyon of the Colorado. From 6 a.m. until 10 p.m. or later, the trading post is a beehive of tourists and Navajos mingling to shop, dine or pick up everything from mail and tack to baled hay. It's mainly the tourists who stay overnight in 62 rooms. Built in 1916, the motel rooms are of native stone and wood architecture (variously called Pueblo style or Victorian territorial) as is the rest of the compound. The rooms tend to be a little funkier than elsewhere on the reservation. ~ Route 89, Cameron; 520-679-2231, 800-338-7385, fax 520-679-2350. MODERATE.

Adjacent to the historic octagonal-shaped Tuba Trading Post is the pleasant, lawn-studded **Quality Inn,** furnished with tan rugs and furniture of Southwestern hand-carved fashion. It has 80 rooms. ~ Main Street, Tuba City; 520-283-4545, 800-644-8383, fax 520-283-4144. MODERATE TO DELUXE.

Students at Tuba City's Greyhills High School are learning the hotel management business by operating the 32-room **Greyhills Inn.** Open year-round to all ages, rooms are comfy and carpeted, with modern interiors. Guests share bathrooms and a TV lounge, and for a modest fee can share meals with Navajo students in their cafeteria. ~ 160 Warrior Drive, northeast of Bashas on Route 160, Tuba City; 520-283-6271, fax 520-283-6604. MODERATE.

If you're not on a cholesterol-free diet, you'll find Indian country food, as with everything else here, an adventure. Fry bread appears at lunch and dinner with taco trimmings as an Navajo taco, or as bread for a sandwich, or as dessert dripping with honey. Other favorites include mutton stew, usually served with parched corn, chili, Mexican food, burgers, steaks, and for breakfast, biscuits with gravy. Note that prohibition is still observed throughout the Hopi and Navajo country. It is illegal to bring or drink alcoholic beverages here.

DINING

Anasazi Gray Mountain Restaurant fills its walls with Southwestern kitsch. Entrées (hamburgers, chicken-fried steak, halibut, pepper steak) come with soup or salad, hot rolls, baked potato, cowboy beans or french fries and salsa. ~ Route 89, Gray Mountain; 520-679-2203. BUDGET TO MODERATE.

A nice surprise is the **Cameron Trading Post Restaurant**. After walking through the typically low, open-beam ceiling trading post, you enter a lofty room lined with windows looking out onto the Little Colorado River. Tables and chairs are of carved oak and the ceiling glimmers silver from its patterned pressed tin squares. Forty-one breakfast choices include Navajo taco with egg, *huevos rancheros* and hot cakes; for dinner, try the deep-fried fish and chicken or steak entrées. ~ Route 89, Cameron; 520-679-2231. BUDGET TO MODERATE.

Poncho's Family Restaurant amid open-beam and wood decor, offers dinners of steak and shrimp, chicken-fried steak, plus the inevitable Navajo taco, and a variety of Mexican entrées. Look for the large historic photos of Charles H. Algert, pioneer Indian trader and founder of Tuba Trading Post, shown on horseback in 1898, and an 1872 photo of the Hopi leader Tuba, standing with arms folded. ~ Main Street, Tuba City; 520-283-5260. MODERATE.

SHOPPING   In business for more than half a century, **Sacred Mountain Trading Post** is often a good outlet for museum-quality Navajo pitch-glazed pottery; also available are glass beads and bead-making materials, Hopi pottery, kachinas and Navajo and Paiute baskets. ~ 23 miles north of Flagstaff on Route 89; 520-679-2255.

The 1916 stone **Cameron Trading Post** is like a department store of Indian crafts, crammed with a good selection of nearly everything—lots of Navajo rugs, cases of jewelry from all Southwestern tribes, kachinas, sandpaintings, baskets and pottery. The adjoining Cameron Gallery offers the most expensive crafts including antique Indian weavings, Apache baskets, Plains beadwork, weaponry and ceremonial garb. ~ Route 89, Cameron; 520-679-2231.

Tuba Trading Post emphasizes Navajo rugs, usually including large pictorials. Also for sale are kachinas, jewelry and the Pendleton blankets Indians like to give one another for births, graduations and other celebrations. ~ Main Street and Moenave Avenue, Tuba City; 520-283-5441.

▼▼▼▼▼▼▼▼▼▼▼▼▼▼

Hopi Indian Country

Three sand-colored mesas stacked and surrounded by a dozen ancient villages form the core of the Hopi Indian Reservation. Completely surrounded by the Navajo Indian Reservation, the villages are strung along 90 miles of Route 264. Home for several centuries to the Hopi, this fascinating high-desert place (about 4000-foot elevation) looks stark and poor one minute, then ancient and noble the next.

SIGHTS   Looking for crafts to buy at the homes of Hopi craftsmakers or attending dances are good reasons to visit the villages. **Hopi Indian Dances**, nearly all of them involving prayers for rain for their dry-farm plots, occur year-round. Dates are rarely announced more than two weeks in advance. Whether or not you can attend will vary with the dance and the village. To ask, call the Hopi Tribal Council Office of Public Relations (520-734-2441). Don't miss a chance to attend one. Instructions for visitors will be posted outside most villages. In all cases, leave cameras, tape recorders and sketching pads in the car. Photography is not permitted in the villages or along Hopi roads.

Two miles southeast of Tuba City at **Moenkopi** ("the place of running water"), a village founded in the 1870s by a Hopi chief from Oraibi, note the rich assortment of farm plots. This is the only Hopi village that irrigates its farmland—water comes from a nearby spring. Elsewhere farmers tend small plots in several locations, enhancing their chance of catching random summer thundershowers. It's also the only one of 12 Hopi villages not situated on or just below one of the three mesas.

It's some 40 miles to the next two villages. **Bacavi**, consisting mostly of prefab homes, was built in 1909 following a political upheaval at Old Oraibi. **Hotevilla**, also a relatively new (built in 1906) village, with its mix of adobe and cinderblock homes at the edge of a mesa, is nonetheless a traditional village known for its dances and crafts. A few miles down the road, on the edge of Third Mesa, **Old Oraibi** is one of the oldest continuously inhabited villages in the United States. Hopis lived here as early as 1150. Try the ten-minute walk from the south edge of the village to ruins of a church built in 1901 by H. R. Voth, a Mennonite minister. It was destroyed by lightning. At Kykotsmovi, "mound of ruined houses," two miles east, then south one mile on Route 2, the **Hopi Tribal Council Office of Public Relations** provides visitor information. ~ Route 2; 520-734-2441.

HOPI CEREMONIAL DANCES

Although some Hopi dances are held in plazas and are open to the public, others are held privately in underground kivas. Many of their dances are appeals for rain or to improve harmony with nature. Starting times are determined by Hopi elders according to the position of the moon, sun and vibrations. The Powamu Ceremony or Bean Dance in late February is a fertility ritual to help enhance the summer harvest, while The Snake Dance is done near the end of August. Live rattlesnakes are used during the ceremony as a form of communication with the Underworld. If you attend a ceremony, remember to respect the proceedings and not take pictures or use tape recorders.

Text continued on page 76.

The Fine Craft of Shopping

While shopping for arts and crafts in Indian Country we've been invited into Hopi homes to eat corn fresh from the field, have discussed tribal politics with college-educated shopkeepers and met traditional basketmakers who spoke no English. At the same time we've longingly admired contemporary Indian-crafted jewelry that would dazzle New York's Fifth Avenue crowd.

Shopping can occur anywhere in Indian Country. Once we bought sandpaintings from the trunk of an Indian artist's car while camping in the Chuskas. But Indian Country's main shopping avenue is Route 264, from Tuba City to Window Rock where you'll find two fine old trading posts. **Tuba Trading Post** offers an assortment of Indian-crafted merchandise. ~ Main Street and Moenave Avenue, Tuba City; 520-283-5441. Expect more of the same at **Hubbell Trading Post**, including the best selection of Navajo rugs along this route. ~ Route 264, Ganado; 520-755-3254.

Throughout Hopi country, shopping is the best way to get to know the locals. Shops line entrances to all three mesas and most villages have at least a few signs in home windows inviting visitors in to look at family-made crafts. (*Note:* Tribal officials caution against making a deposit on any craft you can't take with you unless you know the craftsmaker or have a reliable personal reference.)

What should you be you looking for when shopping? Both Hopi and Navajo offer crafts unique to their tribes.

HOPI CRAFTS

Baskets   Hopi wedding and other ceremonial baskets are still woven by Hopi women. Third Mesa villages are also known for their wicker plaques of colorfully dyed sumac and rabbit brush. Coiled yucca plaques are preferred at Second Mesa. Trays of plaited yucca over a willow ring serve as sifters and are made at First and Second Mesa villages.

Jewelry   The favorite Hopi jewelry form is overlay—designs cut from silver sheets, then soldered onto a second silver piece. Cut-out areas are oxidized black.

Kachinas Kachinas are often carved in dancers' poses, then painted or dressed in cloth, feathers and bright acrylics. The newer trends feature stylized, intricately detailed figures carved from one piece of cottonwood root, then stained. (Navajos now make kachinas too, to the irritation of Hopi carvers.)

Pottery Nampeyo, a First Mesa woman inspired by ancient pottery shards, started the revival of yellow-to-orange Sikyatki pottery a century ago. First Mesa remains a major producer of pottery decorated with black thin-curved-line motifs.

Weaving Traditionally, Hopi men do the weaving in this tribe—mostly ceremonial belts, wedding clothes and some rugs.

NAVAJO CRAFTS

Baskets The most popular basketry of the Navajos is the coiled wedding basket, with its bold-red, zigzag pattern. Other baskets found in Navajo trading posts are likely to be made by Paiutes who also live in the area. During the 1980s, a renaissance resulted in some large, intricately designed coil baskets—both plate and jug-shaped.

Jewelry Since the 1860s, Navajos have engaged in the art of silversmithing, shaping silver to fit turquoise stones. Other popular items are stoneless silver rings, bolos, earrings, necklaces—especially the squash blossom—made by handwrought or sand-cast methods.

Pottery Navajo ceramics are simple, unadorned brown pieces glazed with hot pitch. The pieces look wonderful when made by a master; clunky and amateurish otherwise.

Sandpaintings Medicine men sing curing ceremonies while assistants create elaborate pictures on the ground with sands and crushed minerals in an astonishing assortment of colors. Each is destroyed at the ceremony's end. Similar designs glued onto wood are sold as sandpaintings. Widely available, these are made mainly in the Shiprock, New Mexico, area.

Weaving Thousands of Navajo women and a few dozen Navajo men weave rugs today on the reservation, but only a small percentage of them are considered masterweavers, commanding the highest prices. Still, even a saddle blanket can be a treasured memento.

Continue east on Route 264 a half dozen miles to **Shungopavi**, Second Mesa's largest village, built at a cliff's edge. It's two more miles to the **Hopi Cultural Center**, the biggest social center for Indians and visitors. Hopi staffers of this white, pueblo-style museum-restaurant-motel-gift shop complex always know when and where dances are scheduled; ask at the motel desk. ~ At Second Mesa on Route 264; 520-734-2401.

Tribally owned, the Hopi Cultural Center includes the **Hopi Museum**, exhibiting murals, pottery and historic photos of each mesa. Shop spaces house galleries of Hopi-made crafts. ~ 520-734-6550. Just 100 feet west of the complex at the **Hopi Arts and Crafts Cooperative Guild**, silversmiths work amid the biggest assortment of Hopi-made crafts on the reservation. ~ 520-734-2463.

East of the Cultural Center, the two weathered villages of **Sipaulovi** and **Mishongnovi** are strikingly placed above the desert floor on Second Mesa, many of their dwellings carved from stone. It's a steep climb north to both up an unnamed road from Route 264. Founded in the 1680s, both are known for their dances and are worth a visit for the views. ~ Information: 520-737-2570.

If you have time to make only one stop, visit the trio of villages on First Mesa—**Hano, Sichomovi** and **Walpi**. Perched atop the flat oblong mesa, its sides dropping precipitously 1000 feet to the desert below, the village locations help you understand why the Hopis believe they live at the center of the universe. Accessible only by a thrilling curvy drive up a narrow road with no guardrails (signs off Route 264 point the way), all three villages seem to grow out of the mesa's beige-colored stone. Vistas are uninterrupted for miles amid an eerie stillness. ~ Six miles east of the Secakuku Trading Post; 520-737-2262.

Most awesome is Walpi. Built some 300 years ago on a promontory with panoramas in all directions, Walpi's houses stack atop one another like children's blocks, connected with wooden ladders. From the parking lot (no cars are permitted in Walpi) the village resembles a great stone ship suspended on a sea of blue sky. Leaders keep the village traditional so that neither electricity nor running water is permitted. During the summer, shy schoolgirls lead **tours of Walpi** daily. Sign up at Ponsi Hall. ~ 520-737-2262.

Here, as in the other villages, kivas or ceremonial chambers dug into the earth, serve as they have since Anasazi days, a refuge where clan dancers fast and observe rituals for days prior to dances. Then on dance days, no longer farmers in denims, the Hopis slowly emerge through ladders on kiva roofs to the hypnotic rhythm of drums and rattles. Transformed in feathers, bells and pine boughs, they appear as sacred beings.

Everyday activities include women baking bread out of doors in beehive ovens or tending clay firings. These are excellent pottery villages. Crude signs in windows invite you into homes of kachina and pottery makers, a wonderful chance to get acquainted with these hospitable people.

Hano resembles its neighboring Hopi villages, but in language and custom it remains a Tewa settlement of Pueblo Indians who fled Spanish oppression in the Rio Grande region in the late 1690s.

Continuing east on Route 264, Hopi Indian Country ends at Keams Canyon, the federal government administrative center, with tourist facilities (restaurant, motel, grocery) clustered around **Keams Canyon Trading Post**. Well-chosen crafts are for sale; the finest art is in a side room. ~ Route 264; 520-738-2294.

Follow the canyon northeast into the woods. About two miles in, on the left, near a ramada and a small dam, you'll find **Inscription Rock** where Kit Carson signed his name on the tall sandstone wall about the time he was trying to end Navajo raiding parties.

◄ HIDDEN

Designed by Arizona's award-winning architect Benny Gonzales, Second Mesa offers the only Hopi-owned tourist complex. Here are 33 rooms of the **Hopi Cultural Center Motel** with their white walls, blonde furniture, television, desk, vanity, dusty rose rug and Indian print-wall decor. Check to make sure your room has a door lock; things can be a little casual here! ~ Route 264; 520-734-2401, fax 520-734-2435. MODERATE.

LODGING

Old trailer home modules make up the **Keams Canyon Motel**. The 20 units are a little depressing (with sagging curtains and scratches on wood walls and stains on the carpets), but clean; at affordable rates, they are often sold out during summer. ~ Route 264; 520-738-2297. BUDGET.

Hopi's primary meeting place, the **Hopi Cultural Center Restaurant** with open-beam ceiling and sturdy, wood-carved furniture, offers Hopi options at all meals. Breakfasts include blue-corn

DINING

✔ **CHECK THESE OUT—UNIQUE DINING**

- *Budget:* Satisfy your cravings for *chile rellenos* at **Casa Blanca Café**, a quaint spot that's been celebrated in papers from coast to coast. *page 66*
- *Budget:* Squeeze into the trailer housing the **Tuller Café**—you won't be disappointed with the Navajo sandwiches or Homer's goulash. *page 85*
- *Budget to moderate:* Wander to the rear of the **Cameron Trading Post** and you'll discover a surprisingly good restaurant that boasts 41 breakfast choices. *page 72*
- *Moderate:* Take in panoramic vistas from the tri-level **Stage Coach Dining Room**, where a dinner favorite is roast leg of lamb. *page 90*

Budget: under $8 Moderate: $8–$16 Deluxe: $16–$24 Ultra-deluxe: over $24

pancakes, blue-corn cornflakes with milk and fry bread. For lunch or dinner, Nok Qui Vi—traditional stew with corn and lamb, served with fresh-baked green chiles and fry bread—as well as steak, chicken and shrimp entrées round out the menu. For dessert there's strawberry shortcake. ~ Route 264 at Second Mesa; 520-734-2401 ext. 300. BUDGET TO MODERATE.

Second Mesa Nova-Ki next to the pueblo-style Secakuku Supermarket serves up burgers and grilled pork chops amid mauve walls, wood tables and American Indian paintings. ~ 668 Second Mesa; 520-737-2525. BUDGET TO MODERATE.

Murals depicting Hopi mesa life decorate the exterior at **Keams Canyon Café**. This simple eatery has such entrées as T-bone steak, roast beef, barbecued ribs and enchiladas, all served on formica tables. ~ Route 264 in Keams Canyon; 520-738-2296. MODERATE.

SHOPPING The number of roadside Hopi galleries and shops doubled in the early '90s. Owned by individual families, groups of artists or by craftsmakers with national reputations, all these Hopi crafts enterprises are located on or near Route 264.

Third Mesa's **Monongya Arts and Crafts** has large rooms filled with Indian jewelry, some pottery and kachina doll sculptures. ~ Third Mesa; 520-734-2344.

Driving east a half-mile, follow the Old Oraibi signs south to **Old Oraibi Crafts** specializing in Hopi *dawas*—wall plaques made of yarn. This tiny shop with a beam ceiling also sells stuffed Hopi clown dolls.

Eastbound on 264, **Calnimpetwa's Gallery** looks like a house. Spacious, white-walled rooms are lined with gallery-quality baskets, pots and jewelry made primarily by Hopi, Navajo and Santo Domingo people. Many of the crafts have a sleek contemporary look. ~ Route 264; 520-734-2406.

In Second Mesa, by the Hopi Cultural Center, the pueblo-style **Hopi Arts and Crafts Cooperative Guild Shop** sells work by more than 350 Hopi craftsmakers, often introducing new artists. You'll see fine, reasonably priced samples of all Hopi crafts—coil baskets, wicker plaques, kachina dolls—from traditional to the contemporary baroque and even the older-style flat dolls, plus silver jewelry, woven sashes and gourd rattles. Prices are good. Staff members are knowledgeable about who the best craftsmakers are in any specialty and where to find them. In the shop you'll also see Hopi silversmiths at work. ~ Second Mesa; 520-734-2463.

East of the Hopi Cultural Center one-and-a-half miles, on the left, stop at an unassuming-looking **Tsakurshovi** to find the funkiest shop en route, the only place you can buy sweetgrass, bundled sage, cottonwood root, fox skins, elk toes, warrior paint, dance fans and the oldest-style kachina dolls, amid a delightful hodgepodge of crafts and trade items adored by Hopi dancers. (Owners invented the "Don't Worry, Be Hopi" T-shirts.) ~ Second Mesa; 520-734-2478.

Phil Poseyesva Art Limited sells high-quality kachinas, pottery and jewelry. The jewelry is designed by the owner himself. ~ Six miles east of the Hopi Cultural Center, next to Secakuku Supermarket, Second Mesa; 520-737-9306.

Honani Crafts Gallery, with its stained-glass windows of Hopi dancer designs, sells jewelry by 16 silversmiths from all three mesas plus kachinas, books and concho belts. ~ Five-and-a-half miles east of the Hopi Cultural Center; 520-737-2238.

It's seven more miles to First Mesa, where Walpi residents welcome you to see pottery and kachinas they've made in Hopi's most picturesque village.

Thirteen miles east, visit **McGee's Indian Art Gallery** at Keams Canyon Trading Post, distinctive for its Hopi village murals. For sale are a tasteful variety of Hopi and Navajo crafts—concho belts, silver jewelry, wicker plaques, kachinas, sandpaintings, moccasins and rugs. Be sure to look in the room housing their finest award-winning crafts. ~ Route 24, Keams Canyon; 520-738-2295.

▼▼▼▼▼▼▼▼▼▼▼▼▼▼▼▼▼▼

Central Navajo Country

This is the heart, soul and capital of Navajoland—a strikingly beautiful land of canyons, red rocks, forests and mountains where the Navajos have recorded their proudest victories and most bitter defeats. The longer you stay and explore, the more you'll appreciate the ever-evolving culture that is the Navajo Way.

The ruins of ancient cities you'll see also remind us that long before the Navajo arrived this too was homeland to ancestors of the Hopis—the Anasazi.

SIGHTS

Forty miles east of Keams Canyon, near the small village of Ganado, follow a shaded road a half mile west along a creek to **Hubbell Trading Post National Historic Site,** which still operates as it did when Lorenzo Hubbell, dean of Navajo traders, set up shop here last century. Now owned by the National Park Service and operated by South West Parks and Monuments Associations, Hubbell's remains one of only a few trading posts with the traditional "bullpen" design—shoppers stand outside a wooden arena asking for canned goods, yards of velvet, tack and such. Built in the 1870s, part museum and part gallery, these three stone rooms smell and look their age—the floors uneven from years of wear. Walls are jammed to their open-beam ceilings with baskets, pottery, books, rugs, historical photos, jewelry, postcards, dry goods and grocery items. Tack and tools still dangle from the rafters. ~ Route 264, Ganado; 520-755-3254.

Self-guiding tours of the 160-acre complex and exhibits in the **Visitors Center** explain how trading posts once linked the Navajo with the outside world, and how Hubbell was not just a trader but a valued friend of the Indian community until his death in 1930. The Hubbell family continued to operate the post until it was given to the National Park Service in 1967. Also in the Visitors Center is a good selection of Indian-related books. And for a tip, Navajo weavers and silversmiths demonstrating their crafts will pose for photos. ~ Ganado; 520-755-3475.

Hour-long tours of the **Hubbell House,** with his excellent collection of crafts, give further insights into frontier life and the remarkable trader who lies buried on a knoll nearby.

Navajo-owned ponderosa pine forest lands comprise part of the 30-mile drive to Window Rock, eastward along Route 264. Picnickers may wish to stop a while at **Summit Campground,** where the elevation reaches 7750 feet. ~ Located 20 miles east of Ganado.

Seven miles east of Summit Campground, before entering Window Rock, stop in St. Michaels, on your right, at trailers labeled **Navajo Nation Tourism.** Here you'll be able to obtain Central Navajo Country maps and tourism information. ~ 520-871-6436.

Also here is **St. Michaels Mission Museum** in the white, hand-hewn native stone building that in the late 1890s was four-bedroom living quarters and chapel for Franciscan friars from Cincinnati. (Sleeping must have been tough on such thin mattresses atop box crates!) Other displays—everything from uncomfortable-looking wooden saddles to vintage typewriters—include old photographs that depict their work and life. You'll see pages of the first phonetic systems they made to help create the written Navajo language. Outside, towering cottonwoods and a friar's three-quarter-acre flower garden create a parklike oasis. Open only from Memorial Day to Labor Day. ~ Three miles west of Window Rock off Route 264, St. Michaels; 520-871-4171.

Next door, the **St. Michaels Prayer Chapel** houses a 16-foot wood carving entitled "The Redemption of Mankind," created by German artist Ludwig Schumacher as a gift to Americans Indians.

East on Route 264 three miles, a rare Indian Country traffic light (at Route 12) marks "downtown" **Window Rock,** a growing, modern Navajo Nation capital. West of the Navajo Nation Inn, the **Navajo Nation Museum** and **Navajo Arts & Crafts Enterprise** share space. The former, with sophisticated exhibits, leads visitors through an overview of historic and contemporary Navajo life and traditions. Mannequins were created via plaster casts from real Navajos. One room is devoted to changing exhibits by noted and emerging Navajo artists. The crafts guild encourages innovation among its members and guarantees the quality of everything it sells. ~ East of Route 12 on Route 264, Window Rock; Navajo Nation Museum: 520-871-6673, Navajo Arts & Crafts Enterprise: 520-871-4095.

Travel two miles east from Route 264 north on Indian Route 12, and you will find the **Navajo Nation Zoological and Botanical Park**. In this natural setting roam domestic and wild animals that figure in Navajo culture and folk lore—everything from coyote, wolves, cougars, bears, deer, elk, bobcats, rattlesnakes and prairie dogs to goats. In all, 53 species live here. Look for the Navajo-churro sheep, brought by the Spanish. Herds are being increased because of their proven resistance to disease and the excellent weaving quality of their wool. Displays here include fork-stick and crib-log examples of hogan architecture. A modest botanical garden labels typical high-desert plants: Indian rice grass, Navajo tea, lupine, asters and junipers. ~ Indian Route 12, Window Rock; 520-871-6573.

A row of towering red-sandstone pinnacles that resemble the **Haystacks**, for which they are named, forms the zoo's western boundary. The zoo and pinnacles are part of **Tse Bonito Tribal Park**, where the Navajos camped in 1864 on their "Long Walk" from their homeland. ~ Route 264, Window Rock; 520-871-6573.

When you arrive at the street light at the town of Window Rock, follow Route 12 north past Window Rock's shopping center, then drive right a mile to **Tseghahodzani**—"the rock with the hole in it." Here you'll find a sweeping wall, several stories tall, of vermilion-colored sandstone. Almost dead center is an almost perfectly circular "window" 130 feet in diameter eroded in it, offering views to the mountains beyond. John Collier, Commissioner of Indian Affairs in the 1930s, was so stirred by it, he declared it

JOHN LORENZO HUBBELL—HERO

To American Indians at the turn of the century, John Lorenzo Hubbell was all but a hero. He operated a trading post at Ganado, giving the Indians important contact with the outside world. They traded silver work, wool, sheep and rugs for essentials such as flour, coffee, sugar, tobacco and clothing. To smooth the trading process, Hubbell spoke English, Spanish, Navajo and Hopi. He was also a sheriff and a member of the territorial legislature. Hubbell tried improving the lot of American Indians by bringing in a silversmith from Mexico to teach them silver working. But he really gained their respect during a smallpox epidemic. Having had smallpox, he had developed an immunity to it. So he was able to treat the Navajo without getting the disease himself.

the site for the Navajo administrative center. Visitors can picnic and walk here.

Nearby, visit the octagonal stone **Council Chambers,** designed as a great ceremonial hogan. Murals painted by the late Gerald Nailor depict tribal history. It is here the 88-member Tribal Council meets four times a year to set policy. You'll hear Navajo and English spoken at all proceedings. ~ Window Rock; 520-871-6417.

The prettiest route in Indian Country is **Route 12** from Route 40 through Window Rock and on north another 65 miles. The road hugs red-rock bluffs while skirting pine forests, lakes, Navajo homes and hogans surrounded by pasture, orchards and corn-fields.

Follow signs to the pine-clad Navajo Community College's **Tsaile Campus** and its tall glass hogan-shaped Ned Hatathli Cultural Center with two floors devoted to the **Hatathli Museum and Gallery.** From prehistoric times to the present—dioramas, murals, photographs, pottery, weaponry and other artifacts interpret Indian cultures including the Navajo. Wonderfully detailed murals tell the Navajo story of Creation, but you'll need to find someone to interpret it for you as there's little text. Books and crafts are sold in the adjacent gallery at this two-year college, established in 1957. Visitors are also welcome in the college's library and dining hall. Closed Saturday and Sunday. ~ Route 12, about 60 miles north of Window Rock; college: 520-724-3311, museum and gallery: 520-724-6653.

Route 64, to the left off of Route 12, leads to a favorite spot of tourists from around the world, **Canyon de Chelly National Monument** (access is also available three miles east off Route 191 on Route 7). By the time the Spanish arrived in the 1540s the Navajos already occupied this trio of slick, towering red-walled canyons that converge in a Y. The canyons and rims are still home to Navajo families, their sheep and horses grazing. Water near the surface moistens corn, squash and melon crops, apple and peach orchards.

It's hard to decide if Canyon de Chelly is most impressive from the rim drives, with their bird's-eye views of the hogan-dotted rural scenes, or astride a horse or an open-air jeep, sloshing (during spring runoff) through Chinle Wash. The best introduction for any adventure is the **Visitors Center.** Chinle, the shopping and administrative center for this part of the reservation, is as plain as its famed canyons are spectacular. ~ Along the main road through Chinle; 520-674-5500.

Be sure to stop at the visitors center museum where exhibits on 2000 years of canyon history, plus cultural demonstrations, local artists' exhibits and a ranger-staffed information desk will enlighten you about the area. Next door is a typical Navajo hogan.

The center is also the place to hire Navajo guides—required if you hike, camp, or drive your own four-wheel-drive vehicle into the canyons.

Proud tales of the Navajos' most daring victories are retold daily by guides who also point out bullet holes in the walls from brutal massacres. Thousands of much older ruins leave haunting clues to a people who lived and died here from about 200 A.D. until the late 1300s when prolonged drought throughout the Four Corners region probably caused them to move to the Rio Grande and other regions of Arizona and New Mexico. Each bend in the canyon reveals ever-taller canyon walls, more pictographs and petroglyphs (historic and prehistoric art drawn on rock walls). Each turn showcases vivid red walls and the yellow-green of leafy cottonwoods thriving along the canyon floor.

North and South Rim drives, each 16 miles one-way, take about two hours each to see. (It's a good idea to bring along brochures that point out geological, botanical and historical sites at each overlook.) **South Rim Drive** follows the Canyon de Chelly, which gives the monument its name. Highlights include: **White House Overlook** (located at 5.7 miles; the only nonguided hike into the canyon begins here), to view remains of a multistory masonry village where about 100 persons lived about 800 years ago. On a narrow ledge across the canyon, ancients built retaining walls to try to keep their homes from sliding off the sloping floor into the canyon.

Spider Rock Overlook (at 16 miles) is a vista of the steepest canyon walls, about a 1000-foot vertical drop. Look right to see Monument Canyon; left to see Canyon de Chelly. The 800-foot-tall spire at their junction is **Spider Rock**, where Spider Woman is said to carry naughty Navajo boys and girls. Those white specks at the top of her rock, Navajo parents say, are the bleached bones of boys and girls who did not listen to mother and dad.

> According to the Navajo creation story, Spider Woman wove the world then taught the Navajo to weave.

North Rim Drive explores the **Canyon del Muerto** ("Canyon of the Dead") named in 1882 by Smithsonian Institution expedition leader James Stevenson after finding remains of prehistoric Indian burials below Mummy Cave. Highlights include:

Antelope House Overlook (at 8.5 miles), which is named for paintings of antelope, probably made in the 1830s, on the canyon wall left of this four-story, 91-room ruin. Prehistoric residents contributed hand outlines and figures in white paint. Viewers from the overlook will see circular structures (kivas, or ceremonial chambers) and rectangular ones (storage or living quarters). Across the wash in an alcove 50 feet above the canyon floor is where 1920s archaeologists found the well-preserved body of an old man wrapped in a blanket of golden eagle feathers; under it was a white cotton blanket in such good shape it appeared brand new. It is believed he was a neighborhood weaver. Also here, at Navajo Fortress Viewpoint, the isolated high redstone butte across the canyon was once an important Navajo hideout from Spanish, American and perhaps other Indian raiders.

Mummy Cave Overlook (at 15.2 miles) is site of the largest, most beautiful ruins in Canyon del Muerto. The 1880s discovery of two mummies in cists found in the talus slope below the caves inspired this canyon's name.

Massacre Cave Overlook (at 16 miles) is site of the first documented Spanish contact with Canyon de Chelly Navajos. In the winter of 1805 a bloody battle is believed to have occurred at the rock-strewn ledge to your left, under a canyon rim overhang. Hoping to end persistent Navajo raiding on Spanish and Pueblo Indian villages, Antonio de Narbona led an expedition here and claimed his forces killed up to 115 Navajos, another 33 taken captive.

LODGING

The Navajo Nation's only tribally owned motel, **Navajo Nation Inn** bustles with a mix of Navajo politicians and business people in suits and cowboys in black "reservation hats." The 56 rooms are pleasantly decorated with turquoise carpet, Southwest-style wood furniture and matching bedspreads and curtains with traditional Navajo rural scenes. ~ 48 West Route 264, Window Rock; 520-871-4108, 800-662-6189, fax 520-871-5466. MODERATE.

A parklike scene is the setting for the historic stone and pueblo-style **Thunderbird Lodge**. All 72 adobe-style rooms handsomely blend Navajo and Southwestern architectural traditions. Each features American Indian prints and is an easy walk to the canyon entrance. There's a gift shop and cafeteria. ~ A quarter-mile southeast of Canyon de Chelly National Monument Visitors Center, Chinle; 520-674-5841, 800-679-2473, fax 520-674-5844. MODERATE.

Best Western Canyon de Chelly Motel makes up for its sterile architecture by providing one of Chinle's two swimming pools (indoor, for guests only); 100 rooms, some for nonsmokers. ~ A block east of Route 191 on Navajo Route 7, Chinle; 520-674-5875, 800-327-0354, fax 520-674-3715. DELUXE.

The only enterprise on the entire Navajo Indian Reservation letting you experience life with a rural Navajo extended family is

HIDDEN ► **Coyote Pass Hospitality: Hogan Bed and Breakfast.** Accommodations are primitive: Guests sleep in an authentic dirt-floor log hogan and use old-fashioned outhouses. Scholars, artists and folks eager for a rest from the predictable conveniences have found the Coyote Pass Hospitality a refuge. Special tours (520-674-9655) to favorite backcountry haunts can be arranged. ~ Near Tsaile; 520-724-3383. MODERATE.

Café Sage, located in a two-story, brown stucco building, once the former Presbyterian College campus, welcomes tourists to dine in the Navajo Nation Health Foundation cafeteria where daily dinner specials might include tortellini and chicken with vegetables and garlic toast. Closed Saturday and Sunday. ~ Turn right a half-mile east of Hubbell's on Route 264; in the Sage Memorial Hospital, Ganado; 520-755-3411 ext. 292 or 294. BUDGET.

DINING

A trailer wide enough for two rows of sky-blue booths makes up **Tuller Café.** Here they dish up meat loaf, pork chops, Navajo sandwiches (tortilla or fried bread with roast beef), Navajo stew (mutton, vegetable stew) and Homer's goulash (macaroni, meat, green pepper, tomatoes) with garlic toast. Closed Sunday. ~ Located on the south side of Route 264, St. Michaels; 520-871-4687. BUDGET.

Navajo Nation Inn Dining Room in a modern, spacious room is the Navajo capital's biggest restaurant. Seating 250 and decorated with Navajo art, the menu includes chicken, steak, Navajo sandwiches, Navajo burgers, beef stew, vegetable stew and sometimes a mutton buffet. Lunch is always busy, the restaurant filled with politicians from nearby tribal headquarters offices. ~ 48 West Route 264, Window Rock; 520-871-4108. MODERATE.

Junction Restaurant is one of only two sit-down (nonbuffet) restaurants in Chinle. A mix of peach and blue booths and blonde-wood tables and chairs seat patrons dining on everything from *huevos rancheros* or biscuits and gravy for breakfast to a crab Louis or hot sandwiches for lunch to Mexican specialties for dinner. ~ Adjacent to Canyon de Chelly Motel, a block east of Route 191 on Navajo Route 7, Chinle; 520-674-8443. BUDGET TO MODERATE.

Located in the original 1902 trading post built by Samuel Day, **Thunderbird Restaurant** serves up half a dozen entrées cafeteria-style for each meal. The menu offers a good variety, and changes some each day. You sit in a choice of booths or tables surrounded by walls with top-quality, for-sale Navajo crafts. ~ Thunderbird Lodge, a quarter-mile southeast of Canyon de Chelly National Monument Visitors Center, Chinle; 520-674-5841. BUDGET.

Be sure to stop at the **Hubbell Trading Post,** whose low stone walls, little changed in 90 years, contain the best Navajo rug selection en route, plus several rooms crammed with jewelry, dolls, books, baskets and historic postcards. ~ Route 264, Ganado; 520-755-3254.

SHOPPING

Navajo Arts & Crafts Enterprise sells the work of some 500 Navajo craftsmakers. Selection is excellent and quantity is large—rugs of all styles, Navajo jewelry of all kinds, stuffed Navajo-style dolls. ~ In the same building as the Navajo Nation Museum, Window Rock; 520-871-4095.

The **Thunderbird Lodge Gift Shop** provides a good selection of rugs, many of them made in the Chinle area, as well as kachinas, jewelry, baskets and souvenirs. Some of the fine-quality arts and crafts decorating the neighboring cafeteria walls are also for sale. ~Thunderbird Lodge, a quarter-mile southeast of Canyon de Chelly National Monument Visitors Center, Chinle; 520-674-5841.

PARKS

TSE BONITO TRIBAL PARK Prior to their "Long Walk" to Fort Sumner, New Mexico, in 1864, the Navajo camped here among prominent red-sandstone hills called "Haystacks." The park encompasses the Navajo Nation Zoological and Botanical Park, housing native and domestic animals culturally important to the Navajos. Zoo visitors center with exhibits, restrooms; crib-log hogans; 53 species of animals, birds and other wildlife. ~ Located in Window Rock on Route 264; 520-871-6573.

LAKE ASAAYI BOWL CANYON RECREATION AREA 🏃 ⛵ One of the prettiest of the Navajo fishing lakes, located in the Chuska Mountains known as the "Navajo Alps," Asaayi Lake is popular for fishing (rainbow trout), picnicking and primitive camping. The 36-acre lake and creek are fishable year-round. Picnic areas, barbecue grills, pit toilets. ~ From Window Rock, take Route 12 to Route 134. Drive northeast four miles then south seven miles on a graded dirt road to the lake; 520-871-6647.

▲ Allowed; the $2 permit is available at the recreation area or at the Navajo Forestry and Navajo Fish and Wildlife, both in Window Rock.

CANYON DE CHELLY NATIONAL MONUMENT 🏃 🚲 🐎 The most famous and popular Navajo Indian Reservation attraction is this 130-acre land of piñon and juniper forests cut by a trio of red-walled sandstone canyons. Extending eastward from Chinle to Tsaile, the canyon's rim elevations range from 5500 to 7000 feet while the canyon bottoms drop from 30 feet nearest Chinle to 1000 feet farther east. Cottonwood trees and other vegetation shade farms connected by miles of sandy wash along the canyon bottom. Two major gorges, 27 and 34 miles long, dramatically unveil walls of 250-million-year-old solidified sand dunes in a strata geologists call the Defiance Plateau. There is a motel, restaurant, gift shop, visitors center, museum, crib-log hogan, restrooms, jeep and horse tours, guided hikes. ~ Located in Chinle, via Routes 7 or 64; 520-674-5500. Spider Rock Campground is eight miles east of the visitors center on South Rim Canyon Drive.

▲ There are two campgrounds available. Cottonwood Campground has 97 sites (no hookups); no fee. Spider Rock Campground, run by a private concessionaire, offers 30 sites (no hookups); $10 per night. ~ 520-674-8261.

There's something both silly and irresistible about driving to Four Corners
to stick each foot in a different state

(Colorado and Utah) and each hand in still two others (Arizona
and New Mexico) while someone takes your picture from a scaffolding. But then, this is the only place in the United States where
you can simultaneously "be" in four different states. The inevitable Navajo crafts booths offer up necklaces, bracelets, earrings, T-shirts, paintings, sandpaintings, fry bread and lemonade—
a splendid way to make something festive out of two intersecting
lines on a map.

SIGHTS

To get to Northern Navajo Country from the south, you'll have to
pass by **Teec Nos Pos Arts and Crafts Center**, the usual roadside
gallery of Southwest Indian crafts, with an emphasis on area sandpaintings and Navajo rugs. ~ Routes 160 and 64; 520-656-3228.

Heading westbound on Route 160, even before travelers reach
Kayenta, amazing eroded shapes emerge on the horizon—like the
cathedral-sized and -shaped **Church Rock**. Kayenta, originally a
small town that grew up around John Wetherill's trading post at
5564-feet elevation, today is both Arizona's gateway to Monument Valley and a coal-mining center.

The 24 miles north to Monument Valley on Route 163 is a pre-
lude to the main event, huge red-rock pillars. Half Dome and **Owl
Rock** on your left form the eastern edge of the broad Tyende Mesa.
On your right rise **Burnt Foot Butte** and **El Capitan**, also called
Agathla Peak—roots of ancient volcanoes whose dark rock con-
trasts with pale-yellow sandstone formations.

A half-mile north of the Utah state line on Route 163 is a crossroads; go left two miles to Gouldings Trading Post and Lodge, or
right two miles to **Monument Valley Navajo Tribal Park Headquarters** and Monument Valley Visitors Center. Inside you can see
excellent views from a glass-walled observatory. This was the first
Navajo Tribal Park, set aside in 1958. Within you'll see more than
40 named and dozens more unnamed red and orange monolithic
sandstone buttes and rock skyscrapers jutting hundreds of feet. It
is here that you can arrange Navajo-owned jeep tours into the
Valley Drive. Admission. ~ P.O. Box 360289, Monument Valley,
UT 84536; 801-727-3353.

For a small fee, you can explore the **17-mile Loop Drive** over
a dirt road, badly rutted in places, to view a number of famous
landmarks with names that describe their shapes, such as **Rain
God Mesa**, **Three Sisters** and **Totem Pole**. At **John Ford's Point**, an
Indian on horseback often poses for photographs, then rides out
to chat and collect a tip. A 15-minute round-trip walk from **North
Window** rewards you with panoramic views.

The Navajos and this land seem to belong together. A dozen Navajo families still live in the park, and several open their hogans to guided tours. For a small fee, they'll pose for your pictures. A number of today's residents are descendants of Navajos who arrived here in the mid-1860s with Headman Hoskinini, fleeing Kit Carson and his round-up of Navajos in the Canyon de Chelly area. Hoskinini lived here until his death in 1909.

In all, seven John Ford Westerns were filmed in Monument Valley between 1938 and 1963.

The ultimate cowboy-Indian Western landscape, Monument Valley has been the setting for many movies—*How the West Was Won*, *Stagecoach*, *Billy the Kid*, *She Wore a Yellow Ribbon*, *The Trial of Billy Jack* to name just a few films.

Gouldings Trading Post, Lodge and Museum, a sleek, watermelon-colored complex on a hillside, blends in with enormous sandstone boulders stacked above it. The original Goulding two-story stone home and trading post, now a museum, includes a room devoted to movies made here. Daily showings can be seen in a small adjacent theater. ~ Two miles west of Route 163, Monument Valley; 801-727-3231.

HIDDEN ►

From Gouldings it's nearly 11 miles northwest on paved Oljeto Road to the single-story stone **Oljeto Trading Post**, its Depression-era gas pumps and scabby turquoise door visible reminders of its age. Inside ask to see a dusty museum room filled with American Indian crafts hidden behind the turquoise bullpen-style mercantile. Often you can buy a fine used Navajo wedding basket for a good price. ~ Oljeto; 801-727-3210.

Back to Kayenta and Route 160, it's a scenic 18-mile drive northwest to the turnoff for the **Navajo National Monument**, which encompasses some of the Southwest's finest Anasazi ruins (open only from Memorial Day to Labor Day). This stunning region showcases the architectural genius of the area's early inhabitants.

To gain an overview of the monument, stop by the **Visitors Center and Museum** featuring films and exhibits of the treasures tucked away beneath the sandstone cliffs. You'll be impressed by pottery, jewelry, textiles and tools created by the Kayenta Anasazi who lived in these exquisite canyons. There's also a craft gallery selling Zuni, Navajo and Hopi artwork. ~ Nine and a half miles north of Route 160 on Route 564, or twenty miles southwest of Kayenta; 520-672-2366.

From the visitors center you can hike an undemanding forest trail to **Betatakin Point Overlook**. Here you'll get an overview of Betatakin Ruin and Tsegi Canyon. One of the ruins here, **Inscription House**, is closed to protect it for posterity. However, it is possible to make the strenuous but rewarding hike to **Betatakin Ruin**, located in a dramatic alcove 700 feet below the canyon's rim. On this trip back in time, you'll see a 135-room ledge house that rivals the best of Mesa Verde. Also well worth a visit is remote **Keet Seel**. Even some of the roofs remain intact at this 160-room, five-kiva ruin. You can only reach this gem with a permit obtained at the visitors center. For more information on the ranger-led walks to these two well-preserved ruins, see "Hiking" at the end of the chapter.

Back on Route 160, it's about 28 miles southwest to **Elephant Feet**, roadside geologic formations that resemble legs and feet of a gigantic sandstone elephant.

LODGING

Wetherill Inn has 54 spacious rooms sporting dark-brown furniture, upholstered chairs, multicolored spreads and matching curtains in Southwest style. ~ Route 163, a mile north of Route 160, Kayenta; 520-697-3231, fax 520-697-3233. MODERATE.

Tour buses full of French, German, Italian and Japanese guests frequent the 160-room **Holiday Inn Kayenta**. All guest rooms in the two-story adobe brick buildings offer floral carpets in hallways, cherry-wood furniture, upholstered chairs and spacious bathrooms. There's also an outdoor pool. ~ Route 160 just west of Route 163, Kayenta; 520-697-3221, 800-465-4329, fax 520-697-3349. DELUXE.

The only lodging right at Monument Valley, open since the 1920s, takes brilliant advantage of the views. Sliding glass doors lead to balconies for each of the 62 rooms at **Gouldings Lodge** so guests can enjoy the eroded Mitten Buttes. The indoor pool is for guests only. ~ Four miles east of the tribal park, Monument Valley, UT; 801-727-3231, 800-874-0902, fax 801-727-3344. DELUXE.

Anasazi Inn at Tsegi Canyon, with 57 rooms and a view of the canyon, is the closest lodging to Navajo National Monument. ~ Ten miles west of Kayenta on Route 160; 520-697-3793, fax 520-697-8249. MODERATE.

DINING

An American Indian theme prevails at the **Holiday Inn Restaurant**, complete with Anasazi-style walls and sandpainting room dividers. Tables for four and matching chairs are decorated in Southwest style. There's a continental breakfast buffet for diners in a hurry; a salad bar and burgers, sandwiches, Navajo tacos for lunch or dinner; meat and fish entrées for dinner. ~ On Route 160 just west of Route 163, Kayenta; 520-697-3221. MODERATE.

Old West saloon architecture signals Kayenta's **Golden Sands Café**. Inside, wagon-wheel lamps, miniature stagecoaches and other Old West memorabilia continue the theme. Breakfast specials include omelettes or blueberry pancakes; dinner entrées include rib steak, barbecued chicken, chicken-fried steak and Navajo tacos. ~ Adjacent to the Wetherill Inn on Route 163, a mile north of Route 160, Kayenta; 520-697-3684. BUDGET.

Lively, crowded and cheery, **Amigo** serves fresh (nothing served here comes out of a can) Mexican, American and Navajo entrées. Popular with locals. Closed Sunday. ~ On the east side of Route 163, a mile north of Route 160, Kayenta; 520-697-8448. BUDGET.

Three levels of dining stairstep a bluff so that the **Stage Coach Dining Room** patrons can enjoy the panoramas of Monument Valley. Part of a late 1980s major expansion and remodel, this former cafeteria now offers sit-down service. The peach and burnt umber booths and tables compliment the stunning sandstone bluffs and views outside. A dinner favorite is the roast leg of lamb. Desserts worth a splurge include blueberry pie and cherry pie or a fudge brownie with ice cream. There's a salad bar, and nonalcoholic wine and beer are offered. ~ At Gouldings Lodge, Monument Valley; 801-727-3231 ext. 404. MODERATE.

An all-American menu at **Anasazi Inn Café** offers burgers, steak, chicken and a few Navajo dishes. ~ On Route 160, ten miles west of Kayenta; 520-697-3793. MODERATE.

SHOPPING Ask to see the crafts room at the 1921 **Oljeto Trading Post**, 11 miles northwest of Gouldings near Monument Valley, and you'll be led into a dusty museum-like space. The room is crammed with crafts, some for sale, some for admiring. Best buys here are Navajo wedding baskets popular with today's local brides and grooms. Simple, brown-pitch Navajo pottery made in this area is also sold here as well as cedar cradleboards, popular on the "res" as a baby's safety seat. ~ Oljeto; 801-727-3210.

Yellow Ribbon Gift Shop provides Southwestern tribal crafts and souvenirs for all budgets. ~ Part of Gouldings complex, Monument Valley; 801-727-3231.

PARKS **MONUMENT VALLEY NAVAJO TRIBAL PARK** 🚶 🚲 🏇 Straddling the Arizona-Utah border is the jewel of tribally run Navajo Nation parks. With its 29,816 acres of monoliths, spires, buttes, mesas, canyons and sand dunes—all masterpieces of red-rock erosion—it is a stunning destination. With dozens of families still living here, it is also a sort of Williamsburg of Navajoland. There's a visitors center with museum and shops, showers, restrooms, picnic tables, arts and crafts. ~ On Route 163, 24 miles northeast of Kayenta. The visitors center is east another four miles. The Gouldings complex is west three miles; 801-727-3353.

▲ Mitten View has 100 sites; $10 per night up to six people.

NAVAJO NATIONAL MONUMENT 🚶 🏇 Three of the Southwest's most beautiful Anasazi pueblo ruins are protected in the canyons of this 360-acre park, swathed in piñon and juniper forests at a 7300-foot elevation. Inscription House Ruin is so fragile it is closed. Betatakin Ruin, handsomely set in a cave high up a canyon wall, is visible from an overlook. But close looks at Betatakin and the largest site, Keet Seel, require fairly strenuous hikes permitted between Memorial Day and Labor Day. Visitors center, museum, gift shop, restrooms, picnic areas and barbecue grills. ~ Take Route 160 west of Kayenta, turn right at Route 564 and continue nine miles; 520-672-2366.

▲ There are 45 sites; no fee.

Outdoor Adventures

FISHING

Fishing is permitted year-round in Indian Country with a one-day to one-year Navajo tribal license required at all lakes, streams and rivers in the Navajo Nation. No fishing tackle or boats are for rent on the reservation. Boats are permitted on many of the lakes; most require electric motors only.

WESTERN NAVAJO COUNTRY Get fishing licenses and boating permits from CSWTA Inc. Environmental Consultant. ~ Tuba City; 520-283-4323.

CENTRAL NAVAJO COUNTRY Whiskey Lake and Long Lake are known for their trophy-size trout, located in the Chuska Mountains, a dozen miles south of Route 134 via logging routes 8000 and 8090. Their season is May 1 through November 30.

Popular all-year lakes stocked with rainbow trout each spring include **Wheatfields Lake** (44 miles north of Window Rock on Route 12) and **Tsaile Lake** (half-mile south of Navajo Community College in Tsaile). Tsaile Lake is also popular for catfish.

Good for largemouth bass and channel catfishing is **Many Farms Lake** (three miles via dirt road east of Route 191 in Many Farms). You can get licenses and permits from **Navajo Fish & Wildlife**. ~ Window Rock; 520-871-6451. **Wilkinson's Tsaile Trading Post** also has licenses and gear. ~ Tsaile; 520-724-3484.

NORTHERN NAVAJO COUNTRY The Kayenta Trading Post has fishing licenses and boating permits. ~ Kayenta; 520-697-3541.

JOGGING

Navajos and Hopis, who pride themselves on their long-distance-running traditions that date back to first contact with whites in the

RIDE 'EM COWBOY!

Statisticians claim Navajos host more rodeos per year than all other United States tribes combined. Rarely does a summer weekend pass without Navajo cowboys and cowgirls of all ages gathering somewhere on the reservation. To find one when you visit, call *The Navajo Times*, a weekly, in Window Rock (520-871-6641), the Navajo Tourism Office (520-871-6659), or Navajo Radio Station KTNN (520-871-2666).

1540s, host races at every tribal fair. Races are open to non-Indians as well. And it is common to see American Indian joggers daily along virtually any route, so bring your togs and run too.

CENTRAL NAVAJO COUNTRY   At Canyon de Chelly, try the White House Ruins trail or either of the rim trails.

NORTHERN NAVAJO COUNTRY   The four-mile road leading into Monument Valley or roads to Oljeto and around Gouldings Lodge are good places for a jog.

JEEP TOURS   Jeeps, either with tops down or with air conditioning on (not all jeeps have air conditioning, so ask operators before you pay money) are a popular way to see Navajo Indian Reservation attractions noted for occasional sand bogs and even quicksand pockets. Navajo guides often live in the region and can share area lore and American Indian humor.

At Canyon de Chelly, **Thunderbird Lodge Tours** offer half- or all-day outings in large, noisy, converted all-terrain Army vehicles. ~ Thunderbird Lodge, Chinle; 520-674-5841.

Monument Valley tour operators all offer half-day and all-day tours of Monument and adjoining Mystery Valley. It's the only way visitors can see the stunning back country. Most tours include visits to an inhabited hogan. Some offer lunch or dinner.

Licensed operators include: **Gouldings Monument Valley Tours.** ~ At Gouldings Lodge near Monument Valley; 801-727-3231. **Tom K. Bennett Tours.** ~ 801-727-3283. **Bill Crawley Monument Valley Tours.** ~ Kayenta; 520-697-3463. **Frank and Betty Jackson's Dineh Guided Tours.** ~ Monument Valley Visitors Center. **Navajo Guided Tour Service.** ~ Monument Valley Visitors Center; 801-727-3287.

RIDING STABLES   Horses have been an important icon of Navajo culture since the Spanish introduced them in the mid-16th century. They're a grand way to connect with a Navajo guide while seeing awesome country through his eyes. Most offer one-hour to overnight or longer options; there's flexibility on where you go and how long you stay.

CENTRAL NAVAJO COUNTRY   In Canyon de Chelly, **Justin Tso's Tsegi Stables,** located right at the entrance of the reservation, offers tours to White House Ruins and elsewhere in and beyond the canyon. ~ 520-674-5678. **Twin Trails Tours** depart from the North Rim of Canyon de Chelly, about one mile past Antelope House turnoff. ~ 520-674-8425.

NORTHERN NAVAJO COUNTRY   In Monument Valley, **Ed Black's Horse Riding Tours** can be an hour around The Mittens, or all day or longer into the valley. ~ Located via a dirt road north from the visitors center a quarter-mile; 801-739-4285. **Bigman's Horseback Riding** offers one-and-one-half-hour to overnight rides into the monument's buttes, mesas and canyons. ~ Three-fourths mile east of Route 163; 520-677-3219. Arrange for horse rides to Keet Seel Ruin in Navajo National Monument through the **National Park Service.** Open from Memorial Day to Labor Day. ~ 520-672-2366.

Biking is permitted on any paved roads in Navajo Country, but only on the main paved highways on the Hopi Indian Reservation.

SOUTHERN NAVAJO COUNTRY Petrified Forest National Park routes will often be too hot for daytime summer riding but offer a splendid way to sightsee in cooler spring and fall seasons.

CENTRAL NAVAJO COUNTRY While you'll find no designated bike paths or trails within the reservation, bicycles are well suited to both rim roads at Canyon de Chelly. Cyclists from around the world are attracted to the uphill challenges of the Chuska Mountain Routes 134 (paved), 68 and 13 (partially paved).

NORTHERN NAVAJO COUNTRY Bicycling is popular along the paved, pine-clad nine miles of Route 564 into Navajo National Monument visitors center. Mountain bikes are particularly suited to the 17-mile rutted dirt loop open to visitors in Monument Valley.

BIKING

Because most of the land covered in this chapter is tribally owned or in national parks and monuments, hiking trail options are limited. Hopi back country is not open to visitors; it is, however, on the Navajo Indian Reservation. For the mountains, ask for suggestions from area trading posts, or hire an Indian guide by the hour or overnight or longer. Guides know the way and can share stories about the area.

A hat, sunglasses and drinking water are recommended for all hikes; add a raincoat during the July and August monsoon season.

HIKING

SOUTHERN NAVAJO COUNTRY **Little Painted Desert County Park** has a strenuous one-mile hiking trail descending 500 feet into some of the most colorful hills in all the Painted Desert. Colors are most intense early and late in the day.

Homolovi Ruins State Park offers a one-mile hiking trail leading past two of the largest Anasazi Indian village ruins (the ruins are four miles apart); at each you'll see skeletal walls outlining living quarters and kivas (ceremonial chambers) from villages thought to have belonged to the ancestors of today's Hopi people before they moved to their current mesas.

Petrified Forest National Park's summertime temperatures often soar in the 90s and 100s. Hiking is best early or late in the day. Water is available only at the visitors center at the north and south end of the park, so you're wise to carry extra with you.

A loop that begins and ends at the Crystal Forest stop on the park's 28-mile scenic loop, **Crystal Forest Interpretive Trail** (.5 mile), leads past the park's most concentrated petrified wood stands. You can see how tall these ancient trees were (up to 170 feet), and the variety of colors that formed after crystal replaced wood cells.

An introduction to the Chinle Formation, **Blue Mesa Hike** (1 mile) is a loop interpretive trail that leads past a wonderland of blue, gray and white layered hills. Signs en route explain how the hills formed and are now eroding.

Painted Desert Wilderness Area (unlimited miles) trailhead begins at Kachina Point at the park's north end. A brief trail descends some 400 feet, then leaves you on your own to explore cross-country some 35,000 acres of red-and-white-banded badlands of mudstone and siltstone, bald of vegetation. The going is sticky when wet. Get free backcountry permits at either visitors center.

CENTRAL NAVAJO COUNTRY Canyon de Chelly's only hike open to visitors without a guide is **White House Ruin Trail** (3 miles round-trip), beginning at the 6.4-mile marker on the South Rim Drive. The trail switchback is down red sandstone swirls, crosses a sandy wash (rainy seasons you will do some wading in Chinle Creek; bring dry socks) to a cottonwood-shaded masonry village with 60 rooms surviving at ground level and an additional ten rooms perched in a cliff's alcove above.

Free 9 a.m. to noon, ranger-led hikes of varying lengths elsewhere in the canyon begin most mornings at the visitors center. Navajo guides can be hired at the **Canyon de Chelly National Monument Visitors Center** to take you on short or overnight hikes into the canyon. ~ 520-674-5500.

Hiking is not permitted in **Monument Valley** without a Navajo guide. Hire one at the visitors center (801-727-3287) for an hour, overnight or longer. Fred Cly (801-727-3283, or ask at the visitors center) is a knowledgeable guide especially good for photo angles and best times of day.

Navajo National Monument trails include **Sandal Trail** (.5 mile), a fairly level self-guided trail to Betatakin Ruin overlook; bring binoculars. The ranger-led hike to **Betatakin Ruin**, or "ledge

---

✔ **CHECK THESE OUT—UNIQUE OUTDOOR ADVENTURES**
- Gallup through **Canyon de Chelley** and view the area through the eyes of your Navajo guide. *page 92*
- Head to **Whiskey and Long lakes** in the Chuska Mountains and try for the trophy-size trout. *page 91*
- Join the long-distance-running tradition of the Hopis and Navajos and jog the **White House Ruins trail**. *page 92*
- Descend 500 feet into the technicolor hills on a strenuous hike in **Little Painted Desert County Park.** *page 93*

house" in Navajo (2.5 miles), is strenuous, requiring a return climb up 700 steps. But it's worth the effort for the walk through the floor of Tsegi Canyon. National Park Service guides lead two tours of 25 hikers each day, May through September. Tokens are awarded on a first-come, first-served basis at the visitors center. The hike to **Keet Seel** (8 miles), the biggest Anasazi ruin in Arizona (160 rooms dating from 950 A.D. to 1300 A.D.) is open to hikers for long weekends, May through September. Much of the trail is sandy, making the trek fairly tiresome. You can stay only one night; 10 people a day may hike in. Reservations are made 60 days in advance, call 520-672-2366 or 520-672-2367. Or take your chances and ask for cancellations when you get there.

▼▼▼▼▼▼▼▼▼▼▼▼
Transportation

CAR

This is a land of wide-open spaces, but don't despair. Roads have vastly improved in the last decade, easing the way for travelers. Bounded on the south by **Route 40**, two parallel routes farther north lead east and west through Indian Country: the southern **Route 264** travels alongside the three Hopi mesas and Window Rock; the northern **Route 160**, en route to Colorado, is gateway to all the northern reservation attractions. **Route 89**, the main north-to-south artery, connects Flagstaff with Lake Powell, traversing the Western Indian Reservation. Five other good, paved north-south routes connect Route 40 travelers with Indian Country. **Route 99/2** and **Route 87** connect the Winslow area with Hopi villages. **Route 191** leads to Ganado, Canyon de Chelly and Utah. **Route 12**, arguably the prettiest of all, connects Route 264 with Window Rock and the back side of Canyon de Chelly. This is desert driving; be sure to buy gas when it is available.

AIR

There is no regularly scheduled commuter air service to Hopi or Navajo lands. The nearest airports are Gallup, New Mexico; Flagstaff, Arizona; and Cortez, Colorado.

BUS

Navajo Transit System offers weekday bus service between Fort Defiance and Window Rock in the east and Tuba City in the west. The system also heads north from Window Rock to Kayenta on weekdays with stops including Navajo Community College at Tsaile. ~ Based in Fort Defiance; 520-729-4002.

TRAIN

Amtrak's daily "Southwest Chief" connects Los Angeles with Chicago stops at three Indianland gateway cities: Flagstaff, Winslow and Gallup. ~ 800-872-7245. **Nava-Hopi Bus Tours** out of Flagstaff offers people arriving on Amtrak bus tours to Indian Country. ~ 520-774-5003.

FOUR

North Central Arizona

When it comes to north central Arizona, visitors soon discover that it's a region of vivid contrasts. The many unusual places to be found in this area vary dramatically in everything from altitude to attitude, from climate to culture. Here, you'll find communities that range from Old West to New Age, from college town to artist colony, along with lava cones and red rock spires, American Indian ruins and vast pine forests, even a meteor crater, all just waiting to be explored.

Set at the edge of a huge volcano field, Flagstaff grew up as a railroad town in the midst of the world's largest ponderosa pine forest. The town was founded in 1881, less than a year before the first steam train clattered through, and thrived first on timber and later on tourism. Today, both freight and passenger trains still pass through Flagstaff. The largest community between Albuquerque and the greater Los Angeles area on Route 40, one of the nation's busiest truck routes, Flagstaff's huge restaurant and lodging industry prospers year-round. In fact, casual visitors detouring from the interstate to fill up the gas tank and buy burgers and fries along the commercial strip that is Flagstaff's Route 40 business loop can easily form the misimpression that the town is one long row of motels and fast-food joints. A closer look will reveal it as a lively college town with considerable historic charm. A short drive outside of town will take you to fascinating ancient Indian ruins as well as Arizona's highest mountains and strange volcanic landscapes.

Less than an hour's drive south of Flagstaff via magnificent Oak Creek Canyon, Sedona is a strange blend of spectacular scenery, chic resorts, Western art in abundance and New Age notions. You can go jeeping or hiking in the incomparable Red Rock Country, play some of the country's most beautiful golf courses, shop for paintings until you run out of wall space or just sit by Oak Creek and feel the vibes. People either love Sedona or hate it. Often both.

You'll also have the chance to visit one of the state's best-preserved ghost towns. Jerome, a booming copper town a century ago, was abandoned in the 1950s and then repopulated in the 1960s by artists and hippies to become a tourist favorite today.

Prescott is a quiet little town with a healthy regard for its own history. Long before Phoenix, Flagstaff or Sedona came into existence, Prescott was the capital of the Arizona Territory. Today, it is a city of museums, stately 19th-century architecture and century-old saloons. Change seems to happen slowly and cautiously here. As you stroll the streets of town, you may feel that you've slipped back through time into the 1950s, into the sort of all-American community you don't often find any more.

▼▼▼▼▼▼▼▼▼▼
Flagstaff Area   Visitors who view Flagstaff from the mountain heights to the north will see this community's most striking characteristic: It is an island in an ocean of ponderosa pine forest stretching as far as the eye can see. At an elevation of 7000 feet, Flagstaff has the coolest climate of any city in Arizona. Because of its proximity to slopes in the San Francisco Peaks, Flagstaff is the state's leading ski resort town in the winter. It is also a lively college town, with students accounting for nearly 30 percent of the population.

SIGHTS   Flagstaff has been called "The City of Seven Wonders" because of its proximity to the Grand Canyon, Oak Creek Canyon, Walnut Canyon, Wupatki National Monument, Sunset Crater, Meteor Crater and the San Francisco Peaks. A good place to start exploring the area is downtown, toward the west end of Santa Fe Avenue (the business loop of Route 40). The downtown commercial zone retains its turn-of-the-century frontier architecture. Neither run-down nor yuppified, this historic district specializes in shops that cater to students from Northern Arizona University, on the other side of the interstate and railroad tracks. A building-by-building historic downtown **walking tour brochure** is distributed by the Main Street Foundation. ~ 323 West Aspen Avenue; 520-774-1330.

The **Flagstaff Visitors Center** provides ample information on the Flagstaff area. Take time to stroll through the old residential area just north of the downtown business district. Attractive Victorian houses, many of them handmade from volcanic lava rock, give the neighborhood its unique character. ~ 1 East Route 66; 520-774-9541.

On a hilltop just a mile west of downtown is **Lowell Observatory**. The observatory was built by wealthy astronomer Percival Lowell in 1894 to take advantage of the exceptional visibility created by Flagstaff's clean air and high altitude. His most famous achievement during the 22 years he spent here was the "discovery" of canals on the planet Mars, which he submitted to the scientific community as "proof" of extraterrestrial life. Building the observatory proved to be a great accomplishment in itself, though. The planet Pluto was discovered by astronomers at Lowell Observatory 14 years after Dr. Lowell's death, and the facility continues to be one of the most important centers for studying the solar system. Take a guided tour of the observatory and see Dr. Lowell's original Victorian-era telescope. On some summer evenings, astronomers hold star talks and help visitors stargaze through one of the center's smaller telescopes. Admission. ~ 1400 West Mars Hill; 520-774-3358; recorded schedule information, 520-774-2096.

Overshadowed by Lowell Observatory, the **Northern Arizona University Campus Observatory** actually offers visitors a better chance to look through a larger telescope. Public viewing sessions are held every Friday night when the sky is clear. The campus observatory specializes in studying eclipsing binary stars and pulsating stars. Closed Saturday and Sunday. ~ West side of San Francisco Street on campus; 520-523-7170.

◄ HIDDEN

Another sightseeing highlight in the university area is **Riordan Mansion State Historic Park**, a block off Milton Road north of the intersection of Route 40 and Route 17. The biggest early-day man-

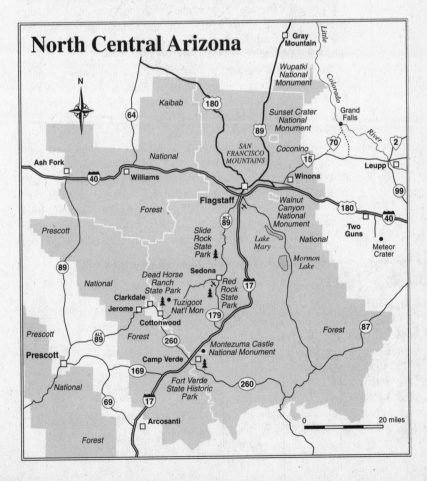

North Central Arizona

sion in Flagstaff, it was built in 1904 by two brothers who were the region's leading timber barons. Constructed duplex-style with over 40 rooms and 13,300 square feet of living space, the mansion blends rustic log-slab and volcanic rock construction with turn-of-the-century opulence and plenty of creative imagination. Tour guides escort visitors through the mansion to see its original furnishings and family mementos. Admission. ~ 1300 Riordan Ranch Road; 520-779-4395.

Just north of town on Route 180, the **Museum of Northern Arizona** is known worldwide for its exhibits of American Indian artifacts, geology, biology and the fine arts of the Grand Canyon region. During the summer months, the museum hosts separate exhibitions of Navajo, Hopi and Zuni artists. Admission. ~ 3001 North Fort Valley Road; 520-774-5211.

Nearby, the **Coconino Center for the Arts** provides space for fine-arts exhibits, musical performances, workshops and a folk-arts program. In summer, coinciding with the Museum of Northern Arizona's Indian artists exhibitions, the Center for the Arts presents a two-month Festival of Native American Arts. Closed Sunday. ~ 2300 North Fort Valley Road; 520-779-6921.

In the same vicinity, the **Arizona Historical Society–Pioneer Museum** exhibits memorabilia and oddities from Flagstaff's past, including a stuffed bear, Percival Lowell's 1912 mechanical computer and early-day photos of the Grand Canyon. Closed Sunday. ~ 2340 North Fort Valley Road; 520-774-6272.

Not far beyond the Museum of Arizona on Route 180 is the turnoff for **Schultz Pass Road**. This unpaved scenic drive offers glimpses of the spectacular San Francisco Peaks, which tower above Flagstaff. About 14 miles long, the road comes out on Route 89 a short distance north of the turnoff to **Sunset Crater National Monument**. Sunset Crater, a bright-colored 1000-foot-tall volcanic cone in the San Francisco Volcano Field, is of recent origin. It first

✔ **CHECK THESE OUT—UNIQUE SIGHTS**

- Stargaze through one of the **Lowell Observatory** telescopes when you visit Flagstaff during the summer. *page 98*
- Look in awe at the 800-year old cliff dwellings built by the Sinagua people and now protected in the **Montezuma Castle National Monument.** *page 108*
- Take time to stroll the streets of historic **Jerome** (population 500), a ghost town that was once a thriving silver-mining town. *page 115*
- Visit **Arcosanti,** the meeting place of architecture and ecology that will be home to 5000 people some day. *page 118*

erupted in the winter of 1064–65 and kept spraying out molten rock and ash until 1250. A one-mile self-guided nature trail, which starts 1.5 miles away from the visitors center, leads through cinder and lava fields. The ice cave along the trail has been closed because of unstable conditions since a 1984 cave-in. Hiking is no longer permitted on the slopes of Sunset Crater, either, since footprints create streaks visible from a great distance and mar the beauty of the perfect cone, but several other volcanic craters in the national forest are open to hikers and off-road vehicles. Admission. ~ Forest Service Road 545; 520-556-7042.

Near Sunset Crater National Monument, **Wupatki National Monument** preserves numerous pueblo ruins on the fringes of the volcano field. They were inhabited in the 12th and 13th centuries, at the same time the volcanic activity was at its peak. Repeatedly, fiery eruptions would drive the American Indians out of the area and volcanic ash would fertilize the land and lure them back. As a result, Wupatki's communities were small, architecturally dissimilar, often designed for defense as different groups competed for use of the rich farmland. A paved 36-mile loop road takes motorists through Sunset Crater and Wupatki national monuments, rejoining Route 89 about 15 miles from its starting point. Admission. ~ Forest Service Road 545; 520-556-7040.

Sinagua Indians (the name is Spanish for "without water," referring to their farming methods) lived from the Grand Canyon southward throughout central Arizona and are thought to be the ancestors of the Hopi people. One of the most interesting Sinagua sites is at **Walnut Canyon National Monument**. Here, the Indians built more than 300 cliff dwellings in the walls of a 400-foot-deep gorge. A paved trail takes visitors around an "island in the sky" for a close-up look at the largest concentration of cliff dwellings, while a second trail follows the rim of this beautiful canyon. Admission. ~ Take Exit 204 from Route 40 just east of Flagstaff; 520-526-3367.

Another fascinating bit of north central Arizona's flamboyant geology is **Meteor Crater**. A shooting star 80 feet in diameter and moving at an unimaginable speed struck the earth here 49,000 years ago and the impact blasted a crater 570 feet deep and a mile across. Geologist Daniel Barringer theorized a century ago that this was a meteor impact crater. Experts scoffed at the idea, especially since volcanic craters, so common east of Flagstaff, suggested a rational explanation for the phenomenon. He staked a mining claim to search for the huge, valuable mass of iron and nickel which, he was convinced, lay buried beneath the crater. An ambitious drilling operation did not strike a mother lode from outer space but did come up with fragments proving the theory and the geologist's family has been operating the claim as a tourist attraction ever since. The visit is worth the fairly steep admission fee if you take time to go on a guided tour along the main trail. Admission. ~ About thirty miles east of Flagstaff, five miles off Route 40 at Exit 233; 520-289-2362.

LODGING   For information on bed and breakfasts throughout Arizona, call or write to the **Arizona Association of Bed & Breakfast Inns.** ~ P.O. Box 7186, Phoenix, AZ 85011; 602-277-0775.

Flagstaff offers a good selection of bed-and-breakfast accommodations. Among the antique-furnished vintage lodgings available in the downtown area is **The Inn at Four Ten**, a beautifully restored 1907 home with nine guest suites and two guest rooms featuring period decor. ~ 410 North Leroux Street; 520-774-0088, 800-774-2008. MODERATE TO DELUXE.

Another bed and breakfast located in the historic district is the homelike **Birch Tree Inn.** ~ 824 West Birch Avenue; 520-774-1042, 800-645-5805. MODERATE.

There is also the **Dierker House**, where the three guest rooms have king-size beds with down comforters and share a common sitting room. ~ 423 West Cherry Street; 520-774-3249. MODERATE.

The large, rather elegant modern **Woodlands Plaza Hotel** has spacious and modern rooms, with pastel color schemes and king-size beds. Facilities for guests include indoor and outdoor whirlpool spas, a steam room, sauna, fitness center and heated swimming pool. Room service, valet service and complimentary shuttle service are also among the hotel's amenities. ~ 1175 West Route 66; 520-773-8888, 800-528-1234, fax 520-773-0597. MODERATE TO DELUXE.

The **Monte Vista Hotel**, a 1927 hotel now listed on the National Register of Historic Places, has spacious rooms that feature oak furniture, brass beds, velvet wall coverings and gold-tone bathroom fittings—a touch of old-time elegance. Movie stars used to stay here in the hotel's glory days and some rooms bear plaques naming the most famous person who ever slept in them: Humphrey Bogart, Cornell Wilde and Walter Brennan, to name a few. ~ 100 North San Francisco Street; 520-779-6971, 800-545-3068, fax 520-779-2904. MODERATE.

Flagstaff has three youth hostels. Especially in the summer months, all three of these affordable accommodations host backpack travelers of all ages from all parts of the world, and solitary travelers are sure to make instant friends here. The **Weatherford Hotel** operates as an AYH hostel and also offers a few very plain private rooms in a historic building downtown. ~ 23 North Leroux Street; 520-774-2731. BUDGET.

You can also try the **Grand Canyon Downtowner Independent Youth Hostel**, which has private and dormitory accommodations.

The hostel offers free pick-up service from both the Amtrak and Greyhound stations. ~ 19 South San Francisco Street, Flagstaff; 520-779-9421. BUDGET.

Also with private and dormitory rooms is the third hostel, **Motel Du Beau International Hostel.** Tours of the Grand Canyon are offered daily in the summer and less frequently during the rest of the year. ~ 19 West Phoenix Avenue, Flagstaff; 520-774-6731, 800-398-7112, fax 520-774-4060. BUDGET.

In the pines just five minutes out of town, the **Arizona Mountain Inn** offers bed-and-breakfast rooms in the main inn and one- to five-bedroom cottages with fireplaces and cooking facilities. Amenities include volleyball, horseshoe and basketball areas as well as hiking and cross-country skiing trails. ~ 685 Lake Mary Road; 520-774-8959, 800-239-5236, fax 520-774-8837. MODERATE.

DINING

For fine dining, one good bet is the small, homey-feeling **Cottage Place Restaurant.** Specialties include châteaubriand and roast duck à l'orange, as well as a vegetarian pasta with pesto. Reservations recommended. Closed Monday. ~ 126 West Cottage Avenue, Flagstaff; 520-774-8431. MODERATE.

Another good place for a romantic dinner is the **Woodlands Café.** There's booth and table seating at this Southwestern dining room with atrium windows and forest views. Navajo white walls are decorated with Navajo rugs and baskets; the chandelier is crafted from deer racks. You can select from such entrées as Gulf shrimp sautéed with onion, garlic, tomato and cilantro, and poached breast of chicken stuffed with wild rice and pepper. Reservations are recommended. ~ 1175 West Route 66, Flagstaff; 520-773-9118. MODERATE.

Yet another of Flagstaff's finest restaurants is **Chez Marc Bistro,** a small, intimate restaurant in a house listed on the National Register of Historic Places. A typical dinner might consist of duck pâté with pistachio hors d'oeuvre, baby greens with dijon vinaigrette and warm goat cheese and sea scallops on black fettuccine with fresh vegetables and saffron sauce. ~ 503 North Humphreys Street; 520-774-1343. DELUXE.

The Apollo astronauts trained at Meteor Crater before their moon landings in the late 1960s.

The **Main Street Bar and Grill** is a favorite among locals serving dishes such as fajitas, Philly cheesesteaks, quiche Lorraine and barbecued ribs. ~ 14 South San Francisco Street, Flagstaff; 520-774-1519. BUDGET TO MODERATE.

Other great little contemporary restaurants in Flagstaff's downtown area, featuring menu selections that emphasize healthy gourmet food, include **Charly's** on the ground floor of the Weatherford Hotel youth hostel. ~ 23 North Leroux Street; 520-779-1919. BUDGET.

Or you can try **Café Espress**, which specializes in vegetarian, poultry and fish selections. Changing exhibits by local artists adorn the walls. ~ 16 North San Francisco Street; 520-774-0541. BUDGET.

As a university town, Flagstaff has a plethora of pizzerias— over 20 of them. We recommend **NiMarco Pizza**. Besides the largest pizza-by-the-slice selection, NiMarco also has Italian-style baked stuffed sandwiches including exceptional stromboli. ~ 101 South Beaver Street; 520-779-2691. BUDGET.

HIDDEN ▶ For an unusual dining environment, head out of town to the **Mormon Lake Lodge Steak House & Saloon**, which has been in operation since 1924 and is reputed to be one of the West's finest steak houses. The restaurant also features ribs, chicken and trout, all cooked over a bed of mountain oak embers. The authentic brands from ranches all across Arizona which have been seared into the wood paneling of the restaurant's walls are said to be the result of one of the wildest branding parties ever. ~ Located 25 miles east of Flagstaff on Mormon Lake Road, Mormon Lake Village; 520-354-2227. MODERATE TO DELUXE.

SHOPPING The **Art Barn**, located next to the Coconino Center for the Arts, offers works of local and reservation artists for sale. A nonprofit, member-supported organization, the Art Barn provides artist facilities including classes, exhibition space and a bronze foundry. Closed Sunday and Monday during winter. ~ 2320 North Fort Valley Road, Flagstaff; 520-774-0822.

Flagstaff also boasts quite a few regional arts-and-crafts galleries, most of them featuring traditional and contemporary Navajo and Hopi work. One of the largest is **Four Winds Traders**. Closed Sunday and Monday. ~ 118 West Route 66; 520-774-1067.

Wander around the downtown area and you will find a number of others. East of downtown is **Jay's Indian Arts**. In operation since 1953, Jay's keeps mobile units on the road throughout the Southwest buying rugs, jewelry, pottery, kachinas and the like direct from artists on the Navajo, Hopi, Papago, Apache and Pueblo indian reservations. ~ 2227 East 7th Avenue; 520-526-2439.

NIGHTLIFE Because of the university, Flagstaff boasts both a busy cultural events calendar and a lively nightclub scene. On the cultural side, the performing arts roster includes the **Flagstaff Symphony Orchestra**. ~ 520-774-5107. Chamber music is the specialty of the **Coconino Chamber Ensemble**. ~ 520-523-3879. Classical fans may also want to attend a performance of the **Master Chorale of Flagstaff**. ~ 520-523-2642. The **Flagstaff Oratorio Chorus** holds performances in Flagstaff as well. ~ 520-523-4760. Also found in town is the NAU **Choir Office**. ~ 520-523-2642. Most performances are held at the **Coconino Center for the Arts**. ~ 2300 North

Fort Valley Road; 520-779-6921. Some are held at the **Northern Arizona University School of Performing Arts**. ~ Corner of Riordan Road and Knoles Drive; 520-523-3731.

The **Theatrikos Community Theatre Group** performs at the Flagstaff Playhouse. ~ 11 West Cherry Street; 520-774-1662. For current performance information, inquire at the **Flagstaff Visitors Center** or tune to the university's National Public Radio station, KNAU, at 88.7 on your FM dial. ~ Visitors center: 101 East Route 66; 520-774-9541.

As for nightclubs, one hot spot is **The Monsoons**, a rock-and-roll club attached to a barbecue restaurant. Cover. ~ 22 East Santa Fe Avenue, Flagstaff; 520-774-7929.

Charly's, on the ground floor of the Weatherford Hotel youth hostel, features jazz and blues. ~ 23 North Leroux Street, Flagstaff; 520-779-1919.

For a more intimate atmosphere, check out **Granny's Closet**. ~ 218 South Milton Road, Flagstaff; 520-774-8331. Another intimate favorite is the **Mad Italian**, known locally as the "Mad I." ~ 101 South San Francisco Street, Flagstaff; 520-779-1820.

The sometimes rowdy **Museum Club**, better known among the locals as the "Zoo Club," is one of the best examples in the West of an authentic cowboy club. The huge log-cabin-style building began as a trading post and taxidermy shop in 1931 and has operated as a nightclub since 1936. Decor includes an ornate 1880 mahogany back bar and an astonishing collection of big game trophies. Legendary country artists who have performed here include Willie Nelson, Bob Wills and the Texas Playboys, Commander Cody and the Lost Planet Airmen and many others. Cover for live bands. ~ 3404 East Route 66, Flagstaff; 520-526-9434.

PARKS

LAKE MARY Actually two long reservoirs, Upper and Lower Lake Mary provide the primary water supply for Flagstaff. They were created by damming Walnut Creek, which explains why there is no longer any water flowing through Walnut Canyon National Monument. The National Forest Service operates picnic areas on the wooded lakeshore and the small Lakeview Campground overlooks the upper lake. Both lakes are popular places to fish for northern pike, walleye pike and catfish. The upper lake is also used for power boating and waterskiing. There are picnic areas. Closed winter and early spring. ~ Located eight miles south of Flagstaff on Lake Mary Road. From Route 40, take Exit 195-B and follow the signs; 520-774-1182.

▲ Lakeview Campground has 30 sites; $7 per night. Pinegrove Campground has 46 sites; $8 per night.

MORMON LAKE The largest natural lake in Arizona, covering over 2000 acres when full, is very shallow, averaging only ten feet in depth and can shrink to practically nothing during spells of dry weather. Because the shoreline keeps changing, there is no boat ramp and anglers must carry their boats to the water by hand. Several hiking trails run along the lakeshore and into the surrounding forest. Nature trail, lodge, restaurant, groceries, winter sports. ~ It's 30 miles southeast of Flagstaff via Lake Mary Road. For information about camping and the lake itself contact the forest service at 520-774-1182. For all other information call 520-354-2227.

▲ There are 27 sites at Dairy Springs and 15 sites at Double Springs; $6 per night. Campgrounds are closed mid-September to Memorial Day.

▼▼▼▼▼▼▼▼▼
Sedona Area

Sedona. The creative and the mystical have always been intrigued by the place. Indians once came here to worship, New Agers to feel the "vibrations," artists to capture the beauty. But no matter the number of its devotees, no one knows exactly why this place has such appeal. Its essence remains elusive. Perhaps part of the seduction are the colors—red rock mountains that rise from the earth to nestle in brilliant blue sky. The landscape is a dreamy mix of fancifully shaped hoodoos, buttes and spires rising above green piñon and juniper trees, low shrubs and stark patches of reddish rock. Adjacent to Sedona is the spectacular Oak Creek Canyon, named after the creek that formed it by carving into the southern edge of the Colorado Plateau. All of these natural elements are highlighted by an intense sunlight that brings out contrast and color.

Sedona is located about halfway between Phoenix and the Grand Canyon. The first to discover this special spot were the Indians. About 800 years ago, the Southern Sinagua Indians settled here, leaving behind a 600-room cliff dwelling ruin called Honaki, which is now on the National Register of Historic Places. If you're out hiking, it's worth a side trip to discover these ruins. However, don't be surprised if you are turned away. The ruins are very fragile and are almost disappearing due to impact. They're located on an alcove on the west side of Loy Butte next to Lincoln Canyon.

More settlers came at the turn of the century. At the time, the economic base of the economy was ranching and farming, and apple orchards dotted the area. Writer Zane Grey was also charmed by the area, drawing attention to it in the book *Call of the Canyon* in the 1920s and publicizing it even more in the film version, which was shot on location.

With all this attention, it was only a matter of time before tourism became the main attraction. Today about 4 million people visit the town annually. They come to shop at the numerous art galleries, to nurture their spirits, and to relax amidst a red rock fantasy.

Capture
the Energy

For years, Sedona has received attention as a place with an unusual energy. Long considered sacred ground by American Indian tribes, the Sedona area has become a haven for New Age followers who are drawn to unique energy points termed "Vortexes."

There are various theories underlying the Vortexes' existence. Some say they are focal points in the earth's "natural energy grid," places where energy, both negative and positive, enter and leave the earth. Others explain the phenomena as electric and magnetic forces or yin/yang energy.

While it's believed there are many such places in the world, this area has become well known within the New Age community. It is commonly claimed that psychic powers, emotions and talents are stronger here, and people say it's a place where you are forced to face yourself—for better or worse. Indeed, some people move to the area expecting to enjoy the heightened energy and, finding Sedona too intense a place, move on.

Before either accepting the Vortexes as real or dismissing them, why not go there yourself and see whether you can feel the power that draws many thousands of people to Sedona every year. It is as good an excuse as any to explore deeper into this stunning Red Rock Country.

While some local visionaries claim to have identified as many as 13 Vortexes, only four are generally recognized. The **Airport Mesa Vortex** is a little more than a mile south of Route 89A on the way to the airport. The **Boynton Canyon Vortex**, one of the area's most popular hiking areas, is several miles north of West Sedona via Dry Creek Road and Boynton Pass Road (for more information see "Hiking" at the end of the chapter).

The **Cathedral Rock Vortex** is by a lovely picnic area alongside Oak Creek, reached from Route 89A in West Sedona via Red Rock Loop Road and Chavez Ranch Road; the rock itself is one of the most photographed places in the area. The **Bell Rock Vortex**, a popular spot for UFO watchers, is just off Route 179 south of Sedona near the Village of Oak Creek. Each vortex reportedly has a radius of ten miles, so you don't need to be standing on one particular spot to feel the force.

SIGHTS   **Oak Creek Canyon** is the most accessible of several magnificent canyons that plunge from the high forests of northern Arizona down toward the low deserts of southern Arizona. A major highway—Route 89A from Flagstaff—runs the length of Oak Creek Canyon, making for a wonderful, though often crowded, scenic drive. After a long, thrilling descent from Flagstaff to the bottom of the canyon, where the creek banks are lined with lush riparian vegetation, the highway passes a number of picnicking, camping and fishing areas.

Midway down the canyon is one of Arizona's most popular state parks, **Slide Rock State Park** (see "Parks" below). At the lower end of the canyon, travelers emerge into the spectacular Red Rock Country, the labyrinth of sandstone buttes and mesas and verdant side canyons surrounding Sedona. The elevation drop from Flagstaff to Sedona is 2500 feet, and the temperature is often 20 degrees higher in Sedona than in Flagstaff.

Sedona is a town for shopping, for sports, for luxuriating in spectacular surroundings. It is not the kind of place where you will find tourist attractions in the usual sense. Other than Oak Creek Canyon, Sedona's most popular tourist spots are spiritual in nature. The **Chapel of the Holy Cross**, south of town on Route 179, is a Catholic "sculpture church" built between two towering red sandstone rock formations. It is open to visitors daily. The **Shrine of the Red Rocks**, on Table Top Mesa two miles off Route 89A on Airport Road, features a large wooden cross and a great view of the Red Rock Country.

And then there are Sedona's **"Vortexes."** The Vortex idea was "channeled" through members of the town's highly visible New Age community several years ago and keeps evolving. For more information, see "Capture the Energy" in this chapter.

A half-hour's drive south of Sedona via Route 179 and Route 17, **Montezuma Castle National Monument** protects 800-year-old

✔ **CHECK THESE OUT—UNIQUE LODGING**

- *Moderate:* Sleep in the room that Humphrey Bogart slept in at **Monte Vista Hotel**, once a popular place among movie stars. *page 102*
- *Moderate:* Brave the night at the **Ghost City Inn**, a Victorian B & B with rooms called "Satin & Spurs" and "Champagne & Propane." *page 115*
- *Deluxe:* Gallup your way to the **Greyfire Farm**, where people *and* horses are welcome to stay overnight. *page 111*
- *Ultra-deluxe:* Treat yourself to the luxury of **Los Abrigados**, a lavish Sedona resort with stylish suites and endless amenities. *page 110*

Budget: under $50   Moderate: $50–$90   Deluxe: $90–$120   Ultra-deluxe: over $120

cliff dwellings built by the Sinagua people, ancestors of the Hopi. The ruins got their name from early explorers' mistaken belief that Aztecs fled here and built the structures after the Spanish conquest of Mexico. Though there is no truth to the old theory, archaeologists now know that several centuries before the Spanish arrived, Toltec traders used to visit the Southwest, bringing with them architectural methods from central Mexico. The main "castle" is a five-story, 20-room residential structure set high on the cliff. Although visitors cannot climb up to the ruin, the view from the nature trail below will tingle the imagination. The visitors center displays artifacts of the Sinagua and Hohokam cultures. Admission. ~ 2800 Montezuma Castle Highway, Camp Verde; 520-567-3322.

South of Montezuma's Castle via Route 17, in the small town of Camp Verde, portions of an old cavalry fort from the Apache Wars in the 1870s and early 1880s are preserved as **Fort Verde State Historic Park.** Visitors can walk through the former surgeons' and officers' quarters, and there is a museum of pioneer and military artifacts. The fort formed the end of the General Crook Trail, the major patrol and supply route during the Apache Wars, which followed the Mogollon Rim west for more than 100 miles from Fort Apache. The trail is used for hiking and horseback riding today. Admission. ~ Hollamon Street, Camp Verde; 520-567-3275.

Near the little town of Cottonwood, en route from Sedona to Prescott a few miles below Jerome, is **Tuzigoot National Monument,** an uncharacteristically large Sinagua Indian pueblo ruin. Once home to about 225 people, the fieldstone pueblo stood two stories high and had 110 rooms. Today its white walls still stand on the hilltop and command an expansive view of the valley. Although the vista is marred by slag fields from a refinery that used to process Jerome's copper ore, the museum at the national monument offers a good look at the prehistoric culture of the Sinagua people. Admission. ~ Route 89A, 520-634-5564.

One of the most beautiful canyons in the area is **Sycamore Canyon,** which parallels Oak Creek Canyon. Sycamore Canyon is a designated wilderness area, meaning that no wheeled or motorized vehicles are allowed. The Parsons Trail takes you up the wild, lushly wooded canyon for most of its 4-mile length, passing numerous small cliff dwellings resting high above. Camping is not permitted in the lower part of Sycamore Canyon. For information, call the Sedona Rangers Station. ~ Turn off at Tuzigoot National Monument and follow the well-maintained dirt road for about 12 miles to the trailhead at the end of the road; 520-282-4119.

As you drive down Oak Creek Canyon from Flagstaff to Sedona, you will notice several privately owned lodges and cabin complexes in the midst of this spectacular national forest area. You can reserve accommodations at these places and enjoy the canyon in

LODGING

the cool of the evening and early morning, avoiding the midday throngs and traffic of peak season and weekends. Several places are located just below Slide Rock State Park.

Top of the line, **Junipine Resort** offers modern suites and one- and two-bedroom "creekhouses." These individually decorated one- and two-story units are all crafted from wood and stone. Offering mountain, forest or creek views, each 1300 to 1500 square foot unit comes with a kitchen and redwood deck overlooking the canyon. ~ 835 North Route 89A, Oak Creek Canyon; 520-282-3375, 800-742-7463, fax 520-282-7402. ULTRA-DELUXE.

Canyon Wren Cabins offers one old-fashioned log cabin and three chalets with loft bedrooms, within walking distance of swimming holes, fishing spots and hiking trails. ~ Route 89A, Oak Creek Canyon; 520-282-6900, 800-437-9736. DELUXE.

In the same part of the canyon, there are more simple accommodations at **Don Hoel's Cabins**. ~ Route 89A, Oak Creek Canyon; 520-282-3560, 800-292-4635, fax 520-282-3654. MODERATE.

Houses, all with fireplaces and fully equipped kitchens, are available at **Forest Houses**. ~ Route 89A, Oak Creek Canyon; 520-282-2999, 520-282-0663. MODERATE TO DELUXE.

Farther down canyon, **Oak Creek Terrace** offers resort accommodations ranging from motel-style rooms with king-size beds, color TV and fireplaces to two-bedroom suites with heart-shaped jacuzzis. ~ Route 89A, Oak Creek Canyon; 520-282-3562, 800-224-2229, fax 520-282-6061. MODERATE TO ULTRA-DELUXE.

Sedona specializes in upscale resorts. Among the poshest accommodations in town is **Los Abrigados**. Situated next to the atmospheric Tlaquepaque shopping area, Los Abrigados features fanciful Mexican-inspired modern architecture throughout and elegantly stylish suites with kitchens, fireplaces and patios or balconies. Guest facilities include tennis courts, swimming pool, weight room and spa. ~ 160 Portal Lane; 520-282-1777, 800-521-3131, fax 520-282-6913. ULTRA-DELUXE.

Another top-of-the-line Sedona accommodation is **L'Auberge de Sedona**. Individually designed guest rooms and cottages are decorated with furnishings imported from Provence, France, to recreate the atmosphere of a French country inn on ten acres of creekside grounds within walking distance of uptown Sedona. ~ 301 L'Auberge Lane; 520-282-1661, 800-272-6777, fax 520-204-5757. ULTRA-DELUXE.

Charming, more affordable lodging in Sedona can be found at the **Rose Tree Inn**, which strives for an "English garden environment" and has patios and a jacuzzi. This small inn is close to uptown. ~ 376 Cedar Street; 520-282-2065, fax 520-282-0083. MODERATE TO DELUXE.

A Touch of Sedona Bed and Breakfast, uphill from uptown, offers five individually decorated theme rooms with corresponding motifs—the "Contemporary Eagle," "Hummingbird," "Kachina," "Roadrunner" and "Wolf's Den." ~ 595 Jordan Road; 520-282-6462, 800-600-6462, fax 520-282-1534. MODERATE TO DELUXE.

Greyfire Farm is one of the area's more unusual bed and break-   ◀ HIDDEN
fasts. Nestled among the pines in a rural canyon between the Red Rock Country and Wild Horse Mesa, near hiking and horseback riding trails in the national forest, the "farm" can accommodate two guest horses. It provides bed and breakfast for human guests as well. Rooms are bright with quilts and have private baths. ~ 1240 Jacks Canyon Road, Sedona; 520-284-2340, 800-579-2340, fax 520-284-2340. DELUXE.

For basic motel rooms in Sedona, the **White House Inn** in West Sedona just before the Dry Creek Road turnoff provides lodging with phone and cable television. ~ 2986 West Route 89A; 520-282-6680. MODERATE.

Near uptown Sedona, the **Star Motel** also offers standard rooms. ~ 295 Jordan Road; 520-282-3641, 800-896-7301. MODERATE.

Visitors seeking to change their lives in Sedona might want to consider staying at the **Healing Center of Arizona**. Rates for accommodations in this dome complex are mid-range, and inexpensive gourmet vegetarian meals are served. Amenities, offered for reasonable fees, include a sauna and a spa. Holistic therapies available to guests at the center include acupressure treatments, herbology, rebirthing, crystal healing, psychic channeling and more. ~ 25 Wilson Canyon Road; 520-282-7710. BUDGET TO MODERATE.

For American Continental cuisine, try **Tray's**. Although it's in a   **DINING**
shopping mall, the restaurant has been cleverly decorated to look like a Mediterranean courtyard. The menu includes filet mignon, duck à l'orange and chicken piccata, as well as vegetarian entrées such as pomodora basilica. ~ 2370 West Route 89A, #10; 520-282-3532. DELUXE.

◆◆

✔ CHECK THESE OUT—UNIQUE DINING

- *Budget:* Join the other folks who go back time and again to the **Dinner Bell Cafe** for the delicious home-style cooking. *page 119*
- *Moderate to deluxe:* Work up an appetite and then head to **Mormon Lake Lodge Steak House & Saloon,** said to be one of the West's best steak houses. *page 104*
- *Moderate to deluxe:* Savor the lamb and poultry served in the **House of Joy,** an elegant restaurant that was once a bordello. *page 115*
- *Ultra-deluxe:* Indulge in fine French prix-fixe dinners at **L'Auberge de Sedona,** where there's a view of Oak Creek. *page 112*

Budget: under $8 Moderate: $8–$16 Deluxe: $16–$24 Ultra-deluxe: over $24

L'Auberge de Sedona has an outstanding French restaurant with a view on Oak Creek and memorable prix fixe dinners. The six-course menu, which changes nightly, typically features pâté, soup, a small baby green salad and entrées such as poached salmon, grilled lamb or chicken. ~ 301 L'Auberge Lane, Sedona; 520-282-1661. ULTRA-DELUXE.

Another outstanding Continental restaurant is **Rene at Tlaquepaque,** which specializes in rack of lamb carved tableside. The most elaborate French Provincial decor in the Southwest makes this restaurant extra special. Open-air patio dining is available. ~ Route 179 at Tlaquepaque, Sedona; 520-282-9225. DELUXE.

A good Mexican restaurant is **Oaxaca,** which has an outdoor deck for dining with a view of uptown Sedona. ~ 321 Route 89A, Sedona; 520-282-4179. MODERATE.

Italian food is featured at the **Hideaway,** with tables on a balcony over the creek, surrounded by a stand of sycamore trees. ~ Route 179 near Route 89A, Sedona; 520-282-4204. MODERATE

For health-conscious Thai food, made with all natural, organic ingredients, try **Thai Spices Natural,** a restaurant located in the White House Inn motel in West Sedona. ~ 2986 West Route 89A, Sedona; 520-282-0599. BUDGET TO MODERATE.

And for a synthesis of ethnic cuisines—European, Mediterranean and Asian cooking techniques used to create highly original, healthy dishes such as red cabbage with goat cheese, hazelnuts and apples or Cajun fish with raspberry glazed cucumbers—head for the **Heartline Café.** ~ 1610 West Route 89A, Sedona; 520-282-0785. MODERATE TO DELUXE.

For just plain good, just-like-mom's food in Sedona, the place to go is **Irene's Restaurant** near the intersection of Route 179 and Verde Valley School Road. Irene's is famous for home-cooked desserts, including apple dumplings, peach cobbler and giant cinnamon rolls. ~ Castle Rock Plaza; 520-284-2240. BUDGET TO MODERATE.

Another good spot is **Phil and Eddie's Diner,** offering all-day breakfasts, burgers and fries, blue-plate specials and soda fountain suggestions in a 1950s nostalgia ambience. ~ 1655 West Route 89A, Sedona; 520-282-6070. BUDGET.

SHOPPING   Sedona's shopping district is one of the three or four best in Arizona. Many of the galleries, boutiques and specialty shops are labors of love, the personal creations of people who spent years past daydreaming about opening a cute little store in Sedona. The town has more than 60 art galleries, most of them specializing in traditional and contemporary American Indian art, "cowboy" art and landscape paintings. Quality is relatively high in this very competitive art market. You can easily spend a whole day shopping your way up and down the main streets of town, leaving your feet sore and your credit cards limp.

Most galleries and boutiques, as well as tourist-oriented shops, are in "uptown" Sedona, on Route 89A above the "Y" (the junction where Route 89A curves right toward West Sedona while the road continuing straight becomes Route 179). Virtually all supermarkets, shopping malls and places where practical things can be purchased are in West Sedona.

The most relaxing and enjoyable place in Sedona to browse is **Tlaquepaque**, a large, eye-catching two-story complex of specialty shops and restaurants below the "Y" on Route 179. Built in Spanish Colonial style with old-looking stone walls, courtyards, tile roofs and flowers in profusion, Tlaquepaque looks more like Old Mexico than the real thing. Representative of the range of stores here are several that deal in animal motifs. **Aguajito del Sol** exhibits animal sculptures. ~ 520-282-5258. **Mother Nature's Trading Company** carries educational toys and games in addition to rocks and minerals. ~ 520-282-5932. The **Cuddly Coyote** presents a selection of stuffed toy animals, books and children's clothing. ~ 520-282-4480. In addition, **Showcase El Mundo**, a working artists' studio for the visual and performing arts, offers demonstrations by the artists in residence. ~ 520-282-1625.

Sedona is named after the wife of the town's first postmaster, Sedona Schnebly.

Across the highway from Tlaquepaque you'll find the **Crystal Castle**, one of the larger New Age stores in this town which, according to many, is the New Age capital of the known cosmos. It carries unusual books, incense, jewelry, runes, visionary art and, of course, crystals. In front of the store, a "networking" bulletin board lets you scan the array of alternative professional services in town—channelers, psychic surgeons, clairvoyants, kinesiologists, numerologists and many more. ~ 313 Route 179; 520-282-5910.

There are many other stores in the same vein in Sedona, such as **Angels, Art & Crystals**. ~ 2445 West Route 89A; 520-282-7089. The **Golden Word Book Centre** offers New Age literature. ~ 3150 West Route 89A; 520-282-2688. Get your chakras aligned at **Crystal Magic**. ~ 2978 West Route 89A; 520-282-1622. Can't get enough? The **Center for the New Age** has Vortex information, networking for New Age activities, psychic readings daily and a "Psychic Faire" every Saturday. ~ 341 Route 179; 520-282-1949.

Shopping enthusiasts will also want to visit **Oak Creek Factory Outlet**, a mall located south of town on Route 179 in the village of Oak Creek. This is factory-direct outlet shopping with a difference. The factories represented include **Capezio** (520-284-1910), **Jones of New York** (520-284-1919), **Mikasa** (520-284-9505), **Izod/Gant** (520-284-9844) and **Anne Klein** (520-284-0407)—designer goods at discount prices.

NIGHTLIFE   Sedona has surprisingly little nightlife. One exception is the **Samba Café**, where you can hear top-notch jazz on Sunday and Monday evenings. This is a favorite gathering spot for locals who come here to relax, socialize and enjoy the tasty *tapas*. ~ 2321 West Route 89A; 520-282-5219.

Other than that, try the lounges in the major resort hotels, or call the **Sedona Arts Center** for their current schedule of theatrical and concert performances. ~ Route 89A at Art Barn Road; 520-282-3809.

PARKS   **SLIDE ROCK STATE PARK** 🏃 ⚓ Very popular with students from the Northern Arizona University, this swimming area midway between Flagstaff and Sedona in the heart of Oak Creek Canyon is almost always packed during warm-weather months. It is like a natural water park, with placid pools, fast-moving chutes and a wide, flat shoreline of red sandstone for sunbathing. The state park also includes the Pendley homestead, listed on the National Register of Historic Places and acres of apple orchards. Visitors are not allowed to pick the apples, but cider made from them is sold at a stand on the trail to the swim area. When rangers are available they lead nature/historical walks on Saturdays. You'll find a picnic area, restrooms, volleyball court, nature trail, snack bar; day-use fee, $5. ~ Located seven miles north of Sedona via Route 89A in Oak Creek Canyon; 520-282-3034.

RED ROCK STATE PARK 🏃 🚲 ⚓ Beautiful Oak Creek runs through this 286-acre park situated in the heart of Red Rock Country. Naturalists offer guided walks daily along the six-mile trail system dotted with sycamore and cottonwood trees. One route leads to a 1948 house that resembles an Indian pueblo and, sitting atop a hill, affords great views of the area. The visitors center has natural history exhibits and videos. Fishing is allowed on Oak Creek, with catches including warm-water catfish and sunfish. There are picnic areas, restrooms and a visitors center; day-use fee, $5. ~ Drive four miles southwest of Sedona on Route 89A, then turn south on Lower Red Rock Loop Road; the park appears in three miles; 520-282-6907.

DEAD HORSE RANCH STATE PARK 🏃 ⚓ This 325-acre park, located along the Verde River, has both desert and lush areas that can be enjoyed by walking the extensive hiking trails. Fishing is allowed in the Verde River and the four-acre lagoon, which is stocked with panfish, catfish, bass and trout. There are picnic tables, restrooms and showers; day-use fee, $5. ~ From Cottonwood, take Main Street to 10th Street, then go north for about a mile; 520-634-5283.

▲ There are 45 sites; $10 per night for no hookups, $15 per night with hookups.

Jerome, located southwest of Sedona on Route 89A, is one of Arizona's most intriguing ghost towns. After having been completely abandoned in the 1950s, it was resettled by hippies in the late 1960s and now has a population of about 500 people—a mere shadow of the 15,000 population it had in the first decades of the 20th century, when it was a rich silver mining district and the fifth-largest city in Arizona.

The history of Jerome's mining era is brought to life in three museums. The old Douglas Mansion in **Jerome State Historic Park** at the lower end of town offers an informative 25-minute video called "Ghost Town of Jerome," a three-dimensional model of Jerome showing the underground shafts and tunnels and a mineral exhibit. Admission. ~ Douglas Road; 520-634-5381.

For a look at mining tools, old photos, and other exhibits about old-time copper mining enter the **Jerome Historical Society Mine Museum.** Admission. ~ Main Street; 520-634-5477.

The **Gold King Mine Museum** has a re-created assay office, a replica mine shaft and a petting zoo. Admission. ~ Perkinsville Road; 520-634-0053.

The real pleasure of Jerome lies in strolling the streets that switchback up Cleopatra Hill, browsing in the shops along the way and admiring the carefully preserved turn-of-the-century architecture. Many of the town's buildings were constructed of massive blocks of quarried stone to withstand the blasts that frequently shook the ground from the nearby mine. The entire town has been declared a National Historic Landmark.

A historic railroad that carries sightseers through some of Arizona's most spectacular country is the **Verde River Canyon Excursion Train.** Revived in November 1990, this train achieved instant popularity as a major tourist attraction. It takes passengers on a 40-mile round trip from Clarkdale, just below Jerome. The diesel-powered train winds along sheer cliffs of red limestone in curve after curve high above the Verde River, through a long, dark tunnel, over bridges, past gold mines and Indian Ruins, to the ghost town of Perkinsville and back. Admission. ~ 300 North Broadway Street, Clarkdale; 520-639-0010.

An 1898 Victorian bed and breakfast, the **Ghost City Inn** features five rooms with shared baths. Visit the Old West in the "Satin and Spurs" room or float away in the "Champagne and Propane" room. There's also a jacuzzi to relax in. ~ 541 North Main Street; 520-634-4678. MODERATE.

In Jerome, the elegant place to dine is the **House of Joy,** a former house of ill repute whose past is recalled in the decor—red lights, red candles, red flowers, red placemats, red everything. The fairly limited menu features veal, lamb and poultry. Seating is by reservation only. Open for dinner on weekends only. ~ Hull Avenue; 520-634-5339. MODERATE TO DELUXE.

For breakfast or lunch, try the **Flat Iron Café**, serving pastries, vegetarian dishes and panini sandwiches along with gourmet coffees and teas in historic surroundings. ~ 416 Main Street; 520-634-2733. BUDGET.

SHOPPING   Many of Jerome's residents are arts-and-crafts people, and a stroll up and down the town's switchback main street will take you past quite a few intriguing shops that offer pottery, jewelry, handmade clothing, stained glass and other such wares.

You can watch jewelers create contemporary designs at **Aurum Jewelry**. About 50 local artists show their work here, which ranges from a sculptured iron spoon and fork to belt buckles, bolo ties, custom knives and jewelry. ~ 369 Main Street; 520-634-3330.

A good place to hunt for a souvenir that recalls Jerome's mining origins is **The Copper Shop**. ~ 130 Main Street; 520-634-7754.

At the **Raku Gallery**, about 30 artists sell raku and contemporary artwork. It's worth stopping by just for the dramatic views from the glass wall facing Verde Valley and Boynton Canyon. ~ 250 Hull Avenue; 520-639-0239.

In the last few years, the heart of the working art movement in town has been centered at the **Old Mingus Art Center**, which is now filled with studios and galleries carrying everything from paintings to blown glass. The biggest is the **Anderson/Mandette Art Studios** One of the largest private art studios in the country, it feels more like a museum as you walk through it. One level contains working studios and a 9' x 17' canvas titled "Arizona." Upstairs, paintings hang by Robin Anderson and Margo Mandette. ~ Route 89A; 520-634-3438.

NIGHTLIFE   The Old West saloon tradition lives on in Jerome, where the town's most popular club is the **Spirit Room** in the old Conner Hotel. There is live music on weekend afternoons and evenings and the atmosphere is as authentic as can be. Cover. ~ 166 Main Street at Jerome Avenue; 520-634-8809.

▼▼▼▼▼▼▼▼▼
Prescott   Continuing southwest on Route 89A, in the next valley, sits the Prescott, the original territorial capital of Arizona from 1864 to 1867. President Abraham Lincoln decided to declare it the capital because the only other community of any size in the Arizona Territory, Tucson, was full of Confederate sympathizers. Today, Prescott is a low-key, all-American city with a certain quiet charm and few concessions to tourism. Incidentally, Prescott is located at the exact geographic center of the state of Arizona.

Built in 1916, the **Yavapai County Courthouse** sits at the heart of **SIGHTS**
Prescott, surrounded by a green plaza where locals pass the time
playing cards and chatting, and tourists rest awhile on park
benches. Surrounding the plaza are many of the town's shops, in
addition to historic Whiskey Row, where at one time some 20 saloons were open day and night.

The major sightseeing highlight in Prescott is the **Sharlot Hall**
Museum, which contains a large collection of antiques from Arizona's territorial period, including several fully furnished houses
and an excellent collection of stagecoaches and carriages. Sharlot
Mabridth Hall was a well-known essayist, poet and traveler who
explored the wild areas of the Arizona Territory around the turn
of the century. In 1909, she became the territorial historian, a position she held until Arizona achieved statehood. Seeing that Arizona's historic and prehistoric artifacts were rapidly being taken
from the state, Ms. Hall began a personal collection that grew
quite large over the next three decades and became the nucleus of
this large historical museum. The museum's collections are housed
in several Territorial-era buildings brought from around the county,
including one governors' mansion, in a large park in downtown
Prescott. The museum is closed Monday during winter. ~ 415
West Gurley Street; 520-445-3122.

Prescott also has some other noteworthy museums. The **Phippen**
Museum of Western Art, six miles north of town, honors cowboy
artist George Phippen and presents changing exhibits of works by
other cowboy artists. It is generally considered one of the best
cowboy art museums in the country. Closed Tuesday. Admission.
~ 4701 Route 89 North; 520-778-1385.

The **Smoki Museum** houses a large collection of Indian artifacts from throughout the Southwest. The museum also houses the

SHARLOT HALL

One of the most admired women in Arizona history was Sharlot Hall, who
arrived in Prescott in 1882. She helped manage the family ranch east of
Prescott, passing time writing poetry and panning for gold. But in 1909
she became the territorial historian and the first woman in Arizona to
hold a political office. In 1924, Hall was asked to go east and represent
Arizona in the electoral college. Originally she turned down the offer,
not having enough money for suitable clothes. But officials at the
United Verde Mine saved the day, buying her a blue silk dress with a
fine copper mesh coat. This "copper dress" was a hit back east and
gave a free shot of publicity to the Arizona copper industry. Today,
you can learn all about her in the Sharlot Hall Museum.

largest collection of Kate Cory's works as well as a library. Closed Wednesday during the summer. Open by appointment only from October through May. Admission. ~ 147 North Arizona Street; 520-445-1230.

Probably the most unusual of Prescott's museums is the **Bead Museum**, displaying a phenomenal collection of beads, jewelry and other adornments from around the world and explaining their uses as trade goods, currency, religious items and status symbols. Visitors to this one-of-a-kind nonprofit museum discover that there's more to beads than they ever suspected. Closed Sunday. ~ 140 South Montezuma Street; 520-445-2431.

Thirty-four miles east of Prescott you'll find **Arcosanti**, a planned city that will eventually be home to 5000 people. Arcosanti was designed by famed Italian designer Paolo Soleri as a synthesis of architecture and ecology. It is pedestrian-oriented, and its unusual buildings with domes, arches, portholes and protruding cubes, make maximum use of passive solar heat. Tours are offered daily. Continuing construction is financed in part by the sale of handmade souvenir items such as Cosanti wind bells. Admission. ~ Route 17, Exit 262 at Cordes Junction; 520-632-7135.

LODGING   Prescott has several historic downtown hotels. The most elegant of them is the **Hassayampa Inn**, a 1927 hotel listed on the National Register. The lobby and other common areas have been restored to their earlier glory and furnished with antiques. The rooms have been beautifully renovated and all have private baths, telephones and color TVs. ~ 122 East Gurley Street; 520-778-9434, 800-322-1927. DELUXE TO ULTRA-DELUXE.

A smaller hotel on a quiet side street is the **Hotel Vendome**. Rooms in this 1917 hotel have been nicely restored and decorated in tones of blue. Some have modern bathrooms, while others have restored Victorian-style baths. ~ 230 South Cortez Street; 520-776-0900. MODERATE.

Sitting atop Nob Hill with a view of Courthouse Square is **The Marks House**, a yellow Queen Anne Victorian bed and breakfast. Built in 1894, the house and its four guest rooms are decorated with antiques; all have feather beds and private baths. Mornings begin with a full family-style breakfast. ~ 203 East Union Street; 520-778-4632. MODERATE TO DELUXE.

More modest rooms, all with private baths, are available at the **Hotel St. Michael**. The location couldn't be better for those who wish to enjoy the Wild West nightlife of Whiskey Row, on the same block. ~ 205 West Gurley Street; 520-776-1999, 800-678-3757, fax 520-776-7318. BUDGET TO MODERATE.

A posh bed and breakfast in a 1902 main house with four guest houses is the **Prescott Pines Inn**. It has 13 Victorian-style guest rooms beautifully decorated in subdued color schemes. Some have fireplaces and others have kitchens. Sumptuous full breakfasts are served on rose patterned china. Reservations are recommended as much as a year in advance for peak season. ~ 901 White Spar Road; 520-445-7270, 800-541-5374, fax 520-778-3665. MODER-ATE TO DELUXE.

Prescott also has more than its share of low-priced, basic lodging from which to explore the wild canyons and forests surrounding the city. The prices can't be beat at the once charming, now somewhat run-down Mediterranean-style **American Motel**, rooms have telephones and wonderful old murals on the walls. ~ 1211 East Gurley Street; 520-778-4322, fax 520-778-1324. BUDGET.

Prescott's finer restaurants include the **Peacock Room** in the Hassayampa Inn. Here you'll find a full menu of Continental and American specialties in an elegant old-time atmosphere. An etched-glass peacock ornaments the front door of this art deco dining room. Choose between seating at tables or semicircular booths. Tiffany-style lamps add to the quaint atmosphere of this high-ceilinged establishment. ~ 122 East Gurley Street; 520-778-9434. MODERATE TO DELUXE.

DINING

A century old general merchandise store that has been transformed into a popular restaurant, **Murphy's** is a walk through history. A leaded-glass divider separates the bar and restaurant sections decorated with photos of Prescott's mining heyday. Mahogany bar booths and a burgundy carpet add to the charm of this establishment. You can also enjoy a drink in the lounge offering views of Thumb Butte. Specialties include mesquite-broiled seafood and prime rib of beef along with fresh home-baked bread. ~ 201 North Cortez Street; 520-445-4044. MODERATE TO DELUXE.

With many plants and a creekside view, the **Prescott Mining Company** is a large, modern restaurant with an entrance styled after a mine shaft. It serves a number of steak and seafood dishes. Closed Monday during winter. ~ 155 Plaza Drive; 520-445-1991. MODERATE TO DELUXE.

For breakfast or lunch in Prescott, a very popular place in the downtown area is **Greens and Things**, which serves an assortment of pancakes, omelettes and homemade soups. ~ 106 West Gurley Street; 520-445-3234. BUDGET.

Also good is the **Prescott Pantry** in the Iron Springs Plaza shopping center. This bakery-deli-wine shop has restaurant seating and offers ever-changing daily specials, hearty sandwiches, espresso and cappuccino and fresh-baked pastries. ~ 1201 Iron Springs Road; 520-778-4280. BUDGET.

For home-style cooking in Prescott head to the **Dinner Bell Café**. It may not look like much from the outside, but give it a try and you'll find out why this is one of the most popular restaurants in central Arizona. For breakfast try the hubcap size pancakes or three egg omelettes. Lunch specials include pork chops, chicken-fried steak, ground round steak and hot roast beef. Be sure to try the homemade salsa. ~ 321 West Gurley Street; 520-445-9888. BUDGET

SHOPPING Because it is old as Arizona towns go, and perhaps because of Sharlot Hall's recognition that it was important to preserve the everyday objects of 19th-century Arizona, Prescott is a good place for antique shopping. As in most antique hunting areas, some items offered for sale do not come from the Prescott area but have been imported from other, less visited parts of the country. Most, however, are the real thing, and antique buffs will find lots of great shops within walking distance of one another in the downtown area, especially along the two-block strip of Cortez Street between Gurley and Sheldon streets.

Most of the bars that line Prescott's Whiskey Row have been in operation since the late 19th century, when this was one of the most notorious sin strips in the West.

Some of the best places to browse are the indoor mini-malls where select groups of dealers and collectors display, such as the **Merchandise Mart Antique Mall.** ~ 205 North Cortez Street; 520-776-1728. **Prescott Antique & Craft Market** is another such mall. ~ 115 North Cortez Street; 520-445-7156. Nearby is the **Deja Vu Antique Mall**, which also features an old-fashioned soda fountain. ~ 134 North Cortez Street; 520-445-6732.

An excellent gallery in town is **Sun West**. Arizona and local artists sell sculpture, pottery, furniture, paintings and jewelry, and there are also rugs woven by the Zapotec people. ~ 152 South Montezuma Street; 520-778-1204.

NIGHTLIFE If old-time saloons appeal to you, don't miss Prescott's **Whiskey Row**, downtown on the block of Montezuma Street directly across from the Yavapai County Courthouse. The saloons remain authentically Old Western, and so do most of the customers.

The fanciest of the bunch is **Big Mike's Palace**, which has live country music Friday and Saturday. ~ 120 South Montezuma Street; 520-778-4227. Another typical bar of the genre is the **Bird Cage Saloon**. Cover on weekends. ~ 148 South Montezuma Street. Or stop by **Billy's Western Bar**. Cover on weekends. ~ 144 South Montezuma Street; 520-445-1244.

PARKS **WATSON LAKE AND GRANITE DELLS** 🏃 ⛵ 🚣 A labyrinth of granite rock formations along Route 89 just outside of Prescott surrounds pretty little Watson Lake, a manmade reservoir that is locally popular for boating and catfish fishing. The area used to be a stronghold for Apache Indians. More recently, from the 1920s to the 1950s, there was a major resort at Granite Dells and some artifacts survive from that era. There are picnic area, restrooms, showers, hiking, rock climbing. ~ Located four miles northeast of Prescott on Route 89; 520-778-4338.

▲ There are 50 sites (25 with electrical hookups); $11 per night with electricity, $8 without.

North Central Arizona is a popular region for both downhill and cross-country skiing.

▼▼▼▼▼▼▼▼▼▼▼▼▼▼
Outdoor Adventures

SKIING

FLAGSTAFF AREA   Arizona's premier downhill ski area is the **Arizona Snowbowl**, located 14 miles north of Flagstaff on the slopes of the San Francisco Peaks. The ski season runs from mid-December to mid-April. ~ Snowbowl Road; 520-779-1951; snow report, 520-779-4577. The small **Williams Ski Area** is located on Bill Williams Mountain, about four miles south of the town of Williams. ~ 520-635-9330.

For cross-country skiers, the **Flagstaff Nordic Center**, 16 miles north of Flagstaff in Coconino National Forest, maintains an extensive system of trails from mid-November through mid-March. The center offers equipment rentals, guided tours and a ski school. ~ Route 180; 520-779-1951. Another great cross-country skiing facility is the **Mormon Lake Ski Touring Center**, 28 miles southeast of Flagstaff off Lake Mary Road. The center is open from December to late February. ~ Mormon Lake Village; 520-354-2240.

BALLOON RIDES

For the most spectacular guided tour in town, sightsee from a hot-air balloon.

SEDONA AREA   See the Red Rock Country from the sky with **Red Rock Balloon Adventure**. ~ 3230 Valley Vista Drive, Sedona; 520-284-0040. Also hovering above is **Northern Light Balloon Expeditions**. ~ P.O. Box 1695, Sedona, AZ 86339; 520-282-2274.

JEEP TOURS

For Sedona visitors who wish to explore the surrounding Red Rock Country, the town has an extraordinary number of jeep tour services, offering everything from general sightseeing journeys to spiritual inner journeys. Trips range from one hour to all day, and are fully guided. They'll usually pick you up at any Sedona lodging.

Pink Jeep Tours runs sightseeing trips in—what else—those flashy pink jobs you see darting around town. ~ 204 North Route 89A; 520-282-5000. **Pink Jeep Tours Ancient Expeditions**, their more low-key operation, uses green jeeps and leads trips to Indian ruins and petroglyphs, which require a little hiking as well as jeeping. ~ 276 North Route 89A; 520-282-2137. Ooh and ahh at the vista from 2000 feet up Schnebley Hill Road, or explore ruins in the Boynton Canyon backcountry with **Sedona Adventures Jeep**

Tours. ~ Uptown Mall; 520-282-3500. Whether you're looking for a Wild West sightseeing tour that traverses private ranchlands, or a New Age "Vortex Tour" where you can absorb the electromagnetic energy that is said to swirl among select stones in Boynton Canyon, the cowboy-garbed guides at **Sedona Red Rock Jeep Tours** can provide it; the emphasis here is educational, so whichever tour you take, you'll doubtless learn as much as you ever wanted to know about the area. ~ 270 North Route 89A; 520-282-6826. **Earth Wisdom Tours** also runs trips to the Vortex, with discussions covering science, myth, personal growth and the secrets of the Medicine Wheel. ~ 293 North Route 89A; 520-282-4714.

GOLF

While you might not be able to golf year-round here, most of the year offers excellent weather for hitting the greens.

FLAGSTAFF AREA   Tee off at **Elden Hills Golf Resort**, closed in winter. ~ 2380 North Oakmont Drive, Flagstaff; 520-527-7997.

SEDONA AREA   Pitch and putt at **Sedona Golf Resort**. ~ 7260 South Route 179; 520-284-9355. Drive a wedge at **Village of Oak Creek Country Club**. ~ 690 Bell Rock Boulevard, Sedona; 520-284-1660. Play the greens at **Canyon Mesa Country Club**. ~ 500 Jacks Canyon Road, Sedona; 520-284-2176. Swing some clubs at **Poco Diablo Resort**. ~ 1752 South Route 179, Sedona; 520-282-7333. Go for a hole in one at **Antelope Hills Golf Course**. ~ 1 Perkins Drive, Prescott; 520-445-0583.

TENNIS

There is not a lot of tennis in this area, but you should be able to find a few open courts.

FLAGSTAFF AREA   Public tennis courts in Flagstaff are located in **Thorpe Park** (Toltec Street) and **Bushmaster Park** (Lockett Road).

SEDONA AREA   Sedona has no public tennis courts. For a fee, courts are available to the public at the **Sedona Racquet Club**. ~ 100 Racquet Drive, off West Route 89A; 520-282-4197. The same is true at **Poco Diablo Resort**. ~ 1752 South Route 179; 520-282-7333.

PRESCOTT   In Prescott, tennis courts are open to the public during the summer months at **Yavapai College**. ~ 1100 East Sheldon Street; 520-445-7300. Public summer courts are also found at **Prescott High School**. ~ 1050 North Ruth Street; 520-445-5400. **Ken Lindley Field** has courts open for summer use. ~ East Gurley and Arizona streets.

RIDING STABLES

The equestrian will find many riding opportunities in this region.

FLAGSTAFF AREA   In Flagstaff, try **Hitchin' Post Stables**. ~ 448 Lake Mary Road; 520-774-1719. Also in Flagstaff is **Ski Lift Lodge Stables**. ~ Route 180 at Snow Bowl Road; 520-774-0729. **Perkins**

Wilderness Trail Rides leads rides in Williams but is closed in the winter. ~ Route 40 Exit 171; 520-635-9349.

SEDONA AREA   **Kachina Stables** offers rides in Sedona. ~ Lower Red Rock Loop Road, Sedona; 520-282-7252.

As in the rest of the state, this region is fast becoming a mecca for biking.

BIKING

FLAGSTAFF AREA   Flagstaff has about eight miles of paved trails in its **Urban Trail System and Bikeways System**, linking the Northern Arizona University campus, the downtown area and Lowell Observatory. Maps and information on the trail system are available upon request from the **City Planning Office**. ~ 211 West Aspen Street; 520-779-7632.

Outside the city, a popular route for all-day bike touring is the 36-mile paved loop road through Sunset Crater and Wupatki national monuments, starting at the turnoff from Route 89 about 20 miles northeast of town.

For mountain bikers, several unpaved primitive roads lead deeper into the San Francisco Volcano Field in **Coconino National Forest**. Check out the forest road that leads to the base of Colton Crater and SP Crater. For complete information, contact the **Peaks Ranger Station**. ~ 5075 North Route 89; 520-526-0866.

The **Flagstaff Nordic Center**, 16 miles north of Flagstaff in Coconino National Forest, opens its extensive trail system to mountain bikers from the end of May through October and offers mountain bike and helmet rentals. ~ Route 180; 520-779-1951.

SEDONA AREA   The same network of unpaved back roads that makes the **Red Rock Country** around Sedona such a popular area for four-wheel-drive touring is also ideal for mountain biking. Get a map from one of the local bike shops and try the dirt roads leading from Soldier Pass Road to the Seven Sacred Pools or the Devil's Kitchen. Or follow the Broken Arrow Jeep Trail east from Route

---

✔ **CHECK THESE OUT—UNIQUE OUTDOOR ADVENTURES**

- Arrive in the winter and you won't be disappointed with the ski runs at **Arizona Snowbowl**, located on the San Francisco Peaks. *page 121*
- Soar above **Red Rock Country** in one of the many colorful hot-air balloons. *page 121*
- Set aside a day to explore the unpaved primitive roads through the **Coconino National Forest** by bicycle. *page 123*
- Hike **Parsons Trail** in Sycamore Canyon and you will be rewarded with vistas of cliff dwellings in the canyon above. *page 109*

179 to Submarine Rock. The Schnebly Hill Road climbs all the way north to Flagstaff, paralleling the Oak Creek Canyon Highway. The upper part of the road is steep, winding and very rough, but the lower part, through Bear Wallow Canyon, makes for a beautiful mountain biking excursion.

Bike Rentals   In Flagstaff, you can rent mountain bikes and obtain trail information at **Absolute Bikes**. ~ 18 North San Francisco Street; 520-779-5969. **Cosmic Cycles** also rents bikes. ~ 113 South San Francisco Street; 520-779-1092. **Mountain Sports** is another Flagstaff store with bikes and information. ~ 1800 South Milton Road; 520-779-5156. In Sedona, you'll find trail information and bike rentals at **Mountain Bike Heaven**. ~ 1695 West Route 89A; 520-282-1312. **Sedona Sports** also rents bikes. ~ 260 Van Deren Street; 520-282-1317.

HIKING   Lovers of the outdoors will delight in the number and variety of hiking trails this area provides.

FLAGSTAFF AREA   Just north of Flagstaff rise the San Francisco Peaks, the highest in Arizona. Numerous trails start from Mount Elden and Schultz Pass roads, which branch off Route 180 to the right a short distance past the Museum of Northern Arizona. Other trailheads are located in Flagstaff at Buffalo Park on Cedar Avenue and near the Peaks Ranger Station on Route 89. Most trails in the Flagstaff area close in winter.

The elevation drop from Flagstaff to Sedona is 2500 feet, and the temperature is often 20 degrees higher in Sedona than in Flagstaff.

From the ranger station, the **Elden Lookout Trail** (3 miles) climbs by switchbacks up the east face of 9299-foot Mount Elden, with an elevation gain of 2400 feet and, waiting to reward you at the top, a spectacular view of the city and the volcano fields around Sunset Crater.

The **Fatman's Loop Trail** (1 mile), branching off of Elden Lookout Trail for a shorter hike with a 600-foot elevation gain, also offers a good view of Flagstaff.

From the Buffalo Park trailhead, the **Oldham Trail** (5.4 miles) ascends the west face to the top of Mount Elden. The longest trail on the mountain, this is a gentler climb. The Oldham Trail intersects Mount Elden Road three times, making it possible to take a shorter hike on only the higher part of the trail. **Pipeline Trail** (2.8 miles) links the lower parts of the Oldham and Elden Lookout trails along the northern city limit of Flagstaff, allowing either a short hike on the edge of town or a long, all-day loop trip up one side of the mountain and down the other.

Perhaps the most unusual of many hiking options in the strange volcanic landscape around the base of the San Francisco Peaks is on **Red Mountain**, 33 miles north of Flagstaff off Route 180. A gap in the base of this 1000-foot-high volcanic cone lets

you follow the **Red Mountain Trail** (1 mile) from the end of the   ◄ *HIDDEN*
national forest access road straight into the crater without climbing. Not often visited by tourists, this is a great place to explore
with older children.

For maps and detailed hiking information on these and many
other trails in Coconino National Forest, contact the **Peaks Ranger
Station.** ~ 5075 North Route 89; 520-526-0866.

SEDONA AREA   While every visitor to Flagstaff or Sedona drives
through often-crowded Oak Creek Canyon, one of central Arizona's "must-see" spots, few stop to explore the canyon's west
fork, a narrow canyon with sheer walls hundreds feet high in
places, which is only accessible on foot. For more information on
trails in this area, call 520-282-4119.

The trailhead for the **West Fork Trail** (14 miles) is in the southwest corner of the Call of the Canyon on the west side of Route
89A, ten miles north of Sedona. There is a small parking area
nearby, often full. The first three miles of the fairly level trail, which
pass through a protected "research natural area," are heavily used
and easy to hike. Farther up, the trail becomes less distinct, requires fording the creek repeatedly and leads into the Red Rock
Secret Mountain Wilderness.

A very popular hiking spot in the Red Rock Country is Boynton Canyon, one of Sedona's four "Vortex" areas. According to
Sedona's New Age community, Boynton Canyon is the most powerful of the Vortexes, emanating an electromagnetic yin/yang psychic energy that can be felt for miles around. Whether you believe
in such things or not, it is undeniably beautiful. From the trailhead
on Boynton Pass Road—a continuation of Dry Creek Road, which
leaves Route 89A in West Sedona—the nearly level **Boynton
Canyon Trail** (2.5 miles) goes up the canyon through woods and
among redrock formations. There are several small, ancient Sinagua Indian cliff dwellings in the canyon. If you visit the ruins be
aware that the dwellings are very fragile and are disappearing due
to impact.

A right turn from Dry Creek Road on the way to Boynton Pass
will put you on unpaved Forest Road 152, which is rough enough
in spots that drivers of low-clearance vehicles may want to think
twice before proceeding. From this road, the **Devil's Bridge Trail**
(1 mile) climbs gradually through piñon and juniper country to a
long red sandstone arch with a magnificent view of the surrounding canyonlands. You can walk to the top of the arch. Located
three miles further, at the end of Dry Creek Road, is the trailhead
for the **Vultee Arch Trail** (2 miles), which follows Sterling Canyon
to another natural bridge.

PRESCOTT   There are many hiking trails in the national forest
around Prescott. One of the most popular is the **Thumb Butte**

Trail (1.7 miles), a loop trip that goes up a saddle west of town, through oak and piñon woods, offering good views of Prescott and Granite Dells. The trail starts from Thumb Butte Park. To get there, go west on Thumb Butte Road, an extension of Gurley Street.

More ambitious hikers may wish to explore the **Granite Mountain Wilderness**. Of its several trails, the one that goes to the summit of the 7125-foot mountain is **Little Granite Mountain Trail** (3.7 miles), a beautiful all-day hike with an elevation gain of 1500 feet. For information on this and other trails in the area, contact the Prescott National Forest—Bradshaw District ranger station. ~ 2230 East Route 69, just east of Prescott; 520-445-7253.

▼▼▼▼▼▼▼▼▼▼
Transportation

CAR

One hundred and thirty eight miles north of Phoenix via **Route 17**, Flagstaff is located on **Route 40**, the main east-west route across northern Arizona. Grand Canyon–bound travelers leaving the interstate at Flagstaff have a choice between the more direct way to Grand Canyon Village, 79 miles via **Route 180**, or the longer way, 105 miles via **Route 89** and **Route 64**, which parallels the canyon rim for 25 miles. These routes combine perfectly into a spectacular loop trip from Flagstaff.

Another scenic loop trip from Flagstaff goes south on **Route 89A**, descending through Oak Creek Canyon to the trendy town of Sedona in the magnificent Red Rock Country, a distance of 26 slow miles. From Sedona, Route 89A continues for 58 more miles through the historic mining town of Jerome, with a steep climb over Cleopatra Hill, to Prescott, the old territorial capital. From there, a 51-mile drive on Route 89 returns travelers to interstate Route 40 at Ash Fork, about 55 miles west of Flagstaff.

AIR

Mesa-America West Airlines flies into the **Flagstaff Pulliam Airport**.

Scenic Airlines (520-282-7935) provides on-demand charter service for travelers between the **Sedona Airport** and Phoenix.

BUS

Nava-Hopi Xpress provides bus service to the Grand Canyon South Rim, as well as Flagstaff, Williams and Phoenix. ~ 114 West Santa Fe Avenue, Flagstaff; 520-774-5003, 800-892-8687.

Greyhound Bus Lines stops at the bus terminals in Flagstaff and Prescott. ~ Reservations: 800-231-2222. Flagstaff: 399 South Malpais Lane; 520-774-4573. Prescott: 820 East Sheldon Street; 520-445-5470.

TRAIN

Amtrak serves Flagstaff and Kingman daily on its "Southwest Chief" route between Chicago and Los Angeles. The westbound passenger train stops in Flagstaff late in the evening, so arriving passengers will want to make hotel reservations in advance with a deposit to hold the room late. Amtrak offers a complimentary shuttle bus service to the Grand Canyon for its Flagstaff passengers. ~ 1 East Santa Fe Avenue, Flagstaff; 800-872-7245.

Flagstaff has about a dozen car-rental agencies, most of them at the airport. Among the airport concessions are **Avis Rent A Car** (800-331-1212), **Budget Rent A Car** (800-499-4888) and **Hertz Rent A Car** (800-654-3131). Located downtown, and more convenient for those arriving by train or bus, is **Budget Rent A Car.** ~ Corner of Humphreys (Route 180 North) and Aspen streets; 800-527-0700. **Triple A Car Rental** will accept a cash deposit in lieu of a credit card. ~ In the lobby of the Knights Inn; 520-774-7394. Also in Flagstaff is an office of **Cruise America**, a nationwide motorhome rental agency. ~ 824 West Route 66; 520-774-4707, 800-783-3768.

    At the Sedona Airport, rentals are available from **Budget Rent A Car** (800-499-4888).

    For rentals in Prescott try **Hertz Rent A Car** (Prescott Municipal Airport; 520-776-1399, 800-654-3131) or **Budget Rent A Car** (1031 Commerce Drive; 520-778-4282, 800-527-0700).

CAR RENTALS

Flagstaff has more than its share of taxi companies because many public transportation travelers stop there en route to the Grand Canyon. These cabs will take you anywhere in central Arizona at any time of day or night. Sedona? Phoenix? No problem. Call **A Friendly Cab** (520-774-4444), **Alpine Taxi Cab Co.** (520-526-4123) or **Harper's Taxi** (520-779-1234). Shop and compare— rates vary.

    Sedona's local taxi companies are **Bob's Sedona Taxi** (520-282-1234) and **Red Rock Taxi** (520-282-3600). Prescott's taxi company, **Ace City Cab** (520-445-1616) offers discounted rates for senior citizens and physically challenged persons. **Reliable V.I.P. Taxi** and **Limousine Service** run out of Prescott Valley.

TAXIS

FIVE

Western Arizona

Heading west, the mighty Colorado River pours out of the Grand Canyon, spreads itself into Lake Mead, proceeds through a succession of scenic lakes, resorts and riverfront coves, then rolls south until it reaches the Gulf of California. In its wake, visitors to the region will discover a number of unusual points of interest and unparalleled recreational opportunities—each one surrounded by a distinctive landscape, each one quite different from the others. Here, you'll find broad expanses of sparkling water, summer breezes whipping up whitecaps, waterskiers cutting crystal wakes, colorful sails curled above catamarans, and miles of sandy beaches—all along the Colorado River on Arizona's "West Coast."

Kingman is a good starting point for exploring Arizona's western edge. Set at the crossroads of Routes 93 and 40, the town is strategically placed for excursions to Lake Mead and Hoover Dam, Bullhead City/Laughlin and Lake Mohave, Lake Havasu and its London Bridge, and the Parker Strip and Quartzsite. Along the way, you can explore gold and silver mining ghost towns such as Oatman and Chloride, which cling to a tenuous existence amid scenic surroundings. From Kingman, there's also a steep road that leads to the alpine greenery of Hualapai Mountain State Park, where you can picnic and camp.

About 80 miles north of Kingman, on Route 93, is manmade Lake Mead, which is shared by Arizona and Nevada. Created in the 1930s when the Colorado River was backed up by Hoover Dam, Lake Mead is a popular recreation area.

In the forbidding, rocky hills of western Arizona's Mohave Desert, real estate promoters used to sell lots in planned communities sight unseen to gullible people in the East. Most of these would-be towns never even came close to reality, but two "cities" set in the middle of nowhere along desolate stretches of the Colorado River have become the twin hubs of a genuine phenomenon.

Bullhead City, the fastest-growing city in Arizona, is an isolated resort and retirement community of about 25,000 people. Founded as the construction camp for Davis Dam, Bullhead City has no visible reason for its existence except daily sunshine, warm weather year-round, boating and fishing access to the Colorado River—and a booming casino strip across the river in Laughlin, at the extreme southern tip of Nevada.

Even more improbable than Bullhead City is Lake Havasu City, which the *Los Angeles Times* has called "the most successful freestanding new town in the United States." Though it enjoys a great wintertime climate and a fine location on the shore of a 45-mile-long desert lake, there is really no logical explanation for Lake Havasu City—except that, in the 1960s, chain saw tycoon Bob McCulloch and partner C. V. Wood Jr., planner and first general manager of Disneyland, decided to build it. Since their planned community had no economic base, they concluded that what it needed was a tourist attraction. They came up with a doozie—the London Bridge. Yes, the *real* London Bridge, bought at auction and moved block by massive granite block across the Atlantic, where it was reassembled over a channel to connect to an island in Lake Havasu. The unprecedented, seemingly absurd plan actually worked, and you can see the result for yourself today.

In addition to London Bridge, Lake Havasu City has an "English Village" to complement it. Nearby, the two sections of Lake Havasu State Park are well-developed recreational areas that take advantage of the lake's 45 miles of shoreline. The Windsor Beach Unit on the upper level of the lake has boat ramps, shaded picnic areas, campsites and more primitive camping areas accessible by boat. The Cattail Cove Unit has similar facilities, plus a marina, restaurant, store and boat rentals.

Near Parker Dam, which impounds Lake Havasu, Buckskin Mountain State Park attracts tube floaters, boaters and waterskiers. Hiking trails into the Buckskin Mountains lead to panoramic vista points, and, for some lucky hikers, sightings of desert bighorn sheep.

About halfway down the "coast," the Bill Williams River empties into the Colorado River just above Parker Dam. Upstream is Alamo Lake State Park, a large man-made reservoir created for recreation and flood control. The lake has bass fishing, swimming, boating, canoeing and views of native wildlife, including the bald and golden eagle.

En route to these unusual Arizona communities, you'll have a chance to visit two of the state's wildlife preservation areas, the Fort Mohave Indian Reservation and Havasu National Wildlife Refuge. Keep a sharp eye and you may glimpse a bald eagle, peregrine falcon or desert bighorn sheep, along with a wide variety of other fauna.

Downriver from Parker Dam, the town of Parker and the Colorado River Indian Reservation serve as trade centers and jumping-off points for more recreation. Farther south, the town of Quartzsite, which is more a sprawling RV park than a city, attracts several hundred thousand people late January and early February for its annual rock and mineral shows.

▼▼▼▼▼▼▼▼▼
Kingman Area

At the crossroads of Routes 40 and 93, Kingman has earned a reputation as a comfortable stopover for travelers hurrying between Phoenix and Las Vegas or Los Angeles and Albuquerque. It is also a natural hub for leisurely trips to nearby ghost towns, Hoover Dam, Lake Mead and other recreational resorts along the Colorado River.

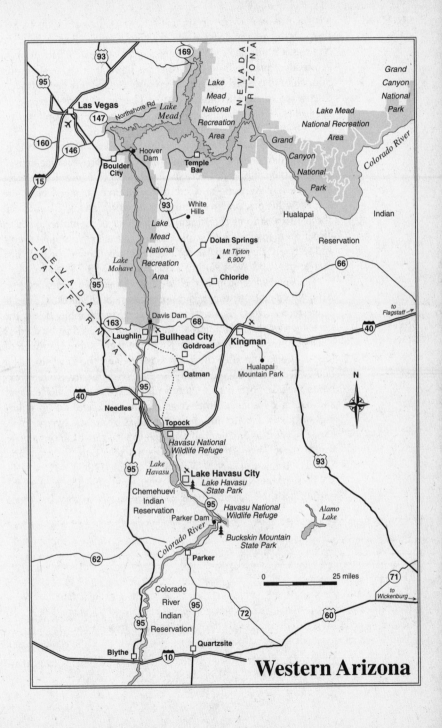

Western Arizona

SIGHTS   Kingman was named for surveyor Lewis Kingman, who passed through the area in 1892 while charting a railroad route between Needles, California, and Albuquerque, New Mexico. The railroad camp subsequently built here took his name, but the town didn't flourish until the early 1900s, when silver and copper deposits were discovered in the surrounding hills. The mines were depleted by the 1940s, but the town survived as an important pit stop for travelers on the Santa Fe railway and old Route 66.

With more than 1500 motel rooms and 50 restaurants, modern-day Kingman continues its tradition as a key provisioning center. Most of the commercial activity has shifted to Motel Row—East Andy Devine Avenue—and suburban shopping centers, but there are a few historical gems around town worth seeing. To find out about them, stop at the **Kingman Chamber of Commerce**, which dispenses maps, brochures and a listing of the area's annual events and festivals. Be sure to ask for a map of downtown's historic district tour. ~ 333 West Andy Devine Avenue; 520-753-6106.

An interesting stop is the **Mohave Museum of History and Arts**, which gives visitors a glimpse of many of the unusual aspects of western Arizona. A mural and dioramas in the lobby depict the settlement of the region and show how camels used to be used as beasts of burden in these parts. Kingman is the source of much of the turquoise mined in the United States, and the museum has a fine collection of carved turquoise objects. American Indian exhibits include portrayals of the traditional ways of the Hualapai and Mohave Indians. Other rooms contain a collection of paintings of U.S. Presidents and their first ladies by artist Lawrence Williams, as well as memorabilia of the town's most famous native son, the late actor Andy Devine. Open 1 to 5 p.m. Saturday and Sunday. Admission. ~ 400 West Beale Street; 520-753-3195.

To see how Kingman's upper crust lived after the turn of the century, visit the **Bonelli House**, an impressive two-story, balconied

---

✔ CHECK IT OUT—UNIQUE SIGHTS

- Fantasize about the rich life when you see all the treasures at the **Bonelli House**, built by a wealthy Kingman family in the early 1900s. *page 132*
- Descend into the bowels of the **Hoover Dam**, an engineering feat that supplies electricity to Arizona, Nevada and southern California. *page 138*
- Travel the Colorado River and learn the history of the area on the paddlewheel steamer named **Little Belle**. *page 140*
- Walk across the **London Bridge**—yes, the original bridge from England that was moved to Lake Havasu City in 1968. *page 144*

mansion constructed in 1915 of native tufa stone. The home was built by Swiss Mormons who made a fortune in the jewelry business. Inside, the rooms are decorated with furnishings and fixtures that reflect the elegance of the era—Victorian brass beds, ornately carved music boxes, antique wall clocks, and an unusual water-jacketed stove. Closed Tuesday and Wednesday. ~ 430 East Spring Street; 520-753-1413.

A drive through the older section of Kingman, away from the chain-store motels and generic coffee shops, reveals a turn-of-the-century downtown area on the brink of fading away. For the time being, you can still admire the architectural splendor the proud buildings once enjoyed, from Victorian mansions to simple adobe shacks. Some of the sights on the chamber's historic district tour include the Spanish Colonial **Santa Fe Railroad Depot** at Andy Devine Avenue and 4th Street; the mission revival-style IOOF building at 5th and Beale streets; the classic Greek-style tufa-stone, glass-domed **Mohave County Courthouse** at Spring and 4th streets; and, just east of the museum, **Locomotive Park**, a collection of early train locomotives, with a 1927 Baldwin steam engine and bright red caboose as the centerpiece.

To step even further into the area's past, drive to the old gold-mining town of **Oatman**, about 25 miles southwest of Kingman via Route 66. Founded in 1906 and mostly abandoned in 1942, Oatman is a funky collection of rickety, Old-West buildings—some look ready to collapse, while others are occupied by souvenir stores and yogurt shops. This is one of the better preserved of Arizona's ghost towns, thanks largely to the fact that it has been used several times as a movie set. A healthy tourist trade also keeps the town going. Weekends are lively with country music and staged shootouts in the streets.

Besides the usual assortment of antique and curio shops, the **Oatman Hotel** features an upstairs museum of old movie posters, rusty mining equipment and period antiques. In 1939, Carole Lombard and Clark Gable spent their wedding night here after getting married in Kingman. One of her dresses is displayed in the honeymoon suite. ~ Route 66; 520-768-4408.

A more pristine example of an Arizona ghost town is **Chloride**, located about 23 miles northwest of Kingman via Route 93. Named for the salt deposits in the surrounding hills, Chloride is a weathered gathering of wood-planked buildings, miner's shacks and processing mills. Although not as rehearsed as Oatman's, the townsfolk put on amateurish skits and shootouts on the weekend. Although the high melodrama would be better accompanied by a player piano, everyone seems to have a good time. The sights here include several galleries and antique shops, and a bed and breakfast next door to Shelp's General Store.

About an hour's drive east of Kingman are the **Grand Canyon Caverns,** limestone caves with selenite crystals and marine fossils dating back three million years. Guided tours begin with a 21-story elevator ride below ground to the cavern floors for a 45-minute walk along lighted trails equipped with handrails. Above ground are a historical museum, gift shop and restaurant. Admission. ~ Route 66 near Peach Springs; 520-422-3223.

LODGING   It seems nearly every motel chain is represented in Kingman. Most are located along East Andy Devine Avenue and West Beale Street, and provide dependable lodging. Among the nicer ones, the **Quality Inn** features modern guest rooms, some equipped with kitchenettes and refrigerators. Fitness buffs will like its pool, sauna and workout room. ~ 1400 East Andy Devine Avenue; 520-753-4747, 800-221-2222, fax 520-753-4747. MODERATE.

In the downtown area, the **Arizona Inn** is within walking distance from the historic downtown sights. Comfortable rooms are decorated with dark-wood furniture and cool pastels. ~ 411 West Beale Street, Kingman; 520-753-5521, fax 520-753-6579. BUDGET.

HIDDEN ►   In the ghost town of Oatman, the old **Oatman Hotel** has reopened as a bed-and-breakfast establishment. The authentic two-story adobe with arched facade and corrugated iron walls and ceilings may induce you to take a room, as it did Clark Gable and Carole Lombard on their wedding night after a surprise ceremony in Kingman. Oatman was on the main highway—Route 66—to Hollywood back then, and a peek into the honeymoon "suite," with its bare hanging light bulb and crumbling walls, will give you an idea of how eager Clark and Carole must have been. Although the light bulb may have been changed, the rates remain inexpensive. ~ Route 66; 520-768-4408. BUDGET.

DINING   Dozens of chain restaurants and coffee shops line East Andy Devine Avenue in Kingman, but for some local flavor try **The Kingman Deli,** where the chili is thick and spicy, and there are over three dozen types of sandwiches. Sample the popular "Sneaky Snake" with ham, turkey, roast beef and swiss cheese or the "Tumbleweed" with cucumber, avocado, sprouts, tomatoes and swiss cheese. Closed Sunday. ~ 419 East Beale Street; 520-753-4151. BUDGET

SHOPPING   Most of Kingman's commercial activity takes place along Beale Street and Andy Devine Avenue, parallel one-way streets that form a loop through the downtown area. The two merge at the eastern end, where there are a pair of regional shopping centers. There's not much in between, except **The Oldtown Coffeehouse,** a country store and café that occupies the historic Kayser House, a quaint 1920s bungalow that's part of the downtown tour. Here, you can

Don't Be Spooked

Arizona has two types of ghost towns—those that have been completely and irrevocably abandoned to the ravages of time and those that have risen into new life thanks to tourism. Good examples of both types can be found along the beat-up old segment of Route 66 that climbs and winds over the mountains between Kingman and Topock near the state's western boundary.

Goldroad, a once-prosperous town whose residents dug $7 million worth of gold ore out of the desert hillsides between 1901 and 1931, is just about gone now. All that remains are mine shafts, a few crumbling adobe walls and stone foundations.

Oatman, just two miles away, was another gold-mining town of about the same size, founded at about the same time as Goldroad and abandoned around the same time. The old buildings still stand. Some are boarded up, but many others have become curio shops and snack bars. People today come from all over the state on weekends to wander through town.

Why the difference? The landowners of Goldroad destroyed their buildings on purpose to reduce their property-tax assessments. In Oatman, though, a small group of "never say die" citizens survived the lean years by selling refreshments to passers-by on the old highway. Eventually, Hollywood discovered Oatman and used it as a set for several Western movies, including *How the West Was Won*. People around Oatman realized early on that one day old buildings might be worth more than the gold ore that some say still lies in the ground beneath both Goldroad and Oatman.

In recent years, Oatman has been declared a National Historic District, as have other famous Arizona ghost towns like the copper-mining towns of **Jerome** and **Bisbee** and the silver boom town of **Tombstone**. Historic status virtually assures their continued survival and prosperity by offering special tax breaks to investors who restore the old buildings and by prohibiting anyone from tearing them down. Bed and breakfasts, cafés and yogurt shops are springing up behind the old storefronts, and parking is becoming a problem.

Without tourism as an economic base and incentive for preservation, we would never have the opportunity to wander the streets of a town from yesteryear. For those travelers with vivid imaginations, a good local history book and an urge to explore away from the well-trodden tourist paths, the nearly vanished towns also have something special to offer. You can find history unadorned in the dusty remains of places like **White Hills** and **Mineral Park** north of Kingman, **Walker** and **McCabe** in the national forest near Prescott and **Stanton** and **Weaverville** north of Wickenburg, as well as dozens of sites in the southeast part of the state. The **Arizona Office of Tourism** publishes a free brochure telling how to find these and other ghost towns. ~ 2702 North 3rd Street, Phoenix, AZ 85004; 602-230-7733, 800-842-8257.

purchase baskets, dried flower arrangements, candles and gourmet coffees, teas and foods. Closed Sunday. ~ 616 East Beale Street; 520-753-2244.

NIGHTLIFE   You won't find Kitty or Festus at the **Long Branch Saloon**, but you can kick up your heels to live country-and-western music nightly. ~ 2255 Airway Avenue, Kingman; 520-757-8756.

Or you can catch a flick at **The Movies**. ~ 4055 Stockton Hill Road, Kingman; 520-757-7985.

PARKS   **HUALAPAI MOUNTAIN PARK** 🏃 This island of forested slopes in the middle of the Mohave Desert is a locally popular picnicking, camping and hiking area. These mountains were once the ancestral home of the Hualapai Indians, who now live farther north on a reservation as the west end of the Grand Canyon. Managed by the Mohave County Parks Department, the park offers cool, protected habitat for wildlife including deer, elk, coyotes and occasional mountain lions. There are picnic areas, restrooms, cabins, softball diamond, hiking trails, winter snow play area. ~ Located 14 miles southeast of Kingman on the paved Hualapai Mountain Park Road; 520-757-0915.

▲ There are 70 tent sites and 11 RV hookups; $6 per night for tent sites, $12 for hookups. Besides tent and RV campgrounds, there are 15 cabins built in the 1930s as part of a Civilian Conservation Corps camp that can be rented for the night at budget prices. Reservations are required. ~ 520-757-0915.

▼▼▼▼▼▼▼▼▼▼▼▼
Lake Mead Area   Downriver from the Grand Canyon, the Colorado River becomes a series of man-made desert lakes formed by the dams of the Colorado River Project, which provides: electricity for Southern California, a steady supply of irrigation water for Imperial Valley agriculture, and flood control for all the communities along the once-raging river. With Nevada and California on the other side, the river and lakes form the Arizona state line.

SIGHTS   The largest of the reservoirs is 110-mile-long **Lake Mead**, about 80 miles north of Kingman on Route 93, not far from Las Vegas. Created when the Colorado River was backed up by Hoover Dam from 1935 to 1938, Lake Mead is a popular destination for boating, fishing, windsurfing, waterskiing, lying on the beach or exploring hidden coves and inlets by houseboat. The sheer size of the lake—822 miles of shoreline and nine trillion gallons of water—and the surrounding jagged canyons and desert sand dunes are reason enough to visit the largest man-made lake in the United States.

The lake is especially popular with anglers, who take a run at largemouth bass, rainbow, brown and cutthroat trout, catfish and black crappie. Striped bass, which can reach 50 pounds, are the most popular game fish in recent years.

A good way to learn about Lake Mead is to stop at the **Alan Bible Visitors Center.** Located midway between Boulder City and Hoover Dam, the center's botanical garden, exhibits and short movie shown periodically throughout the day describe the area's history and attractions. There are also books for sale that can provide more in-depth information on the area's history, flora and fauna. ~ Route 93 and Lakeshore Road, Boulder City, NV; 702-293-8906.

The easiest way to access Lake Mead from the isolated Arizona shore is at **Temple Bar Marina.** There's lodging, a café and provisions here. This is the last outpost for supplies if you plan to boat north of Temple Bar. ~ Reached by a well-marked, paved 28-mile road that turns off Route 93 about 55 miles north of Kingman; 520-767-3211.

Although more remote, **South Cove/Pearce Ferry** is recommended for its scenic vistas of the lake and craggy peaks of Iceberg Canyon, about 46 miles east of Hoover Dam. Take Route 93 north from Kingman about 40 miles to the Dolan Springs turnoff and drive east. After passing Dolan Springs, you'll enter a massive forest of Joshua trees and the retirement resort of Meadview. Soon, you'll begin to catch glimpses of Lake Mead, framed by the jagged peaks of Iceberg Canyon. South Cove has only a boat ramp and toilets, but it offers a serene respite, accented by the deep blue waters of Lake Mead and rough-hewn mountains that frame it. The final four-mile stretch of dirt road to Pearce Ferry drops down through steep canyon walls and granite buttes. At the shoreline are camping facilities, boat ramps and plenty of peace and quiet. If the rocky granite corridors remind you of the Grand Canyon, it's because the park's western boundary is just a mile east of here.

There's also a scenic drive that runs along the Nevada side of the lake, where there are more marinas, a campground, a popular public beach and a few small resorts. Take Route 166 from Boulder City through the washes and canyons above the lake until you reach **Northshore Road** (Routes 147 and 167). You can stay on the highway that follows the shoreline all the way to the Valley of Fire State Park, or drop down to the lake at Callville Bay, Echo Bay or Overton Beach. You'll find food and facilities at all three resorts.

Lake Mead Cruises offers a **Hoover Dam cruise** aboard a three-deck paddleboat, the *Desert Princess.* The 100-foot-long sternwheeler is the largest vessel to ply the waters of the lake, and features a snack bar, two glass-enclosed decks, an open promenade deck, an 80-seat dining room, cocktail lounge and dancefloor. The late afternoon cruise features a sunset dinner and stunning views of illuminated Hoover Dam. Cruises leave several times a day from the Lake Mead Marina. ~ Lake Mead Marina: 322 Lakeshore

Road, Boulder City, NV; 702-293-3484; Lake Mead Cruises: 702-293-6180.

Hoover Dam, which impounds Lake Mead, was a tourist attraction in the area even before the first casino was built on the Las Vegas Strip. This huge dam rises 726 feet above the river and generates four billion kilowatt-hours of electricity in a year. Containing over three million cubic yards of concrete, it was completed in 1935. Its Depression-era origins are evident in the art deco motifs that decorate the top of the dam, including two huge Winged Figure of the Republic statues and a terrazzo floor patterned with mystical cosmic symbols. Guided tours begin at the **Hoover Dam Visitors Center** and take visitors down into the interior of the dam on an elevator. Admission. ~ 702-293-8367.

LODGING & DINING

The only lodging on the Arizona shore of Lake Mead is at **Temple Bar Marina,** where you can rent a room at the modern motel, or one of the older cabins with kitchenettes. There is also a café, cocktail lounge, campground, boat-launching ramp, fuel dock and store. This is the last outpost for supplies if you plan to boat north of Temple Bar. ~ 520-767-3211, 800-752-9669, fax 520-767-3033. BUDGET TO MODERATE.

There's a motel on the Nevada shore of the lake at **Echo Bay Resort and Marina.** Along with a restaurant and lounge, the motel offers modern rooms, an RV village and an airstrip for light aircraft (day-use only). ~ 702-394-4000, 800-752-9669. MODERATE.

About a mile north of the Boulder Beach, **Lake Mead Resort and Marina** has hundreds of boat slips and a popular floating restaurant, coffee shop and cocktail lounge. ~ 322 Lakeshore Road; 702-293-3484.

Farther north, the **Las Vegas Boat Harbor** has more boat slips, a picnic area and campground. ~ P.O. Box 91150, Henderson, NV 89009; 702-565-9111.

◆◆

✔ **CHECK IT OUT—UNIQUE LODGING**

- *Budget:* Stay at the historic **Oatman Hotel** and ask to see the simple room where Clark Gable and Carole Lombard spent their honeymoon. *page 134*
- *Budget to moderate:* Motor up to the **Temple Bar Marina,** the only waterfront accommodations on Lake Mead. *page 138*
- *Moderate:* Cross the Nevada border and check into the **Colorado Belle,** a showy casino-hotel shaped like a Mississippi steamboat. *page 142*
- *Deluxe:* Go sailing, boating and waterskiing until your heart's content when you're a guest at the **Nautical Inn.** *page 145*

Budget: under $50   Moderate: $50–$90   Deluxe: $90–$120   Ultra-deluxe: over $120

You can also camp or park your RV at **Callville Bay Resort Marina**, which also has a coffee shop and cocktail lounge. ~ P.O. Box 100 HCR-30, Las Vegas, NV 89124; 702-565-8958.

BOULDER BEACH   Most of Lake Mead's shoreline consists of rocks and gravel, but you can spread a beach towel at Boulder Beach. The two miles of beach and the clear water of Lake Mead attract year-round sunbathers. The clear water and warm temperatures attract divers, who can explore the ill-fated yachts, *Tortuga*, near the Boulder Islands, and the *Cold Duck*, submerged in 35 feet of water. There are picnic areas, restrooms, ranger station, a snack bar and convenience store are nearby. ~ Located two miles north of the Alan Bible Visitors Center; 702-293-8990.

▲ There are 298 sites in two campgrounds; $10 per night for tents and RVs (no hookups).

PARKS

Bullhead City, 35 miles west of Kingman via Route 68, may be Arizona's fastest-growing city, but it owes its prosperity to Laughlin, Nevada, on the far side of the river. The city of Laughlin is a shimmering riverfront resort that has blossomed into Nevada's third-largest gambling center. Because it has few residential and commercial areas of its own, most of the thousands of people who work there live, shop and send their kids to school in its Arizona sister, Bullhead City. The closest gambling zone to the greater Phoenix area, Laughlin is packed to overflowing every weekend. The rest of the week, the casinos, buffets, lounges and showrooms play host to motorhome nomads who appreciate the opportunity to avoid Las Vegas traffic and avail themselves of Laughlin's vast, free RV parking lots.

▼▼▼▼▼▼▼▼▼
**Bullhead City/
Laughlin Area**

But gambling isn't the only attraction in the Bullhead City/Laughlin area. The Colorado River and nearby Lake Mohave are major draws, offering year-round water sports such as swimming, boating, fishing and waterskiing. Also within short driving distance are ghost towns, historic mines, and intriguing lost canyons waiting to be explored.

Commercial boat cruises are also a popular pastime. Before the bridge across the Colorado River was built in the mid 1980s, visitors used to park on the Arizona side of the river and ride passenger ferries across to the casinos on the Nevada shore. Now, on busy weekends when parking lots in Laughlin are full, the ferries still carry people across the river, making for a brief, fun, and, best of all, free cruise. Several companies also offer longer riverboat sightseeing tours down the river from casino docks. One is **Colorado Belle's Blue River Safaris**, which operates a 40-foot jet boat through the river gorge. Closed Sunday. ~ 2100 South Casino

SIGHTS

Drive, Laughlin; 702-298-0910. Another is **Laughlin River Tours**, which runs the *Little Belle* paddlewheel steamer from the Edgewater Casino dock and even offers on-board weddings. ~ 3080 South Needles Highway; 702-298-1047.

Bullhead City was incorporated in 1984, but it was founded in 1945 when it was the construction camp for Davis Dam, three miles upstream. The town, named for a rock formation now submerged by Lake Mohave, is a collection of lowrise housing tracts, shopping centers and mobile home parks. New housing developments and retirement communities along the Colorado River—Riviera, Fort Mohave and Golden Shores—have extended Bullhead City's outskirts as far south as Topock, at the junction of Route 40.

The best time to visit Bullhead City/Laughlin is in the winter and spring months, when the daytime temperatures range from 65 to 80°. Temperatures in July and August can reach an astounding 120° or more, making this area the hottest spot in the nation.

There's not much to see or do in Bullhead City, unless pre-fab homes and tilt-up shopping centers are your idea of excitement. So it's no surprise that the most-visited attraction in the area is the strip of ten casinos across the water on the river's western shore. Unlike their larger cousins on the famed Las Vegas Strip, the Laughlin hotel/casinos are close together and are easily accessible by a concrete strand that follows the river. The best is the **Colorado Belle**, a 600-foot replica of a Mississippi steamboat, complete with three decks and four black smokestacks. In the evening, the paddlewheel "turns" by strobe light. Inside, the decor is turn-of-the-century New Orleans, with lots of plush red carpeting, glassglobe lamps, brass railings and wrought-iron fixtures. The cluster of shops on the mezzanine level has several restaurants and an old-fashioned candy store. ~ 2100 South Casino Drive, Laughlin; 702-298-4000, 800-477-4837, fax 702-299-0669.

For a bit of Dodge City by the river try the **Pioneer Hotel** next door. The two-story hotel looks like a U-shaped fort, finished with weathered wood panels. The facade of the casino entrance suggests a Wild West boarding house. Swinging doors and a wooden porch lead into a hectic casino, decorated with dark-wood floors and distressed paneling. On the river side of the hotel is a waving neon cowboy—River Rick—Laughlin's version of Vegas Vic. The grounds facing the river include a lush flower garden, green grass and shade trees. ~ 2200 South Casino Drive, Laughlin; 702-298-2442, 800-634-3469.

Also worth visiting is the **Riverside Resort**. Be sure to stop in at the antiques shop just off the casino. The small but interesting collection consists of slot machines, juke boxes, vintage radios and a variety of old neon signs. On display, but not for sale, are antique slots from Don Laughlin's personal collection, including a

1938 vest pocket slot machine and a 1931 slot that paid off in golf balls. ~ 1650 South Casino Drive, Laughlin; 702-298-2535, 800-227-3849, fax 702-298-2695.

The **Davis Dam and Powerplant** was built in 1953 to produce hydroelectric power and regulate water delivery to Mexico. The powerplant, downstream from the dam embankment on the Arizona side of the river, is open daily for self-guided tours, which include recorded lectures, illustrated maps and close-up views of the plant's turbines. ~ About three miles north of Bullhead City; 520-754-3628.

Behind the dam lies **Lake Mohave**, which extends 67 miles upstream to Hoover Dam. The long, narrow lake (four miles across at its widest point) provides a multitude of recreational opportunities, including fishing, boating, waterskiing and windsurfing.

Lake Mohave is accessible at only two points in Arizona: Willow Beach, off Route 93 about 60 miles north of Kingman, and Katherine Landing, six miles north of Bullhead City and Laughlin. **Lake Mohave Resort**, six miles north of Bullhead City, rents houseboats and other craft for use on Lake Mohave. ~ Katherine Landing; 520-754-3245, 800-752-9669, fax 520-754-1125. **Willow Beach Harbor** also provides rentals. ~ 520-767-4747.

LODGING

On Sunday through Thursday nights, rooms cost significantly less in the casino hotels of Laughlin, Nevada, than they do in Bullhead City on the Arizona side of the Colorado River. In fact, on weeknights, you can rent a spacious, modern room with a king-size bed, remote control television, art prints and designer wallpaper in Laughlin for about the same rate as a plain, somewhat threadbare room in an aging mom-and-pop motel by the interstate in Kingman.

Most hotel accommodations in Laughlin are in the budget range during the week and in the moderate-to-deluxe range on the weekend, but they can be in short supply. Reservations are essential on weekends and a good idea at other times. Laughlin's strip consists of ten casino hotels.

Top of the line and the closest to the bridge across the river from Bullhead City, is **Don Laughlin's Riverside Resort Hotel and Casino**. The resort's owner conceived the idea of promoting a casino strip here, founded the town that is named after him, and in 1977 converted the old Riverside Bait Shop on this site into Laughlin's first casino. ~ 1650 Casino Drive; 702-298-2535, 800-227-3849, fax 702-298-2614. BUDGET TO MODERATE.

Some of the other hotels are famous-name spinoffs from well-known Las Vegas and Reno casinos, such as the **Flamingo Hilton**, which is the town's largest with 2000 rooms. ~ 1900 South Casino Drive; 702-298-5111, 800-352-6464, fax 702-298-5777. Or try the **Golden Nugget**. ~ 2300 South Casino Drive; 702-298-7111,

800-950-7700, fax 702-298-7122. Another option is **Harrah's Laughlin,** a very nice hotel over a hill from the others at the south end of Casino Row. ~ 2900 South Casino Drive; 702-298-4600, 800-447-8700, fax 702-298-6896. The **Colorado Belle,** a showy casino hotel shaped like a giant riverboat midway down the strip, was created by the same company that owns Circus Circus and the Excalibur in Las Vegas. ~ 2100 South Casino Drive; 702-298-4000, 800-477-4837, fax 702-299-0669. There is also the **Edgewater Hotel,** a 1450-unit highrise. ~ 2020 South Casino Drive; 702-298-2453, 800-677-4837, fax 702-298-8165. BUDGET TO DELUXE.

For most visitors to the Bullhead City/Laughlin area, there is probably not much point to staying on the Arizona side of the river. Most of the motels in Bullhead City are clean and modern but unexceptional, and room rates tend to run higher than in the Laughlin casino hotels. They seem to thrive on weekend and peak-season overflows. It's hard to believe that many people with aversions to the gambling scene would go out of their way to stay in Bullhead City when they could as easily proceed south to the more family-oriented Lake Havasu City. But if they did, they'd find good noncasino lodging in Bullhead City at the **Bullhead River Motel.** It is an all-suite motel, ideal for families, and has a boat and fishing dock available for use at no charge. ~ 455 Moser Avenue; 520-754-2250. BUDGET TO DELUXE.

It's not the Reading, but you can ride the rails on a mini-passenger train at the **Ramada Express.** The narrow-gauge railroad shuttles you on a 15-minute ride from the parking lot to the casino, decorated like a Victorian railroad station. Guest rooms in the 1500-room towers behind the casino feature deep earth-tone colors, dark-wood furniture and brass lamps and fixtures. ~ 2121 South Casino Drive, Laughlin; 702-298-4200, 800-272-6232, fax 702-298-6403. BUDGET TO MODERATE.

DINING

Along with a nice view of Lake Mohave, Lake Mohave Resort's restaurant **Tail of the Whale** serves a tasty blackened catfish and other seafood dishes, plus steaks and chops. ~ Katherine Landing just above Davis Dam; 520-754-3245. MODERATE.

In Laughlin, hit the casinos for inexpensive feasts. Just about every hotel on Casino Row has an all-you-can-eat buffet featuring 40 or more items, in the budget range for dinner and almost absurdly affordable—no more than you'd spend at a franchise hamburger joint—for breakfast and lunch. To sweeten the deal even more, two-for-one buffet coupons are included in free "fun books" widely distributed in visitors centers and truck stops in Kingman and elsewhere along Route 40. The largest buffet in town is located at the **Edgewater Hotel.** ~ 2020 South Casino Drive; 702-298-2453. BUDGET.

Each casino also has a full-service 24-hour coffee shop, most of them featuring breakfast specials priced between 99 cents and $1.99. Notable among the 24-hour casual places is **Flamingo Diner**, a classic New York–style deli. ~ Flamingo Hilton, 1900 South Casino Drive; 702-298-5111. BUDGET.

Many, though not all, casinos also have slightly more upscale fine dining restaurants. **Harrah's Laughlin** offers an intimate atmosphere and a riverside view at William Fisk's Steakhouse (reservations required) or authentic Mexican fare at La Hacienda. ~ 2900 South Casino Drive; 702-298-4600. MODERATE.

In the **Colorado Belle**, seafood is a specialty in the casually classy Orleans Room. ~ 2100 South Casino Drive; 702-298-4000. MODERATE.

Gold River serves fine American and Continental selections in the Lodge, designed in a hunting lodge theme with wood-beamed ceiling and big stone fireplace, all so convincing that you may forget that you're in a casino. Dinner only. ~ 2700 Casino Drive; 702-298-2242. MODERATE.

NIGHTLIFE

Nightlife on the river all happens in Laughlin where each of the casinos has at least one, often two, cocktail lounges that don't charge for watching musical acts that perform here while practicing for Las Vegas. Only one of the casinos has a showroom where name acts appear: **Don's Celebrity Theater** hosts such performers as the Gatlin Brothers, the Smothers Brothers, the Oakridge Boys, the McGuire Sisters and Willie Nelson. Cover. ~ Don Laughlin's Riverside Resort, 1650 Casino Drive; 702-298-2535.

PARKS

The Colorado River and Lake Mohave provide a multitude of recreational activities, including boating, fishing, waterskiing, scuba diving and windsurfing. Landlubbing hikers will love the desert and canyons surrounding Bullhead City/Laughlin. Lake Mohave above Davis Dam actually resembles the river below the dam—the lake stretches for 67 miles through jagged canyons and rocky mountains. At its widest point, it is only four miles from shore to shore.

KATHERINE LANDING Located just 640 feet above sea level along Lake Mohave, Katherine Landing's flora and fauna is representative of the surrounding Mohave Desert. Short hikes into the area reveal desert shrubs, cacti and roadrunners, as well as views of the Black and Newberry Mountains in the distance. There's striped bass, bluegill and channel catfish for anglers, and there's good swimming at South Telephone Cove. There are restrooms, pay showers, laundry facilities, full-service marina with boat rentals, fishing tackle and waterski rentals, motel, restaurant and grocery store, visitors center. ~ Located just north of Bullhead City off of Route 163; 520-754-3272.

▲ There are 150 dry campground sites, each with a barbecue grill, picnic table and running water; $8 per night.

DAVIS CAMP COUNTY PARK 🏊 ⛵ Here at the only public beach on the Colorado River you'll find a stretch of sandy beach where you can swim, fish or launch a jet ski. You can angle here for striped bass, catfish and trout, and there's a marked off swimming area good for children. At the south end of the park is a marsh that's home to variety of birds and other small wildlife. There are restrooms, showers, laundry facilities, barbecue grills and ramadas with picnic tables; day-use fee, $3. ~ Located about one mile north of Laughlin on the Arizona side of the river; 520-754-4606.

▲ There are 130 sites with full hookups ($15 per night), 30 sites with partial hookups ($11 per night) and an open area for tent camping ($8 per night).

WILLOW BEACH 🚤 ⛵ Nearby, you can tour the Willow Beach National Fish Hatchery that keeps both lakes stocked, and its small exhibit room where you can learn about the Colorado River's history. Bait, tackle and fishing licenses are available at the dock; try for trout and striped bass. There are restrooms, picnic grounds, barbecue grills, boat rentals, fuel, grocery store. ~ On Lake Mohave about 14 miles south of Hoover Dam off of Route 93; 520-767-4747.

▼▼▼▼▼▼▼▼▼▼▼▼▼
Lake Havasu Area

About 20 miles upstream from Parker Dam, **Lake Havasu** may be the prettiest dammed lake along the Colorado River. Cool and bright blue in the heart of the desert, this 46-mile-long lake has become a very popular recreation area.

SIGHTS Lake Havasu's main claim to fame is **London Bridge** in Lake Havasu City. The audacity and monumental pointlessness of the city fathers' moving the bridge here when the city of London decided to replace it draws curiosity seekers in droves. To believe it, you have to see it. Originally built in 1825 to replace a still older London Bridge that had lasted 625 years, this bridge was sold at auction in 1968. Lake Havasu City's promoters bought it for $2,460,000. The 10,000 tons of granite facing were disassembled into blocks weighing from 1000 to 17,000 pounds each, shipped and trucked 10,000 miles to this site and reconstructed on the shore of Lake Havasu when the city was practically nonexistent. Then a canal was dug to let water flow under the bridge. It is 300 feet wide and 2000 feet long, and you can drive or walk across it. Every year, millions do. Is it worth seeing? Absolutely! It's a giant object lesson in the fine line between madness and genius—and one of the strangest things in Arizona.

In **Lake Havasu City**, a number of boats offer sightseeing tours from London Bridge. They include the first cruise boat on the lake, the cute little *Miss Havasupai,* operated by **Lake Havasu Boat Tours.** ~ 520-855-7979. At the other end of the spectrum is the large Mississippi riverboat replica *Dixie Belle.* ~ 520-453-6776. **Bluewater Charters** runs daily boat excursions from London Bridge to Topock Gorge and the Havasu National Wildlife Refuge. ~ 520-855-7171.

In the little town of **Topock**, located midway between Bullhead City and Lake Havasu City at the junction of Route 40 and Route 95 South, Jerkwater Canoe Co. rents canoes to explore otherwise inaccessible areas of the **Havasu National Wildlife Refuge**. The company can also provide directions to the beautiful **Topock Gorge**, ancient petroglyph sites and the **Topock Maze**, where Mohave Indians used to go to cleanse their spirits after long journeys. ~ Jerkwater Canoe Co.: 520-768-7753.

◄ HIDDEN

LODGING

Lake Havasu City boasts many fine resort hotels. The **London Bridge Resort**, with its blend of Tudor and medieval castle–style architecture and beautiful contemporary guest rooms, has its own golf course, lovely green landscaped grounds and a waterfront location right next to London Bridge and the Olde English Village. ~ 1477 Queen's Bay Road; 520-855-0888, 800-624-7939, fax 520-855-2414. MODERATE TO ULTRA-DELUXE.

Across the bridge, on the island, the **Nautical Inn** also has a golf course, as well as a private dock with waterskiing, sailing, boating and jet-skiing equipment for guests. All the rooms are on the waterfront. Each carpeted unit comes with two double beds, a patio and direct access to the lawn and beach. The suites include refrigerators and kitchenettes. ~ 1000 McCulloch Boulevard, Lake Havasu City; 520-855-2141, 800-892-2141, fax 520-453-5808. DELUXE.

Within a mile of the bridge, standard motel rooms are available at the **Windsor Inn**. ~ 451 London Bridge Road, Lake Havasu City; 520-855-4135, 800-245-4135, fax 520-855-5385. The **Shakespeare Inn** also has similar accommodations. ~ 2190 McCulloch Boulevard, Lake Havasu City; 520-855-4157, 800-982-3622, fax 520-453-1514. BUDGET TO MODERATE.

> Except for the Grand Canyon, London Bridge is the most visited tourist attraction in Arizona.

Spacious one- and two-bedroom suites are available at the **Sands Vacation Resort**. Pictures of the Southwest decorate the pastel walls of these courtyard units. Each carpeted suite includes a living room, dining area and kitchenette. ~ 2040 Mesquite Avenue, Lake Havasu City; 520-855-1388, 800-521-0360, fax 520-453-1802. MODERATE.

DINING

Lake Havasu City, oddly, has virtually no high-priced haute cuisine, but it does have a good selection of pleasant, affordable restaurants. A good place for salads, steaks and seafood is **Shugrue's** in the Island Fashion Mall, which has an unbeatable view of London Bridge from the island side through tall wraparound windows. Fresh bakery goods are the specialty. ~ 1425 McCulloch Boulevard, Lake Havasu City; 520-453-1400. MODERATE.

Also on the island, the **Captain's Table**, in the Nautical Inn, serves traditional American menu selections with a lakeside view overlooking the resort's private dock. ~ 1000 McCulloch Boulevard, Lake Havasu City; 520-855-2141. MODERATE.

Away from the water, a local favorite is **Krystal's**, featuring specialties such as Alaskan king crab legs, lobster tails and mahi. ~ 460 El Camino Way, Lake Havasu City; 520-453-2999. MODERATE.

Another long-time local favorite is **Nicolino's Italian Restaurant**, serving 30 varieties of pasta. Closed Sunday. ~ 86 South Smoketree Avenue, Lake Havasu City; 520-855-3484. MODERATE.

In the English Village on the mainland side of the bridge, there's the usually busy **Mermaid Inn**, serving fish and chips, clam strips and hamburgers. ~ 401 English Village, London Bridge, Lake Havasu City; 520-855-3234. BUDGET.

SHOPPING   Arizona's "West Coast" holds a number of enticements for visitors, but shopping isn't one of them. The most interesting shopping district in the area is the **Olde English Village** on the mainland side of London Bridge in Lake Havasu, and the most remarkable thing about it, other than its vast expanse of bright-green lawn in the heart of one of America's most desolate deserts, is that the land on which it was built was owned by the city of London—making the bridge a symbolic link between London and Lake Havasu City. The cute Olde English buildings housing the shops and snack bars remind us that the city and the bridge were the brainchild of the retired general manager of Disneyland. The Olde English Village has about two dozen theme gift shops such as the London Arms Gift Shoppe, the Copper Shoppe, the Gallerie of Glasse and the Curiosity Shoppe, as well as the London Bridge Candle Factory, which claims to be the world's largest candle shop.

At the other end of the bridge, the **Island Fashion Mall** houses a dozen shops selling men's and women's fashions, sportswear and fine jewelry.

NIGHTLIFE   In addition to Lake Havasu City's hotels cocktail lounges, a nice spot for an intimate encounter is **London Arms Pub and Restaurant**, a British-style pub that looks transplanted from Walpole Street. Besides the used-brick facade, curved glass windows, wrought-iron fence and stately carriage lamps, the establishment features private leather-lined booths and a dark-wood bar accented by brass fixtures. ~ 422 Olde English Village; 520-855-8782.

LAKE HAVASU STATE PARK 🏃 🚣 ⛴ 🚤 ⛵ This shoreline
park area in and around Lake Havasu City encompasses most of
the Arizona shore of this broad blue lake nestled among stark,
rocky desert hills. The park has several campgrounds and rocky
swimming beaches in two developed units—Windsor Beach, north
of the center of town, and Cattail Cove, about 15 miles south of
town. Cattail Cove has a state-operated marina. Besides these two
areas, the park encompasses the Aubrey Hills Natural Area, a wild
shoreline that can't be reached by road. Fish for largemouth bass,
striped bass and catfish. There are picnic areas, restrooms, showers,
marina, nature trails; restaurants, groceries and lodging nearby in
Lake Havasu City; day-use fee, $7. ~ The main automobile acces-
sible areas are at Windsor Beach and Cattail Cove 15 miles south
of Lake Havasu City on Route 95. Other areas of the park, which
includes most of the east shore of Lake Havasu, are only accessible by boat; 520-855-2784.

▲ There are 74 sites at Windsor Beach (520-855-2784) and
40 sites with full RV hookups at Cattail Cove (520-855-1223); $10
per night at Windsor, $15 per night at Cattail. Also available are
150 primitive boat-in sites along the shore in the Aubrey Hills
Natural Area south of Lake Havasu City; vault toilets, picnic tables and shade structures; $10 per boat.

HAVASU NATIONAL WILDLIFE REFUGE 🏃 ⛵ Nature buffs will
enjoy this wildlife refuge, which straddles the Colorado River from
Topock, 20 miles north of Lake Havasu City, to Pittsburg Point,
about two miles north of the city. Hikers through the marshy trails
are often rewarded with views of a bald eagle, peregrine falcon,
desert bighorn sheep or a number of winter visitors: snow and
Canadian geese and other waterfowl. There are restrooms, showers, laundry and a visitors center. ~ The visitors center is at 1406
Bailey Avenue, Needles, CA. To get to the park, go ten miles east
on Route 40, exit on Mohave County 227 (Route 95). The exit is
well-marked; 619-326-3853.

▲ There are 40 sites; $7 per night ($14.50 per night with
hookups); information, 520-768-2350.

Downstream from Parker Dam, which impounds ▼▼▼▼▼▼▼▼▼▼▼▼
Lake Havasu, the Colorado River flows through the **Parker Dam Area**
Colorado River Indian Reservation to Parker, a non-
descript trade center about 35 miles south of Lake Havasu City.
Just two miles north of Parker, Headgate Rock Dam impedes the
Colorado to form Lake Moovalya, an 11-mile stretch of water
recreation better known as "The Parker Strip."

Parker was nothing more than a postal stop until the railroad came
through in 1908. Most of the town's development, however, oc-

curred after the river was dammed and tourists began flocking to the lakes upstream. Recreation remains Parker's main reason for existing, along with a moderate climate that attracts several thousand snowbirds, mostly retirees, each winter.

The town itself has little to offer; many of its 3000 citizens live in wall-to-wall RV parks scattered across the scrub-brush hillsides, dotted with an occasional red-tile-roof home. Despite Parker's lackluster appeal, the area is besieged by visitors who enjoy year-round boating, waterskiing and inner-tubing (there's even an annual seven-mile inner-tube race) along the scenic Parker Strip.

The city's main attraction is the **Colorado River Indian Tribes Museum,** a storehouse of prehistoric American Indian artifacts from the Anasazi, Hohokam and other tribes, as well as dioramas of pueblos and other dwellings, crafts and folk art of the more modern Mohave, Chemehuevi, Navajo and Hopi people. Most interesting is the photo gallery of early reservation life and archival library of old manuscripts, books and other documents. Visit the gift shop before leaving; it has a good assortment of American Indian publications, baskets, beadwork and other crafts. Closed Saturday and Sunday. ~ 2nd Avenue and Mohave Road; 520-669-9211.

About 15 miles upstream sits **Parker Dam,** a virtual twin to Davis Dam. One significant difference is you that can see only one-third of Parker Dam; the bedrock foundation is 235 feet below the riverbed. Like its upstream cousin, Parker Dam is open for self-guided tours. Be sure to step into the turbine room and watch the massive generator shaft spinning.

If you'd like a change of pace, drive 34 miles south on Route 95 to the town of **Quartzsite,** the site of one of the strangest reunions in Arizona, and possibly the world. Although the dusty scrub-brush town—if you can call it that—consists of just a few motels, restaurants, and RV parks, each winter its population swells from several hundred to several hundred thousand. The reason? The **Quartzsite Gemborees,** six shows resembling Bedouin bazaars for rock-swappers and gem collectors. Held in late January and early

RIVER OF THE DAMMED

Davis Dam is one of three dams operating to control flooding and produce hydroelectric power along the Colorado River. Along with the other two—**Hoover Dam** to the north and **Parker Dam,** about 80 miles downstream—they form the Lower Colorado River Dams project. They also divert river water to form three lakes: Lake Mead, Lake Mohave and Lake Havasu. Another six large dams in Colorado, Utah and New Mexico also control the waters of the mighty Colorado.

February, the festivals attract droves of rock and gem aficionados for a metallurgical freakout. In addition to the hundreds of booths, where you can buy everything from healing crystals to 5000-pound slabs of quartz, the festivals feature flea markets, antique and collectibles shows, a rodeo, camel and ostrich races, country music, an auto show—all choreographed in the tradition of Hunter Thompson. Started in 1964 by a rag-tag group of rock hounds, the original event has grown to six annual shows, becoming Quartzsite's main reason for existence. For further details about the Quartzsite Gemborees, contact Howard Armstrong at P.O. Box 2801, Quartzsite, AZ 85346; 520-927-5213.

LODGING

You won't find a bellhop in this part of the country, but there are clean rooms at **El Rancho Motel**, along with a few kitchenettes, refrigerators, a pool and in-room coffee. ~ 709 California Avenue, Parker; 520-669-2231, fax 520-453-1514. BUDGET TO MODERATE.

Traveling families will like the **Stardust Motel** because of its oversized rooms and mini-suites, most with refrigerators and microwave ovens, all clean and well maintained. ~ 700 California Avenue, Parker; 520-669-2278, fax 520-669-6658. BUDGET TO MODERATE.

DINING

For home-cooked American dishes, try the **Paradise Café**, a formica-topped, family-run eatery that caters to regular locals who feast on the barbecued chicken, pork ribs, fish and chips and homemade pies. ~ Route 95 at Riverside Drive, Parker; 520-667-2404. BUDGET.

In Quartzsite, the main event is the **Main Event**, a combination restaurant, truck stop, general store, curio shop and gas station. The ponderous dining area is of the neo-coffee-shop genre with vinyl booths and formica tables, but the simple American dishes such as chicken-fried steak, liver and onions, and grits and gravy are served in huge portions. After you've refueled, check out the gift shop, which has a strange collection of carved wooden animals. ~ Route 10 at Exit 17; 520-927-5683. BUDGET.

PARKS

LA PAZ COUNTY PARK You can spread a beach towel or picnic blanket at this grassy recreational area. Located along the Colorado River, the 640-acre park is perfect for a relaxed family outing. Common catches for anglers are bass, catfish, bluegill, striper, flathead and perch. Swimming is good at the sandy beach. There are covered ramadas, barbecue grills, picnic tables, restrooms, showers, tennis courts, baseball field, playground; day-use fee, $2. ~ About eight miles north of Parker via Route 95; 520-667-2069.

▲ About a third of the park is open to tent camping; $8 per night. There are also 30 ramada sites ($10 per night) and 99 RV sites with full hookups ($12 per night). An RV overflow area offers partial hookups ($10 per night). All camping fees are for two people; there's a $2 charge for each additional person.

BUCKSKIN MOUNTAIN STATE PARK This state park located near Parker Dam caters to tube floaters, boaters and waterskiiers. But you can also hike the nature trails in the mountains that surround the eastern edge of the park. In addition to panoramic vistas of the Colorado River, hikers can sometimes catch a glimpse of desert bighorn sheep that roam the area. Fish for bass, bluegill and catfish. There is a picnic ground, restrooms, gas dock, inner-tube rentals and snack bar; day-use fee, $5. ~ Buckskin Mountain is on Route 95, about 11 miles north of Parker. River Island is another one and a half miles north of Buckskin Mountain; 520-667-3231.

▲ Buckskin Mountain has 89 sites (water and electric hookups, $15 per night; cabañas, $20 per night). River Island offers 37 sites (water hookups, $10 per night). Restrooms and showers are available at both campgrounds.

▼▼▼▼▼▼▼▼▼▼▼▼▼▼
Outdoor Adventures

FISHING

This region offers some of Arizona's best fishing. It's open season on all fish year-round at Lake Mead and the abundant Colorado River.

LAKE MEAD AREA There's plenty of catfish, bluegill, crappie and striped bass, often tipping the scales at 30 pounds, at **Lake Mead**. One of the best spots for bass is near the Las Vegas Boat Harbor because of the waste-water nutrients that dump from the Las Vegas Wash. The Overton arm of Lake Mead is one of the best areas for striped bass, whose threadfin shad schools often churn the water in their feeding frenzies. Also worth trying are Calico Basin, Hemenway Harbour the Meadows, Stewarts Point and Meat Hole. For tips on other spots, ask any park ranger or try any of the marinas, which also sell licenses, bait and tackle. For example, there's **Lake Mead Marina**. ~ 322 Lakeshore Road; 702-293-3484. Also on the lake is the **Las Vegas Boat Harbor**. ~ Lake Mead Drive; 702-565-9111. **Callville Bay Resort Marina** has licenses, bait and tackle. ~ HCR 30, Box 100, off Northshore Road; 702-565-8958. **Echo Bay Resort and Marina** is a good spot to fulfill your fishing and boating needs. ~ 702-394-4000. **Temple Bar Marina** is also on Lake Mead. ~ 520-767-3211.

BULLHEAD CITY/LAUGHLIN AREA Fishing is also excellent along the **Colorado River** near the Bullhead City/Laughlin area. Anglers can fill their creels with striped bass, rainbow trout, bass, catfish, bluegill and crappie. A good spot is the cold water below Davis Dam. There's also good fishing above the dam on **Lake Mohave**, noted for its rainbow trout and bass.

This is one of the wettest parts of the state and opportunities for water sports abound.

LAKE MEAD AREA   On Arizona's West Coast, you can skip across Lake Mead in a power or ski boat, or simply relax under sail or on the deck of a houseboat. For rentals in the Lake Mead area, try the **Callville Bay Resort Marina**. ~ HCR 30, Box 100, off Northshore Road; 702-565-8958. **Lake Mead Marina** also has rentals. ~ 322 Lakeshore Road; 702-293-3484. At the north end of Lake Mead try **Overton Beach Resort and Marina** for boat rentals. ~ 702-394-4040. Another place to rent boats at the north end of Lake Mead is **Echo Bay Resort and Marina**. ~ 702-394-4000.

BULLHEAD CITY/LAUGHLIN AREA   In the Bullhead City/Laughlin area, waterskiing is permitted along the Colorado River from Davis Dam to Needles. The sparsely populated area just below Bullhead City is the best choice. You can also waterski on Lake Mohave north of Davis Dam. For boat rentals and equipment, check out **Lake Mohave Resort**. ~ Katherine Landing; 520-754-3245.

LAKE HAVASU AREA   The lower Colorado River and Lake Havasu are a mecca for watersport enthusiasts, and craft of all kinds are available for rent. In Lake Havasu City, pontoon boats are available at **Island Boat Rentals**. ~ 1580 Dover Avenue; 520-453-3260. Another option for rentals in Lake Havasu City is **Rick's Pontoon Boat Rentals & Sales**. ~ 1637 Industrial Boulevard; 520-453-1922. Power boats for fishing and waterskiing are for rent at **Lake Havasu Marina**. ~ 1100 McCulloch Boulevard; 520-855-2159. **Resort Boat Rentals** also has power boats for fishing and waterskiing. ~ English Village; 520-453-9613. Fifteen miles south of Lake Havasu City, **Sand Point Marina** rents fishing boats, pontoon boats and houseboats. ~ 520-855-0549. Waterskiing lessons are offered by **Havasu Adventures Water Ski School**. ~ 1425 McCulloch Boulevard; 520-855-6274.

✔ **CHECK THESE OUT—UNIQUE OUTDOOR ADVENTURES**
- Bring your rod and tackle to **Lake Mead**, where the catfish, bluegill, crappie and striped bass are abundant. *page 150*
- Run the spring rapids on the **Colorado River** in a raft, canoe or kayak. *page 152*
- Set up camp at **Hualapai Mountain Park**, once the ancestral home of the Hualapai people. *page 136*
- Wind your way along the **Mohave Sunset Walking Trail**, and enjoy the commanding views of Lake Havasu. *page 153*

RIVER RUNNING
The stretch of Colorado River from Hoover Dam to Willow Beach is open year-round to rafts, canoes and kayaks, but the best time is spring and fall. River running requires a permit from the **Hoover Dam Police Department**. Advance reservations are required. ~ P.O. Box 60400, Boulder City, NV 89006; 702-293-8204. For canoe and kayak rentals, try **Boulder City Water Sports.** ~ 1108 Nevada Highway, Boulder City, NV; 702-293-7526. It's not exactly white-knuckle rafting, but you can float down the Colorado River from Hoover Dam to Black Canyon and see waterfalls, hot springs and geological formations. For details, contact **Black Canyon, Inc.** ~ 1297 Nevada Highway, Boulder City, NV; 702-293-3776.

GOLF
For information on courses, contact the **Arizona Golf Association**. ~ 7226 North 16th Street, Suite 200, Phoenix, AZ 85020; 602-940-3035.

KINGMAN AREA Kingman visitors won't be disappointed with **Valley Vista Country Club.** ~ 9686 Concho Drive; 520-757-8744. Another option is **Kingman Municipal Golf Course.** ~ 1001 East Gates Road; 520-753-6593.

LAKE MEAD AREA Serving the Lake Mead and Hoover Dam area is the **Boulder City Municipal Golf Course.** ~ 1 Clubhouse Drive, Boulder City, NV; 702-293-9236.

BULLHEAD CITY/LAUGHLIN AREA In Laughlin, tee off at the **Emerald River Golf Course.** ~ 1155 West Casino Drive; 702-298-0061. In Bullhead City play the greens at **Riverview Golf Course.** ~ 2000 East Ramar Road; 520-763-1818. Also in Bullhead City is **Chaparral Country Club.** ~ 1260 East Mohave Drive; 520-758-3939. **Desert Lakes Golf Course** is located about 12 miles south of the Laughlin/Bullhead City bridge. ~ 5835 Desert Lakes Drive, Fort Mohave, AZ; 520-768-1000.

LAKE HAVASU AREA Golfers can choose from two excellent courses around Lake Havasu. The first is the **Queen's Bay Golf Course.** ~ 1477 Queen's Bay Road; 520-855-4777, You'll hope your score is falling down, falling down at the **London Bridge Golf Club.** ~ 2400 Clubhouse Drive; 520-855-9096.

TENNIS
Courts are fairly easy to come by if you want to rally away the endlessly sunny days.

BULLHEAD CITY/LAUGHLIN AREA In Laughlin you can hold court at the **Flamingo Hilton Hotel.** ~ 1900 South Casino Drive, Laughlin; 702-298-5111. The **Riverview RV Resort** also has courts. ~ 2000 East Ramar Road, Bullhead City; 520-763-5800.

LAKE HAVASU AREA Tennis courts are available for a fee in Lake Havasu City at **London Bridge Racquet and Fitness Center.** ~ 1425 McCulloch Boulevard; 520-855-6274.

Hikers will be happy with all the forest and canyons this area has to offer.

KINGMAN AREA Hualapai Mountain Park, 14 miles southeast of Kingman, has an extensive network of hiking trails through piñon, oak, aspen and ponderosa forest teeming with bird and animal life. Six interconnecting trails totaling seven miles, branching from the **Aspen Springs Trail** (1 mile) allow you to custom-design your own hike, whether you want to take an easy walk to **Stonestep Lookout** (.5 mile) or a more ambitious hike to the summit of **Aspen Peak** (2.5 miles with a 3200-foot elevation gain) or **Hayden Peak** (2.75 miles with a 3400-foot elevation gain). The Aspen Springs Trail can also be combined with the **Potato Patch Loop** (2 miles) for a great five-mile loop trip.

BULLHEAD CITY/LAUGHLIN AREA A wonderful, little-known wintertime hike is **Grapevine Canyon** (1 mile). There is no clearly defined trail, but you will have no trouble tracing the tracks of other hikers up the wash along the canyon floor. Some rock scrambling is involved. At the mouth of the canyon are many petroglyphs that nomadic American Indians scratched into the sandstone with their *atl-atls*, or throwing sticks, an estimated 1200 years ago. Farther up the canyon, a thin waterfall flows year-round. The presence of water attracts nocturnal wildlife, and you may see tracks of badgers, skunks, desert bighorn sheep and even mountain lions. The wild grapes that grow here give the canyon its name. Grapevine Canyon is in Nevada, 13 miles west of the Laughlin/Bullhead City bridge on Route 163 and one-and-a-half miles in on the clearly marked, unpaved road to Christmas Tree Pass. There is a parking area near the mouth of the canyon.

◄ HIDDEN

LAKE HAVASU AREA The **Mohave Sunset Walking Trail** in Lake Havasu State Park winds for two miles between Windsor Beach and Crystal Beach through a variety of terrains from lowlands dense with salt cedar to ridgelines commanding beautiful views of the lake. Signs along the sometimes hilly trail identify common Mohave Desert plant life.

▼▼▼▼▼▼▼▼▼▼
Transportation

CAR

On Arizona's "West Coast" along the lower Colorado River, the Bullhead City/Laughlin area is reached by exiting **Route 40** at Kingman and driving 26 miles on **Route 68** through the most starkly stunning scenery in the Mohave Desert, or by exiting Route 40 at Topock, 12 miles east of Needles, California, and driving 35 miles north on **Route 95**. The other major Colorado River resort, Lake Havasu City, is 21 miles south of Route 40 on Route 95. A fascinating back-road route connecting Route 95 with Route 40 at Kingman goes through the historic town of Oatman on its steep climb over Sitgreaves Pass, a drive challenging enough to evoke amazement at the fact that this numberless road used to be part of Old Route 66, the main highway across the Southwest to Los Angeles in the days before the interstate was built.

AIR

The **Bullhead City–Laughlin Airport** is serviced by America West, Reno Air and United Express; the **Kingman Airport** in Kingman and the **Lake Havasu City Airport** are serviced by America West.

BUS

Greyhound Bus Lines stops at the bus terminals in Kingman and Laughlin. ~ Reservations: 800-231-2222. Kingman: 3264 Andy Devine Parkway; 520-757-8400. Laughlin: 1650 South Casino Drive; 702-298-2535.

CAR RENTALS

Car-rental agencies at the Bullhead City–Laughlin Airport are **Avis Rent A Car** (800-331-1212) **Budget Rent A Car** (800-330-9002) and **Hertz Rent A Car** (800-654-3131).

SIX

South Central Arizona

If your image of Arizona is cowboys, ranches and hitching posts, think again, partner. For while the flavor of the West is very much evident in the central band of the state, the trappings of the 20th century are everywhere—indeed, flourishing and growing apace. Head to its major cities—including Phoenix, Scottsdale, Tempe and Mesa—and you'll find a vibrant arts community, professional sports galore, shopping centers and stores as far as the eye can see, a fine college campus, intriguing architecture, enough golf, tennis and other activities to satisfy anyone and everyone. But if you're hankering for a glimpse of the frontier or a taste of the outdoor life, well, they're here, too: miles of virgin desert, rivers to swim and sail, towns more in the past than the present, trails to roam. So saddle up, friend.

Phoenix takes its name from the legendary phoenix bird, and with good reason: The biggest metropolis between southern Texas and California and the ninth largest in the country, Phoenix is a city taking flight. The population of Phoenix proper is 1,335,900 which balloons to 2,251,515 when you include the 23 satellite towns that blend seamlessly along the valley of the Salt River. Some thousand families a month set up homes in the broad river valley as subdivisions and shopping centers mushroom.

Phoenix today is a far cry from the era of the Hohokam Indians. The Hohokam, meaning "those who vanished," built a network of irrigation ditches to obtain water from the Salt River, part of which is still in use today. Then, as now, irrigation was vital to Phoenix. So much water is piped in to soak fields, groves and little kids' toes that the desert air is actually humid—uncomfortably so through much of the summer. Lettuce, melons, alfalfa, cotton, vegetables, oranges, grapefruit, lemons and olives are grown in abundance in the irrigated fields and groves, lending a touch of green to the otherwise brown landscape. Boating, waterskiing, swimming and even surfing—in a gigantic, mechanically activated pool—are splendid byproducts.

Did we mention sports? Whatever your game may be, this is sports heaven. In professional competition, Phoenix has baseball (the Triple-A Firebirds), hockey (the Roadrunners), football (the Cardinals) and basketball (the Suns). Plus, the Arizona State University Sun Devils play football, basketball and baseball. Still other spectator sports include rodeos and horse racing. For the active set, there are 125 golf courses and hundreds of tennis courts, as well as bike, jogging and horse-riding trails, and opportunities for all kinds of other pursuits.

The action here isn't all on the field. The city has completed a $1.1 billion re-development of the downtown that began in 1988. Testimony to the effort are the glitzy Arizona Center, the Mexican-themed Mercado and the 18,000-seat America West Arena next to the Civic Center Plaza.

Metropolitan Phoenix, or the Valley of the Sun, originated in 1850 on the banks of the Salt River and became the capital of the Arizona Territory in 1889. At one time, nearly 25,000 Indians were the exclusive inhabitants of Arizona. The earliest were the Hohokam who thrived from 30 A.D. until about 1450 A.D. Signs of their settlements remain intact to this day. Two other major tribal groups followed: the Anasazi in the state's northern plateau highlands, and the Mogollon People, in the northeastern and eastern mountain belt. Today there are 23 reservations in Arizona, more than any other state, with an estimated 190,091 Indians from 17 different tribes living in sad testimony to the white settlers' land grabs. Some 150 miles east of Phoenix in the White Mountain region of northern Arizona is the Fort Apache Indian Reservation with a million and a half acres of land. Bordering it, with another two million acres, is the San Carlos Apache Indian Reservation. The largest Indian reservation in North America, Navajoland, home to 90,942 Navajos, begins 76 miles north of Flagstaff and extends into northwestern New Mexico and southeastern Utah. Located almost in the center of the Navajo Indian Reservation is the Hopi Indian Reservation, 6500 members strong, who have lived on the same site without interruption for more than 1000 years, retaining more of their ancient traditions and cultures than any other Indian group.

In the mid-1500s, the conquistadors arrived, carrying the banner of Spain. They were looking for gold and seeking souls to save. They found more souls than gold and in the process introduced the Indians to cattle, horse raising and new farming methods, augmenting their crops of beans, squash and maize with new grains, fruits and vegetables. The Spanish-Mexican influence is still strongly evident throughout the Southwest. And the gold prospector eventually became the very symbol of the Old West—an old man with a white beard, alone with his trusted burro, looking to strike it rich. You only have to go 30 miles east of Phoenix into the Superstition Mountains to find the lore and the legend and the lure of gold still very much alive today.

Until about the mid-1880s, the Indians accepted the few white miners, traders and farmers who came West, but as the number of settlers grew, friction arose and fighting resulted. The cavalry was called in and one of the most brutal chapters in the history of the Southwest followed. Black troops of the Tenth Cavalry, known as Buffalo Soldiers because of their dark skin and curly black hair, came in large numbers to protect citizens of the Arizona land where Geronimo, Cochise, Mangus, Alchise and other chieftains had dotted the cactus-covered hills and canyons with

the graves of thousands of emigrants, settlers and prospectors. Numerous sites throughout the entire state bring those days of conflict into vivid focus—Cochise Stronghold in the Dragoon Mountains south of Willcox, hideout of the notorious Apache chief; Fort Bowie National Historic Site, an adobe ruin that was a key military outpost during the Indian wars, and nearby Fort Huachuca, an important territorial outpost that's still in operation today as a communications base for the U.S. Army; and Fort Verde State Historic Park, located in Camp Verde on Route 17 between Phoenix and Flagstaff, yet another military base that played a key role in subduing the Apaches in the 1870s.

Arizona's broad central band stretches across the state in what visiting English author J. B. Priestley once described as "geology by day and astronomy by night."

With the construction of the first railroad in 1887, fast-paced expansion took hold as Phoenix drew settlers from all over the United States. In 1889 it was named the capital of the Arizona Territory, and statehood was declared in 1912.

Once hailed as the agricultural center of Arizona, Phoenix by 1920 was already highly urbanized. Its horse-drawn carriages represented the state's first public transportation. Its population reached 29,053 and the surrounding communities of Tempe, Mesa, Glendale, Chandler and Scottsdale added 8636 to the count. As farmers and ranchers were slowly being squeezed out, these years of Phoenix's development saw a rugged frontier town trying to emulate as best it could famous cities back East. It had a Boston store, a New York store, three New England–style tea parlors and a number of gourmet shops selling everything from smoked herring to Delaware cream cheese. The region's dry desert air also began to attract scores of "health-seekers." The advent of scheduled airline service and the proliferation of dude ranches, resorts and other tourist attractions changed the character of the city still further.

Today, high-tech industry forms the economic core of Phoenix, while tourism remains the state's number-two job-producer. Not surprisingly, construction is the city's third major industry. But Phoenix retains a strong community flavor. Its downtown area isn't saturated with block after block of highrises and apartment houses. The city and all its suburbs form an orderly, 800-square-mile pattern of streets and avenues running north and south and east and west, with periphery access gained by soaring Los Angeles–style freeways. Beyond are the mountains and desert, which offer an escape from city living, with camping, hiking and other recreational facilities.

If the desert isn't your scene, neighboring Scottsdale just might be. Billing itself as "The West's Most Western Town," Scottsdale is about as "Western" as Beverly Hills.

Scottsdale's population of 154,145 appears to be made up primarily of "snow birds" who came to stay: rich retirees from other parts of the United States who enjoy the sun, the golf courses, the swimming pools, the mountains, the bolo ties and the almost endless selection of handicraft shops, boutiques and over 120 art galleries. Actually, retired persons account for only 20 percent of this fast-growing city, whose median adult age is 39. There are far more yuppies than grandmas.

Scottsdale was only desert land in 1888 when U.S. Army Chaplain Winfield Scott bought a parcel of land located near the Arizona Canal at the base of Camelback Mountain. Before long, much of the cactus and greasewood trees here had been replaced by 80 acres of barley, a 20-acre vineyard and 50 orange trees. Scottsdale remained a small agricultural and ranching community until after World War II. Motorola opened a plant in Scottsdale in 1945, becoming the first of many electronics manufacturing firms to locate in the valley.

Less than a quarter-mile square in size when it was incorporated in 1951, Scottsdale now spreads over 150 square miles. Its unparalleled growth would appear never-ending except that the city is now braced up against the 50,000-acre Salt River Indian Reservation, established in 1879 and home of the Pima and Maricopa people who haven't let their juxtaposition with one of the nation's wealthiest communities go unrewarded. The reservation boasts one of the largest shopping areas in the Southwest, a junior college, thousands of acres of productive farmland and future hotel sites.

The network of satellite communities that surrounds the Phoenix-Scottsdale area, like random pieces of a jigsaw puzzle, is primarily made up of bedroom communities. Tempe to the south is home of Arizona State University. Burgeoning Glen

dale, to the northwest, was originally founded as a "temperance colony" where the sale of intoxicants was forever forbidden. Mesa, to the east, covering 100 square miles, is Arizona's third-largest city. Carefree and Cave Creek, to the north, are two communities sheltered by the Sonoran Desert foothills and surrounded by mountains. Carefree was planned for those who enjoy fun-in-the-sun activities like tennis, golf and horseback riding. Cave Creek, a booming ranching and mining center back in 1873, thrives on its strong Western flavor. A bit hokey, but fun. Like fallout from a starburst, these and other neighboring communities all revolve around the tempo, pace and heartbeat of the Phoenix-Scottsdale core.

Beyond the urban centers, you can pull up to a gas station that's the last one from anywhere, visit honky-tonk saloons, skinny-dip in a mountain lake, pan for gold, meet dreamers and drifters. The best way to see the West is to be part of it, to feel the currents of its rivers or the steepness of its hills underfoot. South central Arizona certainly offers ample opportunity.

▼▼▼▼▼▼▼▼
Phoenix

The history of south central Arizona unravels in smooth, easy chapters through Phoenix's museums and attractions, particularly highlighting its Indian heritage. But this is by no means all you'll find here. The city is also a bustling art mecca, evident from the moment visitors arrive at Sky Harbor Airport, with its array of contemporary and Western artworks on display. The airport's program of changing art exhibits, in conjunction with the Phoenix Art Commission, is a model for similar programs at airports throughout the country. Art is everywhere in the city. Along Squaw Peak Freeway, a ten-mile stretch that connects downtown Phoenix with the city's northern suburbs, you may think you're seeing things, and you are. The freeway is lined with 35 giant three- and four-foot sculptures—vases, cups, Indian-style pots and other utensils, all part of the city's public arts project "to make people feel more at home with the freeway." Not everyone in Phoenix loves the idea. Detractors have dubbed the freeway art project "Chamber Pots of the Gods."

Surely the last of the rugged Marlboro men can still be seen astride handsome, well-groomed horses in Phoenix, but they're not riding off into the sunset, never to be seen again. Chances are they're heading into the vast expanse of desert land that still surrounds the city proper to recharge their motors. Long considered a scourge of man, arid and untamable, the desert with its raw awesome beauty is now considered by many as the last vestige of America's wilderness. Numerous tour operators offer guided jeep and horseback tours into the desert, but as any Arizonian will tell you, the desert is best appreciated alone. Southwestern Indians have long known the secrets of the desert. Now the settler man comes to turn his face skyward into the pale desert sun.

But whether the city proper or its environs are your scene, trying to take in all the sights and sounds in one trip is a bit like counting the grains of sand in a desert. We suppose it can be done, but who on earth has the time? To help you on your quest, here are some of this city's highlights.

Phoenix's once lackluster downtown is starting to reap the benefits of some $1.1 billion worth of cultural and architectural enhancements in progress since the late 1980s. A focal point of the new **Phoenix Municipal Government Center**, which includes a new city hall, is one of the city's oldest landmarks—the **Orpheum Theater**, a magnificent 1929 Spanish baroque revival building that was once considered the most luxurious playhouse west of the Mississippi River. Under restoration, the theater gives free public tours of the exterior and by January 1997 will be a showcase for the performing arts, community and civic events, ballet, children's theater, film festivals and other special events. ~ 602-252-9678.

SIGHTS

Other improvements are making downtown more pedestrian-friendly, such as the **Margaret T. Hance Deck Park**, a 29-acre greenbelt stretching from 3rd Street to 3rd Avenue, with wooded areas, fountains and a Japanese garden symbolizing Phoenix's ties to sister city Hemeji, Japan.

Southwestern anthropology and primitive arts are featured at **The Heard Museum**. The eight exhibition galleries on three levels include a Hopi kachina collection, Cochi story-teller figures, pottery by Maria Martinez, silver and turquoise jewelry, basketry, blankets and other American Indian crafts. Indian art demonstrations are frequently presented. Admission. ~ 22 East Monte Vista Road; 602-252-8840.

Phoenix Art Museum, which features exhibits on Western, contemporary and decorative arts, has an outstanding costume collection that includes accessories and textiles. The museum is currently undergoing a major renovation project, due to be completed in September 1996. Until that date, admission to the museum is

---

✔ **CHECK THESE OUT—UNIQUE SIGHTS**

- Bring the kids to the world's largest firefighting museum, aptly named the **Hall of Flame Museum**, where old-time firefighting equipment and hundreds of artifacts are on display. *page 165*
- Stride through **Rawhide-Arizona's 1880 Western Town**, and dodge real sheep and shootouts while exploring rickety Main Street. *page 176*
- Venture into Tonto National Forest and gaze at **Tonto Natural Bridge**, the largest natural travertine bridge in the world. *page 190*
- Delve into the past at **Casa Grande Ruins National Monument**, where you'll see Indian dwellings built in the 1300s. *page 195*

free—however, displays are also limited. Call for specific exhibition information. Closed Monday. Admission. ~ 1625 North Central Avenue; 602-257-1880.

The **Arizona State Capitol Museum** was built in 1900 to serve as the Territorial Capitol. The building has been restored to the 1912 era when Arizona won statehood. Guided tours feature permanent exhibits in the Senate and House Chambers, the Governor's Suite and the Rotunda. A wax figure of the state's first governor, George Hunt, is seated at his partnership desk surrounded by period furnishings. Major artifacts include the original silver service taken from the USS *Arizona* before the battleship was sunk at Pearl Harbor and the roughrider flag carried up Cuba's San Juan Hill during the Spanish-American War. Closed weekends. ~ 1700 West Washington Avenue; 602-542-4675.

Mineral and ores from Arizona and the rest of the world are displayed at the **Arizona Mining and Mineral Museum**, one of the finest of its kind in the Southwest. Closed Sunday. ~ 1502 West Washington Avenue; 602-255-3791.

Over at the **Hall of Fame Museum** you will find rotating exhibits dedicated to the people who made Arizona what it is today. Crammed with artifacts, each section offers insight on the colorful lives of pioneers who built this state. Closed weekends. ~ 1101 West Washington Avenue; 602-255-2110.

The Mercado is composed of half a dozen commercial buildings patterned on a traditional Mexican village. This two-block-long complex includes shops offering Western wear, American Indian jewelry and handicrafts, and is in the process of adding dining and entertainment venues. Beautiful courtyards add to the charm of this eclectic complex. ~ Van Buren Street between 5th and 7th streets; 602-256-6322.

Museo Chicano features changing exhibits ranging from local to international focus. Hispanic culture, arts and history are exhibited, as well as the work of well-known and emerging artists. In addition, the museum offers a popular series of cultural programs and performing arts events, such as the city's Mexican Ballet Folklorico. Closed Sunday and Monday. Admission. ~ 25 East Adams Street; 602-257-5536.

It seems appropriate—a museum of science and technology located in a parking garage! That's where you'll find the **Arizona Science Center**, which features a discovery arcade with hands-on energy, physics and life sciences exhibits, located on the main level of the Hyatt Regency parking garage. The focus is on subjects like computers, gravity, momentum, energy, nutrition and infinity. Also on display are stars of the Southwestern desert such as the iguana, gila monster, python, vine snake and tortoise. The museum will be

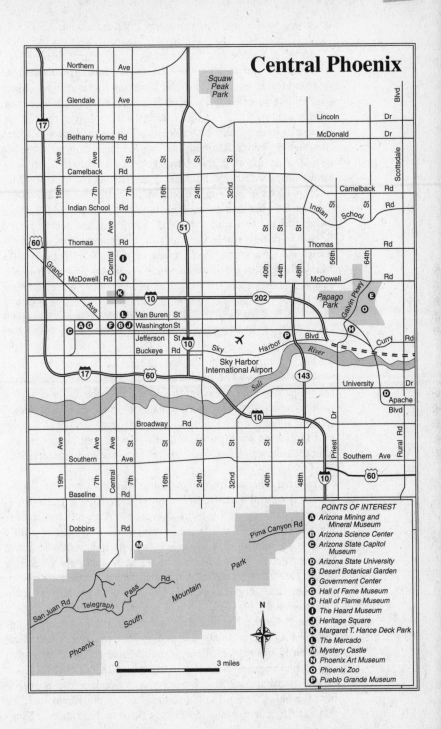

Central Phoenix

POINTS OF INTEREST

- Ⓐ *Arizona Mining and Mineral Museum*
- Ⓑ *Arizona Science Center*
- Ⓒ *Arizona State Capitol Museum*
- Ⓓ *Arizona State University*
- Ⓔ *Desert Botanical Garden*
- Ⓕ *Government Center*
- Ⓖ *Hall of Fame Museum*
- Ⓗ *Hall of Flame Museum*
- Ⓘ *The Heard Museum*
- Ⓙ *Heritage Square*
- Ⓚ *Margaret T. Hance Deck Park*
- Ⓛ *The Mercado*
- Ⓜ *Mystery Castle*
- Ⓝ *Phoenix Art Museum*
- Ⓞ *Phoenix Zoo*
- Ⓟ *Pueblo Grande Museum*

relocating to Heritage Square in early 1997. Admission. ~ 147 East Adams Street; 602-256-9388.

Heritage Square is a Southwestern time warp featuring four turn-of-the-century homes: the **Arizona Doll and Toy Museum**; the **Rosson House**, an 1895 Eastlake Victorian that contains a beautiful collection of period furniture; the **Silva House**, a Victorian-style bungalow that has exhibits ranging from turn-of-the-century swimsuits to origami; and the **Stevens-Haustgen House**, in which the Pueblo Grande Museum (see below) has exhibits on the archaeological history of the Heritage Square area itself. There is an admission at the Rosson House and the Arizona Doll and Toy Museum. ~ Heritage Square: 7th and Monroe streets; 602-262-5071.

The **Phoenix Museum of History** has recently undergone a move and major expansion. Now located in the Heritage and Science Park next to Heritage Square, the museum focuses on the territorial history of Phoenix from the Civil War to the 1930s. Many displays are interactive and involve personal stories and historical figures; others include an impressive printing press exhibit and one of the state's oldest mining locomotives. There is now a library for research and browsing, as well as a gift shop. The building is wheelchair accessible. Admission. ~ 105 North 5th Street; 602-253-2734.

For a glimpse into the Hohokam tribe's past, visit the **Pueblo Grande Museum**. The exhibits include a prehistoric Hohokam ruin, a permanent display on this legendary tribe and a changing gallery featuring Southwestern Indian arts, crafts and archaeology. Of special interest is an outdoor trail that leads visitors to the top of a Hohokam platform mound. There is also an interactive exhibit for children. Admission. ~ 4619 East Washington Street; 602-495-0901.

Located not far from the central Phoenix museums is the **Desert Botanical Garden** where more than 20,000 plants from desert lands of Africa, Australia, North and South America are displayed. You can see this beautiful garden via a self-guided nature walk or a group tour. Featured is a three-acre showcase of native Sonoran desert plants, a saguaro forest, a mesquite thicket, a desert stream and an upland chaparral habitat, complete with historic American Indian dwellings. Admission. ~ 1201 North Galvin Parkway; 602-941-1225.

Nearby is the **Phoenix Zoo** which uses natural settings, including a four-acre African Savanna, to showcase over 1300 mammals, birds and reptiles. Phoenix newcomers are frequently startled to find themselves driving along busy Van Buren alongside a family of trumpeting elephants. For a convenient zoo overview take the Safari Train. Popular highlights are the World Herd of Arabian Oryx, a rare Sumatran tiger exhibit and the Baboon Kingdom. Children will especially enjoy the hands-on participatory exhibit called Wildlife Encounters–Mammals. Be sure to visit the one-acre tropical rainforest, the home of 15 bird and animal species adopted from around the world. Admission. ~ 455 North Galvin Parkway; 602-273-1341.

The largest firefighting museum in the world is the **Hall of Flame Museum**. On display are more than 90 restored hand-drawn, horse-drawn and motorized fire engines and hundreds of artifacts. Special games, exhibits and programs, all stressing fire safety, are offered for children. Admission. ~ 6101 East Van Buren Street; 602-275-3473.

Tucked away in the foothills of South Mountain Park, the **Mystery Castle** is an 18-room extravaganza fashioned from native stone, sand, cement, water, goat's milk and Stutz Bearcat wire-rim wheels. Warmed by 13 fireplaces, the parapeted castle has a cantilevered stairway, chapel and dozens of nooks and crannies and is furnished with Southwestern antiques. It's known as the "mystery" castle because the builder, Boyce Luther Gulley, thinking he was about to die from tuberculosis, ran away from his Seattle home in a Stutz Bearcat and devoted 15 years to the construction project. It was only after his death in 1945 that the missing builder's family learned of his whereabouts and inherited the castle. Closed Monday. Admission. ~ End of South 7th Street; 602-268-1581.

Pioneer Arizona Living History Museum re-creates an Old West town using mostly original buildings—a church, schoolhouse, printing shop and blacksmith shop—and featuring costumed interpreters. Living history exhibitions include cooking, gardening and sewing. At the opera house you'll see melodramas and historic performances all themed to the territorial period, 1858 to 1912. Of special interest is one of our nation's last remaining herds of colonial Spanish horses. You can also enjoy the picnic area and a restaurant. Closed Monday and Tuesday. Admission. ~ Pioneer Road exit off of Route 17; 602-993-0212.

As a major resort and convention center, the Valley of the Sun features some of the most spectacular hotel resorts in the country. It has had the rare distinction of having more *Mobil Travel Guide* Five Star resorts (three of the twelve top-rated resorts nationwide) than any other city in the United States (see "Spoil Yourself" in this chapter). Yet it's not without its share of budget- and moderate-priced hotels and motels, and proliferating bed and breakfasts.

LODGING

An elegant scene of the past is mirrored in the glossy facade of the present with the rebirth of the **San Carlos Hotel** in the heart of downtown. Built in 1927, the seven-story San Carlos was overhauled recently, but its charm was kept intact—a crystal chandelier and period furnishing in the lobby, original bathtubs, basins and furniture in the 113 guest rooms. Deep carpets line the hallways. The San Carlos is one of the largest hotels listed in the National Register of Historic Places. ~ 202 North Central Avenue; 602-253-4121, 800-528-5446, fax 602-523-6668. MODERATE.

The 24-story **Hyatt Regency Phoenix** is across from Civic Plaza downtown. With 712 rooms, it's the city's largest hotel. It has a heated swimming pool, exercise equipment, a café, lounges and revolving roof-top dining room. Rooms are smallish but tastefully furnished in a light, Southwest style. ~ 2nd and Adams streets; 602-252-1234, 800-233-1234, fax 602-254-9472. ULTRA-DELUXE.

A find, price-wise, is the **Nendels Valu Inn**, an attractive two-story brick inn with 30 large rooms—mauve and green color themes predominating—and a swimming pool and free airport shuttle service. ~ 3307 East Van Buren Street; 602-275-3691, 800-547-0106, fax 602-267-0448. BUDGET.

For those interested in meeting fellow budget-travelers try the **Hostel Metcalf House.** Here's what you get: two dormitory-style rooms (men's and women's) with bunk beds for ten in each. Guests may use the kitchen and community room. ~ 1026 North 9th Street; 602-254-9803. BUDGET.

The YMCA has 139 rooms in an seven-story downtown building. It's good old Y-style, nothing fancy, but it's clean. For a dollar extra, full use of the gym facilities is included. ~ 350 North 1st Avenue; 602-253-6181. BUDGET.

If you want to stay in shape while you're away, try the **Lexington Hotel and City Square Sports Club,** a full-service hotel with 180 rooms, a restaurant and a lounge along with a full-scale athletic club facility including basketball and racquetball courts, sauna, steamroom and pool. Rooms are standard Southwestern decor, but the workout's great. ~ 100 West Clarendon Avenue; 602-279-9811, 800-927-8483, fax 602-631-9358. MODERATE.

◆◆

✔ CHECK THESE OUT—UNIQUE LODGING

- *Budget:* Make your pocketbook happy as you bed down at **Nendels Valu Inn,** an attractive two-story brick inn in Phoenix. *page 166*
- *Moderate:* Laze around the pool at **Scottsdale's Fifth Avenue Inn** after a shopping spree in Scottsdale's premier shopping district. *page 180*
- *Moderate to deluxe*: Pick out one of the leather-bound books to read as you relax in **The Maricopa Manor**'s Library Suite. *page 167*
- *Ultra-deluxe:* Lose yourself at **The Boulders,** where 12-million-year-old granite boulders are the backdrop at this luxury resort. *page 190*

Budget: under $50 Moderate: $50–$90 Deluxe: $90–$120 Ultra-deluxe: over $120

Desert Sun Hotel offers 107 guest rooms with modern furnishings and various color themes. It has a 24-hour restaurant, a lounge, swimming pool, and the price is right. ~ 1325 Grand Avenue; 602-258-8971, 800-227-0301, fax 602-256-9196. BUDGET.

The **Maricopa Manor** is a Spanish-style bed and breakfast situated in a garden-like setting of palm trees and flowers in the heart of north central Phoenix. Built in 1928, the inn has five individually decorated suites, all with private baths. Typical is the Library Suite with its canopied king-size bed, private deck entrance, handsome collection of leather-bound books and an antique work desk. Guests may also use the inn's spacious Gathering Room as well as the formal living, dining, music rooms, patio, pool and gazebo spa. ~ 15 West Pasadena Avenue; 602-274-6302, 800-292-6403, fax 602-266-3904. MODERATE TO DELUXE.

◄ *HIDDEN*

Looking for a quick snack? Go to the tony new **Arizona Center** and take the elevator or stairs to the second floor and, voilà! Here you'll find a whole array of attractive fast-food restaurants all sharing a mutual sit-down dining—**Tumbleweed Cafe, Gyros and Grill, Hot Dogs on a Stick, Scotto Pizza, Teriyaki Temple, Chinese Cafe**, and more. ~ Van Buren between 3rd and 5th streets; 602-271-4000. BUDGET.

DINING

At **Sam's Café**, a large patio set amidst fountains is one draw; good Southwestern cuisine is another. Start with *poblano* chicken chowder, then have chile-rubbed shrimp topped with lemon butter and *pico de gallo*, or cheese-filled tortellini with chorizo and black beans. If the weather is inclement (which it rarely is), indoor dining is also nice, with more fountains and terra-cotta colored walls. ~ 455 North 3rd Street; 602-252-3545. MODERATE.

With a dozen aquariums scattered around the lobby and dining room, the **Golden Phoenix** appears to have the largest tropical fish population of any Arizona restaurant. While the decor of this stucco-style establishment offers few Asian touches, the kitchen does wonders with Mandarin dishes like *kung pao* shrimp and hot sizzling beef. ~ 1534 West Camelback Road; 602-279-4447. MODERATE.

The chef at **Eddie's Grill** has elevated cooking to an art form by blending culinary traits from America's diverse ethnic groups into a "New American" cuisine. Try the toasted seafood wontons with raspberry-jalepeño sauce or grilled chicken breast with ginger cream sauce. As multicultural as this restaurant may sound, it's truly American at heart, from the U.S.-produced meats and vegetables to the wines and bottled water. Don't ask for Evian. Dinner only weekends. ~ 4747 North 7th Street; 602-241-1188. MODERATE TO DELUXE.

Christo's specializes in Northern Italian cuisine, which means less pasta in favor of meatier fare—chicken *zingarella*, osso buco veal, rack of lamb—and fish dishes such as halibut topped with goat cheese, olive oil, garlic and sliced tomatoes. Sparkling stemware, crisp peach-and-white tablecloths and table flowers add a festive note. Closed Sunday. ~ 6327 North 7th Street; 602-264-1784. MODERATE TO DELUXE.

HIDDEN ►   A popular neighborhood restaurant, **Texaz Grill** really looks like it was transferred over from Dallas with its neon beer signs, glowing jukebox, antique wall memorabilia (old Texas license plates and the like) and chalkboard menus. Steaks come in a variety of sizes, from an eight-ounce fillet to an 18-ounce Lone Star, but the biggest seller of all is the chicken-fried steak served with heaps of mashed potatoes and buttermilk biscuits, just like in Texas. Dinner only on Sunday. ~ 6003 North 16th Street; 602-248-7827. BUDGET TO MODERATE.

And you thought diners went the way of the dinosaur. Step into **Ed Debevic's** and you'll find yourself back in the 1950s, complete with tabletop jukeboxes, photos of Marilyn, blue-plate specials, burgers, shakes and fries. The servers perform nostalgic dances of the '50s and '60s, and the low prices are right out of the past, too. ~ 2102 East Highland Avenue; 602-956-2760. BUDGET.

Greekfest brings a bit of Mykonos to the desert with a taverna-like atmosphere of white walls, archways, beamed ceilings, hand-crafted wallhangings and marble floors. A tasty meal can easily be made of the mezzes or appetizer, which include panfried calamari, grilled octopus, *hummus*, house-made lamb sausage, phyllo-wrapped meat, cheese and spinach pastries and salads. Dinner only on Sunday. ~ 1940 East Camelback Road; 602-265-2990. MODERATE.

A colorful coffee house with a touch of bohemia is **Dos Barista's Coffeehouse** in the Town & Country Shopping Center. A red neon espresso sign in the window greets people; inside, red, yellow and turquoise colors add to the decor. Don't expect meals here—just good pastry and coffee. A bin of newspapers will keep you enter-

WEATHER OR NOT? WHILE SOME LIKE IT HOT . . .

All of south central Arizona gets hot, despite the seemingly innocuous average annual temperature of 72°F. Winter is cool and clear, in the 60s; spring is breezy and warm, in the 90s; summer is torrid, often topping 100, and that's when the monsoons come, the swift summer rainstorms that usually arrive late in the day with spectacular flashes of lightning and deep, rolling rumbles of thunder; autumn is marvelously dry and clear, in the 80s. Depending on your weather preference, choose your time to visit accordingly.

tained, as will people-watching or the live folk music three nights a week. Some just stare at the unique wall of burlap bags. There are also a handful of outdoor tables. ~ 4745 North 20th Street; 602-957-2236. BUDGET.

Christopher Gross, the chef-owner of **Christopher's** was recently named one of the ten top chefs in the country and now you can hardly get into the place. It's located in the Biltmore Financial Center, which is good; wait 'til you see the bill. Contemporary French food is served in a small (16 tables) candlelit dining room, all new and gleaming. The attentive waiters really know their wines, so helpful advice is available if needed. ~ 2398 East Camelback Road; 602-957-3214. ULTRA-DELUXE.

Adjacent to Christopher's is **The Bistro**, same owner, same kitchen, different entrances, but far more casual, with a marble floor and open kitchen. ~ 2398 East Camelback Road; 602-957-3214. DELUXE.

What it lacks in decor, **Ham's** makes up for in great cooking and affordable prices. Specials change daily and include beef tips and noodles, fried chicken, barbecued beef and meatloaf, all served with heaps of mashed potatoes, veggies and biscuits. Closed Sunday. ~ 3302 North 24th Street; 602-954-8775. BUDGET.

At **Ayako of Tokyo**, teppanyaki chefs grill chicken, scallops, shrimp, filet mignon and lobster at your table. Each entrée comes with soup, salad, rice, vegetables and green tea. Rice paper screens add a Japanese touch to the decor of this restaurant graced with Oriental paintings and panels. There are also sushi and tempura bars, as well as a lounge. Dinner only on weekends. ~ 2564 East Camelback Road, Biltmore Fashion Park; 602-955-7007. MODERATE TO DELUXE.

Wright's is an open, airy dining room at the Arizona Biltmore with a menu featuring New American cuisine. There is raisin and pistachio french toast with warm fruit compote as well as snazzy egg dishes. The lunch and dinner menus are filled with pasta, seafood and meat dishes served with intriguing sauces. For dinner start with an appetizer such as golden tomato and goat cheese tart with black olive oil, and then try an entrée such as seared ahi tuna with ginger sticky rice or smoked venison loin with herb spaetzle and garlic spinach. Save room for one of their fabulous desserts. ~ 24th Street and Missouri Avenue; 602-954-2507. DELUXE TO ULTRA-DELUXE.

Havana Cafe offers the not-too-spicy cuisine of Spain and Cuba in an atmosphere that's more a small, cozy café than in the style of Hemingway's Havana. *Chicharitas*, an appetizer of fried green plantain chips, will get the juices flowing. There's saucy chicken with blends of herbs, spices, rice, tomatoes, vegetables and olive oil and paella (for two), the house specialty, sausage, *sopa de ajo* (garlic soup), *escabeche*, *picadillo* and more. ~ 4225 East Camelback Road; 602-952-1991. MODERATE.

HIDDEN ►   A spot popular with the downtown office workers eager for a touch of home cooking, **Mrs. White's Golden Rule Cafe** offers pork chops, chicken, cornbread and cobbler. Get there early for a table. Closed Sunday. ~ 808 East Jefferson Street; 602-262-9256. MODERATE.

To the west of Phoenix, check out **The Spicery** located in the Catlin Court Shops District, a downtown area where historic homes have been preserved. This eatery is in a charming, 1895 Victorian house. It offers tea service all day as well as food the way mother used to make it—homemade soups, salads, chubby sandwiches, fresh-baked bread and pies. Closed Sunday. ~ 7141 North 59th Avenue, Glendale; 602-937-6534. MODERATE.

SHOPPING   Western wear would seem a natural when hitting the shopping scene—and you're right. There's a herd of places selling boots, shirts, buckles and whatever else you might want. If you're in the market for Western clothes, just to look the part or to get ready for your next rodeo appearance you might start with **Aztex Hats** offering the largest selection of Western hats in Arizona. ~ 15044 North Cave Creek; 602-971-9090. **Frontier Boot Corral** has been in business for over 25 years with a complete line of Western wear. ~ 7th and Van Buren streets; 602-258-2830. **Saba's Western Store**, in business since 1927, includes Barry Goldwater among its clientele. ~ 2901 West Bell Road; 602-993-5948. **Sheplers** is part of the world's largest Western-wear chain. ~ 9201 North 29th Avenue; 602-870-8085.

If you like malls and shopping complexes, get ready. Phoenix has them in abundance. Some of the best are: **Park Central Mall** is the city's best-known shopping center and the oldest. The **Green Woodpecker**, a large novelty gift shop, can be found here. ~ 3121 North 3rd Avenue; 602-264-5575. **Metrocenter** is an enclosed double-deck mall that includes **Robinson's**, **Dillard's** and **Macys**. ~ 9617 Metro Parkway West; 602-997-2641.

The Mercado, located downtown adjacent to the Phoenix Civic Plaza, is a festive mall and Mexican cultural center with colorful buildings, brick-lined streets and outdoor dining. Mexican shops and restaurants feature arts, crafts, fashions and good things to eat of the hot and spicy persuasion. ~ Van Buren Street between 5th and 7th streets; 602-256-6322.

For designer merchandise at legendary low prices, head for **Loehmann's**. ~ 3135 East Lincoln Drive; 602-957-8691.

Museum gifts shops also offer unique finds for selective shoppers. For instance, the **Phoenix Art Museum** offers books, posters, catalogs and art-replica gifts. It also has a special section for children. ~ 1625 North Central Avenue; 602-257-1880.

The **Desert Botanical Garden** has a gift shop offering foods, spices and jellies made from desert plants, as well as nature books and Southwestern souvenirs and crafts; plants are sold in an adjoining greenhouse. ~ 1201 North Galvin Parkway; 602-941-1225.

It was the disappearance of the Hohokam Indians that led settlers to select the name "Phoenix" from the symbol of immortality of the ancient Egyptians.

Don't drop just yet. Because after all those malls and other stores, we come to the farmers' markets! Every Thursday from 9 a.m. to 1 p.m., farmers from around the community sell their freshest produce at low prices in the courtyard at **Heritage Square**. ~ Monroe and 7th streets; 602-262-5071.

For a kicker, **American Park 'N Swap** is the largest open-air flea market in the Southwest, with over 2000 dealers selling or swapping everything from used office furniture and rare antiques to Indian jewelry and rare one-of-a-kind photos of Marilyn Monroe. Open Wednesday, Friday and weekends. ~ 3801 East Washington Street; 602-273-1258.

A small town south of Phoenix is the setting for the **Guadalupe Farmer's Market**. You will find fresh vegetables, exotic fruits and dried chile peppers. ~ 9210 South Avenida del Yaqui, Guadalupe. A few blocks north is **Mercado Mexico** where Mexican *dulces* (sweets) are sold—*ates* (jellied fruit candies), sugared pecans, lightly dusted chocolate balls, jars of *cajeta*, a caramel sauce made from goat's milk, and other sticky delights. You'll find a good range of handicrafts and souvenirs from Mexico here as well. ~ 8212 South Avenida del Yaqui, Guadalupe; 602-831-5925.

◄ HIDDEN

NIGHTLIFE

Nightlife in south central Arizona is as diverse and far-reaching as the area itself, from twanging guitars of country-and-western bands to symphony strings. There are Indian ceremonials and sophisticated jazz as well. To find out what's happening, check the entertainment pages of the *Arizona Republic* and the *Phoenix Gazette*.

If you feel more adventurous, you might try some of the following: **Graham Central Station** where traditional and country-and-western music can be heard nightly, with big-name acts, concerts and live bands. Friday's happy hour is one of the best in town. ~ 4029 North 33rd Avenue; 602-279-4226.

From the sound of things, **America's Original Sports Bar**, on the second level of the Arizona Center, might seem to newcomers like a place for nightly brawls. No way. There is 3-on-3 basketball and even a volleyball court, all in the Valley's trendiest new bar. Food is served, and of course plenty of drinks. With all that action you can work up a thirst. Cover on weekends. ~ 455 North 3rd Street; 602-252-2502.

Also in the Arizona Center, upstairs, is the **Cheyenne Cattle Company** a glitzy country-and-western nightspot with live music, cowgirl waitresses and a goodly share of business-expense-account types (the Convention Center is located nearby) among the loyal crowd of hooters and honkers. Weekend cover. ~ 455 North 5th Street; 602-253-6225.

A valley institution for the two-step crowd, **Mr. Lucky's** has live country music upstairs and recorded Top-40 rock-and-roll downstairs. Live bull-riding(!) Wednesday, Friday and Saturday. Weekend cover. ~ 3660 West Grand Avenue; 602-246-0686.

"Home of the Nashville Stars," **Toolies Country** is a 600-seat frontier Western cabaret with dinner and dancing nightly to the music of big-name country entertainers. Occasional cover. ~ 4231 West Thomas Road; 602-272-3100.

Nightlife here isn't restricted to the bar and two-step scene. A more refined look at the arts flourishes here as well. **The Herberger Theater Center** is an ultramodern theater complex housing two separate theaters, **Center Stage** and **Stage West**, where professional theater performances take place. The Center features the **Ballet Arizona,** and is home to the **Arizona Theater Company,** which has performed in Phoenix for more than 25 years. ~ 222 East Monroe Street; 602-252-8497.

The 2500-seat **Phoenix Symphony Hall** houses the Phoenix Symphony and stages entertainment ranging from opera and ballet to Broadway shows and top-name concert performers. ~ 225 East Adams Street; 602-262-7272.

PARKS   **SOUTH MOUNTAIN PARK** 🚶 🚲 🐎 ⛵ With 17,000 acres, this is the largest municipal park in the world, a vast rugged mountain range that was once American Indian hunting ground. A spectacular view of Phoenix can be seen from Dobbins Lookout, 2300 feet above the desert floor. The park offers over 40 miles of well-marked hiking and riding trails. Its steep canyons reveal evidence of ancient American Indian artifacts and petroglyphs. Facilities include picnic areas, restrooms and a sunken concrete stage for park ranger lectures or impromptu sing-alongs. ~ Located at 10919 South Central Avenue; 602-495-0222.

PAPAGO PARK 🚶 🚲 🐎 ⛵ A part of the Phoenix parks network since 1959, Papago is a neat blend of hilly desert terrain, quiet lagoons and glistening streams. The former American Indian townsite now offers golf, picnic sites, ballfields and fishing. Three lagoons are stocked with bass, catfish, bluegill and trout in winter. (It's free for kids 15 and under but an urban fishing license is required for all others.) Also within its boundaries are the Phoenix Zoo, the Desert Botanical Garden, and the Phoenix Municipal Stadium, where the Oakland A's hold their spring training. You'll also find firepits, restrooms, archery range, bike paths and running courses. ~ Located at 625 North Galvin Parkway; 602-256-3220.

SQUAW PEAK RECREATION AREA 🏃 One of Phoenix's most familiar landmarks with its craggy, easily identifiable pinnacle, Squaw Peak is primarily known for its hiking trails. However, the rocky terrain has been moderately developed for other recreational pursuits as well, whether picnicking or curling up in the shade of a towering saguaro with an Edward Abbey tome on the evils of overdevelopment. The picnic ramadas have electricity. Other amenities include drinking water, firepits, tables, benches and restrooms. ~ Located at 2701 East Squaw Peak Drive; 602-495-0222.

ESTRELLA MOUNTAIN REGIONAL PARK 🏃 🚲 🐎 With 19,840 acres, Estrella offers abundant vegetation and spectacular mountain views, with peaks within the Sierra Estrella Mountains reaching 3650 feet. The park offers excellent areas for hiking and riding, a rodeo arena and a golf course. Horse and hiking trails abound. There's an amphitheater for lectures and gatherings. Picnic areas and restrooms are located in the park. ~ Located 16 miles southwest of Phoenix on Route 10. Exit on Estrella Parkway and follow it five miles south to the park; 602-932-3811.

WHITE TANK MOUNTAIN REGIONAL PARK 🏃 🚲 🐎 Covering 26,337 acres of desert, canyons and mountains, White Tank is the largest park in the Maricopa County Park System. Elevations range from 1402 feet at the entrance to 4083 feet at the park's highest point. White Tank contains an excellent hiking, mountain bike and horse trail system, a seasonal flowing waterfall (reached by a mile-long self-guided hiker's trail) and American Indian petroglyphs scattered throughout. Two newly constructed wheelchair-accessible trails allow visitors with disabilities to view some of the park's petroglyphs. Facilities include picnic sites, restrooms and showers. ~ Located on Dunlap Avenue (which turns into Olive Avenue before reaching the park), 15 miles west of Glendale; 602-935-2505.

▲ There are 38 sites; $8 per night. Backpack camping is allowed (free).

The Phoenix Gay Scene

While gay activities are found throughout Phoenix, the highest concentration centers around the blocks between Camelback and Indian School roads and between 7th Avenue and 7th Street. This area is home to an array of gay lodging, cafés, bars, shops and nightclubs.

LODGING

In central Phoenix, **Windsor Cottage** consists of two English Tudor–style cottages that share an outdoor pool surrounded by gardens. Each has a refrigerator and microwave, a private bath with a large shower built for two, and french doors opening onto a private patio. One cottage is done in an art deco design and the other is painted in colorful shades of blue and lavender. Laundry facilities and massage are available. The clientele is mostly gay and lesbian. ~ Call for directions; 602-264-6309. MODERATE TO DELUXE.

Larry's Bed & Breakfast is centrally located and features three antique-decorated guest rooms. Folks may watch movies and play cards in the spacious living room, or lounge in the clothing-optional outdoor pool and jacuzzi. Women are welcome, but this is primarily a spot for gay men. A full breakfast is served. ~ 502 West Claremont Avenue; 602-264-6309. BUDGET TO MODERATE.

You can stay for a week or a month at the gay-owned **Arizona Royal Villa Apartments**. Both hotel rooms and one-bedroom apartments are available here. All rooms face the courtyard where there is a clothing-optional swimming pool. Continental breakfast is served. ~ 1102 East Turney Avenue; 602-266-6883. MODERATE.

The men-only **Arizona Sunburst Inn** is a L-shaped ranch house with 12 large, comfortable rooms furnished in contemporary designs; some rooms have private baths while others share. Guests have access to a fully equipped kitchen. The outdoor heated pool and jacuzzi are clothing optional. Continental breakfast is served. ~ 6245 North 12th Place; 602-274-1474. MODERATE.

DINING

Dine on all-American food in an art deco atmosphere at the popular gay-owned **Pookie's Cafe**. This lively spot adorned with colorful stained-glass windows features 27 television screens playing music videos. Choose from a menu offering sandwiches, burgers, quesadillas, Buffalo wings and dinner specials such as steak and pasta. ~ 4540 North 7th Street; 602-277-2121. BUDGET.

At the elegantly understated **Options Arizona Bar & Restaurant/Media Lounge**, you can dine on anything from burgers and filet mignon to chicken Marsala and vegetarian entrées. Adorned in shades of mauve and plum with low lighting, this is a popular spot for both gay men and women. The adjoining lounge features live entertainment. ~ 5111 North 7th Street; 602-263-5776. BUDGET TO MODERATE.

Deceptions Restaurant caters to the gay and lesbian crowd with a menu featuring such classics as pasta, steak, pork chops and chicken fried steak. Staying true to its name, this spot is decorated with masks and pictures of clowns and offers cabaret-style dinner shows on Wednesday and Saturday. Check out the after-hours breakfasts every Friday and Saturday from 3 a.m. on. ~ 5025 North 7th Avenue; 602-274-6275. BUDGET TO MODERATE.

SHOPPING

For a selection of 5000 gay, lesbian, bi and transgender titles, check out **Obelisk the Bookstore**. You'll find fiction and nonfiction as well as a variety of magazines. ~ 24 West Camelback Road; 602-266-2665.

At gay-owned **Whangdoodles** an eclectic collection of antique kitsch and knickknacky stuff lines the shelves. International masks, antique toys and voodoo supplies are some of the items for sale. ~ 24 West Camelback Road; 602-264-9496.

Gay-owned **Pink Flamingos Antiques and Collectibles** is an entire house filled with antiques ranging from beautiful bedroom sets to collector's shot glasses and ashtrays. ~ 2241 North 7th Street; 602-261-7730.

Unique on Central is a gay-owned shop offering a large selection of cards, gifts, music, videos, travel books and magazines. ~ 4700 North Central Avenue, Suite 105; 602-279-9691.

Perhaps the most popular gay bar in the city is **Charlie's**, where you can take clogging and square-dancing lessons three nights a week and dance to good ol' country-and-western music nightly. The scene is mostly men, from 21 to 81 years of age. ~ 727 West Camelback Road; 602-265-0224.

NIGHTLIFE

At **Harley's 155** you'll find a mixed crowd dancing to Top-40 and house music every night of the week. ~ 155 West Camelback Road; 602-274-8505.

Foster's is popular with the younger set, mostly male, who come to dance, dance, dance. Pop music plays every night of the week: Friday is '80s night, and Sunday is disco. ~ 4343 North 7th Street; 602-263-8313.

For nightly live entertainment from jazz to male strippers, head to the cocktail lounge at **Wink's Cabaret**. ~ 5707 North 7th Street; 602-265-9002. Cover.

Both men and women frequent **BS West**, a video/dance bar that has an outdoor patio and features house music on most nights. Tuesday is comedy, Thursday is show tunes and Sunday afternoon there's a tea dance. ~ 7125 East 5th Avenue; 602-945-9028.

For a country-and-western bar that caters mostly to women, head to **The Desert Rose**. A large dancefloor and a lively game room are the attractions. Check out the free dance lessons on Thursday night. ~ 4301 North 7th Avenue; 602-265-3233.

Ain't Nobody's Bizness is a very pink women's bar (although men are welcome) with R & B and Top-40 dance music most evenings. Stand-up comedy is featured on a regular basis and Monday is karaoke night. ~ 3031 East Indian School Road; 602-224-9977.

A dance bar humming with live entertainment and eight music video screens, **Nasty Habits** attracts a primarily lesbian following, though gay men are welcome. ~ 3108 East McDowell Road; 602-231-9427.

▼▼▼▼▼▼▼▼▼
Scottsdale

Like neighboring Phoenix, Scottsdale is proud of its frontier heritage, which can be traced at a number of locations in and near the town. In the Old Scottsdale section, where only 35 years ago Lulu Belle's and the Pink Pony were the only two watering holes for miles around, the buildings all have false fronts, handcrafted signs and hitching posts, and horses still have the right of way. Many restaurants feature waiters and waitresses in period dress. The women have teased hairdos, and the men are all called Slim, Ace, Tex, Shorty and Stretch.

But that's about as *Western* as it gets. Otherwise, Scottsdale is chic, elegant and expensive. Amid its ties to the past, Scottsdale is a showplace of innovative architecture. The Frank Lloyd Wright Foundation is located here (at Taliesin West), as is the Cosanti Foundation, design headquarters for the controversial prototype town of Arcosanti, some 30 miles from Prescott, where building and nature are being fused.

SIGHTS

Housed in a building made of adobe blocks mixed with desert plants (for strength), the **Hoo-Hoogam Ki Museum** is located on the Salt River Pima-Maricopa Indian Reservation bordering the city. Here you will find displays of baskets, artifacts, pottery and historical photographs. Closed Sunday. Admission (free to American Indians). ~ 10000 East Osborn Road; 602-941-7379.

Also, don't miss **Rawhide-Arizona's 1880 Western Town** with its colorful variety of rides and attractions, shops, a steakhouse and a saloon—all mostly located along a rickety Main Street where visitors dodge real sheep and goats. Western shootouts, fiddlers, a gypsy fortuneteller, stunt shows, a full-size 1880s-style locomotive, a carriage exhibit, a covered-wagon circle and an Old West museum are all part of the fun. ~ 23023 North Scottsdale Road; 602-563-1880.

After New York City and Santa Fe, Scottsdale is the busiest art center in the country, with more than 200 galleries.

McCormick Railroad Park is a child's and adult's locomotive fantasy. Start by riding around the park on a miniature steam railroad, then take a whirl on the 1929 carousel. Afterward, tour the railroad museum located in a Pullman car that President Eisenhower used during his whistle-stop campaign in 1952. Finally, bring your kids for an eye-level view of trains whizzing along model railroad tracks through tiny villages. ~ 7301 Indian Bend Road; 602-994-2312.

Taliesin West/Frank Lloyd Wright Foundation, a National Historic Landmark owned by the Frank Lloyd Wright Foundation, was the architect's Arizona home and studio. Situated on 600 acres of rugged Sonoran Desert, this remarkable set of buildings still astounds architectural critics with its beauty and unusual forms. A variety of guided tours are offered. There's also a lecture series. Admission. ~ 12621 North Frank Lloyd Wright Boulevard; 602-860-2700.

Fleischer Museum has rotating shows and permanent exhibits devoted to "American Impressionism, California School," with lots of ladies from that stylish period between the turn of the century and the 1940s, plus misty, dreamlike landscapes, architectural and still-life paintings. ~ 17207 North Perimeter Drive; 602-585-3108.

LODGING

Howard Johnson–Scottsdale lifts itself out of the ordinary chain motel category with a stunning landscape of desert palms and a mountain backdrop. It has 216 rooms and suites—lots of yellows and beige, with floral paintings on the walls and bright Southwestern colors for the slipcovers—built around a large swimming pool, spa and patio. Complimentary continental breakfast is available. ~ 5101 North Scottsdale Road; 602-945-4392, 800-446-4656, fax 602-947-3044. DELUXE.

Holiday Inn–Old Town is located in the heart of "Old Town," close to everything. Its 206 rooms have a Southwestern motif. There are a lounge with nightly entertainment, a restaurant, swimming pool and tennis courts. ~ 7353 East Indian School Road; 602-994-9203, 800-695-6995, fax 602-946-8084. DELUXE.

The revamped **Scottsdale Plaza Resort** is a true find. Set within 40 acres, with 404 rooms, 180 of them suites, the resort features Spanish/Mediterranean-style villas throughout, accented with courtyard swimming pools. The rooms are large and styled with Southwestern furnishing and art. Fountains, palm trees, earth-tone tiles, mauve carpeting, acres of fresh-cut flowers and potted greens add cooling touches. There are swimming pools, outdoor spas, tennis courts, indoor racquetball courts, a pro shop, gym and, if you need more, croquet. ~ 7200 North Scottsdale Road; 602-948-5000, 800-832-2025, fax 602-951-5700. ULTRA-DELUXE.

If you're looking for a gem of a mini-resort, try the 56-room **Best Western Papago Inn & Resort**. Amenities include a heated pool, sauna, lounge and dining room. Guest rooms all overlook a treed and flowered interior courtyard and swimming pool. Environmental "green" rooms—nonsmoking rooms with air and water filter systems—are available for a charge. ~ 7017 East McDowell Road; 602-947-7335, 800-528-1234. DELUXE.

Holiday Inn–Sunspree Resort, a Radisson Resort located on 35 lushly landscaped acres in the heart of Scottsdale, has 200 guest rooms (including 17 one- and two-bedroom suites). All reflect the natural colors of the desert and are richly appointed with Southwestern and Indian art. Recreational facilities include tennis courts, a pool, nearby golf, jogging trails and horseback riding. ~ 7601 East Indian Bend Road; 602-991-2400, 800-852-5265, fax 602-998-2261. ULTRA-DELUXE.

Text continued on page 180.

Spoil Yourself

The American West is big and grand: How inconsistent it would be if its great resort hotels were not just a reach beyond all expectation. And Central Arizona is home to some of the biggest and grandest around.

Designed by Frank Lloyd Wright and Albert Chase McArthur, the refurbished **Arizona Biltmore** has maintained an aura of ease and luxury since its opening in 1929. From its palm-lined drive, elaborate high portico and immense lobby to its bright, handsomely furnished guest rooms, the 498-room Biltmore is as dramatic and visually exciting as it is comfortable. "Arizona's Grande Dame" provides a full range of activities: golf courses, tennis courts, pools, a health club and nearby riding facilities. ~ 24th and Missouri streets, Phoenix; 602-955-6600, 800-950-0086, fax 602-954-2548. ULTRA-DELUXE.

Another ultra-deluxe establishment in Phoenix, to say the least, is **The Phoenician**, the most prestigious and talked-about resort in the Valley of the Sun. Sprawled over 130 acres along the sun-dappled flanks of Camelback Mountain, it's set within a tiered oasis of waterfalls and pools, the largest of which is tiled entirely with mother-of-pearl. Its 442 guest rooms are large and lavish with most situated in the main hotel, others in surrounding *casitas*. There are also 107 *casita* units with parlor suites that have hand-carved travertine fireplaces. If you really want to make a night of it, there are two presidential and 30 luxury suites. Recreational facilities run the gamut—a 27-hole golf course, lighted tennis courts, tournament croquet and a health and fitness spa. ~ 6000 East Camelback Road; 602-941-8200, 800-888-8234, fax 602-947-4311. ULTRA-DELUXE.

The Scottsdale Princess, an ultra-luxury resort in the pretty-in-pink tradition of Princess hotels everywhere, has 600 rooms. It's one of the Valley's largest hotels. Set on 450 elaborately landscaped acres with a central courtyard, waterfall, three swimming pools and 18th-century Spanish Colonial architecture, the Princess is one of the most visually arresting of its kind. The rooms are large, decorated in Southwestern furnishing, with a hint of Santa Fe. The grounds include seven tennis courts, a fitness center and two championship golf courses. ~ 7575 East Princess Boulevard; 602-585-4848, 800-344-4758, fax 602-585-9895. ULTRA-DELUXE.

With 423 rooms, **Marriott's Camelback Inn** outside Scottsdale is yet another glorious world-class retreat dramatically nestled in the foothills between the Camelback and Mummy mountains, where landscaped paths wind through gardens of cactus and desert palms. Its Southwestern pueblo architecture and adobe-style *casitas* blend harmoniously into the stunning desert background. For the sportsminded there are championship golf and tennis, swimming, trail rides, weekly cookouts and fitness facilities. ~ 5402 East Lincoln Drive, Paradise Valley; 602-948-1700, 800-242-2635, fax 602-951-5452. ULTRA-DELUXE.

Marriott's Mountain Shadows Resort and Golf Club offers palm trees, sparkling streams and lakes, and that's just the golf course. At the foot of Camelback Mountain, with over a hundred acres of land, Mountain Shadows seems designed for the sports devotee. Along with its pro 54 holes of golf, it has lighted tennis courts, putting greens, and swimming pools. The hotel's 336 guest rooms are designed in muted Southwestern colors, each with a private terrace. The resort has four restaurants. ~ 5641 East Lincoln Drive, Paradise Valley; 602-948-7111, 800-782-2123, fax 602-951-5452. ULTRA-DELUXE.

Who says the West is wild? The **Wigwam** west of Phoenix is an upper-upper-scale resort on 75 acres of what was originally virgin desert. The design is pueblo-style, with 331 desert-brown adobe *casitas* set in a lavish golf and country-club setting—towering palms, green lawns, cascading flowers and fragrant orange trees. Through the use of building materials native to the Southwest, architecture blends with nature. Slate, stone and wood surfaces are accented with Indian themes and desert colors. Championship golf courses, riding, tennis, swimming and other activities keep the body occupied while the mind relaxes. ~ 300 East Indian School Road, Litchfield Park; 602-935-3811, 800-327-0396, fax 602-935-3737. ULTRA-DELUXE.

Scottsdale's Fifth Avenue Inn, a secluded retreat right in the heart of Scottsdale's premier shopping district, sprawls out around a central courtyard with a large heated swimming pool. Its 92 guest rooms feature desert colors, king and double queen beds, and separate dressing areas. Rates includes breakfast. ~ 6935 5th Avenue; 602-994-9461, 800-528-7396, fax 602-947-1695. MODERATE.

The **Best Western Thunderbird Suite** may be a Best Western property, but don't let the chain-affiliation throw you. It's a four-story, all-suite, hotel designed in a courtyard setting with a heated pool and spa and a restaurant on the premises. Each of the hotel's two-room suites is styled in desert mauve and teals with light Southwestern contemporary furnishings. ~ 7515 East Butherus Drive; 602-951-4000, 800-334-1977, fax 602-483-4046. DELUXE.

DINING

Julio G's, established in 1934, somehow manages to combine a '30s art deco, Santa Fe and Mexican truck-stop decor—ceiling fans, black-tile walls and framed vintage-Mexican advertisements—into a trendy contemporary look. The food is much more clearly defined: *pollo magnifico*, beef tacos, bean tostadas, steaming bowls of rice and beans, chili con carne and tortillas. The staff is friendly and attentive. ~ 7633 East Indian School Road; 602-423-0058. BUDGET TO MODERATE.

Any restaurant that combines American decor with traditional Greek flourishes has to be interesting. The food at **Andros** runs from chicken and burgers to rolled grape leaves, rice and olives, and there's all that great Greek music in the background. There's also a monthly Greek night with live music and belly dancing; call for schedule. ~ 8040 East McDowell Road; 602-945-9573. BUDGET TO MODERATE.

Malee's on Main Thai Gourmet is a charming little spot with a bar in one corner, tables inside and a patio, weather permitting, for dining outside. Attractive tableware is set against peach and green tablecloths. Popular with the art crowd (in Scottsdale that covers a wide swath), the restaurant has an extensive menu that comes in various degrees of spiciness. Dinner only on Sunday. ~ 7131 East Main Street; 602-947-6042. MODERATE.

One of the oldest Mexican restaurants in Scottsdale (also considered the finest by many) is **Los Olivos Mexican Patio**. The restaurant was founded in 1945, but the adobe building in which it's located was built in 1928 and is officially listed as one of Scottsdale's historic landmarks. Large and rambling, with viga ceilings, it has several individual dining rooms inside and patio dining outside. The Mexican cuisine served is primarily Sonoran—enchiladas, seasonal green corn tamales, chimichangas, *chile rellenos* and steak picado. The decor is festive (clay pots, flowers and piñatas) and there's live music and dancing on weekends. Aficionados rate its margaritas among the best in the state. ~ 7328 East 2nd Street; 602-946-2256. BUDGET TO MODERATE.

A traditional breakfast spot (it also serves lunch) is **The Original Pancake House,** in business over 40 years, serving up steaming stacks of golden flapjacks, topped with melted butter, honey, maple syrup, berries or whatever's your pleasure. The restaurant is small—eleven tables and ten booths. The decor is Southwestern with light green and tan colors dominating. Large picture windows in front keep it bright and cheerful. ~ 6840 East Camelback Road; 602-946-4902. BUDGET.

Voltaire is a bastion of French gastronomy, all candlelight and crystal. Boned chicken à la Normande with apples, sautéed sand dabs, rack of lamb and sweetbreads sautéed in lemon butter and capers highlight the extensive menu. Closed Sunday. ~ 8340 East McDonald Drive; 602-948-1005. DELUXE.

Don't be surprised if your waiter breaks into song after you've ordered at **Ristorante Sandolo,** an Italian café known for their singing servers. The restaurant dishes out Venetian-style entrées and gourmet pizzas, followed by complementary sandolo (similar to gondola) rides on the waterway winding through the Hyatt Regency Scottsdale. ~ 7500 East Doubletree Ranch Road; 602-991-3388. MODERATE.

The first thing seasoned travelers look for when staking out a new town is a good place to have breakfast. In Scottsdale, **Boman's N.Y. Kosher-style Restaurant & Deli** hits the spot. Small and non-descript, it has a deli counter on one side, separated from the blue formica tables and banquets by a picket fence. Ceiling fans, an advertisement for Dr. Brown's Cream Soda and an indifferent waitress pretty much set the ambience. The focus is on good food at moderate prices—french toast, applejack pancakes, ham and eggs.

♦♦♦

✔ CHECK THESE OUT—UNIQUE DINING

- *Budget to moderate:* Join the fiesta out on the patio at **Los Olivos Mexican Patio,** one of the oldest Mexican eateries in Scottsdale. *page 180*
- *Moderate:* Stare at the weird decor (animal heads next to old farm tools) as you scarf down barbecued delights at **The Satisfied Frog.** *page 192*
- *Moderate to deluxe:* Go American at **Eddie's Grill,** where food from diverse ethnic groups is blended into "New American cuisine" and all the ingredients are U.S. produced, including the wine. *page 167*
- *Ultra-deluxe:* Indulge at **Christopher's,** where contemporary French food is prepared by one of the nation's top chefs. *page 169*

Budget: under $8   Moderate: $8–$16   Deluxe: $16–$24   Ultra-deluxe: over $24

It's also open for lunch and dinner (pastrami on rye, pickles, brisket, chicken in the pot, stuffed cabbage). A sign on the cash register says, "Shalom, Y'all." ~ 3731 North Scottsdale Road; 602-947-2934. MODERATE.

With the success of her popular Tucson restaurant of the same name, chef/owner Donna Nordin has branched out with another **Café Terra Cotta**, this one in Scottsdale's Borgata shopping center. Colorful and casual, with green chairs and little pots of cacti on the tables, this restaurant serves standout dishes such as a chile relleno stuffed with grilled shrimp accompanied by papaya-melon salsa and large prawns stuffed with herbed goat cheese served on a Southwestern tomato *coulis*. ~ 6166 North Scottsdale Road; 602-948-8100. MODERATE TO DELUXE.

House of Yang is small, only a few tables and chairs, and it appears to do a large takeout business. But whether you eat in or take out, the House of Yang is a course in Chinese cuisine, serving Szechwan, Hunan, Mandarin and Cantonese. Shrimp with lobster sauce—shrimp, onions and peppers, stir-fried and topped with a black bean sauce—comes with rice, won tons and an egg roll. Mongolian beef is thinly sliced beef served with egg roll, fried rice and won tons. ~ 13802 North Scottsdale Road; 602-443-0188. BUDGET.

Rawhide Steakhouse and Saloon is the place to belly up to the bar in Scottsdale's popular Old West frontier town. There's good things to eat, too—mesquite-broiled steaks, prime rib, barbecued chicken, baby back ribs and even fried rattlesnake. The saloon section has an antique bar, gambling tables (but no gambling), "crooked" card dealers and live country music. ~ 23023 North Scottsdale Road; 602-563-5600. DELUXE.

Greasewood Flats is a hot dog, chili and beer kind of place housed in an old graffiti-covered wooden shack in what appears to be a Western junkyard, with discarded school desks, wooden wagons, saddle frames, wagon wheels, milk cans and egg crates all around it. But folks line up to get in. Live music Thursday through Sunday. ~ 27000 North Alma School Road; 602-585-9430. BUDGET.

The **Marquesa** is one of the top restaurants in the valley. Even people who normally avoid hotel dining rooms flock to this one in the Scottsdale Princess Resort to soak up all of its Old World Spanish ambience and nibble on tapas before settling down to more serious pursuits. Roast grouse, in season, with brandy sauce and cranberries, for instance, or steaming Mediterranean-style paella for two. The Marquesa is also known for its excellent wine list. Dinner only, plus Sunday brunch. ~ 7575 East Princess Drive; 602-585-4848. DELUXE.

Don't wear a necktie if you're going to the **Pinnacle Peak Patio** because they'll snip it off and hang it from the rafters. That's part of the appeal of this highly informal Western-style steak house where 16-ounce mesquite-broiled steaks, with all the beans and fixin's, top the menu and the walls reverberate with the sounds of live country bands nightly. ~ 10426 East Jomax Road; 602-967-8082. MODERATE TO DELUXE.

Shells Oyster Bar & Seafood is the best known of the four restaurants located at Marriott's Mountain Shadows Resort. Live miniature fish swim in an illuminated aquarium. The decor is bright and airy, with nautical touches, polished brass, etched mirrors and natural wood finishes. Seafood entrées come in a variety of preparations—flame broiled, steamed, sautéed, panfried or blackened Cajun style, accompanied by a selection of special butters and sauces. ~ 5641 East Lincoln Drive; 602-948-7111. MODERATE TO DELUXE.

SHOPPING

For a fine art collection, visit **Elaine Horwitch Galleries**. The late Ms. Horwitch endowed this and her other gallery in Santa Fe with an eye for quality in contemporary art, and a rare sense of humor. ~ 4211 North Marshall Way; 602-945-0791.

The Borgata of Scottsdale may just be a harbinger of a striking new trend in shopping centers—mini-theme-park shopping malls—this one, a 14th-century-style village with medieval courtyards. International fashions, fine jewelry, unusual gifts, a book and music store and a spate of art galleries await. ~ 6166 North Scottsdale Road; 602-998-1822.

Despite the trendy intrusions, **Scottsdale Fashion Square** remains the city's most fashionable shopping complex. It features top-quality stores like **Neiman Marcus** (602-990-2100), **Dillard's** (602-949-5869) and **Robinson's** (602-941-0066). There's even a shop for the kiddies—**The Disney Store** (602-423-5008). ~ 7000 East Camelback Road; 602-990-7800.

Fifth Avenue Shops comprise the landmark shopping area in the heart of downtown Scottsdale, a sprawl of specialty shops, boutiques, bookstores, galleries, jewelry stores, American Indian crafts shops and restaurants, over 200 in all by latest count. ~ 6940 East 5th Avenue; 602-947-5377. Among them: **Sewell's Indian Arts** for American Indian jewelry, kachinas, Pueblo pottery and Navajo sandpaintings. ~ 7087 5th Avenue; 602-945-0962; **Lemonade Folk Art** for Southwestern gifts and decorations. ~ 7121 5th Avenue, #25; 602-945-8853; **Gallery 10** featuring contemporary American Indian and Western ceramic art, jewelry, kachinas and paintings. ~ 7045 3rd Avenue; 602-994-0405.

Elsewhere, mystery lovers should seek out **The Poisoned Pen**, a mystery bookstore specializing in crime, detective and suspense books from American and British publishers. ~ 7100-D East Main Street; 602-947-2974.

For you cowpokes, **Porters** is one of the oldest names in Scottsdale cowboy gear and features top-of-the-line name brands. ~ 3944 North Brown Avenue; 602-945-0868.

Scottsdale's many art galleries offer contemporary works, Indian art, Western and Old Masters. If you're interested in the local art scene, the **Scottsdale Gallery Association** conducts Art Walks every Thursday, from 7 p.m. to 9 p.m., visiting many of the leading galleries. ~ 602-990-3939.

If you want to check out the art scene on your own, consider **Arizona West Galleries**, which specializes in Western and Civil War relics and American 19th- and 20th-century Western art, including works by Frederic Remington, Charlie Russell and Maynard Dixon. Closed Sunday. ~ 7149 Main Street; 602-994-3752.

The **Biltmore Galleries** also has 19th- and 20th-century art, including works by early New Mexico master Nicolai Fechin, Joseph Sharp and Ernest Blumenschein. ~ 7113 Main Street; 602-947-5975.

Buck Saunders Gallery, the oldest gallery in Scottsdale, having long been the exclusive representative of Arizona's best-known, best-loved artist, Ted De Grazia, continues to exhibit his work. ~ 2724 North Scottsdale Road; 602-945-9376.

Glenn Green Galleries uses the elegant grounds of the posh Phoenician Resort (the gallery is in the hotel's retail corridor) to display the mammoth bronze and stone sculptures of famed Indian artist Alan Houser, as well as sculptors Paul Moore and Eduardo Oropeza. ~ 6000 East Camelback Road; 602-990-9110.

J. R. Fine Arts handles serigraphs, lithographs, oils and sculpture, including those by top contemporary painters Leroy Neiman and Earl Biss. ~ 4151 North Marshall Way; 602-945-7856.

NIGHTLIFE   The **Lobby Bar**, features jazz Wednesday through Saturday. ~ Scottsdale Hyatt Regency, 7500 East Doubletree Ranch Road; 602-991-3388.

For beer brewed on the premises, stop by **Hops Bistro & Brewery**. Favorites are the award-winning unfiltered German Wheat Beer or Hops Amber. The decor is high-tech, with glass block partitions, modern paintings and a black, gray and orange decor. ~ 7000 East Camelback Road; 602-945-4677.

J. Chew & Company has live jazz nightly in an intimate, European-style pub with french doors leading to two outdoor patios with fireplaces. ~ 7320 Scottsdale Mall; 602-946-2733.

Scottsdale Center for the Arts, located in the beautifully sculptured Scottsdale Mall, hosts a variety of events, including the Scottsdale Symphony, guest performing artists, concerts, lectures, classic cinema and art exhibitions. During the summer, music lovers flock to the concerts held outside on the grassy lawn at the mall's east end. For a schedule, call 602-994-2787.

The audience gets involved in solving crimes at **Murder Ink Productions,** a murder mystery dinner theater held at various resorts and restaurants in Scottsdale and Phoenix. ~ 602-967-6800.

▼▼▼▼▼▼▼▼▼▼▼▼
Tempe/Mesa Area

Immediately east of Phoenix are the communities of Tempe and Mesa. Continuing out over the desert that stretches on to New Mexico are Apache Junction and Globe. It's as though, heading east, all the big-city sheen dissolves in degrees into the West of the Old West, the pace slows down and you can almost reach up and feel the sky in your hands.

SIGHTS

Bordered by Scottsdale, Mesa, Phoenix and Chandler, **Tempe** was founded in 1872 by Charles Turnbell Hayden who established the Hayden Flour Mill that year, now the oldest continuously operating business in Arizona. **Old Town Tempe** is where Tempe was originally founded, set up around the old Hayden Flour Mill. Today many of the early homes and buildings have been renovated and serve as restaurants, shops, offices and galleries. ~ North of University Street along Mill Avenue; 602-894-8158. Stop by the **Tempe Convention and Visitors Bureau** for maps and information. ~ 51 West 3rd Street, Suite 105; 602-894-8158.

Forming the character of Tempe is **Arizona State University,** located in the heart of the city. Home of the Fiesta Bowl, it has the largest enrollment of any school in the Southwest. With its 700-acre main campus, where strikingly modern buildings rise from a setting of palm trees and subtropical plants, Arizona State provides the chiefly residential city with its main industry. A number of outstanding museums dot the campus and are open to the public. **Arizona State University Art Museum** has an extensive collection of American paintings, prints and crafts as well as artworks from Africa, Latin America and the South Seas. Closed Monday. ~ 602-965-2787. The **Museum of Anthropology** includes archaeological, physical and sociocultural anthropology exhibits. ~ 602-965-6224. Highlight exhibits at the **Museum of Geology** focus on rare geologic specimens, seismographs and earthquake displays. ~ 602-965-7065. Museum hours vary, so call ahead.

FROM PAST TO PRESENT

For a trip back in time, visit the outstanding **Tempe Historical Museum,** which covers the history of Tempe from early Indian days to the present. Two changing galleries offer historic exhibits on the area. There are also hands-on displays for children. Closed Friday. Admission. ~ 809 East Southern Avenue; 602-350-5100.

For art buffs there is the **Tempe Arts Center and Sculpture Garden** which features eight changing gallery exhibits of contemporary arts, crafts and sculpture. Large-scale works are showcased in the adjoining Sculpture Garden, with many of the works for sale. Closed Monday. ~ 54 West 1st Street; 602-968-0888.

Just east of Tempe, you'll come to the town of **Mesa**. Situated on a plateau, Mesa in Spanish means "tabletop." The town was founded by Mormons in 1883 and was long a farming community. Irrigation canals built by the Hohokam Indians were still used in Mesa until fairly recent times. For information on sights and services in Mesa, stop by the **Mesa Convention and Visitors Bureau**. ~ 120 North Center Street; 602-969-1307.

Mesa Southwest Museum covers the history of the Southwest from the time of the dinosaurs to the settlement of the West, with hands-on exhibits inside and a one-room schoolhouse and a gold-panning stream outside. Closed Monday. Admission. ~ 53 North MacDonald Street, Mesa; 602-644-2230.

A find for aviation aficionados, the **Champlin Fighter Museum** has a collection of 30 restored fighters from World War I, World War II and the Korean and Vietnam wars. Historic weaponry is also displayed. An art gallery, video theater and pilot-memorabilia gift shop round out the bill. Admission. ~ 4636 Fighter Aces Drive, Mesa; 602-830-4540.

Twenty minutes north of Mesa is the **Out of Africa Wildlife Park** where lions, tigers, leopards and giant pythons do their things. There are shows, natural habitat viewing, cub-petting and a playground for the kids. There's also a gift shop and restaurant. Closed Monday. Admission. ~ 2 South Fort McDowell Road, Fountain Hills; 602-837-7779.

LODGING   **The Buttes** is a dramatic 353-room, four-story resort built into the mountainsides, with Southwestern styling and art throughout. All guest rooms feature a Southwestern decor or rose and earth tones, cactus and wood furnishings. It has two restaurants, a nightclub, pools, tennis courts and all of the modern trim and trappings associated with luxury resort living in the valley, including cascading waterfalls and four romantic mountainside whirlpools. ~ 2000 Westcourt Way, Tempe; 602-225-9000, 800-843-1986, fax 602-431-2422. ultra-deluxe.

A little bit of Ireland located within walking distance of the ASU campus is found at the **Valley o' the Sun Bed and Breakfast, Tempe**. It has three rooms (two with connecting bath) located in a ranch-style home with a view of the Papago Mountains. The decor and decorations reflect a note of nostalgia. Continental breakfast is included. ~ P.O. Box 2214, Scottsdale, AZ 85252; 602-941-1281, 800-689-1281. BUDGET.

Cornerstone of downtown Mesa, the **Sheraton Mesa Hotel** has 269 rooms, contemporary furnishings, lounge, restaurant and swimming pool. ~ 200 North Centennial Way; 602-898-8300, 800-456-6372, fax 602-964-9279. ULTRA-DELUXE.

Buckhorn Mineral Wells is a motel and natural hot water mineral springs bath house where massages and therapeutic hot soaks are offered. The motel has 14 rooms in contemporary Southwest decor. ~ 5900 East Main Street, Mesa; 602-832-1111. BUDGET.

DINING

Mill Landing is a handsome restaurant housed in a historic building in the downtown Old Town section of Tempe offering a variety of light meals, salads, soups, sandwiches and seafood specialties. There's dining in the patio, weather permitting. ~ 398 South Mill Avenue; 602-966-1700. MODERATE.

In a similar mold and in a similar building (the Andre, built in 1888), **Paradise Bar and Grill** specializes in prime rib and fresh fish. ~ 401 South Mill Avenue, Tempe; 602-829-0606. MODERATE.

Casa Reynoso is one of the better Mexican restaurants in town, despite its modest appearance—vinyl booths and wrought iron. Try the *gollo burro* or *chile rellenos*. Closed Monday. ~ 3138 South Mill Avenue, Tempe; 602-966-0776. BUDGET.

The Coffee Plantation is a Caribbean-style coffeehouse and retail store in a plantation house. Beans are roasted daily in a rustic roasting shack. There's indoor and outdoor seating where espresso, cappuccino and specialty coffees are served, along with pastries and desserts, light lunch and dinner. ~ 680 South Mill Avenue, Suite 100, Tempe; 602-829-7878. BUDGET.

For Italian Continental cuisine, try **John Henry's**. Duck, lamb, steak, seafood and pasta are some of the favorites you can enjoy in this elegant, plant-filled dining room. Live music Tuesday through Saturday. ~ 909 East Elliot Road, Tempe; 602-730-9009. MODERATE TO DELUXE.

The decor is plain and simple and the food is anything but at **Char's Thai Restaurant** where an exotic touch of the East comes to Tempe with such offerings as chicken soup with coconut milk, smoked beef salad, curried duck and seafood combinations in peanut sauce. There's also a good selection of Asian beers. ~ 927 East University Drive, Tempe; 602-967-6013. BUDGET TO MODERATE.

For a good solid breakfast or lunch, they don't come much better than the **Ripe Tomato Café** where it's always wall-to-wall people. It's a great find for breakfast, and the steak, sandwiches and Mexican specialty lunches aren't bad either. ~ 745 West Baseline Road, Mesa; 602-892-4340. BUDGET.

SHOPPING

Historic **Old Town Tempe** exudes ambiance with its old-fashioned red-brick sidewalks and planters, tree-lined streets and quaint street lamps. Walk the area and you'll find dozens of shops and restaurants. With light music floating in the background, you can scan the shelves at the **Changing Hands Bookstore**, which has more than 50,000 new and used books on three floors. Specialties at the bookstore are spirituality, psychology, literature, women's issues and travel. ~ 414 South Mill Avenue; 602-966-0203. For clothing, gifts and accessories from around the world, try **Mazar Bazaar** ~ 514 South Mill Avenue; 602-966-9090.

If you want to wear a souvenir home, try **Arizona Images** which has a large selection of Arizona State University clothing and gift items, as well as Phoenix Cardinal and Phoenix Sun merchandise. ~ 725 South Rural Road, Tempe; 602-829-1743.

For quality American Indian arts, **Apache Arts** in Mesa offers modern paintings. ~ 9919 East Apache Trail, Mesa; 602-986-5450. **Galeria Mesa** features contemporary art from around the country. ~ 155 North Center Street, Mesa; 602-644-2056.

The **Lenox Factory Outlet** offers selected seconds on the company's famous china and crystal products, as well as candles, silver and other tabletop accessories. ~ 2121 South Power Road, Mesa; 602-986-9986.

NIGHTLIFE   **Grady Gammage Memorial Auditorium**, at the Arizona State University campus in Tempe, is a 3000-seat auditorium designed by Frank Lloyd Wright. Its entertainment features range from Broadway productions to symphony orchestra concerts and ballet. Guided tours of the center are offered Monday through Friday. ~ Tour information: 602-965-4050. Gammage Auditorium: 602-965-3434.

Serving dinner, drinks and laughs, the **Tempe Improv**, is a restaurant/comedy club which features a changing lineup of stand-up comics. ~ 930 East University Drive; 602-921-9877.

The Butte's swinging **Top of the Rock Bar** with its 24-foot video screen and live entertainment on weekends is one of the hottest spots in Tempe. ~ 2000 Westcourt Way; 602-225-9000.

Bandersnatch is big with the ASU college crowd, which means lots of beer including four homemade brews. Live jazz and traditional Irish music several times a week. ~ 125 East 5th Street, Tempe; 602-966-4438. **Balboa Café** draws large crowds with live jazz and rock nightly. Occasional cover. ~ 404 South Mill Avenue, Suite 101, Tempe; 602-966-1300. ·

PARKS   **MCDOWELL MOUNTAIN REGIONAL PARK**   This 21,099-acre wilderness expanse 15 miles northeast of Scottsdale is one of the region's most scenic parks with an abundance of vegetation and majestic mountain views. Elevation ranges from 1600 feet at the southeast corner to 2000 feet along the western boundary. The area is ideal for camping, picnicking, horseback riding, hiking and mountain bike riding. Facilities include picnic areas, restrooms and showers. ~ Located via McDowell Mountain Road, four miles northeast of Fountain Hills; 602-471-0173.

▲ There are 76 sites (all with RV hookups); $12 per night.

From cactus flowers to remote mountain lakes, here is a region rich in scenic wonders. Best known for its dude-ranch resorts, mining towns, cool forests and desert playgrounds, this recreational paradise includes the Wild West town of Wickenberg—the Dude Ranch Capital of the World— the three-million-acre Tonto National Forest and some of the Southwest's better ghost towns.

▼▼▼▼▼▼▼▼▼▼▼▼
North of Phoenix

SIGHTS

Established in 1950, **Carefree** is a planned community set in the scenic foothills of the Arizona desert. To the north and east stretches the immense Tonto National Forest. Next door is the old-time town of **Cave Creek**. Once a booming mining camp in the 1880s (gold and silver), Cave Creek wasn't incorporated until a hundred years later. Sheep and cattle were raised here as well. Today Cave Creek leans heavily on its past, with its Frontier Town re-creation and annual spring rodeo. For more information contact **Carefree/ Cave Creek Chamber of Commerce.** ~ 748 Easy Street, Carefree; 602-488-3381.

Cave Creek Museum offers a living-history exhibit of the desert foothills region, with a restored 1920s tuberculous cabin and a 1940s church, as well as displays of pioneer living, ranching, mining, guns and American Indian artifacts. Open October through May, Wednesday through Sunday. ~ 6140 East Skyline Drive, Cave Creek; 602-488-2764.

To the northwest, on Route 89, you will come to the site of the richest gold strike in Arizona. Named after the Austrian settler Henry Wickenburg, who discovered it, **Wickenburg** is primarily known today as a winter resort.

Frontier Street preserves Wickenburg's turn-of-the-century character with its old-time train depot now housing the **Wickenburg Chamber of Commerce** and a number of vintage wood and brick buildings. One, the Hassayampa, was once the town's leading hotel. Maps for a self-guided historic walking tour are available at the chamber office. ~ 520-684-5479.

Before the town jail was built, the nearby **Jail Tree** was used to chain criminals. Friends and relatives brought them picnic lunches. Today the tree is on the property of the Chaparral Ice Cream Parlor, and tykes eat their ice cream cones there now, probably none the wiser. ~ Tegner Street and Wickenburg Way, Wickenburg.

Venture over to the **Desert Caballeros Western Museum** which covers the history of Wickenburg and surrounding area with major exhibits divided into various rooms. "Period" rooms include the Hall of History and a Street Scene representing Wickenburg at the turn of the century. Others focus on 19th- and early-20th-century lifestyles. Its art gallery features American Indian art and Western masters of the past and present. The Museum Park outside offers unique desert landscaping and plants. Admission. ~ 21 North Frontier Street, Wickenburg; 520-684-2272.

> At the peak of the gold rush, Wickenburg had more than 80 mines, with the town growing into what was Arizona's third-largest city at the time.

Those interested in gold mines and ghost towns might want to visit **Vulture Mine**. This is a historic gold mine and ghost town of sorts. The home of the town founder of Wickenburg can be seen, as well as an early assay office, blacksmith shop, stamp mill, a 3000-foot mine shaft and even a hanging tree. Closed Tuesday and Wednesday. Admission. ~ Vulture Mine Road; 602-377-0803.

To the northeast of Phoenix lies **Payson**, district headquarters for the Tonto National Forest. Payson provides a base camp for numerous scenic attractions within the forest primeval. Founded over a century ago as a tiny mining and ranching community, it now thrives on its recreation industry. **Payson Chamber of Commerce** offers information on the area. ~ 100 West Main Street, Payson; 520-474-4515.

Ten miles north of Payson, **Tonto Natural Bridge** in the Tonto National Forest, is the largest natural travertine bridge in the world.

Payson Zoo has 60 animals, many of them trained "movie stars" who have appeared in films shot in and around Payson. The owner takes guests on a personal tour, and some of the animals perform their movie tricks. Closed Thursday. Admission. ~ Lion Spring Road at the intersection of Route 260, Payson; 520-474-5435.

A state historic monument, **Strawberry Schoolhouse**, is the oldest standing schoolhouse in Arizona. Built in 1884, its last class was held in 1916. The small mountain village at 6000 feet was named for the many wild strawberries that covered the area when pioneers first arrived. ~ Village of Strawberry; 520-476-3547.

LODGING   Located just northeast of Scottsdale, **The Boulders** is built directly against a stunning backdrop of 12-million-year-old granite boulder formations that soar hundreds of feet against the desert sky. Situated on 1300 acres, the resort consists of a main lodge and 160 adobe-style *casitas*, each individually designed to fit the sculptured contours of the desert and the rocks. The hotel is designed in broad architectural sweeps and makes dramatic use of American Indian and regional art and artifacts—Navajo blankets, weavings, pottery, ceramics, paintings, stone sculptures and basketry. Guest rooms feature earth-tone furnishings, hand-hewn, viga ceilings, fireplaces, wet bars, ceiling fans and oversized windows for broad desert vistas. ~ 34631 North Tom Darlington Drive, Carefree; 602-488-9009, 800-553-1717, fax 602-488-4118. ULTRA-DELUXE.

Tumbleweed Hotel is a small downtown Cave Creek hotel made of white slumpstone brick, with 16 rooms in the main building and eight *casita*-style guest houses, all with modern Western-style furnishings and decor. The hotel has a swimming pool. ~ 6333 East Cave Creek Road; 602-488-3668, fax 602-488-2936. MODERATE.

Flying E Ranch is a working cattle ranch—and guest ranch—complete with trail rides, hay rides and chuckwagon dinners on its 20,000-acre spread. There are 17 rooms, plus a heated pool, sauna and whirlpool, along with tennis and shuffleboard. Closed May through October. ~ 2801 West Wickenburg Way, Wickenburg; 520-684-2690, fax 520-684-5304. ULTRA-DELUXE.

◄ HIDDEN

Another top-notch dude ranch in Wickenburg (this one's listed in the National Historic Register), the **Key El Bar Ranch** has room for 20 guests in hacienda-style adobe buildings beneath huge salt cedar trees. The lobby has a stone fireplace, and outside there's a heated pool for soaking after those long hours in the saddle. All meals and horseback riding are included. Open October 15 to May l. ~ Off Rincon Road, Wickenburg; 520-684-7593, 800-684-7583. ULTRA-DELUXE.

Best Western Rancho Grande Motel is an 80-room Best Western with a pool, whirlpool and playground. Rooms are furnished in contemporary motif. ~ 293 East Wickenburg Way, Wickenburg; 520-684-5445, 800-854-7235, fax 602-684-7380. MODERATE.

Swiss Village Lodge is a handsome, two-story hotel with lots of Alpine flavor in the midst of a European-style village of shops and restaurants. Its 99 rooms are decorated in contemporary furnishings, plain and simple. Some have fireplaces. A café, bar and swimming pool are on the premises. ~ Route 87, Payson; 520-474-3241, 800-247-9477. MODERATE.

A landmark around these parts for years, **Kohl's Ranch Lodge** sits on the banks of Tonto Creek 17 miles east of Payson. Many of the 49 rooms and cabins overlook the creek and are equipped with outdoor grills and patios. Cabins have stone fireplaces, vaulted ceilings and kitchenettes, but furnishings are rather plain. Rooms in the lodge have rather tacky, but fun, carpeting that resembles a wood-plank floor. Amenities here include a restaurant, lounges, gift shop, pool and horseback riding. ~ Route 260 East, Payson; 520-478-4211, 800-331-5645. MODERATE TO ULTRA-DELUXE.

DINING   The Satisfied Frog captures a bit of the Old West with wood tables, sawdust on the floor and weird things on the walls—animal
heads, posters, old farm tools. House specialties include barbecued
beef, pork and chicken. The Frog has its own microbrewery and
produces four house brands. ~ 6245 East Cave Creek Road, Cave
Creek; 602-488-3317. MODERATE.

Another amphibian-named eatery, **The Horny Toad** is a rustic,
informal restaurant with wooden tables and booths, seating about
150 for lunch and dinner. Specialties include fried chicken and
barbecued ribs. ~ 6738 Cave Creek Road, Cave Creek; 602-997-
9622. MODERATE.

Still ready for more old time Wild West flavor? You'll find it at
the **Gold Nugget**, a bar and restaurant with red-flecked wallpaper,
brass chandeliers and turn-of-the-century decor. Steaks, prime rib
and chicken dominate the menu. ~ 222 East Wickenburg Way,
Wickenburg; 520-684-2858. MODERATE.

HIDDEN ►   Payson offers **Aunt Alice's**, green and blue on the outside, down-
home on the inside. Aunt Alice serves up fish, burgers, chicken-
fried steak and homemade pies in a country-style setting. ~ 512
North Beeline Highway; 520-472-6988. BUDGET.

La Casa Pequeña features chimichangas, burritos and chicken
Acapulco in a pleasant, south-of-the-border atmosphere. There's
music on weekends. Closed Tuesday. ~ 911 South Beeline Highway, Payson; 520-474-6329. MODERATE.

A Western theme dominates at the **Kohl Ranch Restaurant**,
where painted cowboys cook over a campfire on one wall and a
replica of an 1884 hotel, complete with stained-glass windows,
covers another wall. Beneath the glow of a wagon-wheel chandelier, diners can enjoy barbecued ribs, chicken, steaks and seafood.
~ Route 260 East, Payson; 520-478-4211. MODERATE.

Sit out on the screened porch and enjoy the scenery at the
Heritage House Garden Tea Room. In the background, tunes play
from a replica of a 1930s era jukebox. The fare is light, such as
the tarragon chicken sandwich followed by a slice of homemade
pie. There are also soups and salads. Lunch only. Closed Sunday.
~ 202 West Main Street, Payson; 520-474-5501. BUDGET.

SHOPPING   It's hard to miss **Ben's Saddlery & Shoe Repair**, with a life-sized
horse on top of the building. The owner is a roper, and even if
you're not in the market for authentic Western gear, it's fun to
breathe in the heady smell of leather and saddle soap while walking down aisles stocked with spurs, saddles and boots. ~ 174
North Tegner Street, Wickenburg; 520-684-2683.

The **Gold Nugget Art Gallery** is housed in an adobe building
built in 1863 that was once Old Fort Wickenburg, a U.S. Cavalry
base. Inside these historic walls are original Southwestern wood-

carvings, pottery, paintings, sculptures, designer jewelry and American Indian art. ~ 274 East Wickenburg Way, Wickenburg; 520-684-5849.

A fixture for two decades is the **Wickenburg Gallery**, which showcases national and regional fine art including sculpture, paintings and traditional Navajo weavings. ~ 67 North Tegner Street, Wickenburg; 520-684-7047.

It's hard to decide just what's more satisfying at the **Heritage House**—shopping or porch-sitting. Some come to shop in this quaint 1925 house for furniture, handmade tablecloths, picture frames and afghans. Others just sit in the twig and wicker furniture on the porch, watching the world go by just beyond the picket fence. ~ 202 West Main Street, Payson; 520-474-5501.

Antique lovers have several options in Payson, with the majority of shops just off the Beeline Highway. Try **Payson Antiques**, housing dolls, furniture and primitives by a variety of dealers. ~ 1001 South Beeline Highway; 520-474-8988. **Glass Slipper Antiques** has glassware, furniture, estate jewelry, books and linens. ~ 603 South Beeline Highway; 520-474-6672.

NIGHTLIFE

Cozy booths inside and a balcony with tables overlooking Tonto Creek outside draw people to **The Cowboy Bar** at Kohl's Ranch Lodge. The rustic log building has been around for years, as has the huge oak tree that grows through the ceiling. On weekends, bring your boots and dance to live country music. ~ Route 260 East, Payson; 520-478-4211.

PARKS

TONTO NATIONAL FOREST

Ranging from Sonoran Desert to sprawling forests of ponderosa pine, this national forest covers nearly 2.9 million acres. The Payson and Cave Creek districts are outdoor playgrounds for area residents who can enjoy tubing, rafting and fishing on the Verde River. Barlett and Horseshoe reservoirs serve as watersheds, wildlife habitats and recreational sites for camping, swimming, fishing and boating. Tonto Natural Bridge, the largest known travertine bridge in the world, is a popular attraction, as was Zane Grey's cabin until it burned down in 1990. (The Zane Grey Society has plans for its restoration.) The park has picnic areas, restrooms, showers, boat rentals, snack stands, a restaurant, and hiking and riding trails. ~ There is access to the forest via Route 87 north from Phoenix to the town of Payson, in the heart of Tonto National Forest. To reach Horseshoe and Bartlett reservoirs take the Cave Creek Road east from Carefree to the entrance of the forest. From here Forest Service Road 24 takes you north to Seven Springs Campground. Horseshoe Dam Road continues east seven and a half miles until it forks. Forest Service Road 19 (the right fork) takes you to Bartlett Reservoir and Forest Service Road 265 (the left fork) takes you to Horseshoe Reservoir. Cave Creek Ranger district: 602-488-3441. Payson Ranger district: 520-474-7900.

▲ There are 55 campgrounds; free to $12 per night. Group sites are available. Primitive camping is also allowed. Reservations are only needed for group sites; call USFS Reservations, 800-280-2267. The brand-new Houston-Mesa Campground is conveniently located two miles from Payson. There are 75 tent/RV sites; $12 per night. Seven Springs Campground is on a remote spring and has good access to hiking trails. There are 25 tent/RV sites; no fee.

HASSAYAMPA RIVER PRESERVE 𝕏 A green desert oasis, this riparian area along the Hassayampa River features a cottonwood-willow forest and other vital Sonoran Desert habitats that are being protected by the nonprofit Nature Conservancy. Sit by the banks of spring-fed Palm Lake, a four-acre pond and marsh habitat, and you might spot a great blue heron or snowy egret. Birdwatchers also gather to the preserve to see the more than 200 species of birds that pass through this migration corridor. Naturalists offer guided walks along paths ranging from desert areas with cacti to lusher stretches along the river. Tours start at the visitors center; call ahead for schedule. There are restrooms and picnic areas. ~ Located on Route 60, three miles southeast of Wickenburg near mile marker 114; 520-684-2772.

▼▼▼▼▼▼▼▼▼▼▼▼
South of Phoenix
Out beyond the metropolis, where the bright lights give way to American Indian archaeological sites, you'll find the homeland of the Pima and Maricopa Indians, the site of Arizona's only Civil War battlefield and cotton fields that stretch for miles. Also, mountain peaks, great fishing and, for the born-to-shop crowd, factory-outlet malls. It is an intriguing blend of old and new Arizona.

SIGHTS   Gila River Indian Center in the Gila River Indian Reservation has an Indian museum, gift shop and restaurant featuring authentic Indian fry bread and Southwestern food. Here, too, is **Heritage Park**, featuring about half a dozen mini Indian villages. The museum is free and you can also take an interpretive walking tour of Heritage Park conducted by an American Indian. Tours are available upon request; there is a fee. ~ Casa Blanca Road, off Route 10 via Route 387, Exit 175; 520-315-3411.

Farther south is **Casa Grande**, named for the ancient Indian dwellings northeast of town. Casa Grande is known primarily for cotton-growing, industry and the many name-brand factory-outlet stores that have mushroomed there in recent years. For additional information, contact **Casa Grande Chamber of Commerce**. ~ 575 North Marshall Street; 602-836-2125.

Casa Grande Ruins National Monument was originally built by the Hohokam Indians in the early 1300s; the village was abandoned by the end of that century. Four stories high, and covered by a large protective roof, the main structure is the only one of its size and kind in this area. (The monument grounds contain about 60 prehistoric sites.) The structure is easily viewed via a short path on a well-marked self-guided tour. There's a visitors center and museum where ranger talks are presented. Admission. ~ About 20 miles east of Casa Grande on State Route 87; 602-723-3172.

For cowboy fans, the **Tom Mix Monument,** honors the silent-movie cowboy star near the spot where he died in an auto wreck in 1940. "In memory of Tom Mix whose spirit left his body on this spot and whose characterizations and portrayals in life served to better fix memories of the Old West in the minds of living men," reads the inscription. ~ Pinal Pioneer Parkway 18 miles out of the town of Florence; 602-868-9433.

LODGING

Francisco Grande Resort and Golf Club is where it's all at in Casa Grande. The tallest building in Pinal County (eight stories), the hotel's tower building contains most of its 112 rooms, while other rooms, motel style, are located around the patio. Furnishings are Southwestern-style throughout including paintings on the guest-room walls—cowboys and Western landscapes. The hotel has a restaurant, lounge (with nightly entertainment), swimming pool and golf. ~ 26000 Gila Bend Highway; 602-836-6444, 800-237-4238. MODERATE TO DELUXE.

Holiday Inn at Casa Grande, a four-story, Spanish-style stucco building, has 175 rooms in contemporary style, an outdoor pool and spa, restaurant and lounge with live entertainment Friday and Saturday nights. ~ 777 North Pinal Avenue, Casa Grande; 602-426-3500, 800-858-4499, fax 602-836-4728. MODERATE.

DINING

Gila River Arts and Crafts Restaurant features Indian fry bread along with burritos, tacos, hamburgers, homemade pies and coffee. ~ Gila River Indian Reservation; 520-315-3411. BUDGET.

Mi Amigo Ricardo offers up hot and spicy Mexican specialties—chimichangas, enchiladas, frijoles, tamales, flautas and *posole*—with beer and wine to soothe the flames. The decor is Mexican, of course, and quite attractive. ~ 821 East Florence Boulevard, Casa Grande; 520-836-3858. BUDGET.

Bring a big appetite to the **Golden Corral.** It's a traditional Western steak house where owner Vicki Carlson cuts her steaks fresh daily and the salad bar has 150 items. ~ 1295 East Florence Boulevard, Casa Grande; 520-836-4630. BUDGET.

Bedillon's is a restaurant and museum in two separate buildings. The museum features Indian artifacts and Western memorabilia. The menu offers a full range of American cuisine. Closed Sunday and Monday. ~ 800 North Park Avenue, Casa Grande; 520-836-2045. MODERATE.

A small, downtown Casa Grande bakery and café, **The Cook E Jar** serves up breakfast and lunch as well as take-out bakery goods (even wedding cakes) and sandwiches. Closed Sunday. ~ 100 West 2nd Street; 520-836-9294. BUDGET.

SHOPPING   **Gila River Indian Center** has a shop selling traditional American Indian crafts, silver and turquoise jewelry, sandpaintings, kachinas and baskets. ~ Gila River Indian Reservation; 520-315-3411.

Gila River Arts and Crafts sells quality American Indian items, including jewelry, baskets, kachina dolls, rugs and baskets. ~ Casa Blanca Road, Casa Blanca; 602-963-3981.

Casa Grande, the main town along Route 10 between Phoenix and Tucson, is the site of the largest number of factory-owned **outlet stores** in Arizona. More than 70 are located in two sprawling commercial malls off Route 10 (take Exit 194, Florence Boulevard). More than a million shoppers a year come to Casa Grande seeking bargains from such major represented firms as **Liz Claiborne, American Tourister, Bugle Boy, Royal Doulton** and **Westpoint Pepperell.** For information, call Casa Grande Factory Stores at 520-421-0112, or the Tanger Factory Outlet Center at 520-836-0897.

▼▼▼▼▼▼▼▼▼▼▼▼▼▼
Outdoor Adventures

Arizona's climate is ideal for recreational pursuits—most of the time. But in the summer, dry heat can be deceiving and you may think it's cooler than it actually is. Keep summer exertion to a minimum and play indoors, where there's air-conditioning, if you can.

RIVER RAFTING & TUBING   Three main rivers in south central Arizona, the Verde, the Salt and the Gila, all east of Phoenix, offer a wealth of recreational activities year-round. A number of companies provide rafting and tubing expeditions, with pick-ups, meals and guides included.

SCOTTSDALE   To take a wild ride try **Cimarron River Co.** ~ 7714 East Catalina; 602-994-1199. **Desert Voyagers Guided Rafting Tours** also operates out of Scottsdale. ~ P.O. Box 9053, Scottsdale, AZ 85252; 602-998-7238.

TEMPE/MESA AREA   In Mesa, contact **Salt River Recreation Inc.** ~ Bush Highway and Usery Pass Road, Mesa; 602-984-3305.

JOGGING   The Valley's extensive network of canals provides ideal, often shaded tracks.

PHOENIX   If you want to jog during the hot summers stick to cooler early-morning hours. Phoenix's **Encanto Park**, three miles north of the Civic Plaza, is an excellent jogging trail.

SCOTTSDALE Indian Bend Wash Greenbelt is a dream trail for joggers. It runs north and south for the entire length of Scottsdale, including 13 winding miles of jogging and bike paths laid out within the Greenbelt's scenic system of parks, lakes and golf courses.

There are so many swimming pools found in south central Arizona that gathering rain clouds, so it's said, are often colored green from all the chlorine.

SWIMMING

PHOENIX Many public pools are available, over 30 in Phoenix alone. For starters, there's **Cactus Pool**. ~ 3801 West Cactus Road; 602-262-6680. You can also dive into **Grant Pool**. ~ 714 South 2nd Avenue; 602-261-8728. Make a splash at **Starlight Pool**. ~ 7810 West Osborn Road; 602-495-2412. **Washington Pool** will also cool you down. ~ 6655 North 23rd Avenue; 602-262-7198. For additional information and listings, call 602-258-7946. The pools are open only during the summer.

The Adobe Dam Recreation Area also has **Water World** (602-581-8446), featuring a wave pool and waterslides. Open Memorial Day through Labor Day. ~ Recreation area: Northwest of Adobe Dam, on Pinnacle Peak Road and North 43rd Avenue, Phoenix; 602-581-6691.

TEMPE/MESA AREA In Tempe, **Big Surf** includes a 300-foot surf slide and raft-riding in a gigantic, mechanically activated freshwater pool. Open Memorial Day through Labor Day. Admission. ~ 1500 North McClintock Road; 602-947-2477.

For ballooning enthusiasts, the surrounding mountains provide the perfect setting to let it all hang out. Dozens of firms will be happy to take you up, up and away.

BALLOON RIDES & HANG GLIDING

PHOENIX Fly high in Phoenix with **Xanadu Balloon Adventures**. ~ 10610 North 38th Avenue; 602-938-9324. Soar in the skies with **Adventures Aloft**. ~ 14205 North 71st Place, Paradise Valley; 602-951-2650.

For hang gliding, try **Sky Masters School of Hang Gliding**. ~ 1902 East Behrend Drive; 602-582-5904.

SCOTTSDALE The **Unicorn Balloon Co.** will take you floating above Scottsdale. ~ 15001 North 74th Street; 602-991-3666.

Dozens of stables, dude ranches and equestrian outfitters are available for saddling up and heading off into desert wilderness for a few hours or a few days under the supervision of a crusty trail boss. If ever there was a place for horsing around, this is it.

RIDING STABLES

PHOENIX Saddle up in Phoenix at **All Western Stables**. ~ 10220 South Central Avenue; 602-276-5862. **North Mountain Stables** also will get you riding. ~ 25251 North 19th Avenue; 602-581-0103.

SCOTTSDALE For information on riding in Scottsdale, contact Westworld. ~ 16601 North Pima Road; 602-483-8800. **Trail Horse Adventures** also leads rides from a convenient Scottsdale location. ~ 16601 North Pima Road; 602-941-4756. Horses neigh and ninny at **Old MacDonald's Farm.** ~ 26540 North Scottsdale Road; 602-585-0239.

TEMPE/MESA AREA Get back in the saddle at **Papago Riding Stables.** ~ 400 North Scottsdale Road, Tempe; 602-966-9793.

GOLF

More than half of Arizona's 205 golf courses are located in south central Arizona, making Phoenix and environs the undisputed Golf Capital of the Southwest. Some of the country's finest courses can be found among its resorts, parks and country clubs. The **Arizona Golf Association** can supply specifics. ~ 602-944-3035.

PHOENIX One of the most spectacular is the **Wigwam Gold**, in Litchfield Park just west of Phoenix. ~ Litchfield and Indian School roads; 602-935-9414. Among Phoenix's top public links is **Encanto Park.** ~ 2705 North 15th Avenue; 602-253-3963. You can also swing your clubs at public **Papago Golf Course.** ~ 5595 East Moreland Street; 602-275-8428. **Palo Verde Golf Course** is a third public course in Phoenix. ~ 6215 North 15th Avenue; 602-249-9930.

SCOTTSDALE Top public courses include the **Continental Golf Course.** ~ 7920 East Osborn Road; 602-941-1585. Also open for duffers is public **Coronado Golf Course.** ~ 2829 North Miller Road; 602-947-8364. **Tournament Players Club of Scottsdale** welcomes the public to its greens. ~ 17020 North Hayden Road; 602-585-3600. Ditto for the **Villa Monterey Golf Course.** ~ 8100 East Camelback Road; 602-990-7100.

TEMPE/MESA AREA In Tempe try **Ken McDonald Golf Course.** ~ Western Canal and South Rural Road; 602-350-5250. **Pepperwood Golf Course** is also in Tempe. ~ 647 West Baseline Road; 602-831-9457. Or you can bring your clubs to the **Rolling Hills Golf Course.** ~ 1415 North Mill Avenue; 602-350-5275.

✔ **CHECK THESE OUT—UNIQUE OUTDOOR ADVENTURES**

- Ride the river wild as you take an expedition down the Verde, Salt or Gila rivers. *page 196*
- Soar the sky and gaze at painted desert mountains from technicolor hot air balloons. *page 197*
- Saddle up and ride the trails of cowboys past in the Tempe/Mesa area. *page 198*
- Hike up the winding **Squaw Peak Summit Trail** for dramatic views of Phoenix from the 2608-foot vantage point. *page 200*

Almost all of the parks in the valley's vast network have a tennis
court; for information, call the **Parks and Recreation Department**.
~ Phoenix: 602-262-6861. Scottsdale: 602-994-2408. Maricopa
County: 602-506-2930.

PHOENIX City Center Tennis Courts are open to the public. ~
121 East Adams Street; 602-256-4120. The **Hole-in-the-Wall Racquet Club** allows nonmembers to play. ~ 7677 North 16th Street,
at the Pointe at Squaw Peak Resort; 602-906-3811. The **Phoenix
Tennis Center** also has courts. ~ 6330 North 21st Avenue; 602-
249-3712. Another place to play in Phoenix is the **Watering Hole
Racquet Club**. ~ 901-C East Saguaro Drive; 602-997-7237. The
Mountain View Tennis Center is also in the Phoenix area. ~ 1104
East Grovers Avenue; 602-788-6088.

SCOTTSDALE In Scottsdale try the public courts at **Indian School
Park**. ~ 4289 North Hayden Road; 602-994-2740. You can also
swing a racquet at **Chestnut Park**. ~ 4565 North Granite Reef
Road; 602-994-2481. **Mountain View Park** also has courts for
public use. ~ 8625 East Mountain View; 602-994-2584.

TEMPE/MESA AREA Outstanding in Tempe is the **Kiwanis Recreation Center**. ~ 611 South All-American Way; 602-350-5201.

TENNIS

Biking is popular as both recreation and transportation in the valley and outlying areas. A basic bikeway system was set up for
Phoenix in 1987, and since then more than 100 miles of paths have
been added. Unfortunately, there's a lot of traffic, so be cautious.

PHOENIX A free *People and Places* map that also shows the
Phoenix Bikeway System is available at most bike shops, or call
the Parks, Recreation and Library Department. ~ 602-262-6861.
For bicycling events call 602-262-6542. Also for special-event biking activities contact **Arizona Bicycle Association**. ~ 602-990-
7468. Phoenix's **South Mountain Park** (10919 South Central Avenue), **Cave Creek** and **Carefree**, 30 miles northeast of town, offer
great biking conditions. Also popular is **Papago Loop Bicycle Path**
through the rolling hills that border the canal edging Papago Park.

SCOTTSDALE Scottsdale's **Indian Bend Wash Greenbelt** has
miles of excellent bike paths.

Bike Rentals Need to rent a bike? Try **Try Me Bicycle Shop**. ~
1514 West Hatcher Road, Phoenix; 602-943-1785. **Wheels 'n
Gear** has just the bike for you if you need a rental. ~ 7607 East
McDowell Road, Scottsdale; 602-945-2881. **The Bicycle Store**
sells and rents mountain bikes. ~ Mill and University roads, in the
Tempe Center; 602-966-7090.

BIKING

With all that elbow room and knockout scenery, south central
Arizona is a hiker's paradise. Visitors, in fact, have been known to
park their cars on the highway and impulsively hike up the side of

HIKING

a mountain. Note: Be sure to take water with you, and allow plenty of time to get there and back.

PHOENIX AREA   The **Phoenix Mountain Preserve** has 50 miles of trails and almost pristine areas virtually in the center of Phoenix. It stretches from Lincoln Drive in Paradise Valley north to Greenway Boulevard, bordered on the west by 19th Avenue and on the east by Tatum Boulevard. For a free map of the marked trails within the preserve call 602-262-7901 or 602-262-7797.

Its most popular trail is the **Squaw Peak Summit Trail** (1 mile) that wraps its way up Squaw Peak, offering good lookout points along the way, and from its 2608-foot summit, a dramatic view of the city. (The only drawback is the number of fellow hikers you'll meet along the way.)

SCOTTSDALE AREA   **Camelback Mountain** in the Scottsdale area is the valley's best known landmark, and serious hikers truly haven't hiked Arizona until they've conquered it. Part of the Echo Canyon Recreation Area (off McDonald Drive east of Tatum Boulevard; 602-256-3220), Camelback offers sheer red cliffs that in some places rise 200 feet straight up its side. An interpretive ramada near the parking area offers information about the various trails. A relatively easy climb (.8 mile) goes from the ramada to **Bobby's Rock**, a landmark formation of rocks set aside from the cliff and perfect for rock climbers. Also beginning at the ramada, the route to **Praying Monk** is more difficult. A stone formation rises at its summit high above Echo Canyon cliffs. From Praying Monk, the trail continues to the tip of Camelback Mountain, 2704 feet above sea level, 1.3 ever-upward miles.

▼▼▼▼▼▼▼▼▼▼
Transportation

CAR

Visitors driving to Phoenix by car are in for a treat. Arizona's highways are among the best in the country, gas is traditionally cheaper and the scenery in any direction is spectacular—lofty saguaros, magnificent mountains, a cowboy here, a pickup truck there, beer signs blinking faintly in the purple glow of evening. Along the way, small Western towns unfold like storybook pop-ups. **Route 10** traverses the city from the east (El Paso) and west (Los Angeles). From the northwest, **Route 40**, once the legendary Route 66, enters Arizona near Kingman; **Route 93** continues on from there to Phoenix.

AIR

Sky Harbor International Airport is located four miles from downtown Phoenix and is served by Alaska Airlines, America West Airlines, American Airlines, American Trans Air, Arizona Airways, Continental Airlines, Delta Airlines, Frontier, Mark Air, Mesa Air, Northwest Airlines, Scenic Airlines, Skywest Airlines, Southwest Airlines, Trans World Airlines, United Airlines, Shuttle by United, USAir and Western Pacific.

A variety of ground transportation options are available from Sky Harbor Airport. **SuperShuttle** offers airport-to-door service 24 hours a day. ~ 602-244-9000, 800-258-3826. **Courier Transportation** also provides transfers to and from the airport. ~ 602-232-2222. **Arizona Shuttle Service** has service to and from Tucson. ~ 602-795-6771, 800-888-2749. If you're heading north to red rock country, the **Sedona/Phoenix Shuttle Service** departs six times daily from Sky Harbor, making stops in Cottonwood and Sedona. ~ 602-282-2066.

BUS

Greyhound Bus Lines has service to Phoenix from all around the country. Other stations are found in Mesa and Tempe. ~ Reservations: 800-231-2222. Phoenix: 525 East Washington Street; 602-271-7426. Mesa: 1423 South Country Club Drive; 602-834-3360. Tempe: 502 South College Avenue; 602-967-4030.

CAR RENTALS

Rental companies with counters at the airport include **Advantage Rent A Car** (800-777-5500), **Alamo Rent A Car** (800-327-9633), **Avis Rent A Car** (800-331-1212), **Budget Rent A Car** (800-527-0700), **Dollar Rent A Car** (800-800-4000), **Hertz Rent A Car** (800-654-3131), and **National Interrent** (800-328-4567). Agencies with pick-up service are **Courtesy Rent A Car** (602-273-7503), **Enterprise Leasing and Rent A Car** (800-325-8007), **Thrifty Car Rental** (800-367-2277) and **Value Rent A Car** (800-468-2583).

PUBLIC TRANSIT

Valley Metro covers Phoenix and Scottsdale and provides express service to and from other districts within the Valley. It also serves the Phoenix airport. Express buses access Phoenix from Mesa, Tempe and other suburbs. ~ 602-253-5000. **Ollie the Trolley** offers rubber-tire trolley service from 22 Scottsdale resorts and 12 shopping areas on day-pass basis; rides are free within the downtown shopping area mid-October through April. ~ 602-941-2957. **Downtown Dash** serves the downtown Phoenix area with shuttles that depart every six to twelve minutes and loop the downtown area between the State Capitol, Arizona Center and the Civic Plaza weekdays. Rides cost thirty cents. ~ 602-253-5000.

TAXIS

Taxis are expensive in Phoenix since the city sprawls out in all directions. Going from Point A to Point B, at times, may seem like you're crossing the entire state. Some of the major companies in south central Arizona are **AAA CAB** (602-921-8294), **ACE Taxi** (602-254-1999), **Statewide Sedan, Van and Limo Service** (602-252-1277), **Courier Cab** (602-232-2222), **Discount Metro** (602-266-1110) and **Yellow Cab** (602-252-5252). AAA, Courier and Yellow are contracted with the airport in Phoenix.

SEVEN

Eastern Arizona

Perhaps no other region of the state is as geographically diverse as eastern Arizona. The seemingly endless urban sprawl of Phoenix, Tempe and Mesa quickly gives way to breathtaking scenery in the form of desert gardens, jagged river canyons, rolling grasslands and deep pine forests. Venture here and you'll find a wide variety of recreational opportunities, everything from fishing and hunting to hiking and skiing. There's also plenty of history—prehistoric Indian ruins and old mining towns—to be discovered along the way.

The strip of eastern Arizona stretching 203 miles east of Phoenix along Routes 89, 60 and 70 to the New Mexico state line is known as The Old West Highway. Rich in frontier history, it travels a route of the notorious—from Coronado to Geronimo to Billy the Kid.

Anchored on the west by Apache Junction, a growing suburb of the Phoenix metropolitan area and a winter retreat for thousands of snowbirds, the Old West Highway is also the starting point for a scenic detour along the Apache Trail (Route 88). Today's adventurers can wend their way along the trail through the Superstition Mountains, to the reconstructed Goldfield Ghost Town, a series of lakes originating from the Salt River, colorful Tortilla Flat, the Lost Dutchman's Mine and finally Theodore Roosevelt Dam and Lake.

Continue east on the Old West Highway and you'll come to Globe, a quiet town that retains the flavor of the late 1800s. The Old West Highway flattens out east of Globe, and the countryside becomes more arid as you descend into the lower desert. The Mescal Mountains to the south escort you into the Gila River Valley, where the mesas and buttes of the San Carlos Apache Indian Reservation stand out against the sky.

Route 70 branches off Route 60 east of Globe and crosses the southern tip of the 1.8 million-acre San Carlos Apache Indian Reservation, which stretches from the White Mountains to within two miles of Globe, north to the Mogollon Rim and south to Coronado National Forest. An estimated 10,000 Apache live on the reservation, much of it wooded forests that are home to elk, mule deer, wild turkeys, black bear and mountain lions.

On the southern horizon stands Mount Graham, at 10,720 feet one of Arizona's highest peaks. In addition to being a popular fishing, camping and hiking area, the mountain is the site of the Mount Graham International Observatory.

Route 70 continues on to the town of Safford, an important trade center for the Gila River Valley's numerous cotton farmers. From Safford, the Old West Highway cuts through the pastoral Duncan Valley, with its green alfalfa fields, grazing horses and trickling creeks at the eastern edge of Arizona. Duncan, the birthplace of Supreme Court Justice Sandra Day O'Connor, is a fertile source of fire agate, a relatively rare semiprecious stone, which can be picked up right off the ground in designated Bureau of Land Management areas.

North of Duncan on Route 191 is the historic mining town of Clifton, the southern anchor of the Coronado Trail, which climbs through the Apache-Sitgreaves National Forest on its 105-mile journey to Alpine, in the heart of Arizona's Alps.

The Coronado Trail, named for the Spanish explorer who sought the Seven Cities of Gold nearly 500 years ago, practically brushes the Arizona–New Mexico border. The trail runs north-south as Route 191 from St. Johns to Clifton via a winding and twisting paved highway, cutting through rugged mountains and magnificent forests—some of the Southwest's most spectacular scenery.

The White Mountains offer high, cool country dotted with fishing lakes and blanketed in ponderosa pine, spruce, aspen and Douglas fir. At the heart of this area are Pinetop–Lakeside, Show Low and Greer. The main reason folks venture to this part of eastern Arizona is to enjoy the outdoors, whether by fishing, skiing, hiking or simply sitting on a rock with a picnic lunch, breathing in the scent of pine and watching the breeze ripple across a lake. These towns all abound with rustic lodges, inexpensive eateries and plenty of scenic beauty.

▼▼▼▼▼▼▼▼▼▼▼▼▼▼▼▼
Apache Junction Area

At the meeting point of Routes 60, 88 and 89, Apache Junction is in an area of rough lowlands about 30 miles east of Phoenix. Once a sunburned babble of bars, motels and filling stations, it has blossomed into a rustic bedroom community for the Valley of the Sun and a popular snowbird retreat that attracts about 45,000 people each winter, causing local dude ranch operators to complain that there's no range left to ride. A metal impression in the center of the town honors the man believed to have discovered the elusive Lost Dutchman Gold Mine, who died with the secret of its location unspoken. Apache Junction is also the starting point for the 48-mile Apache Trail, Route 88, which slices its way through the Superstition Mountains.

SIGHTS   Apache Junction was unofficially founded in 1922, when a traveling salesman named George Cleveland Curtis put up a tent and sold sandwiches and water to travelers along the highway. A year later he filed a homestead claim and built the Apache Junction Inn. Others soon followed and by 1950 there were enough residents to form a town. They chose the name Superstition City, but because it was a historical site, the Apache Junction name could not be changed.

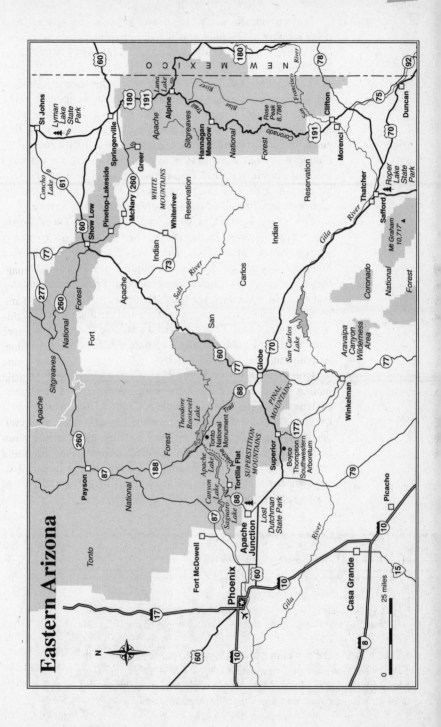

Eastern Arizona

Learn about the area's history and sights at the **Apache Junction Chamber of Commerce**, which dispenses maps and brochures. ~ P.O. Box 1747, Apache Junction, AZ 85219; 1001 North Idaho Road; 602-982-3141.

The **Apache Trail**, Route 88 from Apache Junction to Theodore Roosevelt Lake, is about a 140-mile drive, round-trip, with about 20 unpaved miles above Tortilla Flat. Allow at least three hours for the winding journey. Once past the outskirts of town, the trail enters the dacite cones of the **Superstition Mountains**, formed 20 million years ago when cataclysmic earthquakes and widespread volcanic eruptions pushed land masses thousands of feet into the air and left a depression 20 miles wide. Magma from below the earth's surface flowed in and the Superstitions were formed.

For a taste of the Old West, stop at **Goldfield Ghost Town**, which saw its heyday in the 1890s when gold was discovered at the base of the Superstitions. The weathered-wood buildings that house a restaurant, museum and antique shops look original, but they are actually re-creations, constructed in 1988. The old mining and railroad equipment scattered about are authentic, as are the museum's geology and mining exhibits and the underground mine, which you can tour. Other activities available are jeep tours, carriage rides and gold panning. ~ Route 88, four miles north of Apache Junction; 602-983-0333.

Continuing north on Route 88 you'll find a chain of lakes originating out of the Salt River. They include Saguaro, Canyon and Apache lakes. The most accessible is **Canyon Lake**, which wends its way six-and-a-half miles upstream through one continuous deep canyon. There are boat facilities, beaches, picnic sites, a snack bar and campsites. Recreational activities include fishing (bass and walleye) and waterskiing. There's also a replica of a double-deck sternwheeler that plies the waters with its cargo of tourists and photographers. ~ Route 88; 602-944-6504.

✔ **CHECK IT OUT—UNIQUE SIGHTS**

- Experience the Old West at **Goldfield Ghost Town**, and try your luck as you pan for those little nuggets. *page 206*
- View a piece of history as you wander through the **Besh-ba-Gowah Archaeological Park**, home to the Salado people from 1225 A.D. to 1400 A.D. *page 212*
- Take a dip in the **Kachina Mineral Springs Spa**, set in a mix of Roman-styled tubs and rundown tack. *page 216*
- Stop by the **Little House Museum** for a glimpse into the area's history, including ranching and horse-show memorabilia. *page 226*

Proceeding upstream, you'll pass geodes imbedded in sheer rock walls, deposited by eruptions millions of years ago, on your way to **Tortilla Flat**, which boasts a population of six people. One of the last remnants of the Old West, the town was once a stagecoach stop, complete with a school, general store, restaurant/saloon, hotel and post office, and was home to about 125 people. Today, only the general store, post office and restaurant remain. ~ Located 17 miles from Apache Junction; 602-984-1776.

About five miles east of Tortilla Flat, the paved road surrenders to dirt and gravel and climbs to the top of Fish Creek Hill, which provides spectacular views of the canyon below. Descending the hill, the road twists through a narrow chasm along Apache Lake and finally arrives at **Theodore Roosevelt Dam**. Completed in 1911, this masonry dam, constructed entirely of quarry stone, is the world's tallest. A recent concrete addition, covering the original construction, raised the dam's height to 357 feet and increased the reservoir's surface area by 300,000 acres. A quarter-mile upstream from the dam, a 1000-foot steel arch bridge spans a portion of the reservoir, Roosevelt Lake, giving tourists—and photographers—a better view of the dam. ~ Located 45 miles east of Apache Junction; 520-467-2236.

From Roosevelt Dam you can return to Apache Junction, or continue on Route 88 (which becomes paved again) to **Tonto National Monument**, which contains the remains of the apartment-style dwellings of the Salado people and is one of the state's better-preserved prehistoric archaeological sites. At the visitors center, you can see Salado crafts and tools and an audio-visual program. A highlight of the park itself is a paved but steep, half-mile self-guiding trail that climbs 350 feet up to the 19-room **Lower Ruin**. The 40-room **Upper Ruin** is open for tours from November through April (advance reservations are required). Admission. ~ Route 88, Roosevelt; 520-467-2241.

Back on Route 60, about 25 miles east of Apache Junction near the tiny mining camp of Superior, is the **Boyce Thompson Southwestern Arboretum**. This Eden-like preserve boasts over 1500 specimens, including cacti, succulents and water-efficient trees and shrubs. Home to over 200 kinds of birds and 40 wildlife species, the arboretum has walking trails that wind through 35 acres of outdoor displays and historic buildings. One long-time resident here, a red gum eucalyptus that rises more than 100 feet and boasts a trunk eight feet in diameter, was planted in 1929 as a six-foot sapling. The interpretive center is a 1920s cut-stone house listed on the National Register of Historical Places. Also of interest are the **Clevenger House**, a stone cabin built into a hillside, surrounded by a newly constructed herb garden, and the nearby 26-room mansion, **Picket Post House**, built by copper magnate William Boyce Thompson in 1927. Admission. ~ 37615 Route 60; 520-689-2811.

Heading east from the arboretum, Route 60 gradually climbs through Gonzales Pass until the desert gives way to the Tonto National Forest. The two-lane highway cautiously winds through enchanting **Devils Canyon**, an eerie though picturesque region that seems to change its mood as the day's sunlight progresses. Near sundown, when the shadows grow long, the granite rock formations take on the shape of giant trolls and gnomes, and appear to be crouching, as if to pounce on passing motorists. The canyon and highway are narrow, but there are ample pullouts to photograph or simply enjoy the scenery.

LODGING

The 130-room **Superstition Grande Hotel** stands at the gateway to the Superstition Mountains. The main building is red-brick tile and white stucco. The rooms, brightly colored in pink and green, have modern furnishings. The lobby is contemporary, the bar Western with copper appointments. A favorite of film crews shooting Westerns in the area, the hotel has hosted John Wayne, Ronald Reagan, Richard Boone and other Hollywood stalwarts. Rooms where they stayed bear their names. ~ 201 West Apache Trail, Apache Junction; 602-982-7411. MODERATE.

The small, family-run **Palm Springs Motel** has 11 clean, well-maintained rooms, all with refrigerators, some with kitchenettes. ~ 950 South Royal Palm Road, Apache Junction; 602-982-7055. BUDGET.

In the Superstition foothills, the **Gold Canyon Resort** features chalet-style guest rooms with dark-wood furniture, stone fireplaces, spa tubs, private patios and impressive views of the nearby mountain. There's also a heated pool. ~ 6100 South Kings Ranch Road, Apache Junction; 602-982-9090, 800-624-6445, fax 602-830-5211. ULTRA-DELUXE.

DINING

Lake Shore Restaurant is a rustic, casual dining facility on Saguaro Lake with a deck where you can dine while enjoying a lake view. Shaded by a giant awning, this outdoor eatery is cooled by a mist system and ceiling fans or warmed by outdoor heaters, depending on the season. Start with a strawberry daiquiri and then order from the menu featuring burgers, salads, sandwiches and fried fish (all you can eat on Wednesday and Friday). Dinner-only items include barbecued ribs and pasta dishes. ~ 14011 North Bush Highway, Tonto National Forest; 602-984-5311. MODERATE.

Down Apache Junction way, **Mining Camp Restaurant and Trading Post** is almost as famous as the Lost Dutchman Gold Mine—and it's easier to find. It's worth looking for, offering long wooden tables, planked floors, tin trays and cups, and family-style, all-you-can-eat dining—chicken, beef and barbecued ribs. ~ Route 88, Apache Junction; 602-982-3181. MODERATE.

The Lost Dutchman Gold Mine

With blunted peaks reaching nearly 6000 feet and razor-edged canyons plunging earthward, the Superstition Mountains comprise an area 40 miles long and 15 miles wide— some of the roughest, rockiest, most treacherous territory in the United States. It was in this rugged territory that Dutchman Jacob Waltz was believed to have discovered the Lost Dutchman Gold Mine.

Waltz supposedly found an old Spanish mine in the Superstitions near what is now Apache Junction. He was vigilant about keeping its whereabouts secret, and died in 1891 without revealing the location. For a while people looked for the mine, then it was forgotten for about 30 years.

In the 1930s, Dr. Adolph Ruth came to the area claiming to have a map of the mine. One hot summer day he went into the area to search, and was never seen again. A few months later his skull was found with what looked like a bullet hole in it. Once again, interest in the mine was sparked and people resumed the search. To this day, the treasure has never been found, but prospectors are still looking.

To learn more about this local legend, head to the **Superstition Mountain/Lost Dutchman Museum**, which displays historical artifacts pertaining to the story of the Lost Dutchman Gold Mine. You'll also find exhibits of folk art, prehistoric Indian artifacts, Spanish and Mexican crafts and documents, pottery and relics of early cowboys, prospectors and miners. Admission. ~ Route 88; 602-983-4888.

If you'd like to try your luck in finding the legendary Lost Dutchman Gold Mine, there are a number of companies that offer three-day to seven-day—or longer—treks into the Superstitions. With the help of experienced guides, you will lash your gear to packhorses and mount up for a trip where you can pan for gold or simply ride the wilderness trails, camp, cook, bathe in icy streams and sleep out under the stars. For information, contact **Superstition Stables** in Apache Junction. ~ 2151 North Warner Road; 602-982-6353. You can also try the **Superstition Mountain Guide Service**. ~ Apache Junction; 602-982-4040.

Lakeside Restaurant and Cantina is a tri-level restaurant and lounge with a deck built out over the Canyon Lake. The decor—mauves and teal—is more Californian than Arizonan. Out of the kitchen come burgers, sandwiches, chicken and grilled rib eye steaks with mushrooms and onions. Featured is an all-you-can-eat fish fry on Wednesday, Thursday and Friday. ~ Route 88, Apache Junction; 602-380-1601. BUDGET TO MODERATE.

For true Western flavor, hitch your horse up at the always-crowded **Los Vaqueros** and settle down to a rib-eye or T-bone, barbecue, baked potato, biscuits and beans. There's foot-stomping music and occasionally a brawl at the bar. Los Vaqueros means "the cowboys," and there are plenty of them here. ~ 285 North Apache Trail, Apache Junction; 602-982-3407. MODERATE.

SHOPPING   If you plan to go looking for the Lost Dutchman Gold Mine, or even if you're not, **Pro-Mack South** sells mining equipment, gold pans, lanterns, picks, rope, boots, supplies and just about everything but the treasure map. ~ 940 West Apache Trail, Apache Junction; 602-983-3484.

NIGHTLIFE   A live country band stomps away Wednesday through Sunday at **Los Vaqueros**; that's where everybody goes. ~ 285 North Apache Trail, Apache Junction; 602-982-3407.

PARKS   **USERY MOUNTAIN RECREATION AREA** 🚶🚴🐎🛶🚣 This 3324-acre recreational area is just northwest of the Superstition Mountains. It has an extensive hiking, mountain bike and horse trail system. Throughout the park you will find restrooms, showers and horse-staging areas. ~ It's east of Phoenix via Apache Boulevard or Superstition Freeway (Route 360). Head east to Ellsworth Road and turn north. At McKellips Road, Ellsworth becomes Usery Pass Road. Continue north to the entrance.

▲ There are 73 sites, all with RV hookups; $12 per night; information, 602-984-0032.

LOST DUTCHMAN STATE PARK 🚶 Located in the foothills of the Superstition Mountains, this 292-acre park features eight miles of hiking trails through saguaro, palo verde and other desert flora. Interpretive tours by park rangers are conducted October through April. Facilities include a visitors center, portable toilets, picnic tables, drinking water and barbecue grills. ~ 6109 North Apache Trail, about five miles north of Apache Junction; 602-982-4485.

▲ There are 35 sites (no hookups); $8 per night. There is a dump station.

TONTO NATIONAL FOREST 🚶🚴🐎🛶🚣🏊🚣🛶 To explore the national forest northeast of Apache Junction, travel the famed Apache Trail (Route 88). The scenic drive follows the trail originally used by Apache Indians as a shortcut through the Superstition Mountains, eventually leading to the Salt River chain of lakes—Saguaro Canyon, Apache and Roosevelt lakes. The lakes have been developed for fishing, boating, picnicking, hiking, biking and camping. The Salt River itself is a favorite spot for tubing.

There are several privately run marinas in the forest offering a variety of services. The **Saguaro Lake Marina** has boat rentals, storage, fuel, tours and a restaurant. There are tent-camping sites around the lake. ~ Route 88; 602-986-5546. The **Apache Lake Marina** offers boat rentals, storage and gas. Two motels and a restaurant are also located here. There are RV sites, and tent-camping is allowed all around the lake. ~ Route 88; 520-467-2511. Also a full-service marina with a restaurant and camping facilities, the **Canyon Lake Marina** is situated 15 miles northeast of Apache Junction. ~ Route 88; 602-984-0032.

Throughout the forest you'll find picnic areas, restrooms and hiking and riding trails. ~ The main access road from Apache Junction is Route 88 (Apache Trail). Tortilla Campground is on Route 88 about 11 miles from Apache Junction. Cholla Campground is on Route 188, eight miles north of Roosevelt Dam in Roosevelt. Mesa Ranger District: 602-379-6446. Tonto Basin Ranger District: 520-467-3200.

▲ There are 55 campgrounds; free to $12 per night. Primitive camping is also allowed. Reservations are only needed for group sites; call USF Reservations, 800-280-2267. Located near Canyon Lake, Tortilla Campground has 70 tent/RV sites ($10 per night) and is open from October through March. Cholla Campground on Roosevelt Lake has 200 tent/RV sites ($10 to $16 per night).

▼▼▼▼▼▼▼▼

Globe

East of Devils Canyon, the Pinal Mountains rise to dominate the horizon, until the historic old copper-mining town of Globe wrests control of the horizon. This quiet old copper town, with its many Victorian homes dotting the hillsides, retains the flavor of the late 1800s with a turn-of-the-century main street, complete with an old-fashioned F. W. Woolworth store. Here, you'll find one of the finest American Indian archaeological sites in the state.

Globe began as a mining town in the 1860s after silver was discovered on the Apache reservation. It is named for a spherical silver nugget with markings that resemble the continents. After the silver mines were depleted, copper was discovered, but those mines, too, were shut down by the Great Depression. The town has been dozing in the sun ever since.

On your drive into **Globe** (if arriving from the west), you'll notice massive man-made hills of bleached-out dirt, a by-product of the

SIGHTS

copper mining operations here. The white mesas, which stretch for a couple of miles, are what's left after the ore has been bleached, crushed and smelted. Attempts to grow vegetation in the miniature moonscape have been all but futile, so the mountains of residue remain, perhaps to be recycled as new mining techniques allow extraction of more copper from them.

For local information, visit the **Greater Globe–Miami Chamber of Commerce.** Be sure to ask for the walking tour of downtown Globe, and directions to the archaeological sites. ~ 1360 North Broad Street; 520-425-4495.

Besh-Ba-Gowah Archaeological Park was the home of the Salado people from 1225 A.D. to 1400 A.D., who built a great pueblo containing 300 rooms that once housed an estimated 300 to 400 people. A period of excavation, restructuring and stabilization began in 1985, and three years later the park was open to the public. Along with the impressive structure, the park has a visitors center and museum displaying artifacts, models and photographs relating to the site. There is also a botanical garden that demonstrates how the Salado utilized the surrounding vegetation. Admission. ~ The Globe Community Center, Jess Hayes Road; 520-425-0320.

After leaving the archaeological park, you can get an eagle's eye view of the area by making a right turn on Jess Hayes Road, then driving to Ice House Canyon Road and Kellner Canyon, where you will circle up through the beautiful Pinal Mountains for 15 miles. At the 7850-foot level you'll pass through ponderosa pine, ferns and thick foliage. Pull out anywhere and the overlooks will give you sweeping views of Globe and Miami below.

In town, the rip-roaring days of the early miners come to life at the **Gila County Historical Museum** with exhibits of early artifacts, mining equipment and Salado Indian relics. The museum is housed in the former Old Dominion Mine Rescue and First Aid Station. Closed weekends. ~ Route 60; 520-425-7385.

The **Old Dominion Mine,** across from the museum on Broad Street, is what's left of what was once the world's richest copper mine. In the 1930s, the depressed price of copper, coupled with increasing water seepage into the mine shafts, forced the closure of the mine. Today the mine belongs to Magma Copper Company and is a valuable source of water, which is vital to the company's other operations in the area.

In downtown Globe stands the **Historic Gila County Courthouse** built in 1906. This stately stone structure now houses the Cobre Valley Center for the Arts and a small theater. Climb the 26 stone steps and enter the carved wooden doors to find finished hardwood floors, arched passways, grand rooms with high ceilings and tall windows, and a staircase accented with copper banisters and overhead skylight. ~ 101 North Broad Street.

Also worth visiting is the **Globe Elks Lodge,** the world's tallest three-story building, built in 1910. ~ 155 West Mesquite Avenue; 520-425-2161. You can also check out the old **Gila County Jail** (behind the Gila County Courthouse), constructed of reinforced concrete in 1909, with cell blocks transported from the Yuma Territorial Prison. The **Gila Valley Bank and Trust Building,** with its white terra-cotta facade, is an unusual example of the Beaux-Arts neoclassical style of 1909. The building was the pioneer branch of what is now Valley National Bank. ~ Mesquite Avenue and Broad Street.

The **Country Corner Antique Store** was the town's grocery and mercantile when built in 1920. If the shape of the building seems odd it's because the structure was designed in the shape of the state of Arizona. ~ 383 South Hill Street; 520-425-8208. The **F. W. Woolworth** is part of the Sultan Building, originally built as a two-story brick structure in 1909. ~ 151 North Broad Street; 520-425-7115. Next door, the art deco–style **Globe Theater** was built in 1918 and features copper-covered pillars under the marquee. ~ 141 North Broad Street; 520-425-5581. Nearby is old **Engine No. 1774,** one of only seven remaining steam locomotives in existence. Originally, 355 were built between 1899 and 1901. ~ Pine and Oak streets.

Globe is the commercial gateway to the **San Carlos Apache Indian Reservation,** the 1.8 million-acre expanse that's home to nearly 10,000 Apache Indians. Rambling and remote, lush and rustic, the land is a natural habitat for javelina, elk, bear, mountain lions, bighorn sheep, antelope, waterfowl, grouse, quail, rabbits and a variety of freshwater fish. Camping, hunting and fishing are permitted, with licenses. Contact the Recreation and Wildlife Department, 520-475-2343.

In Globe you'll find the **Copper Manor Motel,** a 62-room, two-story motel with contemporary furnishing, pool and all-night café. ~ 637 East Ash Street; 520-425-7124. BUDGET. **LODGING**

✔ **CHECK IT OUT—UNIQUE LODGING**

- *Budget:* Drop your fishing line in the lake at **Judd's Ranch** after waking in your small log cabin with creaky hardwood floors. *page 225*
- *Moderate:* Spend the night where the likes of John Wayne and Ronald Reagan bedded down—**Superstition Grande Hotel.** *page 208*
- *Deluxe:* Snooze in a true wilderness setting at **Southwest Research Station,** run by the American Museum of Natural History. *page 217*
- *Deluxe:* Get away to the serene and pastoral **Greer Lodge,** built by hand more than 45 years ago. *page 227*

Budget: under $50 Moderate: $50–$90 Deluxe: $90–$120 Ultra-deluxe: over $120

Copper Hills Inn is another Globe caravansary—a 70-room Best Western with basically nondescript contemporary furnishing, a dining room, coffee shop and lounge, a gift shop and a swimming pool. ~ Globe-Miami Highway; 520-425-7151, 800-825-7151. MODERATE.

One of the nicer motels is the **Cloud Nine Motel,** which offers ultra-clean guest rooms decorated in cool pastels, some with refrigerators and spa tubs. There is a pool and a jacuzzi. ~ 1699 East Ash Street; 520-425-5741, 800-256-8399. MODERATE.

DINING

El Rey Café is an authentic Mexican restaurant, small in size but big in flavor, with enchiladas, *chile rellenos*, tacos and chimichangas. Closed Tuesday. ~ Route 60/70; 520-425-6601. BUDGET.

Blue Ribbon Cafe, located in the heart of Globe's old historic district, isn't called "blue ribbon" for nothing. A popular breakfast spot, it's also busy at lunchtime serving sandwiches, salads, burgers and pasta. Closed weekends. ~ 474 North Broad Street; 520-425-4423. BUDGET TO MODERATE.

If you prefer Chinese cuisine, the **Jasmine Tea House** serves Mandarin and Szechuan dishes of pork, beef, chicken and seafood. ~ 1097 North Broad Street; 520-425-2503. BUDGET TO MODERATE.

SHOPPING

The **Cobre Valley Center for the Arts,** located in the historic Gila County Courthouse, houses arts and crafts produced by local members of the Cobre Valley Fine Arts Guild (*cobre* is Spanish for copper). Media represented include stained glass, ceramics, painting (oil, acrylic, watercolors), sculpture (stone, metal, wood, plastic), photography, jewelry (silver, stone, beaded) and mixed media. There are also prints, batik silk scarfs and gift items such as Southwestern-designed soap and stationary, books and painted furniture. ~ 101 North Broad Street; 520-425-0884.

Bacon's Boots and Saddles represents the last of the great saddle makers. Owner Ed Bacon has been hand-crafting saddles for more than 50 years. His store also features a full range of Western wear. Closed Sunday. ~ 290 North Broad Street; 520-425-2681.

F. W. Woolworth's, opened in 1916 and housed in the Sultan Building, is the oldest continuously operating Woolworth's west of the Mississippi. ~ 151 North Broad Street; 520-425-7115.

NIGHTLIFE

Not much happens after dark, but you can see current movies at the **Globe Theater.** ~ 141 North Broad Street; 520-425-5581. Or if you prefer an evening nightcap go to **Under the Palms Cocktails.** ~ 230 North Broad Street; 520-425-2823.

PARKS

TONTO NATIONAL FOREST 🚶 🚴 🐎 ⛵ 🎣 🛶 The Globe district, located in the southeast corner of Tonto National Forest, is a popular escape from the desert heat. The Upper Salt River boasts some of the country's best white water as well as fishing and swimming at the calmer stretches. The Pinal Mountains offer endless opportunities for hiking, biking and horeseback riding. The park has picnic areas, restrooms and hiking and riding trails. ~ Main access to the Globe district is Route 60. To reach Upper and Lower Pinal campgrounds from Globe head west on Route 60. Turn south on Jess Hayes Road and follow signs to the campgrounds. Oak Flat Campground is located right off of Route 60, four miles east of Superior. ~ 520-402-6200.

▲ There are 55 campgrounds; free to $12 per night. Group sites also available. Primitive camping is also allowed. Reservations are only needed fro group sites, call USFS Reservations, 800-280-2267. At a cool 7500 feet Upper Pinal Campground (8 tent sites; no fee) and Lower Pinal Campground (12 tent sites; no fee) are popular in the summer. At a lower elevation, Oak Flat Campground (12 tent/RV sites; no fee) is conveniently located four miles east of Superior.

SAN CARLOS LAKE 🏃 🛥 ↙ The lake, created by the construction of the Coolidge Dam, has 158 miles of shoreline when full. The fishing is good for catfish, bass and crappie. Boat rentals are available in the park. There's a general store (fishing licenses and hiking permits available here). The only other facilities are pit toilets. For information about camping and hiking on tribal lands and fishing in San Carlos Lake, call 520-475-2756. ~ Located 30 miles east of Globe.

▲ There are 11 sites, some with hookups; $15 per night for RVs needing hookups, otherwise camping is included with the $7 fishing license.

Lying low in the fertile Gila River Valley is Safford, a trade center for the valley's numerous cotton farmers, and jumping-off point for outdoor recreation in the Coronado National Forest. Just west of town are the adjoining communities of Thatcher and Pima. Named to commemorate a Christmas visit by Mormon apostle Moses Thatcher, the town is home to Eastern Arizona College; nearby Pima is the site of the Eastern Arizona Museum.

▼▼▼▼▼▼▼▼
Safford Area

Safford's main highway is lined with modern shopping centers, but the downtown district, with its wood-frame and mason buildings, suggests a Midwestern borough. Despite the arid climate, the valley is irrigated by the Gila River and cotton is king here. The **Safford Valley Cotton Growers** has one of a handful of gins in the area that you can tour during season, typically September through January. Call ahead for reservations. ~ 120 East 9th Street; 520-428-0714.

SIGHTS

◄ HIDDEN

HIDDEN ▶ Underground hot springs are another natural resource in Safford. To take a dip, stop by **Kachina Mineral Springs Spa** where you can soak in springs funneled into tiled, Roman-styled tubs. Other amenities include massages, sweat wraps and reflexology (therapeutic foot massage). Although it's a tacky, run-down place, the baths are wonderful and the tubs are clean. ~ Cactus Road just off Route 191; 520-428-7212; charge for services.

A good first stop is the **Safford–Graham County Chamber of Commerce** for brochures and maps. ~ 1111 Thatcher Boulevard, Safford; 520-428-2511.

One of Safford's main landmarks is the **Safford Courthouse**, a neo-colonial brick building with white pillars built in 1916. ~ 8th Avenue at Main Street. Across the intersection is the 1898-vintage **city hall**, which was the town's original schoolhouse. ~ 717 Main Street.

Just outside of town, the quiet residential neighborhoods are dotted with elegant old homes. One of them is the **Olney House**, built in 1890 for George Olney, a former sheriff of Graham County. The two-story home features a plantation-style upper and lower front veranda. It is currently a bed-and-breakfast inn (see "Lodging" below for more information). ~ 1104 Central Avenue, Safford.

HIDDEN ▶ Archaeology buffs can check out the **Museum of Anthropology** on the Eastern Arizona College campus. Artifacts of southeastern Arizona are the focus. Exhibits include pottery and jewelry, a stratigraphic depiction of Gila Valley prehistory and dioramas of the late Ice Age in Arizona, a prehistoric Salado village and of the agriculture of the early Indians. The museum is only open weekdays during the school year. ~ 345 College Avenue, Thatcher; 520-428-8310.

If you feel like getting spaced out in Safford, stop by **Discovery Park**. This complex contains exhibits on the origins of the universe, the history and science of astronomy and radio astronomy, as well as a multimedia room where displays of real lightning are produced. There is also a 20-inch telescope for daytime and nighttime observations, and perhaps most exciting of all, a full-motion flight simulator. Closed Tuesday. Admission. ~ 1651 32nd Street, Safford; 520-428-6260.

Nearby 10,720-foot **Mount Graham** makes for good scenic drives, and its unique ecosphere provides a succession of climate zones, each with its own ecology. The main access road to the mountain is Swift Trail, which at first passes through stands of prickly pear, mesquite, creosote and ocotillo in the lower foothills. As you rise in elevation, the dominant trees are various types of oak, alligator juniper and piñon pine. At a higher elevation (8000 feet) you'll find a profusion of ponderosa pine, Douglas fir, aspen and white fir, some of them dating to 1200 A.D. Botanists say the Douglas firs have survived because the rocky cliffs of the mountains have protected them from the harsh environment. On the drive up the mountain is an apple orchard maintained under a special use permit from the U.S. Forest Service. In late summer and early fall you can purchase fruit at roadside stands. While the orchard survived the extensive May 1996 fires, 6000 acres on Mount Graham were not as lucky; you'll pass through a number of burned out areas on your trek up the Swift Trail. The first 24 miles of Swift Trail are paved, the last 13 are gravel.

The **Mount Graham International Observatory** on Emerald Peak outside of Safford features a 1.8-meter Lennon Telescope and a Submillimeter telescope. A 12-meter binocular telescope is currently under construction (it will be the world's largest of its type when completed in 1998). Further expansion of the facility will add four other telescopes including an eight-meter class infrared/optical telescope. Access to the observatory is by guided tour only. For information, contact Discovery Park. ~ 520-428-6260.

Olney House Bed and Breakfast, a Western Colonial Revival home, has three antique-filled guest rooms, all of which share a bath. In addition to rooms in the main house, there's a one-bedroom cottage and a circa-1890 studio cottage. Scattered throughout are Asian decorations from the owners' travels, and in the dining room is a mural painted by an Apache artist. Guests start the morning with a Southwestern breakfast. Before leaving, be sure to see the pecan tree, which they claim is the tallest in Arizona. ~ 1104 Central Avenue, Safford; 520-428-5118, 800-814-5118, fax 520-428-2299. MODERATE.

LODGING

◄ *HIDDEN*

For beautiful scenery in the middle of true wilderness, the **Southwest Research Station,** run by the American Museum of Natural History, provides a haven for the layperson as well as the scientist. Rooms are furnished simply and three meals a day are included in the tab. Cave Creek Canyon is known for its fabulous birdwatching. A swimming pool, volleyball court and horseshoes are available for the guests. Open to the public from mid-March through October. ~ Take Route 80 to Portal, then follow Cave Creek Canyon for five miles; 520-558-2396. DELUXE.

The rest of Safford's lodgings are mostly chain motels. You won't be disappointed with the **Sandia Motel,** which features rooms with refrigerators and microwaves, a pool, hot tub and even an outdoor basketball court. There's also a restaurant and a lounge with live music on weekends. ~ 520 East Route 70, Safford; 520-428-5000, 800-578-2151, fax 520-428-3779. BUDGET.

The best restaurant in town is **El Coronado,** a friendly place with blue-vinyl booths, ceiling fans and a deep narrow dining room. The tasty Mexican specialties include green chile chimichangas and quesadillas stuffed with green chile, meat, chicken, chorizo and

DINING

chopped green chile. American dishes include chicken-fried steak, shrimp and sandwiches. Closed Tuesday. ~ 409 Main Street, Safford; 520-428-7755. BUDGET.

El Charro Restaurant is a local hangout with formica tables and local artwork on the wall. Mexican specialties include cheese crisps with green chile con carne, green or red chile burritos and Sonora enchiladas. Closed Sunday. ~ 601 Main Street, Safford; 520-428-4134. BUDGET.

Adjacent to the Country Manor Motel, **The Country Manor Restaurant** is open 24 hours a day. Old farm implements hang on the walls and you're likely to see a table of old timers in here shooting the breeze and eating home-cooked meals such as Black Angus beef, Mexican dishes, homemade soups and pies, chicken fried steak, liver and onions and meatloaf. ~ 420 East Route 70, Safford; 520-428-3200. BUDGET.

The **Branding Iron Restaurant** is a ranch-style building flanked by large trees. They serve Western broiled steaks, chicken, seafood, barbecued ribs in a dining room that overlooks the Gila Valley. Closed Monday. ~ 2346 North Branding Iron Lane, Safford; 520-428-6252. MODERATE.

SHOPPING   **Brown's Turquoise Shop Inc.** has rough and cut natural Morenci turquoise and handmade American Indian jewelry. Closed Sunday. ~ 2248 1st Street, Safford; 520-428-6433.

You can't miss **Pollock's Western Outfitters** with its distressed-wood exterior and horse statue on the roof. Inside, there are the latest Western fashions, accessories and tack. Suppliers include Levi, Rocky Mountain, Justin, Tony Lama, Stetson and Resistol. You'll also find Murphy leather goods and King ropes. ~ 610 5th Street, Safford; 520-428-0093.

Behind Pollock's Western Outfitters, **Pollock's Outback Outlet** offers merchandise at discounted prices.

✔ **CHECK IT OUT—UNIQUE DINING**

- *Budget:* Dine on Mexican or American cuisine at **El Coronado**, a friendly place with the best eats in Safford. *page 217*
- *Budget to moderate:* Stroll through Globe's historic district and stop for breakfast at the **Blue Ribbon Cafe**, a celebrated eatery. *page 214*
- *Moderate:* Feast on New Zealand lamb or marinated quail at the intimate **Snowy Mountain Inn.** *page 229*
- *Moderate:* Look for **Mining Camp Restaurant and Trading Post** and its all-you-can-eat dining in Apache Junction. *page 208*

Budget: under $8   Moderate: $8–$16   Deluxe: $16–$24   Ultra-deluxe: over $24

The small shops on downtown's Main Street are fun to explore. In addition to T-shirt and thrift shops, jewelry stores and Western-wear boutiques, you'll find **Toys n' Tools**, a funky little shop where you can buy a stuffed animal, Barbie doll or torque wrench. ~ 419 Main Street, Safford; 520-348-9490.

Trophies n' Tees/Safford Book and Framing has an interesting selection of Southwestern books, maps and cards as well as Arizona souvenirs and T-shirts. Closed Sunday. ~ 513 Main Street, Safford; 520-428-1529.

Locals converge on **Smokey Bob's American Club**. ~ 503 Main Street, Safford; 520-428-2727.   **NIGHTLIFE**

MOUNT GRAHAM The highest peak of the Pinaleño Mountains at 10,720 feet is Mount Graham. Drive the 37-mile-long Swift Trail and you'll leave the cactus and mesquites at the base and travel to a forest of ponderosa pine, aspen and white fir, punctuated by charred areas consumed by the May 1996 forest fire. At the top is 11-acre Riggs Lake, which is stocked with trout (license plus trout stamp required) and also available for boating (electric motors only). The park's facilities are limited to water faucets, restrooms, picnic areas and a visitor station. ~ Go south from Safford for seven miles on Route 191 and turn west at the Mount Graham sign. The first 24 miles of the Swift Trail are paved; the last 13 are graded dirt; 520-428-4150.   **PARKS**

▲ There are six developed campgrounds; $5 per night except at Riggs Flat and Cunningham Corrals ($6 per night). Primitive camping is allowed free below 9800 feet.

ROPER LAKE STATE PARK In addition to swimming in a 30-acre lake with a beach, you can soak outside in a rock tub filled with hot springs bubbling up from the ground. The 240-acre park also includes a refuge for endangered fish in two ponds. The park is home to non-endangered fish as well: catfish, bass, bluegill, trout and crappie. You can fish for them from a shady dock. For meals, sit out on the peninsula's grassy picnic area under a grove of shade trees. You'll find restrooms and showers. ~ Located six miles south of Safford off Route 191; 520-428-6760.

▲ There are 95 sites, 20 with RV hookups; $8 per night for standard sites and $13 per night for hookups.

ARAVAIPA CANYON WILDERNESS Aravaipa Creek flows through an 11-mile-long canyon bordered by spectacular cliffs. Lining the creek are large sycamore, ash, cottonwood and willow trees, making it a colorful stop in fall. You may spot javelina, coyotes, mountain lions and desert bighorn sheep, as well as nearly every type of desert songbird and more than 200 other bird species.   ◄ HIDDEN

There are no facilities whatsoever. ~ To get to the West Trailhead, drive on Route 77 about 12 miles south of Winkelman. Go east on Aravaipa Road; it's 12 miles to the trailhead. To get to the East Trailhead, drive on Route 70 about 15 miles northwest of Safford, then turn off on Klondyke Road. Or follow Route 191 about 19 miles south of Safford and turn on the Fort Grant Road, then follow the signs. It's advisable to check on road conditions with the Safford District Office before setting out.

▲ Primitive camping allowed. The maximum stay is three days/two nights. Permits are required and can be obtained from the Bureau of Land Management's Safford District Office. ~ 711 14th Avenue, Safford; 520-428-4040.

Clifton–Morenci Area

To begin the 44-mile drive from Safford to Clifton, continue east out of Safford on Route 70. The road passes along the edge of Roper Lake State Park, and parallels the Gila River for a few miles. Soon after the river parts ways with the road, take a left turn onto 191 North—otherwise, you'll promptly end up in New Mexico. The route is scenic, traveling between the Gila Mountains to the north and the Whitlocks to the south. As you pass the appropriately named Thumb Butte on your right, you'll cross from Graham County into Greenlee County; finally, the road rejoins and crosses over the Gila River, and takes you into Clifton.

The Clifton–Morenci area is a region shaped by its mining past. Today, the continent's second-largest copper mine operates in Morenci, while the copper industry's heyday is preserved along Clifton's historic Chase Creek Street.

SIGHTS Route 191 follows the San Francisco River, much the way Francisco de Coronado and his conquistadors did, around the bend and into the historic little mining town of **Clifton**, built along the banks of the river.

All around Clifton, the red sandstone cliffs paint a brilliant contrast to the grays and tans of the shale and the tin-and-brick buildings which are reminiscent of the town's golden days at the turn of the century, when copper was king.

The town was founded around 1865, but didn't prosper until copper deposits were discovered in 1872. At first, copper ore had to be shipped to Swansea, Wales, for smelting. Then miners built their own crude adobe smelters along Chase Creek Street, and set up a narrow-gauge railroad to transport the ore from the mines on the surrounding hillsides.

Many of the remnants of early mining operations remain, along with dozens of old buildings—47 are on the National Register of Historical Places—in turn-of-the-century architecture. You'll find most of them along **Chase Creek Street**, which was once the town's main thoroughfare, lined on both sides with stores, saloons, brothels, churches and even an opera house. Today, the four-block-long street, plus a few narrow alleys, parallels Coronado Boulevard (Route 191), separated by a rudimentary brick wall. But you can still walk among the buildings, many of which have been damaged by time and natural disasters. Most, however, retain their architectural splendor.

> At the Greenlee County Historical Museum is the baby chair and doll once belonging to Supreme Court Justice Sandra Day O'Connor, who was born in nearby Duncan.

For instance, the **Catholic Church**, which was rebuilt in 1917 after being destroyed by flood and fire, features leaded and stained-glass windows, a marble altar and porcelain figures imported from Italy. Down the street is Clifton's first **Town Jail**, which is carved into the side of a granite cliff. Next door is the **Copper Head**, a 19th-century locomotive that once carried ore to the smelters. Across the river, the **Carmichael House** is now headquarters for mine officials. It was built in 1913 for mine president James Carmichael, who once had to flee through the home's storm sewer system to escape a mob of angry strikers.

The **Greenlee County Chamber of Commerce**, which has its offices in the old Southern Pacific train depot, dispenses maps and information about the sights and history of the area. Be sure to ask for the walking-tour map of historic Chase Creek. If you have any questions about the history of the area, ask Charles Spezia, who put together the tour. ~ North Coronado Boulevard, Clifton; 520-865-3313.

You'll notice a few caves in the mountain above the south side of Chase Creek. These were built by merchants to store valuables such as whiskey, meat and vegetables. They often had rugged steel doors and sometimes were vented with a vertical shaft.

The renovated **Greenlee County Historical Museum** on the west end of Chase Creek, has assembled an impressive collection of early Clifton memorabilia, including recollections of Geronimo's birth near the Gila River about four miles from downtown. Also on display are a photo gallery of the region's history and paintings by Ted De Grazia, one of Arizona's most famous artists and a native of Morenci. Open Tuesday, Thursday and Saturday afternoons. ~ 315 Chase Creek, Clifton; 520-865-3115.

Phelps Dodge Corporation became a major player in Clifton's development in the 1880s, when it took over most of the local mining operations, about four miles north of town. At the time, the mining camp was called Joy's Camp, but was later renamed **Morenci**, after a town in Michigan. Over the next 50 years, Phelps Dodge, or "PD" as the locals call it (often confused with "Petey"), became one of the largest producers of copper in the world.

Today's Morenci was built by Phelps Dodge in 1969. It consists of a motel/restaurant, a school, library, two shopping centers, bowling alley and the Phelps Dodge Mercantile, a combination supermarket and discount department store. Phelps Dodge operates the open-pit copper mine here, the second largest in North America and open to public tours.

The **Morenci Open Pit Mine** is an awesome sight from the overlooks along Route 191, but you can get a closer look into the depths of the mine through tours offered by Phelps Dodge. Most impressive are the earth moving equipment with tires so huge they dwarf a man, the scoop shovels that can unearth 40 cubic tons of ore with one bite, and the futuristic dump trucks with wedge-shaped bays that haul 190 tons of ore. The tour also includes the mine's crushers, concentrators and electrochemical extraction operation, which processes the copper ore into three-foot-square sheets, each weighing about 200 pounds. The tours, which last about three-and-a-half hours, are conducted by retired miners who explain the state-of-the-art electro-winning process, which has replaced outdated smelting and refining. Closed weekends. ~ 4521 Route 191, Morenci; 520-865-4521.

Continuing north, the highway ascends a series of switchbacks into a high desert climate zone, with juniper trees seemingly growing from the red rock formations.

About halfway to Alpine, you can stop at **Rose Peak**, which offers panoramic vistas of the Escudilla Mountains. For even better views, you can hike to the forest lookout tower, about a half-mile off the highway.

LODGING   Each town has its own motel. **Rode Inn Motel** is in the traditional motel-style, with rooms decorated in a sort of modern Southwest style with antique-white walls and furnishings in pastel greens and blues. Rooms are well kept and offer in-room coffee, microwaves, refrigerators and color cable television. ~ 186 South Coronado Boulevard, Clifton; 520-865-4536, fax 520-865-2654. BUDGET.

The more modern **Morenci Motel** sits on a hill overlooking Clifton and features an adobe brick exterior, wrought-iron fixtures, adobe tiled lobby, restaurant, lounge and gift shop. The large rooms are decorated with dark-wood, Mediterranean-style furnishings and pastel colors. ~ Route 191, Morenci; 520-865-4111, fax 520-865-5525. BUDGET.

DINING   **PJ's Restaurant**, a storefront hole-in-the-wall near the old section of town, is popular with locals who feast on hamburgers, steak dishes or Mexican entrées like chile cheese crisps and green chile plates or red enchiladas. Seating is at the counter or formica dinettes, but the food is tasty and plentiful. ~ 307 South Coronado Boulevard, Clifton; 520-865-3328. BUDGET.

The best place in town to eat is the **Copperroom Restaurant and Lounge,** a somewhat plain but cavernous dining room with ceiling fans, wooden tables, captain chairs and a brick fireplace used during the winter. The house specialties include steaks, prime rib, chicken, liver and onions, halibut and several Mexican dishes. ~ Morenci Motel, Route 191, Morenci; 520-865-4111. BUDGET TO MODERATE.

Not much here, but if you run out of toothpaste try **Phelps Dodge Mercantile,** a combination grocery and discount department store. ~ Morenci Plant Site shopping center, Morenci; 520-865-4121.

SHOPPING

For contemporary surroundings, try the **Copperroom Restaurant and Lounge,** a small but surprisingly active bar with a handful of wooden tables and copper memorabilia hanging from the ceiling. ~ Morenci Motel, Route 191, Morenci; 520-865-4111.

NIGHTLIFE

The long and winding road from Clifton up to Alpine is a beautiful one—just make sure you have plenty of gas and supplies before you begin, because there are no facilities along the 105-mile stretch. Starting from Clifton, you'll first need to make the 1300-foot climb to Morenci, then bid civilization farewell as you continue the ascent into Apache-Sitgreaves National Forest. Your progress through the Blue Range towards Alpine will be marked by the increasing height of the peaks you pass: Mitchell Peak at just under 8000 feet, Rose Peak at almost 8900 feet and Sawed Off Mountain at 9346 feet.

▾▾▾▾▾▾▾▾
Alpine Area

Be aware that this road is subject to closure during winter snow storms. If the road is closed by snow or mudslides, you can drive to Alpine via Routes 78 and 180 through western New Mexico. The detour adds only 20 miles to the trip.

Twenty-two miles before you reach Alpine is **Hannagan Meadow,** a grassy clearing framed by stately ponderosa pine and blue spruce forests. In addition to excellent hiking trails, there's a rustic mountain lodge, and, in winter, cross-country skiing and snowmobiling. ~ Route 191.

SIGHTS

The mountain village of **Alpine** is located in the heart of the Apache-Sitgreaves National Forest, or the "Arizona Alps," as it is called locally. The town was founded in 1879 by Mormon settlers who originally named it Frisco, after the San Francisco River. The name was later changed to Alpine because residents thought the area resembled the Alps. The Arizona Alps don't attract the large number of tourists who flock to the Grand Canyon, the Colorado River or other state attractions, but nature buffs will love the region's abundance of outdoor activities—hiking, camping, hunting, fishing and cross-country skiing.

Alpine has no traffic lights or video stores, just a handful of year-round residents and even fewer commercial attractions. Actually it's nothing more than an intersection of Routes 191 and 180, but there are dependable services and lodging. More important, within a 30-mile radius there are 200 miles of trout streams, 11 lakes, numerous campgrounds, plus a country club and golf course.

In winter, Alpine doesn't hibernate with the black bear, but keeps busy offering cross-country skiing, sledding and ice fishing opportunities.

The region is also a favorite with hunters because it is home to nine of Arizona's ten big game species, including mule deer, elk, black bear, bighorn sheep and mountain lion. Small-game hunters stalk blue grouse, wild turkey, Gambel's quail and a host of waterfowl. The forest is also habitat for a wide variety of rare and endangered birds, including the Mexican spotted owl, bald eagle and peregrine falcon.

From Alpine, you can strike out in any direction and discover unspoiled forests of tall pines, shimmering aspens, trickling streams, wildflower meadows and clear blue lakes. For detailed maps and descriptions of the area, stop at the **U.S. Forest Service**, where rangers can also advise on current road conditions. The office lobby is now open 24 hours, with an interactive video display giving out tourist information when rangers aren't available. ~ 42634 Route 180; 520-339-4384.

A picturesque spot is **Williams Valley**, an unspoiled wilderness area located seven miles northwest of Alpine via Route 191 and Forest Road 249. Here, you can explore 15 miles of hiking trails through wooded forests, or drop a line in tiny Lake Sierra Blanca, which is stocked with rainbow and brook trout.

A nice scenic drive from Alpine is the **Blue River–Red Hill Loop**. Drive east three miles from Alpine on Route 180 to Forest Road 281 (the Blue Road turnoff). As you make this turnoff, you'll see the western tip of **Luna Lake**, 80 acres of crystal-clear waters surrounded by green meadows and pine forests. Facilities include a boat dock and small store.

From Route 180, Blue Road winds south through ten miles of rugged hills until it descends past a few horse ranches into Box Canyon, where the road follows the **Blue River**. Continue downstream past jagged Maness Peak nine miles to the junction with Forest Route 567 (Red Hill Road). Along the way, are tributaries, such as Centerfire Creek, which are home to small schools of rainbow and brook trout. Drive west on Red Hill Road, which twists and climbs out of the valley, often following ridges with panoramic vistas back to Route 191, about 14 miles south of Alpine.

LODGING   The wood-paneled **Tal-wi-wi Lodge** offers clean, comfortable rooms featuring rustic furnishings, some with Swedish fireplaces and spa tubs. There's a seasonal outdoor sauna. The restaurant serves breakfast and dinner, and the lounge often has live music or karaoke on weekends. ~ Route 191, four miles north of Alpine; 520-339-4319. BUDGET TO MODERATE.

If you came to the mountains seeking a cozy retreat, try the **Alpine Cabins**, which feature fireplaces, kitchenettes and four-poster beds. Closed during winter. ~ 42650 Route 180, Alpine; 520-339-4440. BUDGET.

About a mile north of town, **Judd's Ranch** rents small log cabins that feature creaky hardwood floors, knotty-pine walls and small kitchens. You can drop a line in the fishing lake or horseback ride along 15 miles of forested trails. Closed from November to mid April. ~ 42576 Route 180, Alpine; 520-339-4326. BUDGET.

Surrounded by pine forests, the **Coronado Trail Cabins** offers a few cozy single-room cabins fully furnished with kitchenettes and bed covers. Barbecue and picnic areas are outside the units. ~ 25302 Route 191, Alpine; 520-339-4772. BUDGET.

A pair of Alpine motels offer clean, well-maintained rooms—some with kitchenettes—at reasonable prices. One is the **Mountain Hi Lodge**. ~ 42698 Route 180; 520-339-4311. Your other choice is the **Sportsman Lodge**. ~ 42627 Route 191, Alpine; 520-339-4576. BUDGET.

About 22 miles south of Alpine, **Hannagan Meadow Lodge** rents rustic cabins with fireplaces and antique furnishings, and has a dining room (which closes in winter). One of the oldest inns in the state, the lodge also has a general store. ~ Route 191 at Hannagan Meadow; 520-339-4370. MODERATE.

DINING

You'll find home cooking at the **Bear Wallow Café**, a converted house that exudes a casual, friendly atmosphere. Traditional favorites here include T-bone steak, chicken-fried steak, homemade bread and pies. ~ 42650 Route 180, Alpine; 520-339-4310. MODERATE.

SHOPPING

One-stop shopping is the specialty at **The Tackle Shop**, where you can fill your tank, restring your cross-bow, buy a canoe, eat lunch or rent a video. ~ 25373 Route 191, Alpine; 520-339-4338.

If you need to stock up on groceries (other than tortilla chips and bean dip), head to **Alpine Market** for a standard selection of meat, produce and canned goods, as well as the latest gossip circulating the mountain village. ~ 42651 Route 180, Alpine; 520-339-4914.

▼▼▼▼▼▼▼▼▼▼▼▼▼▼
Pinetop–Lakeside Area

Where Route 60 intersects with Route 191 and the Coronado Trail, you'll come to the town of Springerville, where you can make a detour and head west to the recreation and ski area of Pinetop–Lakeside, a winter resort popular with Phoenix residents.

SIGHTS   In the Springerville area, there are two places of interest worth stopping for. Situated on a rim of volcanic rock overlooking the Little Colorado River's Round Valley is **Casa Malpais Pueblo**. Tours originate at the museum in Springerville. Here, you'll learn that the Mogollon people abandoned the pueblo in 1400 A.D., and now the archaeological dig is open to the public. For the best pueblo views, take the guided tour up a steep basalt staircase to the top of the mesa. A tour highlight is the **Great Kiva** made of volcanic rock. Admission. ~ 318 Main Street, Springerville; 520-333-5375.

Follow a dusty, bumpy road for several miles and the unlikely reward is the **Little House Museum** on the X Diamond Ranch. Inside the two-story building are exhibits relating to the area's history, including ranching and horse show memorabilia. Beside it are two restored cabins more than 100 years old. One contains antique musical instruments ranging from a player piano to a Wurlitzer circus organ. Another building has recently been built to house the expanding instrument collection as well as a new exhibit on John Wayne, who had a ranch next door. Advance reservations are suggested. Admission. ~ Located just over three miles south of Route 260 on South Fork Road, near Springerville; 520-333-2286.

Climbing the steep incline of the Mogollon Rim leads to **Show Low**, **Pinetop** and **Lakeside**, forested hamlets of cabins, motels, resorts and campgrounds in a pine woods setting. Most of the commercial activity takes place in Show Low along Route 60. The population of Show Low swells from about 5500 year-round residents to more than 13,000 during the summer, when the big attractions are excellent trout fishing and big game hunting in the Mogollon Rim country and White Mountains. Also popular are hiking, horseback riding, golf and scenic drives. Many Arizonans also keep summer homes at the 6400-foot-elevation town to escape the blistering summer temperatures in Phoenix and other "flatlander" communities. During winter, the Sunrise ski resort on the White Mountain Apache Reservation is famous for its downhill runs and cross-country trails.

SALT RIVER CANYON

Nicknamed the miniature Grand Canyon, the **Salt River Canyon** is a spectacular sight that you can drive right through on Route 60 about 50 miles south of Show Low. There's a bridge where Route 60 crosses the Salt River, which carved the canyon millions of years ago. Seven miles downstream from the bridge via a paved road are fascinating salt banks sacred to the Apache and colored with green, red and orange minerals and algae.

Southeast of Show Low lie the mountain resort twins of Pine-top and Lakeside, and beyond, the Indian towns of Whiteriver and Fort Apache. Lakeside is a starting point for hiking, fishing, camp-ing and backpacking in and near the three resort communities, which are connected by a highway lined with motels, restaurants, gas stations and small businesses.

Built in 1916, the **Lakeview Lodge** is one of the oldest lodges in Arizona. The rustic lounge has a fireplace, high-beamed ceilings and Indian rugs hanging from the second-story railing. The nine rooms and cabins are simply furnished and come with a compli-mentary bottle of wine. Fishermen can use the private pond, then grill their catch on the premises. ~ 2251 Route 260, Pinetop-Lakeside; 520-368-5253. MODERATE.

LODGING

One step short of camping out is staying at the **Lake of the Woods Resort**. Twenty-seven log cabins are scattered amidst pine trees beside a private lake. All of the cabins have fireplaces,TVs, microwaves, kitchen and dining areas and outdoor barbecues. Although some cabins are geared toward honeymooners, most are more family oriented. Amenities include shuffleboard, horseshoes, spas, a sauna, playground, ping-pong, pool tables and boats for rent. ~ 2244 West White Mountain Boulevard, Pinetop-Lakeside; 520-368-5353. MODERATE.

Located on Sunrise Lake near the ski resort four miles south of Route 260 is **Sunrise Park Resort**, owned and operated by the White Mountain Apache Tribe. Guests come to fish in summer and ski in winter, staying at one of the 94 modern, nicely furnished hotel rooms. Amenities include an indoor pool, indoor and out-door spas and restaurant and lounge. ~ Route 273, McNary; 520-735-7676, 800-554-6835, fax 520-735-7339. MODERATE.

A beautiful setting amidst pine trees, rather than luxurious ac-commodations, are what you pay for at **Hawley Lake Resort**. The resort is remote—12 long, winding miles off Route 260—and sit-uated on a lake in one of the highest points in the White Moun-tains. Open from May through November, the resort offers twelve motel rooms and eight cabins overlooking the lake. If you get lucky fishing, grills are available outside and cabins have kitch-enettes. The resort is located on the White Mountain Apache Indian Reservation. Amenities include a café, boat rentals, gas and a store. ~ Route 473, 16 miles east of McNary; 520-335-7511, fax 520-335-7434. MODERATE.

Pastoral is the only word for the setting at **Greer Lodge**, lo-cated on the Little Colorado River with a view of meadows and mountains. To many, it is *the* place to stay. Built by hand as a church retreat 45 years ago out of ponderosa pine and aspen, it now is a charming getaway with nine rooms in the main lodge and eight cabins. The lounge/restaurant area has comfy couches, a huge fireplace, vaulted ceilings and almost floor-to-ceiling windows where guests can look out at the snow falling in winter. Country furnishings warm up the rooms, along with cozy rocking chairs and quilts on the beds. Upon arrival, guests receive a wine and fruit basket; at night, homemade cookies. Horse-drawn sleigh rides and ice skating also available in winter; flyfishing in stocked ponds in summer. ~ Route 373, Greer; 520-735-7216. DELUXE.

Molly Butler Lodge is the oldest lodge in Arizona, built in 1910. Rooms are tiny and a bit run-down, but prices are inexpensive. A nice touch are the plaques on each door with the name and information about a local pioneer. The restaurant on premises serves dinner only. ~ Route 373, Greer; 520-735-7226. BUDGET.

Snowy Mountain Inn is a bed and breakfast nestled in the forest near a trout-stocked pond. Accommodations consist of seven separate log cabins and four knotty-pine bedrooms with private baths located inside the main building of the inn. All the cabins have brick fireplaces (gas-log) in the living room, housekeeping kitchens and lofts with queen beds and a sitting area. There is also a spa and a spacious common room furnished with soft, red leather couches and artifacts from the owner's travels. The gourmet restaurant surrounds a large rock fireplace. Hiking trails can be accessed from the property, which borders on National Forest land. ~ 38721 Route 373, Greer; 520-735-7576, fax 520-735-7705. MODERATE TO DELUXE.

DINING

The **Lakeview Lodge Steakhouse** has salads, sandwiches and hamburgers. Closed Tuesday; breakfast and lunch only on Sunday and Monday. ~ Lakeview Lodge, 2251 Route 260, Pinetop–Lakeside; 520-368-5253. BUDGET.

Charlie Clark's Steak House has been around since 1938. A Western theme predominates, with stuffed bear and deer, a glass-topped, wagon-wheel coffee table and wildlife paintings. There's even a silver saddle once used by movie stars and politicians. Prime rib, steak and seafood are the primary offerings, but vegetarian dishes are available upon request. Dinner can be followed by off-track betting in the front bar. ~ 1701 East White Mountain Boulevard, Pinetop–Lakeside; 520-367-4900. MODERATE.

Catch your own rainbow trout in Fred's Lake, just outside the door at **Farmer Dunn's Vittles**, and they'll cook it for you! An adjoining concession rents fishing equipment. Fridays are fish fry nights; otherwise, the fare is burgers, sandwiches and chicken. Inside the cheery, barnlike building, farm implements hang on the walls. A cow-colored clawfoot bathtub holds the salad bar, while soup warms on a wood-burning stove. Closed Monday and Tuesday. ~ 1543 East Fir Lane, Pinetop–Lakeside; 520-367-3866. BUDGET.

For gourmet dining, try the **Snowy Mountain Inn**. Cuisine includes spinach ricotta flan, New Zealand lamb and marinated quail. The knotty pine walls adorned with creative artifacts give this elegant restaurant a cozy, intimate aura. ~ 38721 Route 373, Greer; 520-735-7576. MODERATE.

SHOPPING

Antiquing is popular in this area. Choices include **The Orchard Antiques** with quality furniture, Nippon china, vintage clothing and primitives; the shop is located in an old house. ~ 1664 West White Mountain Boulevard, Pinetop–Lakeside; 520-368-6563.

In Pinetop–Lakeside, **Sherry's Jewelry & Antiques** has gold and silver estate jewelry, Depression ware, china and furniture. ~ Route 260, Ponderosa Plaza; 520-367-5184.

Primitives, pine and oak furniture, quilts, gifts and gourmet coffee beans are what you'll find at **Billings Country Pine Antiques and General Store**. ~ 103 West Yaeger Street, Pinetop–Lakeside; 520-367-1709.

NIGHTLIFE

Watch classic comedies and musicals at Pinetop–Lakeside's live community **Theatre Mountain**. Located in an old movie house, the theater leans toward family-oriented productions, which patrons enjoy while slurping down ice-cream sundaes and snacks. Admission. ~ 537 Woodland Road, Pinetop–Lakeside; 520-368-8888.

PARKS

WOODLAND LAKE PARK 🚶 🚴 🐎 ⛵ This small but scenic park located in the middle of Pinetop–Lakeside, offers hiking, equestrian and mountain biking trails, volleyball courts, softball fields, boating and playgrounds. People can fish for trout from the shore and pier; a second newly constructed pier is wheelchair accessible. Tall, thin pine trees surround the lake and a one-mile paved loop trail encircles it. The park is also connected with the White Mountain Trailsystem (see "Hiking" at the end of the chapter). Other facilities you'll find in the park are restrooms, picnic tables, barbecues and ramadas ($10 reservation fee). Restaurants and groceries are one mile away in Pinetop. ~ Located a quarter-mile south of Route 260 off Woodland Lake Road; 520-368-6700.

▼▼▼▼▼▼▼▼▼
St. Johns Area

From Show Low, head east on Route 60 and northeast on Route 61 to arrive at St. Johns. Built along the banks of the Little Colorado River, St. Johns, with a population of about 3500, serves as the Apache County seat. The Coronado Trail (Route 180/191), named after the Spanish explorer who first sojourned here, begins innocently enough in the high desert area near St. Johns.

SIGHTS

St. Johns has few sights, except for the **St. Johns Equestrian Center**, which is rapidly becoming one of the premier equestrian facilities in the Southwest, attracting horses and riders from New Mexico, Colorado and Utah, as well as throughout Arizona. Surrounded by rolling hills and juniper-studded deserts, amenities include an 80-acre cross-country course, rodeo arena, show and dressage rings, six-furlong race track, stables and RV sites. In spring and summer, the center hosts local and regional events, both Western and English, rodeos and other horse competitions. ~ Adjacent to St. Johns Airport; call City Hall at 520-337-4517 for more information.

You can find out about the area's history at the **Apache County Historical Society Museum**, which houses displays that include pioneer memorabilia and a log cabin, as well as a set of prehistoric woolly mammoth tusks and a camel's leg bone, both estimated to be about 24,000 years old. Closed weekends. ~ 180 West Cleveland Avenue; 520-337-4737.

The northern part of the **Coronado Trail** meanders through a region of juniper-dotted hillsides, alfalfa pastures, grazing cattle and a few sandy-topped buttes about 44 miles southeast of Petrified Forest National Park. The trail then heads south through Apache-Sitgreaves National Forest to Clifton.

As the Coronado Trail climbs on its journey south, chaparral gives way to pine and aspen, and you pass **Nelson Reservoir**, a 60-acre lake stocked with rainbow, brown and brook trout. If you're ready for a break, there are picnic grounds, restrooms and a boat ramp, but no overnight camping.

South of the reservoir are the rolling **Escudilla Mountains**, a 5000-acre wilderness area with forests of spruce, fir, pine and aspen, and nature trails where hikers are often rewarded with raspberries, elderberries and gooseberries, and glimpses of elk and deer in their natural habitat.

LODGING   St. Johns' lodging scene is unexceptional, but you'll find well-maintained rooms at **Trail Riders Inn**, a trailer-court type of motel with old-fashioned casement windows and adobe-like walls. A restaurant and lounge adjoin the motel. ~ 125 East Commercial Street, St. Johns; 520-337-4422, fax 520-337-2821. BUDGET.

The always-dependable **Whiting Motor Inn** offers all the standard amenities including phones, coffee and cable color TV. ~ 75 East Commercial Street, St. Johns; 520-337-2990, fax 520-337-4478. BUDGET.

DINING   A popular local hangout and city landmark is **Katy's Kountry Kitchen**, which features a stagecoach and wagon wheels at the entrance. Inside, the Western atmosphere is punctuated by dark-wood paneling and cast-iron utensils on the walls, not to mention the stuffed deer and wild boar. Seating is of the early dinette variety, but the unpretentious American fare is plentiful. Specialties include chicken-fried steak, roast beef and rib-eye steaks. ~ 106 West Cleveland Street, St. Johns; 520-337-2129. BUDGET TO MODERATE.

For a more varied menu, try the **Rhino's Horn**, which orchestrates a good rendition of several Italian dishes including lasagna and calzones. You can also feast on frisbee-sized burgers, a slab of barbecue ribs or fresh catfish. ~ 855 West Cleveland Street, St. Johns; 520-337-2223. BUDGET.

PARKS

CONCHO LAKE This lake, stocked with rainbow and brook trout, is a peaceful spot to drop a line. Or you may choose to play a round of golf at the neighboring public course. The only facilities in the park are restrooms. ~ The lake is ten miles west of St. Johns off of Route 61; 520-337-4644.

▲ Free camping permitted.

LYMAN LAKE STATE PARK A small herd of buffalo greets visitors at the entrance to the park. Farther on, a 1500-acre lake lures both fishing and boating enthusiasts. In fact, it is the only lake in the White Mountains where powerboating is allowed, so waterskiers and jetskiers flock to Lyman Lake. This is also a good place to swim as there's a cove especially marked off for swimming. Anglers fish offshore for rainbow trout, catfish, bluegill and widemouth bass. The lake was formed by damming the Little Colorado River and is fed by snowmelt from the slopes of Mount Baldy and Escudilla Mountain. Other attractions include hiking the three trails, which range from a half a mile to one mile in length, and are dotted with Indian petroglyphs. This 1180-acre park was the first recreational state park in Arizona and sits at an elevation of 6000 feet. Facilities include restrooms and hot showers. ~ Ten miles south of St. Johns off Route 191; 520-337-4441.

▲ There are 45 RV sites with electrical and water hookups and 18 developed sites for tents, complete with picnic tables and barbecue grills. Beach and wilderness camping are allowed. Fees are $8 per night for tents, $11 per night for RV hookups.

Outdoor Adventures

FISHING

Eastern Arizona is an angler's paradise with numerous lakes dotting the area around Pinetop–Lakeside and Greer. Anglers will also find plenty of challenge—and game fish—along the Old West Highway.

APACHE JUNCTION AREA In the Apache Junction area, **Saguaro, Canyon, Apache** and **Roosevelt lakes** are popular year-round fishing meccas.

GLOBE **San Carlos Lake** near Globe is the biggest fishing draw in this area.

SAFFORD AREA **Roper Lake** in Safford attracts anglers from all over Arizona.

ALPINE AREA   In the Alpine area, **Bear Wallow Creek**, a tributary of the Black River, is famous for Arizona Native trout. Also on the **Black River** at different stops you can try for rainbow trout, while trout and catfish can be found in **Eagle Creek**. East of Alpine and dropping off into the Blue Primitive Area, rainbow trout can be found in **Luna Lake** and the ruggedly remote **Blue River**. North of Alpine you'll find rainbow, brown and brook trout in **Nelson Reservoir**. More casual anglers can seek catfish in the **San Francisco River** near Clifton. You can buy bait, tackle and a license at the **Alpine Tackle Shop**. ~ 25373 Route 191; 520-339-4338.

PINETOP–LAKESIDE AREA   To fish at the lakes on the White Mountain Apache Indian Reservation, which are stocked with rainbow and brown trout, contact the **Game and Fish Department**. ~ Route 73, Whiteriver; 602-338-4385. For general fishing information in the White Mountains, stop by the **Arizona Game and Fish Department**. ~ 2878 East White Mountain Boulevard, Pinetop–Lakeside; 520-367-4281.

For private fly-fishing, catch and release, try **X Diamond Ranch**. ~ Springerville; 520-333-2286. There are quality waters with rainbow, brown and Apache trout as well as boat rentals and camping May through October at **Hawley Lake**. ~ McNary; 520-335-7511. For fishing and camping supplies or a license, check with **Western Drug**. ~ 105 East Main Street, Springerville; 520-333-4321.

ST. JOHNS AREA   In the St. Johns area, 1500-acre **Lyman Lake** is a good spot for catfish, largemouth bass, walleye, crappie and northern pike. Or try 60-acre **Concho Lake** for rainbow and brook trout (shore fishing only). **Lyman Lake State Park** has a lake stocked with trout, bass, catfish and bluegill. ~ Route 191, St. Johns; 520-337-4441.

RIVER RAFTING   During the spring run-off, the Upper Salt River offers some of the country's best whitewater rafting opportunities. **Sun Country Rafting** operates out of Phoenix but runs single and multiday trips on the Upper Salt River. ~ 602-493-9011.

WINTER SPORTS   Eastern Arizona increasingly attracts recreationally minded tourists, and not just in the summer. Locals are somewhat stunned by the growing number of winter visitors here in recent years.

ALPINE AREA   Cross-country skiing, sledding and snowmobiling are popular at **Hannagan Meadow**, 22 miles south of Alpine on Route 191, where there are over 11 miles of machine-packed trails, which are serviced after each storm. The snowmobiles in the area are prohibited from designated ski trails. Another good spot for cross-country skiers is **Williams Valley**, which features nine miles of groomed ski trails, plus an additional five-and-a-half miles of marked trails. From Alpine, drive one-and-a-half miles north on

Route 191 to the Williams Valley turnoff, Forest Road 249, and continue for five miles.

PINETOP–LAKESIDE AREA **Sunrise Park Resort** has 800 acres of skiable area on three mountains and 11 lifts. ~ 20 miles east of McNary on Route 260; 520-735-7669.

Hunters love the forests around Alpine because of the abundance of both big and small game—such as mule deer, whitetail deer, elk, javelina, black bear, mountain lion, Merriam's turkey, bighorn sheep, pronghorn antelope, blue grouse, Albert's squirrels, cottontail rabbits, mourning doves, Gambel's quail and many waterfowl.

HUNTING

You can buy a license and supplies at **The Alpine Tackle Shop.** ~ 25373 Route 191; 520-339-4338. For maps and information about the area, check at the **U.S. Forest Service Office.** ~ 42634 Route 180, Alpine; 602-339-4384.

If you feel the need to tee off in the mountains, greens are scattered throughout the region. Most are nine-hole courses; keep in mind that many are closed in the winter.

GOLF

APACHE JUNCTION AREA In Apache Junction, try **Gold Canyon Golf Club.** ~ 6100 South Kings Ranch Road; 602-982-9090.

GLOBE **Cobre Valley Country Club** has a nine-hole course. ~ Route 88 north of Globe; 520-473-2542.

SAFFORD AREA In the Safford area, the **Mount Graham Golf Course** offers an 18-hole course for year-round play, a pro shop, cart rentals and lounge. ~ Two miles south of Safford at Daley Estates; 520-348-3140.

ALPINE AREA You can tee off at the **Alpine Country Club,** which features a 18-hole course, restaurant and lounge. ~ 58 North County Road 2122; 520-339-4944.

PINETOP–LAKESIDE AREA Pinetop–Lakeside offers **Silver Creek Golf Club.** ~ 2051 Silver Lake Boulevard; 520-537-2744. Also in the area is the **Pinetop Lakes Golf & Country Club.** ~ 4643 Buck-

✔ **CHECK IT OUT—UNIQUE OUTDOOR ADVENTURES**
- Sleep close to the stars at 10,720 feet atop **Mount Graham**, the highest point in the Pinaleño Mountains. *page 219*
- Cross-country ski through **Hannagan Meadow** with its 11 miles of machine-packed trails. *page 232*
- Get back in the saddle and ride the trails through spectacular **Gold Canyon**. *page 234*
- Escape the desert heat and try your luck at landing a rainbow trout at **Hawley Lake**. *page 232*

springs Road; 520-369-4184. North of Pinetop–Lakeside is the **Show Low Country Club.** ~ 860 North 36th Drive, Show Low; 520-537-4564.

RIDING STABLES
This is the real Wild West; there's no better place to saddle up and take to the hills. If you're lucky, you may even find the legendary Lost Dutchman Mine and strike it rich—but if you don't, a ride in this beautiful backcountry is its own reward. Giddyup!

APACHE JUNCTION AREA   Get back in the saddle at **Don Donnelly Stables at Gold Canyon.** ~ 6010 South Kings Ranch Road, Gold Canyon; 602-982-7822. Also in the area is **Superstition Mountain Guide Service.** ~ Apache Junction; 602-982-4040.

PINETOP–LAKESIDE AREA   In Greer you can saddle up at **Lee Valley Outfitters.** ~ Main Street; 520-735-7454.

HIKING
If you don't get a chance to go horseback riding, at least take the opportunity to hoof it along some of Eastern Arizona's wilderness trails. Bird and animal enthusiasts should keep an eye peeled for samples of western wildlife; everyone should keep an eye on the panoramic views.

APACHE JUNCTION AREA   Usery Mountain Recreation Area offers the well-maintained **Wind Cave Trail** (1.5 mile), which is moderately challenging and popular with local climbers. **Pass Mountain Trail** (7 miles) takes about four hours to complete.

SAFFORD AREA   **Arcadia Trail** (5.1 miles), located in the Piñalenos Mountains, passes through a forest of Douglas fir, aspen and pine trees, along with wild raspberry vines. As the highest range in southern Arizona, hikers will see a panoramic view of the area.

Swimming is ideal at Canyon, Apache and Roosevelt lakes.

ALPINE AREA   The 450,000-acre Apache-Sitgreaves National Forest is a hiker's paradise, with terrain ranging from piñon and juniper woodlands to high-elevation forests of spruce and fir, meadows and alpine lakes.

About 14 miles south of Alpine, hikers can explore the **Red Hill Trail No. 56** (10 miles), a trek along a dirt road that leads into the Blue Range Primitive Area. From the upper trailhead at the Right Fork of Foote Creek, just off Forest Route 567 a mile east of Route 191, the trail traces the ridges of the Red Hill mountains, then descends along Bush Creek on its way to the Blue River. The lower trailhead is at Blue Camp, an old Civilian Conservation Corps (CCC) camp that's now a school, just off Forest Route 281. (If you like to do your hiking by horseback, corrals have recently been built at the upper trailhead.)

In the **Blue Range Primitive Area,** you'll find spectacular rock formations with steep escarpments, along with thick forests of spruce, fir and ponderosa pine. Keep a sharp watch for black bear,

Rocky Mountain elk, bighorn sheep, javelina, mule deer, mountain lions and bobcats. The area is excellent for birdwatching; keep your binoculars trained for the Arizona woodpecker, aplomado falcon, American peregrine falcon and southern bald eagle.

West of the Coronado Trail (Route 191), the **Bear Wallow Wilderness** contains 11,000 acres including one of the largest stands of virgin ponderosa pine in the Southwest. **Bear Wallow Trail No. 63** (7.6 miles) traces Bear Wallow Creek downstream from the K. P. Cienega Campground (about 26 miles south of Alpine) through jagged canyons of juniper, west to the San Carlos Apache Indian Reservation's eastern boundary. Two shorter trails connect with the main trail and creek from the north: **Reno Trail No. 62** (1.9 miles) and **Gobbler Point Trail No. 59** (2.7 miles).

There's excellent hiking in the **Escudilla Wilderness Area**, an alpine forest with peaks over 10,000 feet, ten miles north of Alpine. The **Escudilla National Recreation Trail** (3 miles) from Terry Flat takes you to the summit of Escudilla Mountain through aspen groves, pine forests and grassy meadows. The trailhead is along Forest Route 56, four and a half miles east of Route 191. Rangers at the **U.S. Forest Service** (42634 Route 180, Alpine; 520-339-4384) will provide detailed trail maps and advice on current conditions.

There area many guides and outfitters in the Alpine area. Operating out of Alpine is the **Neal Richards Alpine Guide Service**. ~ P.O. Box 596, Alpine, AZ 85920. Also in Alpine is the **Tackle Shop and Alpine Garage**. ~ P.O. Box 125, Alpine, AZ 85920; 520-339-4338. In Eager you'll find **Chris Isaacs Escuidilla Outfitters**. ~ P.O. Box 945, Eager, AZ 85925. **Scott Haggitt Primitive Outfitters** operates out of Lakeside. ~ P.O. Box 324, Lakeside, AZ 85929.

PINETOP–LAKESIDE AREA The **White Mountains Trailsystem** contains about 180 miles of trails from Vernon in the east to Pinedale in the west. For a map of trails, stop by the **Lakeside Ranger District**. ~ 2202 South White Mountain Boulevard (Route 260); 520-368-5111. The Trailsystem has recently been completed and consists of ten loop trails. Some highlights are **Blue Ridge Trail** (9.5 miles) in Pinetop–Lakeside, which is easy to moderate. It passes Billy Creek and climbs through tall pines to the top of Blue Ridge with vistas along the way. The newly completed **Ghost-of-the-Coyote Trail** (14 mile loop) begins near Pinedale. The fairly flat trail winds through juniper and pine forests.

The **Mogollon Rim Overlook** (1 mile) is an easy hike with interpretive placards along the way and beautiful views of the valley below the Mogollon Rim. It's two miles north of Pinetop–Lakeside off Route 260.

ST. JOHNS AREA There are a couple of short trails that pass by ancient petroglyphs in **Lyman Lake State Park**. Along the way, you'll be able to enjoy views of the lake below.

▼▼▼▼▼▼▼▼▼▼▼▼
Transportation

CAR

The western anchor of the Old West Highway, Apache Junction, is about 30 miles east of Phoenix via **Route 60**. On its eastern end you can join the Highway at Safford via **Routes 191** from Clifton, or **Route 70**, which crosses to Lordsburg, New Mexico. **Route 180/191** links the Coronado Trail towns of St. Johns, Alpine and Clifton. You can get to the Pinetop–Lakeside area from the west via Route 60, turning onto **Route 260** at Show Low. From the east, Route 260 connects to Route 180 at Springerville.

BUS

The closest **Greyhound Bus Lines** terminal to Coronado Trail towns is in Safford about 30 miles southwest of Clifton. ~ Reservations: 800-231-2222. Safford: 404 5th Street; 520-428-2150.

CAR RENTALS

Along the Old West Highway, you can rent a car or van at **Cobre Valley Motors**. ~ Route 60, Globe; 520-425-4487. There is also **Hatch Brothers Auto Center**. ~ 1623 Thatcher Boulevard, Safford; 520-428-6000.

EIGHT

Southern Arizona

Southern Arizona is a vast region of grasslands and desert punctuated by some of the state's most beautiful mountains. Four ranges have peaks higher than 9000 feet—the Santa Catalinas, Santa Ritas, Huachucas and Chiricahuas. At the heart of the region is Tucson, an urban metropolis rising out of the Sonoran Desert. A rich cultural tradition ranging from the Pima tribe to the Jesuits reflects this community's close ties to neighboring Mexico.

Scattered east of Tucson are portions of the Coronado National Forest. To the southeast, the rolling grasslands and woodland hills around Patagonia are some of the state's best cattle and horse ranchland, while the Elgin area has acres of green vineyards where local wines are produced. Farther east is Sierra Vista, whose claim to fame is Fort Huachuca, a historic military base whose troops defeated Apache leader Geronimo. Some 11,400 soldiers and civilians are still based here. Nearby Tombstone and Bisbee are old mining towns. Tombstone, the town "too tough to die," survives by selling its history. There are museums and exhibits on every corner—each, of course, charging for the pleasure of your company. Visitors flock here to relive the rowdy life of the Old West, from the shootout at O.K. Corral to the gambling at Birdcage Theater. Bisbee has become a quiet artists' colony with a more bohemian flavor. Here, visitors can shop in historic buildings along Main Street, tour old mines and walk along the narrow, hilly streets dotted with Victorian architecture. Up around Willcox are orchards teeming with fruit and vegetables. In autumn, you can pick your own or stop at one of the many roadside stands.

South of Tucson is the most populated portion of southern Arizona. Off Route 19 is Tubac, an artists' community with about 100 studios and galleries. Farther south is the border town of Nogales, where you can bargain for Mexican crafts and sample authentic cuisine. Southwest of Tucson is a large, scarcely populated area containing the Papago Indian Reservation, Cabeza Prieta National Wildlife Refuge and Organ Pipe Cactus National Monument. In the westernmost corner of the state is Yuma, a historic town on the Colorado River that attracts residents with its lush, subtropical climate, farmlands fertile with vegetables, citrus trees and groves of date palms.

Although Tucson and southern Arizona abound with history, the real reason people visit is for the natural beauty—for the meditative solitude of a desert that seemingly rolls on endlessly, creating vast spaces for the imagination.

▼▼▼▼▼▼▼▼▼
Tucson

The ultimate insult to a Tucson resident is to say his town is just like Phoenix. Like bickering siblings, the two cities have never gotten along well and each is proud of its unique personality. While Phoenix is a vast, sprawling city that welcomes booming development, Tucson would just as soon stay the same size and keep developers out—especially those who would alter the environment. Phoenix thrives on a fast pace; Tucson is informal, easygoing and in no great rush to get anywhere.

Surrounded by five mountain ranges and sitting in a cactus-roughened desert, Tucson is an arid, starkly beautiful place with wide-open skies and night silences broken only by the howling of coyotes. The highest mountains are powdered with snow in winter; the desert is ablaze with cactus blooms in spring.

Most of Tucson's 12 inches of annual precipitation arrives during the late summer monsoon season when afternoon thunderstorms roll through the desert with high winds and dramatic lightning shows. During summer, the average high temperature hovers around 98. In winter, average highs are about 65, making the city a popular spot for winter visitors, who come to golf and relax in the balmy weather.

Basically, Tucson is an affable, unpretentious town that feels comfortable with itself. There's no need to impress anyone here with high fashion—blue jeans are good enough for most places. Nor do wealth and conspicuous consumption have a large following. Most Tucsonans don't come here to make lots of money, but rather to live in a beautiful, natural area that's within driving distance of more of the same.

The cultural heritage of Tucson is a mix of Spanish, Mexican and American Indian. The city is only 60 miles from Nogales and the Mexican border, but you don't have to go that far to find Mexican food, artwork and culture. The red-tiled adobe homes spread across the valley reflect the residents' love of Spanish and American Indian architecture.

The Hohokam people were the first in the area. Father Eusebio Francisco Kino, a Jesuit priest, came to work with them and established a chain of missions, including Tucson's famous Mission San Xavier del Bac.

Later, the Spanish flag flew over the city, as did the Mexican, Confederate and United States flags. In 1867, Tucson was the capital of the Arizona Territory. But when the capital moved north, disgruntled Tucson was given the University of Arizona as compensation. This increased the population, and it jumped again just

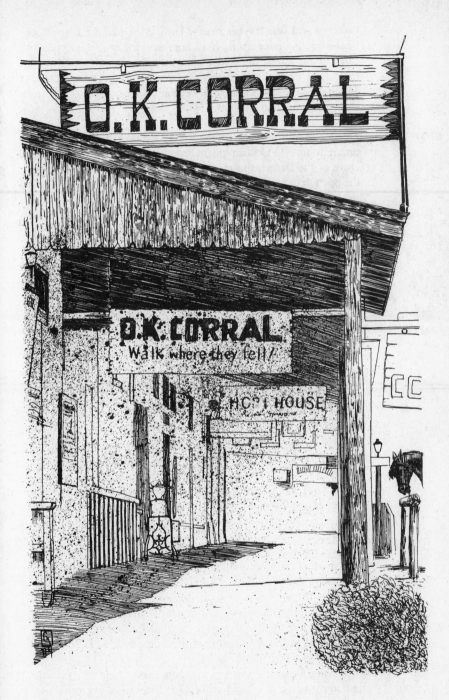

before World War II when nearby Davis-Monthan Air Force Base began training pilots to fly B-17 bombers. Today 750,000 people call Tucson home and live within the metro area's 500 square miles. The university has grown to 35,000 students, and Davis-Monthan is still an active military base with more than 7767 military personnel and civilians.

SIGHTS

Nine miles southwest of Tucson is the **Mission San Xavier del Bac** on the Tohono O'Odham Indian Reservation. Known as the White Dove of the Desert, this stunning white adobe church rises from the open desert floor and is picturesquely framed by blue sky and the mountains beyond. Although the Jesuits founded the mission in the 1600s, the present building was built between 1783 and 1797. It is a combination of Spanish, Byzantine and Moorish architecture. Visitors can walk in through weathered mesquite doors, sit on the worn wooden pews, and feast their eyes on the ornate statues, carvings, painted designs and frescoes. In addition to touring the facility, you can attend mass Tuesday through Friday, which is open to the public, or visit during one of the celebrations. ~ Signs appear as you drive south on Route 19; 602-294-2624.

Across the square in the **San Xavier Plaza**, American Indians sell fry bread and crafts.

Drive north to Speedway Boulevard, turn left and you'll reach Gates Pass, where the road begins to twist and you'll have splendid panoramic views of Tucson and the saguaro-dotted landscape of Tucson Mountain Park. This is where you'll find **Old Tucson Studios**, a re-creation of an old Western frontier town. Columbia Pictures created Old Tucson Studios in 1939 as a movie location for the film *Arizona*, and since then more than 300 films and television episodes have been shot here including *Rio Bravo*, *Gunfight at the O.K. Corral* and *El Dorado*. The studios are temporarily closed due to a fire. They will reopen at the end of 1996. Call ahead for information. Admission. ~ 201 South Kinney Road; 602-883-0100.

Just a few minutes down Kinney Road, **The Arizona-Sonora Desert Museum** is a cross between a zoo and a botanical garden with more than 300 different animals and 1400 plant species indigenous to the Sonoran Desert. Visitors can inspect the aquatic exhibits and the animals in their desert habitats, or walk inside an aviary and a re-created limestone cave (all exhibits are wheelchair accessible). Definitely worth a visit. Admission. ~ 2021 North Kinney Road; 602-883-2702.

Tucson Botanical Gardens contains a small field of American Indian crops, a cactus and succulent garden, a tropical greenhouse, an herb garden, a sensory garden and a xeriscape (arid landscaping) demonstration garden. Perhaps most unusual is the historic

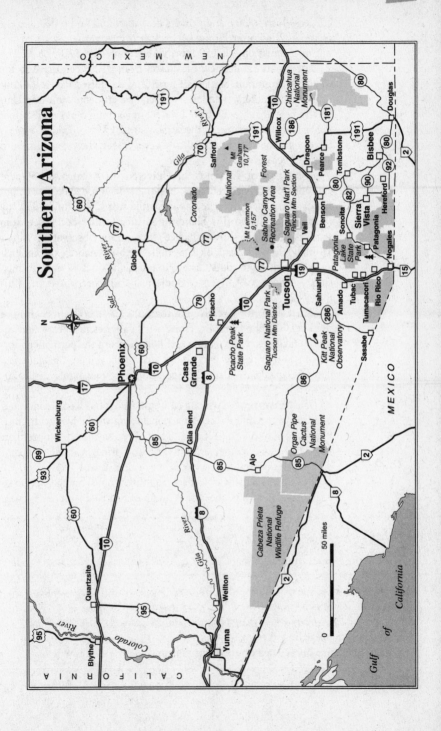

Southern Arizona

garden—lush foliage and flowers that surround and reflect the era of the 1920s Porter House. A backyard bird garden is a new addition. Admission. ~ 2150 North Alvernon Way; 520-326-9255.

For a panoramic view of Tucson from 3100 feet, drive to the top of **A Mountain**. Settlers of territorial days used it as a lookout for Apache raiders. The latest raiders are students from the University of Arizona, who have been whitewashing the A on it before the first football game of the season since 1915. ~ Take Congress Street exit west off Route 10 to Cuesta Street, then go south onto Sentinel Peak Road.

A big part of Tucson is the **University of Arizona**, a 350-acre campus dotted with red-brick buildings. If you decide to explore the campus, there are a few worthwhile stops. ~ 520-621-2211.

One definite stop is **Flandrau Science Center & Planetarium** with its laser light shows, science store, public observatory with a 16-inch telescope available for public use and science exhibits such as a walk-through model asteroid and night skies exhibit. Admission. ~ Corner of University Boulevard and Cherry Avenue; 520-621-7827.

The **Center for Creative Photography** has a collection of more than 50,000 photographs, along with galleries, a library and research facilities. Photography exhibitions from the permanent collection and traveling exhibitions are displayed in the galleries. Closed Saturday. ~ Park Avenue and Speedway Boulevard; 520-621-7968.

The **University of Arizona Museum of Art** has Renaissance and later European and American art, including works by Rembrandt, Picasso, Rothko and O'Keeffe. The collection includes more than 3000 paintings, sculptures, drawings and prints. Closed Saturday. ~ Park Avenue and Speedway Boulevard; 520-621-7567.

El Presidio Historic District, running from Church Avenue to Alameda Street, was once the Presidio of San Augustin del Tucson,

✔ CHECK IT OUT—UNIQUE SIGHTS

- Bask in the beauty of **Mission San Xavier del Bac's** ornate statues, carvings and frescoes. *page 240*
- See Georgia O'Keefe originals and 3000 other pieces of European and American art at the **University of Arizona Museum of Art.** *page 242*
- Bring your binoculars when you visit the **Ramsey Canyon Preserve—** the birdlife is colorful and plentiful. *page 260*
- Wander the ruins and cemeteries of **Duquesne** and other **ghost towns** off Route 82. *page 271*

which the Spanish army enclosed with a 12-foot-high adobe wall in 1783. Today, the main attraction in El Presidio is the **Tucson Museum of Art**, a complex specializing in pre-Columbian, modern American and Southwestern art, along with several historic houses and the Plaza of the Pioneers—a showplace for the museum's sculpture collection. Admission. ~ 140 North Main Avenue; 520-624-2333.

Fort Lowell Museum is a reconstructed commanding officers' quarters from the days when it was a key military post during the Apache Indian wars of the 1870s and 1880s. Life on a military post in frontier Arizona is revealed through furnishings, artifacts and displays of military equipment. Closed Sunday through Tuesday. ~ 2900 North Craycroft Road; 520-885-3832.

◀ *HIDDEN*

The late Ted De Grazia gained fame painting impressionistic-style portrayals of the Southwest and its people. Today his home and galleries, the **De Grazia Gallery in the Sun**, are open to the public. Skylights in the adobe structures bathe his paintings in light. Walking through, you pass underneath brick archways and go through landscaped courtyards that he so lovingly tended when he lived here. The unusual architecture, including an iron gate inspired by the historic Yuma Prison, is worth a visit in itself. ~ 6300 North Swan Road; 520-299-9191.

Arizona's oldest historical museum, the **Arizona Historical Society Museum**, has everything from a full-scale reproduction of an underground mine tunnel to an exhibit on the history of transportation. ~ 949 East 2nd Street; 520-628-5774.

Pima Air and Space Museum contains one of the largest collections of historic aircraft in the world. Among the 200 aircraft are the Boeing B-29 Superfortress, the type of plane that dropped the first atomic bomb on Japan, and the SR-71 Blackbird, the world's fastest aircraft. Admission. ~ 6000 East Valencia Road; 520-574-0462.

For a truly unusual experience, stop by **Biosphere 2**, a controversial three-acre miniature replica of the earth with a tropical rainforest, savannah, marsh and desert. There are small greenhouses where different ecosystems are displayed. Research focus has shifted from sustainable agriculture to global climate changes. Although you can't go inside the airtight structure, you can see the outside of this high-tech, space-age glass and steel monolith, look through its glass walls and stop by the visitors center. Tours are offered every day on the hour. Admission. ~ Route 77 Mile Marker 96.5, Oracle; 520-896-6200.

Although Tucson is known for its upscale, full-service resorts—a haven for those escaping cold winters elsewhere—it also has a number of budget and mid-range accommodations.

LODGING

Built in the 1930s, the **Arizona Inn** is a historic gem. Although it's in the middle of town, it feels like a lush oasis with 14 acres of lawns and gardens thick with orange trees, native cypress and date palms. No two of the resort's 80 rooms are alike, but all are decorated to the 1930s period and some have antiques. The inn also has a swimming pool, tennis courts, a restaurant and a cocktail lounge decorated with 19th-century Audubons. ~ 2200 East Elm Street; 520-325-1541, 800-933-1093, fax 520-881-5830. ULTRA-DELUXE.

Hotel Congress is a piece of Tucson's history. The block-long classical brick and marble structure was built in 1919 to serve Southern Pacific railroad passengers, and John Dillinger's gang were among its guests. Geometric Indian designs add character to the lobby, which also provides seating for the Cup Café and overflow from the nightclubs. The renovated hotel rooms are decorated with black-and-white-tile bathrooms, black headboards and salmon-colored walls. Of the hotel's 40 rooms, seven are hostels with bunk or single beds and private baths. None of the rooms have televisions, but they *do* have a rarity nowadays—windows that open. Gay-friendly. ~ 311 East Congress Street; 520-622-8848, 800-722-8848, fax 520-792-6366. BUDGET.

Bed and breakfasts are proliferating in Tucson. Built in 1905, the **Peppertrees Bed and Breakfast Inn** is a red-brick Territorial home. There are two, two-room Southwest-style guest houses and three main rooms furnished with period pieces from England. French doors lead outside to a beautifully landscaped patio. ~ 724 East University Boulevard; phone/fax 520-622-7167, 800-348-5763. DELUXE.

La Posada del Valle is a stucco-and-adobe inn built in 1929. A novelty is afternoon tea, served in a living room furnished with art deco antiques from the '20s and '30s. The 1920s theme carries over to the five guest rooms, and each is named after famous women of that era. Sophie's Room is a favorite with an 1818 king-size Victorian bedroom set. Karen's Cottage, separate from the main house, is an early 1900s suite with an African motif. ~ 1640 North Campbell Avenue; phone/fax 520-795-3840. DELUXE.

Centrally located, **North Campbell Suites Hotel** offers four-room suites with kitchens. The 11 suites aren't fancy, but are homey and functional with adequate furnishings and a hide-a-bed in the living room for extra sleeping space. A swimming pool and trees help soften the look of the motor court. ~ 2925 North Campbell Avenue; phone/fax 520-323-7378. DELUXE.

Best Western Tanque Verde Inn and Suites is a hacienda-style inn with rooms overlooking a lush courtyard dotted with Mexican fountains. The 90 guest rooms are clean and comfortable; some are kitchenettes. There is a pool and complimentary breakfast. ~ 7007 East Tanque Verde Road; 520-298-2300, 800-882-8484, fax 520-298-6756. DELUXE.

For an assortment of affordably priced motels, drive down Miracle Mile, once the main thoroughfare through the city. The area is a bit seedy with several strip joints, but there are a few decent places. One is the **Best Western Ghost Ranch Lodge**. Today, the property has 83 rooms housed in brick buildings surrounded by grassy lawns, palm trees and cactus gardens. The theme is Western, with a cow skull over the lobby fireplace and Western memorabilia throughout. There's also a restaurant, bar, pool and whirlpool. ~ 801 West Miracle Mile; 520-791-7565, 800-456-7565, fax 520-791-3898. MODERATE.

The Lodge on the Desert is a garden resort hotel with 40 adobe-colored buildings grouped around patios that open to lawns and gardens. Rooms have beamed ceilings, handpainted Mexican tile accents, Monterey furniture, and many have mesquite-burning beehive fireplaces. Other amenities include a restaurant and a pool with mountain views. ~ 306 North Alvernon Way; 520-325-3366, 800-456-5634, fax 520-327-5834. MODERATE TO ULTRA-DELUXE.

The resorts are expensive during winter high season, but most slash prices during the hot summer months. Among the best resorts is the **Westin La Paloma**. The 487 Southwest-style rooms have private balconies or patios, a sitting area, oversized closet and a stocked fridge. Many of the suites have wood-burning fireplaces and sunken spa tubs. There are three swimming pools including one with swim-up bar, Jack Nicklaus golf course, tennis and racquetball courts, a health center and, for tired parents, day care for the small fry! ~ 3800 East Sunrise Drive; 520-742-6000, 800-876-3683, fax 520-577-5886. ULTRA-DELUXE.

Located in the foothills of the Santa Catalina Mountains, **Loews Ventana Canyon** is another 93-acre, luxury resort. Highlights are an 80-foot waterfall cascading down into a pond, and secluded paths lined with mesquite, squawbush and blue palo verde. Many of the

▸▸▸

✔ CHECK IT OUT—UNIQUE LODGING

- *Budget:* Glide down the solid white Italian-marble staircase in the lavish lobby of **The Gadsden Hotel**, a National Historic Monument. *page 266*
- *Moderate to deluxe:* Perch yourself on Ajo's highest hill at **The Mine Manager's House Inn**, where you can see downtown's Spanish-style plaza. *page 273*
- *Deluxe:* Enjoy afternoon tea amid art deco antiques after you check into **La Posada del Valle**. *page 244*
- *Ultra-deluxe:* Pretend you're in paradise at the **Arizona Inn**, where 14 acres of lush gardens surround you. *page 244*

Budget: under $50 Moderate: $50–$90 Deluxe: $90–$120 Ultra-deluxe: over $120

398 Southwest-style rooms have original artwork, burnished-pine furnishings, private balconies and bathrooms with marble floors. Amenities include five restaurants and lounges, tennis, golf, fitness trails, pools, a health club and shops. ~ 7000 North Resort Drive; 520-299-2020, 800-234-5717, fax 520-299-6832. ULTRA-DELUXE.

Just north of town is **The Triangle L Ranch**, an 1880s homestead on an 80-acre ranch. The four private cottages include an ivy-covered adobe cottage with a clawfoot tub in the bathroom and screened sleeping porch, and one with a stone fireplace, rose arbor entry and private patio. Two of the cottages have kitchens and multiple bedrooms. A wood-burning stove warms the kitchen for breakfast, which consists of eggs from the owner's chickens and other homemade treats. The ranch rents the cottages September through June. ~ 2805 Triangle L Ranch Road, Oracle; 520-896-2804, fax 520-896-9070. MODERATE TO DELUXE.

Picacho Motel and Restaurant has been around since the 1930s. Waitresses in the lobby restaurant often double as receptionists to check guests into this casual motel. Just outside the 26 rooms are palm and fruit trees, while inside is somewhat worn wood paneling hung with country pictures, along with bureaus and desks. ~ 6698 Eisenhower Street, Picacho; 520-466-7500. BUDGET.

For information on bed and breakfasts throughout Arizona, contact the **Arizona Association of Bed & Breakfast Inns**. ~ P.O. Box 7186, Phoenix, AZ 85011; 602-277-0775.

DINING

There is an eclectic mix of cuisine in Tucson, but Southwest- and Sonoran-style Mexican fare are the specialties. You can't beat **Janos** for American nouvelle cuisine with a Southwestern twist. The adobe house shares a courtyard with the Tucson Museum of Art, and inside displays of original art hang below ocotillo ceilings on 20-foot-high walls. Menus are seasonal, but typical entrées are pepito-roasted lamb loin with wild mushroom spoon bread and ancho chile sauce, or sesame-crusted ahi with stir-fried Napa cabbage and mango sauce. Closed Sunday in winter. Closed Sunday and Monday in summer. ~ 150 North Main Avenue; 520-884-9426. DELUXE TO ULTRA-DELUXE.

Café Magritte is an intimate, artsy café located in the heart of the arts district. The two-story eatery has large skylights and brick walls hung with local artwork. The food is eclectic, but has a hint of the Southwest. Specialties include various pasta dishes, like the tortellini Sonora with cilantro, roasted red peppers and pistachios and pesto sauce. Closed Monday. ~ 254 East Congress Street; 520-884-8004. BUDGET TO MODERATE.

Walk into **Café Poca Cosa** and you're bombarded with festive color. Green paint covers the ceilings, red chile peppers dot the walls, lights hang on indoor trees, and purple, green and red tiles

cover the tables. The menu changes two or three times daily, and
is written on a blackboard that's brought to the table. Dishes are
homestyle Mexican. Specialties include chicken breast in mango
sauce, *pollo en chipotle* (chile) sauce and pork marinated in beer.
Closed Sunday. ~ 88 East Broadway Boulevard; 520-622-6400.
MODERATE.

For the innovative in pizza, try **Magpies Pizza**. Examples of
their fare include The Greek with spinach, basil, garlic, piñon nuts,
feta cheese, cheese and sundried tomatoes, or Cathy's with garlic,
stewed tomatoes, mushrooms, artichokes, roasted red peppers and
Romano cheese. Located in a small strip center, Magpies has a
contemporary look with a black-and-white-tile floor, red chairs
and modern art on the walls. ~ 605 North 4th Avenue; 520-628-
1661. BUDGET TO MODERATE.

In the next block is **Delectables**, decorated with brass chandeliers and turn-of-the-century oak antiques. Inside are wood tables,
wood-beamed ceilings and curving tinted windows that look out
onto 4th Avenue, while outside are somewhat rundown green

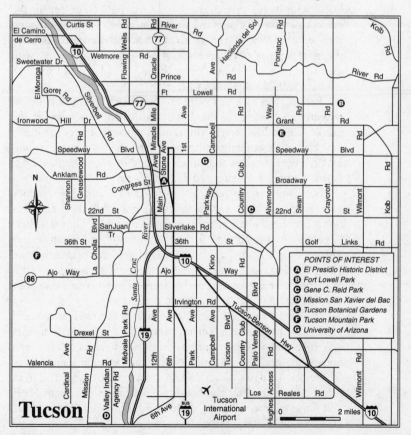

POINTS OF INTEREST
A El Presidio Historic District
B Fort Lowell Park
C Gene C. Reid Park
D Mission San Xavier del Bac
E Tucson Botanical Gardens
F Tucson Mountain Park
G University of Arizona

Tucson

metal tables with matching chairs. This eatery offers fresh ruby trout and chicken piccata plus salads and sandwiches. ~ 533 North 4th Avenue; 520-884-9289. BUDGET TO MODERATE.

At the **Arizona Inn**, you choose the ambience: formal dining room, casual patio or courtyard ablaze with tiny lights in the trees. The fare includes Continental, Southwestern, nouvelle and traditional selections. One treat is the fresh steamed fish, enhanced with ginger and leeks, and served at your table from a bamboo steamer. ~ 2200 East Elm Street; 520-325-1541. DELUXE.

HIDDEN ►

Located in the warehouse district, **Tooley's** is little more than a glorified taco stand with good food. Customers order food at an outdoor window, then sit at one of the handful of tables on the sidewalk or perch on the curb. The menu boasts that Tooley's is home of the turkey taco, and turkey is used instead of chicken in all their entrées. If you're watching your wallet, you can't beat the super low prices. Closed Sunday. ~ 299 South Park Avenue; 520-882-9758. BUDGET.

At the **Blue Willow Restaurant,** you can either dine inside the house with its light peach walls and artsy posters, or opt for the brick, vine covered courtyard. Either choice is a winner. Although they serve sandwiches and salads at lunch and dinner, breakfast is the most popular meal here with 24 omelettes, including one with avocados, jack cheese and green chiles. ~ 2616 North Campbell Avenue; 520-795-8736. BUDGET.

Two minutes away is **Coffee Etc.,** where it's best to skip the entrée and go straight for the dessert and coffee. Favorites are the Snicker cheesecake served with Danish nutcream or cocoa almandine coffee. Resembling an open air café, the restaurant has umbrellas over the tables and clouds painted on the ceilings. ~ 2700 North Campbell Avenue; 520-881-8070. BUDGET.

For Southwestern food, try **Café Terra Cotta**. The outdoor patio is lit by miniature white lights at night, while the indoor section is decorated in turquoise and terra cotta colors. Entrées include large prawns stuffed with herbed goat cheese and Southwestern tomato coulis, stuffed red and green chiles, and pizzas that are cooked in the woodburning oven and topped with ingredients such as herbed mozzarella, lime and cilantro. ~ 4310 North Campbell Avenue; 520-577-8100. MODERATE TO DELUXE.

The casually elegant **Daniel's Restaurant** has received national acclaim for its Northern Italian cuisine since opening several years ago. Inventive appetizers such as sweet-potato chips layered with housemade gravlax, red-onion capers and chive oil lead the way for traditional pasta dishes and an array of lamb, veal and fresh fish entrées. The menu also boasts an extensive wine, grappa, beer and single malt scotch list. ~ 4340 North Campbell Avenue, Suite 107; 520-742-3200. DELUXE TO ULTRA-DELUXE.

It's hard to beat dining at **Anthony's in the Cantina** with its top-notch views and ambience. The almost floor-to-ceiling windows look over the city lights in this hacienda-style building. Dinner is served on elegant china with pale pink linens, fresh flowers and classical music playing in the background. Chandeliers hang from the vaulted, beamed ceiling and a large fireplace warms the room in winter. The Continental specialties include veal scaloppine in a citrus bourbon sauce, lamb Wellington and chicken tantano. Wash it down with a bottle from the extensive selection of about 1300 wines. Closed Saturday and Sunday for lunch only. ~ 6440 North Campbell Avenue; 520-299-1771. DELUXE.

Mi Nidito Café is a tiny, tacky, crowded Mexican joint with great food, from enchiladas to menudo. Portions are generous and there are always plenty of locals lining up to fatten their waistlines. Walls are covered with murals of palm trees. Closed Monday and Tuesday. ~ 1813 South 4th Avenue; 520-622-5081. BUDGET.

Micha's is a larger restaurant owned by the Mariscal family for many years and whose portrait is just inside the door. You won't leave here hungry—even the flour tortillas are about a foot in length. Don't miss the chimichangas, topopo salad or grilled shrimp fantasia. ~ 2908 South 4th Avenue; 520-623-5307. BUDGET.

If you'd rather stay away from high-calorie Mexican food, try **The Good Earth**, the local choice for health foods. The extensive menu has salads, hot and cold sandwiches, pasta, seafood, chicken, vegetarian dishes and breakfast items that are served all day long. Although spacious, the atmosphere is nevertheless cozy with earth toned decor, solid wood tables, lots of hanging plants, and a cactus garden to add a touch of the Southwest. ~ 6366 East Broadway Boulevard; 520-745-6600. BUDGET TO MODERATE.

The two boulevards boasting the largest concentration of restaurants in Tucson are Broadway and Speedway.

As the name suggests, diners at **Van Gogh's Ristorante Italiano** eat Italian food amid reproductions of Van Gogh's artwork. Along with traditional fare, you'll find more imaginative specials such as roast duck stuffed with smoked oysters and pine nuts, served with a Grand Marnier sauce. Diners can also hear live music on the enclosed patio. ~ 7895 East Broadway Boulevard; 520-722-5518. MODERATE.

The **Olympic Flame** offers something rare in a Greek restaurant—white tablecloths and fresh flowers. They serve flaming *saganaki* at the table amid a chorus of opas, as well as pastitsio, moussaka, gyro, steaks and Greek-style salads. Closed Sunday. ~ 7970 East Broadway Boulevard; 520-296-3399. MODERATE.

Jamaica Bay Café has, as one would expect, a tropical setting with high ceilings, plants and colorful carpeting. Specialties include veal Madagascar, cayenne salmon and shrimp scampi. ~ 6350 East Speedway Boulevard; 520-296-6111. MODERATE.

The **Presidio Grill** offers dishes with a Southwestern flavor. Try an appetizer of roasted whole garlic and brie with marinated peppers, followed by Presidio chicken pasta prepared with browned garlic, poblano chiles, prosciutto, fresh basil, roma tomatoes and olive oil. Decor here is postmodern with an unusual color scheme of black, green, orange and yellow. And for those booth aficionados among us, it's nice to find a place with more booths than tables. The Silver Room offers a more formal setting with white tablecloths and metal accents. ~ 3352 East Speedway Boulevard; 520-327-4667. DELUXE.

Farther down the road is **Szechuan Omei Restaurant,** a Chinese restaurant where you can choose from more than 135 entrées, including lunch specials. Decor is nothing fancy, just red tablecloths and chairs and the usual Chinese lanterns and paintings. ~ 2601 East Speedway Boulevard; 520-325-7204. BUDGET.

HIDDEN ► Marie A. Sinbres, Rosita's daughter, presides over **El Arte de Rosita,** cooking all of their tasty Mexican food. On the walls hang photographs of Rosita with the late artist and friend Ted De Grazia, along with some of his prints. Handmade crocheted curtains hang between the portal and the porch, and outside Christmas lights line the porch year-round and plants take root in clawfoot tubs. Eclectic home-style best describes the atmosphere. Closed Sunday and Monday. ~ 1944 East Prince Road; 520-881-5380. BUDGET.

Don't let the shopping center location stop you from visiting **Boccata,** whose main draws are city views and good Northern Italian/Southern French food. The ambience is simple and sophisticated, with plum and yellow walls dotted with contemporary art. Among the choices are the *penne ciao bella* with grilled chicken, roasted peppers, artichoke hearts and pine nuts in white wine sauce,

✔ **CHECK IT OUT—UNIQUE DINING**

- *Budget to moderate:* Look no farther than the **Longhorn Restaurant** for the biggest hot dog in Cochise County. *page 267*
- *Moderate:* Don't miss the opportunity to dine at **The Montura,** a 150-year-old horse stable that is now an elegant restaurant. *page 274*
- *Deluxe:* Select one of the 1300 wines at **Anthony's in the Cantina,** then sit back and enjoy Tucson's sparkling lights. *page 249*
- *Deluxe to ultra-deluxe:* Admire the Tucson Museum of Art's collection, then dine at neighboring **Janos,** where pepito-roasted lamb loin is among the offerings. *page 246*

Budget: under $8 Moderate: $8–$16 Deluxe: $16–$24 Ultra-deluxe: over $24

or the grilled rib-eye steak in a merlot sauce served with fried crispy onions and roasted-garlic mashed potatoes. ~ River Center, 5605 East River Road; 520-577-9309. MODERATE.

Tork's Café is a tiny, family-run place with only a handful of tables and delicious Middle Eastern food. The *shawerma* plate with beef, chicken or lamb contains strips of meat cooked with onions and bell peppers. Other choices are the vegetarian falafel plate, humus dip, tabouleh and kabobs. Closed Sunday. ~ 1701 North Country Club Road; 520-325-3737. BUDGET.

Webb's Old Spanish Trail Steak House specializes in delicious ◄ HIDDEN barbecue ribs and chicken, as well as steaks. Old tools decorate the walls of this rustic-style restaurant. At night, settle down by the picture window and you're likely to see javelinas stop by to feed. There's also outdoor patio dining. ~ 5400 South Old Spanish Trail; 520-885-7782. MODERATE.

Walk through antique, hacienda-style doors and you're inside **Tohono Chul Tearoom**, located in a rustic, 52-year-old house in ◄ HIDDEN the midst of Tohono Chul Park. Unless the weather is bad, opt for outdoor dining on a patio that sits amid palo verde trees and cactus, and offers free entertainment from the birds and other critters that come to nibble. For lunch, innovative sandwiches are served on croissants or sourdough bread. Other choices are breakfast, Sunday brunch and afternoon tea complete with finger sandwiches, scones and pastries. No dinner. ~ 7633 North Paseo Del Norte; 520-797-1711. MODERATE.

Although it's in the lobby of the Picacho Motel, the **Picacho Restaurant** is a cozy affair with dark-wood ceilings and booths and a Southwestern flavor with cow skulls and Indian rugs on the wall. People come mainly for the oversized hamburgers, although they also serve sandwiches and steaks. ~ 6698 Eisenhower Street, Picacho; 520-466-7500. MODERATE.

SHOPPING

If you want anything with a Southwestern flair, Tucson is where you'll find it. In addition, you'll find shops catering to almost every need, with the majority of the artsy and antique shops downtown and various specialty shopping plazas scattered throughout the town.

For shopping mixed with entertainment, head for the **Tucson Arts District** on the first and third Saturday of the month when "Downtown Saturday Night" is held. During this event, stores, restaurants and galleries stay open late, musicians perform in the streets, and the area becomes a hot night spot for entertainment-seekers and shopaholics. There are over 40 galleries, in addition to antique, novelty and specialty shops. Every Thursday an "Artwalk" is held in the district, making stops at exhibit rooms, galleries and artists' studios (call ahead for a brochure). ~ Located downtown roughly between Congress and Cushing streets, and Main and 4th avenues; 520-624-9977.

Huntington Trading Co. Inc. carries American and Mexican-Indian Art—pottery, baskets, masks, carvings and paintings. ~ 111 East Congress Street; 520-628-8578. **Berta Wright Gallery Shops** has a wide range of ethnic and contemporary crafts including jewelry, clothing and high-quality Mexican and South American imports. ~ 260 East Congress Street; 520-882-7043. For the tykes, there's **Yikes!**, a toy store with unusual gifts, small toys and books. Connected to Yikes! and sharing the same phone number, **Picante** sells various imported gift items, T-shirts, ethnic clothing and jewelry. ~ 300–302 East Congress Street; 520-622-8807.

Nearby is **4th Avenue** with over 100 shops and restaurants. Shops in this older neighborhood contain vintage clothing, unique fashions, jewelry, books and art. Don't be surprised to find touches such as incense burning in the shops.

Antigone Books specializes in books by and about women as well as gay and lesbian literature. ~ 411 North 4th Avenue; 520-792-3715. **The Jewel Thief** offers a huge selection of earrings, with most hanging on large boards around the shop and many priced at under $10. ~ 557 North 4th Avenue; 520-623-7554. For clothing, try **Jasmine** with its natural fiber clothing, some handwoven in Morocco. ~ 423 North 4th Avenue; 520-629-0706. **Del Sol** carries Southwestern clothes, scarves and jewelry, and a huge selection of rugs made by the Zapotecs of Mexico. ~ 435 North 4th Avenue; 520-628-8765. On the vintage side, stop by the **Tucson Thrift Shop**, which specializes in vintage clothing from the 1960s. ~ 319 North 4th Avenue; 520-623-8736. Another thrift store is **Loose Change**, a funky place with clothes from different eras that you try on in rooms closed off with refrigerator doors. ~ 417 North 4th Avenue; 520-622-5579.

In the El Presidio Historic District downtown is **Old Town Artisans**, an 1850s restored adobe structure with surrounding shops that fill an entire city block. In the outdoor courtyard hang chile peppers and handmade hummingbird feeders, along with Mexican fireplaces. Inside the 13-room marketplace is Southwestern folk art made by Arizona artisans, American Indian tribal art and imports from Latin America. ~ 186 North Meyer Avenue; 520-623-5204. Another worthwhile stop in this area is the **Tucson Museum of Art gift shop** with contemporary pottery and other artistic gifts. ~ 140 North Main Avenue; 520-624-2333.

For Mexican imports, check out what is unofficially called the Lost Barrio Warehouse District—a group of shops located in old, red-brick warehouses. **Rustica** sells Southwestern and Mexican furnishings and accessories. ~ 200 South Park Avenue; 520-623-4435. **Magellan Trading Company** has great buys on Mexican

HIDDEN ►

HIDDEN ►

glassware as well as handicrafts, artifacts and furniture from Mexico, New Guinea, Indonesia and Africa. ~ 228 South Park Avenue; 520-622-4968.

St. Philips Plaza is a cluster of Southwest-style shops with red-tile roofs that include art galleries, clothing stores and restaurants. ~ Corner of River Street and Campbell Avenue. **Bahti Indian Arts** offers American Indian crafts such as drums, jewelry, rugs, pottery and kachina dolls. ~ 4300 North Campbell Avenue; 520-577-0290. **El Presidio Gallery Inc.** is a fine-arts gallery with original Southwestern art in a variety of media. ~ 4340 North Campbell Avenue, Suite 62; 520-529-1220.

Drive farther down River Road and you'll see **River Center**, a Southwest-style shopping plaza. The stores surround a brick courtyard with a fountain and waterway. **Totally Southwest** (520-577-2295) has Southwestern gifts while **The West** (520-299-1044) has cookbooks, cards, kids gifts and needlework supplies, with proceeds going to local women's and children's charities. ~ River Center: corner of River Street and Craycroft Road.

Built in 1939, **Broadway Village** was one of the first shopping centers in Arizona. It houses a variety of shops in whitewashed red-brick buildings. ~ Corner of Broadway Boulevard and Country Club Road. The more unusual includes a tiny mystery bookshop called **Clues Unlimited**. ~ 123 South Eastbourne; 520-326-8533. ◄ *HIDDEN* There's also an expensive, fashionable children's boutique called **Angel Threads**. ~ 350 East Broadway; 520-326-1170.

B&B Cactus Farm has more than 600 varieties of cacti and succulents from around the world. ~ 11550 East Speedway Boulevard; 520-721-4687.

For antiques outside of the downtown area, browse through **Unique Antique**, a 90-dealer antique mall that owners claim is the

TED DE GRAZIA

One of Arizona's most renowned artists was Ted De Grazia, who depicted the Southwest in paintings, prints, bronzes and collector's plates. His distinctive, impressionistic-style works, with their signature bright colors and featureless faces, hang in Tucson's De Grazia Gallery in the Sun. Born in Morenci, Arizona, in 1909, De Grazia spent his life traveling through Mexico and the Southwest, learning the lore of the Apache, Navajo, Yaqui and Papago tribes and collecting three art degrees. One of his most surprising moves came in 1976. To protest the severe taxes on heirs of artists, he burned 150 of his paintings—valued at $1.5 million. He was irate that his wife would have to sell most of these paintings to pay the inheritance tax on their value whenever he died. In 1982, De Grazia died of cancer.

largest in Southern Arizona. ~ 5000 East Speedway Boulevard; 520-323-0319. You can also check out **Sandy's Antiques**, which specializes in gold and silver jewelry from Navajo and Zuni people, as well as furniture, collectibles, costume jewelry, clocks and dolls. ~ 4500 East Speedway Boulevard, Suite 78; 520-327-0772.

Casas Adobes Shopping Center is yet *another* Southwest-style shopping plaza with a variety of specialty shops. ~ 7051 North Oracle Road. A favorite is **Antigua de Mexico**, a Latin American import store with Mexican Colonial and Southwestern furniture, folk art, pottery, glassware, tinware and sterling silver from Taxco. ~ 7037 North Oracle Road; 520-742-7114.

North Campbell Avenue has a number of shopping venues. One of the most popular, judging by the ever crowded parking lot, is **Bookman's**—*the* place for bibliophiles to browse. The owner claims the largest selection of used books and new magazines in the Southwest. Bookman's also has a rare-book room and sells used magazines, records, tapes, video games, computer software and CDs. ~ 1930 East Grant Road; 520-325-5767.

NIGHTLIFE **THE BEST BARS** **Bum Steer** is a casual place in a large, barnlike building containing a restaurant, several bars, a video arcade, volleyball court and small dancefloor. Inside, everything from cannons to airplanes hang from the vaulted roof. Entertainment includes live rock bands and karaoke night. Cover some evenings. ~ 1910 North Stone Avenue; 602-884-7377.

The **Outback** offers a whole complex for evening entertainment—cocktails in an outdoor patio, dancing in the Thunderdome, light dining in the Outback Café, and billiards and darts in the Boomerang Bar. Cover. ~ 296 North Stone Avenue; 602-622-4700.

Even if you don't plan to eat or drink, the **Solarium Restaurant and Lounge** is worth a visit just to see the architecture. The best description defies description, but the three-story wood structure is a cross between a ship and a greenhouse. Enter through large floral iron doors, and inside are lots of windows, plants and wood planks. An acoustical guitarist performs Thursday through Saturday. ~ 6444 East Tanque Verde Road; 520-886-8186.

The **Chicago Bar and Grill** offers a heady mix of music. There's rock-and-roll on Monday and Tuesday, reggae on Wednesday and Thursday, and blues on Friday, Saturday and Sunday. Chicago memorabilia covers the walls, from White Sox parking signs to hometown banners. Cover Wednesday through Saturday. ~ 5954 East Speedway Boulevard; 520-748-8169.

Berkey's Bar is another good place to hear the blues with live music all week long. An older crowd hangs out here, ordering drinks from the glass block bar, dancing and shooting pool. Cover on weekends. ~ 5769 East Speedway Boulevard; 520-296-1981.

Gentle Ben's Brewing Co. is a microbrewery near campus with delicious European-style ales. If you're there at the right time of the day, you can actually see workers brewing. This two-story building is furnished with recycled tables and chairs, and there's outdoor seating where you can see and be seen. There's live reggae and rock-and-roll Thursday through Saturday. Cover for live bands. ~ 865 East University Boulevard; 520-624-4177.

Laffs Comedy Café hosts everything from national to local acts. Tuesday is open mike night, Wednesday is ladies night and Thursday is college and military I.D. night. Cover. ~ 2900 East Broadway Boulevard; 520-323-8669.

Decorated with lots of oak and brass, **Suite 102** is where lawyers and other professionals meet. There's an outdoor dining area and background contemporary tunes. ~ 5350 East Broadway Boulevard; 520-745-9555.

Follow the cowboy hats and neon lights and you'll end up at **Cactus Moon**, a huge place specializing in country music. Western artwork hangs on the walls and rodeos roll on movie screens. A glittering, colored light shines on the dancefloor, which is big enough for two-steppers not to be toe-steppers. Weekend cover. ~ 5470 East Broadway Boulevard; 520-748-0049.

Cactus Moon is tiny compared to **A Little Bit of Texas**, a music hangout that sprawls over an entire acre. Inside are a country and a rock-and-roll bar, each with their own dancefloor. Around the perimeter of A Little Bit of Texas are stores selling items from cowboy hats to photographs. There is live music on occasion. Cover on weekends. ~ 4385 West Ina Road; 520-744-7744.

For live salsa and traditional jazz, stop by **Café Sweetwater**, a narrow bar squeezed next door to the restaurant of the same name. ~ 340 East 6th Street; 520-622-6464.

Trophies is a popular sports bar offering pool, darts, satellite TV and casual fare. ~ Hotel Park Tucson, 5151 East Grant Road; 602-323-6262.

Graffiti on the tables and walls is the decor at **Bob Dobbs' Bar & Grill**, a local hangout for the college and older crowd. A bright, noisy place, it has indoor and outdoor seating and plenty of televisions for catching the latest sports coverage. ~ 2501 East 6th Street; 520-325-3767.

◄ *HIDDEN*

For alternative music—and alternative crowds—peek into **Club Congress** adjoining the Hotel Congress. Tucson's unconventional set mixes with the college crowd at this cavernlike place with a red-and-brown-tile floor and dark walls. Cover. ~ 311 East Congress Street; 520-622-8849.

Tucson McGraws is a Mexican cantina with a bar and dining room serving steaks and ribs. Step outside, walk down the steps and you'll land on the terrace ramada that looks toward the Santa

Rita Mountains and Tucson's beautiful sunsets. An outdoor fireplace warms customers on cold evenings, and a guitarist entertains on weekends. ~ 4110 South Houghton Road; 520-885-3088.

THEATER   Arizona Theater Company has been unofficially called the State Theater of Arizona and performs six varied productions in Phoenix and Tucson from October to May. ~ 330 South Scott Avenue; 520-622-2823. Plays by the Arizona Theater Company and other groups are performed in the restored Spanish Colonial revival **Temple of Music and Art** in Tucson and the **Herberger Theater Center** in Phoenix.

Gaslight Theatre offers corny musical melodramas. Patrons eat free popcorn while hissing at the villain and cheering for the hero or heroine. Many of the comedies are original, written especially for the theater. ~ 7010 East Broadway Boulevard; 520-886-9428.

Invisible Theatre has classics, musicals and Off-Broadway plays by Arizona playwrights and contemporary dramatists from September through June. During the lunch hour they offer brown-bag play festivals. ~ 1400 North 1st Avenue; 520-882-9721.

OPERA, SYMPHONY AND DANCE   Ballet Arizona is the state's professional ballet company that performs in both Tucson and Phoenix. They perform a repertoire of classical and contemporary works including world and national premieres from September through April. ~ 520-882-5022.

Southern Arizona Light Opera Company performs four Broadway musicals a year at the Tucson Convention Center Music Hall September through May. ~ 908 North Swan Road; 520-323-7888.

Arizona Opera serves both Tucson and Phoenix and produces Grand Opera. The season runs from October through March, and productions have included *Don Giovanni*, *Otello* and *Madame Butterfly*. ~ 3501 North Mountain Avenue; 520-293-4336.

For classical, pops and chamber concerts there is the **Tucson Symphony Orchestra**. Performances run from September through May. ~ 443 South Stone Avenue; 520-792-9155.

Centennial Hall hosts a full lineup on an international scale, from Chinese acrobatics to African dances to Broadway shows. Past performers include Itzhak Perlman, the Prague Symphony Orchestra and George Winston. ~ University of Arizona, Building 29; 520-621-3341.

A professional modern dance company, **Tenth Street Danceworks** performs about four times a year and specializes in mixed media videography, or projecting video images on a screen or the dancers. ~ 3233 South Pinal Vista; 520-795-6980.

PARKS   **GENE C. REID PARK** 🚶 🚲 ⛵ This 131-acre park is a lush oasis in the desert with grassy expanses dotted with mature trees. There are a wide variety of recreational facilities here, including a recreation center, two golf courses, a swimming pool, pond, paddle boat rentals, tennis and racquetball courts and Hi-Corbett field where major league baseball teams come for spring training. Other attractions are Reid Park Zoo and a rose garden with more than 2000 plants. The park has restrooms, picnic tables and ramadas. ~ Located between Broadway Boulevard and 22nd Street, Country Club Road and Alvernon Way; 520-791-4873.

TUCSON MOUNTAIN PARK 🚶 🚲 🐎 Winding, hilly roads take you through this 20,000-acre, high-desert area brimming with ocotillo, palo verde, mesquite and saguaros and punctuated by mountains with rugged volcanic peaks. A popular spot is the Gates Pass overlook just past Speedway where you can pull off the road and get a panoramic view of Tucson, Avra Valley, Kitt Peak and watch Arizona's renowned sunsets. The park also includes the Arizona-Sonora Desert Museum and Old Tucson; there is an admission fee to both sites. There are established picnic areas throughout the park. The park also features archery and rifle ranges. (Archery hunting is allowed in season with proper permit.) ~ Located about ten miles west of the city limits off Gates Pass Road (no recreational vehicles are allowed on the road). Another entrance is on Kinney Road off Ajo Way; 520-740-2690.

▲ Gilbert Ray Campground has 160 sites, all with electric hookups; $7 per night for tents and $9 per night for RVs; information, 520-883-4200.

FORT LOWELL PARK 🚶 🏊 With its blend of history and recreation, Fort Lowell Park is an ideal family getaway. Fort Lowell was once a major military post and supply depot. Stroll between the trees on Cottonwood Lane, and you'll see a number of ruins, including that of the adobe post hospital built in 1875. Farther down is a museum in the reconstructed officers' quarters. The 59-acre park also has a pond with a fountain and plenty of hungry ducks around the perimeter, and a trail with marked exercise stops along the way. The park also includes tennis and racquetball courts, pool, picnic areas, lighted ball fields and shade ramadas. ~ Located at 2900 North Craycroft Road; 520-791-4873.

SAGUARO NATIONAL PARK Established to protect the saguaro cactus, found mainly in Arizona, the park is divided into two segments on opposite sides of Tucson. For general information, call 520-733-5100.

Rincon Mountain District 🚶 🚲 🐎 The more popular segment of Saguaro National Park is the Rincon Mountain District east of town, a 70,000-acre chunk established in 1933. Begin your tour at the visitors center, with dioramas and other exhibits of the geological and botanical history of the park. Then drive along Cactus Forest Drive, a scenic eight-mile-loop showing off tall saguaro cacti with their splayed arms. This district has more than 100 miles of hiking and equestrian trails. You'll also find picnic areas, restrooms and barbecue grills. ~ Drive east on Old Spanish Trail about three miles beyond city limits; visitors center: 520-733-5153.

Tucson Mountain District 🚶 🚵 🐎 The 20,738-acre Tucson Mountain District to the west has a newly expanded visitors center with orientations to the park, exhibits, maps and books, and features the six-mile-long Bajada Loop Drive that passes dense saguaro forests and American Indian petroglyphs. There are 12 miles of hiking and equestrian trails. Amenities include picnic areas, restrooms and barbecue grills. ~ Located two miles beyond the Arizona-Sonora Desert Museum off Kinney Road; visitors center: 520-733-5158.

SABINO CANYON RECREATION AREA 🚶 🚵 One of the most scenic spots in the region is a route that cuts through the Santa Catalina Mountains in the Coronado National Forest. You can either hike, bike or take the shuttle on a seven-and-a-half-mile round trip that climbs a road lined with cottonwoods, sycamores, ash and willow trees. Along the route flows Sabino Creek with its pools and waterfalls that tumble underneath arched stone bridges. The shuttle makes nine stops along the way, so you can jump on or off as you go. For the romantically inclined, the shuttle has moonlight rides during the full moon from April to June and September to December. The shuttle will also take you on the two-and-a-half-mile trip to Bear Canyon Trail, where you then hike two more miles to Seven Falls, which cascade almost 500 feet down the side of a hill. Facilities in the park are limited to restrooms and a visitors center. ~ Located at the north end of Sabino Canyon Road shortly before it dead-ends near the intersection with Sunrise Drive; general information, 520-749-8700 or shuttle information, 520-749-2327.

MOUNT LEMMON 🚶 🚵 🎿 In the hour's drive from Tucson to the top of Mount Lemmon, you travel from a lower Sonoran Desert zone to a Canadian zone forest, or from cacti to pine forests. For this reason, Tucsonans flock there in summer to escape the heat, and in winter to ski at Mount Lemmon Ski Valley, the southernmost ski area in the United States. If you take Catalina Highway to the top, the steep and winding mountain road will pass Rose Canyon Lake stocked with trout, and the town of Summerhaven with its handful of shops and restaurants. Once on Mount Lemmon, you can hike on 150 miles of trails. There are restrooms and picnic areas. ~ Mount Lemmon is within the Coronado National Forest. Drive east on Tanque Verde Road to Catalina Highway, then head north 30 miles to Summerhaven; 520-749-8700.

▲ There are tent and RV sites (no hookups) with toilets and drinking water at Rose and Spencer canyons; $9 per night. Molina

Basin has tent sites; $5 per night. General Hitchcock campground also has tent sites; no charge. Rose and Spencer canyons are closed in winter.

TOHONO CHUL PARK Few tourists know about this treasure hidden in northwest Tucson. But walk down the winding paths of the 37-acre park and you'll discover about 400 species of arid climate plants, many of which are labeled, along with water fountains, grotto pond areas and a greenhouse with plants for sale. In addition, you'll find an exhibit hall, two gift shops and a tea room as well as picnic tables, ramadas and restrooms. ~ Located off Route 89 at 7366 North Paseo del Norte, about six miles north of the Tucson city limits; 520-742-6455.

◀ HIDDEN

CATALINA STATE PARK 🚶🚴🐎 This 5500-acre preserve sits in the Santa Catalina foothills. Highlights include Romero Canyon, a beautiful area with clear pools shaded by sycamore and oak trees, and adjacent Pusch Ridge Wilderness, home to desert bighorn sheep. The Hohokam once farmed the area, and as you walk through the park you can still see some of the pit houses and ball court ruins. Facilities include restrooms, showers, picnic tables and grills; day-use fee, $3. ~ Off Route 77, about nine miles north of the city limits at 11570 North Oracle Road; 520-628-5798.

▲ Catalina State Park Campground has 48 tent and RV sites; $8 per night without hookups, $13 with hookups.

PICACHO PEAK STATE PARK 🚶 The most dramatic part of the park is Picacho Peak, a landmark formation that rises 1500 feet above the desert floor and can be seen for miles around. The peak is believed to be 22 million years old—or four times as old as the Grand Canyon—and was used as a landmark by early explorers. It was also the site of the battle of Picacho Pass during the Civil War. The 4000-acre park has seven miles of developed hiking trails that wind past saguaro cacti as well. Facilities include picnic areas, ramadas and restrooms; day-use fee, $3. ~ Located 40 miles north of Tucson just off Route 10; 520-466-3183.

▲ There are 85 sites ($8 per night) and 12 RV hookups ($13 per night).

▼▼▼▼▼▼▼▼▼
East of Tucson

The Wild West comes to life in this area of Arizona where murder and lynching were once considered leisure activities, poker was more popular than Sunday church services and whiskey was king. While this region is best known for infamous spots like Boot Hill and the O.K. Corral, it's also the home of historic mining towns like Bisbee, mineral spas and a cowboy hall of fame.

Get on Route 10 heading east and one of the first attractions you'll pass is **Colossal Cave**, one of the largest dry caverns in the world.

SIGHTS

Set in the Rincon Mountains, it was once home for Indians and outlaws. During 50-minute tours, hidden lights illuminate formations such as the Silent Waterfall and Kingdom of the Elves. Admission. ~ Off Old Spanish Trail in Vail; 520-647-7275.

HIDDEN ►

Farther east on Route 10 is Benson, where the **Arts & Historical Society** tells the story about how Benson grew along with the arrival of the railroad. Inside are antiques, artifacts and an old grocery store. A gift shop offers local arts and crafts. Closed Sunday and Monday. ~ 180 South San Pedro Street; 520-586-3070.

On your way to the Old West towns of Bisbee and Tombstone, take a detour toward Elgin. You will enter what at first seems an oxymoron—Arizona **wine country**. But there are several wineries out here, and it's a pretty drive through the vineyards.

HIDDEN ►

In the town of Elgin you'll find **The Chapel of the Blessed Mother, Consoler of the Afflicted**, a small chapel set amid grasslands, vineyards and cottonwood trees that is administered by the Monks of the Vine, a Wine Brotherhood of area vintners.

Head south on Route 90 and you can't miss **Fort Huachuca**, a National Historic Landmark founded in 1877 to protect settlers from Apache raiders. The Fort Huachuca soldiers eventually tracked down and defeated Apache leader Geronimo. Today, this 73,000-acre installation is home to the U.S. Army Intelligence Center. One highlight is the Fort Huachuca Museum, located in a turn-of-the-century building first used as a bachelor officers' quarters. Inside are military artifacts, dioramas and the history of the fort. For a panoramic view of the fort and town, drive up Reservoir Hill Road. If you'd prefer picnicking, there are plenty of scenic spots amid large, old trees. For a map, stop at the visitors center at the entrance. ~ Sierra Vista; 520-538-7111.

Take Route 92 south and you'll find a place known to birders worldwide. **Ramsey Canyon Preserve** is home to a variety of birds, including 14 species of hummingbirds from April to mid-September. Also commonly spotted here are white-tailed deer, gray squirrels and coati. The Nature Conservancy owns this 280-acre wooded gorge set in the Huachuca Mountains. The preserve is often full so call in advance for reservations. ~ Route 92, five miles south of Sierra Vista; 520-378-2785.

Hop on Route 90 again for the quick trip to **Bisbee** near the Mexican border. An old mining town and now an artists' enclave, the town is full of Victorian architecture perched on hillsides, along with funky shops and restaurants. For the full history of the town, start at the **Bisbee Mining & Historical Museum**, located in the former General Office Building of the Copper Queen Consolidated Mining Co. On the front lawn is old mining equipment, while inside the 1897 red-brick building are photo murals, artifacts and walk-in environments that highlight Bisbee's history. Admission. ~ 5 Copper Queen Plaza; 520-432-7071.

For a firsthand view of mining history, put on a slicker, hard hat and battery-pack light and hop on the underground train at the **Queen Mine Underground Tour**. An ex-miner narrates as he takes you through the Copper Queen Mine, which prospered for more than 60 years before it closed in 1944. The journey is a cool one, so bring a jacket. From here you can also take the **Lavender Open Pit Mine Tour**, a narrated, 13-mile bus tour around a 300-acre hole where more than 380 million tons of ore and waste have been removed. In conjunction with this, the **Historic District Tour** travels through the old section of Bisbee spotlighting such buildings as the Copper Queen Hotel and the Phythian Castle. Admission. ~ 478 North Dart Road, Bisbee; 520-432-2071.

Continue your time travel to the Old West at **Slaughter Ranch**, located near the Mexican border. Now a National Historic Landmark, it was once the home of John Slaughter, a former Texas Ranger, sheriff of Cochise County and one of the founders of Douglas. He bought the fertile grassland in 1884 and developed it into a cattle ranch. Slaughter's house and half a dozen other buildings furnished to reflect the era are still on the 140-acre site. Closed Monday and Tuesday. Admission. ~ Geronimo Trail, 16 miles east of Douglas; 520-558-2474.

Northwest of Douglas is **Tombstone**, the town too tough to die. Prospector Ed Shieffelin staked a silver claim there in 1877 and it became a Wild, Wild West town. Unfortunately, today the town is extremely touristy and every attraction is out to make a buck, but there are a few worthwhile stops.

The **Tombstone Courthouse** has a restored courtroom and two floors of historic exhibits that reflect the ups and downs of this once rowdy town. Now part of the Arizona State Park system, the red-brick building was the town's courthouse from 1882 until 1929. Admission. ~ 3rd and Toughnut streets, Tombstone; 520-457-3311.

A huge rosebush that spreads across 8000 feet of supports is the main attraction at the **Rose Tree Inn Museum**. Planted in 1885, the bush is an especially awesome sight if you come in spring when it's covered with white blossoms. You can also tour the historic adobe home with local artifacts and period rooms. Admission. ~ 4th and Toughnut streets, Tombstone; 520-457-3326.

Allen Street is the heart of Tombstone. At one end is the **Bird Cage Theatre**, a famous night spot in the late 1800s that is now a National Historic Landmark. Overlooking the gambling casino and dance hall are birdcage-like compartments where prostitutes plied their trade. Never a dull place, the theater was the site of 16 gunfights. If you bother to count you'll find 140 bullet holes riddling the walls and ceilings. Also, the longest poker game in the history of the West reputedly unfolded here . . . it lasted nine years. Is this an ace attraction or what? Admission. ~ 6th and Allen streets; 520-457-3421.

The most famous of Tombstone's many gunfights occurred in 1881 at **O.K. Corral** down the street from the Bird Cage. Lifesize figures stand in the corral as a narrator describes the shootout. An adjacent building showcases old Tombstone photos and other historic items. Admission. ~ Allen Street, Tombstone; 520-457-3456.

The losers of the shootout and other gunslingers lay buried at **Boot Hill Graveyard**. Enter the graveyard through the gift shop to see rows of graves—little more than piles of rocks with white metal crosses to mark them—as well as a spectacular view of the area. ~ Route 80 West, Tombstone; 520-457-9344.

Founded in 1880, the **Tombstone Epitaph** is still being published. In one corner of the newspaper office is the original press and other printing equipment. As residents say, every Tombstone should have an Epitaph. ~ 9 South 5th Street, Tombstone; 520-457-2211.

After looping off Route 10 to see Sierra Vista, Bisbee and Tombstone, get back to Route 10 and go east to Dragoon, home of the **Amerind Foundation** and little else. This is a real treasure tucked away amidst the rock formations of Texas Canyon. The research facility and museum have been devoted to American Indian culture and history since they opened in 1937. Visitors walk through the Spanish Colonial revival-style buildings to see American Indian pieces, such as beadwork, costumes, ritual masks and weapons, as well as Western artwork, including works by Frederic Remington and William Leigh. Closed Monday and Tuesday in summer. Admission. ~ Dragoon Road, Dragoon; 520-586-3666.

More Western history is farther east on Route 10 in Willcox at the **Museum of the Southwest** adjoining the Cochise Information Center. There's a bust of Chief Cochise, Indian artifacts and a mineral and rock collection. Open Sunday 1 to 5 p.m. ~ 1500 North Circle I Road, Willcox; 520-384-2272.

The most famous cowboy of the area was Rex Allen, born in Willcox in 1920. **The Rex Allen Arizona Cowboy Museum** features mementos of Rex Allen's life, from his homesteading and ranch life in Willcox to his movies and television shows. Another section features the pioneer settlers and ranchers of the West. Admission. ~ 155 North Railroad Avenue, Willcox; 520-384-4583.

LODGING   The majority of accommodations in Sierra Vista are along Fry Boulevard—the main commercial thoroughfare through town—and on South Route 92. **Sierra Suites** is a two-story, red-brick hotel that lures guests with complimentary breakfast. The 100 rooms face courtyards, and inside are mirrored sliding glass closet doors, glass tables, a chest of drawers, refrigerators and microwaves. The price includes use of the pool and whirlpool. ~ 391 East Fry Boulevard, Sierra Vista; 520-459-4221, fax 520-459-8449. MODERATE.

Thunder Mountain Inn is a two-story, beige-colored brick building with 102 rooms, a dining room, café and lounge. Lower-level guest rooms facing the pool have sliding-glass doors. Most accommodations have double beds and a desk. ~ 1631 South Route 92, Sierra Vista; 520-458-7900, 800-222-5811, fax 520-458-7900. MODERATE.

For a really secluded getaway, venture out to **Ramsey Canyon Inn** located in the Huachuca Mountains along a winding mountain stream and adjacent to the Nature Conservancy's Mile Hi/Ramsey Canyon Preserve and the Coronado National Forest. Accommodations consist of two cabins decorated in a rustic Southwest style and six rooms furnished with country antiques. ~ 31 Ramsey Canyon Road, Hereford; 520-378-3010, fax 520-378-0487. MODERATE TO DELUXE.

◄ *HIDDEN*

Built in 1917, **The Bisbee Inn** overlooks Brewery Gulch, once one of the Southwest's wildest streets. Each of the 18 rooms has handmade quilts on the beds, antique dressers with mirrors, and its own sink. Guests share bathrooms in the hall. This red-brick inn offers an all-you-can-eat breakfast. ~ 45 OK Street, Bisbee; 520-432-5131. BUDGET TO MODERATE.

School House Inn Bed & Breakfast is a large, restored, 1917 red-brick schoolhouse just above Garfield Park. The nine rooms are fairly large, and each has a private bath with a large tub. A full breakfast is served. ~ 818 Tombstone Canyon, Bisbee; 520-432-2996, 800-537-4333, fax 520-432-2996. BUDGET TO MODERATE.

The Copper Queen Mining Co. built the **Copper Queen Hotel** just after the turn of the century when it was a gathering place for politicians, mining officials and travelers, including the young Teddy Roosevelt. A plaque on one door marks the room where John Wayne stayed. The hotel is in the midst of an ongoing restoration, so ask for the restored rooms when you go. These are decorated Victorian style with floral wallpaper and tile bathrooms. The four-story building contains 45 guest rooms, along with the Copper Queen Saloon and Dining Room. ~ 11 Howell Avenue, Bisbee; 520-432-2216, 800-247-5829, fax 520-432-4298. MODERATE.

The **Bisbee Grand Hotel** is ideally located in the main shopping area in town. The original hotel was built in 1906. There are three suites and eight rooms; all rooms have private baths. All rooms reflect the era with floral wallpaper, red carpeting, brass beds and antiques. They also have sinks and ceiling fans. The rooms are upstairs, while downstairs is the old Western saloon, Victorian Ladies Lounge and billiards room. ~ 61 Main Street, Bisbee; 520-432-5900, 800-432-1909. MODERATE TO DELUXE.

The **Jonquil Motel** is a small motor court with seven clean, comfortable rooms. The rooms have televisions but no telephones. ~ 317 Tombstone Canyon, Bisbee; 602-432-7371. BUDGET.

Text continued on page 266.

Calling All
City Slickers!

Fueled by romantic images of Western heroes and desert sunsets and indulging in the fantasy of an escape to simpler times, more people than ever are opting to hang their saddles at dude ranches. In Southern Arizona, cowpokes have more than their fair share of choices. Guest ranches here range from resorts where you're more likely to overheat in the jacuzzi than the saddle, to working ranches where wranglers round 'em up and dine on beans and burgers. Whatever the orientation, most have horseback riding, a whole range of outdoor activities, and a casual, secluded atmosphere. Some are closed during the hot summer months, so call ahead.

One of the most luxurious getaways is **Tanque Verde Ranch**, which has been around since the 1880s. It comes complete with indoor and outdoor swimming pools, tennis courts, an exercise room and, of course, horseback riding. Guests stay in one of 65 *casitas* and patio lodges, some with beehive fireplaces, antiques and Indian bedspreads. Sliding glass doors offer stunning desert views. To relax, cozy up in the lobby with a good Western novel by the stone fireplace. ~ 14301 East Speedway Boulevard, Tucson; 520-296-6275, 800-234-3833, fax 520-721-9426. ULTRA-DELUXE.

White Stallion Ranch sprawls across 3000 acres—grazing land for their herd of Longhorn. Guests take breakfast rides, watch rodeos every Saturday afternoon, and pet deer, sheep and pygmy goats at the on-site zoo. Rooms at this ranch are rustic with Western decor. Closed May through October. ~ 9251 West Twin Peaks Road, Tucson; 520-297-0252, 800-782-5546, fax 520-744-2786. ULTRA-DELUXE.

Don't look for televisions or telephones inside the 23-room **Lazy K Bar Ranch**, because here you're meant to leave the outside world behind. Ranch-style meals are served in a dining room, and Saturday night is set aside for steak cookouts beside a waterfall. Afterward, you can relax in the comfortable library with wood paneling and beams, bookshelves, a fireplace and card table. Rooms are comfortable, carpeted and decorated in a Southwestern motif. ~ 8401 North Scenic Drive, Tucson; 520-744-3050, 800-321-7018, fax 520-744-7628. DELUXE.

Price Canyon Ranch in the Chiricahua Mountains is a working cattle ranch with one- and two-room bunk houses with baths. Meals are served in the 113-year-old main ranch house. Visitors can either ride on short trips or go on longer overnight pack trips for two to ten nights. Overnight trips require a month's notice and a party of four. Accommodations include meals and horseback riding. ~ Route 80 to 400-mile marker, go left at cattle guard into dirt road and drive seven miles, Douglas; 520-558-2383. DELUXE.

Grapevine Canyon Ranch offers accommodations in guest rooms with country-ranch furnishings and American Indian touches and include three meals. Visitors also lounge in the sitting room, a cozy place with a wood-beamed ceiling, Indian-design rugs and steer horns over the fireplace. At this working cattle ranch, horseback riding is the main attraction. ~ Highland Road, Pearce; 520-826-3185, 800-245-9202, fax 520-826-3636. ULTRA-DELUXE.

Rancho Santa Cruz Guest Ranch is a 112-acre ranch that opened in the 1920s. The ten adobe and stucco rooms are modest, but comfortable, and two of the three suites have fireplaces. A grassy courtyard with chairs beckons visitors to relax, as does the outdoor pool. ~ Off the Route 19 frontage road, Tumacacori; 520-281-8774. BUDGET TO MODERATE.

Circle Z Ranch in the foothills of the Santa Rita Mountains is a colorful, unpretentious place built in the early 1920s. It accommodates no more than 45 people at a time. The ranch's adobe cottages are decorated with brightly painted wicker furniture and Mexican crafts, but don't have TVs or telephones. Instead, recreation centers around the heated pool and tennis court and, in the evening, the lodge with its massive stone fireplace and bookshelves filled with classics, including Zane Grey titles. The ranch has a three-night minimum, and is open from November 1 through May 15. ~ P.O. Box 194, Patagonia; 520-394-2529. ULTRA-DELUXE.

Sitting in the foothills of Baboquivari Peak near the Mexican border, **Rancho De La Osa** is a 200-year-old Territorial-style ranch. Made of handmade adobe block, rooms have fireplaces and Indian and Spanish furnishings. Activities include riding purebred quarter horses and swimming, or sampling cocktails in the Cantina, an old Spanish/Indian mission. ~ 28201 West La Osa Ranch Road, Sasabe; 520-823-4257, 800-872-6240, fax 520-823-4238. DELUXE.

Another ranch of note is **Triangle T Guest Ranch**. ~ Dragoon Road, Dragoon; 520-586-7533. BUDGET TO MODERATE. **Rex Guest Ranch** is also worth checking out. ~ 131 East Mado Montoso Road, Amado; 520-398-2914, 800-547-2696, fax 520-398-9696. DELUXE TO ULTRA-DELUXE.

The Gadsden Hotel is a National Historic Monument that opened in 1907 as a hotel for cattlemen, miners and ranchers. Many of the hotel's 160 rooms have been furnished with period antiques, and the lobby is magnificent; there's a solid white Italian-marble staircase, four marble columns with capitals decorated in 14K gold leaf, and vaulted stained-glass skylights that run its length. Several Hollywood movies have been filmed here. Amenities include a lounge, dining room and coffee shop. ~ 1046 G Avenue, Douglas; 520-364-4481, fax 520-364-4005. BUDGET.

The eight-room Tombstone Boarding House Bed and Breakfast Inn is housed in an adobe building constructed around 1879. Rooms are tastefully decorated in pastel colors with lacy curtains and Victorian-era furnishings. A full breakfast is served in the country kitchen. ~ 108 North 4th Street, Tombstone; 520-457-3716, 520-457-3038. MODERATE.

DINING

HIDDEN ▶

Horseshoe Café is a family-owned restaurant that has been around for more than 50 years. On the walls are Western murals by artist Vern Parker, and the posts in the café display cattle brands of Southern Arizona. A neon horseshoe on the ceiling helps light the room. Entrées include chili, sandwiches, omelettes, burgers, steaks and Mexican specialties. ~ 154 East 4th Street, Benson; 520-586-3303. BUDGET.

Peking Chinese Cuisine is located in a small strip center with neon signs in the windows. The best deal here is an all-you-can-eat lunch buffet. The place is casual with red booths and tables, and Chinese-type lanterns and fans hanging from the ceiling. ~ 1481 East Fry Boulevard, Sierra Vista; 520-459-0404. BUDGET.

Speaking in relative terms, the Thunder Mountain Inn Restaurant is one of the more expensive places in town. Diners eat prime rib and seafood atop white tablecloths in booths divided by etched glass. ~ 1631 South Route 92, Sierra Vista; 520-458-7900. MODERATE TO DELUXE.

Fine Continental cuisine is the last thing you'd expect to find out here, but Karen's fits the bill. The menu changes weekly, but a typical entrée is grilled chicken breast stuffed with mozzarella and herbs, then covered with a sundried tomato sauce. ~ Route 82, Sonoita; 520-455-5282. MODERATE TO DELUXE.

Bisbee has a number of small eateries that almost defy description. One is Café 18 Steps which resembles a charming European café. There are just seven tables in this tiny restaurant. The menu is on a blackboard and features delicious homemade specialties such as shrimp and fennel pasta and trout with roasted garlic and pecans. Open for dinner on Saturday only. ~ 51 Main Street, Bisbee; 520-432-5155. BUDGET.

A sleek bistro-style restaurant designed to please urban cowboys, **Café Roka** offers a wide variety of flavorful pastas and house specialties such as smoked salmon with Gorgonzola. Open weekends only in the summer and Wednesday through Saturday the rest of the year. ~ 35 Main Street, Bisbee; 520-432-5153. MODERATE.

The **Renaissance Café** is a tiny, no-frills place where the locals hang out. Local artists' works hang on the walls, bulletins paper the front window, and a radio station plays in the background. There are a few tables inside, and a few out on the sidewalk. Offerings include sandwiches, hot bagel melts, pizza, salads and desserts as well as tasty coffee, espresso and herbal teas. ~ 10-A Lyric Plaza, Bisbee; 520-432-4020. BUDGET.

The **Nellie Cashman Restaurant** is housed in an 1879 building with decor to reflect the era including a stone fireplace, high wood ceilings and photos of bygone years. Although they serve sandwiches and burgers, they're best known for their homemade berry pies. ~ 121 South 5th Street, Tombstone; 520-457-2212. MODERATE.

If you're in the mood for the biggest hot dog in Cochise County, weighing in at half-pound and measuring a foot long, then saunter over to the **Longhorn Restaurant** and order a Longhorn Dog. If that's not what you crave, they offer a wide selection of Italian, Mexican and American food. The decor is Western with longhorns hanging over the door and yellowing wanted posters of characters such as Billy the Kid laminated on the tables. ~ 501 East Allen Street, Tombstone; 520-457-3405. BUDGET TO MODERATE.

SHOPPING

◄ *HIDDEN*

Singing Wind Bookshop is in the *really hidden* category. From Route 10, turn north on Ocotillo Road, then go for two-and-one-quarter miles and turn right on West Singing Wind Road until you see the chained green gate. Don't let it stop you—just open it and drive on in and down to the ranch house. Here, there are two huge rooms full of new books about the Southwest, Western Americana and other categories. ~ West Singing Wind Road and North Ocotillo Road, two-and-a-quarter miles north of Route 10, Benson; 520-586-2425.

In downtown Benson, **Zearings Mercantile Store** is a narrow, high-ceilinged place that has been around as long as anyone can remember. Inside you'll find guns, gifts, candies from around the world, relics and every imaginable kind of knickknack. ~ 305 East 4th Street, Benson; 520-586-3196. For trendier items, stop in **Kiva Gifts**, where they sell "a little bit of everything." Located next to the Chamber of Commerce, they have Southwestern, American Indian and Mexican arts, crafts and clothing, jams, jellies and honeys, books on the Southwest and so on. ~ 363 West 4th Street, Benson; 520-586-9706.

Head south to Sierra Vista and you'll discover **Misty's Gift Gallery**, one of the largest collectors' galleries in the Southwest with names that include Goebel, Hummel, Lladro, Gorham, De Grazia and Perillo. There is also a gallery with original artwork, lithographs and bronzes. ~ 228 West Fry Boulevard, Sierra Vista; 520-458-7208.

The **Johnson Gallery** is a huge place with a variety of imports including American Indian serigraphs, lithographs and etchings, American Indian masks, Tarahumara Indian artifacts, American Indian arts and Quezada family pottery. ~ 69 Main Street, Bisbee; 520-432-2126. **The Gold Shop** features innovative, contemporary jewelry created by about a dozen craftspeople from Bisbee and the Southwest. ~ 9 Howell Avenue, Bisbee; 520-432-4557.

Poco Loco features striking hand-painted dinnerware and other pottery plus Western collectibles, furniture and jewelry. ~ 81 Main Street, Bisbee; 520-432-7020.

Allen Street is the heart of shopping in Tombstone, where you'll find lots of souvenir shops mixed in with higher-quality jewelry and clothing stores. **Arlene's Southwest Silver & Gold** is a large place with American Indian jewelry and artwork including pottery, baskets, kachina dolls and rugs. ~ 404 Allen Street, Tombstone; 520-457-3344.

Gabe's Victorian Shop and Doll Museum is one of the oldest shops in Tombstone. The place is crammed full of dolls, dollhouse pieces, Victorian cards, collectibles and more than 150 paper dolls. In the back of the shop is a museum with dolls dating back to the 1830s. Admission to museum. ~ 312 Allen Street, Tombstone; 520-457-3419.

The **Territorial Bookstore** has a huge selection of titles on Wyatt Earp and the Old West. ~ 401 Allen Street, Tombstone; 520-457-3170.

Looking for antique African clamshell discs, camel bone beads or yak bone beads handcarved in Pakistan? Even if you aren't, the **Tombstone Bead Co.** has them, and one of the largest selections of beads in the country. They import from all over the world and also make their own beads. ~ 416 Allen Street, Tombstone; 520-457-2323.

Medicine Bow has leathers and Western wear including handmade belts, hats, buckles and knives. ~ 509 Allen Street, Tombstone; 520-457-3805.

Near the tiny ghost town of Gleeson, you'll find rattlesnake regalia galore at **John & Sandy's Rattlesnake Crafts**. Hatbands and belts made from the hide, and jewelry made from the vertebrae are just a few of the items created from the rattler that this amazing little store carries. The owners do all the hunting and craftwork themselves. ~ 15 miles east of Tombstone on Gleeson Road; 520-642-9207.

The time to travel out to the Willcox area is fall, when farms and roadside stands are selling their produce. The Willcox Chamber of Commerce has a brochure listing 27 orchards and mills where you can stop. One is **Stout's Cider Mill**, where you can buy apples, cider, dried fruit, nuts, peaches, apple pies, chile peppers and Arizona desert preserves. ~ 1510 North Circle I Road, Willcox; 520-384-3696.

NIGHTLIFE

◄ HIDDEN

Arena Bar & Rodeo Grounds overlooks the rodeo grounds—a plus when there's something to watch, but that's not too often. Inside a Western theme dominates. A lasso hangs on the door, cow skulls decorate walls, and you can warm yourself by the big rock fireplace. There are also a pool table and dancefloor, along with outdoor picnic benches. ~ 250 North Prickly Pear Street, Benson; 520-586-9983.

Established in 1902, **St. Elmo Bar and Grill** in historic Bisbee is a tradition around here. Memorabilia such as old maps hang on the walls, and seating is mainly stools at the counter. On weekends there's live music and dancing. Entertainment during the week is supplied by the CD jukebox or pool tables and dart board. ~ 36 Brewery Avenue, Bisbee; 520-432-5578.

Adjoining the Copper Queen Hotel, the **Copper Queen Saloon** is a small, dark, intimate place with some turn-of-the-century furnishings and live music on weekends. ~ 11 Howell Avenue, Bisbee; 520-432-2216.

At the **Stock Exchange Bar**, almost one whole wall is covered with an original board from the New York stock exchange. This historic building has a pressed tin roof and worn wooden floors. There's live rock and blues every weekend. Downstairs is the Brewery Restaurant. ~ 15 Brewery Avenue, Bisbee; 520-432-9924.

Walk through swinging doors of **Big Nose Kate's Saloon** and you step back into the Old West. Waitresses dressed as saloon gals serve drinks in the same place where Lily Langtry and Wyatt Earp once tipped their glasses. Lighted, stained-glass panels depict Tombstone's characters, and old photographs hang on the walls. On weekends you'll find live country-and-western music and skits of Western brawls. ~ 417 East Allen Street, Tombstone; 520-457-3107.

At one time, Tombstone reputedly had saloons and gambling halls making up two of every three buildings.

The Crystal Palace Saloon has been restored to look like it did when it was built in the 1880s. The long, narrow room has old wood tables and red drapes underneath a copper ceiling. Live music is performed every day except Monday. ~ 420 East Allen Street, Tombstone; 520-457-3611.

Johnny Ringo's Saloon is a historic, intimate bar where the main attraction is the collection of more than 600 military patches on the walls. ~ 404 Allen Street, Tombstone; 520-457-3961.

PARKS

CHIRICAHUA NATIONAL MONUMENT 🏃 The Chiricahua Apaches called this area the Land of the Standing-Up Rocks because throughout the park are huge rock spires, stone columns and massive rocks perched on small pedestals. Geologists believe that these formations were created as a result of explosive volcanic eruptions. For an overview of the park, drive up the winding, eight-mile-long Bonita Canyon Drive. You'll pass pine and oak-juniper forests before reaching Massai Point at the top of the Chiricahua Mountains where you can see the park, valleys and the peaks of Sugarloaf Mountain and Cochise Head. You can also explore the park on foot via about 20 miles of trails. Other attractions include historic Faraway Ranch and Stafford Cabin. There are picnic tables, restrooms and a visitors center with exhibits; day-use fee, $4. ~ From Willcox, go east on Route 186 for 35 miles; 520-824-3560.

▲ There are 24 sites; $7 per night. No backcountry camping is allowed within the monument.

▼▼▼▼▼▼▼▼▼▼▼▼▼▼
South/West of Tucson

Far off the beaten track, southwestern Arizona is home to the world's leading astronomical center, remote ghost towns, wildlife preserves and a sanctuary dedicated to the unusual organ pipe cactus. This is also where civilization disappears and the desert blooms.

SIGHTS

Heading south on Route 19, you will pass the retirement community of Green Valley and arrive at the **Titan Missile Museum**, the only intercontinental ballistic missile complex in the world that's open to the public. Here you'll be taken on a one-hour guided tour into the bowels of the earth, experience a countdown launch of a Titan missile and view a silo. It's an eerie excursion. Closed Monday and Tuesday in summer. Admission. ~ 1580 West Duval Mine Road; 520-791-2929.

To get away from the high-tech missiles and delve deeper into the area's history, continue farther south on Route 19 to Tubac. Here, the Spanish founded a presidio in 1752 to protect settlers from the Indians. At **Tubac Presidio State Historic Park** visitors can see the remains of the original presidio foundation, the foundation of the Spanish captain's house from the military garrison in 1750, an 1885 schoolhouse and a museum detailing the history of Tubac. Admission. ~ Route 19, 520-398-2252.

A few more minutes down Route 19 are the adobe ruins of a Spanish frontier mission church at the **Tumacacori National Historical Park**. Along with the museum, visitors walk through the baroque church, completed in 1822, and the nearby ruins, such as a circular mortuary chapel and graveyard. Since little has been built in the vicinity, walking across the grounds feels like a walk back in time. Admission. ~ Route 19, Exit 29, Tumacacori; 520-398-2341.

Continuing south, Route 19 hits the Mexican border. **Nogales, Mexico,** is a border town offering bargain shopping, restaurants and some sightseeing. On the other side is Nogales, Arizona. Photographs and artifacts detail the town's history at the **Pimeria Alta Historical Society Museum,** a 1914 mission-style building that once housed the city hall, police and fire departments. Closed Monday and Tuesday. ~ 136 North Grand Avenue; 520-287-4621.

Just off of Route 82 you'll pass by some **ghost towns,** including Harshaw and Duquesne. **Duquesne** was a mining center established around the turn of the century with a peak population of 1000 residents, including Westinghouse of Westinghouse Electric. **Harshaw** was settled around 1875 and operated about 100 mines. Today all that's left are ruins and graveyards. Some of the roads en route are extremely rugged and bumpy, so be prepared.

◄ *HIDDEN*

Tucson and the surrounding area is known as the Astronomy Capital of the World with more astronomical observatories than anywhere else. One of the most famous is the **Kitt Peak National Observatory.** Drive up a mountain road and you'll come across the observatory's gleaming white domes and its 21 telescopes. During tours you can step inside some of the telescopes, including the 18-story-high four-meter telescope. There's also a museum with exhibits on the observatory. If you're planning on staying awhile, bring food—it's a long haul up the mountain and there's nothing to nibble on at the top. ~ Located 56 miles southwest of Tucson off Route 386; 520-318-8600.

Continuing to the west about 100 miles on Route 85 you'll come to **Ajo,** a small scenic town whose center is a green plaza surrounded by Spanish Colonial-style buildings. It is also an old copper mining town and as such shows its scars. The **New Cornelia Copper Mine** is one of the largest open-pit copper mines in the world, stretching a full mile in diameter. Although operations ceased in 1984, you can go to the pit lookout and learn about mining operations at the adjacent visitors center. Closed Saturday and Sunday. ~ La Mina Road; 520-387-7451.

From the mine you can see the **Ajo Historical Society Museum** located in what was once St. Catherine's Indian Mission, a stucco church built in 1942. Inside are artifacts from Ajo's history, including a blacksmith shop, dentist's office, printing shop and American Indian artifacts such as old saddles found on graves. ~ 160 Mission Street, Ajo; 520-387-7105.

From Ajo, drive north on Route 85 until you reach Route 8; proceed west and you'll eventually hit Wellton. Don't blink, or you'll miss the **McElhaney Cattle Company Museum** with its amusing collection of antiquities including buggies, carriages, a popcorn wagon, an old hearse, several stagecoaches, a fire wagon and antique cars. Closed Sunday. ~ Avenue 34; 520-785-3384.

◄ *HIDDEN*

Much farther west, near the California border, is **Yuma**. Once a steamboat stop and major crossing on the Colorado River, today it's a bustling city that supports farming and basks in a subtropical climate. The first major construction here was the **Yuma Territorial Prison**, a penitentiary built between 1876 and 1909 and now a state historic park. Known as the Hell-hole of Arizona, life inside the walls were rough, and prisoners who escaped were faced with hostile deserts and the currents of the Colorado River. Today visitors walk through the gloomy cells and climb the guard tower, where one can see the Colorado River and surrounding area. Admission. ~ 1 Prison Hill Road; 520-783-4771.

For an excursion on the Colorado River, try a jetboat tour. **Yuma River Tours** offers rides past petroglyphs, homesteads, steamboat landings and mining camps. ~ 1920 Arizona Avenue; 520-783-4400.

Just across the river from the prison is **The Quechan Indian Museum**, one of the oldest military posts in the area. Currently it is headquarters for the Quechan Indian Tribe and houses their artifacts. Closed Sunday. Admission. ~ Indian Hill Road, Yuma; 619-572-0661.

The military supply hub for the Arizona Territory was the **Yuma Crossing Quartermaster Depot**, which served the Southwest until it closed in 1883. Several of the original buildings remain, including the commanding officer's quarters and Office of the Quartermaster. Costumed interpreters provide tours of the complex. Admission. ~ 201 North 4th Avenue, Yuma; 520-329-0404.

More of Yuma's history comes to light in the **Arizona Historical Society Century House Museum**. Once the home of pioneer merchant E. F. Sanguinetti, it now has artifacts, photographs and furnishings of Arizona's territorial period. Just outside are colorful gardens and aviaries with exotic birds. ~ 240 South Madison Avenue; 520-782-1841.

The **Yuma Art Center** features changing exhibits by contemporary Southwestern artists. Closed Sunday. ~ 377 Main Street; 520-783-2314.

LODGING   Located in Madera Canyon, **Santa Rita Lodge Nature Resort** is a perfect birders' getaway. Just outside the large windows in each of the 12 rooms are feeders that attract a number of bird species. Inside the rooms, charts hang with pictures of different types of hummingbirds. The lodge also offers nature programs that meet in the patio area, and staff birders will take guests on birding walks. ~ Located 13 miles southeast of Green Valley in the Coronado National Forest; 520-625-8746, fax 520-648-1186. MODERATE.

Bing Crosby founded the **Tubac Golf Resort** back in 1959. The 33 rooms and suites have wood-burning fireplaces, Mexican furniture, tiled bathrooms and patios facing the mountains. The resort has a golf course, tennis court, pool and spa, hiking trails and a full service restaurant and bar. ~ 1 Avenida de Otero, Tubac; 520-398-2211, 800-848-7893, fax 520-398-9261. DELUXE.

Rio Rico Resort & Country Club is a beautiful resort in the Cayetano Mountain range. Many of the rooms have wood-beamed ceilings, sliding glass doors overlooking the pool or mountains, and contemporary Southwestern decor in pastel colors. Amenities include a golf course, horse stables, jacuzzi, exercise room, restaurant and lounge. ~ 1069 Camino Caralampi, Rio Rico; 520-281-1901, 800-288-4746, fax 520-281-7132. DELUXE.

The Stage Stop Inn is a 43-room hotel with a restaurant and clean, comfortable rooms (some with kitchenettes) facing the pool in the middle. Movie casts and crew often stay here while filming in the area. The Western lobby showcases a moose skull above the fireplace, cattle brands on the tile floor and Western paintings on the walls. ~ 303 McKeown Avenue, Patagonia; 520-394-2211. BUDGET.

A tiny treasure, **The Little House** offers a guesthouse with two rooms. Each has a sitting area with corner fireplace, a private bath and patio, and contemporary Southwestern furnishings. Guests are invited for complimentary continental or full breakfasts with eggs, sausage, fruits and breads. ~ 341 Sonoita Avenue, Patagonia; 520-394-2493. MODERATE.

◄ **HIDDEN**

Looking like a miniature dollhouse, **The Guest House Inn** is a charming white house with blue trim and a long front porch dotted with white wicker furniture for lazing away the hours. Phelps Dodge once entertained dignitaries here, and breakfast is now served on the 20-foot-long walnut dining table where these guests once ate. Inside the setup is unusual, with a living room in the middle and guest rooms lining either side of the house. Each of the four bedrooms has a private bath and its own decorating scheme. ~ 3 Guest House Road, Ajo; 520-387-6133. MODERATE.

Located atop the highest hill in Ajo, **The Mine Manager's House Inn** was built in 1919 for the mine manager's family. You can see the mine from the house, and inside old photos of the mine hang in the cozy living room. Instead of reflecting the house's history, room furnishings are modern. But breakfast is served at the huge pecan table original to the house. During free time, stop in the reading room or soak in the outdoor hot tub. ~ 1 Greenway Drive, Ajo; 520-387-6505, fax 520-387-6508. MODERATE TO DELUXE.

Built during the space races with the Russians, the theme at the **Best Western Space Age Lodge** is obvious. Guest rooms have pictures of rockets blasting off into space and contain whitewashed wood furniture, pastel colors and large, well-lighted mirrors above the counter. There's also a pool and coffee shop. ~ 401 East Pima Street, Gila Bend; 520-683-2273, 800-528-1234, 520-683-2273. MODERATE.

La Fuente Inn has 96 Southwest-style rooms decorated in pastels. Rooms face the grassy interior courtyard and pool. Prices include a complimentary continental breakfast, happy hour and use of the fitness room. ~ 1513 East 16th Street, Yuma; 520-329-1814, 800-841-1814, fax 520-343-2671. MODERATE.

DINING

HIDDEN ▶

Even though there's not much in Amado, it's worth a stop to eat at **The Cow Palace**, a local landmark that has been around since the 1920s. While in town to shoot movies, Western stars have frequented the place, and their photos hang on the walls. Decor is rustic Western, with a wagon wheel for a chandelier and red tablecloths, carpet and curtains. Entrées carry on the theme with names such as The Trail Boss porterhouse steak and Chuck Wagon barbecue beef sandwich. ~ 28802 South Nogales Road, Amado; 520-398-2201. BUDGET TO MODERATE.

If you've never dined in a 150-year-old horse stable, stop in at **The Montura** restaurant at The Tubac Golf Resort. Actually, the place is quite nice. Inside are arched windows, cobblestone floors and pottery made by Mexicans and American Indians. Look closely and you might find Apache Indian arrowheads embedded in the restaurant's adobe walls. Dinner focuses on steak, pasta, seafood and Mexican specialties with a Southwestern twist. ~ 1 Avenida de Otero, Tubac; 520-398-2211. MODERATE.

Opened in the 1940s as a coffee shop in someone's home, **Wisdom's Café** is now a restaurant crammed with old photographs, farming tools, velvet paintings, patchwork rugs and other odds and ends. You can spot it on the road by the two gigantic imitation chickens in front. If you can get by the chickens, try some of their Mexican food. Closed Sunday. ~ Route 19 frontage road, Tumacacori; 520-398-2397. BUDGET.

San Cayetano in the Rio Rico Resort & Country Club offers Southwestern cuisine as well as a Sunday champagne brunch. Two walls have floor-to-ceiling windows with panoramic views of the mountains. The interior has tables and booths decorated in blue, tan and maroon to fit a casual Southwestern look. ~ 1069 Camino Caralampi, Rio Rico; 520-281-1901. MODERATE.

HIDDEN ▶

Home Plate is a greasy spoon where the locals meet to chow down on burgers and hot and cold sandwiches. Civic-club banners circle the room and partially cover the brick walls. Open for breakfast and lunch only. ~ 277 McKeown Avenue, Patagonia; 520-394-2344. BUDGET.

The dining room at the **Stage Stop Inn** has the hotel's Western theme with cattle brands on the floors and a chuckwagon containing a salad bar. Other offerings are sandwiches, hamburgers, steaks, Mexican food and homemade desserts. ~ 303 McKeown Avenue, Patagonia; 520-394-2211. BUDGET TO MODERATE.

Although the exterior of **Dago Joe's** is rather plain, the owners have livened up the interior with contemporary decor—framed posters, plants, and a peach-accent wall with matching tablecloths. The menu is varied, but they're known for steaks. Closed Tuesday. ~ 2055-A North Route 85, Ajo; 520-387-6904. MODERATE.

A Yuma tradition for more than a decade, **Hensley's Beef Beans and Beer** is the place for prime rib, lobster and hamburgers. Dishes are served amid walls covered with cowboy pictures and cow horns. ~ 2855 South 4th Avenue, Yuma; 520-344-1345. MODERATE.

About 80 shops and restaurants make up the town of **Tubac**. Although it's geared to tourists, they've managed to avoid the rubber-tomahawk syndrome and you'll find high-quality artwork. All of the shops are within walking distance and are evenly distributed along Tubac Road, Plaza Road and Calle Otero.

SHOPPING

Tortuga Books, known throughout the Southwest, specializes in philosophy, psychology, children's books, Southwestern literature, greeting cards, CDs and cassettes. ~ 19 Tubac Road, Tubac; 520-398-2807. **The Pot Shop Gallery** features signed lithographs by R. C. Gorman, as well as prints, pottery and clay artwork created by Arizona artisans. ~ 16 Tubac Road, Tubac; 520-398-2898. The **Chile Pepper** and **Chile Pepper, Too!** offer Southwestern gourmet foods, chile food products, chile wreaths, coffees, teas, clothing and jewelry. ~ 201 Tubac Road, Tubac; 520-398-2921. For handcrafted American Indian jewelry, kachinas, sandpaintings, baskets and pottery, stop in **Old Presidio Traders**. ~ 27 Tubac Road, Tubac; 520-398-9333.

Owned and operated by American Indians, **Cloud Dancer Jewelry Studio** offers custom-designed jewelry with turquoise and precious gems in gold, silver and platinum settings. ~ 4 Tubac Road; 520-398-2546.

To shop in the older, more historic section of town, go to Calle Iglesia. In this area you'll find **Hugh Cabot Studios & Gallery** housed in a 250-year-old adobe building that used to be a hostelry for Spanish soldiers. This internationally known artist creates Southwestern and general-interest works in several mediums and makes his home in Tubac. ~ Calle Iglesia, Tubac; 520-398-2721.

A handful of shops line the main street in Patagonia, including **Southwest Silver and Gold**. The specialty here is silver jewelry, including earrings somehow made out of snowflakes using silver as a medium. They also offer jewelry crafted with local materials such as turquoise, malachite, azurite and Patagonia red jasper. ~ 520-394-2033.

◄ *HIDDEN*

Housed in a long, narrow, 1916 building on the Plaza, **Kliban's Variety Store Inc.** offers an eclectic mix of hardware, clothing, baby stuff and old knickknacks. ~ 29 Plaza, Ajo; 520-387-6421.

Another Ajo stop is the **Ajo Art Gallery** with a mixture of contemporary paintings by artists from across the United States. ~ 661 North 2nd Avenue, Ajo; 520-387-7525.

NIGHTLIFE Scenic mountain views from picture windows draw people to **Calabasas Lounge** at the Rio Rico Resort & Country Club. The contemporary, Southwest-style bar has live Top-40, jazz and dance music on weekends. ~ 1069 Camino Caralampi, Rio Rico; 520-281-1901.

Lutes Casino is one of the oldest continually owned and operated pool and domino parlors in the state. Open since 1920, the place is crammed full of farm implements, paintings and historic memorabilia. ~ 221 Main Street, Yuma; 520-782-2192.

PARKS **PATAGONIA LAKE STATE PARK** The largest recreational lake in Southern Arizona (265 acres) is located in this park. Patagonia Lake, nestled amid rolling hills, was created by the damming of Sonoita Creek in 1968. It's stocked with bass, crappie, catfish, bluegill and, in the winter, trout. A small, sandy beach lures swimmers. You can windsurf here although it's not allowed on weekends from May through October. Because of its elevation of 3750 feet, the 645-acre park sometimes offers temperatures cooler than Tucson. The park provides picnic areas, restrooms, showers and a marina with boat rentals; day-use fee, $5. ~ Located off Route 82 about 12 miles north of Nogales. Follow the signs to the park; 520-287-6965.

▲ There are 119 sites, including 34 RV hookups and 13 accessible by boat only; hookups are $15 per night, all other sites $10 per night.

PATAGONIA SONOITA CREEK PRESERVE Nine miles north of Patagonia Lake State Park is a 312-acre sanctuary in a narrow flood plain between the Santa Rita and the Patagonia mountains. This preserve encompasses a one-and-a-half mile stretch of Sonoita Creek lined with large stands of cottonwoods—some a hundred feet tall—as well as Arizona walnut, velvet ash, willows and Texas mulberry. Birdwatchers from all over the world come here because more than 200 species of birds have been seen. It is also home to white-tailed deer, bobcat, javelina, coyotes and the most endangered fish in the Southwest, the Gila Topminnow. Closed Monday and Tuesday. There are no facilities in the park; groceries are available in nearby Patagonia. ~ From Patagonia, turn northwest off Route 82 onto 4th Avenue, then go left on Pennsylvania Avenue. When the pavement ends, cross the creek and follow the dirt road for two miles. There will be an entrance with the visitors center on your left; 520-394-2400.

CORONADO NATIONAL FOREST The Coronado National Forest in Arizona has 1.7 million acres of public land in 12 sky islands, or mountain ranges that jut above the surrounding desert. Following are three of the highlights:

Madera Canyon 🚶 🚲 🐎 This spot is a great place for bird-watching, with more than 200 species including several varieties of woodpeckers, hawks, wrens and vultures. Driving up through the canyon the desert changes from grassland to forest. Trees on the lower slopes of the Santa Rita Mountains are mesquite, and farther up are live oaks, alligator junipers, cottonwoods and syca-mores along Madera Creek. There are more than 70 miles of trails. You'll find restrooms, picnic areas and grills; day-use fee, $5. ~ Located 49 miles south of Tucson. Take Route 19 south from Tucson to Green Valley's Continental Road, then go southeast for 13 miles; 520-281-2296.

▲ There are 13 sites at Bog Springs Campground; $5 per night per vehicle.

Pena Blanca Lake 🚶 🐎 🚤 🛥 🎣 This is a 49-acre lake sur-rounded by oak, cottonwood and mesquite trees and light-colored bluffs. The lake is situated at 4000 feet—making it higher and somewhat cooler than Tucson. Fishing is good for bass, bluegill, crappie, catfish and rainbow trout. A trail leads around the lake. Also located here are picnic areas, restrooms and picnic tables. Pena Blanca Lake Resort (520-281-2800) has a lodge, restaurant, fishing supplies and boat rentals. ~ Located five miles north of the Mexican border. Take Route 19 south from Tucson to Ruby Road, then go west for about nine miles; 520-281-2296.

▲ There are 13 sites at White Rock Campground (a quarter-mile from the lake), although there are no lake views; $5 per night per vehicle.

Parker Canyon Lake 🚤 🛥 🎣 Parker Canyon Lake is an 130-acre fishing lake west of the Huachuca Mountains and surrounded by grassy, rolling hills. Bluegill, bass, perch, trout and catfish are the common catches. To assist with the fishing there are boat rentals, bait and a fishing dock. There are also restrooms, picnic areas and a grocery store; day-use fee is $5. ~ From Sonoita, take Route 83 south for 30 miles until it runs into the park; 520-378-0311.

▲ There are 64 sites and an overflow area in the summer that accommodates 50 to 75 self-contained vehicles; $8 per night.

ORGAN PIPE CACTUS NATIONAL MONUMENT 🚶 🚲 This 330,000-acre refuge became a national monument in 1937 to pro-tect the Sonoran desert plants and animals and the unique organ pipe cactus. Start at the visitors center 17 miles south of the north-ern entrance. Here you can see exhibits and pick up a self-guided tour pamphlet. A good tour is the Puerto Blanco Scenic Drive, a

53-mile graded dirt loop with numbered stops described on the tour. The only paved road through the park is Route 85. While exploring the monument, you'll pass mountains, plains, canyons, dry washes and a pond surrounded by cottonwood trees. Picnic areas and restrooms are the only facilities in the park. Groceries are in Lukeville, five miles south; day-use fee, $4. ~ The monument is located 35 miles south of Ajo, and the visitors center is at the 75-mile marker on Route 85; 520-387-6849.

▲ There are 208 sites in the main campground; $8 per night. Fresh water is available at the dump station and at the visitors center. Primitive camping is allowed at four sites in the Alamo campground and anywhere in the backcountry as long as you're a half mile from the road; you can pick up the free permits for backcountry camping at the visitors center.

CABEZA PRIETA NATIONAL WILDLIFE REFUGE Established in 1939 to protect wildlife and wildlife habitat, the 860,000-acre refuge is an arid wilderness rife with cactus and mountains. Passing through the park is the 250-mile El Camino del Diablo (Highway of the Devil) that was pioneered by Spanish Conquistador Captain de Anza in 1774—and stretches from Mexico to California. Along the way you pass Cabeza Prieta Mountain with its lava-topped granite peak, and Mohawk Valley with sand dunes and lava flows. Since roads here are rugged and unimproved, four-wheel-drive vehicles are required. Also, beware of the six species of rattlesnakes. Limited hunting for desert bighorn sheep is allowed. There are no facilities in the refuge; the closest groceries are in Ajo, seven miles east. The refuge is sometimes closed for military use or inclement weather; call ahead to see if it's open. ~ You'll need explicit directions, which you can get when you pick up the Refuge Entry Permit at the refuge office in Ajo (611 North 2nd Avenue). It's advisable to call ahead; 520-387-6483.

▲ There are three primitive campgrounds with no facilities; no wood fires allowed; no water. Permit required.

▼▼▼▼▼▼▼▼▼▼▼▼▼▼
Outdoor Adventures

BOATING

Although water isn't plentiful in Southern Arizona, there are a few lakes where boats are available to rent.

TUCSON You can rent paddle boats in Tucson at **Gene C. Reid Park**. ~ Between Broadway Boulevard and 22nd Street, Country Club and Alvernon Way, Tucson; 520-791-4560.

EAST OF TUCSON Boat rentals are available at **Parker Canyon Lake**. ~ Off of Route 83, 30 miles southwest of Sierra Vista; 520-455-5847.

SOUTH/WEST OF TUCSON **Patagonia Lake State Park** offers boat rentals. ~ Patagonia; 520-287-6965. **Pena Blanca Lake** also has boats for rent. ~ Off Route 289, Nogales; 520-281-2800.

For a retreat from the heat take a plunge at one of Southern Arizona's public pools.

SWIMMING

TUCSON Fort Lowell Park has a pool. ~ 2900 North Craycroft Road; 520-791-2585. Dive in at **Himmel Park**. ~ 1000 North Tucson Boulevard; 520-791-4157. Get wet at **Morris K. Udall Park**. ~ 7200 East Tanque Verde Road; 520-791-4004. **Joaquin Murieta Park** has a public pool. ~ 1400 North Silverbell Road; 520-791-4752. Cool yourself down in **Jacobs Park**'s pool. ~ 1010 West Lind; 520-791-4358.

For those without a fear of heights, there's nothing like floating above it all. Ballooning is a great way to escape the heat and get a magnificent view at the same time.

BALLOON RIDES

TUSCON To see Tucson from on high, call **A Balloon Experience**. ~ 15115 North Airport Drive, Scottsdale; 602-820-3866. **A Southern Arizona Balloon Excursion** also ascends from the Tucson area. ~ 520-624-3599. A third company hovering above is **Balloon America**. ~ 520-299-7744.

There's only one place to ski in these parts—the **Mount Lemmon Ski Valley**. The southernmost ski-area in North America, Mount Lemmon offers 15 runs, equipment rental, ski school and restaurant. ~ Mount Lemmon; 520-576-1400.

SKIING

If you prefer to let someone else do the walking, there are several horseback riding outfitters in the area.

RIDING STABLES

TUCSON A Western town like Tucson wouldn't be the same without opportunities to go riding. Dudes and dudettes can saddle up at **Desert-High Country Stables Inc**. ~ 6501 West Ina Road; 520-744-3789. You'll be riding high at **El Conquistador Stables**. ~ 10000 North Oracle Road; 520-742-4200. Mount a steed at **Pusch Ridge Stables**. ~ 13700 North Oracle Road; 520-297-6908. Saddle up at **Pantano Riding Stables**. ~ 4450 South Houghton Road; 520-298-9076. Get into the Western spirit at **Wild Horse Ranch Resort**. ~ 6801 North Camino Verde; 520-744-1012.

SOUTH/WEST OF TUCSON *Montar a caballo* at **Rio Rico Stables**. ~ 320 Stable Lane, Rio Rico; 520-281-7072.

Mild winters make this region ideal for golfers, and aficionados can choose between a wide range of private and public courses.

GOLF

TUCSON In the Tucson area, try **Tucson National Golf Club**. ~ 2727 West Club Drive; 520-575-7540. Swing your clubs under the sunny skies at **Starr Pass Golf Club**. ~ 3645 West Starr Boulevard; 520-622-6060. Create your own version of the Skins Game at **Sun City Vistoso Golf Club**. ~ 1495 East Rancho Vistoso Boulevard, Tucson; 520-825-3110. Work on your game at **Randolph Golf**

Course. ~ 600 South Alvernon Way; 520-791-4161. Improve your handicap at **El Conquistador Country Club–Sunrise Course**. ~ 10555 North La Canada Drive; 520-544-1800. Be the best that you can be at **Dorado Golf Course**. ~ 6601 East Speedway Boulevard; 520-885-6751. Go for a hole in one at the **Arthur Pack Desert Golf Course**. ~ 9101 North Thornydale Road; 520-744-3322. Play the manicured greens at **Ventana Canyon Golf & Racquet Club**. ~ 6200 North Club House Lane; 520-577-1400. Beware the hazards at **Cliff Valley Golf Course**. ~ 5910 North Oracle Road; 520-887-6161. Tee off at **El Rio Golf Course**. ~ 1400 West Speedway Boulevard; 520-791-4229. Take aim at the greens at **Fred Enke Golf Course**. ~ 8251 East Irvington Road; 520-296-8607. Pitch and putt at **Silverbell Golf Course**. ~ 3600 North Silverbell Road; 520-791-5235.

EAST OF TUCSON A prime golfing spot east of Tucson is the **Turquoise Valley Golf Course**. ~ Off Naco Highway, Bisbee; 520-432-3091. In Douglas, play the **Douglas Municipal Golf Course**. ~ Leslie Canyon Road North; 520-364-3722.

SOUTH/WEST OF TUCSON At the Resort Rio Rico, play the greens at the **Rio Rico Golf Course**. ~ Rio Rico; 520-281-8567. **Tubac Valley Country Club** is the premier spot in Tubac. ~ 1 Otero Road; 520-398-2211. In Yuma you can tee off at **Mesa Del Sol Golf Club Ltd.** ~ 10583 Camino Del Sol Avenue; 520-342-1817.

TENNIS

The dry, hot climate provides excellent court conditions all year.

TUCSON When it's not too hot to serve, try the public tennis courts in Tucson. **Fort Lowell Park** has public courts. ~ 2900 North Craycroft Road; 520-791-2584. Or you can swing a racquet at **Himmel Park**. ~ 1000 North Tucson Boulevard; 520-791-3276. You can work on your serve at **Jesse Owens Park**. ~ 400 South Sarnoff Drive; 520-791-4821. Or try the **Randolph Tennis Center**. ~ South Alvernon Way; 520-791-4896. **Pima Community College** also has courts available for public use. ~ 2202 West Anklam Road; 520-884-6005.

BIKING

In the mountains or along a river, on asphalt or dirt, through residential areas or among the mighty saguaro, Tucson is bicycle-friendly. If you haven't brought one, rent one in town and take to the road or trail.

TUCSON Tucson is a very popular area for bicycling. Some favorite routes include riding on **Oracle Road** north of Ina Road where cyclists find wide shoulders and beautiful mountain views. Ride about 15 miles to Catalina, where the road narrows and is best left to experienced riders. On the way back turn into Sun City Vistoso, a large retirement community where the roads are wide and the scenery pretty.

Another popular ride is parallel to the Santa Catalina Mountain foothills along **Sunrise Drive** to Sabino Canyon, where you can climb up a challenging, four-mile road through the mountains. Because of the trolley, Sabino Canyon is only open to bicyclists before 9 a.m. and after 5 p.m., except Wednesday and Saturday when it is closed to bicyclists entirely. For more information, call 520-749-8700.

Starting on North Campbell Avenue and running along the banks of the dry Rillito River is a multi-use **asphalt trail.** Currently it's about four miles long, although it's still under construction and more trails are added annually. The **Santa Cruz River Park** has another trail that runs along a riverbank. About four miles long, the trail currently breaks for a short gap just over three miles, then continues.

The **Saguaro National Monument,** both east and west, also offers a number of good trails, both for mountain and road bikes, as does the hilly **Tucson Mountain Park.** Both are in scenic areas studded with cactus and mountains. Another enjoyable route is along the **Old Spanish Trail** from Broadway Boulevard to Colossal Cave.

For more information and maps on bicycling in the area, contact the **City of Tucson bicycling coordinator** at 520-791-4372.

Bike Rentals   There are a handful of places in Tucson where you can rent bicycles, including **The Bike Shack.** ~ 940 East University Boulevard; 520-624-3663. You can also rent a two-wheeler at **Broadway Bicycles.** ~ 140 South Sarnoff Drive; 520-296-7819. Equipment and rentals are available at **Tucson Bicycles.** ~ 4743 East Sunrise Drive; 520-577-7374. **Full Cycle** also will help you get set up with rentals. ~ 3232 Speedway Boulevard; 520-327-3232.

EAST OF TUCSON   Good areas for bicycling can also be found outside of Tucson. Bikeable roads east of the city are **Route 90,** which you can take to Sierra Vista and then on to Bisbee, and **Route 80** through Tombstone.

✔ CHECK IT OUT—OUTDOOR ADVENTURES

- Breathe the pine-filled air as you hike **Heart of Rocks Trail** and pass rock formations called Totem Pole and Big Balanced Rock. *page 283*
- Check out the 15 ski runs at the southernmost ski-area in North America—**Mount Lemmon Ski Valley.** *page 279*
- Cool your feet in refreshing Sabino Creek after cycling **Sabino Canyon** in the foothills of the Santa Catalina Mountains. *page 281*
- Pack a picnic lunch, then spend the day at **Patagonia Lake State Park** fishing, boating and swimming. *page 276*

SOUTH/WEST OF TUCSON A good ride is to take **Route 83** from Colossal Cave, past Sonoita and Patagonia to Nogales. This road has little traffic and wide shoulders.

HIKING With trails lacing its many national monuments, recreation areas and state parks, Southern Arizona is built for hiking. You can view old adobe ruins, lime kilns, ancient petroglyphs and geological marvels, or scale one of the many peaks, for a stellar view of your surroundings.

TUCSON In the Rincon Mountain District in Saguaro National Monument is the **Freeman Homestead Nature Trail** (1 mile), a loop that starts off the spur road to the Javelina picnic area and descends from a saguaro forest to a small wash filled with mesquite trees. Along the way you pass the ruins of an adobe house built in the 1920s.

The **Cactus Forest Trail** (2.5 miles) takes you though a saguaro forest between Broadway Boulevard and Old Spanish Trail. You also pass the remains of the first ranger station built in the monument, and two kilns used to manufacture lime around the turn of the century.

For a trek on **Mount Lemmon** follow the **Wilderness of Rocks Trail** (5.2 miles). The trailhead is a mile and a half past Ski Valley. On the way are pools along Lemmon Creek and thousands of eroded and balanced rocks.

Pima Canyon Trail (7.1 miles) in the Santa Catalina Mountains is a difficult trail that climbs from 2900 to 7255 feet through a bighorn-sheep management area. Along the way you'll pass Pima Canyon Spring and good views of Tucson and A Mountain. To get there, follow Christie Drive north until it dead-ends at Magee Road. Go right and park.

In the **Tucson Mountain District** the **King Canyon Trail** (3.5 miles) begins off of Kinney Road across from the Arizona-Sonora Desert Museum, then climbs up to a picnic area and beyond to the top of Wasson Peak (elevation 4687), the highest point in the area.

The short **Signal Hill Petroglyphs Trail** (.25 mile) goes up a winding path along a small hill off Golden Gate Road. At the top are rocks with ancient Indian petroglyphs on them.

The **Valley View Overlook Trail** (.75 mile) on the Bajada Loop Drive descends into two washes and ends on a scenic ridge overlooking most of Avra Valley.

Hunter Trail (2 miles) in **Picacho Peak State Park** offers scenic lookouts as it climbs from 2000 to 3374 feet in height. It was named for Captain Sherod Hunter, a Confederate officer who placed lookouts at Picacho pass and was involved in the battle that occurred here in 1862.

EAST OF TUCSON   To find **Lutz Canyon Trail** (2.9 miles), drive 12 miles south of Sierra Vista on Route 92 to Ash Canyon Road. Hikers walk past old mine workings in a narrow, deep canyon with oak, juniper and Douglas fir.

Crest Trail (10.6 miles) in the **Coronado National Memorial** runs along the crest of the Huachuca Mountains which affords a great view of northern Mexico on clear days.

Within the **Chiricahua National Monument** you'll find **Massai Point Nature Trail** (.5 mile), which starts at the geology exhibit at Massai Point and takes you past a large balanced rock, a board with a description of the park's geologic story and views across Rhyolite Canyon.

The **Sugarloaf Trail** (.9 mile) takes you to the top of Sugarloaf Mountain, the highest point within the monument.

Natural Bridge Trail (2.5 miles) begins at the Bonita Canyon scenic drive, then passes a natural rock bridge and climbs through oak and juniper woodlands to a pine forest.

Heart of Rocks Trail (3.5 miles) winds through pine and fir forests and some of the park's most impressive rock formations, including Big Balanced Rock, Punch and Judy and Totem Pole.

Built as a supply artery for fire fighters stationed in the high Chiricahuas, **Greenhouse Trail** (3.75 miles) ascends 3000 feet. Along the way you'll pass Cima Cabin, the fire fighters' headquarters, and Winn Falls, which flows at a peak during the summer. To get there, go north off Cave Creek Spur Road onto Greenhouse Road and drive half a mile.

The **Coronado National Forest** offers the **South Fork Trail** (6.8 miles). Beginning off Cave Creek Road at the road end in South Fork Forest Camp 3.5 miles above Portal, Arizona, it passes South Fork Cave Creek, one of the most famous bird-watching canyons in the Chiricahua Mountains, and a 70-foot-tall finger of red rhyolite called Pinnacle Rock. It starts in a forest of sycamores, cypress and black walnut trees and leads to huge Douglas fir trees and the small bluffs above the South Fork Cave Creek.

SOUTH/WEST OF TUCSON   **Kent Springs–Bog Springs Trail Loop** (5.7 miles) within the Santa Rita Mountains climbs from 4820 feet to 6620 feet. Along the way are three springs, which create an unusually lush area with large sycamore and walnut trees. Exit off of Route 19 at Madera Canyon and park near the Bog Springs campground.

From Tucson, **Route 10** runs north toward Phoenix, then crosses **Route 8** which heads west toward Gila Bend and Yuma. **Route 85** from Gila Bend goes south, turns into **Route 86**, cuts through the Papago Indian Reservation and goes to Tucson. South of Tucson is **Route 19** to Nogales, while the main

▼▼▼▼▼▼▼▼▼▼
Transportation

CAR

thoroughfare east from Tucson is Route 10 toward New Mexico.
Jutting south off Route 10 are **Route 83** to Sonoita, **Route 90** to
Sierra Vista, **Route 191** to Douglas and **Route 186** to Chiricahua
National Monument.

AIR

Aeroliteral, AirMexico, America West Airlines, American Airlines,
Arizona Airways, Continental, Delta Air Lines, Northwest Airlines, Reno Air, Southwest and United Airlines fly into **Tucson International Airport.**

Yuma International Airport is served by America West Ex-
press, Mesa Airlines, Skywest, and United Express while **Sierra
Vista Municipal Airport** is served by America West Express and
Mesa Airlines.

TRAIN

Amtrak services area with the "Texas Eagle" and the "Sunset
Limited." ~ Reservations: 800-872-7245. Tucson: 400 East Toole
Street. Benson: 4th and San Pedro streets. Yuma: 281 Gila Street.

BUS

Greyhound Bus Lines services Tucson from around the country.
Other stations in Southern Arizona include Nogales, Yuma, Benson and Willcox. ~ Reservations: 800-231-2222. Tucson: 2 South
4th Avenue; 520-792-3475. Nogales: 35 North Terrace Avenue;
520-287-5628. Yuma: 170 East 17th Place; 520-783-4403.

**CAR
RENTALS**

At Tucson International Airport are **Avis Rent A Car** (800-331-
1212), **Dollar Rent A Car** (800-800-4000), **Hertz Rent A Car**
(800-654-3131) and **National Interrent** (800-227-7368).

Car-rental agencies at the Yuma International Airport are **Avis
Rent A Car** (800-331-1212), **Budget Rent A Car** (800-227-3678),
and **Hertz Rent A Car** (800-654-3131).

Enterprise Rent A Car (800-325-8007) and **Rent A Ride** (800-
982-4960) serve the Sierra Vista Municipal Airport.

**PUBLIC
TRANSIT**

For extensive bus service throughout Tucson, call **Sun Tran** (520-
792-9222). Local bus service in Nogales is **Dabdoub Bus Service**
(520-287-7810).

TAXIS

Leading cab companies in Tucson include ABC **Cab Co.** (520-623-
7979), **Allstate Cab Co.** (520-888-2999), **Checker Cab Co.** (520-
623-1133) and **Yellow Cab Co.** (520-624-6611).

In Sierra Vista try **Call A Cab** (520-458-5867) or **Cochise Cab
Co.** (520-458-3860).

NINE

Santa Fe Area

Native cultures scoff at the notion that Christopher Columbus discovered this continent. Even as the Europeans tread through the Dark Ages, the Anasazi Indians were well into their building of intricate Chaco Canyon in northwestern New Mexico. In fact, the Pueblo Indians are thought to have come to Santa Fe around 1200 or 1300 A.D., although they were preceded for centuries by the Anasazi, well before Europeans dreamed of a New World.

The first Spanish settlers claimed this aptly named "Kingdom of New Mexico" in 1540 and the Spanish made Santa Fe a provincial capital in 1610. Over the next seven decades, Spanish soldiers and Franciscan missionaries sought to convert the Pueblo Indians of the region. Tribespeople numbered nearly 100,000, calling an estimated 70 burnt-orange adobe pueblos (or towns) home.

In 1680 the Pueblo Indians revolted, killing 400 of the 2500 Spanish colonists and driving the rest back to Mexico. The Pueblos sacked Santa Fe and burned most of the structures (save the Palace of the Governors), remaining in Santa Fe until Don Diego de Vargas reconquered the region 12 years later.

When Mexico gained independence from Spain in 1821, so too did New Mexico. But it wasn't until the Mexican-American War that an American flag flew over the territory. In 1848 Mexico ceded New Mexico to the United States and by 1912 New Mexico was a full-fledged state.

Why have people always flocked to this land of rugged beauty? The absolute isolation provided by the fortresslike hills in Los Alamos appealed first to the American Indians, later to scientists. The natural barriers surrounding sky-high Santa Fe, coupled with its obvious beauty, have always made it a desirable city and deserving capital, located at the crossroads of north and south.

Some maintain the lands around Santa Fe are sacred. Each year there's a pilgrimage to the modest Santuario de Chimayo church, said to be constructed on sacred and healing ground. The American Indians, who successfully rejected white man's attempts to force-feed them organized religion, have blessed grounds and rituals that remain secret to all outsiders. The spirituality takes many forms. For example, semifrequent supernatural occurrences are reported as straight news.

There's also the magic light and intense colors that artist Georgia O'Keeffe captured so accurately on canvas. The high-altitude sun beaming on the earth tones helps to create shadows and vibrancies not to be believed, from subtle morning hues to bold and empowering evenings. Watching a sunset unfold over the Sangre de Cristo and Jemez mountains can be a spiritual experience as oranges, pinks and violets, chalk-colored pastels and lightning-bolt streaks of yellow weave together a picture story with no plot. Color even emerges in everyday life, as blood-red chile *ristras* line highway stands against a big blue sky.

Many newcomers, like the region's tourists, are here because of the climate. These high, dry mountain towns are pleasingly warm during spring and fall. Summer can bring intense heat and the winters are cold enough to make Santa Fe and nearby Taos viable ski areas. Summer and fall are particularly popular among vacationers.

Others come for the Santa Fe area's cultural mix, which is as colorful and varied as the weather. Anglo, Indian and Spanish peoples coexist, each group more accepting of the others' beliefs yet holding on strong to their own time-honored traditions. New generations living on the pueblos seem less apt to follow the old ways and more interested in the outside world. Whether this is prompted by materialism, survival of the race or both remains to be seen. Still, where other regions have been homogenized by prosperity, in no way are the pueblo peoples tossing aside their proud heritage.

The same goes for the physical remains in the centuries-old cities. Rigorous zoning laws maintain Santa Fe's image by restricting architecture to either the adobe brick or Territorial styles. Fortunately, ordinances make it difficult for developers to raid and tear down. Las Vegas (New Mexico, not its glittering namesake in Nevada) has nine historic districts, with architecture ranging from adobe to Italianate.

The city of Los Alamos, birthplace to the atomic bomb, remains an interesting contrast to the old and new. Modern in its technology and scientific findings, Los Alamos' laboratories co-exist within a stone's throw of ancient ruins and Indian pueblos.

Modern art and literature also meld with the entrenched traditions of pottery and jewelry-making. By 1915 Ernest Blumenschein and Bert Phillips had convinced others of the Taos' "brilliant light" and formed the now-famous art colony known as the Taos Society of Artists. New York heiress Mable Dodge Lujan, a flamboyant fireball and ardent patron of the arts, attracted D. H. Lawrence, Georgia O'Keeffe, Willa Cather and Aldous Huxley to the area as well, leaving a lasting legacy of writers and painters inspired by the region's artistic soul.

Tradition also blends well with modern culinary influences as evidenced in Santa Fe's original cuisine. New styles of cooking in many of the exciting restaurants of the region rely upon old recipes, with a twist. Piquant food is distinctive and uses home-grown chiles and family recipes, blue-corn tortillas and Navajo bread. Rejection of Anglo-izing has made the area unique. Whether it's in the names, lifestyles or biting scents of sage and piñon, in the Santa Fe area, everything has an accent to it.

Above all, however, this is still a land of "mañana," where a majority lives by the philosophy that "if it doesn't get done today, there's always tomorrow." On Sundays, life moves markedly slower than in the rest of the country. This can translate into a frustrating experience as the laissez-faire attitude carries over onto roads that seemingly change numerals in midstream. (The truth is that roads here follow ditches and arroyos and other natural land features.) But if you find yourself lost or learn that your laundry wasn't done on time, just remember: In the Santa Fe area, there's always tomorrow . . . and tomorrow.

Santa Fe

A trivia game asks what's the oldest state capital in the United States. The answer of Santa Fe, which has been home to a government seat since 1610, is always a stumper. Not only does the "City Different" defy the government center stereotype (a domed capitol building and proper tree-lined streets), but unlike most state capitals, it's not easy to get to.

You can't take a commercial jet or even a train into Santa Fe. Albuquerque, an hour's drive south, is the closest large airport, and the city of Lamy, about 17 miles south, is the nearest Amtrak stop. But the independent Santa Feans seem to like it this way. And once you arrive, you'll find it's well worth the trouble.

Strict guidelines mandate the Territorial and Spanish Colonial architecture that characterizes the well-known Santa Fe style. Thanks to city codes, there are no highrises blocking the mountain views or the ever-changing colors at dawn and dusk. This attractive capital, situated at 7000 feet elevation and backdropped by the spectacular Sangre de Cristo Mountains, is becoming desirable to more and more people who are fleeing their urban homes for Santa Fe's natural beauty and culture.

Those rushing to relocate here either part or full time have driven housing prices to outer-space levels. Fledgling artists aren't being represented in galleries, as owners can only afford to stock their high-rent shops with proven names. Chain stores are sneaking into the commercial core and around the popular Plaza area looking for the all-too-important tourist dollar.

Some worry that Santa Fe may become victim to its own success, but a city that has survived numerous invasions and changes of flag can surely endure this most recent influx.

By digging a little deeper, it's still possible to find a soul amid Santa Fe's slickening veneer. Avoiding summer holiday weekends, such as Memorial Day or Labor Day, will find favorite tourist spots less crowded and Santa Feans more willing to have a chat. The city is quite beautiful in the fall, when the leaves are changing and the days are still balmy.

SIGHTS   There is plenty to see in Santa Fe, from palaces of worship to galleries to the Indian Market, but save time for the **State Capitol**, one

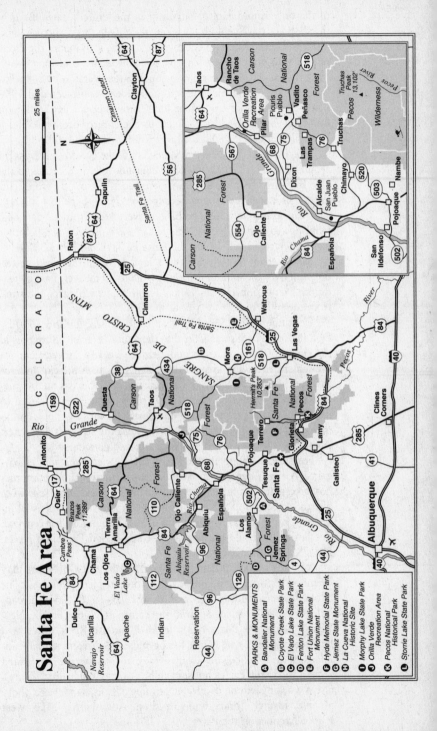

Santa Fe Area

25 miles

N

COLORADO

SANGRE DE CRISTO MTNS

Rio Grande

Navajo Reservoir
Jicarilla Apache Indian Reservation

Brazos Peak 11,289'
Hermit's Peak 10,263'
Truchas Peak 13,102'

Raton
Capulin
Clayton
Cimarron
Watrous
Las Vegas
Mora
Questa
Taos
Rancho de Taos
Taos
Picuris Pueblo
Peñasco
Vadito
Las Trampas
Truchas
Chimayo
Dixon
Alcalde
San Juan Pueblo
Ojo Caliente
Española
San Ildefonso
Pojoaque
Nambe
Santa Fe
Tesuque
Los Alamos
Abiquiu
Ojo Caliente
Tierra Amarilla
Chama
Dulce
Los Ojos
El Vado Lake
Abiquiu Reservoir
Jemez Springs
Galisteo
Lamy
Glorieta
Pecos
Terrero
Clines Corners
Albuquerque
Antonito
Osier
Cumbre Pass
Santa Fe Trail
Cimarron Cutoff
Pecos River
Pecos River
Rio Chama
Rio Chama
Rio Grande

Carson National Forest
Santa Fe National Forest
Pecos Wilderness
Orilla Verde Recreation Area
Pilar

Roads: 64, 87, 56, 25, 64, 159, 522, 38, 434, 518, 75, 76, 68, 110, 84, 96, 112, 126, 44, 4, 502, 41, 285, 40, 161, 518, 554, 567, 285, 75, 503, 520, 518

PARKS & MONUMENTS

- Ⓐ Bandelier National Monument
- Ⓑ Coyote Creek State Park
- Ⓒ El Vado Lake State Park
- Ⓓ Fenton Lake State Park
- Ⓔ Fort Union National Monument
- Ⓕ Hyde Memorial State Park
- Ⓖ Jemez State Monument
- Ⓗ La Cueva National Historic Site
- Ⓘ Morphy Lake State Park
- Ⓙ Orilla Verde Recreation Area
- Ⓚ Pecos National Historical Park
- Ⓛ Storrie Lake State Park

of the only round capitol buildings in the United States. Built in the shape of the Pueblo Indian Zia, the three-story structure, with a red-brick roofline and whitewashed trim, symbolizes the circle of life: four winds, four seasons, four directions and four sacred obligations. It also resembles a much larger version of a Pueblo Indian ceremonial kiva. The roundhouse was constructed in 1966 to replace an older capitol building (now known as the Bataan Building) down the block. Tours of the capitol are available. ~ Paseo de Peralta and Old Santa Fe Trail; 505-986-4600.

The Tlaxcala people from Mexico built the **San Miguel Mission** around 1610, making it the oldest continuously used church in the U.S. But this was probably considered sacred ground before that, as there is evidence of human occupation dating back to 1300 A.D. San Miguel is an amazing archive of everything from pyrographic paintings to buffalo hides. Included in the collection is a bell that dates back to 1356! ~ 401 Old Santa Fe Trail; 505-983-3974.

Meander up the **Old Santa Fe Trail** through the parklike setting and over the mountain-runoff-fed Santa Fe River. Pass by traditional irrigation ditches called *acequias*, which carry moisture from the hills found throughout the city.

Continue up the Santa Fe Trail to the **Plaza**, built in 1610 by Don Pedro de Peralta as an end to the Santa Fe Trail. (A marker in the Plaza commemorates its completion.) There's always plenty of excitement revolving around this town square. American Indians roll out their blankets and hawk their wares to tourists on the sidewalks surrounding the Plaza. Their prices have been adjusted to meet Santa Fe's ever-increasing popularity. Groups of young Latino men crowd into big cars and slowly cruise the square's perimeter. If you're lucky, there will be live music and dancing.

For serious shoppers, the Plaza offers little in the way of bargains. A Plaza department store's transformation into boutiques bothered many Santa Feans. **Woolworth's Five and Dime** sells wool Indian blankets and Santa Fe souvenirs in addition to its usual inventory, but with rising rents and a lease coming up for renewal, this landmark could go, too. ~ 60–62 East San Francisco Street; 505-982-1062.

America's oldest public building, the **Palace of Governors** may be more historically significant than the artifacts it houses. The adobe fortress, built by the Spanish in 1609–1610, served as capital of Nuevo Mexico, Spain's northernmost colony in the New World, before the Pilgrim's landed at Plymouth Rock. Once held by Pueblo Indians, the Palace has been used as governmental headquarters for Mexico, the Confederacy and the territorial United States. Today the Palace houses exhibits of regional history. There's also a working exhibit of antique printing presses, as well as a photo archive, history library and gift shop. Admission. ~ 105 West Palace Avenue, on the Plaza; 505-827-6483.

Situated west of the Palace of Governors, the **Museum of Fine Arts** is a prototype of the architectural revival style called Spanish-Pueblo. The building is a reproduction of New Mexico's "Cathedral of the Desert" exhibit at the 1915 Panama-California Exposition in San Diego. Completed in 1917, it embodies aspects of the Spanish mission in the region. Notice the ceilings of split cedar *latillas* and hand-hewn vigas. Housing more than 7000 pieces of art, the museum is a repository for works of early Santa Fe and Taos masters as well as contemporary artists. Admission. ~ 107 West Palace Avenue, on the Plaza; 505-827-4455.

Before leaving the Plaza area, you'll want to pop into the **La Fonda Hotel**, which calls itself the inn at the end of the trail, for a drink in the popular bar or a meal in its impressive dining room. You can glean as much information about what's going on at La Fonda as at the chamber of commerce. ~ 100 East San Francisco Street; 505-982-5511.

If you're interested in attending church services, consider the beautiful Santa Fe **Cathedral of St. Francis of Assisi**, whose cornerstone was laid in 1869 by Archbishop Lamy. With its stained-glass windows, bronze panels and smaller Sacrament Chapel, it's certainly the grandest church in the Southwest. In a corner is the sacred La Conquistadoria ("Lady of the Conquest"), the oldest representation of the Madonna in the United States. Devotion has been maintained to the woodcarved statue for more than 300 years. In the early morning light, La Conquistadoria appears positively heavenly. ~ 131 Cathedral Place; 505-982-5619.

Santa Fe's most significant new sightseeing highlight is the **Institute of American Indian Arts Museum**. This downtown museum is part of the only federally chartered Indian college-level art school. Exhibits are arranged to place contemporary artwork within a context of tribal tradition. For instance, located just beyond the main entrance is the welcoming circle, a circular space symbolic of the cycles of nature and the continuity of the American

✔ **CHECK IT OUT—UNIQUE SIGHTS**

- Don't miss the **Museum of International Folk Art**, with its 125,000 artifacts from around the world. *page 292*
  - Sit beneath the stars and listen to arias performed by the country's finest summer opera company, the **Santa Fe Opera**. *page 310*
    - Step into the **Bradbury Science Museum** to learn the story behind the atomic age. *page 316*
      - Spend time exploring the over 30,000 acres of **Bandelier National Monument**'s scenic wilderness, which is dotted with ancient Indian ruins. *page 317*

Indian people. Here, before viewing the exhibits, visitors can gather their thoughts in the quiet, contemplative manner in which American Indians have traditionally approached art appreciation. Admission. ~ 108 Cathedral Place; 505-988-6211, 800-858-4214.

Those who believe in miracles must make a point of stopping by the tiny **Loretto Chapel**, patterned after France's Saint Chappelle, which holds the beautiful "magic staircase." When the chapel was built, craftsmen failed to install any way to reach the choir loft. Short on funds, the nuns prayed for a solution to the problem. The story goes that a man came armed with only a saw, hammer and hot water to shape the wooden staircase. He worked for months and built a staircase that makes two 360-degree turns but has no visible means of support. When it came time for payment, the man mysteriously disappeared. Admission. ~ 211 Old Santa Fe Trail; 505-988-5531.

Impressive is a good way to describe the privately owned **Wheelwright Museum of the American Indian**. Though the collection has a lot of Navajo weavings, changing exhibits feature historic and contemporary American Indian art. ~ 704 Camino Lejo; 505-982-4636.

The nearby **Museum of International Folk Art** houses the world's largest collection of folk art—125,000 artifacts from around the globe. Toys, textiles, ritual and religious art are colorfully displayed in the Girard Wing. The Hispanic Heritage Wing looks at the traditions of New Mexico's Hispanic folk culture including a huge Spanish Colonial collection. Video interaction monitors help visitors learn more about the history and craft of various artifacts. The museum parking lot also affords a spectacular view of the Jemez Mountains, southwest of Santa Fe, and the Sangre de Cristos to the north. Admission. ~ 706 Camino Lejo; 505-827-6350.

During the summer and pre-Christmas season, hundreds of art lovers participate in the Canyon Road Art Walks, held each Friday from 5 to 7 p.m. and sponsored by Canyon Road galleries.

Southwestern American Indians are the focus of the **Museum of Indian Arts & Culture**, with exhibits drawn from extensive collections of the museum's Laboratory of Anthropology. For a treat spend time in the Resource Center, where you can do traditional beading, use a Pueblo drum, card wool and touch various artifacts and learn about powwows, feast days and other events in the area. Admission. ~ 710 Camino Lejo; 505-827-6344.

Wandering up to **Canyon Road** (see "Shopping" below), you'll pass by historic haciendas and witness firsthand the center of Santa Fe's burgeoning arts community.

If you continue up Canyon Road beyond the galleries and shops and the broad, green neighborhood park, you'll come to **Cristo Rey Church**. Don't be deceived by the historic look of this adobe church. It was actually built in 1940 in the style of Spanish

Colonial mission churches (such as those in Chimayo, Las Trampas and Truchas on the High Road to Taos) to house a stone altarpiece dating back to 1760. This treasure, one of the finest works of early New Mexican religious sculpture, depicts God and a number of saints. ~ 1120 Canyon Road; 505-983-8528.

Randall Davey Audubon Center is named for a painter known for his horse-racing themes. When he died in the early 1980s, Davey left his 135-acre estate to the National Audubon Society. As you stroll the easy walking trails that circle the oak and piñon terrain, you may encounter a wide variety of animal life, including rabbits, skunks, raccoons and deer. Birdwatchers are likely to spot magpies, piñon jays, ravens and dozens of songbird species. A visitor center inside the home includes a bookstore with an excellent selection on the natural history of New Mexico. The rest of the home, including Davey's studio and an exhibition of his works, opens for tours on an irregular basis. Closed Sunday during winter. Admission. ~ 1800 Upper Canyon Road; 505-983-4609.

The Downs at Santa Fe hosts quarter-horse and thoroughbred racing on Wednesdays, Fridays and weekends in-season. For a more uptown experience, pay a few extra dollars for entrance to the Jockey Club. Admission. ~ Route 25; 505-471-3311.

Settle into a private hot tub under the starlit evening at **Ten Thousand Waves**. This authentic Japanese health spa also offers full-body massages and facials. Admission. ~ Ski Basin Road; 505-982-9304.

To take in the whole picture of Santa Fe, hoof it up to the **Cross of the Martyrs**, located in the city's Marcy Park section. There are stairs by Paseo de Peralta and Washington Avenue that you climb to earn the bird's-eye view of the city.

About 15 miles southwest of Santa Fe is **Rancho de Las Golondrinas**, a restored Spanish hacienda dating back to 1710. It was once the last *paraje* (inn) before Santa Fe on the grueling journey along El Camino Real, the "Royal Highway," which brought traders and settlers from Mexico City to Northern New Mexico. The 200-acre grounds still operate as a working farm, growing Indian corn and raising sheep. Coming here is like stepping back in time. Rancho de Las Golondrinas is closed to the public November through March. Admission. ~ Route 25, Exit 276, go to Los Piños Road; 505-471-2261.

HIGH ROAD TO TAOS   When it comes time to leave Santa Fe, drive up Bishop's Lodge Road through the upscale village of Tesuque and connect with Route 76 to take the High Road to Taos. While traveling this way takes an hour longer than taking Route 76, it is a memorable drive with stunning vistas of the Sangre de Cristo Mountains. Several small towns and pueblos along the way offer many opportunities for sightseeing.

En route, if you can keep from being intrusive, visit Archbishop Lamy's private chapel at the **Bishop's Lodge**. Small, private and very holy are words that characterize this sanctuary along the Little Tesuque Stream. Vigas have replaced the former rafters in this intimate chapel, but the archbishop's cloak, hat and crucifix remain. Enter by way of an old church key! It's quite possible a visit here will inspire you to read Willa Cather's classic, *Death Comes for the Archbishop*. ~ Bishop's Lodge Road, Tesuque; 505-983-6377.

Also in Tesuque is the **Shidoni Foundry**, where bronze pourings take place on Saturdays. The art foundry, gardens and contemporary gallery are world-renowned among purveyors of fine art. ~ Bishop's Lodge Road; 505-988-8001.

When light shines through colored glass, wonderful things happen. The **Dunbar Stained Glass Studio and Gallery** sparkles with glasswork. Call ahead for an appointment. ~ P.O. Box 769, Tesuque; 505-984-8515.

Just outside the village is the **Tesuque Pueblo**. Considered one of the most traditional of the pueblos, Tesuque continues to have a strong agricultural emphasis, which results in natural food products for sale. Bright designs characterize their pottery. The pueblo also has a casino. ~ Route 285; 505-983-2667.

Farther north, at Pojoaque, go left on Route 502 to **San Ildefonso Pueblo**, where you'll see beautiful burnished black matte pottery in the tradition of the late Maria Martinez. Current potters here continue to create artistic wonders. There's also a museum on site displaying jewelry, costumes and religious artifacts. Admission. ~ Route 502; 505-455-2273. **Pojoaque Pueblo**, the smallest of the Tewa pueblos, hosts special fiesta days and has a tourist center where handcrafted items are sold, plus an on-site RV park. ~ Route 285; 505-455-2278.

Through Pojoaque to Route 503 turn right and wind past the cottonwoods to **Nambe Pueblo** and the sparkling Nambe Falls picnic site. This area was once a Spanish province where early settlers developed their communal land grants. Many Nambe residents are descendants of those early settlers. Photography fee. ~ Route 503, Nambe; 505-455-2036.

Turn left on Route 520 and head through the Chimayo Valley to **Chimayo**. Located between the Sangre de Cristos and the Rio Grande Valley, the Chimayo Valley is a fertile area at the confluence of three streams.

HIDDEN ►   Within the village of Chimayo is the **Santuario de Chimayo**, the place of countless miracles. Legend has it that in the early 1800s a man who saw a shining light coming from the ground dug and found a crucifix. The cross was moved to a church nearby and placed on the altar. The next morning the crucifix was gone, and

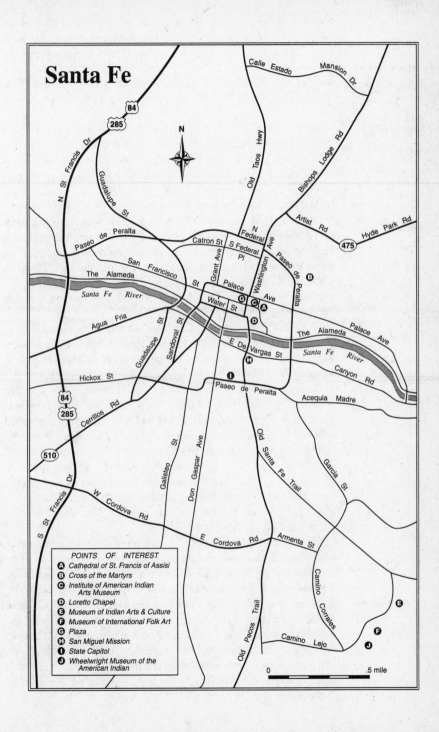

Santa Fe

POINTS OF INTEREST
- **A** Cathedral of St. Francis of Assisi
- **B** Cross of the Martyrs
- **C** Institute of American Indian Arts Museum
- **D** Loretto Chapel
- **E** Museum of Indian Arts & Culture
- **F** Museum of International Folk Art
- **G** Plaza
- **H** San Miguel Mission
- **I** State Capitol
- **J** Wheelwright Museum of the American Indian

0   .5 mile

found in its original location. The crucifix was moved back to the church, but again disappeared and ended up in its original location. This kept happening until people realized that someone or something wanted it to remain at this site. So, a church was built in Chimayo between 1814 and 1816. This is probably one of the reasons why people believe the Santuario's dirt is blessed.

El Santuario, "The Shrine," remains a magic place where people with ailments come to feel God's healing touch. There's an annual pilgrimage to the church beginning on Good Friday. Testaments to its healing powers are everywhere, as discarded crutches, braces and *retablos* (Christ drawings) fill the church's side rooms. ~ County Road 98; 505-351-4889.

> The tough little town of Truchas was home to John Nichol's *The Milagro Beanfield War.*

After visiting Chimayo, head north on Route 76 to the town of Truchas with its little weaving and woodcutting shops. It is a burgeoning arts center whose people are undoubtedly inspired by the splendid scenery of the Sangre de Cristos and New Mexico's second-highest mountain, 13,102-foot Truchas Peak.

Stop by the **Hand Artes Gallery** for folk and fine art. ~ Route 76, Truchas; 505-689-2443.

Also in Truchas is the **Cardona-Hine Gallery**, featuring the contemporary paintings of Alvaro Cardona-Hine and his wife, Barbara McCauley, as well as a dozen other New Mexican artists. ~ Route 76; 505-689-2253.

Continue north on Route 76 to **Las Trampas**. Once a walled adobe village—to protect it from "wild" Indians—Las Trampas is home to the 18th-century **Church of San Jose,** an oft-photographed mission church with mud plastering and early paintings. ~ Route 76.

After passing through Las Trampas you'll come to Peñasco. Turn on Route 75 through the **Picuris Pueblo** to see the native pottery, weaving, silversmithing, beadwork and remains of a pueblo from the 13th century. Picuris, with its standing round house, remains the smallest of New Mexico's pueblos. Admission. ~ Route 75, Peñasco; 505-587-2519.

From Picuris, rejoin Route 76 for a few miles until you connect with Route 3 and pass over the landmark U.S. Hill Vista, an early, tortuous trading route. After driving over hill and dale, when Route 3 meets with Route 68, head straight to the Ranchos de Taos.

HIDDEN ►

There you'll find **San Francisco de Asis,** a Spanish Colonial adobe church that was the favorite of artists Georgia O'Keeffe and Ansel Adams. It's home to Henri Ault's amazing *The Shadow of the Cross,* which some say is miraculous. Ault's painting depicts Christ carrying a cross when observed from one angle. In different light, however, the cross cannot be seen. ~ Route 68, Ranchos de Taos; 505-758-2754.

RIVER ROAD TO TAOS   If you opt not to take the High Road to Taos and want to continue north out of Santa Fe on Route 285, you'll come across the jolly sandstone **Camel Rock Monolith.** Primitive camping is allowed near the distinctive rock; $16 per night. ~ 505-455-2661.

Continuing north past Española, where the highway divides, drive a little farther on Route 68 to Route 70 and the San Juan Pueblo sign. **San Juan Pueblo** was the site of the first capital of New Mexico in 1598. Geometric designs and luster define the red-incised pottery. Woodcarvings and weavings are also for sale on site. ~ 505-852-4400.

Another 15 miles or so north on Route 68 takes you to the turnoff to the verdant town of **Dixon** where artists hold studio visits the first weekend in November. ~ Route 75; information on studio visits: 505-579-4111.

In this fragrant valley is the **La Chiripada Winery**, which has a tour and tasting room. ~ Route 75, Dixon; 505-579-4437.

From there it's just a couple more miles on the "river road" to Pilar and the **Orilla Verde Recreation Area,** a nice rest stop on the river's edge. Admission. ~ Route 68.

If you return to Route 68 to travel north toward Taos, you'll discover the highway was built by the U.S. Army and first called Camino Militar. Completion of this road helped end centuries worth of isolation in Taos.

LODGING

The sparkling **Inn of the Anasazi** prides itself on the personal touch, from the homemade juice and introduction letter at check-in to the escorted tour of the hotel by a bellman and thoughtful turn-down service and dimming of lights in your bedroom. Its understated elegance has made the Anasazi a favorite among well-heeled visitors. Decor throughout the small inn is decidedly low key—neutral tones prevail. Rooms are bedecked with four-poster beds, viga ceilings, cast-iron furniture, angelic figurines and handknitted cotton blankets. Instead of "do not disturb" signs, hotel attendants place leather-tied blocks over doorknobs. ~ 113 Washington Avenue; 505-988-3030, 800-688-8100, fax 505-988-3277. ULTRA-DELUXE.

Red-brick coping and windows trimmed in white signal the traditional Territorial-style architecture of **Hotel Plaza Real**. Situated around a central courtyard, the hotel's 56 rooms feature massive wood beams and Southwest-style furniture. Nearly all the units have a fireplace and most have a patio or balcony. But, a word to the wise: some rooms are small and second-floor units feature steep, narrow staircases. Rates include a hearty continental breakfast and underground parking, a plus considering the likelihood (or lack thereof) of finding a spot near the Plaza. ~ 125 Washington Avenue; 505-988-4900, 800-279-7325, fax 505-983-9822. ULTRA-DELUXE.

Considering the noise on the street it fronts, rooms at the **Inn on the Alameda** are surprisingly quiet. Everything emphasizes sunny and clean—from the white adobe walls to the blue and pink bathroom tiles and the modern lines of the artwork. Many rooms are decorated with wicker and wood-cane furniture; all come with fluffy robes for guest use. Breakfast is included. ~ 303 East Alameda Street; 505-984-2121, 800-289-2122, fax 505-986-8325. ULTRA-DELUXE.

If you find bigger is always better, then be sure to book a room at the looming, yet lovely, 218-room **Eldorado Hotel.** Lovers of classic Santa Fe architecture about choked when this monolith was constructed. Yet few who venture inside find fault with the brass-and-chrome-fixtured lobby bar, heated rooftop pool, two cocktail lounges and adjacent shops. Medium-size double rooms are done in mauves and earth tones. Those with bucks to burn might opt for the Presidential Suite with five rooms, two fireplaces, a wet bar and balcony. Even non–Gold Card holders will appreciate the rooms with fireplaces—a valet lights the fire for you. ~ 309 West San Francisco Street; 505-988-4455, 800-648-5966, fax 505-945-4543. ULTRA-DELUXE.

How many different ways can you say sweet? The **Grant Corner Inn** is a turn-of-the-century restored Colonial manor transformed into a wonderful bed and breakfast famous for its morning repasts. Looking more like a New England inn than a Southwestern abode, the Grant Corner is filled with gorgeous white wicker furnishings, brass beds, quilts and a collection of oh-so-cute bunny art. ~ 122 Grant Avenue; 505-983-6678, fax 505-983-1526. DELUXE TO ULTRA-DELUXE.

Afternoon tea attracts a high-tone crowd to the **Hotel St. Francis,** one of the prettiest properties in town. Each of the 81 rooms and suites is unique with high ceilings, casement windows, brass and iron beds and cherrywood furniture. Original hexagonal tile and porcelain pedestal sinks give the bathrooms a lush yet historic feel. A spacious lobby hosts the famous afternoon tea, complete with finger sandwiches and scones. ~ 210 Don Gaspar Avenue; 505-983-5700, 800-529-5700, fax 505-989-7690. DELUXE TO ULTRA-DELUXE.

Literally "the inn at the end of the Santa Fe Trail," **La Fonda Hotel** is a Santa Fe institution. Though the original 1610 adobe hotel is gone, the latest incarnation still caters to weary travelers in search of pleasant lodging and fine food. Each room is unique, with hand-painted wooden furniture and room accents; many feature balconies and fireplaces. A central meeting spot for area sightseeing tours and recreational activities, La Fonda hums with excitement. A newsstand, art gallery, shops, restaurant and cantina all add to the bustle. ~ 100 East San Francisco Street; 505-982-5511, 800-523-5002, fax 505-982-6367. ULTRA-DELUXE.

The scent of piñon wood pervades the polished and contemporary **Hotel Santa Fe,** located on the edge of Santa Fe's historic   ◄ HIDDEN
Guadalupe district. Large rooms, many of which have a separate sitting area, are handsomely decorated in those oh-so-familiar Southwestern colors and hand-carved furniture. The first off-site Indian project in the state, the hotel is half-owned by the Picuris Indian Pueblo. The Picuris run its gift shop, while other American Indians work in the rest of the hotel. ~ 1501 Paseo de Peralta; 505-982-1200, 800-825-9876, fax 505-984-2211. DELUXE TO ULTRA-DELUXE.

Not to be confused with the neighboring Hotel Santa Fe, the **Santa Fe Motel** has bungalow-style dwellings, standard lodge rooms as well as a large adobe house for rent. Each unit has its own personality; some are peppy while others are a little on the shady side. Given its prime location, within walking distance of the Plaza, the Santa Fe Motel is probably the best value for the money. ~ 510 Cerrillos Road; 505-982-1039, 800-999-1039. MODERATE.

Typically, the farther you move away from Santa Fe's Plaza, the more hotel prices drop. But one must guard against a few of the 1950s-style hotels lining Cerrillos Road—some are dives!

The **El Rey Inn,** with its lush garden property filled with fountains and patios, stands tall against neighboring hotels. Decor varies between Indian pueblo, Victorian and Spanish. Some rooms have Oriental rugs; others feature brick floors. Omnipresent in all units is an attention to detail and cleanliness. ~ 1862 Cerrillos Road; 505-982-1931, 800-521-1349, fax 505-989-9249. MODERATE.

Just down the road is a standout in the chain hotel department. **Quality Inn's** predictably decorated rooms are spacious and spot-

---

✔ CHECK IT OUT—UNIQUE LODGING

- *Budget to moderate:* Leave the hotel scene behind and check into the **Orange Street Inn,** where the frozen yogurt in the fridge will make you feel at home. *page 320*
  - *Moderate:* Step out your back door for a day of trout fishing when you settle in at the **Oso Ranch and Lodge.** *page 323*
    - *Deluxe:* Envelop your tired body in a feather bed in a room decorated à la various animals at **Inn of the Animal Tracks.** *page 300*
      - *Ultra-deluxe:* Retreat from the world at **The Bishop's Lodge,** once the private dwelling of Archbishop Jean Baptiste Lamy. *page 300*

Budget: under $50 Moderate: $50–$90 Deluxe: $90–$120 Ultra-deluxe: over $120

less. All top-floor rooms have balconies. Formica showers and tile floors are found in the bathrooms. ~ 3011 Cerrillos Road; 505-471-1211. MODERATE.

HIDDEN ► Lions and tigers and bears, oh my! At the **Inn of the Animal Tracks** each of the five rooms uses a different animal theme. In the Playful Otter quarters, for example, stuffed dolls keep the guests company as platform feather beds envelope tired bodies. There's a select library of books from which to choose. All breakfast and high-tea delectables are baked on the premises. Not surprisingly, there's a resident cat. ~ 707 Paseo de Peralta; 505-988-1546. DELUXE.

Romance blooms at **La Posada de Santa Fe**. In the spring, the lush grounds burst forth with tulips and sweet peas; flower fancy decor mimics the natural setting. Wood floors and viga ceilings adorn the cozy *casitas*, many of which have kiva fireplaces. The hotel's Victorian bar is a natural place for whispering sweet nothings. ~ 330 East Palace Avenue; 505-986-0000, fax 505-982-6850. DELUXE TO ULTRA-DELUXE.

On the northern edge of town are two rather rural alternatives to the city lodging experience. **The Bishop's Lodge** is the better of the two primarily because of its rich history. The property along the Little Tesuque Stream was once the private retreat of Archbishop Jean Baptiste Lamy. The bishop's sacred, private chapel still stands behind the main lodge and can be entered by borrowing a special key from the front desk. Since 1917, the 1000-acre ranch has hosted guests who choose from horseback riding, meditative hikes and tennis. Rather simple but well-kept rooms are bedecked with older furnishings. ~ Bishop's Lodge Road, off Route 285, Tesuque; 505-983-6377, 800-732-2240, fax 505-989-8739. ULTRA-DELUXE.

A similar resort experience is offered at the more modern **Rancho Encantado** which has fancier accommodations but less overall ambience and attention to service than the Bishop's Lodge. Handsome tree-lined grounds are criss-crossed with cobblestone paths linking the main building to the *casitas*, corral, tennis courts and cantina. Victorian touches prevail in some of the spacious and thoughtfully furnished rooms and cottages, the latter featuring fireplaces. ~ Route 4, Tesuque; 505-982-3537, 800-722-9339, fax 505-983-8269. ULTRA-DELUXE.

Located on the famed high road to Taos, **Hacienda Rancho de Chimayo** is a splendid seven-room retreat. Antique beds made of mahogany and iron, as well as traditional Chimayo hand-woven draperies and rugs give the rooms a homey feel. Many have fireplaces crafted from adobe as well as pine floors and vigas. All the rooms adjoin a beautiful courtyard, and the inn itself is adjacent to a popular New Mexican restaurant. This place is a real gem. ~ County Road 98, Chimayo; 505-351-2222. MODERATE TO DELUXE.

Homemade granola and goat's milk yogurt start the day at the **Inn of the Anasazi**. The innovative kitchen creates indescribable cuisine that blends many elements, flavors, exotic grains and organic ingredients. Homemade breads, seafoods and wild game feature prominently in the menu. The Inn's beautiful 96-seat dining room alone is worth a visit. ~ 113 Washington Avenue; 505-988-3236. DELUXE TO ULTRA-DELUXE.

◄ *HIDDEN*

Tongues smile at the thought of the **Santacafé**, where herbs are exalted and only the freshest of foods find their way to the table. The combination of flavors never disappoints, from the starter to the grand finale. What's best about Santacafé is it doesn't try too hard when delivering its Southwestern/Asian cuisine. It doesn't have to. ~ 231 Washington Avenue; 505-984-1788. DELUXE.

Though the wait for a table can be long, don't pass up the opportunity to breakfast or brunch at **Grant Corner Inn**. Locals flock to this intimate restaurant (it only seats 30) located within one of the city's most popular bed and breakfasts. While the regular menu has first-rate fare (waffles, egg dishes, soufflés), your best bet is the full brunch special, which includes a fruit frappe, a choice between two entrées, pastries and fresh-ground Colombian coffee or Crabtree & Evelyn tea. Fresh flowers adorn every table and service is extremely attentive. Reservations a must! ~ 122 Grant Avenue; 505-983-6678. MODERATE.

Get the scoop on the world with your café mocha and dessert at the **Galisteo News**. A sophisticated selection of newspapers, including the *International Herald Tribune*, fills the racks. Galisteo is a fine, fine place for people-watching. ~ 201 Galisteo Street; 505-984-1316. BUDGET.

Caffe latte never tasted so good as in the Bohemian atmosphere of the **Aztec Street Café**, where you'll find lively conversation, tasty bagels and art worthy of discussion but, alas, too much cigarette smoke. ~ 317 Aztec Street; 505-983-9464. BUDGET.

Sopapilla translates to "pillow," an apt description for the light, puffy fried dough typically served drizzled with honey.

Modern American cuisine in a hip setting makes **Zia Diner** a fine place to come on your own. Sit at the counter or come with pals and the kids and grab a big table. There's food here for everyone, like meatloaf, burgers, pizza and a Mount Everest–size pile of fries. Zia moves a good crowd through and provides a "window of reading" for delay times. The adjacent Zia bar hops, too. ~ 326 South Guadalupe Street; 505-988-7008. BUDGET TO MODERATE.

In the old railroad station is **Tomasita's**, which on the surface looks like a tourist trap. But the food—Tomasita's wins raves for its green chile and *chile rellenos*—and the margaritas wipe away any disparaging thoughts. ~ 500 South Guadalupe Street; 505-983-5721. BUDGET TO MODERATE.

Text continued on page 304.

Colorful Cuisine

Chances are the one question you'll be asked after a New Mexico vacation is, "How was the food?" Like Cajun cooking in Louisiana or spicy Szechuan dishes in China, authentic New Mexican cooking can delight the senses as much as any scenic panorama. Odds are, long after you've left the state, your palate will still savor the flavorful (sometimes fiery) tastes of New Mexico.

Bottom line . . . New Mexican cooking is not Mexican or Tex-Mex. It is distinctive cuisine with strong roots in the state's Indian culture as adapted by Spanish and Anglo settlers. From flavors to cooking techniques, all are delicately balanced, with the result a literal feast of tastes, textures, smells and colors: green chiles, yellow cheese, blue corn.

This mélange dates back hundreds (maybe even thousands) of years. New Mexico's early inhabitants dined on rabbit and venison. But these meats were quickly replaced by beef, *chorizo* (a spicy pork sausage) and mutton after the Spanish arrived. Corn, beans, squash and nuts originated with American Indians. Europeans brought wheat, rice, fruit, onions, garlic and grapes. From Mexico came tomatoes, avocados and chocolate.

Today's New Mexican cooking uses such unusual fruits and vegetables as jicama, chayote (or vegetable pear), *nopales* (the flat green pads of the prickly pear cactus), tomatillos (with their tart lemon flavor) and plantains. Cumin is the predominant spice, though oregano, cilantro, *epazote*, mint, cinnamon and coriander are also utilized.

Traditionalists will tell you there are four basic elements to a true New Mexican meal—chile, corn, cheese and beans. If all four aren't served, you aren't getting an authentic dinner.

Ah, yes, the chile: heart and soul of New Mexican cooking. Politics, religion, who'll win the Super Bowl, no topic generates more dispute than red versus green and hot versus mild. New Mexicans consume more chiles per capita than any other state and it's the state's second-largest cash crop. If you compared chiles to grapes, New Mexico would be the champagne capital of the world. Local experts estimate more than 35,000 tons are exported within a single year.

The chile (not to be confused with chili powder or chili in a bowl) may have existed as early as 700 B.C. Columbus found "chile" (the Aztec name for the wrinkled, fiery pods) in the West Indies in 1493 and brought them to the New World. Pueblo Indians were growing a mild version along the banks of the Rio Grande when the Spanish arrived in the 1500s.

Nowadays, some still believe a hot dose of chiles will clear the sinuses. True or not, chiles are high in vitamins A and C. Most of us recognize at least a few of the many varieties—green bell pepper, *poblano* (a large, dark green chile), jalapeño, serrano and *chipotle* to name a few. Almost everyone quickly recognizes the New Mexico red chile strung in wreaths and chains called *ristras*.

Part of the nightshade family (which includes tomatoes and potatoes), chiles used before they are ripe are green. Once ripe, they're red. They can be picked and eaten in both stages. Not all chiles are "hot." The amount and variety of chile and whether it is fresh, dried or ground determines the hotness.

One of the best ways to learn all there is about New Mexican cooking is at the **Santa Fe School of Cooking**. Here, expert chefs demonstrate the history and techniques of New Mexico cuisine. Best of all, students get to sample the finished product. ~ 116 West San Francisco Street, Upper Level, Plaza Mercado, Santa Fe; 505-983-4511.

If enrolling in a two-and-a-half hour class isn't your idea of a vacation, it's at least a good idea to master a few Spanish terms for the basic dishes. For example, *carne asada* means roasted meat (though it now sometimes includes grilled meat). *Carne adovada* refers to meat marinated in red chile. Chicken in chile sauce is known as *mole*.

A traditional tamale is minced meat and red pepper rolled in corn meal, wrapped in corn husks and baked or steamed. The ever-popular *chile rellenos* refers to a large, battered, fried green chile, stuffed with either cheese, avocado, shrimp, pork, etc. *Chile con queso* is a chile and cheese pie. A side order of *frijoles* will get you a plate of pinto beans. *Sopapilla* translates to "pillow," an apt description for light, puffy fried dough served with honey. And *flan* is smooth, creamy caramel custard.

Tortillas are the "bread" of New Mexico. Usually made of white cornmeal, they come hot and fresh with almost every dish. Some cooks favor flour or blue cornmeal for preparing tortillas. And yes, blue corn is really "blue." Finally, never be embarrassed to ask questions or request your chile on the side. New Mexicans take great pride in their cooking and want you to enjoy all the flavors (and surprises) it holds.

Southwestern cuisine and Continental-style entrées with a tangy Creole snap dominate the menu at **Pink Adobe**, where the favorite entrée is steak served with green chiles and mushrooms. ~ 406 Old Santa Fe Trail; 505-983-7712. MODERATE TO DELUXE.

The only place for prime beef in town, the **Bull Ring** is an upscale steak house with white linen tablecloths and an exclusive wine list. ~ 150 Washington Avenue; 505-983-3328. MODERATE TO DELUXE.

HIDDEN ►

One of Santa Fe's most romantic restaurants is found in, surprise, surprise, an old convent! **La Tertulia** never disappoints. The nuns must be watching over their former residence because from the chips to soups to main courses and rich desserts, the food is heavenly. A pitcher of sangria is a must, as is the steak smothered in green chile. A Spanish Colonial art collection bedecks the walls of this former Dominican order house turned eatery. ~ 416 Agua Fria Street; 505-988-2769. MODERATE.

Of the three Japanese restuarants in Santa Fe, **Shohko Café** has the freshest food and best sushi bar. Sake and tempura ice cream are very viable accompaniments. ~ 321 Johnson Street; 505-983-7288. MODERATE TO DELUXE.

The Coyote Café made a big splash when it first opened and was soon ranked among the top 100 restaurants in the country. The ever-evolving menu typically includes griddled buttermilk corn cakes with chile shrimp and salsa fresca and New Mexico Angus rib chop with red-chile onion rings. Some locals feel the Coyote is overrated, but it remains a favorite among the visiting crowd. ~ 132 West Water Street; 505-983-1615. ULTRA-DELUXE.

The Compound Restaurant is where you'll probably want to go for a very special evening. Foie gras, lamb, caviar and fresh fish are attentively served in this restored hacienda. The impressive wine cellar has some rare vintages. Closed Monday and the month of January. ~ 653 Canyon Road; 505-982-4353. ULTRA-DELUXE.

Locals still love **El Farol**, which serves hot and cold Spanish tapas and entrées. Try one of the house specialties—paella, cold curry chicken or shrimp sautéed in garlic, lime and sherry—for an inexpensive and filling meal. El Farol's ambience is as good as its food. ~ 808 Canyon Road; 505-983-9912. MODERATE.

Considered one of Santa Fe's finest restaurants, **La Casa Sena** boasts both a main dining room and a smaller cantina. The restaurant, part of a restored 1860 adobe casa, covers its walls with paintings by early Santa Fe masters. Fine, fresh ingredients are used (even the water is from their own well), resulting in fabulous dining adventures. Entrées take regional favorites and give them a creative twist like grilled Colorado lamb chops with a tropical fruit insalata, and grilled herb-crusted sea bass served with a legume mushroom sauté. Don't miss the avocado-lime cheesecake with piñon crust. Outrageous! ~ 125 East Palace Avenue, Sena Plaza; 505-988-9232. DELUXE.

Lines form early at the accompanying **La Casa Sena Cantina** because no reservations are accepted. But in this bustling crowded space, everything from food to song is artistically presented. In fact, nowhere else in Santa Fe does the blue corn chicken enchilada come with a rousing rendition of "Phantom of the Opera." The limited menu includes such specialties as country-fried rib eye with garlic basil mashed potatoes accompanied by corn and white bean succotash. Waiters and waitresses perform excerpts from popular musicals, then follow with a sampling of show tunes. Patrons come and go between sets, making their way among the tiny butcher-block tables and baby grand piano. ~ 125 East Palace Avenue; 505-988-9232. MODERATE TO DELUXE.

If an old Mexico-style huge lunch followed by a siesta are what you're after, then seek out the venerable **Shed**, where wise eaters come before noon to avoid the lines. Blue-corn tortillas wrapped around cheese and onion specialties are served on sizzling plates with *posole* on the side. Consider starting your meal with some fresh mushroom soup and ending it with lemon soufflé. ~ 113½ East Palace Avenue; 505-982-9030. BUDGET TO MODERATE.

Somewhere you'd definitely not think to stop for a snack is **Woolworth's**. But this particular franchise store sells a tasty, though messy, Frito pie (a chip and bean concoction) that's fun to munch on while sitting in the Plaza. ~ 60–62 East San Francisco Street; 505-982-1062. BUDGET.

An inexpensive downtown favorite is **Tia Sophia's**, a long-established restaurant known for its breakfast burrito. This spicy entrée consists of scrambled eggs and chili rolled in a tortilla, a com-

✔ **CHECK IT OUT—UNIQUE DINING**

- *Budget:* Sniff the arousing aromas emanating from **Vera's Mexican Kitchen**, then savor the spicy native dishes. *page 323*
- *Moderate:* Take brunch at **Grant Corner Inn**, where the attentive service matches the fabulous food. *page 301*
- *Deluxe:* Whet your appetite at the **Landmark Grill**, and indulge in exotic cuisine in a refined setting. *page 314*
- *Ultra-deluxe:* Feast on wild game, homemade bread and other delectables at the **Inn of the Anasazi**. *page 301*

Budget: under $8 Moderate: $8–$16 Deluxe: $16–$24 Ultra-deluxe: over $24

bination that has gained popularity throughout the west. You can't beat the original version pioneered right here. Choose from breakfast and lunch daily specials as well as a wide variety of traditional New Mexican selections. The Southwestern-style decor is bright and homey. Closed Sunday. ~ 210 West San Francisco Street; 505-983-9880. BUDGET TO MODERATE.

With the unlikely name of **Dave's Not Here**, this great little neighborhood spot serves typical Mexican food and a yummy Greek salad. But it's the burgers that keep people coming back. You can have them with guacamole, green chile, onions or just plain naked. By the way, namesake Dave really isn't here—he sold the restaurant a long time ago. ~ 1115 Hickox Street; 505-983-7060. BUDGET.

When you gotta have a pizza fix, head for **Il Primo Pizza** for some cheesy, Windy City–style deep dish. ~ 234 North Guadalupe Street; 505-988-2007. BUDGET.

Breakfast lovers head to the **Tecolate Café** for omelettes bursting with gooey filling, thick flapjacks and baskets of biscuits and muffins. For lunch, the burgers, enchiladas and burritos are popular. ~ 1203 Cerrillos Road; 505-988-1362. BUDGET.

HIDDEN ► Before it gets too trendy, check out the **Tesuque Market** and its casually chic atmosphere. The Tesuque chile-cheeseburger, stir-fry veggie plate and salads are highly recommended. There's a full wine cellar and good choices by the glass. ~ Route 591 and Bishop's Lodge Road, Tesuque; 505-988-8848. BUDGET.

Tucked into the mountains about 40 minutes north of Santa Fe, **Restaurante Rancho de Chimayo** serves authentic New Mexican meals in an adobe house. Bill of fare includes tamales, enchiladas, tacos and flautas plus specialties like marinated pork cutlets served in a red-chile sauce and chicken breasts topped with chile sauce and melted cheese. Leave room for the homemade *sopapillas* and honey. During summer months, ask for the outdoor patio seating. Closed Monday from November through May. ~ Country Road 98, Chimayo; 505-351-4444. BUDGET TO MODERATE.

SHOPPING In a city known for its history and architecture, what everyone remembers about Santa Fe is . . . the shopping. Myriad arts and crafts shops plus 225 galleries crowd the Plaza and nearby Canyon Road, a two-mile street lined with fine art stores.

For silver jewelry, pottery and handwoven blankets of exquisite detail, look no further than beneath the portal of the Palace of Governors on the Plaza where Indian artisans gather to market their wares.

HIDDEN ► Always exciting images by well-known 19th- and 20th-century shooters can be viewed at **Andrew Smith Fine American Photography Gallery**. ~ 203 West San Francisco Street; 505-984-1234.

Fenn Gallery features folk art, early and contemporary Taos and Santa Fe painters as well as American Indian jewelry. Fenn's sculpture garden and fountains only add to the atmosphere. ~ 1075 Paseo de Peralta; 505-982-4631. The **Elaine Horwitch Gallery** is modern, hooked into "the scene" and always worth your time. ~ 129 West Palace Avenue; 505-988-8997.

Laura Carpenter Fine Art is the place for contemporary art. Carpenter's gallery is quite well regarded internationally. ~ 309 Read Street; 505-986-9090. Another well-known gallery here is **Gerald Peters**. ~ 439 Camino del Monte Sol; 505-988-8961. **Allene Lapidus** is a purveyor of collectible art. ~ 217 Johnson Street; 505-984-0191.

Stunning Southwestern scenes of adobes and more are found at **Ventana Fine Art**. ~ 211 Old Santa Fe Trail; 505-983-8815.

Well-priced casual Southwestern clothing makes **Chico's** a good place to purchase wearable souvenirs. ~ 328 South Guadalupe Street; 505-984-1132.

Bodhi Bazaar has contemporary casual and dressy clothing. ~ 500 Montezuma Street; 505-982-3880. Cotton garments for men and women fill the shelves at **Pinkoyote**. ~ 315 Old Santa Fe Trail; 505-984-9911. Hand-appliquéd shirts and women's Western wear are found at **Three Sisters**, one of several good shops located at the Inn at Loretto. ~ 211 Old Santa Fe Trail; 505-988-5045.

An unusual bookstore, **The Ark** is found well off the beaten track in a hideaway hacienda. Books on healing and UFOs, crystals and incense fill this New Age haven. ~ 133 Romero Street; 505-988-3709.

Find gold jewelry and brilliant earth stones like sugilite at **Spirit of the Earth**. ~ 211 Old Santa Fe Trail; 505-988-9558. Ear cuff king and master jeweler **Ross LewAllen** has branched out into safari bracelets, pendants, beading and wildlife-theme wearables. ~ 105 East Palace Avenue; 505-983-2657.

Silver buckles shake hands with serpent and leather belts as well as snazzy custom-made Western boots at **Tom Taylor**. ~ 100 East San Francisco Street; 505-984-2231.   ◄ HIDDEN

For outrageous greeting and postcards, try the **Marcy Street Card Shop**. ~ 75 West Marcy Street; 505-982-5160. The **Chile Shop** has pottery, *ristras*, chile powders and cookbooks. ~ 109 East Water Street; 505-983-6080.

For tribal arts there are numerous choices, including **La Fonda Indian Shop**. ~ La Fonda Hotel, 100 East San Francisco Street; 505-988-2488. You can also try **Tin-Nee-Ann**. ~ 923 Cerrillos Road; 505-988-1630.

CANYON ROAD While art abounds everyday in the City Different, from public sculpture to stylishly dressed Santa Feans, one of the greatest concentrations of galleries can be found on Canyon

Road. High rents have made the old artist-working-in-the-back-room an anomaly and turned Canyon Road into a rather exclusive enclave. There are plenty of beautiful things to be viewed here—from clothing and jewelry to furniture and paintings—satisfying most palates if not every pocketbook.

The past decade has seen Santa Fe emerge as a collectors market for ethnic art from all over the world.

Start your Canyon Road journey out at **Mabel's**, a gift emporium where the slippers, bathrobes, doorknockers and stationery all have animal and nature themes. ~ 201 Canyon Road; 505-986-9105.

Lovers of bronze sculpture should check out **Meyer Gallery** and its huge selection of impressionist paintings by well-known artists. ~ 225 Canyon Road; 505-983-1434. **Mariposa Santa Fe** displays contemporary gold and silver inlaid jewelry. ~ 225 Canyon Road; 505-982-3032. In the same building is one of the country's oldest galleries, **Munson Gallery**, featuring paintings, sculpture and graphics. ~ 225 Canyon Road; 505-983-1657. The **Hahn Ross Gallery** features the whimsical contemporary art—paintings, sculpture, monoprints—of 20 artists. ~ 409 Canyon Road; 505-984-8434.

Important American regionalists and contemporary painters are shown at **Cline Fine Art Gallery**. ~ 526 Canyon Road; 505-982-5328.

Bellas Artes is an intriguing gallery featuring significant works in painting, clay, sculpture, fibers as well as African and pre-Columbian art. ~ 653 Canyon Road; 505-983-2745. **Quilts Ltd.** sells just what its name promises. Some are traditional, others contemporary. ~ 652 Canyon Road; 505-988-5888.

Antique American Indian kachinas, basketry and textiles are among the artifacts found at **Kania-Ferrin Gallery**. ~ 662 Canyon Road; 505-982-8767. At the **Phil Daves Studio/Gallery**, landscapes, figurative paintings and nudes are shown by appointment only. ~ 669 Canyon Road; 505-982-4867.

Carol LaRoche Gallery has monotypes, abstract and representational art that was created by LaRoche herself. ~ 708 Canyon Road; 505-982-1186.

Natural-fiber clothing designs and handmade garments have made **Judy's Unique Apparel** popular. ~ 714 Canyon Road; 505-988-5746.

Folk art, 19th-century American Indian art and vintage photos are found at **Alan Kessler**. ~ 836 Canyon Road; 505-986-0123.

HIDDEN ►

When you're writing a guidebook it's hard to decide whether the **Trader Jack's Flea Market** belongs in the shopping or sightseeing section. Just as every flea market reflects its surrounding community, this northern New Mexico gathering place contains Spanish, Anglo and American Indian traders alike. Pull your pickup truck over to the side of the road, shuffle through the dust and you'll find everything from pinto beans to auto parts to fine turquoise jewelry. The flea market is open every Friday, Saturday and Sunday. ~ To get there head six miles north from Santa Fe on Route 84; turn left after the opera house.

For eight generations the Ortega family has been weaving brilliant sashes, vests, purses and jackets at their wonderful little shop, **Ortega's Weaving.** ~ Route 76, Chimayo; 505-351-4215.

Next door, the **Galeria Ortega** is a good place to check for Southwestern gifts (pottery, kachinas, paintings, candles) and books on regional topics. ~ 505-351-2288.

Operated by Joseph Sisneros, great-grandson of the Jaramillo pioneer family, and his wife, Myakel, **Rancho de Chimayo Showroom** specializes in 14- and 18-karat gold. Look for Cochiti storyteller dolls, sterling silver bracelets and Hopi/Apache clay kachinas. The Navajo vases are exquisite. ~ County Road 98, Chimayo; 505-351-4444.

NIGHTLIFE

O sole mio: **La Casa Sena** has singing waiters and waitresses and one heck of a wine list. ~ 125 East Palace Avenue; 505-988-9232.

For a nightcap, try the gracious Victorian bar in **La Posada de Santa Fe** with its chandeliers and leather chairs and cushy couch by the fireplace. In the summer, take a sip on the outdoor patio. ~ 330 East Palace Avenue; 505-986-0000.

A mix of politicians, tourists and just plain old working folks can be found at the **Pink Adobe,** a handsome watering hole around the corner from the State Capitol. ~ 406 Old Santa Fe Trail; 505-983-7712.

Get ready to kick up your heels at **Rodeo Nites,** a rowdy nightclub for lovers of country-and-western music. Cover Thursday through Saturday. ~ 2911 Cerrillos Road; 505-473-4138.

El Farol is a dark cantina where locals love to hang out and drink. With a spirit all of its own, El Farol attracts real people. You can hear live music here every night, including flamenco, R&B and country. ~ 808 Canyon Road; 505-983-9912.

Even more down home is the macho **Evangelo's,** where the beer is cheap, cheap, cheap. ~ 200 West San Francisco Street; 505-982-9014.

The lounge in the **La Fonda Hotel** during happy hour gurgles with the energy of locals and visitors. Hot hors d'oeuvres and music are fine accompaniments to the loaded margaritas. ~ 100 East San Francisco Street; 505-982-5511.

The Palace Restaurant offers piano music, well-poured drinks and reliable service. ~ 142 West Palace Avenue; 505-982-9891.

For a relaxed atmosphere, ease into the guitar or piano music at the **Ore House.** ~ 50 Lincoln Avenue; 505-983-8687.

OPERA, THEATER, SYMPHONY AND DANCE   Music and moonlight fill the **Santa Fe Opera,** one of the country's most famous (and finest) summer opera companies. Blending seasoned classics with exciting premieres, the Opera runs from late-June through August in the open-air auditorium. Though some seats are sheltered, warm clothing and raingear are suggested, since evenings can be cold and/or wet. ~ Route 84-285; 505-982-3855.

Community theater of the highest order is found at **Santa Fe Community Theater,** which produces musical comedies, plays, a Fiesta Melodrama and a one-act series. ~ 142 East De Vargas Street; 505-988-4262.

The beautiful Paolo Soleri Outdoor Amphitheatre of the Santa Fe Indian School campus serves as home to the **Santa Fe Summer Concert Series,** which brings big-name acts to town. ~ Cerrillos Road; 505-256-1777.

The **Santa Fe Symphony** (505-983-3530) performs both traditional and contemporary classical works at Sweeney Center (201 West Marcy Street).

Founded in 1980, the **Pro Musica Santa Fe** (505-988-4640) performs from September through May at the Lensic Theater (211 West San Francisco Street) and the Loretto Chapel (211 Old Santa Fe Trail).

Saint Francis Auditorium (inside the Museum of Fine Arts) plays host to the **Santa Fe Concert Association** (505-984-8759) and **Santa Fe Chamber Music Festival** (505-983-2075).

The sizzling **Teatro Flamenco** (505-983-8477) returns to Santa Fe each summer for a series of flamenco dance concerts under the direction of Maria Benitez. Performances are held at the Radisson Picacho (750 North St. Francis Drive).

PARKS   **HYDE MEMORIAL STATE PARK** 🏃 🏠 A small park (350 acres) in the foothills high above Santa Fe, Hyde Park's woodsy and sheltered feeling gives one the impression they're light years away from the city. A good base for cross-country skiing or hiking in the Santa Fe National Forest. There are picnic areas, restrooms and a general store with limited supplies; day-use fee, $3. ~ On Route 475, just over seven miles northeast of Santa Fe; 505-983-7175.

▲ There are 50 tent sites ($7 per night) and seven sites with electric hookups ($11 per night).

▼▼▼▼▼▼▼▼▼▼
Las Vegas Area   The slow-paced town of Las Vegas, with its refreshingly real central plaza, is the county seat of three-million-acre San Miguel County. A practically undiscovered gem, it reflects the heritage of northern New Mexico. The surrounding region takes in the Pecos River, rushing from the high peaks of the Pecos Wilderness down a deep canyon and past ancient Indian

ruins, as well as the magnificent mountain country around Hermit's Peak. To the north lies the strangely silent land around Mora, one of a small cluster of traditional villages that are slowly turning into ghost towns. Few travelers take the time to explore the Las Vegas area, just an hour's drive from Santa Fe; for those who do, a wealth of history and natural beauty awaits.

By driving the back road (Routes 84 and 85), which follows the Santa Fe Trail, between the capital city and Las Vegas, you'll first pass the **Glorieta Battlefield**, the site of the westernmost skirmish of the Civil War, the 1862 Battle of Glorieta Pass. This engagement was triggered by a Texas unit of the Confederate Army that tried to capture Santa Fe as a base for seizure of the Colorado and California goldfields. Defeat of the rebels at Glorieta Pass put an end to this audacious plan.

SIGHTS

Seven miles from Glorieta (just a few miles off of Route 25 midway between the capital and Las Vegas) is **Pecos** (population 1500), a tiny town that consists of a gas station, a general store, a National Forest Service ranger station and two places typical of every New Mexican village: a Catholic mission church and a bar. Much of the predominantly Spanish-speaking population ekes out a living in the surrounding national forest, cutting vigas, *latillas* and firewood or grazing small herds of cattle, horses and goats. Unpaved roads (many of them passable by passenger car—check at the ranger station for suggestions) lead into the forest in all directions from the village; it's a beautiful area, full of spotted, rolling hills.

When the late actress Greer Garson and her husband donated 365 acres to preserve a postclassic pueblo civilization, they made possible the creation of **Pecos National Historical Park**. Walk among ruins dating back to 1200 A.D., a pueblo thought to have stood four to five stories back in 1451 when it had a population of 2000 (more than live in the Pecos area today). By the 17th century the Franciscan monks had taken over the pueblo and built a pair of mission churches. You can still see the remains of the huge church, *convento* and garden walls alongside the ancient pueblo ruins. Rampant disease and famine coupled with Comanche Indian raids in the mid-1800s led to the pueblo's abandonment, but survivors moved to Jemez Pueblo, where even today they form a separate clan and speak a dialect distinct from other Indians at the pueblo. When visiting, be careful to respect the privacy of the spirits that may haunt this incredible site. The ancient pueblo people were quite leery of strangers, forbidding them to set foot on pueblo land even when Pecos Pueblo was a center for trade with the Plains people. Trading parties actually had to camp outside the city wall. Admission. ~ Route 63, two miles south of Pecos; 505-757-6032.

Going west from the park and Pecos village, the road winds along a scenic river canyon painted with scrub oak. Along the way you'll pass a lake where the locals fish for dinner, a trout hatchery, monastery and clusters of summer cabins. The upper Pecos River is renowned for its catch-and-release fly fishing, and on summer weekends you'll find the riverbanks lined with fishermen.

North of Pecos on Route 63 is the settlement of **Terrero**, site of a long-abandoned refinery that used to process gold and other ores from the surrounding mountains. The pavement ends about four miles north of Terrero, and the unpaved road, steep and rough in spots, continues to a series of trailheads and large, well-developed campgrounds at the south portal of the Pecos Wilderness.

About 50 miles from Pecos is the country's original **Las Vegas**. The area's modern-day roots go back to the railroad's heyday, when Las Vegas was an important mercantile center. Las Vegas' destiny to become a major port of entry for supply wagons on the Santa Fe Trail began in 1835, when the Mexican government gave land grants to 29 individuals. By 1879, railroad tracks were laid east of the Gallinas River in "New Town"; not surprisingly, Railroad Avenue and the neighborhood boomed. But by 1905, railroad traffic was diverted south and the once-expanding city, whose population in the late 1800s rivaled Denver's, dwindled.

The diverse origins of people who came during Las Vegas' prime left an architectural legacy of everything from Territorial and Italianate styles to Victorian designs. In fact, Las Vegas has nine historic districts and more than 900 historically designated buildings. Movie buffs may recognize the distinctive-looking town as the setting of numerous silent films.

As you enter the city, you'll want to first head to the historic **Plaza**, the center of Old Town. The Plaza dates back to the 1600s

DAY TRIP TO LA CUEVA

La Cueva National Historic Site, part of the Mora land grant of 1835, is an exceptionally beautiful sight in the springtime. Built around a hacienda completed in 1863, La Cueva was a major agricultural center and the home of an adobe mill that ground flour for generations. Electricity was generated here until 1949. You can visit the old mill and the Mercantile Building, now the **Salman Ranch Store**, a peaked-roof adobe that sells locally produced jams, syrups and the like, along with dried flowers and wildflower seeds. Northeast of the store is **San Rafael Mission Church**, a building graced with handsome French Gothic windows.
~ Route 518, 25 miles north of Las Vegas; 505-387-2900.

with the Spaniards, although archaeological digs in Las Vegas show that the Paleo Indians lived here as early as 8000 B.C.

Afterward, stop by the **Las Vegas–San Miguel Chamber of Commerce** for maps of walking tours, hiking trails and information on Las Vegas' history. ~ 727 Grand Avenue; 505-425-8631.

Next door is the **Rough Rider's Museum**, which has mementos of the Spanish American War, American Indian artifacts and other historical items, many of which were donated by Rough Riders. ~ 729 Grand Avenue; 505-425-8726.

Pretty buildings line the street of **New Mexico Highlands Campus**, which was established in 1893 bridging the rivaling Old and New Towns. The school is known for its fine arts, performing arts and technical programs. ~ National Avenue; 505-425-7511.

Yet the pride of the area is the **United World College**, a beautiful red-slate structure that looks like a castle, complete with turrets. The school's unique setting and approach to learning draw gifted students from around the world. To find the college, drive up pretty Hot Springs Canyon past painted barns, a picturesque little church and a couple of colorful wall murals. ~ Near the former spa of Montezuma; 505-454-4200.

Well-marked **natural hot springs baths**, located right off the highway in view of the United World College, are offered in varying temperatures.

For a splendid drive, continue on Route 65 through Gallinas Canyon into the heart of the Sangre de Cristos and on up to the hiker's paradise of 10,263-foot **Hermit's Peak**.

Backtracking to Las Vegas and then north on Route 518 takes you to the boardsailing-haven **Storrie Lake State Park**. A short drive farther north on scenic Route 518 puts you in **Mora**, known as the breadbasket of the area during the heyday of the Santa Fe Trail, when it grew wheat.

In the nearby town of Cleveland is the **Cleveland Roller Mill Museum**, a turn-of-the-century flour mill that operated until 1947. The building, which is on the National Register of Historic Places, has original mill equipment. Open May through October. Admission. ~ 505-387-2645.

Northeast of Las Vegas via Route 25 is **Fort Union National Monument**, which beginning in 1851 and throughout most of the 19th century was the largest military post in the region and headquarters for soldiers who protected Santa Fe Trail travelers from Indian raids. A self-guided trail and visitors center explains its rich history. Admission. ~ Route 161, Watrous; 505-425-8025.

Victoriana is alive in the center of Las Vegas at the historic **Plaza Hotel**. Originally built in 1882 in the Italianate bracketed style, the Plaza was the first major inn constructed after the railroad's ar-

LODGING

rival. A century later, original features such as tin ceilings and window bracketing were uncovered. Rooms are decorated in period furniture, antiques and floral accents typical of late-19th-century buildings in the West. ~ 230 Old Town Plaza, Las Vegas; 505-425-3591, 800-328-1882, fax 505-425-9659. MODERATE.

HIDDEN ▶

Or drive just a few miles to the "new" section of town to the hacienda-style **Inn on the Santa Fe Trail** for the best rooms for the price in the area. Completely gutted and redone in 1991, the property is handsomely decorated in oak and whitewashed pine furniture crafted by a Las Vegas artisan. Southwestern paintings cover pink walls. Fiberglass tubs are found in the bathrooms. ~ 1133 Grand Avenue, Las Vegas; 505-425-6791, 800-425-6791, fax 505-425-0417. BUDGET TO MODERATE.

There's no belfry at the **Carriage House Bed and Breakfast,** but if you're outside at sundown, you might spot the bats that live in the attic—that's when the furry creatures tend to emerge. Bats are only one of the attractions at this circa 1893 Victorian inn, the perfect base for exploring historic Las Vegas. The six rooms and two suites are furnished with bird's-eye maple chests and chenille bedspreads; elegant public areas complement the accommodations. This charming establishment is on the National Register of Historic Places. ~ 925 6th Street, Las Vegas; 505-454-1784. MODERATE.

DINING

The **Landmark Grill,** the most elegant restaurant in Las Vegas, has an English look highlighted by Corinthian columns and floral-patterned tablecloths. Indulge in the curried chicken coyote, the grilled king salmon marinated in a raspberry chipolte sauce or the rib-eye steak served with red or green chile. The intimate setting has been known to whet appetites of all kinds. ~ Plaza Hotel, 230 Old Town Plaza, Las Vegas; 505-425-3591. MODERATE.

Located between a used-car lot and a gas station, **The Mexican Kitchen** is the kind of place you'd normally pass right by. But we made our way past the PacMan machines in the entryway, took a seat at one of the formica tables and noticed signed autographs from *General Hospital* soap opera stars who stopped by this re-decorated drive-in while shooting an episode nearby. Perhaps the word-of-mouth reviews had already started. For excellent burritos, tacos and enchiladas at inexpensive prices, we wouldn't hesitate to return. ~ 717 Grand Avenue, Las Vegas; 505-454-1769. BUDGET.

For a real slice of Americana, wander into the formica-filled **Spic and Span Bakery and Café,** where homemade donuts and sweet rolls jam the glass cabinets. Mexican specialties are served in the café. A natives' hangout, heads swivel when a newcomer enters the sanctum. ~ 713 Douglas Avenue, Las Vegas; 505-425-6481. BUDGET.

Don't be deterred by the shabby exterior of **Estella's Café.** Thoughtfully prepared American and Mexican cuisine dominate the menu. The green chile comes highly recommended. ~ Bridge Street, Las Vegas; 505-454-0048. BUDGET.

On the historic Plaza in Las Vegas is the **La Galeria de los Artesanos Book Store**, where you'll find New Mexican and Southwestern guidebooks, fiction and nonfiction housed in a former law office. ~ 220 North Plaza; 505-425-8331.

In Las Vegas, try a spot that was named after a ghost, **Byron T's Saloon** for a selection of libations. ~ Plaza Hotel, 230 Old Town Plaza; 505-425-1455.

STORRIE LAKE STATE PARK   A pretty mountain lake that's favored by gung-ho windsurfers who like the consistent breezes and families that enjoy the jewel of a setting. Swimming is also allowed here. There is a visitors center, picnic area, toilets and showers; day-use fee, $3. ~ Located on Route 518, four miles north of Las Vegas; 505-425-7278.

▲ There are 54 sites (22 with RV hookups); tent sites are $7 per night and hookups are $11 per night. Primitive camping is allowed along the lake's shore; $6 per night.

MORPHY LAKE STATE PARK   A scenic mountain lake and park that's a popular fishing spot for everyone and a swimming hole for only the very hearty. Unspoiled barely does justice to this little jewel. There are restrooms; day-use fee, $3. ~ Located on Route 94, four miles west of Ledoux; 505-387-2328.

▲ There are 50 primitive sites; $6 per night.

COYOTE CREEK STATE PARK   Fishing and camping are the main attractions in this compact 80-acre park. But there are also hiking trails, picnic sites and a playground as well as a visitors center. The park has restrooms and showers; day-use fee, $3. ~ Located on Route 434, 17 miles north of Mora; 505-387-2328.

▲ There are 73 sites including ten RV hookups and 23 primitive sites. Fees per night are $6 for primitive sites, $7 for standard sites and $11 for hookups.

▼▼▼▼▼▼▼▼▼▼▼
Los Alamos Area

The Pajarito Plateau, a broad, pine-forested shelf of lava and ash, spans the eastern slope of the Jemez Mountains. This unusual mountain range is circular because some 200,000 years ago it was the base of a single volcano larger than any active volcano on earth today. The elements have carved the plateau into canyons with sheer orange-and-white walls where ancient cliff-dwellers made their homes.

This geological labyrinth made the plateau a perfect place for the government to hide its top-secret A-bomb laboratory during

World War II. Throughout the Cold War, as the brains behind the bomb continued to move into the area, Los Alamos boomed to become the wealthiest town in the state. Today, the future of this community surrounded by wilderness is uncertain as it slips into post–Cold War history.

In fact, history is an ever-present reality throughout the land between Santa Fe and Taos. It can be captured in such places as Bandelier National Monument, with its ruins of Indian pueblos and cliff dwellings from the 13th century, as well as still-inhabited Indian pueblos and Spanish mountain villages where the ways of life still endure from centuries past.

SIGHTS   **Los Alamos** was developed in the early 1940s by the U.S. government for scientists working on the highly secretive Manhattan Project. The isolated town in the high-altitude Jemez Mountains boasted a spectacular setting, with scenery of dense forest and Indian pueblos; an extinct volcano formed a natural barrier on the other side. About the only thing here was the private Los Alamos Ranch School for Boys, but it was easily closed and the Manhattan Project, an experiment that would change the course of history, was set underway.

Bright young minds were imported to create the first atomic bombs—nicknamed "Fat Man" and "Little Boy"—that eventually helped end World War II. But, alas, the inventors and their families were forced to live behind a wall of secrecy, where mail was subject to a censor's pen and passes were needed for leaves. It was physicist Robert Oppenheimer, architect of the atomic bomb, who once said: "The notion of disappearing into the New Mexico desert for an indeterminate period disturbed a good many scientists."

Los Alamos National Laboratory remains the major presence in the city and accounts for the lion's share of local jobs. The Department of Energy still owns the laboratory that employs more than 7000 for national security studies, metallurgy, genetics information, geothermal and solar research. Los Alamos, obviously, still attracts the intelligentsia.

Los Alamos is warming (no pun intended) to visitors after decades as an ultrainsular community. The bomb was invented under a veil of secrecy; people in Santa Fe (only about 35 miles away) didn't even know what was going on "up there."

HIDDEN ▶   No matter how you feel about the atomic age, a visit to the **Bradbury Science Museum** is a must. Three dozen exhibits are interspersed with photographs, a timeline, films and letters, including one from Albert Einstein to President Roosevelt. The Robert Oppenheimer story is detailed. The museum is alternatingly frightening and enlightening. A recent exhibit discussed laboratory research to protect the environment. ~ 15th and Central streets, Los Alamos; 505-667-4444.

To understand a little more about this unique town, be sure to stop at the **Los Alamos Historical Museum,** which covers pre-bomb history dating back to the Pleistocene era, artifacts from the defunct boy's school and items from the World War II era. ~ 1921 Juniper Street, Los Alamos; 505-662-6272.

Adjacent to the historical museum is a 1928 log building that's home to the **Fuller Lodge Art Center.** This national landmark, once the recreation hall for ranch school students, hosts exhibits by native and visiting artists. ~ 2132 Central Avenue, Los Alamos; 505-662-9331.

Nearby is the gleaming **Larry R. Walkup Aquatic Center,** the highest-altitude Olympic-size indoor pool in the United States, serving athletes and recreational swimmers who enjoy a splash. ~ 2760 Canyon Road, Los Alamos; 505-662-8170.

The earth is hot around Los Alamos less because of radioactivity than its volcanic history, and hot springs bubble forth to the delight of those who enjoy a refreshing and relaxing dip. In their natural state are the **Spence Hot Springs** (Route 4, about seven miles north of Jemez Springs) and **Battleship Rock Warm Springs** (Route 4, about five miles north of Jemez Springs). Short, well-trod foot paths take off from the respective parking areas.

At the more developed **Jemez Springs Bathhouse** nudity is not an option. Admission. ~ Route 4 near the town of Jemez Springs, about 40 miles southwest of Los Alamos; 505-829-3303.

One mile north of the city of Jemez Springs is the **Jemez State Monument.** The monument, officially recognized in 1935, honors pre-Columbian Indian ruins, including the ruins of a pueblo, and the remains of a Spanish mission, the Church of San Jose de los Jemez, which was built in 1621–22. A tiny museum explains some of the Jemez tradition. Admission. ~ Route 4; 505-829-3530.

Valle Grande was created about a million years ago when a volcano's summit seemingly crumbled and spewed ash as far east as Kansas. It left a broad basin called a caldera (thought to be the largest of its kind) that stretches about 15 miles in diameter. ~ Route 502, 14 miles west of Los Alamos.

Bandelier National Monument encompasses 32,737 acres of scenic wilderness. The Anasazi people, who settled in the Jemez

TSANKAWI

Bandelier National Monument has miles of maintained hiking trails in a wilderness area known as **Tsankawi,** which is located in a separate section of the monument. Largely unexcavated, Tsankawi is accessible by a trail that goes to the top of the mesa and passes by some interesting Anasazi drawings.

Mountains between 1100 to 1550 A.D., centuries before white men arrived, farmed this comparatively lush area in Frijoles Canyon. The canyon walls bear their symbols. Most of Bandelier, named for ethnologist Adolph Bandelier, is wild backcountry, with several riparian oases. Strenuous climbs up steep cliffs are required to explore much of the backcountry. (Note: Much of the backcountry was impacted by a forest fire in May 1996. Contact the visitors center for updated information.) Admission. ~ Route 4, ten miles south of Los Alamos; 505-672-3861.

Start your perusal of the park at the visitors center with a ten-minute slide show of "The Bandelier Story." The short, self-guided Main Loop Creek Trail takes off from the visitors center near the Frijoles Creek and passes **Tyuonyi** ("Meeting Place"), a circular village believed to have once stood three stories high. Its single entrance has led to speculation that this large and impressive structure was used for defending the village.

Behind Tyuonyi is **Talus House**, which has been completely reconstructed to give visitors an idea of what the homes along the cliff would have looked like. The trail continues to the longest structure at Bandelier aptly named **Long House Ruin**, nestled under a cliff. It's full of ancient pictographs and petroglyphs.

You can continue on the trail for a half mile and scramble up several somewhat scary ladders to the **Ceremonial Cave**, which affords a great overall view of the canyon. Backtracking to the visitors center, hike down Frijoles Canyon across the creek to the **Upper Falls** and then view yet another waterfall about a half-mile down the path.

If your appetite is whet for ruins, then drive a few dozen miles northwest to the **Puye Cliff Dwellings**, a fascinating little ancient city. Inhabited by up to 1500 people between the years of 1250 to 1577, Puye is currently operated by the neighboring Santa Clara Pueblo, who are probably descendants of the original settlers. The excavated ruins of the ancient apartmentlike complexes are evident from miles away as you approach the site. Upon arrival, choose either the Cliff Trail or the Mesa-Top Trail for exploring. Admission. ~ Route 5, 11 miles west of Route 30, Española; 505-753-7326.

The **Cliff Trail** takes off from above the parking lot and offers the you a chance to walk through cavelike rooms and past petroglyphs and the outlines of buried masonry dwellings for more than a mile along the south face of the Puye mesa. Rock inscriptions of spirals and masks, serpents and humans are carved along the caves and cliffs. You'll also see outlines of buried masonry dwellings known as talus rooms. Stepping places and hand grips lead to kivas and the grand Community House from the cave rooms (or cavate rooms) below. Near the base of the cliffs are two kivas. But there may be more ceremonial chambers and other treasures lying undiscovered, well-beneath the earth's surface.

It's possible to drive up to the second trail, appropriately called **Mesa Top**, by following the road past the visitors center. From there, the Puye's 740-room pueblo, with its restored room, can be examined. Historians imagine the structure loomed as high as three stories tall. When perusing the remains, take a look around at the splendid views of the Rio Grande region. Puye villagers of so long ago likely enjoyed a similar panorama.

After exploring the cliff dwellings, drive six miles west to gorgeous Santa Clara Canyon, a nice place for a picnic or fishing stop.

Returning to Route 30 and continuing north toward the city of Española takes one to the **Santa Clara Pueblo**, which is known for its highly polished black and red pottery. A stream, several lakes and picnic areas are open to the public. There is no admission fee, but paid permits are required for photography and filming. ~ Route 30, Española; 505-753-7330.

> Roughly 7000 archaeological sites are said to surround the Los Alamos area.

Passing through **Española**, founded in the 1880s as a railroad stop (although it was discovered by the Europeans as early as 1598), you'll notice the community remains true to its Hispanic heritage in everything from culture to churches. Although it has evolved into a bedroom community for Santa Fe, Española's claim to fame has always been as the "Low-Rider Capital" of the world. Cruise Main Street on a Saturday night to see the spiffed-up vehicles and macho young men.

Turning west on Route 84 takes the traveler through the ink spot of a town called Hernandez. Stop at **Romero's Fruit Stand** to pick up authentic *ristras* (strings of chiles), local honey and tart apple cider before continuing your trip north. ~ Routes 84 and 285; 505-753-4189.

After sitting in the car all day, one's neck tends to stiffen and the shoulders develop knots. It's time for a soak in some mineral hot springs and maybe a massage. About a half hour drive from Española is the no-frills spa called **Ojo Caliente Mineral Springs**. Soak in the springs or perhaps take an herbal wrap. Five minerals—iron, soda, lithia, sodium and arsenic—bubble from the ground. One of the oldest health resorts in the country, Ojo Caliente still looks as it did oh-so-many years ago. Admission. ~ Route 285; 22 miles north of Española; Ojo Caliente; 505-583-2233.

The scenery of sage-filled hills and open vistas will probably start to look more and more familiar as you continue north on Route 84. This is Georgia O'Keeffe country with its blue-bird skies, yucca plants and red-brushed hills in the high desert. The muddy, red-tinged Rio Chama sidles along the highway.

The small town of **Abiquiu**, which was settled in the 1700s on an American Indian ruin at the river's bend, was O'Keeffe's home for many years. When steep, pastel-colored cliffs, part of the shifting formation called the Gallina Fault Zone, come into view, you'll

HIDDEN ▶ know you're nearing the **Ghost Ranch Living Museum**. Environmental education is a theme at this unique learning center. Operated by the U.S. Forest Service, the living museum's short walking tours showcase the native plants and animals. An outdoor refuge is home to orphaned and injured animals. Gateway to the Past, an outdoor museum, has exhibits regarding the culture and peoples of the region. Also here is the one-acre Beaver National Forest, the smallest national forest in the country. The Rio Chama Information Center at the museum provides current and useful facts on the river. Admission. ~ Route 84, Abiquiu; 505-685-4312.

A few miles north again on Route 84 takes you to the trails and natural wonder of **Echo Canyon Amphitheater**. Years of erosion have hollowed out this gargantuan sandstone theater. A picnic area and campground are available.

LODGING They'll loan you golf clubs, tennis rackets or bikes, recommend hikes and heap up plenty of free advice at the **Orange Street Inn,** a quiet alternative to the hotel scene. The suburban-looking house— one almost expects to see June Cleaver at the door—offers eight rooms, four of which share two baths. Each room is furnished differently; some have a Southwest style, others have antiques, and all have thick comforters on the beds. Not only is the morning meal included, but the fridge is open for frozen yogurt during the day and wine in the afternoon. ~ 3496 Orange Street, Los Alamos; phone/fax 505-662-2651, 800-662-3180. BUDGET TO MODERATE.

At the **Los Alamos Inn**, the 115 rooms are bright and pleasant with pastel bedspreads and art class–variety paintings. The inn is in a wooded area of town. Sitting by the swimming pool and sauna will make you feel miles away from the city. ~ 2201 Trinity Drive, Los Alamos; phone/fax 505-662-7211, 800-279-9279. MODERATE.

A dwelling of the same variety is the **Hilltop House Hotel,** which caters to businesspeople with mini-suites and executive suites with full kitchens, a hot tub and sauna, an indoor heated pool and a 24-hour deli. ~ Trinity Drive and Central Street, Los Alamos; 505-662-2441, 800-462-0936, fax 505-662-5913. MODERATE.

DINING Satisfy all kinds of taste demands by dining at **De Colores**, where the menu features native cuisine, grilled chicken and steaks. ~ 820 Trinity Drive, Los Alamos; 505-662-6285. MODERATE.

For lighter fare such as croissants, sandwiches, pastries and espresso, pay a visit to **Café Allegro**. ~ 800 Trinity Drive, Los Alamos; 505-662-4040. BUDGET.

NIGHTLIFE They roll up the sidewalks early in Los Alamos; a big night out may consist of a brew at the corner pub (the likes of which are admittedly few and far between).

BANDELIER NATIONAL MONUMENT 🏃 Nestled in the Jemez
Mountains are cave and cliff dwellings and Pueblo ruins abandoned
about 450 years ago by the farming ancestors of the present Pueblo
people. Hiking trails lead the curious visitor around this secret
honeycombed world. Much of the backcountry was ravaged by a
forest fire in May 1996, so check with the visitors center for updated information. There's a visitors center to get you started.
Food service in the park; a supermarket is nearby; day-use fee, $5.
~ Take Route 502 to Route 4, about ten miles south of Los Alamos;
505-672-0343, 505-672-3861.

▲ There are 94 sites during the summer, about 30 sites during the off-season; $8 per night for individual sites, $35 per night
at group sites. Closed December through February.

FENTON LAKE STATE PARK 🚴 🛶 🚣 🛥️ 🚤 Sheltered in a   ◄ *HIDDEN*
ponderosa pine forest below 1000-foot red cliffs, the park surrounds a 35-acre trout lake that allows no motorboats or swimming. (But nonmotorized boats are allowed and there is access.) In
winter, cross-country skiers appreciate the two miles of groomed
trails and enjoy gliding around the frozen lake through deep snow.
Campsites fill early in the summer, in spite of the fact that Fenton
Lake's 7800-foot elevation makes for cool, cool nights. There are
picnic areas and restrooms throughout the park; day-use fee, $3.
~ Take Route 4 until you reach Route 126, 45 miles west of Los
Alamos; 505-829-3630.

▲ There are 30 developed tent sites, $7 per vehicle; and five
sites with electricity, $11 per vehicle.

ABIQUIU RESERVOIR 🏊 🛶 🏄 🛥️ 🚤 All water sports are
permitted in this 4000-acre reservoir, an Army Corps of Engineering project, which was created by damming the Rio Chama. The
colors of the day, especially sunsets, are splendid in the wonderfully pastel-colored country that artist Georgia O'Keeffe loved so
much. Facilities include picnic areas. ~ On Route 84, seven miles
northwest of Abiquiu; 505-685-4371.

▲ There are 53 tent sites, $6 per night.

It was a forgotten town near where a little-used backcountry   ▼▼▼▼▼▼▼▼
highway crossed the Colorado state line—until the railroad   **Chama Area**
returned. Now thousands of visitors each summer come to
Chama to ride the narrow-gauge steam train into the aspen forests
of the Colorado mountains and back. Although Chama has only
about 1000 residents, it is the largest town in this wild mountain
area where most of the population lives scattered in tiny, traditional Spanish villages or down narrow dirt roads into the solitary
reaches of the Apache lands.

SIGHTS   At an altitude of 8000 feet, **Chama**, located in the southern San Juan Mountains just nine miles from the Colorado border, is becoming more and more popular as a recreation area. Summer is still high time, but with more than 300 miles of trails in the Carson National Forest, snowmobile safaris are common in the little town that bills itself as the "Snowmobile Capital of the Southwest."

Tourism, ranching and lumbering are the lifeblood of Chama, which experienced its first population explosion in the early 1880s with the building of the railroad. The train served mining camps that were digging into this rich region. Records show those were wild times, as saloons and gambling halls lined the main drag.

Like most Wild West towns, Chama had its bust, too. But in 1974 the governments of Colorado and New Mexico purchased 64 miles of rail and restored the coal-fired steam train as a historic tourist attraction. The "double-header" (twin engine) narrow

HIDDEN ▶   gauge **Cumbres and Toltec Scenic Railroad** leaves Chama daily between Memorial Day weekend and mid-October, to chug over hill and dale, through meadows and past groves of piñon, oak, aspen and juniper. Admission. ~ Main Street; 505-756-2151.

Nestling against the river's edge, fording a trestle and hugging high passes, the train makes a 64-mile one-way trip to Antonito, Colorado (you ride a van back) or shorter round-trips to Osier, Colorado. It travels through the valley of Los Piños River, which bursts with iris and sunflower and Indian paintbrush. The steam train moves along up the four percent grade of 10,015-foot Cumbres Pass and burrows through two tunnels to the Toltec Gorge. Autumn is a nice time to see the aspen trees alight the forest. No matter what the season, the ride may be chilly and snow always a possibility. It's not a ride for anyone in a hurry. The 64-mile one-way trip takes six-and-a-half hours.

Ten miles south of Chama on Route 84 is **Los Ojos**, a town that was founded around 1860. Plenty of Los Ojos' original houses remain standing. The architecture combines traditional adobe construction with turn-of-the-century pitched roofs,

◆◆◆◆◆◆◆◆◆◆◆◆◆◆◆◆◆◆◆◆◆

In the 1700s, some people used red chile as a meat preservative, while others rubbed it on their gums for toothaches.

Victorian influences and gingerbread trim. Here you can visit the **Tierra Wools Cooperative Showroom**, where artisans try to revitalize the once-thriving native tradition. ~ Route 84; 505-588-7231.

The **Brazos Cliffs** abut the skyline south of Chama, and for about three weeks each spring a waterfall of snow runoff cascades off 11,289-foot Brazos Peak. ~ Route 512, seven miles east of Route 84.

The tribal members residing on the unspoiled Jicarilla Apache Indian Reservation (505-759-3242) open up their lands for hunting, fishing and camping on the mountain lakes. The Jicarilla's commercial center of **Dulce**, located on Route 64, 25 miles west of

Chama, is where you'll find a tribal arts-and-crafts shop and a small museum.

LODGING

Train buffs holing up in the Chama area for a few days would be wise to make their nest at the homey **Demasters Lodge**. Five enormous rooms with private baths are clean as a whistle. The hot tubs—both indoor and outdoor—help cut the chill of Chama's nights. During hunting season or winter, a huge fire roars in a shared family room that's watched over by a den of animals—bear, elk and mountain lion—bagged locally. Hearty, made-to-order country breakfasts are included in the room price. Dinner (at an extra cost) is available for guests, as well. ~ Route 17, Chama; 505-756-2942. MODERATE.

◄ HIDDEN

Just a few steps out the back door from the **Oso Ranch and Lodge** is the Chama River and Oso Lakes for rainbow trout fishing. The log bed and breakfast has a real outdoorsy feel, from the leather and pine bedrooms to the wild turkeys, elk and deer that are regularly sighted. Guests can choose from breakfast only to full meal plans. ~ Seco Drive, Chama; 505-756-2954, 800-882-5190, fax 505-756-2854. MODERATE TO DELUXE.

DINING

Let your nose lead you: The spicy, peppery smell of native cuisine hails from **Vera's Mexican Kitchen**, where *rellenos*, burritos and enchiladas await. ~ Route 84, Chama; 505-756-2557. BUDGET.

American standards and Mexican favorites are offered at the **High Country Restaurant and Lounge**, where you can choose between such entrées as filet mignon, a seafood platter, steak *asada* or *pico de gallo*. ~ Route 84, Chama; 505-756-2384. BUDGET TO MODERATE.

SHOPPING

The **Narrow Gauge Gift Shop** sells engineers caps (naturally!) and T-shirts at fair prices. ~ Main Street, Chama; 505-756-2963.

Attempting to revitalize the timeless art of weaving are the wool growers and artisans of **Tierra Wools**, who gladly offer their wares through a cooperative showroom. ~ Route 84, Los Ojos; 505-588-7231.

NIGHTLIFE

Catch a little summer melodrama with the weekend gun shows and the 100-year-old soap opera at **Foster's Hotel, Restaurant and Saloon**. The historic hotel, where you'll want to stop for a beverage on any other night, has been in business since 1881. ~ 4th and Terrace streets, Chama; 505-756-2296.

PARKS

EL VADO LAKE STATE PARK This is a beautiful mountain lake for waterskiing and fishing (the latter of which is popular year-round). A fishing derby is held here during the summer; in the winter, ice fishermen head for the frozen waters. There are picnic areas and playgrounds; day-use fee, $3. ~ On Route 112, 14 miles southwest of Tierra Amarilla; information through State Parks Department, 505-827-7465.

▲ There are 43 developed sites ($7 per night) and 30 primitive sites ($6 per night) and 21 RV sites ($11 per night).

▼▼▼▼▼▼▼▼▼▼▼▼▼▼▼
Outdoor Adventures

FISHING

Use bait or fly, but don't head home without some tall fish tales from your trip to the Enchanted Circle. Pack your pole and perambulate over to the Pecos River or one of the area's lakes.

SANTA FE In the Santa Fe area, the fish are probably biting at **Morphy Lake State Park** and **Storrie Lake**, as well as at the **Pecos River**. Try **High Desert Angler** for your fly-fishing guide service. ~ 435 South Guadalupe Street, Santa Fe; 505-988-7688.

BOATING & WIND-SURFING

Some prefer playing on the water when it's not rushing over large rocks. If you don't have your own windsurfing or boating equipment, you can hunt down one of the Storrie Lake sailboard-rental outfits, or go with a boat rental on scenic Heron Lake.

LAS VEGAS AREA On the shores of Storrie Lake north of Las Vegas are the **North Shore Windsurfing Centre** and **G&G Sailboards**, ready to supply you with boards and wetsuits. Neither company has a phone or a permanent building.

CHAMA AREA In the Chama area, hire vessels from **Stone House Lodge**. ~ Heron Lake Road, Rutheron; 505-588-7274.

RIVER RUNNING

Shooting the rapids is an increasingly popular activity around here, so get your feet wet on a tame or tumultuous guided tour of the Rio Grande or the Rio Chama. Many outfitters are ready and willing to help immerse you in the fun of wave riding.

SANTA FE **Rocky Mountain Tours** will take you whitewater rafting. ~ 217 West Manhattan Street; 505-984-1684. **New Wave Rafting Co.** also leads tours from Santa Fe. ~ Route 5 Box 302-A; 505-984-1444. Another outfitter for the region is **Santa Fe Rafting**. ~ 1000 Cerrillos Road; 505-988-4914.

SWIMMING

Swim with the bigshots at the most elevated Olympic-size pool in the country (altitude-wise, that is). Or just splash around in one of the several public pools in the area.

SANTA FE Take a Santa Fe splash at the **Salvador Perez Pool**. ~ 601 Alta Vista Street; 505-984-6755. Also in the area is the the **Tino Griego Pool**. ~ 1730 Llano Street; 505-473-7270. The **Alto/Bicentennial Pool** opens in late May for summer swims. ~ 1121 Alto Street; 505-984-6773.

LAS VEGAS AREA The junior Olympic–size pool at **New Mexico Highlands University** is open to the public on a limited basis. ~ 2118 8th Street, Las Vegas; 505-425-7511.

LOS ALAMOS AREA The **Larry Walkup Aquatic Center** has the highest altitude Olympic-size indoor pool in the nation (athletes use it for endurance training). It's open to the public for lap swimming. ~ 2760 Canyon Road, Los Alamos; 505-662-8170.

SKIING

Don't be fooled by the seemingly dry New Mexico landscape: the mountains are situated in a moisture belt that in an average year receives more snow than the Colorado Rockies. When storm clouds part, be prepared for warm, sunny days in the high desert.

SANTA FE How many capital cities have a full-service ski area within a 30-minute drive? **Santa Fe Ski Area** is located up a winding, twisting road, approximately 15 miles northeast of downtown Santa Fe. ~ Route 475; 505-982-4429.

CHAMA AREA In Chama, the community-trail system maintains nearly four miles of groomed cross-country tracks in the Rio Grande National Forest.

Ski Rentals For ski rentals in Santa Fe, try **Alpine Sports.** ~ 121 Sandoval Street; 505-983-5155. In Los Alamos, try **Trail Bound Sports.** ~ 771 Central Avenue; 505-662-3000. Telemark and cross-country ski rentals, backcountry supplies and repairs, and maps of the Cumbres Pass are available through **Chama Ski Service.** ~ 1551 Alamo Drive, Chama; 505-756-2492.

GOLF

Believe it or not, the New Mexico desert harbors great golfing. Lush courses provide a cool respite from summer heat and primo playing conditions even in the dead of winter. (And there's no charge for the fabulous scenery.)

SANTA FE Practice your swing at the **Santa Fe Country Club.** ~ Airport Road, Santa Fe; 505-471-0601. Play the manicured greens at the **Quail Run Golf Course.** ~ 3101 Old Pecos Trail, Santa Fe; 505-986-2255.

LAS VEGAS AREA In Las Vegas, tee off at **New Mexico Highlands University Golf Course.** ~ Country Club Drive; 505-425-7711.

LOS ALAMOS AREA Duffers in Los Alamos play at the **Los Alamos Golf Club.** ~ 4250 Diamond Drive; 505-662-8139.

TENNIS

There's plenty of space to serve and volley in the Enchanted Circle. Hit one of the area sports stores and head for the parks.

SANTA FE Santa Fe vacationers can take a swing at the **Salvador Perez Complex** (St. Francis Drive and Alta Vista Street), **Herb Martinez Park** (Carlos Rey Street), **Dr. Richard Angle Tennis Courts**

(Old Pecos Trail and St. Michael's Drive), the **Fort Marcy Complex** (Old Taos Highway and Morales Road) and **Larrigoite Park** (Agua Fria Street and Avenida Cristobal Colon). Court information is available at 505-473-7228.

LOS ALAMOS AREA   In Los Alamos, there's **Urban Park** (48th and Urban streets) and **East Park** (110 East Road). ~ 505-662-8170.

RIDING STABLES

Wondering how to acquire that true Western swagger? Hop in the saddle and ride the range—or just take a lesson—with one of the several outfitters in the area.

SANTA FE   Trail rides, lessons and outfitting are available through **B Bar C Training & Boarding Stables.** ~ Route 10, Santa Fe; 505-471-3331. You can also saddle up at **Bishop's Lodge.** ~ Bishop's Lodge Road, Santa Fe; 505-983-6377. Trail rides and pack trips can be taken through the **Llano Bonito Ranch.** ~ 129 Upper Llano Road, Llano; 505-587-2636.

LAS VEGAS AREA   In Las Vegas, try **Enchanted Journeys.** ~ Mineral Hill Road; 505-425-3324.

LOS ALAMOS AREA   **Round Barn Stables** offers trail rides and archaeological horseback tours. ~ Route 285, Ojo Caliente; 505-583-2233.

BIKING

If you haven't noticed the high altitude yet, why not get in touch with your environment by going for a two-wheeled spin? You'll be amply rewarded for your huffing and puffing with breathtaking views.

SANTA FE   From the Santa Fe Plaza, pedal to **Ski Area Basin Road,** which takes cyclists up a windy and at times steep 15-mile two-lane road through heavily wooded national forest land to the Santa Fe Ski Area. To enjoy a shorter trip at a more forgiving altitude (the ski area is at 10,400 feet), just ride the eight miles to Hyde State Park.

A killer ten-mile ride for mountain bikers starts north of the Picacho Hotel on St. Francis Drive, crosses Dead Man's Gulch and Camino La Tierra before heading into the foothills of **La Tierra.** Circle back to the hotel via Buckman Road.

CHAMA AREA   About five miles south of Jemez Springs, take Route 485, which cuts northwest for about ten miles through the hills and two narrow gauge railroad tunnels. Join the Crimson Rock dirt road that follows the river up to **Fenton Lake State Park** and its headwaters. Once you get to Fenton Lake, there are miles of dirt roads within these environs.

Bike Rentals   To get rolling in Santa Fe, try **City Different Bicycle.** ~ 1611 St. Michael's Drive; 505-983-4473. **Trail Bound Sports** is Los Alamos' center for bike rentals and equipment. ~ 771 Central Street; 505-662-3000.

HIKING

When it comes time to travel without wheels, rest assured that the hiking trails in this region offer plenty of incentive for lacing up your boots. Just outside the city limits of Santa Fe, national forest land beckons and the hiker can disappear almost immediately into the dozens of trails that dip around peaks and to mountain lakes. All distances are one-way unless otherwise noted.

SANTA FE The Winsor Trail (9 to 14 miles) meanders at 11,000 feet, sidling along Big Tesuque Creek and the Nambe River. Start at the top of Ski Basin Road and traipse through stands of aspen and evergreen and, finally, above timberline to 12,000-foot-plus Santa Fe Baldy. If you prefer a longer hike, begin in Tesuque along the creek. The gentle Borrego Trail branches off of Winsor.

LAS VEGAS AREA A trail to **Hermit's Peak** (4 miles) gains nearly 3000 vertical feet after starting at 7500 feet. A narrow and rocky path, the view from atop is spectacular. Find it by following Route 65 to the parking lot at El Porvenir, 15 miles northwest of Las Vegas.

LOS ALAMOS AREA The majority of Bandelier National Monument is considered undisturbed backcountry. A large forest fire in May 1996 had a considerable impact on the backcountry; check with the visitors center before you venture out. ~ 505-672-3861.

Plenty of gratification without a whole lot of effort is found on the **Main Loop Trail** (1 mile) in Frijoles Canyon at Bandelier National Monument. Start from the visitors center and walk past the big kiva and the condominium-style dwelling (known as Long House) built into the canyon wall.

Trail to the Falls (1.5 miles) crosses Rio de los Frijoles, follows the creek and passes some impressive cliffs and tent rocks before arriving at the falls.

The trail to the detached **Tsankawi Ruins** (1.5 miles) starts from a trailhead near the intersection of Routes 4 and 502 and winds through lush piñon-juniper woodland, past petroglyphs to a high mesa and the unexcavated Tsankawi Ruins, a condo-style site and nearby cliff dwellings. The trail provides spectacular views of the Española Valley.

✔ **CHECK IT OUT—UNIQUE OUTDOOR ADVENTURES**
- Paddle down stream, with the help of skilled guides, on a whitewater thrill down the tumultuous **Rio Grande**. *page 324*
- Don your skis at **Santa Fe Ski Area**, a quick 30-minute drive from New Mexico's state capital. *page 325*
- Saddle up pardner, and take an archaeological horseback tour in **Ojo Caliente**. *page 326*
- Wander the **Cliff Trail** in Bandalier National monument for sights of petroglyphs, buried buildings and cavelike rooms. *page 318*

▼▼▼▼▼▼▼▼▼▼
Transportation

CAR

Route 25 is the favored north-south road through New Mexico, accessing Las Vegas and Santa Fe. **Route 68** heads south from Taos to Santa Fe, while **Route 285/84** heads north from Los Alamos through Española all the way to Chama and the New Mexico/Colorado border.

Route 64 skirts across the northern edge of New Mexico passing through the Four Corners Area and across to Chama.

AIR

Most visitors to the Santa Fe area fly into Albuquerque (see "Transportation" in Chapter Twelve). **Santa Fe County Municipal Airport** has daily flights via Mesa Airlines from Albuquerque and Denver, Colorado. **Shuttlejack** departs the Albuquerque airport on a regular basis for Santa Fe. ~ 505-982-4311.

BUS

TNM&O Coaches services Santa Fe and Las Vegas. ~ 858 St. Michaels Drive; 505-471-0008.

TRAIN

Amtrak's "Southwest Chief" serves Santa Fe via the village of Lamy, 17 miles from town. ~ 800-872-7245. The **Lamy Shuttle** can take you into Santa Fe. ~ 505-982-8829.

CAR RENTALS

Avis Rent A Car (800-331-1212) and **Hertz Rent A Car** (800-654-3131) have offices both at the airport and in town. **Enterprise Rent A Car** (800-325-8007) offers free shuttle service from the airport. **Budget Rent A Car** (800-527-0700) has an office in town.

PUBLIC TRANSIT

With their chic tan and turquoise paint jobs designed by local artist Sally Blakemore, the natural gas–propelled **Santa Fe Trails** buses are a great way to navigate Santa Fe. Bus #6 takes you from downtown to the Indian Arts, Folk Art and Wheelwright museums as well as to St. John's College. Route #2 serves the motels along Cerrillos Road and goes to the Villa Linda Mall on the far west side of town. This bus also makes it possible to avoid downtown parking problems by leaving your car at the De Vargas Mall (St. Francis Drive at Paseo de Peralta) and taking a 50-minute bus ride downtown. Buses run every half-hour from 6:30 a.m. to 7:00 p.m. on all routes. ~ 505-984-6730.

In Los Alamos, the **Los Alamos Bus System** provides regularly scheduled bus service on a variety of routes. ~ 505-662-2080.

TAXIS

In Santa Fe try **Capital City Cab Co.** ~ 505-438-0000.

WALKING TOURS

Perhaps the most down-to-earth method of touring cities like Santa Fe and Taos is via a walking tour. Local guides provide rich historical and personal insight to their communities as you stroll ancient streets and narrow lanes. Most tours last about two to three hours and may include visits inside area museums. Call **Santa Fe Walks.** ~ Eldorado Hotel lobby, 309 West San Francisco Street; 505-988-2774. You can also try **Taos Walking Tours.** ~ 505-758-4020.

TEN

Taos and the Enchanted Circle

Painters Ernest Blumenschein and Bert Phillips were on their way to Mexico in 1898 when their wagon broke an axle and they found themselves stranded in Taos. In the end, however, it mattered very little. For in the people, the landscape and the crisp mountain light they found subject matter so compelling that their paintings inspired a generation of artists from the East and Europe to follow in their talented footsteps.

The Sangre de Cristo Mountains ("Blood of Christ") abut the town of Taos, which sits at an altitude of nearly 7000 feet above sea level on the east, and the Rio Grande River forms the city's western boundary. The Enchanted Circle is the name commonly given to an 80-mile loop route from Taos that crosses the crest of the Sandre de Cristos and circles all four sides of Wheeler Peak (elevation 13,161 feet), the highest mountain in New Mexico. The drive along the Enchanted Circle affords incomparable vistas of the heart of the high country, perspectives that could hardly help but inspire great works of art.

By the 1920s, Taos enjoyed a reputation as one of the greatest artists' colonies in America, thanks in large part to the sponsorship of local grand dame Mabel Dodge Luján, an East Coast heiress who married a man from Taos Pueblo and invited guests such as D. H. Lawrence, Georgia O'Keeffe and Ansel Adams to visit. (Her house is now a bed-and-breakfast inn.)

In the late 1960s, Taos gained brief notoriety for its hippie communes, where young people from the city joined in attempts to return to the Pueblo Indian way of life. The best known of the old-time communes, New Buffalo, revealed to the outside world in Taos filmmaker Dennis Hopper's '60s epic *Easy Rider*, has now been converted into a bed-and-breakfast establishment.

But the fact that artists and idealists have taken to this part of New Mexico has hardly disrupted the deep cultural traditions that have characterized this area for thousands of years. Powwows, for instance, began in the days when Taos was one of the most distant outposts of the Rio Grande Pueblo Indians. These intertribal gatherings provided opportunities for trade, dancing and politics between the Pueblo Indians and the nomadic Arapahoe and Ute people who roamed the plains and mountains to the north. Today, powwows at Taos Pueblo attract participants from as far away as Canada. The pueblo itself draws throngs of non-Indian travelers from around the world each year to see this tiny, five-story town where residents continue to live without electricity or running water in accordance with ancient custom.

After the first Spanish settlers came, Taos served as a marketplace for trade between the colonists and the Indians. In the 1820s, it became the outpost where mountain men emerged from the southern Colorado Rockies to trade for supplies. (At least one legendary frontiersman, Kit Carson, settled down in Taos, where he lived out his later years as one of the few Anglos in the Spanish and Indian community.) Today, tourism is the town's main industry. It seems that Taos residents (native Pueblo people, descendants of Spanish settlers and contemporary artists and sculptors alike) still support themselves in the same time-honored traditions—trading with visitors from the outside world.

▼▼▼▼▼▼▼▼▼▼
Taos Area

Just as Santa Fe is a unique city, with all the social and economic complexity that term implies, Taos (population 4000) is a unique small town, not exactly easy to understand but certainly direct in its unconventionality. Painters and writers form the backbone of this peaceful yet eccentric frontier outpost, where American Indians, graying hippies and Spanish villagers alike walk in extraordinary beauty. The hodgepodge of architectural styles—Victorian-era frame houses, now stuccoed over in hues of tan, clustered with adobe haciendas from the Spanish Colonial period and Indian houses stacked like honeycombs—only serves to enhance the town's compelling landscape.

SIGHTS

Surrounded by mesas, canyons and mountain peaks, **Taos** has plenty of outdoor recreation year-round. The Taos Box, a wilderness canyon through which the Rio Grande tumbles and roars, offers plenty of whitewater rafting in early summer. Visitors who rent horses from the stables at Taos Pueblo can ride into the reservation's forested mountain highlands, which are otherwise off-limits to non-Indians. Hikers and backpackers find an alpine wonderland among the 13,000-foot summits of the Wheeler Peak area. For those who prefer more conventional sports, the biggest challenge to playing any of the area's golf courses and tennis courts is focusing on the ball instead of the stunning mountain scenery.

Given the superb natural setting, it's ironic that stifling gridlock and auto pollution plague Taos' main artery, Paseo del Pueblo, in all but the slowest seasons. But there's really no other way to get to Taos, and given the large local opposition to airport expansion, it could remain this way for a while. So be ecologically minded, leave your car at your residence and walk around the compact commercial core.

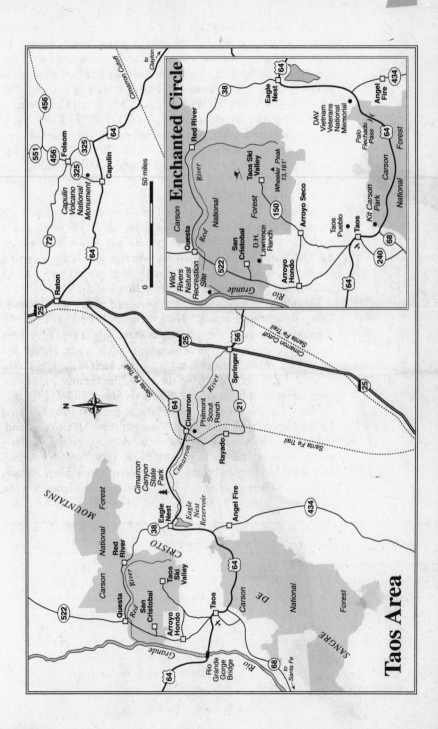

Taos Area

SANGRE DE CRISTO MOUNTAINS

Carson National Forest

to Clayton

Cimarron Cutoff

456

64

551 456 Folsom 325

72 325 Capulin

Capulin Volcano National Monument

64

Raton

25

Santa Fe Trail

N

25 56 Springer

Cimarron Cutoff Santa Fe Trail

25

64 Cimarron

Cimarron River

Philmont Scout Ranch

21 Rayado

Santa Fe Trail

Cimarron River

Cimarron Canyon State Park

Eagle Nest 38

Eagle Nest Reservoir

Angel Fire

434

64

Red River

Questa

Carson National Forest

Red River

San Cristobal

Taos Ski Valley

Arroyo Hondo

522

Taos

Rio Grande Gorge Bridge

Grande

68 to Santa Fe

64

Enchanted Circle

64

38 Red River

Eagle Nest

434 Angel Fire

DAV Vietnam Veterans National Memorial

Palo Flechado Pass

Red River

Carson National Forest

Taos Ski Valley

Wheeler Peak 13,161'

150 Arroyo Seco

Kit Carson Park

68

240

Carson

Questa

Wild Rivers Natural Recreation Site

522 San Cristobal

D.H. Lawrence Ranch

Arroyo Hondo

64

Taos Pueblo

Taos

Rio Grande

50 miles

0

The **Historic Taos Plaza**, as is true in so many Southwestern towns, is its lifeblood. The Plaza has for centuries remained the commercial center for tourism and throughout the centuries, three flags—Spanish, American and Mexican—have flown over the stucco buildings. Plaza galleries and shops merit at least a day's visit. Pick up sightseeing information at the **Taos Chamber of Commerce**. ~ 1139 Paseo del Pueblo Sur; 505-758-3873, 800-732-8267.

Kit Carson Park is a 22-acre verdant park in the center of town that houses the grave of frontiersman Kit Carson. There are picnic areas, a playground, restrooms and an outdoor ice-skating rink (mid-November through February only). ~ 209 Paseo del Pueblo Norte, Taos; 505-758-8234.

Mountain man and scout Kit Carson purchased half of a 12-room adobe home in 1843 as a wedding gift for his bride, Josefa Jaramillo. Today the **Kit Carson Home and Museum** showcases the Old West, with a living room, bedroom and kitchen that re-create the period when Carson's family lived there. There is also a gun exhibit. Admission. ~ Kit Carson Road; 505-758-0505.

Blending the sophistication of European charm with a classic Taos adobe, the **Ernest L. Blumenschein Home** showcases the paintings of Blumenschein (co-founder of the Taos Society of Artists); his wife, Mary Greene Blumenschein; their daughter, Helen; and other Taos artists. The fully restored home, built in the late 1700s, is filled with furnishings from the early 20th century, plus European antiques. Admission. ~ 222 Ledoux Street; 505-758-0505.

Two blocks southwest of the Plaza, at the west end of historic Ledoux Street, is the **Harwood Museum**, New Mexico's second-oldest museum. A Pueblo Revival–style adobe compound, the Harwood showcases the brilliant work of the Taos Society of Artists, core of the local artists' colony. A collection of 19th-century *retablos* (religious paintings on wood) will also fascinate. Closed Sunday. From April through November 1996, the museum will be closed

---

✔ CHECK THESE OUT—UNIQUE SIGHTS

- Visit stunning **Taos Pueblo**, backdropped by the Sangre de Cristo Mountains, and witness daily life as it has been lived for 800 years. *page 335*
- Learn about weaving, quilting, wood carving and other century-old crafts when you stop by the **Martinez Hacienda**, a restored Spanish Colonial hacienda. *page 335*
- Pay tribute to the author of *Sons and Lovers* at the **D. H. Lawrence Ranch**, a memorial built by Lawrence's widow Frieda. *page 345*
- Glance inside the legendary **St. James Hotel**, a Cimarron landmark where shootouts in the saloon were commonplace. *page 348*

for renovations, but the collection will temporarily relocate to other galleries around Taos. Admission. ~ 238 Ledoux Street; 505-758-9826.

The **Fechin Institute** is full of handcarved woodwork in the former adobe of Russian artist Nicolai Fechin, who also designed the building. Open Wednesday through Sunday afternoons from late May through early October. Open in winter by appointment only. Admission. ~ 227 Paseo del Pueblo Norte; 505-758-1710.

Governor Bent's House and Museum has American Indian artifacts and war-era memorabilia from the first governor of New Mexico. It's worth about 15 minutes of your time. Admission. ~ 117 Bent Street; 505-758-2376.

You'll likely see a lot of art while in New Mexico, but as gallery rents continue to rise, finding locally produced pieces becomes more difficult. That's why the **Stables Art Center,** with its accent on local artists, is so refreshing. It's the only gallery run by the Taos Art Association. ~ 133 Paseo del Pueblo Norte; 505-758-2036.

Two miles north of the city, the distant past endures at the **Taos Pueblo,** oldest of the New Mexican Indian pueblos open to the public. This complex houses old adobe buildings that appear much as they did when Spanish explorers first viewed them in 1540. Five stories of adobe structures tower over the site, which allows no electricity or running water for its 50 or so remaining families living in the pueblo buildings. Traditional ways are followed—food is cooked in an outdoor *horno* (oven) and water is drawn from the stream that breeches the heart of the pueblo. Local artisans sell mica-flecked pottery, silver jewelry, moccasins, boots and drums here. Authentic Indian fry bread, hot and drizzled with honey, is a firsthand way to sample American Indian cooking. Closed mid-February through early April. Admission; camera and artist sketching fees. ~ Route 64; 505-758-8626.

Just north of the pueblo turn right on Route 150 for a trip to the **Taos Ski Valley.** The road rises and rolls past churches and tiny hotels through the sleepy towns of Arroyo Seco and Valdez. Making the 12-mile trip at dusk, when the light reflects from the aspen trees in ever-changing hues, can be a magical experience.

American Indian and Hispanic art fill the **Millicent Rogers Museum,** a memorial to the late Standard Oil heiress. Within the 15 galleries are rare examples of jewelry, textiles, basketry, paintings and pottery, as well as exhibits by contemporary artists. Closed Monday from November through April. Admission. ~ Four miles north of Taos off Route 522; 505-758-2462.

South of Taos, at the **Martinez Hacienda** you might discover craftsmen chinking the dark wooden walls of a sheep barn to ward off winter's cold. One of the only fully restored Spanish Colonial adobe haciendas in New Mexico, the fortresslike home is constantly being replastered to maintain its structural integrity. Inside, area artisans who perpetuate century-old skills through a living history program demonstrate weaving, quilting, wood carving and other folk arts. Admission. ~ Ranchitos Road, Route 240; 505-758-1000.

LODGING   Epicenter of Taos activity is the enormously popular **Historic Taos Inn**. A National Historic Landmark, the inn is comprised of several separate houses from the 1800s. Thirty-seven rooms are decorated in a Southwestern motif with Mexican tile, locally designed furniture and hand-loomed Indian bedspreads; most have hand-painted fireplaces. If the inn is booked, which it may very well be, set aside an evening to enjoy a drink in the lobby, which is as comfortable as any living room. A favorite hangout for locals, also known as "Taoseños," the inn's lobby is showplace to the recurring "Meet the Artist Series." ~ 125 Paseo del Pueblo Norte, Taos; 505-758-2233, 800-826-7466. MODERATE TO ULTRA-DELUXE.

The **Laughing Horse Inn** is a century-old hacienda transformed into a European-style pension. As the name implies, it helps to have a sense of humor when staying here. One guest room has chile pepper–motif lights and the inn's floor varies between old wood and varnished dirt. The communal kitchen offers light snacks for next-to-nothing prices. ~ 729 Paseo del Pueblo Norte, Taos; 505-758-8350, 800-776-0161, fax 505-751-1123. MODERATE.

A hermit could easily hole up for an extended period of time in the **Sonterra Condominiums**, a special little side-street retreat. Quiet, comfortable and decorated in bright contemporary New Mexican style, most of the Sonterra units have fireplaces, separate sitting space and private patios. ~ 206 Siler Road, Taos; 505-758-7989. MODERATE TO DELUXE.

From the friendly "welcome home" greeting by the front-desk clerk to the hearty skillet breakfasts, the **Ramada Inn Taos** is big on comfort and warmth. Refurbished in nouvelle-adobe style and pastel colors, the Ramada capably handles groups—even in the hot tub, where après ski is often shoulder to shoulder—without neglecting individuals. ~ 615 Paseo del Pueblo Sur, Taos; 505-758-2900, 800-659-8267, fax 505-758-1662. MODERATE TO DELUXE.

A distinctive Pueblo-style architecture marks the **Holiday Inn Don Fernando de Taos**. Rooms are designed around central courtyards and connected by walkways that meander through landscaped grounds. Standard rooms are oversized, while suites have living rooms, fireplaces and hospitality bars. All feature Southwestern styles, including hand-carved New Mexican furniture. A large heated pool, hot tub, tennis court and on-site restaurant and lounge add to the friendly ambience. ~ 1005 Paseo del Pueblo Sur, Taos; 505-758-4444, 800-759-2736, fax 505-758-0055. DELUXE.

Back to
New Buffalo

Back in the 1960s, young people from all over the country abandoned city life and migrated to the mountains of New Mexico. Soon, over 3000 hippies set up house in the Taos area.

Clearing the land and building adobe communal homes, they sought to create a simple lifestyle in tune with nature. Simple it wasn't. Besides the hard physical labor they experienced, these freewheeling pioneers had to cultivate their own food, debate communal politics and wrestle with the problems and possibilities of their new-found sexual freedom. Life became a grand experiment.

In the forefront of this back-to-the-land movement was the New Buffalo Commune. Rick Klein, using an inheritance, purchased 80 acres of land in the ancient valley of Arroyo Hondo, just outside Taos. It was 1967, the Summer of Love. With a commitment to change, Klein gave the land to the commune. New Buffalo became the ultimate counter-cultural experience. Celebrities Dennis Hopper, Peter Fonda, Timothy Leary and Janis Joplin reportedly stayed here at one time.

The nation was exposed to the lifestyle of New Buffalo through essays in *Look* and *Life* magazines, as well as *Playboy*, *Newsweek* and *Esquire*. An exact replica of the commune was fashioned for the movie *Easy Rider*. Craft industries thrived here—pottery, tie-dying, weaving, leather and jewelry making. Communing with nature and American Indian spirits, many New Buffalo residents discovered spiritual connections. But it was the nudity, rock-and-roll and drugs that made the headlines. By the 1980s the commune collapsed; and in 1989 the land reverted back to Klein and his wife.

What happens to defunct communes? They become bed and breakfasts, of course! Now at the **New Buffalo Bed and Breakfast**, Rick and Terry Klein still offer a communal feeling at their former hippie retreat. With a family atmosphere, complete with common rooms and shared baths, it's a unique hostelry. There are five guest rooms, some decorated in subdued Southwestern fashion and one that is done up in a tie-dye scheme that, according to the owners, is "really crazy." There are also four tepees (all with beds and lit by candles) available May to October, and an "alternative campground" that allows anyone to walk in and pitch a tent.

While the days of drugs and free love are long since vanished, the pursuit of spiritual enlightenment and the blending of counterculture and American Indian culture endure. There is a communal center where meals are served, and where music and drumming workshops regularly take place. If you yearn for a trip back to another era, a stop at the New Buffalo Bed and Breakfast is your ticket. ~ Arroyo Hondo; 505-776-2015, fax 505-776-1053. BUDGET TO MODERATE.

The exterior of the **Sagebrush Inn** looks just like that of any other Pueblo-style hotel. But open the hefty front door and it's a totally different world. Rooms are dark and romantic, usually decorated with Navajo rugs and pottery and equipped with fireplaces. A pool and hot tubs are nice amenities. Breakfast is included in the room price. ~ 1508 Paseo del Pueblo Sur, Taos; 505-758-2254, 800-428-3626. MODERATE TO DELUXE.

Set among the cottonwood trees in a parklike setting is the **El Monte Lodge**. Refrigerators are standard issue in the traditionally appointed Southwestern-style rooms. Some of the units sport kiva fireplaces and kitchenettes. ~ 317 Kit Carson Road, Taos; 505-758-3171, 800-828-8267. MODERATE TO DELUXE.

Taos bed and breakfasts are extraordinary and becoming ever more popular. Hidden on a lovely lane about three blocks south of the Plaza is **Casa de los Chimeneas**, a guesthouse for those who love being pampered. The largest of the four units has a study and living room, with a collection of books and magazines. The rooms have oak furniture, tiled bathrooms and views of the formal garden and fountains. There's a hot tub on site and a large common area. ~ 405 Cordoba Road, Taos; 505-758-4777. DELUXE TO ULTRA-DELUXE.

El Rincón Bed and Breakfast is a remarkable inn with 13 units, each a treat in itself. Built around a patio overflowing with flowers, each room features a spiral staircase, vigas, an American Indian fireplace and cowboy motifs. The whimsical Sonrisa Room has a canopied bed with a wedding-ring quilt, while the Paisley Room has an East Indian touch complete with a Byzantine headboard and hand-carved teak. This inn includes a wheelchair-accessible unit. ~ 114 Kit Carson Road, Taos; 505-758-4874, fax 505-758-4541. MODERATE TO DELUXE.

HIDDEN ► Every room at **Casa Benavides Bed & Breakfast Inn** is unique, but they share a common quality—luxury. Several meticulously restored buildings, including an old trading post and an artist's studio, make up the 31-room complex. This crème de la crème property is elegantly furnished with tile floors, handmade furniture, kiva fireplaces, down comforters and a bevy of unusual antiques. The sumptuous breakfasts are served in a bright, airy dining room. ~ 137 Kit Carson Road, Taos; 505-758-1772, fax 505-758-5738. MODERATE TO ULTRA-DELUXE.

One of the area's original bed and breakfasts, **La Posada de Taos** provides a homey atmosphere in its huge book-filled living room and open, sunny dining room. The 100-year-old house has been lovingly remodeled with six guest units, each with tiled baths and antique furnishings. Five of the units are inside the inn itself, the sixth is a honeymoon cottage across the adobe-walled courtyard. All but the Taos Room have private patios and wood-burning stoves or adobe fireplaces. ~ 309 Juanita Lane, Taos; 505-758-8164, 800-645-4803. MODERATE TO DELUXE.

Still think "there's no place like home"? Then visit **The Ruby Slipper**. Even Dorothy could find a room to suit her needs at this bed and breakfast. Choose from a room with a sunken bedroom or one with willow furniture. Oak floors, kiva fireplaces, traditional viga ceilings and private entrances also characterize some of the seven quiet rooms. ~ 416 La Lomita Road, Taos; 505-758-0613. MODERATE TO DELUXE.

Close to the Taos Ski Area, with outrageous views of the Sangre de Cristo Mountains, is luxurious **Salsa Del Salto**. Goose-down comforters warm the king-size beds. Leather couches in the common area are placed in front of the two-story stone fireplace—a good place for getting horizontal after a long day on Taos' tough slopes. The pool, tennis courts and hot tub help take the edge off, as well. ~ Route 150, one mile north of Arroyo Seco; phone/fax 505-776-2422, 800-530-3097. DELUXE TO ULTRA-DELUXE.

Skiers, hikers and other adventuresome spirits looking for an ultra-cheap experience should seek out the **Hostelling International—Taos**, also known as the **Abominable Snowmansion**. The hostel has six dorm rooms with large closets and dressing areas (any can be converted into private family rooms). A piano, fireplace and conversation area are also available. There are Indian tepees or a bunkhouse for additional sleeping arrangements. Showers and use of the solar kitchen are included in the price. ~ Taos Ski Valley Road, Arroyo Seco; 505-776-8298. BUDGET.

It's hard not to get lost while walking around the compound known as the **Quail Ridge Inn**. Low-slung buildings containing fully equipped apartment-size rooms dot the landscape. A casual, country-club variety of clientele clogs the pool, tennis and squash courts and fitness center. The self-contained resort offers so many on-site amenities and diversions that you need not ever leave the complex, which would be a crying shame considering all there is

---

✔ CHECK THESE OUT—UNIQUE LODGING

- *Budget:* Request one of the three authentic tepees at the **Abominable Snowmansion**, where you'll be well positioned for days of hiking or skiing. *page 339*
- *Moderate:* Get cozy in one of the **Laughing Horse Inn**'s unique rooms, then join the other guests for a snack in the communal kitchen. *page 336*
- *Moderate to deluxe:* Hole up in a rustic cabin at **Rio Colorado Lodge**, located just minutes from the Red River. *page 346*
- *Deluxe to ultra-deluxe:* Return to **Salsa Del Salto** after a day on the slopes and ease away the pain soaking in the hot tub. *page 339*

Budget: under $50 Moderate: $50–$90 Deluxe: $90–$120 Ultra-deluxe: over $120

to see in Taos. ~ Taos Ski Valley Road, Taos; 505-776-2211, 800-624-4448, fax 505-776-2949. DELUXE TO ULTRA-DELUXE.

If long days of skiing and multicourse meals are enough to satisfy you, consider a stay in the Taos Ski Valley at one of the European-flavored lodges like the simple but comfortable **Hotel St. Bernard.** Location, location, location and a family atmosphere prevail at this 28-room chalet-style dwelling. Reservations are usually made by the week only; all meals are included in the price. Closed early April through Thanksgiving. ~ Taos Ski Valley Road, Taos; 505-776-2251. DELUXE.

About one mile from the ski area is the **Austing Haus Hotel,** the largest timber-frame building in North America. As the name implies, this charming 24-unit bed and breakfast has an Austrian ambience. The glass dining room is truly elegant. ~ Taos Ski Valley Road, Taos; 505-776-2649, 800-748-2932. MODERATE TO DELUXE.

DINING

You could eat three meals a day in the Taos Inn's award-winning restaurant **Doc Martin's** and never get bored. Blue-corn and blueberry hotcakes at breakfast make the mouth water, as do shrimp burritos for lunch. But it's at dinnertime that the kitchen really shines. Savor the grilled ahi tuna and specials like the piñon-crusted lamb chop and try to save room for dessert. ~ 125 Paseo del Pueblo Norte, Taos; 505-758-1977. MODERATE TO DELUXE.

HIDDEN ►

Delicious whole-grain breads, fresh-squeezed juices, plus tarts and pies to undo all the good you've put in your body are common at the **Main Street Bakery.** If you're shy about garlic, don't order the home-style potatoes. This is a great place to catch up on local gossip. Dinner—mostly sandwiches and pasta dishes—is served Wednesday through Sunday. ~ 211 Doña Luz Road, Taos; 505-758-9610. BUDGET TO MODERATE.

The funky sign on local institution **Michael's Kitchen** might grab you, but the sweets' cabinet could lock you into a stranglehold. Spill-off-your-plate-size breakfasts pack 'em in on ski mornings; diner-type meals are served the rest of the day. ~ 304 Paseo del Pueblo Norte, Taos; 505-758-4178. BUDGET.

Lamb entrées top the list of house specialties at **Lambert's of Taos.** Established in 1989 by the former chef at Doc Martin's, Lambert's serves imaginative presentations of mahimahi, salmon and swordfish in the parlor rooms of a refurbished Territorial-era house that exudes an atmosphere of gracious frontier living. The menu also includes beef, veal and poultry selections. ~ 309 Paseo del Pueblo Sur, Taos; 505-758-1009 MODERATE.

The emphasis is on fresh at the **Apple Tree,** a charming house converted to a restaurant. The Apple Tree offers innovative interpretations of standard poultry, fish and meat dishes. Killer desserts top off the menu. ~ 123 Bent Street, Taos; 505-758-1900. MODERATE TO DELUXE.

Pizza Emergency has great Sicilian and New York–style pizza and a name you won't quickly forget. Also on the menu are baked pastas and hot meatball sandwiches. They have free delivery in the Taos area, but only until 9:30 p.m.—well before the pizza bug typically strikes. ~ 316 Paseo del Pueblo Sur, Taos; 505-751-0911. BUDGET.

Housed in an old adobe building, **Roberto's** specializes in Northern New Mexican cuisine. The entrées include tacos, enchiladas, homemade tamales and *chile rellenos*. Closed Tuesday in summer; closed every day but weekends and holidays November through May. ~ Kit Carson Road, Taos; 505-758-2434. MODERATE.

Taos has no shortage of newsstand cafés. **Caffe Tazza** makes for a wonderful stop in the middle of the day. ~ 122 Kit Carson Road; 505-758-8706. **Dori's** is a pleasant place to sip espresso and munch on a sweet or just kick back and work on your novel. ~ 402 Paseo del Pueblo Norte, Taos; 505-758-9222. BUDGET.

For outstanding *chile rellenos*, blue-corn tortillas and other regional food in a fun and rowdy atmosphere, try the **Chile Connection**. ~ Mile Marker 1, Taos Ski Valley Road, four miles north of Taos; 505-776-8787. MODERATE.

Those looking for a special evening in an intimate setting would be well advised to try **Casa Cordova**, where the Continental cuisine includes such dishes as grilled quail with raspberry glaze and prawns broiled with olive oil and garlic. R. C. Gorman lithographs decorate the walls and the big Mexican chairs seem to suck you up when the tequila and sangria start doing their number. Closed Sunday. ~ 150 Taos Ski Valley Road, Arroyo Seco; 505-776-2500. MODERATE TO DELUXE.

Amid an Old World kind of atmosphere, the **Rathskeller Restaurant** features homemade soups, sandwiches, stews and chili. Closed early April through Thanksgiving. ~ Hotel St. Bernard, Taos Ski Area; 505-776-2251. BUDGET TO MODERATE.

✔ **CHECK THESE OUT—UNIQUE DINING**

- *Budget:* Go to **Michael's Kitchen** for a bounteous breakfast that will sustain you on the Taos slopes. *page 340*
- *Moderate:* Choose **The Lodge at Red River**, in the heart of town, for a relaxing, filling meal. *page 347*
- *Moderate to deluxe:* Check out the bullet holes in the ceiling when you dine on escargot or veal marsala at **Lambert's**. *page 340*
- *Ultra-deluxe:* Reserve a table at **St. Bernard's** for a scrumptious *prix-fixe* dinner in a chalet-style ambience. *page 342*

Budget: under $8 Moderate: $8–$16 Deluxe: $16–$24 Ultra-deluxe: over $24

Seatings for nonguests are tough to come by (and are only by reservation) at **St. Bernard's** set-menu restaurant but well worth the cajoling to enjoy a typical dinner of rack of lamb or bouillabaisse, topped off by raspberry melba. Closed early April through Thanksgiving. ~ Taos Ski Area; 505-776-2251. ULTRA-DELUXE.

For après-ski nibbles, mosey on down the hill to **Tim's Stray Dog Cantina**. Quaff multiple varieties of margaritas while chowing down on the rich tequila shrimp, homemade green-chile stew and mud pie that will push your cholesterol count off the Richter scale. ~ Cottam's Alpine Village, Taos Ski Valley; 505-776-2894. BUDGET TO MODERATE.

SHOPPING   The Taos "mystique" has always lured artists and craftsmen, so expect to find lots of shops and galleries around the Plaza and surrounding streets.

For a deal on moccasins, stop by the **Taos Moccasin Factory Outlet Store**. ~ 216 Paseo del Pueblo Sur; 505-751-0032. **Old Mexico Shop** is a traditional favorite for American Indian prints and native clothing. ~ McCarty Plaza, Taos; 505-758-2531.

Gourmets will find stoneware, Southwestern foods, linens and more at **Taos Cookery**. ~ 113 Bent Street, Taos; 505-758-5435.

Antiques and beautiful Oriental rugs fill the front and back yards of **Patrick Dunbar Rugs and Antiques**, which is interesting to visit even if you can't afford a single thing. ~ 222 Paseo del Pueblo Norte, Taos; 505-758-2511.

Touristy, yes, but wonderful too, is R. C. Gorman's **Navajo Gallery**, which specializes in Gorman's paintings and sculpture of Navajo women. ~ 210 Ledoux Street, Taos; 505-758-3250.

Taos has a plethora of art galleries. Here's a sampling of what you'll find. **Rod Goebel Gallery** features interpretive portraiture, landscapes and still lifes. ~ 110 Paseo del Pueblo Norte; 505-758-2181. **The Clay and Fiber Gallery** has beautiful bowls, jewelry, textiles and clothing. ~ 126 West Plaza Drive; 505-758-8093. **Stables Art Center** carries the work of many area artists. ~ 133 Paseo del Pueblo Norte; 505-758-2036. The **New Directions Gallery** specializes in contemporary Taos painting and sculpture. ~ 107-B North Plaza, Taos; 505-758-2771. Another gallery that merits a visit is **Wade Gallery of Taos**. ~ 208 Paseo del Pueblo Norte; 505-758-7500. Also stop by the **Taos Traditions Gallery**. ~ 221 Paseo del Pueblo Norte; 505-758-0016.

There are many great bookstores in Taos. A favorite is **Moby Dickens Bookshop**, which has plenty of places to sit and read. A watch cat guards the door. ~ 124-A Bent Street; 505-758-3050. **Brodsky Bookshop** has a large selection of American Indian and Southwestern titles as well as poetry and literature. ~ 218 Paseo del Pueblo Norte; 505-758-9468. The **Taos Book Shop** purports to be the oldest book shop in the state. ~ 122-D Kit Carson Road; 505-758-3733.

Taos Artisans Gallery is an impressive cooperative of iron sculpture, jewelry, leather, pottery and woven clothing. ~ 107-A Bent Street; 505-758-1558. Another gem of an art cooperative is **Open Space Gallery**, where more than a dozen local artists show their work. ~ 103-B East Plaza, Taos; 505-758-1217.

The Jordans Magic Mountain Gallery features contemporary ceramics, inlaid boxes, jewelry, bronze sculpture and oil paintings. ~ 107-A North Plaza, Taos; 505-758-9604.

Those heaven-bound should wing their way to **Angel's**, where the clothing is feminine and romantic, and the gift items are angelic. ~ 113 Bent Street, Taos; 505-758-7571. The owners of Angel's run a trendy store called **10½ for Men** featuring casual and out-on-the-town duds for dudes. ~ 109 Bent Street, Taos; 505-758-1226.

LaLana Wools uses fine natural fibers to make sweaters and coats, yarns and jackets. ~ 136 Paseo del Pueblo Norte, Taos; 505-758-9631. **Taos Mountain Outfitters** sells garb and equipment for trekking into the high country. ~ 114 South Plaza, Taos; 505-758-9292.

NIGHTLIFE

Movies, live theater and other performances can be enjoyed at the **Taos Community Auditorium**. ~ Paseo del Pueblo Norte, Taos; 505-758-2052.

To taste the local flavor or take a gander at the recurring local artists' series, swing by the **Taos Inn's Adobe Bar**. ~ 125 Paseo del Pueblo Norte, Taos; 505-758-2233.

Hot times are had at the **Sagebrush Inn Bar**, with nightly live music and country-and-western dancing. ~ 1508 Paseo del Pueblo Sur, Taos; 505-758-2254.

Live music also can be heard at the **Ramada Inn**. ~ 615 Paseo del Pueblo Sur, Taos; 505-758-2900.

Taos' best sports bar, complete with brew pub and a boisterous crowd, the **Chile Connection** is a busy hot spot. ~ Mile Marker 1, Ski Valley Road, Taos; 505-776-8787.

For a drink in the Taos Ski Valley, check out the margaritas at **Tim's Stray Dog Cantina**. ~ Cottam's Alpine Village, Taos Valley Ski Area; 505-776-2894. The **Thunderbird Lodge** is another good bet. ~ 3 Thunderbird Road; 505-776-2280.

On the road back to Taos, **Casa Cordova** is a natural stop for après-ski drinks. ~ 150 Taos Ski Valley Road, Arroyo Seco; 505-776-2500.

PARKS

ORILLA VERDE RECREATION AREA ⌐ Situated on the banks of an ultrascenic stretch of the Rio Grande, the park is renowned for its trout fishing but equally popular for day outings and weekend camping. The only facilities are picnic areas and restrooms. ~ Located on Route 68, 14 miles southwest of Taos; 505-758-4060. ▲ There are 32 campsites; $5 to $7 per night.

▼▼▼▼▼▼▼▼▼▼▼▼▼▼▼▼
Enchanted Circle Area

The Enchanted Circle is the name given to the 84-mile loop formed by Routes 522, 38 and 64. From Taos, the paved route winds through subalpine evergreen forests around the base of Wheeler Peak, the highest mountain in New Mexico (elevation 13,161 feet). Along the way you'll find ski resorts, a recreational lake in a basin surrounded by mountain peaks, and a moving tribute to the men and women who served in the Vietnam War.

SIGHTS

After you've "done" Taos and want to tour the area known as the **Enchanted Circle**, drive south of downtown Taos to Route 64 and cruise over scenic Palo Flechado Pass, which was used by American Indians and Spaniards who came from the plains via the Cimarron River. Along the way are several places to pull over for a picnic or snapshot.

Upon reaching the intersection of Route 434, turn south for a quick visit to the resort town of **Angel Fire**. In winter it's a favorite destination for intermediate skiers, while in summer, golfers, hikers and lovers of chamber music flock to Angel Fire.

The DAV **Vietnam Veterans National Memorial** pays tribute to soldiers who fought in Vietnam. Set against the backdrop of the Sangre de Cristo Mountains, this 24-acre monument is one of the largest in the country. It includes a visitors center with extensive exhibits dedicated to the memory of those who lost their lives as well as access to computerized archives of KIA (killed in action) and MIA (missing in action) soldiers. There's also an interdenominational chapel on the premises. Closed Monday in summer; closed Monday and Tuesday in winter. ~ Route 64, Angel Fire; 505-377-6900.

Back on Route 64 you'll soon come to **Eagle Nest Reservoir,** a fine sailing, windsurfing and fishing lake that affords a spectacular lookout. Be sure to get a good look at **Wheeler Peak**, the state's highest peak at 13,161 feet above sea level.

At the lake's north shore is the village of **Eagle Nest**, with a handful of restaurants and shops. From there it's 24 windy miles to Cimarron through the Cimarron Range (one of the easternmost ranges of the Sangre de Cristo Mountains), the Colin Neblett Wildlife Area and Cimarron Canyon.

Three miles east of Eagle Nest are the towering walls of **Cimarron Canyon State Park**. Be sure to watch your speed, and after dark be on the lookout for deer as you travel through the narrow canyon. ~ Route 64; 505-377-6271.

Return to Eagle Nest; just north of the town (where Route 64 becomes Route 38) is an open and pretty valley ringed with high mountains. Drop down Bobcat Pass into **Red River**, yet another Wild West village. Though touristy, this turn-of-the-century gold-mining town retains a certain charm from its rip-roaring gambling, brawling and red light district days. A ski area rises out of its center and national forest land surrounds it completely.

Taos Ski Area is so popular that Taos has become the only town in New Mexico where winter, not summer, is the peak tourist season.

Winnie's Museum Park is a special find. Your tour begins at the office where guide Winnie Hamilton leads the way down to the early 1900s Oldham Cabin. After being introduced to a sheriff named "Big Jim," your charming docent, who has an encyclopedic grasp of local history, will tell you the story of early settlers, including her own family. Early mining tools, historic documents, turn-of-the-century furniture and toys all enhance the story. Closed November through March (or any other snow-heavy days, or whenever Winnie feels like it). Admission. ~ Upper Red River Canyon Road, 1.5 miles east of Red River; 505-754-6404.

Continuing east on the Enchanted Circle, which hugs Red River, you'll drive past plenty of forest and camping spots until you reach the honey-producing town of Questa. Just 11 miles northeast of Questa is the **Wild Rivers Natural Recreation Site**, the ideal place to see the Rio Grande and Red River in their natural state. The Art Zimmerman Visitors Center features geologic exhibits, interpretive displays and rangers who will help you make the most of this scenic area. Most visitors flock to La Junta Point overlooking the junction of these free-flowing rivers. Self-guiding nature trails show you how the Rio Grande Gorge was etched out over the centuries by wind and water. The numerous hiking trails in this area include several steep climbs leading down to the water. Proceed with caution. ~ Located on Route 378; 505-758-8851.

Thirteen miles south of Questa is the **D. H. Lawrence Ranch**, a memorial to the British writer built by his widow, Frieda. Now a field center for the University of New Mexico, it can be readily visited during the daytime hours. ~ Located off Route 522, San Cristobal; 505-776-2245.

Another 13 miles south is the junction of Routes 522 and 64. Go west on Route 64 until you reach the **Rio Grande Gorge Bridge**. You may want to hold your breath while crossing this suspension bridge, 650 feet over the Rio Grande.

Bring the family to the full-service **Legends Hotel and Conference Center** where ultraspacious guest rooms, bedecked in pastel colors and Southwestern styles, offer plenty of closet space and can easily accommodate rollaway beds. ~ North Angel Fire Road, Angel

LODGING

Fire; 505-377-6401, 800-633-7463, fax 505-377-4200. MODER-ATE TO DELUXE.

The Inn at Angel Fire offers 28 clean and sensible motel rooms plus a game room, sauna and skiers' packages (including breakfast, dinner and lift tickets) during the snowy season. ~ Route 62, Angel Fire; 505-377-2504, 800-666-1949. MODERATE TO DELUXE.

Prices drop even more at the Laguna Vista Lodge, just 12 miles north of Angel Fire on the pretty road to Eagle Nest. Motel rooms and suites are available. ~ Route 64, Eagle Nest; 505-377-6522, 800-821-2093. BUDGET TO MODERATE.

For a laid-back vacation complete with rustic cabins, a small private fishing lake and easy access to the Red River, head for Rio Colorado Lodge. Paneled with tongue-and-groove knotty pine, the 21 one- to three-bedroom units come with full kitchens and chenille bedspreads. Many offer fireplaces, and most are fully carpeted. Families especially appreciate the large picnic areas (with barbecue pits) and playground for the kids. ~ 515 East Main Street, Red River; 505-754-2212, 800-654-6516. MODERATE TO DELUXE.

The Telemark Bed and Breakfast and Townhouses offers comfortable units. All six rooms are furnished with wicker pieces and antiques. Each of the two-story townhouses offers its own fireplace and two bedrooms. Private decks and porches plus a hot tub overlooking the river add to the enjoyment. Children under seven stay free. Highly recommended. Closed early April through mid-May. ~ River Street, adjacent to Caribel Trail on the river; Red River; 505-754-2534. MODERATE TO DELUXE.

A short walk to the ski slopes, Lifts West Condominium Resort Hotel features contemporary, two-story units, all with fireplaces and wall-to-wall carpeting. Many have complete kitchens and balconies or decks. A heated pool, restaurant and shopping mall are on the premises. ~ 201 Main Street, Red River; 505-754-2778, 800-221-1859, fax 505-754-6617. MODERATE TO ULTRA-DELUXE.

On the banks of the Red River by the ski lifts is the Alpine Lodge. Rooms and apartments are well maintained, all with porch or balcony. On-site restaurant and nearby ski rental make the Alpine a convenient spot for skiers. ~ 417 Main Street, Red River; 505-754-2952, 800-252-2333. BUDGET TO MODERATE.

The 26 rooms at The Lodge at Red River are rustic, but the central location is appealing. ~ 400 East Main Street, Red River; 505-754-6280, 800-915-6343, fax 505-754-6304. MODERATE.

DINING   Try fresh trout with piñon nuts or a double-decker pizza at the Coyote Creek Cafe after you've worked up an appetite on the slopes. Closed Monday April through November. ~ Route 434, Angel Fire; 505-377-3550. BUDGET TO MODERATE.

Eager to trade fast-food drive-ins for a table set with white linen? Then take a seat in the beam-ceilinged dining room at **The Lodge at Red River**. Specialties like rainbow trout, fried chicken and charbroiled pork chops will make up for all the cheeseburgers you've suffered. All entrées come with salad, mashed potatoes and vegetables, and extra helpings on these items are available at no extra charge. The bar is a pleasant après-ski stop. ~ 400 East Main Street, Red River; 505-754-6280. MODERATE.

In the town of Red River, you can't top **Angelina's** for chicken-fried steak, enchilada plates and a generous soup and salad bar. The Southwest-style pastel decor includes ceiling fans and booth seating. Closed Monday April through November. ~ 112 West Main Street, Red River; 505-754-2211. BUDGET TO MODERATE.

Corny as it may sound, you won't waddle away hungry from **Texas Red's Steakhouse**, which specializes in slabs of beef, big hamburgers and other hearty Western-style meals. Closed Tuesday and Wednesday April through November. ~ 111 Main Street, Red River; 505-754-2964. MODERATE TO DELUXE.

Over the mountain in Red River, stop in at **Bull o' the Woods Saloon**, with live country music on weekends. Cover. ~ Main Street; 505-754-2593. Another bar with live country-and-western on weekend nights is the **Motherlode**. Occasional cover. ~ 400 East Main Street, Red River; 505-754-6280.   **NIGHTLIFE**

Melodramas are staged in season at the **Red River Inn**. ~ Main Street, Red River; 505-754-2930.

CIMARRON CANYON STATE PARK 🚶🛶 Granite formations tower above a sparkling stream where brown and rainbow trout crowd the waters and wildlife congregates. Rock-climbing is permitted within these environs with a special use permit (available at the park). There are some hiking trails, but fishing is the most popular park activity. Facilities are limited to picnic areas and restrooms. ~ Located on Route 64, 20 miles west of Cimarron; 505-377-6271.   **PARKS**

▲ There are 104 developed sites ($7 per night).

Known as *Los Llanos*, "the plains," the wide-open country spills from the edge of the mountains across the empty northeastern corner of New Mexico and on   ▼▼▼▼▼▼▼▼▼▼▼▼ **East of Cimarron**
into Oklahoma and the Texas Panhandle. Those who take the time to visit Capulin Volcano can stand at the top of this extinct, solitary cone that rises out of the prairie and appreciate the vastness of this land. Most travelers, however, hurry through the area on the interstate without realizing that the two-lane highway from Raton through Cimarron and through the Sangre de Cristo Mountains is

SIGHTS

a beautiful shortcut to both Taos and Santa Fe. Both Cimarron and Raton preserve their frontier heritage in historic buildings and small museums full of Old Western artifacts.

The settlement of **Cimarron**, where plain and pasture meet rugged mountains, was founded in 1848 with entrepreneur Lucien Maxwell's land grant. Life was cheap back at this outpost on the mountain branch of the Santa Fe Trail and death from a gunfight was not uncommon. Cimarron the town and Cimarron the river certainly lived up to the Spanish translation of their name—wild and untamed. While that may have described Cimarron a century ago, these days it's a pretty mellow small town. The rambling river waters too have been calmed by the establishment of Eagle Nest Reservoir.

A trip to Cimarron wouldn't be complete without a peek inside the historic **St. James Hotel,** with its partly renovated interior and completely authentic funkiness. Built in 1880 by one of Abraham Lincoln's chefs, some say the St. James is haunted by outlaw ghosts of the past. ~ Route 1; 505-376-2664.

Originally built as a grist mill, the **Old Mill Museum** now offers a panoramic view of local history from chuckwagons to regional paintings. And while the collection does include sleighs and American Indian pottery shards, it focuses on ranching, mining and homesteading in the Cimarron area. You'll find yourself surrounded by treasures of the past. This exhibit is not to be missed. Closed October through May. Admission. ~ Route 21, Cimarron.

More down to earth is the **Philmont Scout Ranch**, the nation's largest scouting camp. In 1922, the Tulsa oil baron Waite Phillips bought a 300,000-acre ranch south of Cimarron. In 1941, he donated a total of 136,000 acres to the Boy Scouts of America. Today, a small museum features local artifacts and works of Ernest Thompson-Seton, one of the founders of the Boy Scouts. Also here

◆◆◆

THE MANSION IN THE MIDDLE OF NOWHERE

Dorsey Mansion may be a long way from anywhere, but it's definitely worth the excursion. The stone and log mansion was once the heart of a ranch that extended 60 miles in length. Now it's a landmark—listed on the National Register of Historic Places—adorned with an Italian marble fireplace and a number of intriguing gargoyles. Carved rattlesnakes and bobcats lunge from the intricate stone fountain. Don't try visit in inclement weather; the clay roads are exceptionally slick when wet. Reservations required. Admission. ~ Located 24 miles east of Springer on Route 56, then 12 miles north on a dirt road; 505-375-2222.

is **Villa Philmonte** (admission), the former home of Waite Phillips. Guided tours of the mansion can be arranged at the museum. ~ Route 21, about four miles south of Cimarron; 505-376-2281.

Seven miles south of the Philmont Scout headquarters is **The Kit Carson Museum**, an intriguing living-history exhibit illustrating the life of 1850s–era settlers like Kit Carson (who lived here). Operated by the Boy Scouts of America, this old adobe compound is a terrific place to learn pioneer arts and crafts; it even has a working blacksmith and candlemakers. Open June through August. ~ Route 21, Rayado; 505-376-2281.

Continuing another 38 miles northeast of Cimarron on Routes 64 and 25, you'll come to **Raton** (elevation 6666 feet), a small New Mexican city located on the original Santa Fe Trail. Raton, with its scenic mesas, sits at the foot of Raton Pass and was first founded as a railroad outpost. Visits to Raton should begin with a walking tour of the **Raton Downtown Historic District**, one of New Mexico's most distinguished Main Street districts. Some of the buildings have been completely restored, others are in the midst of rehabilitation and a few cry out for love and care. This is an opportunity to see an array of styles and period pieces from the late 19th to the early 20th centuries—truly an architectural timeline. This area is on the National Register of Historic Places. Pick up the walking-tour brochure at the **Raton Chamber and Economic Development Council**. ~ 100 Clayton Road; 505-445-3689, 800-638-6161.

The most worthwhile area attraction is the **Capulin Volcano National Monument**. Now dormant, the mile-wide cone of the volcano rises 1400 feet above the flat plains. The volcano is believed to be 60,000 to 100,000 years old. A visitors center and small museum provide information on the natural wonder. ~ Located 30 miles east of Raton on Route 64, Capulin; 505-278-2201.

Route 325 leads north from here to the town of **Folsom**. This short (seven miles) and beautiful trip is backcountry New Mexico driving at its best. Winding through picturesque valleys you'll descend to this little hamlet, worth visiting if only to see the turn-of-the-century native stone Catholic church and the 1888 Folsom Hotel. There are also a number of intriguing old adobe houses.

Hop on Route 325 until you reach the junction with Route 64 at Des Moines. Forty-five miles east on Route 64 will bring you to the town of Clayton. Rich in dinosaur history, this area of northeastern New Mexico has plenty of giant tracks to prove it. If you yearn to play amateur paleontologist, visit the **Clayton–Union County Chamber of Commerce**, where they make dinosaurs their business. The kind folks at the COC will no doubt direct you to **Clayton Lake State Park** (12 miles north of Clayton via Route 370), where you can see 500 dinosaur tracks. A web-footed dinosaur created another trail. First found in 1982, the tracks here are etched in Dakota sandstone. ~ Chamber of Commerce: 1103 South 1st Street; 505-374-9253.

LODGING   Best bet by far in Cimarron is the spooky **St. James Hotel,** where famous residents such as Buffalo Bill Cody and Annie Oakley hung their Wild West duds. Built in 1880 and then lovingly restored and reopened a century later, this landmark has rooms with cast-iron beds, period furniture and wildcat rugs. Each unit is unique and ghosts haunt the hallways, so you may ask to inspect your room before renting. ~ Route 21, Cimarron; 505-376-2664, fax 505-376-2623. MODERATE TO DELUXE.

Casa del Gavilan is a charming white adobe bed and breakfast. Period antiques are omnipresent; all seven guest rooms have private baths. ~ Route 21, Cimarron; 505-376-2246, fax 505-376-2247. MODERATE TO DELUXE.

The **Travelodge Cimarron** offers 39 guest rooms made homey with quilts and comforters. These Southwestern-style units also have large vanity/dressing areas and desks if you happened to bring work along. A grassy play area provides welcome relief on hot days for kids and adults. ~ Route 64, Cimarron; 505-376-2288, fax 505-376-9214. BUDGET TO MODERATE.

Spend the night on the old Santa Fe Trail at **Cimarron House Bed and Breakfast,** a pleasant alternative to the motel scene. Five cedar-paneled rooms are appointed in contemporary Southwest style, with king-size beds and fireplaces. The inn, within walking distance of the Old Mill Museum and a historic Catholic church, has picture-window views of the Cimarron River. After seeing the sights, you can relax in the indoor heated pool. ~ 600 18th Street, a block west of Route 21, Cimarron; 505-376-2616, 800-637-3354. MODERATE.

Our top choice in Raton is no contest. It's the **Red Violet Inn,** a turn-of-the-century red-brick Victorian. Four charming rooms are furnished with Hopi rugs and four-poster and brass beds covered with Priscilla-style quilts, while the newly added downstairs room is done in French Provincial style. Guests are welcome to lounge in the Victorian parlor or out in the sunny backyard, but whether they choose to wear an antique hat from the inn's collection is up to them (the wide array includes pill box, Sherlock Holmes and ostrich feather). Breakfast is served in the formal dining room. Closed February. ~ 344 North 2nd Street, Raton; 505-445-9778, 800-624-9778. MODERATE.

Quiet and well priced, **Melody Lane Motel** is convenient to Raton's historic downtown district and adjacent to a popular lounge. Each of these 27 units offers king-size or double beds with floral print spreads. ~ 136 Canyon Drive, Raton; 505-445-3655, 800-421-5210. BUDGET.

Among the least expensive lodging in town, the circa 1902 **El Portal** offers spacious older units with hardwood floors and double beds. Painted Southwestern furniture creates a cheery setting, and the upper stories have nice views. ~ 101 North 3rd Street, Raton; 505-445-3631. BUDGET.

Clayton Motel is a 24-unit motor court that's been fully modernized. The older units now have fresh paint, wall-to-wall carpeting and contemporary oak furniture. Photos of the Southwest decorate the walls. This low-priced establishment is an excellent choice for a good night's sleep. ~ 422 Monroe Street, Clayton; 505-374-2544. BUDGET.

DINING

The knotty pine–paneled **Kit Carson Restaurant** offers frontiersman-size breakfasts, as well as chile burgers, taco salads, steaks and enchilada plates for lunch. If you're watching your waistline, there's a generous salad bar. The paneling in the adjacent lounge is stamped with local cattle brands—all in the spirit of the Old West. ~ Route 64, Cimarron; 505-376-2288. BUDGET TO MODERATE.

Heck's Hungry Traveler is an unpretentious coffee shop where you'll enjoy tripledecker club sandwiches, half-pound hamburgers and cheese enchiladas. Booth and table seating are available. Be sure to try the homemade soups and pies. ~ Route 64, Cimarron; 505-376-2574. BUDGET.

The bullet holes in the ceiling are the last reminders of **Lambert's** days as a saloon and gambling hall. Today, the chandeliers, upholstered chairs, dusty rose tablecloths and candles set the mood for elegant dining. Escargot, veal marsala, buffalo filets and chicken sautéed in an orange sauce are a few selections from the diverse menu. Closed Monday and Tuesday in winter. ~ St. James Hotel, Route 1, Cimarron; 505-376-2664. MODERATE TO DELUXE.

For morning coffee and hot-out-of-the-oven cinnamon rolls, go to **Eva's Bakery**. A variety of sandwiches on homemade bread are also available at lunchtime and dinner. ~ 134 North 2nd Street, Raton; 505-445-3781. BUDGET.

Founded by Jim Pappas and Gus Petritsis in 1923, **Pappas' Sweet Shop Restaurant** was such a popular candy store and soda fountain that the owners added a full-fledged restaurant. Run today by Jim's son, Mike, the Territorial-style establishment overflows with memorabilia: historic photos, train sets, classic car models and gilt-framed mirrors. The eclectic menu ranges from child-sized portions of spaghetti and meatballs to lobster tail, prime rib and stuffed jalapeños. Baklava, toasted coconut pie and fried ice cream are just a few of the choices for dessert. Closed Sunday. ~ 1201 South 2nd Street, Raton; 505-445-9811. MODERATE TO DELUXE.

Eating at **La Palomita** is a bit like being invited to a friend's house (an adobe-style bungalow, to be specific) for dinner. Mexican art and artifacts decorate this intimate setting. Adults can choose from among *sopapilla* burgers, enchiladas, salads and steaks, while the kid's menu offers Mexican and American selections. Closed Tuesday. ~ 1022 South 1st Street, Clayton; 505-374-2127. BUDGET.

If it's atmosphere you are looking for, it's hard to beat the velvet-cushioned banquettes at the **Eklund Dining Room and Saloon**. Built in 1892, this two-story rock-walled landmark is a real find. Mounted game oversee the hand-carved bar, one of the most beautiful in the state. Appointed with gold floral wallpaper, a marble fireplace and historic photographs, the dining room may tempt you to take out your camera. The menu emphasizes New Mexican specialties, though it also offers surf and turf, prime rib and butterfly pork chops. ~ 15 Main Street, Clayton; 505-374-2551. MODERATE TO DELUXE.

SHOPPING   Don't be deceived by the name. **Cimarron General Store** is more than just a place to buy boots, provisions and saddles. A wide variety of antiques, watercolors, Southwestern books and handwoven blankets are also here. ~ 9th and Lincoln streets, Cimarron; 505-376-2244. Next door is **Studio 64**, an intriguing art gallery where you'll find mixed media, oil on canvas, watercolors and ceramic bowls. ~ Cimarron; 505-376-2937.

For a special treat and a wide selection of pottery (including Mesa Verde bowls and turquoise fetish pots), visit the **Cimarron Art Gallery**. Books on the Southwest, jewelry, and earrings are also found here. And it is probably the only gallery in the Southwest with a working 1937 soda fountain—yes, they *do* serve ice cream in the gallery. ~ 337 9th Street, Cimarron; 505-376-2614.

Cowboys and cowgirls (and Western wanna-bes) will find all the proper accessories at **Solano's Boot and Western Wear**, one of the largest shops of its kind in northern New Mexico. Saunter on in and "git" yourself a custom-made hat or an embroidered shirt. A wide selection of jackets, rugs, blankets and belt buckles completes the inventory. Look for cowboy poetry in the book section. ~ 101 2nd Street, Raton; 505-445-2632.

As you could no doubt guess from the name, the **Heirloom Shop** carries antiques and collectibles, including advertising signs. This shop also boasts an excellent array of quilts, Depression glass and china. ~ 132 South 1st Street, Raton; 505-445-8876.

From prints and books to vintage movie posters, **The Little Gallery** is an early-20th-century showcase. The historic two-story store is full of antiques and memorabilia. (Be sure to look up at the painted frescoes bordering the pressed-tinwork ceiling.) ~ 100 South 1st Street, Raton; 505-445-9736.

One way to beat Santa Fe's high prices for American Indian artifacts and collectibles is to head for **Santa Fe Trail Traders**. The

Navajo, Hopi and Zuni artwork, from fetishes and sandpaintings to kachinas and blankets, is well priced for such high-quality merchandise. ~ 100 South 2nd Street, Raton; 505-445-2888.

If you're planning to fish, camp, hike or golf in beautiful northeastern New Mexico, head over to **Knott's Sportsman Supply.** Just about everything you need for life in the outback is on sale here, including maps, regional guides and athletic equipment. Anglers will appreciate the complete selection of fishing rods, lures and flies. ~ 1015 South 1st Street, Clayton; 505-374-8361.

NIGHTLIFE

Murder on the Santa Fe Trail may be your only opportunity to act out a little of the late-19th-century history so prevalent in New Mexico. The focus of your visit is to solve one or more mysterious killings. Guests are cast as investigator, suspect, victim or murderer in this drama, which runs from Friday night through Sunday brunch. Wild West entertainment, sing-alongs, Robert W. Service ballads and St. James ghost stories are all part of the fun. The proceedings occur once or twice a month October through April. ~ St. James Hotel, Route 1, Cimarron; 505-376-2664.

The **Raton Arts and Humanities Council** presents an impressive season that includes adult and children's drama, musical soloists, symphony orchestras and touring dance companies. Most of the events are staged in the rococo Shuler Theater (131 North 2nd Street), opened in 1915 and restored in the early 1970s. Original show curtains remain in use today and the lobby murals are a must-see. ~ 140 South 1st Street, Raton; 505-445-2052.

Outdoor Adventures

FISHING

Anglers find the fishing grand in these parts. Near Taos, head for the Rio Grande. Roads run to the river at Orilla Verde and Wild Rivers Recreation Areas. More adventuresome anglers can hike down the steep volcanic cliffs of the Rio Grande Gorge to remote stretches of the river in search of trophy-size rainbow and brown trout.

TAOS AREA For tackle, advice and guide services in Taos, try **Los Rios Anglers.** ~ 226 Paseo del Pueblo Norte; 505-758-2798.

ENCHANTED CIRCLE AREA In Eagle Nest, there's **Dos Amigos Trading Co.** ~ 247 Therma Drive; 505-377-6226.

RIVER RUNNING

West of Taos, the Rio Grande flows through a spectacular 400-foot-deep gorge nicknamed the Taos Box. Both the Rio Grande and the Chama River, which flows into the Rio Grande midway between Taos and Santa Fe, have been designated by the United States government as Wild and Scenic Rivers, with environmental protection similar to federal wilderness areas. Both are full of river rafts and kayaks during the late spring and early summer when the rivers are swollen with runoff from snow melting in the nearby mountains.

TAOS AREA   There are several rafting guide services in the Taos area, such as **Los Rios River Runners**. ~ Taos Ski Valley Road; 505-776-8854, 800-544-1181. Also in Taos is **Native Sons Adventures**. ~ 715 Paseo del Pueblo Sur; 505-758-9342, 800-753-7559. **Far Flung Adventures** operates out of El Prado. ~ P.O. Box 707, El Prado, NM 87571; 505-758-2628, 800-359-2627.

SKIING

This area boasts New Mexico's best alpine skiing.

TAOS AREA   Granddaddy of New Mexico's alpine ski resorts is **Taos Ski Valley**, with a summit elevation of nearly 12,000 feet above sea level. Taos boasts more than 1000 acres of bowls and chutes served by ten chairs and one surface lift. ~ Route 150/Taos Ski Valley Road; 505-776-2291. Snow conditions at Taos Ski Valley are available 24 hours a day by calling 505-776-2916.

ENCHANTED CIRCLE AREA   Novice skiers will find a lot to like at **Angel Fire**. ~ Route 434; 505-377-6401, 800-633-7463. Just a mountain away from Taos as the crow flies is **Red River Ski Area**, towering above a funky little Western-style town of the same name. ~ Route 38, Red River; 505-754-2382. Cross-country skiers who prefer the peaceful sounds of nature will enjoy gliding through the **Enchanted Forest**, which has no services save for a warming hut. ~ Route 38, Red River. For rentals, lessons or a moonlight ski tour, check in at **Miller's Crossing**, a shop which runs the ski area at Enchanted Forest. ~ West Main Street, Red River; 505-754-2374. **Ski Rentals**   To rent your sticks in Taos, visit the **Los Rios White Water Ski Shop**. ~ 23 Ski Valley Road; 505-776-8854. **Cottam's Skiing and Outdoor Shop** will also set you up with equipment. ~ 207 Paseo del Pueblo Sur; 505-758-2822. **Terry Sports** also rents downhill gear. ~ 314 Paseo del Pueblo Norte; 505-758-8522. You'll find cross-country equipment at **Taos Mountain Outfitters**. ~ 114 Taos Plaza South; 505-758-9292. **Los Rios Whitewater Ski Shop** also specializes in cross-country skis. ~ 23 Ski Valley Road; 505-776-8854, 800-544-1181.

✔ CHECK THESE OUT—OUTDOOR ADVENTURES

- Climb the granite formations at **Cimarron Canyon State Park**, where you could easily spend the whole day. *page 347*
- Raft the **Rio Grande** near Taos and experience the Taos Box, a thrilling 400-foot deep gorge. *page 353*
- See the **Enchanted Forest** when it's most tranquil; go on a moonlight nordic tour. *page 354*
- Challenge yourself to hike the strenuous but rewarding **Wheeler Peak Trail**, which leads to New Mexico's highest peak. *page 356*

In Angel Fire, try **Angel Fire Ski Rentals** at the mountain base. ~ 505-377-4290. **Ski Tech** is also convenient to Angel Fire. ~ North Angel Fire Road, Village Center; 505-377-3213. Get your gear in Red River at **River City Sports** near the mountain base. ~ 505-754-2428. **Miller's Crossing** also rents equipment in Red River. ~ 212 West Main Street; 505-754-2374.

Beautiful terrain and varied trails make this a great area to see on horseback. There are several ranches in the region that outfit trips, including one run by a local tribe that leads trips on reservation land.

RIDING STABLES

TAOS AREA   Ride with the American Indians on the Great Spirit's property at the **Taos Indian Horse Ranch**. ~ 1 Miller Road, Taos Pueblo; 505-758-3212. Also try **Shadow Mountain Guest Ranch** for horseback riding in the Sangre de Cristos. ~ Taos Canyon Road, Taos; 505-758-7732.

ENCHANTED CIRCLE AREA   East of Taos, trail rides are offered by **Roadrunner Tours Ltd.** ~ Route 434, Angel Fire; 505-377-6416.

The scenic mountain roads lend themselves to bicycle rides of all lengths and levels.

BIKING

TAOS AREA   A relatively difficult five-mile loop trail called **Devi-sadero** allows for a good view of the town of Taos. Start across from the El Nogal picnic area on Route 64 and get ready to climb 1300 vertical feet of elevation.

ENCHANTED CIRCLE AREA   **La Jara Canyon** (Route 64, on the horseshoe between Taos and Angel Fire) is a meandering two-mile climb to an alpine meadow that appeals especially to those new in the (bike) saddle.

Wait until late afternoon to take the three-mile **Cebolla Mesa Trail** (Route 522, about 18 miles north of Taos) for the splendid sunsets. Pedal near the rim of the 800-foot Rio Grande Gorge at Cebolla Mesa. Start the trip at the intersection of Cebolla Mesa road and Route 522 and ride to the campground.

Bike Rentals   In Taos try **Native Sons Adventures Gearing Up Bicycle Shop.** ~ 129 Pasco de Pueblo Sur; 505-751-0365. **Taos Mountain Outfitters** also rents two-wheeled steeds. ~ 114 Taos Plaza South; 505-758-9292.

From a gentle trail following a creek to a challenging ascent of New Mexico's highest mountain, 13,161-foot Wheeler Peak, the Enchanted Circle is filled with enchanting hiking possibilities. All distances are one-way unless otherwise noted.

HIKING

ENCHANTED CIRCLE AREA   The **Carson National Forest** near Taos has more than 20 marked trails of varying difficulty that wind in and around some of the state's more magnificent scenic spots.

Yerba Canyon Trail (4 miles) begins in the aspens and willows, but snakes through fir and spruce trees as you approach the ridge. As its name would suggest, the trail follows Yerba Canyon for most of its length and climbs some 3600 feet in elevation before reaching Lobo Peak. The trailhead is on Taos Ski Valley Road, a mile up the hill from Upper Cuchilla Campground.

From roughly the same access point as the Yerba Canyon Trail is the **Gavilan Trail** (2.4 miles), a colorful hike that primarily follows alongside Gavilan Creek. Steep in its early section, the trip flattens out as it opens into meadows near the ridge.

In the Red River area you'll find the trail to **Middlefork Lake** (2 miles), which climbs 1200 vertical feet to a glacier lake. **Wheeler Peak Trail** (7 miles), leading to New Mexico's highest peak, is for conditioned hikers only.

▼▼▼▼▼▼▼▼▼▼

Transportation

CAR

From Santa Fe, head north on **Route 285/84**. Near Española, **Route 68** picks up the trail north to Taos. **Route 64** weaves across the northern area of the state, passing through Taos and Cimarron. Note: Parts of the highway that cross high through Carson National Forest are closed during the winter.

AIR

Most visitors to the Taos area usually fly into Albuquerque International Airport (see "Transportation" in Chapter Twelve). Both **Faust's Transportation** (505-758-3410) and **Pride of Taos** (505-758-8340) provide shuttle service to Taos from the Albuquerque airport.

BUS

TNM&O Coaches provides service to Taos from Albuquerque via Santa Fe. The line continues northeast to Eagle Nest, Cimarron and Raton. ~ South Santa Fe Road and Raton Bypass, across from the Taos Chamber of Commerce; 505-758-1144.

CAR RENTALS

If you'd like to rent a car in Taos, try **Dollar Rent A Car**. ~ Taos Airport; 505-758-3500. **United Chevrolet and Toyota** rents cars in Raton. ~ 505-445-3644.

PUBLIC TRANSIT

You need a car in this region because public transportation is nearly nonexistent. Most visitors flying into Albuquerque will rent a vehicle there.

WALKING TOURS

Call **Taos Walking Tours** if you're interested in strolling about the ancient streets of Taos with a local guide. Tours leave at 10 a.m. from the Mable Dodge Luhan House at 240 Morada Lane. Available Monday to Saturday from June through September. ~ 505-758-4020.

ELEVEN

Northwestern New Mexico

Half-wild horses gallop across the sagebrush desert around Chaco Canyon in northwestern New Mexico, a land of timeless mystery and profound loneliness. These beautiful creatures are owned, in a loose way, by Navajo herders, none of whom are seen. Traditional Navajo people choose to live in isolation, building their homes out of sight of main roads and other houses. The only signs of human habitation are the strange, scarecrowlike effigies marking the turnoffs to hidden dwellings.

Although deserted now, the San Juan Basin was the site of one of the great capital cities of the Americas nearly a thousand years ago. An Anasazi city stood at the center of this trade empire that spanned the Southwest, linked by an impressive network of ancient "highways." Travelers who venture on dusty washboard roads across the Indian lands to Chaco Canyon will discover mysterious ruins, all that is left of this enigmatic ancient site. Chaco Canyon's fame has spread in recent years, enough to draw hundreds of visitors in a single day, but why the Anasazi chose to build in this desolate place remains a mystery (and why they abandoned it likewise a puzzle). A visit still provides an experience best described as mystical.

The Navajo nation, the largest and fastest-growing Indian tribe in the United States, controls most of the northwestern quadrant of New Mexico. Royalties from coal mining on the reservation provided the means of purchasing vast sprawls of arid rangeland east and south of the official reservation boundary. And while overpopulation, air pollution and economic depression characterize this part of the state, it also boasts colorful people, an incomprehensible language and fascinating folk ways. In short, Navajoland is a true Third World country within the borders of the wealthiest nation on earth.

Other tribes inhabit the region, as well. The Jicarilla Apache Indian Reservation lies to the east of the Navajo lands, and farther south are a string of pueblos that have been occupied since the first Spaniard, a shipwrecked accountant named Cabeza de Vaca ("Cow's Head"), stumbled upon them after trekking clear across Texas in

1527. Among the pueblos are Acoma, with its fairytale setting overlooking an enchanted landscape of strange rock formations from the top of a steep, isolated mesa, and ancient Zuni, where the people speak a language utterly unlike any other on earth. The American Indians have been here so long that their legends, passed on by spoken word from each generation to the next, contain eyewitness accounts of the volcanic eruptions that created the huge malpais, or lava badlands, on the outskirts of the town of Grants.

Nowhere is the memory of the Spanish soldiers who explored this region in the mid-1500s as vivid as in the mesas south of Route 40 between Grants and Gallup. Here, in the poor and remote villages of the Zuni Indian Reservation, lies the reality behind the "golden cities of Cibola" legend that lured the first explorers northward from Mexico City. Here, too, stand the cliffs of El Morro, where Indians, Spanish explorers and Anglo settlers alike carved messages in stone to create a "guest register" spanning 800 years.

The town of Grants, formerly the center of the uranium boom that swept northwestern New Mexico in the 1950s, and died in the 1970s, is now little more than an inexpensive place for interstate truckers to spend the night. Yet its location, sandwiched between the lava badlands and the forested slopes of Mt. Taylor, is ideal for taking advantage of the wonders of the surrounding lands.

Near the western boundary of New Mexico, Gallup is the largest border town adjoining the Navajo Indian Reservation. It presents a cultural contrast as striking as any to be found along the Mexican border, as the interstate highway brings the outside world to the doorstep of the largest Indian nation in the United States.

▼▼▼▼▼▼▼▼
Grants Area
Just over an hour's drive west of Albuquerque on Route 40, Grants is situated at the center of an intriguing array of places—the most ancient continuously inhabited pueblos in New Mexico, a vast and forbidding lava bed with ice caves that bear the marks of centuries of explorers, and a mountain held sacred in Navajo tradition.

SIGHTS
More than 4500 native people reside in **Laguna Pueblo**, a pueblo that dates back to the turn of the 17th century. Old Laguna is situated on a hillside overlooking the interstate midway between Albuquerque and Grants; the centerpiece is **San Jose de Laguna Church**, a mission church in use since the pueblo's founding. Most Laguna residents live in modern villages scattered across the reservation. ~ 505-552-6654.

Travelers in no particular hurry and tired of dodging trucks on the interstate can catch a remnant of **Old Route 66** at Laguna. The road parallels Route 40 and plays peekaboo with it all the way to the Acoma reservation.

Acoma Pueblo (Sky City) has been inhabited continuously since it was built on a solitary mesa top above a valley of stone pillars in the 12th century—earlier than the pueblos at Salinas, Bandelier or Pecos. New houses are still being built on the roofs of houses

centuries old. There is no school bus service, electricity or running water on the mesa, so today only 15 families live in the Sky City year-round. Most work as potters or pottery painters. More than 400 well-maintained homes in the old pueblo are used as spiritual retreats and summer houses by their owners, who live in modern reservation towns near the interstate. Shuttle buses carry visitors up the steep road, built by a motion-picture crew in 1969, for an hour-long guided tour of the pueblo. Those who choose to can hike back down on the short, steep trail used by Acoma residents for at least 800 years before the road was built. For schedule information, call the **Acoma Visitors Center**. ~ Located 15 miles east of Grants on Route 40 and another 15 miles south on a marked tribal road; 505-470-4966 or 505-470-4967.

Grants got its start as a railroad stop back when the region's major industry was carrot farming. In 1950 a Navajo sheepherder discovered a strange yellow rock that turned out to be radioactive, and Grants suddenly became the center of a uranium mining boom. Today, despite its prime location amid many of western New Mexico's best sightseeing highlights, Grants is a low-key highwayside town with few of the trappings of a tourist mecca.

Those who wish to learn more about the uranium era can do so at the **New Mexico Museum of Mining at Grants** where visitors ride an elevator down from the museum's main floor to explore an underground mine replica. Open every day of the week between May and September. Closed Sunday the rest of the year. Admission. ~ 100 Iron Street; 505-287-4802.

Route 53, a quiet secondary highway, leads south and west of Grants to two national monuments—the first ever established in the United States and one of the newest. The highway continues across the Ramah Navajo and Zuni Indian reservations. Near the pueblo of Zuni, Route 602 goes north and returns to Route 40 at Gallup.

Malpais is Spanish for "bad land," and the 115,000-acre **El Malpais National Monument** protects one of the largest lava beds in New Mexico. The highways that border the lava flow—Route 53 on the north and Route 117 on the east—are connected by a rugged dirt road that runs along the west and south perimeters; these roads should only be attempted in a high-clearance vehicle. Since the monument was created in 1988, federal funding has not been available for campgrounds, interpretive exhibits, paved roads or other facilities. Hiking opportunities in the national monument are discussed in the "Hiking" section at the end of the chapter. ~ Visitors center: Off Route 53 between mile markers 63 and 64; 505-783-4774.

The most rewarding stop on a quick visit to El Malpais is **Bandera Crater and Ice Cave**, a privately owned tourist concession that eventually will be acquired as part of the monument. Separate easy trails take visitors to the crater of one of the volcanoes that made the lava field and to a subterranean ice cave, a lava tube where the temperature stays below freezing even on the hottest summer days. Admission. ~ 505-783-4303.

At **El Morro National Monument,** a 15-minute drive west on Route 53 from Bandera Crater, a white-sandstone bluff marks the location of a 200,000-gallon waterhole. Atop the high bluff are the ruins of Atsina, a 13th-century pueblo where about 1500 people lived. The Indians carved petroglyphs along the trail between the pueblo and the waterhole, starting a tradition that would last 800 years. When conquistador Don Juan de Oñate camped by the pool in 1605, returning after his discovery of the Gulf of California, he scratched an inscription in the sandstone to memorialize his passing. Spanish explorers added their often-lengthy messages to the rock face until 1774. The absence of inscriptions for 75 years bears

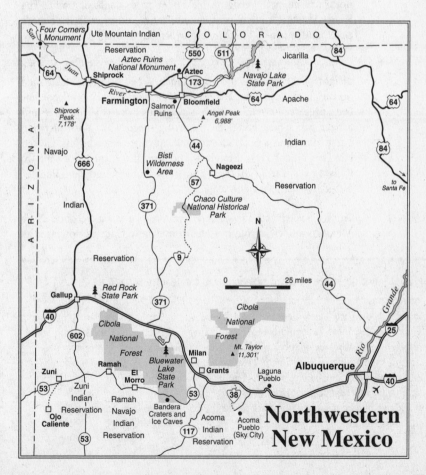

mute witness to the social turmoil surrounding the Mexican Revolution and the Mexican War. The first English inscription appeared in 1849, and soldiers, surveyors and pioneers continued to carve their names in the cliff until 1904. Two years later, President Theodore Roosevelt declared El Morro the nation's first national monument, and defacing the rock with its historical graffiti has been prohibited ever since. Admission. ~ Route 53; 505-783-4226.

LODGING   There are about 15 motels in town. The more modern franchise motels, located near the easternmost Grants exit from Route 40, include the **Best Western The Inn** with large rooms as well as amenities like an indoor swimming pool and sauna. ~ 1501 East Santa Fe Avenue, Grants; 505-287-7901, 800-600-5221, fax 505-285-5751. MODERATE.

Farther west along Santa Fe Avenue are a number of independent motels, all budget. Several of them formerly belonged to national chains, still recognizable under fresh coats of paint. The **Sands Motel** is a block off the main route and offers a little more peace and quiet. ~ 112 McArthur Street, Grants; 505-287-2996, 800-424-7679. BUDGET.

Accommodations are almost nonexistent in Zuni country. One delightful exception is the **Vogt Ranch**, a bed and breakfast listed on the National Historic Register. The home's original decor has been preserved complete with Navajo rugs, a rustic fireplace and a bear pelt which hangs on the living room wall. With just two guest rooms, it's a good idea to make advance reservations. Closed late December to mid-March. ~ The turnoff is just east of Ramah, midway between El Morro National Monument and Zuni Pueblo; 505-783-4362. MODERATE.

DINING   Grants has several low-priced restaurants that serve good New Mexican food. The family-style **Monte Carlo Café** is known for its

UNIQUE NORTHWESTERN NEW MEXICO EXPERIENCES

- Rove among ancient structures at **Aztec Ruins National Monument**, a major pre-historic settlement full of 12th-century pueblo ruins. *page 370*
- Tuck yourself in at **El Rancho Hotel**, the temporary residence for such notables as Katherine Hepburn, Humphrey Bogart and Kirk Douglas during the filming of old-time Westerns. *page 364*
- Pull up where local truckers stop, **The Iron Skillet**, and dine on what's said to be the best food around. *page 363*
- Walk the pathway of the ancients through an extensive lava field on the **Zuni-Acoma Trail**. *page 375*

sheepherder sandwich—a steak on a tortilla with chili and cheese. ~ 721 West Santa Fe Avenue, Grants; 505-287-9250. BUDGET.

Jaramillos Mexi-Catessen, a hole-in-the-wall local favorite, offers a choice of eating on the premises or ordering take-out for a spicy picnic lunch. Closed Saturday and Sunday. ~ 213 North 3rd Street, Grants; 505-287-9308. BUDGET.

Fancier, but still inexpensive, is El Jardin, featuring more sophisticated Mexican entrées such as chimichangas, flautas and *machaca* burritos. Closed Sunday. ~ 319 West Santa Fe Avenue, Grants; 505-285-5231. BUDGET.

For simple good food and plenty of it, consider the Iron Skillet at the Petro Truck Stop west of Grants. This is one of the largest truck stops along the length of Route 40, and the restaurant confirms the adage that the best food is the place with the most semi-trailers parked out front. Open 24 hours daily, the Iron Skillet offers both full family menus and an impressive all-you-can-eat buffet and salad bar as well as daily specials. Each booth has a telephone. ~ Route 40 at Horizon Boulevard, Milan; 505-285-6621. BUDGET.

BLUEWATER LAKE STATE PARK   Secluded in a valley halfway between Grants and Gallup, this picturesque reservoir dates back to the 1920s. The lake is said to have one of the highest fish-catch rates of all New Mexican lakes. (It's stocked with trout.) There are several hiking trails. One begins near the campground and leads down to a lush side canyon. Facilities include picnic tables, restrooms and showers; groceries near the entrance. ~ Located on Route 412, seven miles south of the Prewitt exit from Route 40, which is 19 miles west of Grants; 505-876-2391.

▲ There are 150 sites (15 with RV hookups); primitive camping is allowed near the lake. Fees per night are $6 for primitive sites, $7 for developed campsites and $11 for hookups.

RAMAH LAKE   Mormon settlers created this small lake in the 1880s for irrigation. It operated for generations as a private fishing lake and has been open to the public since 1987. Fishing is good for bass and bluegills; there are also a few trout. There are no facilities here. ~ Located just north of Ramah on Route 53. Ramah is near the eastern boundary of the Zuni Indian Reservation, 55 miles southwest of Grants.

PARKS

▼▼▼▼▼▼▼▼
Gallup Area

Gallup is the largest town on the boundary of the Navajo Indian Reservation, which sprawls across vast tracts of New Mexico, Arizona and Utah. Most of the 200,000 Navajo people live scattered across the land, no home within view of another— on a reservation larger than the states of Connecticut, Vermont and Massachusetts put together. The Navajo people come to Gallup to shop, sell their jewelry, rugs and other handicrafts to traders, and to drink. Alcoholic beverages are prohibited on Navajo land, so people who live on the reservation must do their drinking in Gallup—a reality that most visitors find impossible to ignore. A town trapped between two worlds, Gallup has been poverty ridden and somewhat rundown for generations. Today, as savvy collectors are visiting Gallup in search of bargains on high-quality work by Navajo and Zuni artisans, the previously decrepit downtown area is being gentrified and occupied by fine art galleries and shops.

SIGHTS

The main feature at **Red Rock State Park** is its rodeo grounds nestled in a sheer-walled canyon. A small museum exhibits ancient, historic and contemporary American Indian arts and crafts, including pottery, kachinas, baskets, masks and oil paintings, by artists from various tribes in the region. The park also contains archaeological sites dating back over a thousand years. Open seven days a week in summer. Closed Saturday and Sunday in winter. ~ Off Route 40, just east of Gallup; 505-722-3839.

Gallup rests astride old Route 66 (called Historic 66 in Gallup) just 22 miles from the Arizona border. Located near both the Navajo and Zuni indian reservations, this historic town of 20,000 bills itself as the "Gateway to Indian Country." Pawn shops, bars and a row of neon motels lend a hard edge to the local ambience, but the annual Inter-Tribal Ceremonial and large concentration of American Indians make it a prime place to view native crafts.

Red Rock Canyon State Park is the site of the annual Inter-Tribal Ceremonial, the largest pow-wow in the U.S.

Situated on Route 53 about 30 miles west of El Morro and 40 miles south of Gallup is **Zuni Pueblo**, the largest pueblo (population approximately 7000) in New Mexico. The modern town of Zuni has evolved from a pueblo called Halona, which had been established for centuries when Coronado arrived in 1540, believing it to be one of the fabulously wealthy, mythical "Seven Golden Cities of Cibola." The town does not look like anything special at first glance, but the more you wander the back streets, the more antiquity reveals itself. Stone foundations 800 years old support many modern buildings in Zuni Pueblo, and crumbling stone storage sheds in people's yards may have been built long before Christopher Columbus first set sail. Keep your ears perked here, for the Zuni people speak a language unlike any other known American Indian dialect. ~ Route 53; 505-782-4481.

LODGING

Gallup has more motels comparable in quality and price to those in Grants. It also has one unique historic hotel that is both rustic and elegant. The **El Rancho Hotel** was built in 1937 by the brother of film producer D. W. Griffith. This is where movie stars stayed while shooting Westerns in the surrounding red-rock canyon country. Ronald Reagan (surely you remember him before he was president) checked in here half a century ago. Other illustrious guests included John Wayne, Humphrey Bogart, Spencer Tracy, Katharine Hepburn, Alan Ladd and Kirk Douglas. Rich, dark wood polished to a gleam predominates in the larger-than-life two-story lobby. Rates in the old hotel are moderate; budget-priced motel rooms are available in a modern annex next door. ~ 1000 East Historic 66; 505-863-9311, 800-543-6351, fax 505-722-5917. BUDGET TO MODERATE.

DINING

In Gallup, an unusual eatery is the restaurant in the historic **El Rancho Hotel**. The food is fairly conventional American fare, but movie stars like John Wayne, Humphrey Bogart and Ronald Reagan once ate here and now have menu items named after them as well as publicity photos on the walls—a little bit of old Hollywood in Indian country! ~ 1000 East Historic 66; 505-863-9311. BUDGET TO MODERATE.

New Mexican food is served at **Genaro's**, a well-hidden café specializing in stuffed *sopapillas*. Closed Sunday and Monday. ~ 600 West Hill Avenue, Gallup; 505-863-6761. BUDGET.

New Mexican beef dishes such as *carne adovada* and green-chile steak appear on the menu alongside Italian food at **Panz Alegra**. Closed Sunday. ~ 1201 East Historic 66, Gallup; 505-722-7229. BUDGET TO MODERATE.

Another popular mid-range restaurant is the **Ranch Kitchen**, where waiters in American Indian garb serve American and Mexican fare in an atmosphere defined by Indian art and motifs. ~ 3001 West Historic 66, Gallup; 505-722-2537. BUDGET TO MODERATE.

SHOPPING

American Indian jewelry is said to be the leading industry in Gallup. The number of wholesalers, galleries and pawn shops specializing in jewelry (and rugs) supports this claim, as does the presence of buyers and collectors from all over the world. As the biggest town on the edge of the Navajo Indian Reservation and the nearest town to Zuni (the largest of New Mexico's Indian pueblos), Gallup is the natural location for trading companies dealing directly with American Indian artists and craftsworkers.

Prices for American Indian wares are normally lower in Gallup than in Santa Fe or Albuquerque, but quality varies. State law protects American Indians and collectors alike from fraud in the sale of American Indian–made goods, but it can still require a discerning eye to distinguish handmade crafts from those made in factories that employ American Indians or determine which items are genuinely old as opposed to "antiqued." Still, the region has been a major American Indian arts-and-crafts trading center for more than a century, and it is possible to find valuable turn-of-the-century

Germantown blankets and forgotten pieces of "old pawn" turquoise and silver jewelry.

The largest concentration of American Indian traders is along Historic 66 between 2nd and 3rd streets. The oldest shop on the block is **Richardson's**, where the modest facade gives little hint of the treasures in several large rooms inside. This is one of several downtown pawn shops that serve as "banks" for the Navajo people, continuing the tradition whereby the American Indians store their individual wealth in the form of handmade jewelry, using it as needed for collateral and redeeming it for ceremonials. ~ 222 West Historic 66, Gallup; 505-722-4762.

Another highly reputable American Indian trading company is **OB Enterprises**. ~ 3330 East Historic 66, Gallup; 505-722-5846.

Those interested in the materials and techniques of making American Indian jewelry can learn about them on a visit to **Thunderbird Jewelry Supply**. ~ 1907 West Historic 66, Gallup; 505-722-4323.

Recently, galleries have been appearing along Coal Street, Gallup's main drag a block south of Historic 66. Several of them emphasize contemporary American Indian and Southwestern arts.

Zuni Pueblo has several well-stocked American Indian galleries, particularly **Shiwi Trading Post** ~ 1173 West Route 53; 505-782-5501. Another such place is **Turquoise Village** ~ Route 53; 800-748-2405.

PARKS

ZUNI LAKES The Zuni tribe operates seven fishing lakes in the hills of the reservation. (A permit must be obtained from tribal headquarters in Zuni.) Boating is allowed, though gasoline motors are prohibited. Blackrock Lake has picnic facilities and a playground. ~ Blackrock Lake is three miles east of Zuni off Route 53. Eustace Lake is also just east of Zuni. Galestino Lakes are eight miles south of Route 36 on an unpaved road. Nutria Lakes are seven to eleven miles north of Route 53 on an unpaved road. Ojo Caliente is ten miles south of Zuni on Tribal Route 2. Pescado Lake is 17 miles east of Zuni off Route 53; 505-782-5851.

▲ There are primitive campsites at Blackrock Lake, Ojo Caliente, Nutria Lakes, No. 4 and Eustace Lake. Campgrounds at six of the lakes are open all year; $3 overnight or $8 for a stay up to eight days.

RED ROCK STATE PARK Named for the red-sandstone cliffs that lend an austere beauty to the surrounding area, the 640-acre park's main feature is its rodeo grounds nestled in a sheer-walled canyon. There are also picnic tables, restrooms, showers, museum and trails. The park is the site of several important Indian events, concerts and community activities. Closed Saturday and Sunday in winter. ~ Located just off Route 40 east of Gallup; 505-722-3839.

▲ There are 145 sites with hookups; $8 to $12 per night.

Farmington is the natural base camp for sightseeing in the Four Corners area, the sole hub in the
continental United States where four states—New
Mexico, Arizona, Colorado and Utah—meet. Three rivers, the San
Juan, Animas and LaPlata also converge here, dispelling the notion that this is dry, dusty desert country. In fact, Farmington was
founded on farming, hence its name, although the laid-back town
now has industry and mining at its financial base.

Four Corners Area

Start your sightseeing tour of the region on Route 550, about 30
miles southwest of Farmington at the **Shiprock Peak**. Solidified
lava and igneous rock comprise this neck of a volcano, which can
be seen by air from more than 100 miles away. The towering
Shiprock rises from a great stretch of nothing but sand and rock.
(American Indians called it a "rock with wings.") The site has a
roadside picnic area available, but little else in the way of services.
~ Route 550, off Route 666.

SIGHTS

When you're done admiring the natural beauty at Shiprock
pinnacle, head north on Route 666 until you reach the town of
Shiprock. From here, it's another 30 miles east on Route 64 to the
laid-back town of Farmington. Get your fill of literature at the
very helpful **Farmington Convention and Visitors Bureau.** Closed
Sunday in summer. ~ 203 West Main Street; 505-326-7602, 800-
448-1240.

Take your brochures and maps to **Orchard Park**, in the center
of downtown, where you can peruse your options. ~ Main and
Orchard streets.

For an overview of the area's cultural and outdoor offerings,
check in at the **Farmington Museum**, where there's a replica of
New Mexico's fifth-largest city during frontier days, a children's

FOUR CORNERS MONUMENT

There's something both silly and irresistible about driving to **Four Corners**
to stick each foot in a different state (Colorado and Utah) and each hand
in still two others (Arizona and New Mexico) while someone takes your
picture from a scaffolding. But then, this is the only place in the United
States where you can simultaneously "be" in four different states. The
inevitable Navajo crafts booths offer up necklaces, bracelets, earrings,
T-shirts, paintings, sandpaintings, fry bread and lemonade—a splendid
way to make something festive out of two intersecting lines on a
map. ~ To get to Four Corners from Farmington, head west on
Route 64 until you cross the Arizona/New Mexico border. At Teec
Nos Pos, Arizona, head north on Route 160 for about ten miles.

Text continued on page 370.

Chaco Culture National Historical Park

Prehistoric life existed grandly in Chaco Canyon as is evidenced by the most amazing ancient buildings and art forms at **Chaco Culture National Historical Park**. Admission. ~ Located 54 miles south of Bloomfield via Route 44 and Route 57; 505-988-6716.

An intricate highway system, irrigation ditches and 13 great house ruins have led archaeologists to speculate that Chaco was once a center for the Anasazi civilization. The canyon has remained in a comparatively pristine state largely because access is difficult on rutted dirt roads. A debate continues on whether the road should be upgraded, but those who believe Chaco remains in better shape because of its inaccessibility have prevailed so far. Unless you're driving an expensive sports car or the road is slippery from rain, it's worth the bumpy ride to view 13 major ruins and the remains of a culture suspected to have begun in Chaco around 900 A.D. Note: Services are virtually nonexistent, so come fully prepared with food, water and gas.

The fascinating civilization of 1000 years ago has left in its wake traces of advanced art forms like pottery and weaving. The Chaco Anasazi were farmers who probably fled the drought-stricken area in the 13th century. Chaco is considered to be the center of Anasazi culture (the developed road network tells us that) and religious ceremony (as all the kivas left behind indicate). Site excavation began in the late 1890s and continues today through the University of New Mexico's Chaco Research Institute.

Park rangers conduct informational walks through Chaco Canyon, or you can grab a map from the visitors center and chart your own path through this eerily silent land. Self-guided trails are found at Pueblo Bonito, Chetro Ketl and Casa Rinconada.

Closest to the visitors center is the partially excavated **Una Vida** ruin, with its five kivas and 150 rooms. Because it was built on a mound, Una Vida appears higher than it actually is. Petroglyphs and remains from hogans huddle in the surrounding rock. From the paved park road is the **Hungo Pavi** ruin, an easy trek from the car. Farther down the road is **Chetro Ketl**, with its estimated 500 rooms and 16 kivas one of the largest Chacoan villages. Chetro Ketl's expansive plaza section is thought to be typical of great houses from that time.

A short jaunt in the other direction from the same trailhead brings you to the amazing **Pueblo Bonito**, which was probably the heart and soul of Chaco. The four-story stone masonry complex is obviously the product of painstaking craftsmanship. Consider it to have been the New York City of its day with multiple rooms and kivas crammed into a relatively tight space.

Pueblo del Arroyo, a high-standing D-shaped house, with its 280 rooms and 20 kivas, is found nearby along the paved road. **Kin Kletso**, which was built in two stages, had 100 rooms and five kivas. It may have risen as high as three stories. Take the trail that begins here to the prehistoric **Jackson Stairs**, one of the more impressive stairways in the Anasazi world, and try to figure out the farming terraces of the Anasazi.

Past Kin Kletso is Casa Chiquita, where the hike from the central canyon to the unexcavated great house of **Peñasco Blanco** is well worth the effort. On the south side of paved park road is **Casa Rinconada**, one of the largest kivas in the Southwest. A trail that begins here winds to the South Mesa and the great house of **Tsin Kletsin**, a structure seven rooms strong.

The more adventurous and archaeological-minded can wander in search of "outlier" sites of Chaco Canyon, like Pueblo Pintado and Kin Ya-ah. Free backcountry permits (required before setting out) and directions are available from the visitors center. Camping is also permitted but be prepared: Campers in Chaco Canyon must come equipped with plenty of provisions, especially water. The Gallo campground is located about one mile east of the visitors center. There are 64 sites; $8 per night.

gallery, a reconstruction of a 1930s trading post and an exhibit of the geologic history of the San Juan Basin. Closed Sunday and Monday. ~ 302 North Orchard Street; 505-599-1174.

Next you'll find **Salmon Ruin**, which has remains from an 11th-century pueblo, including a large kiva, built by the Chaco people. Ongoing stabilization of the site's exposed structures continues to this day. Admission. ~ 6131 Route 64; 505-632-2013.

At Salmon Ruin is **Heritage Park**, a re-creation of habitation units, from sand dune campgrounds to tepees and hogans, representing man's occupation in the San Juan Valley. The on-site museum houses regional artifacts, too.

Less than 15 minutes by car from Farmington northeast on Route 550 brings the traveler to the charming town of **Aztec**, with its ancient Indian ruins and turn-of-the-century buildings. Aztec's modern-day renaissance took place in the 1890s, and influences and flavor of that Victorian era prevail. Evidence is found in the neighborhoods surrounding downtown. ~ Chamber of Commerce: 505-334-9551.

There's only one trail in Chaco Canyon where you can ride nonmotorized bikes, and that's the mile-and-a-half Wijiji. Keep your eyes peeled for petroglyphs.

Your first stop on a whirlwind tour of Aztec should begin at the old City Hall, where the **Aztec Museum** displays all kinds of bric-a-brac, like minerals and rocks, Victorian fashions, sleighs and buggies, tools used by the early settlers, an oilfield exhibit and a pioneer village with an authentically furnished post office, general store, bank and log cabin. Closed Sunday. Admission. ~ 125 North Main Street; 505-334-9829.

Strolling along Aztec's **Main Street**, you'll see many turn-of-the-century buildings, including the Odd Fellows Hall (107 South Main Street) and Miss Gail's Inn (300 South Main Street). On a side street is the Presbyterian Church (201 North Church Street), which was built of adobe brick in 1889.

Another building worth a look-see is the **Denver & Rio Grande Western Railway Depot**. No tracks remain on the site of this commercial building turned residence, but the 1915 structure is a classic reminder of the railway's heyday. ~ 408 North Rio Grande.

Aztec's buildings seem perfectly modern in comparison to the ancient **Aztec Ruins National Monument**, a major prehistoric settlement chock full of 12th-century pueblo ruins, including a restored kiva. (Despite its misleading name, no Aztec Indians ever inhabited this area.) Both the Chaco civilization to the south and the Mesa Verde settlement to the north probably influenced Aztec's development. Admission. ~ Ruins Road; 505-334-6174.

A visit to Aztec is a must, for its sheer accessibility as much as for its wonders. First take the self-guided trail that begins outside the visitors center. You'll come upon the **West Ruin** and the magnificently restored **Great Kiva**. West Ruin could be compared to a present-day apartment building because as many as 300 people may have lived there at a single time. The kiva, an underground chamber that's traditionally used for religious ceremonies, was carefully constructed of sandstone blocks from materials that were hand-carried from quarries miles away. Most unusual is a line of green sandstone on one outer wall. Few doors and openings exist, probably to prevent interlopers from breaking into this main building. The kiva was excavated in 1921 and reconstructed about 12 years later.

The open plaza area was the center of daily life in Aztec. Wandering north out of the main ruins takes you to the **Hubbard Site**, a kiva that's unique in that it has three concentric circular walls. Presumably this building was used for religious ceremonies (it's now back-filled for protection). Another tri-walled kiva, largely unexcavated, exists in a nearby mound.

Off the beaten path is the **East Ruin** and its annex, thought to be the second and later civilization at Aztec. Both are largely unexcavated and must be viewed from a distance. Adjacent to the Aztec ruins is a tree-lined picnic area, a nice shady place for a snack or repose after wandering through the ancient playground.

To return to ruin sightings like desolate Angel Peak, you must backtrack to Aztec or take Route 64 east to Bloomfield and then turn south on Route 44 for 17 miles to the turnoff.

Angel Peak, a multimillion-year-old geologic formation, is a sacred dwelling place to the Navajos. A five-mile unpaved, dirt road along the rim offers great views of the pastel-hued mesas and buttes. Camping and picnicking are allowed, though no water is available. After Angel Peak, continue on to Chaco Canyon, the epicenter of Anasazi life, but first consider stopping at the **Navajo trading posts** along Route 44 for jewelry, rugs, necessary supplies and plenty of local gossip.

LODGING

Cast-iron sculptures honoring the "ancient ones" decorate the walls of the pink-hued rooms at the **Anasazi Inn**. Handsome quilt prints in a Southwestern scheme and spotless bathrooms are reason enough to try this centrally located lodge. ~ 903 West Main Street, Farmington; 505-325-4564, fax 505-326-0732. BUDGET TO MODERATE.

If bigger is better, then **Best Western The Inn** has something over its chain competitors on the same street. Extra-large rooms are great for families and help give the inn a leg up. A sizable indoor pool in a tropical setting may make you forget you're in desert country. ~ 700 Scott Avenue, Farmington; 505-327-5221, 800-528-1234, fax 505-327-1565. MODERATE.

With just 33 rooms, the **Farmington Lodge** falls into the small, no-frills category. Most of the well-maintained rooms have refrigerators; a pool opens during the summer. ~ 1510 West Main Street, Farmington; 505-325-0233, fax 505-325-6574. BUDGET.

Its location on a busy highway is definitely a drawback, but you can shut out most of the world's noise in the tidy rooms of the **Enchantment Lodge**. ~ 1800 West Aztec Boulevard, Aztec; 505-334-6143, 800-847-2194, fax 505-334-6144 ext. 225. BUDGET.

Most people come to Aztec for the mysterious ruins. But a visit to its historic Main Street is well worth your time. Smack in the middle of the main drag is **Miss Gail's Inn**, a palace of funk built around 1905. The woodsy rooms—some with partial kitchens—are large enough for multiday living. Weekly rates are a bargain. While this isn't appropriate for everyone, it is a good place to hang your hat if you plan on thoroughly exploring the Four Corners. ~ 300 South Main Street, Aztec; 505-334-3452. MODERATE.

HIDDEN ►

On the edge of the road leading to the mysterious Chaco Canyon ruins is a welcome respite from the dust and heat. The **Chaco Inn at the Post** is a bed and breakfast that promotes a family-style atmosphere—the innkeepers live on the premises and pride themselves in keeping the guests comfortable. Rooms are quaint, with clean lines and wooden floors. Guests can use a pool table in the shared space if there's time away from sightseeing. ~ Route 44, Nageezi; 505-632-3646, 800-962-4226. MODERATE.

DINING

HIDDEN ►

Spinach and feta cheese croissants served piping hot out of the oven, raspberry granola bars and multigrain breads are only a few of the healthy, homemade delectables at **Something Special Bakery & Tea Room**. It's open for breakfast and lunch. Closed Sunday. ~ 116 North Auburn Avenue, Farmington; 505-325-8183. BUDGET.

Among the many restaurants offering wholesome "American cuisine" that dot downtown Farmington, **TJ's Downtown Diner** is just a tad better. Closed Sunday. ~ 119 East Main Street; 505-327-5027. BUDGET.

How hot do you like your green chile? For authentic Mexican cuisine, try the **El Charro Café**. ~ 737 West Main Street, Farmington; 505-327-2464. BUDGET. Its primary competition is the **Los Rios Café**. Closed Sunday. ~ 915 Farmington Avenue, Farmington; 505-325-5699. BUDGET.

While the name suggests a trip back to merry old England, the menu is closer to south-of-the-border. Still, **Chelsea's London Pub** is a good choice for an ale and sandwich, steak or enchilada. Sorry, no kidney pie. ~ 4601 East Main Street, Farmington; 505-327-9644. BUDGET TO MODERATE.

A lunch buffet brings in local nine-to-fivers, but specialties such as sweet and sour pork are favored by diners frequenting the **China House**. Closed Saturday and Sunday. ~ 104 South Main Street, Aztec; 505-334-8838.

Try the **Foutz Trading Co.** for splendid Navajo crafts such as silver jewelry and beaded barrettes. ~ Route 64, Shiprock; 505-368-5790.

If you've been on the road for awhile and could use some "herbal fitness," stop in at **Herbal Alternatives** and pick up natural remedies for all that ails you. ~ 6510 East Main Street, Farmington; 505-327-3205.

American Indian and Western arts and crafts are found at **Echoes.** ~ 103 South Main Street, Aztec; 505-334-9302.

Farmington is not exactly a late-night town, but it does boast a few nightclubs with live music. Check out the **Top Deck Bar** for country tunes. Weekend cover. ~ 515 East Main Street; 505-327-7385. The **Lariat** offers rock and country tunes spun by a DJ. Weekend cover. ~ 1835 East Main Street, Farmington; 505-327-9193.

The **San Juan Stage Company** holds court at the Totah Theatre for a six-play season. ~ 317 West Main Street, Farmington; 505-327-7477.

A lively and colorful musical drama, *Anasazi, the Ancient Ones*, is performed each summer at the **Lions Wilderness Park Amphitheater.** ~ College Boulevard, Farmington; 505-326-7602.

NAVAJO LAKE STATE PARK New Mexico's largest lake offers boating, fishing, swimming and even scuba diving at three recreation areas—Pine, Sims Mesa and the San Juan River. Navajo Lake's sparkling waters and nearly 200 miles of shoreline is chock full of cold and warm water species of game fish, including trophy trout, catfish, pike and bass. The park features a visitors center, marinas, picnic sites and restrooms; groceries are available 20 miles away in Bloomfield or Aztec. ~ Take Route 173 to Route 511, 23 miles east of Aztec; 505-632-2278.

▲ There are 178 sites at Pine (55 with hookups), 46 at Sims Mesa (23 with hookups) and 47 (23 with hookups) at San Juan River. Fees are $7 per night for standard sites, $11 to $13 per night for hookups.

ANGEL PEAK RECREATION AREA A heavenly looking 40-million year-old geologic formation appears to be suspended within a lovely colored canyon. The five-mile-long road around the canyon rim offers fine vistas of the buttes and badlands in this land of the "sacred ones." The only facilities are picnic tables and restrooms. ~ Take Route 44 to the Angel Peak turnoff, about 19 miles southeast of Bloomfield; 505-599-8900.

▲ There are eight sites (no fee); no water.

BISTI WILDERNESS AREA Nearly 4000 acres of eroded shale, clay and sandstone spires, mesas and sculpted rock that defy description were naturally sculpted in this former inland sea. Large reptiles and mammals were thought to walk these lands about 70 million years ago; fossils and petrified wood are all that remain in the desolate area of badlands. No developed trails, facilities or signs mar this protected wilderness. ~ Located on Route 371, 36 miles south of Farmington; 505-599-8900.

▲ Primitive camping allowed (no fee); no water.

▼▼▼▼▼▼▼▼▼▼▼▼▼▼▼
Outdoor Adventures

FISHING

A variety of catches are found in the lakes of the Four Corners area, so try your luck for the plentiful trout or one of the other fish often caught here. Equipment is available as some sites; others are more remote.

FOUR CORNERS AREA The San Juan River at the base of the Navajo Dam in **Navajo Lake State Park** is the site of quality waters teeming with trout. One of the largest lakes in New Mexico, Navajo provides angling opportunities for bluegill, bass, trout, pike and catfish. Try **Born-n-Raised on the San Juan River** for equipment. ~ 1791 Route 173, Navajo Dam; 505-632-2194. **Rizuto's Fly Shop** is also convenient to the lake. ~ 1796 Route 173, Navajo Dam; 505-326-0664.

Another popular trout lake is **Asaayi Lake.** ~ 11 miles east of Navajo, New Mexico, on a dirt road; 520-871-6647. **Morgan Lake** produces trophy largemouth bass, and is also a great catfish lake. ~ Four miles south of Kirtland, next to Four Corners Power Plant.

SKIING

Who needs a resort? Excellent cross-country skiing can be found on county and national forest roads—minus the crowds and lift lines.

GRANTS AREA Primitive roads on **Mt. Taylor** in the Grants area are used for cross-country skiing in the winter. For information on routes and conditions, contact the Cibola National Forest–Mt. Taylor District Ranger Station in Grants. ~ 1800 Lobo Canyon Road; 505-287-8833.

BIKING

Opportunities for mountain biking abound in a region with beautiful scenery and many unpaved roads.

GRANTS AREA Mountain biking is allowed on trails and roads throughout the **Cibola National Forest.** Many bikers recently have been testing their skills on the **Mt. Taylor summit trail** and the **McGaffey region.** Trails in the BLM **Conservation Area** on Route 117 near El Malpais National Monument are also open to bikers. **Bike Rentals** Rentals and ride recommendations can be found at **Scoreboard Sporting Goods.** ~ 107 West Coal Avenue, Gallup; 505-722-6077.

HIKING

Northwestern New Mexico boasts several national forests and monuments with trails for hiking. From 11,000-foot peaks to fascinating archaeological sites to rugged, trailless wilderness areas, there's something for everyone to explore. All distances are one-way unless otherwise noted.

GRANTS AREA   Unpaved roads lead through **Cibola National Forest** to within a mile of the summit of **Mt. Taylor**, the 11,301-foot mountain that dominates the skyline north of Grants. A trail that starts near the junction of Forest Roads 193 and 501 climbs more than 2000 feet up the southwest side of the peak to the mountaintop in three miles. Another begins near La Mosca Peak Overlook and ascends the north ridge to reach the summit of Mt. Taylor in a mile.

In the spring and fall months, **El Malpais National Monument** south of Grants presents some unusual hiking possibilities. The **Zuni-Acoma Trail** (7.5 miles one-way) crosses the lava fields between Routes 53 and 117. Said to be part of a trade route that linked the Zuni and Acoma pueblos in ancient times, the trail is level, but the lava is so rough and uneven that even a short walk from either trailhead will prove quite strenuous.

Other trails into El Malpais start along unpaved Route 42, which skirts the western and southern edges of the monument. The road requires a high-clearance vehicle. The **Big Lava Tubes Trail** (.5 mile) leads to Big Skylight Cave and Four Window Cave, both entrances to the same immense lava tube, part of a system that is 17 miles long. For more information, call 505-783-4774.

▼▼▼▼▼▼▼▼▼▼▼
Transportation

CAR

To the west of Albuquerque on **Route 40**, it is a two-hour drive to Grants and another hour to Gallup. From Gallup, head north on **Route 666** which meets with Route 64 near Shiprock. **Route 64** skirts across the northern edge of New Mexico passing through the Four Corners area and across to Chama.

BUS

Greyhound Bus Lines provides service to Grants and Gallup. ~ Reservations: 800-231-2222. Grants: Singin' Flea Market, 1781 West Santa Fe Avenue; 505-285-6268, 800-588-6268. Gallup: 105 South Dean Street; 505-863-3761, 800-231-2222.

TNM&O Coaches services the Four Corners area. ~ 505-325-1009.

TRAIN

Amtrak's "Southwest Chief" stops in Gallup at the Santa Fe Station. ~ Reservations: 800-872-7245. Gallup: 201 East Historic 66; 800-872-7245.

CAR RENTALS

A car is essential to touring this area. If you are flying in and out of Albuquerque, rent a car there (see Chapter Twelve for information). For rental cars in northwestern New Mexico, try **Avis Rent A Car** in Gallup. ~ 2111 West Highway 66; 800-331-1212. Also in Gallup is **National Interrent**. ~ Gallup Municipal Airport; 800-736-8227.

Henosh Motors has rentals in Grants. ~ 1313 East Santa Fe Avenue; 505-287-4451.

For rentals in Farmington try **Avis Rent A Car**. ~ 1300 West Navajo Avenue; 800-331-1212. **Budget Rent A Car** also has an office in Famington. ~ 1300 West Navajo Avenue; 800-527-0700. Another rental agency in Farmington is **Emergency Rent A Car**. ~ 2937 East Main Street; 505-327-2277. You can also try **Hertz Rent A Car**. ~ 1300 West Navajo Avenue; 800-654-3001. **National Interrent** is another place in Farmington. ~ 1300 West Navajo Avenue; 800-227-7368.

TWELVE

Albuquerque and Central New Mexico

Billy the Kid once roamed this area. Now you can, too. The vast ranchland plains east of the Rocky Mountains haven't changed much since the Kid rode into legend more than a century ago. But Albuquerque is another story. Just another small town on the banks of the Rio Grande downriver from Santa Fe in the heyday of the Wild West, it has been transformed into a bustling metropolis boasting a unique mosaic of lifestyles and cultures. This is the central New Mexico that intrigues the traveler: a mixture of the wild and the sublime, the cowboy and the Indian, the small town and the big city, the past and the present.

History is part of the enchantment of Albuquerque and its environs; geography is another. In fact, the setting is one thing the residents love most about their home. Sandia Peak towers a mile above the eastern city limit. Rural farmland follows the Rio Grande south. And to the west is a wide and beautiful emptiness. Visitors are often surprised by the abruptness with which the city gives way to wilderness at Albuquerque's edge. Route 40 plunges into a parched, overgrazed, alkaline high-desert wasteland that gradually reveals its stark beauty in twisting arroyos and jagged black-lava fields with fortresslike rock mesas and solitary mountains rising like islands from an arid sea.

Central New Mexico is a compelling combination of the high, cool forests of the Rocky Mountains to the north and the rocky, sunbaked Chihuahuan Desert stretching a thousand miles to the south. As a result, if you don't like the weather, you can just move on. In June, the hottest month of the year, when air-conditioning becomes essential in Albuquerque, a short drive into the mountains offers shade, cool streams and occasional patches of unmelted snow. In January, skiers can enjoy nearby slopes and then return to lower elevations where snowfalls are infrequent and light.

The mix of mountain coolness, desert dryness and southern latitude produces evening temperatures that drop to about 50 even in mid-summer and daytime highs above freezing in the dead of winter. In autumn, people watch the month-long procession of bright-gold foliage gracefully descending from the mountain heights to the cottonwood bosquet along the rivers. In springtime, new greenery spreads slowly up the slopes toward the sky.

If you're headed toward Santa Fe from Albuquerque, consider taking the Turquoise Trail (Route 14), a more relaxed and less congested route that crosses the rugged San Pedro Mountains and offers a handful of interesting sights, including a restored old mission church and an old mining town.

Cultural contrasts are equally dramatic. This is a melting pot of Navajo and Pueblo Indians whose lifestyles were upset by the Spanish exploration that began in the 1500s. Also mixed in are Norteño descendants of Spanish and Mexican colonists (New Mexico was a province of Mexico from 1821 until the 1848 treaty that ended the Mexican War with the United States) and Anglos who began settling here in the early 1800s. All these cultures come together in modern-day Albuquerque, a polyglot of a city where ancient ceremonies and futuristic technological research, fiestas and hot-air-balloon races and cowboys and entrepreneurs exist side-by-side.

Equally fascinating sights await beyond Albuquerque's city limits. The eastern plains, where most travelers stop only to exit the interstate for gasoline and a bite to eat, offer beaches and water sports on several large, manmade lakes along the Pecos and Canadian rivers. You'll find the grave of Billy-boy himself in the town of Fort Sumner, along with sites long abandoned to wind, weather and wildflowers (but just aching to be discovered).

Near the small town of Mountainair at the foot of the Manzano Mountains, sightseers can explore Spanish and Indian ruins from centuries past, one-time American Indian trade centers and headquarters for missionary efforts during the colonial era. Outside Socorro, located just off the interstate, nature-lovers visiting between November and March can witness the spectacular congregation of tens of thousands of snow geese, Canadian geese and sandhill cranes.

Faint remnants of conquest can be found throughout the area, left by Spanish soldiers who explored central New Mexico in the first half of the 16th century. These reminders of the past include the site of Coronado's bridge near Santa Rosa and the ruins of the massacred pueblo of Kuaua at Coronado State Monument near Albuquerque.

This sounds like a lot to see and do, and it is. But the astonishing news is that every place described in this chapter is within three hours' drive of Albuquerque. What more incentive do you need?

▼▼▼▼▼▼▼▼▼▼
Albuquerque

If you plan to explore central New Mexico, make Albuquerque your starting point. You'll find that much of the sightseeing here is rooted in the past, but the city also offers a fine collection of art museums and nightspots. Many scenic wonders of nature are within the city limits or nearby. And when the day is done, there are plenty of places to eat and sleep.

SIGHTS

Perhaps the best place to begin is **Old Town**, the original center of Albuquerque during the Spanish colonial and Mexican eras. West

GLENN KIM '22

of the modern downtown area, this low-rise district can be reached by taking Central Avenue west from Route 25 or Rio Grande Boulevard south from Route 40. Situated around an attractive central plaza with a bandstand, many buildings in Old Town date as early as 1780. After 1880, when the railroad reached Albuquerque and the station was built at a distance from the plaza, businesses migrated to the present downtown and Old Town was practically abandoned for half a century.

Revitalization came when artists, attracted by bargain rents, established studios in Old Town. Galleries followed, as did gift shops, boutiques and restaurants. Today, it's easy to while away half a day exploring the restored adobe (and more recent "pueblo-ized" stucco) structures, hidden patios, brick paths, gardens and balconies of Old Town, mulling over the handmade jewelry and pottery offered by American Indian vendors or just people-watching from a park bench.

Home of the largest public exhibition of rattlesnakes in the world, the Old Town's **American International Rattlesnake Museum** could surprise you with some interesting facts about what may be the world's most misunderstood reptile. Bet you didn't know that our founding fathers almost elected the timber rattlesnake instead of the bald eagle as the national symbol. And while it may not have any hands-on exhibits, this museum overflows with rattlesnake artifacts and artwork. Admission. ~ 202 San Felipe Street Northwest, Albuquerque; 505-242-6569.

Two of the city's best museums lie on opposite sides of Mountain Road, three blocks north of Old Town Plaza. The **Albuquerque Museum** contains art and history exhibits, including the permanent "Four Centuries: A History of Albuquerque" display that features the largest collection of Spanish colonial artifacts in the United States. See armor and weapons that belonged to the conquistadors, medieval religious items brought by early missionaries and ordinary household items that evoke the lifestyle of early settlers along the Rio Grande. ~ 2000 Mountain Road Northwest; 505-243-7255.

Nearby, the **New Mexico Museum of Natural History** is the newest major natural-history museum in the United States. It features unique and imaginative exhibits that let visitors walk through time, explore an Ice Age cave, stand inside an erupting volcano and sit on the back of a dinosaur. Admission. ~ 1801 Mountain Road Northwest; 505-841-2800.

East of the downtown, the **University of New Mexico** offers a varied choice of on-campus museums and cultural events. ~ The campus is bordered by Central Avenue, Girard Boulevard, University Boulevard and Indian School Road; 505-277-0111.

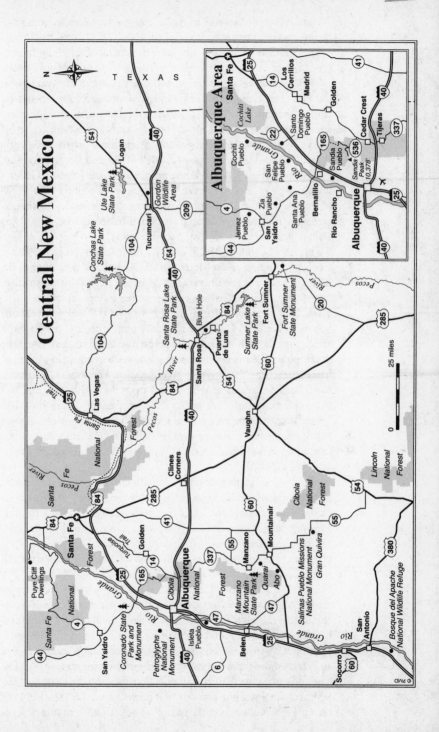

Central New Mexico

Albuquerque Area

The **Maxwell Museum of Anthropology** displays selections from the university's huge international collection of artifacts. Its "People of the Southwest" exhibit simulates an archaeological dig in progress. ~ Grande Avenue and University Boulevard; 505-277-4404.

Current-events information and a campus map are available at the **Fine Arts Center** (505-277-4001). Besides performing-arts facilities, the Fine Arts Center contains the **University Art Museum**, a museum with limited space but an outstanding collection of works by such well-known Southwestern visual artists as Georgia O'Keeffe and Ansel Adams. ~ Cornell Street and Central Avenue.

The university has a separate art museum, the **Johnson Gallery**, which displays selections from a 2000-piece collection of the works of early-20th-century New Mexico artist Raymond Johnson, as well as works from contemporary New Mexico artists. ~ 1909 Las Lomas Boulevard Northeast; 505-277-4967.

Northrop Hall (505-277-4204), the geology building, has a **Geology Museum** and a **Meteoritics Museum,** and next door in the Biology Annex is the university's **Museum of Southwestern Biology** (505-277-5340), which can be toured by appointment.

Across the street from the International Nuclear Weapons School at Kirtland Air Force Base is Albuquerque's scariest tourist attraction, the **National Atomic Museum**. Exhibits here trace the development of nuclear weapons, from Albert Einstein's original letter (suggesting the possibility) to President Franklin D. Roosevelt to replicas of various atomic bombs from the 1940s and '50s and videos of nuclear tests. Missiles, a B-52 bomber, a B-29 and an F-105 are all displayed in an outdoor exhibit. The museum also covers the development of atomic-power plants and contemporary problems of nuclear-waste disposal. ~ Wyoming Boulevard and M Street; 505-284-3243.

Enclosures at the clean, imaginatively designed **Rio Grande Zoological Park** are designed to resemble the animals' natural habitats as much as possible. The most unusual residents are a pack of Mexican lobos, a small wolf subspecies that is extinct in the wild. Of the two dozen lobos that survive in a federal captive-breeding program, the majority has been bred at the Rio Grande Zoo. Admission. ~ 903 10th Street Southwest; 505-843-7413.

The **Indian Pueblo Cultural Center**, jointly owned and operated by all 19 of New Mexico's pueblos, has one of the finest American Indian museums in the state. Through artifacts and dioramas, it traces the history of New Mexico's native population over a span of 20,000 years. Exhibits of traditional pottery and other arts and crafts show the stylistic differences between the various pueblos. The museum also features a collection of photographs from the Smithsonian Institution taken of Pueblo people in the late 19th century. The cultural center has retail galleries, a restaurant serv-

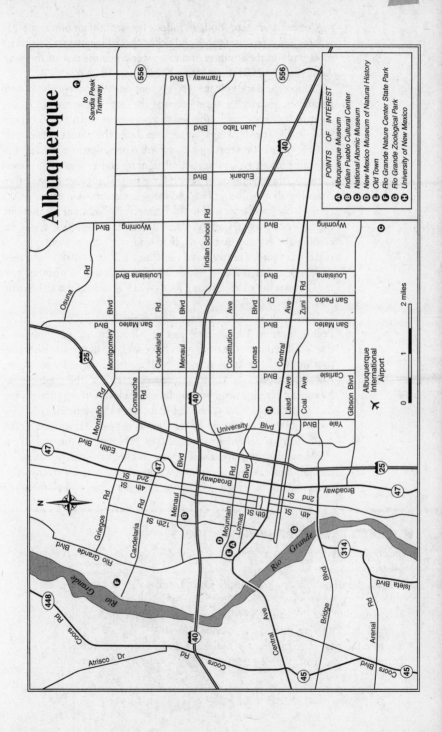

Albuquerque

to Sandia Peak Tramway

Albuquerque International Airport

0   1   2 miles

N

ing American Indian food, an indoor theater and an outdoor plaza where dance performances and other special events are staged almost daily in the summer and most weekends the rest of the year. Admission. ~ 2401 12th Street Northwest; 505-843-7270.

Along the dark volcanic escarpment on Albuquerque's western perimeter, visitors can find perhaps the largest assemblage of ancient Indian rock art in the Southwest—more than 10,000 specimens in all. The drawings were chipped into the patina of rock surfaces 800 to 1000 years ago. Some are representational pictures of animal, human and supernatural figures, and others are abstract symbols, the meanings of which have provided generations of archaeologists with a fertile topic for speculation. A portion of the petroglyphs can be viewed in the **Petroglyphs National Monument**. In the Boca Negra Canyon there are three self-guided trails, including the Mesa Point Trail, that lead you past petroglyphs. To reach the visitors center, take the Unser exit from Route 40, then drive north for three miles. Boca Mesa Canyon is another two miles down the road. Parking fee. ~ 4735 Unser Boulevard Northwest; 505-839-4429.

For many travelers, the ultimate experience is a trip up **Sandia Peak** (elevation 10,378 feet) east of Albuquerque. The mountain rises so sharply on the city's eastern boundary that from either bottom or top it looks as if a rock falling from the cliffs along the ridgeline would land in someone's yard in the fashionable Northeast Heights neighborhood a mile below. On a typically clear day, you can see almost half the state from the summit.

While the summit can be reached by car (see "Turquoise Trail" sights section below) or on foot (see "Hiking" at the end of the chapter), the most spectacular way to climb this mountain is via the **Sandia Peak Tramway**, the world's longest aerial tramway. It takes just 15 minutes to ascend the 2.7-mile cable, and all the while

---

✔ CHECK THESE OUT—UNIQUE SIGHTS

- Stand inside an erupting volcano at the **New Mexico Museum of Natural History**. *page 380*
- Zoom up Sandia Peak on the **Sandia Peak Tramway** for a spine-tingling ride with eagle-eye views of the rugged canyon. *page 384*
- Kid around at the **Billy the Kid Museum**, where a jail cell that once housed the notorious gunman is located. *page 403*
- Explore the past of the ancient peoples at **Salinas Pueblo Missions National Monument**, which preserves the ruins of three Anasazi pueblos. *page 411*

you'll enjoy eagle's-eye views of rugged canyons in the Sandia Wilderness Area; you may even catch a glimpse of Rocky Mountain bighorn sheep grazing on a distant promontory. At the summit are an observation deck, a deluxe restaurant, a gift shop, a snack bar a short walk away at the end of the auto road, the Four Seasons Visitors Center (open April through October) and breathtaking views in every direction. The tram close twice a year (once in April, once in October) for regular maintenance. ~ 10 Tramway Loop Northeast; 505-856-6415.

LODGING

As New Mexico's largest city, Albuquerque has lodgings for every taste. One downtown grand hotel that predates World War II has been restored to the height of luxury. The emerging bed-and-breakfast scene features small, homey places that range from Victorian mansions to contemporary suburban guest houses. Rates for Albuquerque accommodations are much lower than the cost of comparable lodging in Santa Fe or Taos. Note: Reservations are advised for all bed and breakfasts.

Native New Mexican Conrad Hilton started his hotel chain in Albuquerque. The second Hilton hostelry, built in 1939, has been lovingly restored as the city's showpiece downtown historic hotel, **La Posada de Albuquerque**. The lobby, with its vaulted ceiling and Indian murals, sets the tone—a blend of old-fashioned elegance and unique New Mexican style. Handmade traditional New Mexico furniture graces the modern guest rooms. ~ 125 2nd Street Northwest; 505-242-9090, 800-777-5732, fax 506-242-8664. MODERATE TO DELUXE.

Located within walking distance of Old Town and Route 66, the **W. E. Mauger Estate** is a historic Queen Anne home with high ceilings, flowered wallpaper and hardwood floors. The estate has eight bedrooms, each with a private bath, and offers full breakfast as well as wine and hors d'oeuvres in the afternoon. ~ 701 Roma Street Northwest; 505-242-8755, fax 505-842-8835. MODERATE TO DELUXE.

Staying at the **W. J. Marsh House** may make you feel like you are staying in New England instead of the Southwest. The bed and breakfast is housed in and 1892 Victorian located in the Huning Highland historic district. From 1910 to 1920 and during World War II the building was used as a boarding house. (It is also rumored that the house once served as a brothel.) Today it has been restored in its original 1890s style and offers six guest rooms furnished with antiques. Keep and eye out for the resident ghosts. A full breakfast with several courses is served. Gay-friendly. ~ 301 Edith Boulevard Southeast; 505-247-1001. MODERATE TO DELUXE.

The **Old Town Bed & Breakfast** is actually east of Old Town in a quiet residential neighborhood within easy walking distance of the New Mexico Museum of Natural History and the Albuquerque Museum. It features adobe and viga architecture, a patio and two guest quarters. The bottom two-room suite has a separate sitting area and a kiva fireplace, and shares the jacuzzi with the owner. ~ 707 17th Street Northwest; 505-764-9144. MODERATE.

Dave's B&B is located in a quiet, residential neighborhood just a mile from the Old Town area. The Southwestern-style house has two guest rooms both with private baths and entrances to the patio, which features a hot tub. Both the patio and the hot tub are clothing optional. Guests also have access to the kitchen. Dave's caters primarily to the leather crowd, but lesbians are welcome as well. ~ 505-247-8312. MODERATE.

Casas de Sueños is a unique bed and breakfast three blocks from Old Town Plaza. The cluster of small houses and duplexes surrounding courtyard gardens began as an artists' colony in the 1940s. Each living unit is individually designed and furnished, and many have kitchen facilities, fireplaces or hot tubs. Over the entrance to the main house is a large protuberance, which the innkeepers refer to as "the snail." The sight of this architectural curiosity stops cars on the street as drivers gawk. It was originally designed as a nonlinear law office by young architect Bart Prince. ~ 310 Rio Grande Boulevard Southwest; 505-247-4560, 800-242-8987, fax 505-842-8493. DELUXE TO ULTRA-DELUXE.

Closer to the plaza, the **Böttger Mansion Bed and Breakfast** is in a 1910 Victorian home listed on the National Register of Historic Landmarks. The seven guest rooms are individually decorated with Victorian furnishings; one includes a jacuzzi. ~ 110 San Felipe Street Northwest; phone/fax 505-243-3639. DELUXE TO ULTRA-DELUXE.

Strolling among the Territorial-style low rises of Old Town, it would be easy to imagine yourself in an earlier century were it not for the towering presence of the 11-story **Sheraton Old Town** a block away. The grounds preserve natural desert landscaping, while the large lobby bursts with Southwestern designs and colors and the restaurant features improbable nautical decor. Views from the upper floors are arguably the most spectacular in town. ~ 800 Rio Grande Boulevard Northwest; 505-843-6300, 800-237-2133, fax 505-842-9863. DELUXE.

Families traveling together who appreciate the extra space and amenities of a suite can find weekend bargain rates at several of Albuquerque's all-suite hotels. For example, the **Barcelona Court All-Suite Hotel** off Route 40 has suites with separate bedrooms and kitchen facilities that include microwave ovens. ~ 900 Louisiana Boulevard Northeast; 505-255-5566, 800-222-1122, fax 505-255-1611. MODERATE.

The **Holiday Inn Pyramid** is easy to spot; just look for its stepped pyramid shape along Route 25 in the commercial zone north of the city. Inside you'll find an atrium with a 50-foot waterfall, a glass elevator and Mayan and Aztec motifs. The 311 rooms are of the standard hotel variety. ~ 5151 San Francisco Road Northeast; 505-821-3333, 800-465-4329, fax 505-828-0230. DELUXE.

Also on the city's north side off Route 25, and catering to a business clientele, the **Wyndham Garden Hotel** offers some classy touches, from the sunny atrium lobby to the bright, contemporary Southwest–style guest rooms, not to mention the indoor-outdoor swim-through pool. ~ 6000 Pan American Freeway Northeast; 505-821-9451, 800-996-3426, fax 505-858-0239. MODERATE.

Step back into Southwest history by taking a room at the **Hacienda Antigua**. The 200-year old adobe hacienda was built in the Spanish colonial era and still retains its 19th century ambience. The five guest rooms are individually decorated with antiques including iron beds, kiva fireplaces and a 100-year old clawfoot tub. There are plenty of opportunities to relax whether you choose to take a dip in the pool, a soak in the outdoor hot tub or a turn in the orchard. The gourmet breakfast is a real treat. Gay-friendly. ~ 6708 Tierra Drive Northwest; 505-345-5399, 800-201-2986. DELUXE.

Visitors looking for budget accommodations should take Central Avenue east beyond the University of New Mexico campus. Central used to be Route 66, the main east-west highway through Albuquerque before the interstates were built. Although the old two-lane highway has become a wide commercial thoroughfare, several tourist courts dating back to that earlier era still survive along Central between Carlisle and San Mateo boulevards.

The affordably priced **De Anza Motor Lodge** is a prime example. Something about its pueblo styling and tepee-shaped sign recalls that small-town, halfway-from-home-to-California mystique that many people nostalgically associate with Old Route 66.

▲▲▲

✔ CHECK THESE OUT—UNIQUE LODGING

- *Budget:* Unpack your bags at the whimsical **Shaffer Hotel**, a hardware store-turned-hotel, crafted by local folk artist Clem "Pop" Shaffer. *page 412*
- *Budget:* Bed down in a former hacienda at **Casa Grande**, a rustic adobe overlooking a beautiful arroyo. *page 401*
- *Moderate to deluxe:* Check in at Conrad Hilton's second ever Hilton hostelry, **La Posada de Albuquerque**, built in 1939 and lovingly restored. *page 385*
- *Deluxe to ultra-deluxe:* Soak in a hot tub or warm yourself by the fireplace at **Casas de Sueños**, a B&B near Old Town Plaza. *page 386*

Budget: under $50 Moderate: $50–$90 Deluxe: $90–$120 Ultra-deluxe: over $120

Caution: This part of Central Avenue is considered a "bad neighborhood" because a few of the old motels are frequented by prostitutes. ~ 4301 Central Avenue Northeast; 505-255-1654, fax 505-255-7459. BUDGET.

On the east edge of town, near the Central Avenue/Tramway Boulevard exit from Route 40, is another concentration of franchise lodgings. Although this area is a long way from central destinations like Old Town and the university, it is a convenient location from which to ride the tramway or drive up Sandia Peak.

One option is **Best Western American Motor Inn**. ~ 12999 Central Avenue Northeast; 505-298-7426, 800-366-3252, fax 505-298-0212. Another hostelry is **Econo Lodge**. ~ 13211 Central Avenue Northeast; 505-292-7600, 800-424-4777, fax 505-298-4536. MODERATE.

Contemporary in style, the **Albuquerque Hilton** is the finest of several major hotels that cluster northeast of the Route 25 and Route 40 interchange. ~ 1901 University Boulevard Northeast; 505-884-2500, 800-445-8667, fax 505-889-9118. MODERATE TO DELUXE.

> Native New Mexican Conrad Hilton started his hotel chain in Albuquerque.

Casita Chamisa has two units, each with private bath, in a 19th-century adobe home. The shady, forested acreage that is the Casita Chamisa's setting is also an archaeological site, and the innkeepers are happy to show a video that explains all about it. ~ 850 Chamisal Road Northwest; 505-897-4644. MODERATE.

Several first-rate, moderately priced, suburban bed and breakfasts are located in the Paseo del Norte area of Albuquerque and on the other side of the Rio Grande. **Adobe and Roses** rents an adobe guesthouse and a suite. The traditional New Mexico architecture features brick floors, Mexican tiles and vigas. Both units have fireplaces as well as private entrances and kitchenettes. ~ 1011 Ortega Road Northwest; 505-898-0654.

Nearby, **Casa del Granjero** sits on three-and-a-half acres that are accentuated by a gazebo, lily pond, waterfall and hot tub that faces the Sandia Mountains, barn cats, chickens, and horses. Three of the seven guest rooms are in the Main House, an adobe hacienda from the territorial era that features a lovely enclosed courtyard. The Guest House is where the other accommodations are located. Kiva fireplaces, canopy beds, handmade willow furniture, French doors and Mexican-tiled bathrooms are highlights throughout all the rooms. ~ 414 C de Baca Lane Northwest; 505-897-4144, 800-701-4144, fax 505-897-9788. DELUXE TO ULTRA-DELUXE.

DINING

A popular Mexican restaurant is **La Hacienda**. The Spanish colonial atmosphere, with *ristras*, and a big kiva fireplace and lots of Southwestern art on the walls, fits right into the Old Town experience. The menu includes steak and seafood dishes as well as local cuisine such as fajitas. ~ 302 San Felipe Street Northwest; 505-243-3131. MODERATE.

Arguably Albuquerque's most beautiful restaurant, **Maria Teresa** is located in the Salvador Armijo House, a National Historic Landmark dating back to the 1840s and elegantly furnished with Victorian-era antiques. Besides local specialties, the menu includes fine contemporary American and Continental dishes. ~ 618 Rio Grande Boulevard Northwest; 505-242-3900. MODERATE TO DELUXE.

In one of Old Town's oldest buildings, circa 1785, **High Noon** serves enchiladas and burritos as well as steaks, seafood and game to the strains of live flamenco guitar music. A house specialty is the pepper steak served with a pepper and cream cognac sauce. ~ 425 San Felipe Street Northwest; 505-765-1455. MODERATE TO DELUXE.

While the decor of **The Original Garcia's Kitchen** raises a lot of questions (like what's that huge diamondback rattlesnake skin doing over the entry way to the dining room, and who decided to put all the family trophies in the window?), no one ever second guesses the kitchen. Take a table, booth or counter seat and feast on the blue-corn enchilada plate, green-chili stew or *chicharrones* and beans. It's packed during the breakfast hour, when *huevos a la Mexicana* (scrambled eggs, jalapeños, tomatoes and onion) and *huevos locos* (eggs with shredded beef or ham) are among the entrées. Gringo breakfasts like French toast are also served. ~ 1113 4th Street Northwest, Albuquerque; 505-247-9149. BUDGET.

New Southwestern cuisine—traditional New Mexican ingredients imaginatively used in Continental dishes or New Mexican specialties prepared with improbable ingredients—is appearing in quite a few Albuquerque restaurants these days. For example, the menu at **McGrath's**, the restaurant at the Hyatt Regency Hotel, features chicken quesadillas, a filet mignon brushed with Hatch red chile and grilled marinated lamb served with skewered vegetables over saffron rice. ~ 330 Tijeras Avenue Northwest; 505-766-6700. MODERATE TO DELUXE.

A different kind of local cuisine can be found at the restaurant in the **Indian Pueblo Cultural Center.** Open for lunch only, this restaurant serves traditional Pueblo Indian dishes such as fry bread, Indian tacos and *posole.* ~ 2401 12th Street Northwest; 505-843-7270. BUDGET.

For what many consider the best homemade green-chile stew in Albuquerque, visit the 180-seat **Sanitary Tortilla Factory.** ~ 403 2nd Street Southwest; 505-242-4890. BUDGET.

The **Hyperion Café** is an intimate European-style café serving breakfast and lunch. Relax in one of the comfy couches or chairs in the lounge or take a seat at one of the sidewalk tables. For breakfast you can choose from bagel sandwiches, breakfast burritos or one of their many pastries. Lunch offerings include sandwiches, salads, soup and a daily special. Gay-friendly. Closed Sunday. ~ 215 Central Avenue Northwest; 505-242-7766. BUDGET.

A favorite Albuquerque restaurant for unusual food is the **Artichoke Café.** Here the menu changes frequently to take advantage of fresh, seasonal ingredients. Choices are wide ranging, including all of your basic meats, pastas and salads. As one might expect, the first item on the menu is an artichoke—steamed and served with three dipping sauces. Paintings by local artists brighten the walls. ~ 424 Central Avenue Southeast; 505-243-0200. MODERATE.

Farther out on Central Avenue, you can get a green-chile cheese dog, a rich, thick chocolate shake and a big dose of nostalgia at the **66 Diner** a 1950s-style roadside diner designed with Historic Route 66 buffs in mind. ~ 1405 Central Avenue Northeast; 505-247-1421. BUDGET.

If seafood is your preference, try the **Café Oceana.** Entrées served in a friendly neighborhood atmosphere. Shrimp comes prepared in any of a half dozen ways. The menu also features a daily fresh catch—for example, mahimahi sautéed with garlic, ginger, bell peppers, jalapeños and red chile. Closed Sunday. ~ 1414 Central Avenue Southeast; 505-247-2233. MODERATE.

A place where the green chile will knock your socks off (or maybe burn them off) is **Sadie's Dining Room.** This establishment is as local as it gets, with a view of a bowling alley. ~ 6230 4th Street Northwest; 505-345-5339. BUDGET.

New Southwestern cuisine is the specialty at **Casa Chaco.** Formerly the Albuquerque Hilton's coffee shop, Casa Chaco has become a full-scale restaurant featuring such delicacies as shrimp and

---

✔ **CHECK THESE OUT—UNIQUE DINING**

- *Budget:* Pull up to the **Comet II,** one of the last original Route 66 restaurants—in operation for 46 years. *page 408*
- *Moderate:* Sidle up to the state's longest stand-up bar then take a table for dinner at the **Mine Shaft Tavern.** *page 402*
- *Deluxe:* Hop the tram to **High Finance** at the top of the Sandia Peak Tramway, and feast on the incomparable view. *page 392*
- *Deluxe to ultra-deluxe:* Dine at the foot of the Sandia tramway at **Firehouse Restaurant at the Tram,** and order a drink at the antique fire-engine-turned-bar. *page 392*

Budget: under $8 Moderate: $8–$16 Deluxe: $16–$24 Ultra-deluxe: over $24

sea scallops sautéed with a leek and tomato *beurre* sauce and served in a pastry shell, roasted pork tenderloin marinated in herbs and served over angel hair pasta with a peanut and prickly pear cactus glaze, grilled Rocky Mountain lamb served with Dijon mustard, bread crumbs and a green-chile sauce, and pâté seasoned with cilantro, jalapeño and piñon nuts. ~ 1901 University Boulevard Northeast; 505-884-2500. MODERATE.

For inexpensive fare in a lively student environment blending intellectual conversation, video games and general rowdiness, a long-time favorite spot is the **Frontier Restaurant** across the street from the main entrance to the University of New Mexico campus. Food choices include burgers, spicy dishes such as *huevos rancheros* (served any time of day) and giant, sticky, delicious cinnamon rolls. ~ 2400 Central Avenue Southeast; 505-266-0550. BUDGET.

Firehouses seem to be a popular theme for Albuquerque restaurants. The **Monte Vista Firestation** is located in what was once a real fire station and today stands as one of the city's finest surviving examples of the "Pueblo Deco" architecture that sprang up along Old Route 66 in the 1930s. The fare at this restaurant is highly imaginative. The menu changes daily, but a typical dinner might include an ostrich fajita or sea scallops marinated in tequila and lime and served with ancho chile and julienne potatoes. ~ 3201 Central Avenue Northeast; 505-255-2424. MODERATE.

Located in the heart of the Nob Hill district, **Double Rainbow Bakery Cafe** is a popular hangout for gays who want to see and be seen. Grab a seat inside or at a table on the sidewalk anytime from 6:30 a.m. to midnight and anyone from university students to military personnel to neighborhood gay residents will be your neighbor. Famous for the goodies produced at their on-site bakery and for their coffee, which is roasted in-house daily, Double Rainbow also has a café menu with delicious homemade items. On the weekend there is an extended brunch menu. Gay-friendly. ~ 3416 Central Avenue Southeast; 505-255-6633. BUDGET.

Don't be put off by the unpretentious exterior of the **Adobe Rose**, located near the state fairground. This longstanding local favorite featuring New Mexican and Tex-Mex food is renowned for its great fajitas. ~ 6724 Central Avenue Southeast; 505-255-7673. BUDGET.

The homemade Italian fare at **Chianti's** keeps locals coming back again and again. Veal, fish, chicken, pasta and other traditional Italian dishes are served in a romantic candlelit setting. Despite the romantic atmosphere, the clientele is mostly families. Gay-friendly. ~ 5210 San Mateo Avenue Northeast; 505-881-1967. BUDGET TO MODERATE.

Progressive for Albuquerque, **Woody's Cafe and Coffee Bar's** interior has lots of corrugated steel and full wall mural of a Mardi

Gras scene. For breakfast there are pastries, and the lunch and dinner menus have an array of sandwiches. The coffee bar features locally roasted coffee that can also be purchased by the pound. Gay-friendly. Closed Sunday. ~ 11200 Montgomery Avenue Boulevard Northeast, Eldorado Square; 505-292-6800. BUDGET.

One of the city's better Asian establishments, **ABC Chinese Restaurant** is entered through a lacquered dragon and phoenix archway. Bas relief Buddhas and colorful paper lanterns make this Chinese and Korean restaurant a delight. Specialties include boneless tenderloin pork marinated in a spicy Korean bean sauce and barbecued duck with lychee nuts, pineapple and a sweet orange sauce. ~ 8720 Menaul Boulevard Northeast; 505-292-8788. MODERATE.

One of the finest restaurants in these parts is the **High Finance**. It's the setting that makes this restaurant so special. At the top of the Sandia Peak Tramway, the restaurant affords an incomparable view of Albuquerque glistening in a vast, empty landscape a mile below. Entrées include prime rib, steaks and lobster. Guests with dinner reservations here receive a discount on their tramway fares. ~ Sandia Crest; 505-243-9742. DELUXE.

Steaks and seafood are also served at the lower end of the tramway in the **Firehouse Restaurant at the Tram**. Other specialties include mesquite-barbecued ribs and chicken. The view of the city is impressive even from the foot of the mountain, and those with dinner reservations at the Firehouse receive discounts on tram tickets. The Firehouse has a converted antique fire engine for a bar. ~ 38 Tramway Road; 505-856-3473. DELUXE TO ULTRA-DELUXE.

SHOPPING   Shoppers can buy directly from American Indian craftspersons along San Felipe Street across from the plaza in **Old Town,** which is also Albuquerque's art gallery and boutique district. Almost 100 shops can lure visitors into making Old Town an all-day expedition.

Possibly the only candy store in America to be picketed by anti-pornography forces, **The Candy Lady** is an Old Town institution. This adobe-style candyland tempts sweet tooths with 21 brands of fudge, plus dipped strawberries, bonbons and other sugary yummies. But it's the X-rated section doubling as a human anatomy lesson that has caused all the ruckus. Candy molded into the shape of breasts and cakes with spicy frosting designs—even erotic sculptures—actually prompted the city of Albuquerque to attempt a crackdown. ~ 524 Romero Street Northwest; 505-243-6239.

The **Santo Domingo Indian Trading Post,** specializing in jewelry, is owned and operated by a resident of Santo Domingo Pueblo—a bit ironic, since the trading post at the pueblo is operated by non-Indians. ~ 401 San Felipe Street Northwest; 505-764-0129.

The Good Stuff displays an array of American Indian and Western antiques. ~ 2108 Charlevoix Street Northwest; 505-843-

6416. At the **Christin Wolf Gallery** you'll see the artist's fine jewelry as well as Southwestern art and furniture. Metal and paper sculpture and raku-fired pottery in a American Indian motif is also sold here. ~ 206½ San Felipe Street Northwest, Albuquerque; 505-242-4222. **Perfumes of the Desert** carries unusual perfumes blended locally using desert-flower scents. ~ 208 San Felipe Street Northwest; 505-243-0859.

The **Chile Pepper Emporium** has the largest and most complete selection in New Mexico—and the world, probably—of chile items, ranging from spices, sauces and jellies to chile-motif T-shirts and chile-shaped Christmas tree lights. ~ 328 San Felipe Street Northwest; 505-242-7538.

The **Indian Pueblo Cultural Center** has a series of galleries surrounding the central dance plaza. All operated by the cultural center, the galleries differ by price ranges from curio items to museum-quality collectors' objects. Because the cultural center is owned by a coalition of Indian pueblos, authenticity is assured, making this one of the best places to shop for American Indian pottery, sculpture, sandpaintings, rugs, kachinas and traditional and contemporary jewelry. ~ 2401 12th Street Northwest; 505-843-7270.

For Southwestern furniture, kachinas and American Indian jewelry at discount prices, stop by **Albuquerque's Indoor Mercado**, across from the Indian Pueblo Cultural Center. With more than 200 merchants hawking chile products, sandpaintings and dozens of other souvenirs, you're bound to find something to take home. ~ 12th Street at Route 40; 505-243-8111.

Spend some time browsing in **Page One**, the largest independently run bookstore in New Mexico. The friendly staff is always ready to help you find what you need. ~ 11018 Montgomery Boulevard Northeast; 505-294-2026.

For more practical shopping needs, Albuquerque's major shopping malls are **Winrock Center**, located at Louisiana Boulevard Northeast and Indian School Road Northeast, near the Louisiana Boulevard exit from Route 40, and **Coronado Center**, located at Louisiana Boulevard Northeast and Menaul Boulevard Northeast.

GAY STORES   It might not be a San Francisco or New York, but Albuquerque does have a growing gay and lesbian community. While there isn't a strictly gay area, the trendy Nob Hill neighborhood, home to several gay and lesbian bookstores and establishments, is probably where you'll find the closest thing to a "scene."

Full Circle Books has been serving Albuquerque's feminist and lesbian community for over two decades. Several nights a week the bookstore holds special events such as workshops, forums, readings and poetry slams. ~ 2205 Silver Avenue Southeast; 505-266-0022.

For gay and lesbian books which may be out of print try **Tulane Exchange**. The discount bookstore has a section of used gay and lesbian books as well as an excellent selection of gay videos to rent. ~ 111 Tulane Drive Southeast; 505-260-0792.

Sisters' and Brothers' Bookstore touts itself as New Mexico's only lesbian/bisexual/gay community bookstore. In addition to an endless selection of books, they also stock jewelry, flags, videos and anything with a rainbow on it. ~ 4011 Silver Avenue Southeast; 505-266- 7317.

Next door in the Common Bond Community Center is **Blue Angel Video**, which rents films with gay and lesbian themes in a variety of genres including documentaries, experimental, feature films and erotica. ~ 4031 Silver Avenue Southeast; 505-266-8041.

Martha's Body Bueno Shop carries cards, gifts, lingerie, adult novelty items and a wide selection of calendars. ~ 3105 Central Avenue Northeast; 505-255-1122.

In Crowd sells folk art by local and Mexican artists. The back room features adult cards and T-shirts and some leather accessories. ~ 3106 Central Avenue Southeast; 505-268-3750.

NIGHTLIFE   A contemporary pianist tickles the ivories Wednesday through Friday at **La Posada de Albuquerque Lounge**. On weekends a band plays jazz and rhythm-and-blues. Weekend cover. ~ 125 2nd Street Northwest; 505-242-9090.

Wind down after a strenuous day of sightseeing at **Brewster's Pub**, where a balcony bandstand packs them in at happy hour. Dance on the hardwood floor to reggae, rhythm and blues or jazz sounds or just sip a cocktail at the mirrored bar, the hub of a popular single's scene. Come early enough and you may even land a table. Occasional cover. ~ 312 Central Avenue Southwest, Albuquerque; 505-247-2533.

Mariachis were singing away the last time we dropped by **The Dingo Bar**, a cavelike nightclub with muraled walls and footprints on the ceiling. Live bands play blues, jazz, zydeco and alternative rock. Cover. ~ 313 Gold Avenue Southwest; 505-243-0663.

The most popular bar in the university district is the **Fat Chance Bar and Grille** where both students and professors come to socialize and listen to live music. ~ 2216 Central Avenue Southeast; 505-296-5653.

The dancefloor is always busy at **Caravan**. Hollywood-style lighting brightens this beam-ceilinged club which features two country bands nightly. Weekend cover. ~ 7605 Central Avenue Northeast; 505-265-6994.

At **Babe's Sports Bar**, 42 television sets ensure that you'll never miss any of the big games. If you aren't a sports fan, you can dance to the deejay's Top-40 tunes. Cover on weekends. ~ 8904 Menaul Boulevard Northeast; 505-293-9001.

The top comedy club in Albuquerque is **Laffs**, featuring local and national stand-up comedians as well as Tuesday open-mike amateur nights. ~ 3100-D Juan Tabo Boulevard Northeast; 505-296-5653.

Cadillac Ranch Nite-Club, with a dancefloor as big as the Texas horizon and live country music, is a happening place Tuesday through Saturday nights. Cover. ~ 9800 Montgomery Boulevard Northeast; 505-298-2113.

For jazz aficionados there's the **Gulf Coast Jazz Club**. Jazz trios and jam sessions play Thursday through Saturday. ~ 5809 Juan Tabo Boulevard Northeast; 505-293-2922.

With room for 2000 guests, **Midnight Rodeo** has 17 well bars and a racetrack-shaped dancefloor. A disc jockey spins country tunes if there isn't a live act. After you've two-stepped to your heart's content, take a breather in the comfortable Western-style lounge. Cover. ~ 4901 McLeod Road Northeast; 505-888-0100.

GAY NIGHTLIFE   If you're looking to dance, head for the high-tech, gay hot-spot, **Pulse**, located in the Nob Hill district. Designated danceclub nights feature a live deejay playing high-energy and retro music. Cover for special events. ~ 4100 Central Avenue Southeast; 505-255-3334.

The vast **Albuquerque Mining Co.** offers something for everyone with four bars under one roof, volleyball on Sunday and special events. The dance bar is the most popular with its retro and dance music. To take a break from dancing, kick back either on the patio or in the lounge. Enter the Pit at your own risk. The clientele is both gay and lesbian. Cover. ~ 7209 Central Avenue Northeast; 505-255-4022.

Another place to dance the night away is **Foxes Booze n Cruise**. The gay, lesbian and straight clientele boogey to deejay disco music. They also host occasional drag shows. Cover for drag shows. ~ 8521 Central Avenue Northeast; 505-255-3060.

A leather bar is only one of the attractions that makes **The Ranch** a hit with the gay community. This Western-style club also features a wide-open dancefloor and a deejay operating out of a chuckwagon. If you're a little rusty on the Tennessee waltz, you can always work on your pool game. Cover on weekends. ~ 8900 Central Avenue Southeast; 505-275-1616.

OPERA, SYMPHONY AND DANCE   There's a lively performing-arts scene in Albuquerque, most of which centers around the University of New Mexico. Productions at the university's **Popejoy Hall** (505-277-3824) include plays by touring Broadway shows, performances of the **Albuquerque Civic Light Opera** (505-345-6577) and concerts by the **New Mexico Symphony Orchestra** (505-881-8999).

Other theaters on campus include the Theatre Arts Department's **"X" Theatre** in the basement of the Fine Arts Center and the **Rodey Theater** adjoining Popejoy Hall. For schedule information on both theaters, call the Public Events office. ~ 505-277-3824.

The New Mexico Jazz Workshop hosts over 30 concerts a year at locations around the city including the Albuquerque Museum and the zoo. ~ 505-255-9788.

Another important performing-arts venue in Albuquerque is the historic KiMo Theater, which hosts performances by groups including the Riverside Repertory Theater (505-265-2704), the Ballet Theater of New Mexico (505-888-1054) and the Albuquerque Children's Theater (505-888-3644). ~ KiMo Theater: 423 Central Avenue Northwest; 505-848-1370.

PARKS **PASEO DEL BOSQUE** 🏃 🚴 🏇 The bosque, or cottonwood forest, lining the banks of the Rio Grande is protected for future park development all the way through the city of Albuquerque. Most of this area remains wild, undeveloped and inaccessible to motor vehicles. A ten-mile paved trail for joggers, cyclists and horseback riders leads along the edge of the bosque, following the river north from the Rio Grande Zoo to Paseo Del Norte Boulevard in the North Valley. ~ Trail access from Campbell Road, Mountain Road or Rio Grande Nature Center on Candelaria Boulevard Northwest.

▼▼▼▼▼▼▼▼▼▼▼▼▼▼▼

Outside of Albuquerque

Exploring the area surrounding Albuquerque proper is well worth any visitor's time. Traveling north of Albuquerque on Route 25, motorists can explore a number of ancient and modern Indian pueblos, including the largest of the Rio Grande Indian pueblos.

SIGHTS Thirteen miles south of Albuquerque in the South Valley, Isleta Pueblo is a labyrinthine mixture of old and new houses comprising one of New Mexico's larger pueblos. Visitors who wander the narrow streets of the town will eventually find their way to the mission church, one of the oldest in the country. The pueblo operates a fishing lake, campground and bingo parlor. Several shops around the plaza sell the local white, red and black pottery. Photographing ceremonies is prohibited. ~ Route 25; 505-869-3111.

The two nearest pueblos to Albuquerque—Sandia Pueblo and Santa Ana Pueblo—are so small that they often go unnoticed. Sandia Pueblo has an arts-and-crafts market and a Las Vegas–style bingo operation. The Sandia people number about 300 and speak Tiwa, a different language from that spoken at other pueblos in the vicinity. They claim descent from the inhabitants of Kuaua at nearby Coronado State Monument. ~ Route 313, about seven miles north of Albuquerque; 505-867-3317.

Just up the road, Santa Ana Pueblo has about 500 tribal members; nearly all live here, away from the old pueblo off Route 44. The tribe owns a golf course nearby and operates an arts-and-crafts cooperative. ~ Route 313, two miles north of Bernalillo; 505-867-3301.

Founded beside the Rio Grande around the year 1300, Kuaua was a thriving pueblo when a Spanish expedition led by Francisco Vasquez de Coronado arrived in 1540. The 1100 explorers spent the winter there and at first found the people of Kuaua hospitable, but as supplies ran short and demands on the pueblo increased, the Indians became uncooperative and Coronado destroyed the pueblo.

Today, the ruins of Kuaua are preserved at **Coronado State Monument,** 15 miles north of Albuquerque. The unique feature of this ruin is a round ceremonial kiva (an underground chamber) that, when excavated, was found to have murals around its interior—the only pre-Columbian pueblo kiva paintings known to have survived the centuries. Archaeologists carefully removed and mounted the painted layers, and the original murals are now displayed in a room adjoining the visitors center along with diagrams that explain their meanings. The kiva itself has been fully restored and ornamented with replicas of the paintings, and visitors are welcome to climb down into it. The visitors center also contains exhibits about both the pueblo people and the Spanish conquistadors. Admission. ~ Located on Route 44, one mile west of Route 25 from the town of Bernalillo; 505-867-5351.

The Mexican name for the Rio Grande is "Rio Bravo."

Tradition is strong at **San Felipe Pueblo,** ten miles from Bernalillo north on Route 25. The pueblo is known for spectacular dances (the bowl-like central plaza has actually been worn down three feet below ground level by centuries of ceremonies) and beadwork. The pueblo's artisans specialize in *heishi* (disclike beads used for necklaces). Photographs and sketching are strictly prohibited. ~ One and a half miles west of Route 25 at Exit 252; 505-867-3381.

Adventuresome motorists will find an unpaved road running between San Felipe Pueblo and **Santo Domingo Pueblo.** Each pueblo is within a few miles of Route 25, but the road between them seems a world apart from the interstate as it winds through tribal farmland unchanged by time. Santo Domingo is the largest of the Rio Grande Indian pueblos and one of the most conservative. After admiring the horses and other ornate designs painted on the church facade, visitors may wish to stroll through the narrow, old streets and hear the residents speaking in the native Keresan language. There's a small museum and outdoor arts-and-crafts market near the interstate. ~ Five miles west of Route 25 Exit 259; 505-465-2214.

A few miles from the pueblo off of Route 25 is the picturesque **Santo Domingo Trading Post,** the granddaddy of Indian curio shops. The faded storefront, brightly painted back in the 1940s, proclaims the trading post to be one of the Southwest's top attractions—as seen in *Look* magazine.

The mission church at **Cochiti Pueblo** dates back to 1628 and is among the oldest on the Rio Grande. Cochiti artisans originated

◄ HIDDEN

the pottery storyteller figures that now are popular collectibles. The pueblo leases the tribal real estate on which Albuquerque's water supply and recreational reservoir, Cochiti Lake, as well as the town of Cochiti Lake, is situated. There is a campground and other lake services, and fishing is permitted in the Rio Grande with a fishing license. Cochiti Pueblo is farther removed from the interstate than any of the other pueblos between Albuquerque and Santa Fe. ~ To get there, travel north on Route 25, then take the marked tribal road for about 15 miles; 505-465-2244.

American Indians have lived in **Zia Pueblo** since the middle of the 13th century, though diseases introduced by European settlers caused their population to dwindle from 6000 to less than 100 by the end of the 19th century. But today this reservation, located 35 miles east of Albuquerque off Route 44, is thriving once more, with about 700 American Indians making their home here. Spread across 190 acres of piñon-juniper and ponderosa pine woodlands, the Zia reservation features a small cultural center that showcases arts and crafts. And Zia Lake, on the north side of the James River, is a popular fishing spot. ~ Route 44, San Ysidro; 505-867-3304.

In the vicinity, **Jemez Pueblo** is only open to tourists on special feast days in August and November. ~ On Route 4 just north of Route 44; 505-834-7359. But if you'd care to do some shopping for Jemez pottery, sculpture or woven blankets, you can visit the **Red Rock Scenic Area** during summer. Turquoise jewelry, moccasins and drums are also sold here, and with advance permission from the game warden, you can fish the pueblo's Dragonfly lakes after you've spent all your money. ~ Off Route 4, three miles north of Jemez Pueblo.

LODGING

Corrales, a rural North Valley community located near Bernalillo and Coronado State Monument, is home to some of the Albuquerque area's best small bed and breakfasts. **Yours Truly Bed and Breakfast** offers four guest rooms in a modern adobe house with fireplaces, a spa and nearby hiking trails. ~ 160 Paseo de Corrales, Corrrales; phone/fax 505-898-7027, 800-942-7890. MODERATE TO DELUXE.

The **Corrales Inn Bed & Breakfast** has six rooms, private baths and a cozy library with 2000 volumes, primarily regional art and travel. ~ 58 Perea Road, just off Corrales Road, Corrales; 505-897-4422, fax 505-890-5244. MODERATE TO DELUXE.

La Mimosa Bed & Breakfast is a private one-bedroom adobe guest house secluded in a shady courtyard. ~ 1144 Andrews Lane, Corrales; 505-898-1354. MODERATE.

DINING
HIDDEN ►

The elegant **Prairie Star** is 15 minutes north of the city off Route 25 in a sprawling, mission-style adobe house. Menu items include entrées such as marinated flank steak flambéed with bourbon as well as New Southwestern dishes like Pasta Sudoeste (red-chile fettuccine). Closed Monday in winter. ~ Jemez Dam Road, Bernalillo; 505-867-3327. MODERATE TO DELUXE.

RIO GRANDE NATURE CENTER STATE PARK 🏃 This urban wildlife refuge is one of several access points to the bosque and riverbank. The visitors center has exhibits on the river's ecology. Observation windows on one side of the building overlook a three-acre pond frequented by ducks, geese and herons, especially during migration seasons—November and April. The park is a favorite spot for birdwatching in all seasons. Two nature trails, each a mile-long loop, wind through the bosque, and one of them leads to several peaceful spots along the bank of the Rio Grande. Other facilities here are restrooms and a gift shop; day-use fee, $1. ~ The park is located at 2901 Candelaria Road Northwest, where Candelaria ends at the river a few blocks west of Rio Grande Boulevard; 505-344-7240.

PARKS

CORONADO STATE PARK 🏃 🛶 Below the visitors center for the pueblo ruins at Coronado State Monument are pretty camping and picnic areas set amid stands of cottonwood, tamarisk and cholla cactus along the bank of the Rio Grande. Sandia Peak provides a spectacular backdrop. There's a spot for fishing on the Rio Grande although it's not very rewarding. Facilities here include a picnic area, restrooms, showers, a museum, a playground and a short hiking trail; restaurants and groceries nearby in Bernalillo; day-use fee, $3. ~ Located 15 miles north of Albuquerque. Take the Bernalillo exit north from Route 25 and cross the bridge over the Rio Grande; 505-867-5589.

▲ There are 56 sites (38 with RV hookups); $7 per night for standard sites, $11.50 per night for hookups.

COCHITI LAKE 🚶 🏕 🎣 🚤 🛶 At the confluence of the Santa Fe and Rio Grande rivers lies Albuquerque's flood-control reservoir and also its local recreation beach. Windsurfing on the lake is popular, and some people paddle kayaks. Power boating is permitted but is restricted to no-wake speed. Fishing is good for largemouth and smallmouth bass, catfish and walleye. It's also a good place to swim. Facilities here include a picnic area and restrooms; groceries nearby in town of Cochiti Lake. ~ Located 36 miles north of Albuquerque on Route 25 and then 15 miles northwest on Route 22; 505-465-0307.

▲ There are two campgrounds overlooking the lake, operated by the Army Corps of Engineers. Cochiti has 55 sites (34 with RV hookups) and Tetilla Peak has 50 sites (34 with RV hookups); $6 per night for standard sites, $10 per night for hookups.

▼▼▼▼▼▼▼▼▼▼▼
Turquoise Trail

A number of historical sights make the Turquoise Trail a rewarding route from Albuquerque to Santa Fe—and it takes just 15 minutes more driving time than the interstate. To find the Turquoise Trail (Route 14), take Route 40 eastbound from Albuquerque to the Tijeras/Cedar Crest exit, a distance of about ten miles from the city center, and turn north.

SIGHTS

At Cedar Crest, a few miles from the interstate exit, a well-marked paved road, steep in places, forks off from the Turquoise Trail and leads up the eastern slope of the Sandias to **Sandia Peak** summit with its spectacular views of central New Mexico.

HIDDEN ►

About a mile from the Turquoise Trail on the Sandia Peak road is a small wonder for those traveling with children—the **Tinkertown Museum**, which exhibits a miniature Western community entirely hand-carved from wood with mechanical people and moving vehicles. The museum is easily recognized by its fence made of glass bottles. Open April through October. Admission. ~ Route 536; 505-281-5233.

Midway between Albuquerque and Santa Fe, the Turquoise Trail crosses the San Pedro Mountains, a small but rugged range that was the site of major gold-mining operations from the 1880s to the 1920s. Once the area's residential hub, **Golden** is now practically a ghost town. Beside the highway, the ruins of an old stone schoolhouse and other collapsing buildings can still be seen. There is also a beautifully restored mission church dating back to 1830.

Eleven miles away, on the other side of the pass, the town of **Madrid** (pronounced "MAD-rid") owes its existence to coal mining. The all-wood buildings, atypical of New Mexico architecture, give the community a look reminiscent of Appalachian coal towns. Abandoned after World War II, Madrid has since been partly repopulated by artists and historic-district entrepreneurs, but growth is limited due to a lack of water. Attractions in Madrid include a mining museum, a summertime melodrama and a baseball field where concerts are presented regularly.

You won't have trouble discovering Madrid's roots if you go to the **Old Coal Mine Museum**. This block-long memorial pays tribute to an industry that peaked here in 1928. Your self-guided tour includes a visit to a coal mine shaft, a wide array of mining machinery, vintage railroad equipment and antique trucks—look in the parts storage building for a Model T pickup truck. There's a working blacksmith on the premises in summer. Admission. ~ Route 14; 505-473-0743.

A third old mining town along the Turquoise Trail, **Cerrillos** still retains the appearance of an old Spanish village. While silver, gold, copper, zinc and lead have all been mined in the hills north of town—and Thomas Edison once built a $2 million laboratory here in an unsuccessful attempt to develop a method for refining gold without water—Cerrillos is best known for turquoise. American Indians mined turquoise here as early as 500 A.D. Later, the people of Chaco and other Anasazi pueblos traveled from hundreds of miles away to dig pit mines for the stone, which was their most precious trade commodity. Others, from Spanish colonists to modern-day prospectors, have likewise wandered the maze of the Cerrillos hills in search of turquoise.

> When Madrid was a thriving mining town, water was brought in by train; today the train no longer runs and residents buy bottled drinking water.

Featuring a collection of gems, cattle skulls and pottery, the **Turquoise Museum** is a good place to learn about the region's geologic history. The offbeat, sometimes whimsical collection of artifacts is highlighted by guides who are more than happy to fill you in on local lore. The turquoise collection ranges from prehistoric pieces to locally mined Cerrillos turquoise. Take your children next door to the **Petting Zoo**, where they can feed the llamas, burros and goats. Admission. ~ 17 Waldo Street, Cerrillos; 505-438-3008.

The Turquoise Trail intersects Route 25 at the western edge of Santa Fe, where it becomes Cerrillos Road, a busy main street.

LODGING

◀ HIDDEN

For those seeking a remote setting, still within easy commuting distance of Albuquerque's attractions, **Elaine's** is the ideal choice. This bed and breakfast, nestled among ponderosa pines, adjoins Cibola National Forest near Cedar Crest (where the auto road up Sandia Peak turns off from the Turquoise Trail). Outdoor enthusiasts have ample opportunities for hiking, biking, skiing and horseback riding. There's even a resident golden retriever to accompany guests on walks through the foliage. The three-story log house has three guest rooms, big balconies, a grand country fireplace and European antiques everywhere you look. ~ 72 Snowline Estates, Cedar Crest; 505-281-2467, 800-821-3092. MODERATE.

Once a hacienda, the 30-room **Casa Grande** rents guest rooms with kitchenettes. This white adobe is rustic at best: those who aren't accustomed to using an outhouse will have to make some adjustments. But the setting is exceptional, on the edge of a cliff overlooking an arroyo. Rooms come with kitchenettes and showers. ~ 17 Waldo Street, Cerrillos; 505-438-3008. BUDGET.

DINING

At the beginning of the Turquoise Trail is one of the largest restaurants in the Southwest, the **Bella Vista**. This establishment seats 1200 guests in ten separate dining rooms. A generous buffet is served in a split-level dining room as well as out on an adjacent veranda. Other dining rooms are decorated with wrought iron, hanging plants and red tablecloths. Specialties such as flounder with fresh mushrooms and lemon sauce, fettuccine with pesto sauce and *enchiladas rancheras* bring in the masses from Albuquerque half an hour away. ~ Route 14, Cedar Crest; 505-281-3914. BUDGET TO MODERATE.

The oak floor and tables, New Mexican murals and a beam ceiling add to the charm of the historic **Mine Shaft Tavern**, home of the state's longest stand-up bar, 40 feet total. Mingle with the locals at the lodge-pole pine slab or take a table and order a chef's salad, enchiladas or rib-eye steak. For dessert, try the Mine Shaft Sundae, a towering concoction that includes homebaked chocolate fudge brownies, tin roof ice cream and crème de menthe. ~ Route 14, Madrid; 505-473-0743. MODERATE.

Located in the historic company store building, **Madrid Old Fashioned Soda Fountain** is known for its sodas, shakes and root beer floats. A loyal clientele packs the black formica counter. ~ Route 14, Madrid; 505-473-3641. BUDGET.

SHOPPING   **Sin Nombre** is a good place to browse. From antiques and religious art to Mexican blown glass, this curio shop is filled with the exotic and the unusual. At Sin Nombre you'll find turquoise and silver jewelry, old *Life* magazines and postcards promoting the wonders of fallout shelters. ~ Route 14, Madrid; 505-473-0407.

Al Leedom Studio specializes in crystalline porcelain, wood-fired stoneware, horsehair pots, raku and blown and beveled glass. ~ Route 14, Madrid; 505-473-2054.

For Guatemalan clothing and crafts as well as new and used books, head to **Maya Jones**, a colorful shop with all sorts of inexpensive items. The handmade jackets and jewelry are particularly noteworthy. ~ Route 14, Madrid; 505-473-3641.

NIGHTLIFE   **Madrid Melodrama** offers two memorable plays at the Engine House Theater in the Old Coal Mine Museum next to the Mine Shaft Tavern. Alternating in the summer months are *Blazing Guns At Roaring Gulch* and *He Ain't Done Right By Nell*. ~ Route 14, Madrid; 505-473-0743.

A solo guitarist plays weekend afternoons at the **Mine Shaft Tavern**. There's live R&B on Friday evenings. ~ Route 14, Madrid; 505-473-0743.

▼▼▼▼▼▼▼▼▼▼▼
Santa Rosa Area

Drivers crossing eastern New Mexico on Route 40 may find the experience brain-numbing in its monotony—flat and featureless with an endless flow of speeding semi trucks. Those who venture a short detour from the main route, however, will discover a little bit of the special character of Santa Rosa, Fort Sumner and the other communities that dot the boundless prairie. This area is of particular interest to history buffs, for this is where the legend of Billy the Kid is rooted, and indeed, this is where the young outlaw is buried.

Located along the Pecos River, the town of **Santa Rosa** (population 3000) lies 110 miles east of Albuquerque at the junction of Routes 40 and 54. It was settled by Spanish farmers during the 1860s, but its historic roots extend back to 1541, when Spanish explorer Vasquez de Coronado built a bridge across the Pecos River at **Puerto de Luna,** ten miles south of present-day Santa Rosa—or so the story goes. In the 1880s, Puerto de Luna was the largest community in the southeastern quarter of New Mexico Territory; today it is virtually a ghost town. But even though the bridge no longer exists and the stone county courthouse is beginning to crumble (along with a rock-faced church and a saloon where Billy the Kid hung out from time to time), Puerto de Luna still makes for an interesting short excursion off the interstate.

Santa Rosa's main vacation attractions are lakes, to the point that it calls itself "The City of Natural Lakes." Those who find the claim improbable for a town in the arid high plains of New Mexico will be even more surprised to learn that Santa Rosa is a mecca for scuba divers. (See the "Parks" section below.)

New Mexico was a province of Mexico from 1821 until the 1848 treaty that ended the Mexican War with the United States.

If you want to Kid around, drive 46 miles south to **Fort Sumner,** where Billy the Kid happened to be hiding out when the law caught up with him for the last time. You might expect that "Billymania" would be more prevalent in the outlaw's hometown of Lincoln, 100 miles to the south, where most of his escapades took place. But the fact is, Fort Sumner is the Billy the Kid capital of the Southwest. It was here (or at least at a ranch on the outskirts of town) that he was shot to death in 1881.

Two privately owned museums pay tribute to Billy the Kid's life and legend. Each is interesting enough to occupy the curious for an hour or two and spur speculations about whether Billy was a frontier Robin Hood, a psychopathic killer or a product of media hype. There is some duplication between the two museums, since a number of the documents on exhibit are photocopies of originals in the state archives.

The **Billy the Kid Museum,** which showcases a large collection of ranch antiques and a jail cell in which Billy is said to have been locked up once, is located near the eastern edge of town on the way to Fort Sumner State Monument. Closed the first two weeks of January. Admission. ~ 1601 East Fort Sumner Avenue; 505-355-2380.

The **Old Fort Sumner Museum** displays letters written by Billy to the governor to negotiate a pardon, letters from Sheriff Pat Garrett to his wife describing his search for the outlaw, a history of impostors who have claimed to be the real Billy the Kid and a chronology of more than a dozen motion pictures about his brief,

Text continued on page 406.

Be a Road Warrior

Albuquerque residents know it as the "Big I"—the congested freeway interchange in the middle of the city where two famous routes of bygone eras meet.

Interstate Route 25 follows the path of the oldest highway still in use in the United States. Originally known as El Camino Real de Tierra Adentro ("the Royal Road to the Inner Land"), it was established in 1598 to link Mexico City with New Mexico, the northernmost province of the Spanish empire in America. El Camino Real spanned a distance of 1700 miles, crossing brutal expanses of desert and venturing through lands guarded by hostile Apache warriors. Spanish soldiers in armor traveled its length, as did hooded monks on foot. Horses, cows and *vaqueros* (cowboys) first came to the American West via the old Royal Road.

Interstate Route 40 traces Old Route 66, the first paved highway connecting the eastern United States and the West Coast. Route 66 was the kind of highway dreams are made of. It ran across vast, sun-baked, brightly colored desert inhabited by cowboys and Indians all the way to Hollywood, capturing America's imagination as it went. John Steinbeck wrote about it. Glenn Miller immortalized it in song. The television series *Route 66* was one of the most popular programs of the 1960s. Old Route 66 became practically synonymous with the mystique of the open road.

Before the two-lane, blacktop road was replaced by today's high-speed, limited-access highway, travelers had no alternative to driving down the main street of each small town along the route—places like Tucumcari, Santa Rosa, Laguna and Gallup. Today, chambers of commerce in these towns enthusiastically promote Route 66 nostalgia, and what used to be cheap roadside diners and tourist traps are now preserved as historic sites.

While both El Camino Real and Old Route 66 have been paved and straightened into modern interstate highways, travelers willing to take the extra time can still experience much of what it must have felt like to travel either of these roads in times past.

Alternate highways, usually traffic-free and often out of sight of the busy interstate, parallel Route 25 almost all the way from the Indian pueblos north of Albuquerque to El Paso and the Mexican border. These secondary highways trace El Camino Real more exactly than the interstate does, and the New Mexico state government has put up historical markers along them to identify important landmarks from Spanish colonial days such as the stark landscape of the Jornada del Muerto ("Journey of Death").

Good Camino Real alternatives to the interstate include Route 313 from Albuquerque north to San Felipe Pueblo; Routes 47 and 304 south of Albuquerque on the opposite side of the Rio Grande from the interstate, serving old rural communities such as Bosque Farms, Valencia and Belen; Route 1 from San Antonio through Bosque del Apache Wildlife Refuge to Elephant Butte Reservoir; Route 187 from Truth or Consequences to Las Cruces; and Route 28 from La Mesilla, just west of Las Cruces, to El Paso and the border.

Most of Old Route 66 has been obscured by interstate Route 40. Only a few sections of frontage roads and old secondary highways—notably Route 124 from Mesita through the villages of the Laguna Indian Reservation to Acoma—give any hint of the road that used to carry travelers across the desert. The place to look for remnants of Old Route 66 is along the main streets of towns that the interstate has bypassed. Deco-style diners, quaint ma-and-pa motels and old-fashioned curio shops with concrete Indian tepees out front and signs like "Last Chance Before the Desert!" and "See the Baby Rattlers!" can still be found on Route 40 business loops all across New Mexico, from Tucumcari to Albuquerque's Central Avenue to Gallup where the main street was recently renamed Historic 66.

Traveling any of these alternate routes takes twice as long as driving straight down the interstate. The rewards are several—avoiding busy truck routes, discovering the off-beat charm of small-town New Mexico and sampling what cross-country travel used to be like in the American Southwest.

violent career. Admission. ~ Billy the Kid Road, Fort Sumner; 505-355-2942.

Billy the Kid's Grave, in the Maxwell family cemetery behind the Old Fort Sumner Museum, is locked securely behind iron bars because the headstone has been stolen twice. ~ Billy the Kid Road, Fort Sumner.

Just down the road from Billy the Kid's grave, **Fort Sumner State Monument** marks the site of the army outpost for which the town was named. By the time Billy the Kid came to town, the fort had been converted to a ranch headquarters, and it was here that Sheriff Pat Garrett killed him. Just a few years earlier, the fort was the scene of larger and more infamous events. Colonel Kit Carson, after forcing the entire Navajo tribe to walk 400 miles from their homeland to this place, ordered them to build Fort Sumner as a concentration camp. More than 8500 Navajo lived in captivity here for six years, and 3000 of them died of starvation and disease. Finally the government concluded that keeping the Navajo at Fort Sumner was too expensive and that their homeland was without value to the white man. Then the surviving Navajo people were allowed to walk back home. No trace remains of the original fort, but you can see some of the subterranean ruins of the main fort buildings. The most moving part of the monument is a simple shrine of stones brought from all over the Navajo Indian Reservation and left here by American Indians in memory of those who lived and died here. Admission. ~ Billy the Kid Road; 505-355-2573.

From Fort Sumner, it's about an hour-and-a-half drive to the border town of Tucumcari. Drive 11 miles east on Route 60/84 to Taiban. From here, Route 252 climbs the corner of Llano Estacado, a high mesa that covers much of eastern New Mexico, and heads northeast until the town of Ragland. At Ragland, the road drops

LOOK WHAT'S COOKIN'

As every visitor discovers immediately, New Mexico boasts a distinctive culinary style. The two regional specialties that set it apart from Mexican food familiar in other regions are blue corn, grown by the Pueblo Indians and considered sacred in their traditions, and green chile. New Mexico produces virtually all the chile peppers grown in the United States, and while most chiles are exported to the rest of the country in the form of red chile powder, the local preference is to pick the chiles while green, then roast, peel and eat them as a vegetable—chopped as a stew, breaded and fried as *rellenos* or poured as a sauce over just about any entrée.

off from the Llano Estacado into the Canadian River Basin and merges with Route 209. The view of the bluffs as you descend the mesa is quite dramatic and unusual for this characteristically flat area. Take Route 209 north until you reach Tucumcari.

Tucumcari, created by the Rock Island Railroad at the turn of the century and named for a Comanche lookout, is actually best visited during the day when the **Tucumcari Historical Museum** throws open its doors. What you'll see at this Richardsonian Romanesque complex is a compilation of American Indian artifacts, gems, a still from prohibition days and other odd items donated by locals. Pioneer wagons and a pre-1900 windmill highlight the outdoor displays. Closed Monday from September to June. ~ 416 South Adams Street; 505-461-4201.

LODGING

Santa Rosa has more than a dozen budget-priced motels—most of them locally owned and operated. The exception is the **Best Western Adobe Inn,** which straddles between the budget and moderate price ranges for its spacious, modern rooms. ~ Will Rogers Drive at Route 40 Exit 275; 505-472-3446, fax 505-472-5759. BUDGET TO MODERATE.

A cruise down the main street, Will Rogers Drive, reveals that close to half the commercial buildings in Santa Rosa are motels. A good bet is the **Shawford Motel,** which has double-room units for families and operates one of the town's best restaurants next door. ~ 1819 Will Rogers Drive; 505-472-3494. BUDGET.

Billy the Kid fans might consider spending the night in Fort Sumner at one of the two motels, both budget-priced. **The Oasis Motel** is a standard roadside motel. ~ 1704 East Sumner Avenue; 505-355-7414, fax 505-355-7478. The **Coronado Motel** also has the basic amenities of motels everywhere. ~ 309 West Sumner Avenue; 505-355-2466. BUDGET.

Motels have been an important industry in Tucumcari since the 1940s, when the town was a natural stop along Old Route 66 because it was the only place for many miles. Today, billboards along Route 40 for hundreds of miles in each direction tout the fact that Tucumcari has 2000 beds for rent. A number of motels in town still offer the authentic flavor of roadside America half a century ago. Even their names—Buckaroo, Lasso, Palomino, Apache—evoke a notion of the West in an earlier era.

Lovely gardens, a big pool and generous patios make the **Best Western Pow Wow Inn** an ideal choice in the moderate price range. Sixty-two contemporary rooms and suites appointed with American Indian prints and kachina-style lamps offer king- and queen-size beds as well as large vanity areas. ~ 801 West Tucumcari Boulevard, Tucumcari; 505-461-0500, 800-527-6996, fax 505-461-0135. MODERATE.

DINING Settle into one of the red booths at the **Comet II**, one of the last original Route 66 restaurants in town. The Comet is a '50s classic, well-known for its Chimayo-style New Mexican specialties, particularly the blue-corn chicken and smothered *chile rellenos*. Gringos may want to stick with burgers and the like, but everyone can enjoy the homemade pies. ~ 217 Parker Avenue, Santa Rosa; 505-472-3663. BUDGET.

Santa Rosa also has a dozen other restaurants of more recent vintage, most of them either nationwide franchises or motel restaurants and all of them in the budget range. For Mexican food, we recommend **Mateo's Family Restaurant**. ~ Old Route 66, Santa Rosa; 505-472-5720. BUDGET.

The best salad bar in town, along with steaks and seafood, is found at **Joseph's Restaurant**. ~ 865 Will Rogers Drive, Santa Rosa; 505-472-3361. BUDGET.

One of the most attractive dining rooms on this side of the state, **Pow Wow** features a Navajo storm design motif. Hand-painted lamps and American Indian blankets add a handsome touch to this cheery restaurant. Choose from New Mexican specialties like *carne adovada* or stick with the more standard rib-eye steak and rainbow trout. ~ 801 West Tucumcari Boulevard, Tucumcari; 505-461-0500. MODERATE.

If you've maxed out on New Mexican fare, why not head over to the **Golden Dragon** for a bowl of wonton soup and a generous serving of Mongolian beef. This Asian restaurant overflows with shrines and Buddhas. Hamburgers and chicken-fried steak are also available, if you're with the finicky eaters. ~ 106 East Tucumcari Boulevard, Tucumcari; 505-461-2853. BUDGET.

SHOPPING We were so put off by the billboards advertising **Clines Corners** that we almost took a pass. Talk about a blight on the landscape! But like just about everyone else whistling along the interstate, we hit the brakes and drove on in to New Mexico's largest souvenir shop. The operating definition of kitsch, this tourist mecca warehouses thousands of moccasins, silkscreen lamps and baja jackets. It just might be the ultimate tourist trap. On the other hand, the prices aren't bad and there's plenty of selection. ~ 1 Yacht Club Drive, Clines Corners; 505-472-5488.

The last of the original Route 66 curio shops, **The Tee Pee**, a stucco tepee built in the '40s, offers a great photo opportunity for students of this region's recent past. Whether you're shopping for worrystones, twig baskets or authentic Navajo designs, this gift shop is a fun place to browse. If nothing else, buy a wooden postcard to send to your colleagues back at the office. ~ 924 East Tucumcari Boulevard, Tucumcari; 505-461-3773.

Joseph's Cantina has a deejay on Friday and Saturday nights who plays country-and-western and rock. On weeknights, sports fans gather around the big-screen television to cheer on their favorite teams. ~ 865 Will Rogers Drive, Santa Rosa; 505-472-3361.

You can hear live country tunes on weekends at the kachina-style **Pow Wow** lounge. ~ 801 West Tucumcari Boulevard, Tucumcari; 505-461-0500.

BLUE HOLE The amazingly clear water at this spot attracts dive-club caravans from Texas, Oklahoma and Colorado on most weekends. Formed by a collapsed cave and fed by a subterranean river, the lake is deeper (81 feet) than it is wide. Carp live in the dark reaches far below the surface. Swimming is popular, and on hot summer days teenagers can often be seen cannonballing into Blue Hole from the cliffs above even though the water temperature is a very chilly 61. Facilities are limited to restrooms and a dive shop. ~ It's located at the southeast edge of Santa Rosa on Blue Hole Road. Follow the signs from Will Rogers Drive (the business loop from Route 40); 505-472-3370.

JANES-WALLACE MEMORIAL PARK This park is really no more than a local fishing hole. But don't be put off. It's a great place to drop a line and is stocked with what may just be your dinner. Expect to catch bass, catfish and rainbow trout. There are no facilities. ~ Follow 3rd Street, which becomes Route 91, south from Will Rogers Drive.

SANTA ROSA LAKE STATE PARK A flood-control reservoir along the Pecos River, Santa Rosa Lake provides so much irrigation water to the surrounding farmlands that some years it can practically disappear in late summer. (Phone ahead to make sure the lake has water in it.) In wet years, the extensive shallows make for some of the best fishing in the state. Especially known for walleye pike, the lake is also stocked with catfish and bass. Most fishing here is done from boats. Waterskiing is also popular. A short "scenic trail" starts from the state park's Rocky Point Campground. There is no shade anywhere around the lake. The park has picnic tables, restrooms, showers, a playground and a visitors center; day-use fee, $3. ~ From Santa Rosa, take Exit 277 from Route 40. Turn left on 2nd Street; continue for two blocks. Turn right on Eddy Avenue and continue north for seven miles; 505-472-3110.

▲ Rocky Point has 50 sites (16 with RV hookups) and Juniper has 25; $7 per night for standard sites, $11 per night for hookups.

SUMNER LAKE STATE PARK On the Pecos River between Santa Rosa and Fort Sumner, this irrigation reservoir is one of New Mexico's most underused fishing lakes, with the added bonus of several quiet side canyons and a little village of summer cabins. The Y-shaped lake offers good spots for fishing from the shore in shallow, medium or deep water. Crappie, catfish, bluegill, northern pike and walleye are the common catches. State park areas below the dam provide access to both banks of the river. Swimming is permitted. There are picnic tables, restrooms and showers; day-use fee, $3. ~ Located six miles off Route 84. The marked turnoff is 35 miles south of Santa Rosa and ten miles north of Fort Sumner; 505-355-2541.

▲ There are 23 tent sites ($7 per night) and 18 RV hookups ($11 per night).

BOSQUE REDONDO This Fort Sumner city park consists of a series of small lakes on 15 acres. The grassy shore, shaded by cottonwood trees, is a nice picnic spot. It's also a good place to fish. Ducks live on the lakes year-round. The park has restrooms. ~ Located two miles south of Fort Sumner on a marked road from the east edge of town.

CONCHAS LAKE STATE PARK Conchas Lake, on the Canadian River north of Tucumcari, is one of the most popular recreation lakes in New Mexico. Most of the 50-mile shoreline is privately owned, so the only easy public access to the lake is the state park, which includes developed areas on both sides of the dam. It's a good spot to fish and swimming and scuba diving are also permitted. There are picnic tables, restrooms, showers, marinas and groceries; restaurants, lodging, golf course and air strip nearby; day-use fee, $3. ~ It's 25 miles north of Route 40 from the Newkirk/Route 129 exit, which is 27 miles east of Santa Rosa, or 31 miles northeast of Tucumcari on Route 104; 505-868-2270.

▲ There are 100 sites (33 are full RV hookups). Primitive camping available. Fees per night are $6 for primitive sites, $7 for standard sites and $11 for hookups.

GORDON WILDLIFE AREA Tucumcari has a municipal wildlife refuge on the edge of town where a number of lucky birdwatchers have actually seen eagles. The 770 acres of wetlands provide a rest stop for migrating ducks and geese. There are hiking trails as well as an auto road. ~ Located just east of town, marked by a sign on Tucumcari Boulevard (Route 40 Business Loop); 505-461-1694.

UTE LAKE STATE PARK This reservoir was created in 1963 specifically for recreational purposes to bring tourism to the Tucumcari area. Records have been set here for the largest smallmouth bass ever caught in New Mexico. The park has picnic tables, restrooms, showers, a marina with boat rentals and hiking trails; restaurants, lodging and groceries in the lakeshore community nearby; day-use fee, $3. ~ It's 25 miles northeast of

Tucumcari on Route 54, or three miles west of Logan via Route 540; 505-487-2284.

▲ There are 200 standard sites (75 with electric and water hookups) and three primitive camping areas. Fees per night are $6 for primitive sites, $7 for standard sites and $11 for hookups.

▼▼▼▼▼▼▼▼▼▼▼▼
Mountainair Area

For centuries, the Mountainair area was one of New Mexico's most populous regions. Three large Anasazi pueblos, dating back to the 1200s, flourished here. Salt from nearby dry lakebeds was gathered and traded to other pueblos and to the Plains Indians as well. The communities still flourished in 1598, when the first Spanish soldiers and priests arrived and began building their missions. The Spanish colonial presence lasted less than 80 years before famine, drought, disease and Apache raids forced priests and Indians alike to abandon all the pueblos in the area, moving to Isleta and other Rio Grande pueblos. Today, the Mountainair Area is sparsely populated but serves as the backdrop for exploring the ruins of these ancient peoples.

SIGHTS

East of Route 25, 39 miles from Belen via Routes 47 and 60, the quiet little town of **Mountainair** used to call itself the "Pinto Bean Capital of the World." Today it serves the local ranching community and provides travelers a base for exploring the widely separated units of **Salinas Pueblo Missions National Monument**. The national monument preserves the ruins of three large Anasazi pueblos that date back to the 1200s. Massive, crumbling walls of Franciscan churches adjoin each pueblo site. ~ Corner of Broadway and Ripley Street; 505-847-2585.

The Abo unit of the national monument is just off Route 60, nine miles west of Mountainair. Unexcavated pueblo ruins and the remains of the Mission of San Gregorio de Abo fill the small park area sandwiched between private farms. A traditional Anasazi ceremonial kiva built within the church *convento* at Abo puzzles archaeologists, since elsewhere in the Salinas pueblos priests destroyed kivas to halt native religious practices.

The red-walled Franciscan mission at **Quarai**, eight miles north of Mountainair on Route 55 was in operation from 1630 to the late 1670s. Today, in its tranquil setting alongside big cottonwoods at the foot of the Manzano Mountains, Quarai is perhaps the most photogenic of the three Salinas mission ruins. The adjoining pueblo remains are thoroughly buried and difficult to see. A small museum displays relics found at the site.

Gran Quivira presents the national monument's most extensively excavated Anasazi ruins. One of the largest pueblos in New Mexico, the limestone complex was home to about 2000 people at its height. Facilities include a visitors center with interpretive displays and a picnic area. There is no camping at any of the Salinas

◄ *HIDDEN*

Pueblo Missions National Monument sites. ~ Located 25 miles south of Mountainair via Route 55; 505-847-2585.

Mountainair's **Shaffer Hotel** stands as a monument to the whimsical imagination of Clem "Pop" Shaffer, the town blacksmith in the 1920s and 1930s. Inside and out, the hotel's unique handcrafted ornamentation continues to impress visitors. Indian symbols are everywhere, and colored stones have been set into concrete walls to form animal shapes. The Shaffer Hotel now operates as a bed and breakfast, restaurant, art gallery and gift shop. ~ 505-847-2888.

HIDDEN ▶

Those who would like to see more of "Pop" Shaffer's work can do so at **Rancho Bonito**, south of Mountainair on the road to Gran Quivira. The ranch is owned by Shaffer's heirs, who are working to restore it gradually. Walking tours are available in summer provided the "open" sign hangs on the front gate. In the original ranch cabin are examples of the fanciful animals Shaffer carved from tree roots. The state of New Mexico used to make an official gift of one of his wooden animals to each newly elected U.S. president. Both the Shaffer Hotel and Rancho Bonito are on the National Register of Historic Places. ~ 505-847-2832.

LODGING

The place to stay in Mountainair is the **Shaffer Hotel**. Originally built as a hardware store in 1923, it was converted into a hotel soon afterward by renowned local folk artist "Pop" Shaffer for his wife. Shaffer spent the next ten years ornamenting the hotel with his unique, self-taught designs in paint, wood and stone. It closed in 1943 due to lack of help and remained closed until 1982, when restoration of the hotel began. The Shaffer offers simple, pleasant guest rooms reminiscent of an Old West hotel. The room rates include a complimentary breakfast. As for the address, you can't miss the place—it's the biggest building in town. ~ 505-847-2888. BUDGET.

DINING

The **Shaffer Dining Room** in Mountainair's Shaffer Hotel serves sandwiches and tasty full meals at low prices. The unique decor alone makes it worth planning a meal stop here. "Pop" Shaffer painted the ceiling panels with bright Indian designs, each one different. The furniture is also handpainted, and old newspaper and magazine articles pertaining to the hotel hang framed on the walls. ~ 505-847-9911. BUDGET.

PARKS

MANZANO MOUNTAIN STATE PARK 🏃 This small state park provides the most convenient camping for visitors to the Salinas Pueblo Missions National Monument. Located in the foothills near the village of Manzano and the Quarai Unit of the monument. The forest road that continues past the state park turnoff leads to the

Red Canyon trailhead at the Manzano Mountain Wilderness boundary. There are picnic tables, restrooms, playgrounds and nature trails; day-use fee, $3. ~ Located 13 miles northwest of Mountainair off Route 55, follow the highway signs; 505-847-2820.

▲ There are 20 sites (five with RV hookups); $7 per night for standard sites, $11 per night for hookups.

Socorro Area

Seventy-five miles south of Albuquerque just off Route 25 is Socorro, a town so small that the strip of motels and gas stations along the interstate business loop overshadow its distinctive character. But take the time to look around; it will be worth it. This sleepy municipality of 8000 souls is actually one of the oldest towns in the state, dating back to 1615 when Franciscan priests began building a mission. A couple of detours off the interstate will pique the interest of birders and history buffs.

SIGHTS

Socorro's plaza is surrounded by a small, attractive historic district a short distance west of California Street on Manzaneras Avenue. Noteworthy are the restored **San Miguel Mission** (505-835-1620) at 403 El Camino Real, built in 1820 on the site of the church that was destroyed during the Pueblo Revolt of 1680, the old **Valverde Hotel** at 203 Manzaneras Avenue East, built in 1919 and now used as apartments, and the **Garcia Opera House**, one of two opera houses in town during the 1880s. The **Hilton Block**, near the opera house, is named for a relative of hotel tycoon Conrad Hilton, who operated a drugstore there in the 1930s. Hilton was born and raised in San Antonio, a town about nine miles south of Socorro that is so tiny it has no hotel or motel.

Northwest of Socorro's downtown area is the **New Mexico Mineral Museum** at the New Mexico School of Mines. The museum's possessions have been combined with specimens donated by prominent mining speculator C. T. Brown to form one of the largest rock collections on earth. The more than 10,000 pieces include gems and mining artifacts. ~ 801 Leroy Place; 505-835-5154.

An 18-mile drive south of Socorro, **Bosque del Apache National Wildlife Refuge** is especially worth visiting between November and March when it presents one of the most spectacular birdwatching opportunities around. The refuge was established during the 1930s to protect the sandhill crane, which had nearly vanished along the Rio Grande. Local farmers grow corn on refuge land during the summer months and leave one-third of the crop for the birds. Today more than 12,000 cranes spend the winter at the refuge. Besides the four-foot-tall sandhill cranes and a couple of rare whooping cranes that were introduced into the flock in an unsuccessful breeding experiment, the refuge provides a winter home for about 40,000 snow geese. The white geese often rise en masse from the manmade wetlands to fill the sky in a noisy, dazzling display. Admission. ~ Off of Route 25; 505-835-1828.

HIDDEN ►

Of several ghost towns in the Socorro area, perhaps the most interesting is old **San Pedro**, across the river from San Antonio where visitors exit the interstate to go to Bosque del Apache. An abandoned mission church and ruins of several adobe houses in Mexican and early Territorial styles are about all that remain of San Pedro, a town where people once grew grapes and produced champagne. Tamarisks have grown up through the floors of the houses to conceal much of the village. ~ To get to San Pedro, drive east from San Antonio for 1.4 miles on Route 380 and turn south on an unpaved road.

Contrary to many visitors' misconceptions, green chile is *not* milder than red chile.

Forty-six miles west of Socorro is the unusually named **National Radio Astronomy Observatory Very Large Array**. These 27 giant parabolic dish antennas, each weighing 235 tons, are used to search deep space for faint radio waves emitted by celestial objects. Together, the antennas can "see" as well as a telescope with a lens 20 miles in diameter. The Very Large Array is also used in combination with other radio observatories around the world to explore the far limits of the universe. A visitors center at the site explains how it works, and a one-hour, self-guided walking tour lets visitors see the antennas up close. ~ Route 60; 505-772-4011.

LODGING

Every motel in Socorro falls within the budget range. Accommodations are found in two clusters along California Street, the business loop from Route 25. The best in town is the **Best Western Golden Manor Motel**, about a block from San Miguel Mission. ~ 507 North California Street, Socorro; 505-835-0230, fax 505-835-1993. BUDGET.

Representative of the good, clean independent motels in Socorro is the **Motel Vagabond**. ~ 1011 North California Street, Socorro; 505-835-0276.

DINING

Don Juan's Mexican Food serves the standard New Mexican fare. ~ 118 East Manzaneras Avenue, Socorro; 505-835-9967. BUDGET.

The **Valverde Steak House** serves steaks, seafood, enchiladas and other Southwestern dishes—all with a salad bar. It is housed in an old hotel listed on the National Register of Historic Places. ~ 203 East Manzaneras Avenue, Socorro; 505-835-3380. MODERATE.

Located in the center of the small town of San Antonio nine miles south of Socorro, the **Owl Bar & Café** offers everything from inexpensive sandwiches to moderately priced seafood dinners. Their claim to serve the best green-chile cheeseburgers in the world may well be accurate. ~ Route 380, Main Street, San Antonio; 505-835-9946. MODERATE.

Although there aren't many options for skiing in the area, the easy access and reliable snowpack offered by the primary resort makes up for the lack of choices. You'll find both cross-country and downhill skiing right next to Albuquerque in the Sandia Mountains, and equipment rentals are readily available in town.

▼▼▼▼▼▼▼▼▼▼▼▼▼
Outdoor Adventures

SKIING

ALBUQUERQUE   An average annual snowfall of 183 inches makes Sandia Peak one of the most popular ski slopes in New Mexico. **Sandia Peak Ski Area** can be reached either by car or by the Sandia Peak Aerial Tramway. Sandia Peak also offers great cross-country skiing, especially on the Crest and 10-K trails, which begin near the Sandia Crest House at the top of the auto road. ~ 505-242-9133.
Ski Rentals   In Albuquerque, nordic skis are available for rent at **The Bike Coop Ltd.** Closed Sunday. ~ 3407 Central Avenue Northeast; 505-265-5170. Downhill skis are rented by several sporting-goods stores, including the **Ski Service Center.** ~ Hoffmantown Square, 2225-A Wyoming Boulevard Northeast; 505-292-4401.

New Mexico may not conjure up thoughts of windsurfing, but sailboards do shred the water at many of the state's lakes. Grab your board—or rent one—and hoist your sail The sport is most popular at **Cochiti Lake.** Windsurfing is also permitted on **Santa Rosa Lake, Conchas Lake** and **Ute Lake** in the eastern part of the state. Sailboards can be rented in Albuquerque at **Action Sports.** ~ 7509 Menaul Boulevard Northeast; 505-884-5611.

WIND-SURFING

Home of the annual balloon festival, Albuquerque has practically become synonymous with ballooning—at least, the sport is one of the city's major tourist attractions. If you rise early enough on a clear day (and most of them are), you'll see the multicolored creatures making their graceful ascent. Those who want to see what it's like to float above the city on the breeze can do so by contacting a local company like **Cameron's Balloons.** Closed Saturday and Sunday. ~ 2950 San Joaquin Avenue Southeast 505-265-4007. The **World Balloon Corporation** also takes to the air over Albuquerque. Closed Saturday and Sunday. ~ 4800 Eubank Boulevard Northeast; 505-293-6800, 800-351-9588.

BALLOON RIDES

Central New Mexico is a great place to spend a day on the greens— whether you stay in Albuquerque or head to the outlying areas, you'll find a nice spot to swing your clubs. For information on golf courses statewide, contact the **Sun Country Golf Association.** ~ 10035 Country Club Lane Northwest, Suite 5, Albuquerque, NM 87114; 505-897-0864.
ALBUQUERQUE   Tee off in Albuquerque at the **University of New Mexico South Course.** ~ 3601 University Boulevard Southeast;

GOLF

505-277-4546. The **Arroyo del Oso Golf Course** is also popular. ~ 7001 Osuna Road Northeast; 505-884-7505.

OUTSIDE OF ALBUQUERQUE Many Albuquerque golfers travel 40 miles north to play in a lovely setting below the rugged volcanic canyons of the Jemez Mountains at the Indian-owned **Cochiti Lake Golf Course.** ~ 505-465-2239.

SANTA ROSA AREA Work on your line drives at the **Santa Rosa Golf Club.** ~ 505-472-3949. The **Tucumcari Municipal Golf Course** also is open for public golfing. ~ 505-461-1849. You can also play the greens at **Conchas Lake Golf Course.** ~ 505-868-2988.

SOCORRO AREA In Socorro, tee off at the **New Mexico Tech Golf Course.** ~ 1 Canyon Road; 505-835-5335.

TENNIS

Tennis courts are very rare outside of Albuquerque in central New Mexico. If you want to keep up your backstroke while on vacation, sign up for a court in Albuquerque at **Arroyo del Oso Park.** ~ Wyoming Boulevard and Spain Street Northeast. You can also serve and volley at **Los Altos Park.** ~ 10300 Lomas Boulevard Northeast. **Jerry Cline Park** has public courts in Albuquerque. ~ Constitution Boulevard at Louisiana Boulevard Northeast; 505-256-2032. You can also play a match at the **Albuquerque Tennis Complex.** ~ 1903 Stadium Boulevard Southeast; 505-848-1381.

RIDING STABLES

Whether you rent a horse or go on a guided tour, the mountains, rivers and canyons around Albuquerque are ideal for riding.

ALBUQUERQUE Albuquerque has two popular areas for horseback riding—the Rio Grande bosque and the foothills of Sandia Peak. Near the river, **Sandia Trails** rents horses and offers guided tours. ~ 10600 4th Street Northwest; 505-898-6970. Individual rentals and group tours are also available at **Turkey Track Stables,** east of the city near Route 40. ~ Sedillo; 505-281-1772.

BIKING

Central New Mexico is a popular place to pedal, with both on-road and off-road riders. Hit the trails to explore petroglyphs on an extinct volcano, or simply use your wheels to explore the urban outback of Albuquerque.

ALBUQUERQUE A well-developed system of bike trails runs throughout Albuquerque. **Paseo del Bosque** is a paved bike and horse trail running for five miles along the Rio Grande from the Old Town area to the northern edge of town, passing through the Rio Grande Nature Center. **Paseo del Noreste,** a six-mile trail, allows residents of the fashionable Northeast Heights area to commute downtown by bicycle. **Paseo de las Montañas,** a 4.2-mile biking and jogging trail between Tramway Boulevard Northeast and the Winrock Shopping Center on the northeast side of the city, offers grand views of Albuquerque. For complete information about these and other bike trails and bike routes, contact the **Outdoor Recreation Division of Cultural and Recreation Services.** ~ 505-768-3550.

A favorite mountain-biking area is the series of five extinct volcanoes that make up a city-owned open space on **West Mesa**, the western skyline of the city. Dirt roads ramble all around the volcanoes and lead to petroglyphs at the edge of the West Mesa Escarpment.

SOCORRO AREA   Outside Albuquerque, popular cycling trips include the level, unpaved 15-mile tour loop at **Bosque del Apache National Wildlife Refuge** near Socorro. ~ 505-835-1828.

MOUNTAINAIR AREA   The roads in the vicinity of **Fourth of July Campground** in the Manzano Mountains are popular with mountain bikers.

Bike Rentals   **Rio Mountain Sports** rents various sizes of mountain bikes (as well as rollerblades) and does repairs, too. ~ 1210 Rio Grande Boulevard Northwest, Albuquerque; 505-766-9970. For information on bike routes, call or pass by **Two Wheel Drive**, a good shop although they don't rent bikes. ~ 1706 Central Avenue Southeast, Albuquerque; 505-243-8443.

HIKING

The trails of Central New Mexico, with their varied elevations, let you explore a variety of terrain—and your hike can be as convenient to Albuquerque or as remote as you wish. Hike in a lush north-facing valley or on a barren western slope, in a forest of Douglas fir, maple or quaking aspen—or in no forest at all. Climb 10,000-foot peaks or do a bit of spelunking underground, the choice is yours. Just be prepared for changeable weather . . . and breathtaking views.

ALBUQUERQUE   **Sandia Peak**, the 10,378-foot mountain that fills Albuquerque's eastern skyline, offers hiking trails for every preference, from gentle strolls to ambitious ascents.

The easiest way to hike Sandia is to either drive or take the aerial tramway to the crest of the mountain and walk the well-worn trail between the restaurant at the top of the tramway and the gift shop at the end of the auto road, a distance of about a mile with continuous views of the city below. The **Crest Trail** continues along the top ridge through the Sandia Wilderness Area all the way down to Canyon Estates, 25 miles to the south near Route 40, and Placitas, a similar distance to the north near Route 25.

Temperatures on the crest of Sandia Peak run about 20° cooler than on Albuquerque's downtown streets.

The **10-K Trail** (6 miles) starts at a trailhead two miles down the road from the crest and reaches the top ridge at the broadcast towers north of the gift shop. The hike to the summit leads through shady forests of Douglas fir, aspen and spruce with a 1000-foot elevation gain. A continuation of the trail follows the road back down to the trailhead to close the loop.

A trailhead midway up the Sandia Peak road marks the **Tree Spring Trail** (2 miles), which climbs to the top ridge, joining the Crest Trail a mile and a half south of the tram station. It is a 1400-foot climb from the trailhead to the crest.

One of the most challenging trails on Sandia Peak is **La Luz Trail**, which takes expert hikers up the seemingly sheer west face of the mountain from Juan Tabo Picnic Ground to the tram station on the crest. It's a 7.5-mile climb from 7060 feet elevation at the foot of the mountain to 10,378 at the summit. You can ride the tram to the top and hike back down the trail. The **Pino Canyon Trail** is newer—and even more difficult some hikers say. It's about nine miles in length and rises 4000 feet from Elena Gallegos Campground to the summit. The hike is quite scenic and shadier than La Luz Trail.

On the north side of Sandia Peak, lush **Las Huertas Canyon** is accessible by the road that leads from Route 25 through the village of Placitas or by a steep, narrow road that descends from the Sandia Crest auto road. Near the upper end of the canyon, an easy .75-mile trail takes hikers along the canyon wall to **Sandia Man Cave**, where University of New Mexico archaeologists found artifacts left by Indians during the last Ice Age. A flashlight is needed to reach the inner recesses of the cave—plan on getting dirty. For more information on these and on trails in the Sandia area, call 505-281-3304.

MOUNTAINAIR AREA   A profusion of bigtooth maple trees makes Fourth of July Campground near Tajique, located about 30 miles south of the Tijeras exit from Route 40, a favorite for fall hiking.

✔ CHECK THESE OUT—UNIQUE OUTDOOR ADVENTURES

- Float high above the city for a bird's-eye view in a kaleidoscopic **hot air balloon**. *page 415*
- Ride your mountain bike on **West Mesa**, and meander around five extinct volcanoes. *page 417*
- Follow the creek strewn with small waterfalls along the **Red Canyon Trail** in the Manzano Mountain Wilderness. *page 419*
- Scuba dive at **Blue Hole**, where a collapsed cave and subterranean river create an unusual spot for underwater viewing. *page 409*

Two trails leave from the campground. The **Fourth of July Trail** (5 miles) makes a loop to the south, along the edge of the Manzano Mountain Wilderness, affording great views of the Rio Grande and Estancia valleys. The **Albuquerque Trail** runs north to the Isleta Indian Reservation boundary and turns back south to make a six-mile loop.

The southern Manzano Mountains offer excellent hiking opportunities. Two of the best trails here start from the unpaved road past Manzano Mountain State Park near the town of Manzano, just north of the Quarai unit of Salinas Pueblo Missions National Monument.

The **Red Canyon Trail** follows a creek with small waterfalls into the Manzano Mountain Wilderness for three miles to within scrambling distance of the summit of Gallo Peak, elevation 10,003 feet. It is a strenuous climb with a 2000-foot altitude gain.

The **Kaiser Mill Trail** climbs 2000 feet in two miles to intersect the **Manzano Crest Trail**, which runs along the top ridge of the Manzanos. To reach the summit of Manzano Peak, elevation 10,098 feet, follow the Crest Trail for about a mile south of the intersection. Those who plan to hike only the lower portion of one of these trails should choose the Red Canyon Trail, since the first part of the Kaiser Mill Trail, outside the wilderness boundary, has been heavily logged. For more information, call 505-847-2990.

SOCORRO AREA   From the upper ridges of the Magdalena Mountains, you can see Sandia Peak in the distance. Notice the difference. While hiking any of the Sandia trails on a summer day can be a very social experience, few people visit the Magdalenas. **North Baldy Trail** (6 miles), the best hiking access, is a challenge to reach. Beyond Water Canyon Campground, which is off Route 60 about 16 miles west of Socorro, eight miles of unpaved, narrow, often rocky road lead to the trailhead. The trail starts near the summit where the state operates a laboratory to study thunderstorms. After a short, steep climb, the main trail runs along a ridgeline of high mountain meadows to the North Baldy summit (elevation 9858 feet).

▼▼▼▼▼▼▼▼▼▼
Transportation

CAR

Two major interstate highways, **Route 25** and **Route 40**, cross near the center of Albuquerque, an intersection known locally as the "Big I." Santa Rosa is on Route 40, two hours east of Albuquerque, and Tucumcari is another hour east of Santa Rosa.

The most direct way to reach Mountainair from Albuquerque is by exiting Route 25 at Belen and taking **Route 47**, which merges into **Route 60** and runs through Mountainair. Route 60 parallels Route 40 across eastern New Mexico and runs through Fort Sumner.

A straight and very empty two-lane highway through pronghorn antelope country, **Route 41** is the most direct route between Santa Fe and the Mountainair area. Driving south of Albuquerque on Route 25 will bring you to Socorro.

AIR

Albuquerque International Airport is the only major commercial passenger terminal in the state. Carriers include America West, American Airlines, Continental Airlines, Delta Airlines, Frontier, Mesa Airlines, Northwest Airlines, Southwest Airlines, TWA, United Airlines and USAir.

Taxis and hotel courtesy vans wait for passengers in front of the airport terminal. The **Shuttlejack** provides hourly bus transportation to and from Albuquerque and Santa Fe. ~ 505-243-3244. **Sun Tran**, Albuquerque's public bus system, also serves the airport. ~ 505-843-9200.

BUS

Greyhound Bus Lines provides service to Albuquerque, Tucumcari, Fort Sumner and Socorro. ~ Reservations: 800-231-2222. Albuquerque Bus Transportation Center: 300 2nd Street Southwest; 505-243-4435. Tucumcari: 2618 South 1st Street; 505-461-1350. Fort Sumner: 1018 Sumner Avenue; 505-374-9300. Socorro: 202 South California Street; 505-835-1930.

TNM&O Coaches, a regional carrier, also serves Albuquerque. ~ 505-243-4435.

TRAIN

Amtrak's "Southwest Chief," which chugs between Chicago and Los Angeles, stops daily at the Albuquerque passenger station. ~ Reservations: 800-872-7245. Albuquerque: 214 1st Street Southwest; 505-842-9650.

CAR RENTALS

Agencies at Albuquerque International Airport include **Advantage Rent A Car** (800-777-5500), **Avis Rent A Car** (800-331-1212), **Budget Rent A Car** (800-527-0700), **Dollar Rent A Car** (800-800-4000), **Hertz Rent A Car** (800-654-3131) and **National Interrent** (800-328-4562). Located just outside the airport, **Alamo Rent A Car** (800-327-9633) offers free shuttle service to and from the terminal.

Any of the more than 60 agencies listed in the Albuquerque yellow pages can arrange car pickups and drop-offs at the airport or a hotel.

PUBLIC TRANSIT

Sun Tran, Albuquerque's metropolitan bus system, has routes covering most parts of the city, including the airport, the bus depot, Old Town, the University of New Mexico and all major shopping malls. ~ 601 Yale Boulevard Southeast; 505-843-9200.

Taxi services in Albuquerque include **Albuquerque Cab Co./Duke City Cab Co.** (505-883-4888), **Checker Cab Co.** (505-243-7777) and **Yellow Cab Co.** (505-247-8888).

TAXIS

Greyline of Albuquerque offers daily tours to Acoma Pueblo, Santa Fe and Sandia Peak Tramway as well as city tours of Albuquerque; package and charter services are available. ~ 505-242-3880.

TOURS

THIRTEEN

Southern New Mexico

Southern New Mexico has little in common with the northern part of the state. In pre-Columbian times, when the Anasazi Indians were building cities in the Four Corners area, Mimbres people occupied the southern region, living in small cliff-dwelling communities. Their pottery has long been famed for the imaginative artistry of its animal motifs, but scientists are only now realizing what a sophisticated knowledge of astronomy the Mimbres possessed. They vanished without explanation centuries before nomadic Apaches moved into the region and the first European settlers arrived in New Mexico.

The Spanish colonists who settled Santa Fe avoided the south, where the land was parched and arid, and Apache Indians terrorized any outsider who set foot in their territory. Most of the development in southern New Mexico has come in the 20th century, from air force bases to ski resorts and huge boating reservoirs. Today descendants of the Apaches operate exclusive recreation facilities at the edge of the Mescalero Apache Indian Reservation near Ruidoso.

With the exception of Carlsbad Caverns National Park, southern New Mexico is less visited by vacationers than other parts of the state. That's surprising, and somewhat disappointing, for this region boasts enough outdoor sports and roadside sightseeing to fill a two-week vacation easily. Cool islands of high mountain forest offer relief from the scorching summers of the Chihuahuan Desert. On top of this, they're great for winter skiing. The lowlands enjoy a much longer warm season for spring and fall outdoor activities than Albuquerque, Santa Fe or Taos, making the entire region an attractive year-round destination.

Southern New Mexico is divided into several geographic regions. The area east of the mountains is, for all practical purposes, indistinguishable from west Texas. Carlsbad Caverns is closer to the Texas state line than to any New Mexico town. Ruidoso, the horse racing and skiing town in the mountains west of Roswell, caters almost exclusively to visitors from Texas. South of Ruidoso, memories of the Wild West live on in Lincoln, once among the most lawless towns on the frontier, now a low-key historic district.

South central New Mexico encompasses several barren mountain ranges and the vast, unpopulated desert area known as the Jornado del Muerto ("Journey of Death"), so desolate that the United States government chose it as the place to test the first atomic bomb. Today the population of this region lives along two main north-south routes separated from each other by the huge White Sands Missile Range, which is off-limits to all nonmilitary persons.

Driving on Route 25 or the older highway that parallels it, motorists find an empty landscape flanking a series of large recreational lakes. Taking Route 52 through the Tularosa Basin, the sights are more unusual—a giant lava field, many ancient Indian petroglyphs, and miles of pure white sand dunes. In the mountains just west of Alamogordo, charming little Cloudcroft is a bustling ski town in the winter and a cool, quiet haven the rest of the year.

The southwestern part of the state is filled with national forest. Driving to the boundary of the roadless Gila Wilderness, the largest wilderness area in the lower 48 states, you won't find any gas stations or grocery stores along the route, but you will discover many scenic lookouts, mountain lakes and hiking trails. Travel within the Gila Wilderness is restricted to horseback riders and hikers. A driving trip from Gila Cliff Dwellings National Monument in the canyonlands at the heart of the wilderness to the Catwalk on the western perimeter and then north through the ghost town of Mogollon to Snow Lake on the high mountain slopes can take several scenic, pleasurable and adventurous days.

▼▼▼▼▼▼▼▼▼▼▼▼▼▼▼▼▼▼▼
Southeastern New Mexico

Best known for Carlsbad Caverns and the legacy of Billy the Kid, southeastern New Mexico is a land filled with new discoveries for the traveler. Lincoln National Forest's White Mountain Wilderness; Sierra Blanca, New Mexico's highest peak; Bitter Lake National Wildlife refuge and a living memorial to that firefighting icon Smokey the Bear are some of southeastern New Mexico's primary attractions. Technicolor sunsets, secluded mountain lakes, and great skiing and mountain biking are just the extra attractions.

SIGHTS   **Carlsbad Caverns National Park** takes you 750 feet underground inside a limestone reef in the foothills of the Guadalupe Mountains, where ancient standing groundwater dissolved and hollowed out a spectacular honeycomb of caves. Eons of dripping dampness decorated the cave with an amazing display of natural mineral spires, curtains, crystals and lace. Bottomless pits, fairy temples and alien landscapes challenge your imagination. There are more than 80 known limestone caves in the park, ten of which are open

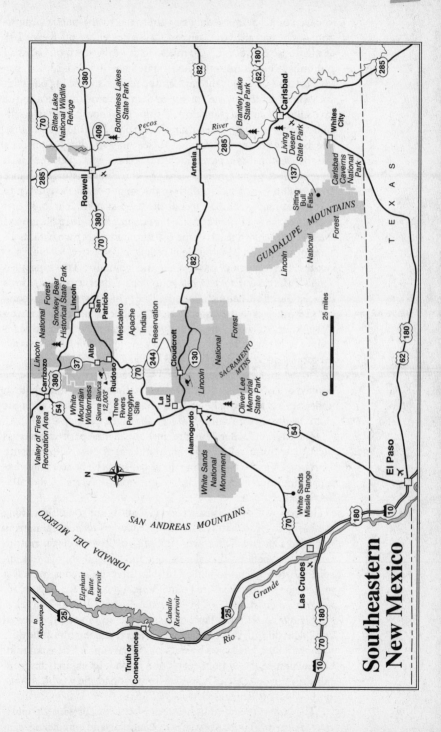

Southeastern
New Mexico

to cavers with permits; only two are open to the public. Admission. ~ The entrance to Carlsbad Caverns is either off Route 285 or off Route 62-180. It is 20 miles south of the town of Carlsbad and only 17 miles from the Texas state line; 505-785-2232.

Carlsbad Cavern is the cave most people visit, the big one with the visitors center on the surface and an elevator that runs to the cave's Big Room 750 feet below. Visitors can choose from two self-guided tours or a ranger-led tour. On the easy Big Room Tour, they ride both ways on the elevator to see only the Big Room on a mostly level one-mile paved loop trail. Those who pick the much more strenuous—and more rewarding—three-mile Natural Entrance Tour walk a switchback trail from the mouth of the cave down to a depth of more than 830 feet at the deepest point, climb 80 feet back up to the Big Room and ride the elevator back up to the ground level. However you reach it, the Big Room inspires awe with its 14 acres of floor area, 200-foot-high ceiling and massive, looming stalactites and towering stalagmites and columns. The ranger-led King's Palace Tour takes visitors to four different rooms: King's Palace, Queen's Chamber, Papoose Room and Green Lake Room.

HIDDEN ►   The other cave that is open to the public is **Slaughter Canyon Cave,** in an isolated part of the park backcountry reached via a county road that is gravel part of the way. Though it has been open for tours since its discovery in 1937, Slaughter Canyon Cave is undeveloped and can only be toured with a ranger. Tours must be booked a day in advance at the main visitors center, and children under age six are not allowed. The hardest part of the tour is the climb to the cave entrance 500 feet above the parking lot.

The **Million Dollar Museum,** just outside the park entrance, is the largest historical museum in southeastern New Mexico, with 12 rooms of exhibits including dolls, guns, music boxes, ranch antiques and mummified Indians. Admission. ~ White's City; 505-785-2291.

In the town of **Carlsbad,** a marked auto tour route runs along the Pecos River, which is partially dammed to form long, narrow Carlsbad Lake through town. At **Carlsbad River Village** you can rent paddleboats on the lake or visit the mineral springs that inspired early residents to name Carlsbad after the famous spa resort in Germany. Closed Saturday and Sunday (except for large party advance reservations). ~ 711 Muscatel Avenue; 505-887-0512.

Living Desert State Park offers a close-up look at the animal and plant life of the Chihuahuan Desert. Inhabitants include a mountain lion, a bear, wolves, bison and javelinas. There is a mineral exhibit in the visitors center and an indoor exhibit that contains giant tropical cactus species from around the world. Admission. ~ Just off Route 285; 505-887-5516.

The largest town in southeastern New Mexico, with a population of nearly 50,000, **Roswell** is the shipping and commercial center for thousands of square miles of ranchlands in the region. At first glance, Roswell does not look like the kind of place that would have much to offer vacationers. But explore a bit and you'll discover some little-known sightseeing treasures. Bottomless Lakes State Park and Bitter Lake National Wildlife Refuge are described in the "Parks" section below.

The **Roswell Museum and Art Center** is one of the best in the state, with collections ranging from Western art and Indian artifacts to early rockets. The museum's highlight is a collection of paintings by famed landscape painter and portraitist Peter Hurd, who was born in Roswell and spent most of his life on his ranch nearby. Other artists represented here include Georgia O'Keeffe and Marsden Hartley. Open Sunday only, 1 to 4 p.m. ~ 100 West 11th Street; 505-624-6744.

What do football great Roger Staubach and New Mexico artist Peter Hurd have in common, other than that they're good with their hands? Both were students at New Mexico Military Institute, an institution that has sent more than 2800 graduates into combat duty since the Spanish American War. The proud heritage of NMMI is captured at the **General Douglas L. McBride Museum**. Grouped by war, the exhibit areas showcase many little-known treasures, including a machine-gun-toting Harley Davidson used by one of General Pershing's squadrons in the assault on Pancho Villa in 1916. Closed Saturday, Sunday and Monday. ~ 101 West College Boulevard, Roswell; 505-624-8220.

Experience turn-of-the-century New Mexican life at the **Historical Center for Southeast New Mexico**, a museum that spans the period from 1865 to 1940. It's located in a grand 1910 prairie-style structure and is decorated with pioneer antiques and Victorian furniture. The collection of artifacts is drawn from local Chaves County residents. Children will be fascinated by the dis-

---

✔ CHECK THESE OUT—UNIQUE SIGHTS

- Bring the kids—or the kid within—to **Smokey Bear Historical State Park** and trace the career of America's best-known fire-preventing bear. *page 428*
- Climb aboard the gleaming five-story space exhibit at the **International Space Hall of Fame**, and view the collections of moon rocks, space suits and capsules at this fascinating museum. *page 438*
- Drive through **White Sands National Monument** and watch as the ever-changing gypsum dunes dazzle the eyes and boggle the mind. *page 439*
- Journey to **Shakespeare**, an 1870s ghost town where dramatic re-enactments of the Bard's murders and hangings are staged. *page 450*

play of vintage toys. Open Friday, Saturday and Sunday, 1 to 4 p.m. Admission. ~ 200 North Lea Avenue, Roswell; 505-622-8333.

Ruidoso is a year-round resort with plenty of skiing and horse racing. The race track, **Ruidoso Downs**, is located five miles east of town. Quarter horses and thoroughbreds run here each afternoon during the summer season, which climaxes with the All-American Futurity, the world's richest quarter horse race with a $2 million purse. At the end of the racing season, mule races and high-priced horse auctions provide a last burst of excitement. Closed Saturday and Sunday in winter. Admission. ~ Route 70 East; 505-378-4431.

Adjacent to the racetrack is a noteworthy collection of horse memorabilia at the **Museum of the Horse**. An upstairs gallery traces 30,000 years of equine history and offers some surprising insights on the development of the West. Exhibits explain horse breeding, biomechanics and racing. Downstairs, there is a collection of other horse-drawn vehicles. There's also a saddle exhibit, featuring the best in Tibetan, Cossack and Charro design. Closed Monday from November through April. Admission. ~ Route 70 East; 505-378-4142.

The village of **Lincoln** would have faded from the map generations ago had it not been the scene of an infamous "war" between two competing groups of storekeepers and ranchers in 1878. After the leader of one faction was assassinated, one of his employees, a professional gunman known as Billy the Kid, avenged him by killing all the participants in the ambush and their bosses. The Lincoln County War ultimately brought down the territorial government of New Mexico and made Billy the Kid a legend.

The whole village and its surrounding area are now a historic district, giving Lincoln the authentic feel of a late-19th-century town. The focal points of a walking tour of Lincoln are several units of **Lincoln State Monument** as well as other structures. The Old Courthouse contains exhibits explaining the Lincoln County War and an actual bullethole made by Billy the Kid during a jailbreak. The Historical Center Museum displays Victorian-era frontier artifacts and has exhibits about "buffalo soldiers" (black troops stationed in the West after the Civil War) and the Apaches they fought. Admission. ~ Off Route 380; 505-653-4372.

A few miles west of Lincoln, the sightseeing highlight in the small town of Capitan is **Smokey Bear Historical State Park**. A must for kids and anyone interested in the history of advertising, this small museum traces the career of America's best-known bear from early artist's sketches through more than 40 years of forest service propaganda, children's comics and commercial kitsch. A film tells the story of the "real" Smokey the Bear (1950–1976), who was rescued by rangers from a fire in Lincoln National Forest and sent to live in a Washington, D.C. zoo. The live bear was named after the imaginary character, not vice-versa as legend suggests. Admission. ~ Route 380; 505-354-2748.

Visitors to Carlsbad Caverns may choose to stay at White's City by the national park entrance or in the town of Carlsbad, a 20-minute drive away.

LODGING

In White's City, the **Best Western Cavern Inn**, the **Walnut Canyon Inn** and the **Guadalupe Inn**, all offer fairly standard motel accommodations. Walnut Canyon is open in the summer only. ~ 505-785-2291, 800-228-3767, fax 505-785-2283 for all three establishments. MODERATE.

In the town of Carlsbad, the **Quality Inn** offers spacious rooms surrounding a courtyard patio and pool. ~ 3706 National Parks Highway, Carlsbad; 505-887-2861, 800-321-2861, fax 505-887-2861 ext. 310. BUDGET TO MODERATE.

Roswell's lodging scene is unexceptional. The top of the line is the **Best Western Sally Port Inn**, with its tropical atrium, spa facilities and guest rooms with tall picture windows and some with refrigerators. ~ 2000 North Main Street, Roswell; 505-622-6430, 800-528-1234, fax 505-623-7631. MODERATE.

One of the better low-priced motels is the **Frontier Motel**. ~ 3010 North Main Street, Roswell; 505-622-1400, 800-678-1401, fax 505-622-1405. BUDGET.

At the **Roswell Inn**, spacious landscaped grounds complement 121 rooms with contemporary Southwestern decor. These units have comfortable sitting areas and oak furniture. The fireplace lounge and swimming pool make this a good choice. ~ 1815 North Main Street, Roswell; 505-623-4920, 800-323-0913, fax 505-622-3831. MODERATE.

✔ CHECK THESE OUT—UNIQUE LODGING

- *Budget:* Bed down at **The Palace Hotel**, a former bank building circa 1882 turned bed and breakfast. *page 450*
- *Moderate:* Spend the night at **Inn of the Arts Bed & Breakfast**, where the units are named for New Mexican and American Indian artists. *page 441*
- *Moderate to deluxe:* Turn in at the **Lodge at Cloudcroft**, an elegant hotel in operation since the turn of the century. *page 440*
- *Deluxe:* Check into the **Inn of the Mountain Gods** on the Mescalero Apache Indian Reservation and horseback ride, fish, play tennis, canoe or visit the spa. *page 432*

Budget: under $50 Moderate: $50–$90 Deluxe: $90–$120 Ultra-deluxe: over $120

Text continued on page 432.

On the Trail
of Billy the Kid

No other character in New Mexico's history captures the imagination like Billy the Kid. He was the west's enigmatic "live fast, die young" character, a sort of 19th-century James Dean who has lived on in novels and movies. More than a century after his violent death at the age of 21, Billy the Kid's legend seems stronger than ever. Travelers can explore throughout southern New Mexico, from Lincoln to Mesilla to Silver City and beyond, following historical markers that recall the outlaw's exploits.

Lincoln is where the foundation was laid for Billy the Kid's immortality. There, visitors learn about the 1878 Lincoln County War, a violent conflict between a naive newcomer and a ruthless cattle baron that spread to involve the whole county in gunfights and arson for months and finally toppled the government of territorial New Mexico. Billy the Kid was on the side of the "good guys," legally deputized to capture the gunmen who had murdered his employer. Instead of arresting them, however, he shot them to death, causing modern scholars to believe that he was a violent sociopath.

After ridding Lincoln County of its nest of cattle rustlers, robber barons and corrupt politicians, Billy was granted amnesty by the new governor of New Mexico, Lew Wallace. Many people throughout the county reputedly saw him as a Robin Hood character. Yet he became the region's leading cattle rustler himself before he was hunted down for the murders of two sheriffs and a deputy and shot to death by the newly appointed Lincoln County sheriff, his old friend Pat Garrett.

One of the things Billy the Kid did best was escape. Two of his most daring escapes—one from a burning house under siege by a local posse and federal troops, the other from a makeshift jail cell in the old courthouse that houses the Lincoln State Monument headquarters today—took place in Lincoln.

South of Lincoln, in Ruidoso, visitors can see the water wheel of Dowlin's Mill, where gunmen cornered Billy the Kid seeking revenge for a friend he had shot. Billy escaped by hiding in a flour barrel. Located south of Ruidoso, Blazer's Mill near Mescalero was the site of a furious shootout during which the leader of the band of gunmen known as the Regulators was killed, after which Billy, the youngest and wildest member of the gang, took command.

Billy the Kid enthusiasts—and southern New Mexico sees its fair share of them—can find traces of the outlaw and his legend all across the state. On the outskirts of Fort Sumner (see Chapter Twelve for more information) is the site of Billy the Kid's grave near the ranch where Pat Garrett caught up with him. Fort Sumner also has the two biggest Billy the Kid museums in the state. An outdoor theater production recounting Billy's exploits is presented during the summer months in San Juan (located east of Tucumcari).

On Route 70 east of Las Cruces, a state sign marks the spot where Garrett himself was later killed in a dispute over goat grazing. In old Mesilla, just outside of Las Cruces, visitors can see the courthouse where Billy was convicted and sentenced to hang for murdering a lawman. (He escaped.)

North of Carrizozo on the way to the town of Corona, a marker tells of yet another siege in which Billy and his gang were trapped by a posse inside a burning stagecoach station but escaped in the confusion after a deputy sheriff was killed in the crossfire while trying to negotiate a surrender.

Before the Lincoln County War began, Billy the Kid worked in a general store at Seven Rivers. The townsite is lost beneath the waters of Brantley Dam, but details can be found in the small historical museum in Artesia. Earlier, Billy spent part of his boyhood and attended school briefly in Silver City. His childhood cabin and his mother's grave are there, along with the first jail he ever escaped from—at the age of 15 while in custody for robbing a Chinese laundry.

Populist hero or psychopathic killer? Historians and Hollywood scriptwriters are still guessing. But one thing's for sure: Billy the Kid wandered far and wide across some of the prettiest country anywhere.

HIDDEN ▶   For more than half a century **Dan Dee Cabins** has been the quintessential cottage resort, a tradition among families who know this mountain region well. Fourteen pine-paneled cabins—with one to three bedrooms each—spread across five nicely landscaped acres with picnic and barbecue areas. Equipped with kitchenettes, fireplaces, wicker and pine furniture, these units are just steps away from a fishing stream and convenient to year-round resort activities. Dan Dee Cabins is one of the friendliest places we found in New Mexico. ~ 310 Main Road, Ruidoso; 505-257-2165, 800-345-4848. MODERATE.

The **Inn of the Mountain Gods** on the Mescalero Apache Indian Reservation near Ruidoso is one of New Mexico's most exclusive resorts. It is owned by the Mescalero Apaches, whose mountainous reservation extends from Ruidoso south to Cloudcroft. Rooms are in buildings scattered through the pine forest above a manmade lake used for fishing and canoeing. Other facilities include a golf course, indoor and outdoor tennis courts, a horseback riding stable, archery and skeet shooting ranges and a spa. Many activities are open to nonguests for a fee. Most of the facilities are closed in winter. ~ Carrizo Canyon Road, Mescalero Apache Indian Reservation; 505-257-5141, 800-545-9011, fax 505-257-6173. DELUXE.

Other accommodations in Ruidoso range from condominiums to cabins and come in all price ranges. The **Carrizo Lodge** is a historic inn featuring Spanish-style stucco architecture in a canyon setting shaded by old trees. ~ 900 Carrizo Canyon Road, Ruidoso; 505-257-9131, 800-227-1224, fax 505-257-5621. MODERATE.

Several complexes near the Ruidoso River rent cabins in the pines with kitchens and fireplaces, including **Story Book Cabins**. ~ Upper Canyon Road, Ruidoso; 505-257-2115, fax 505-257-7512. **Whispering Pines Cabins** is another such establishment. ~ Upper Canyon Road, Ruidoso; 505-257-4311. MODERATE.

Lower-priced motels in the Ruidoso area cluster east of town on Route 70 near the Ruidoso Downs racetrack. For low-cost lodging, try the comfortable **Stagecoach Motel**. ~ 301 Sudderth Drive, Ruidoso; 505-257-2610. Similar prices are found at the nearby **Economy Inn**. ~ 2019 Route 70, Ruidoso; 505-378-4706, fax 505-378-4398. Both are clean and simple and have color televisions. BUDGET.

Monjeau Shadows Bed & Breakfast Establishment is an attractive B&B in the mountains. A four-story Victorian farmhouse located on ten wooded acres with walking paths, this seven-room inn is furnished with antiques and heirlooms. There's a big gameroom on the premises and the owners can arrange historic tours of Billy the Kid country, as well as skiing, horseback riding and golf. ~ Located 12 miles north of Ruidoso on Route 37 at the turnoff to Ski Apache, Alto; 505-336-4191. MODERATE TO DELUXE.

Lincoln has a small selection of memorable places to stay. Advance reservations are essential at all of them. Located in the oldest building in Lincoln, **Ellis Store Bed & Breakfast**, a Territorial-period adobe, offers rooms with private and shared baths. ~ Lincoln; 505-653-4609, 800-653-6460, fax 505-653-4610. MODERATE.

Casa de Patron Bed & Breakfast is nestled between two hillsides in the Bonita River Valley. There are three moderate-priced rooms in the main house, and two deluxe-priced *casitas*. New additions to the bed and breakfast are the Vaquero room decorated in a Spanish cowboy theme and the Eastburn room, which has a country garden flavor. They are located in the Trailhouse behind the main house. ~ Lincoln; 505-653-4676, fax 505-653-4671. MODERATE TO DELUXE.

Art lovers should seek out the **Hurd Ranch Guest Homes**, where artist Michael Hurd designed the four adobe one-bedroom *casitas* with a blend of traditional Southwestern and contemporary furniture. Part of the 2500-acre Sentinel Ranch, both units—with Saltillo tile, antique cabinetry and American Indian rugs—come complete with kitchens and patios. Also available is the more expensive contemporary suite in the Hurd–La Rinconada Gallery. This two-story unit, which features a private balcony, is decorated with original paintings by members of the famous Hurd family. ~ Mile Marker 281, Route 70, San Patricio; 505-653-4331, 800-658-6912, fax 505-653-4218. DELUXE TO ULTRA-DELUXE.

DINING

Carlsbad Caverns Restaurant serves inexpensive cafeteria-style fare in the national park visitors center. It is often crowded enough to make hungry sightseers wish they'd brought a picnic lunch. Inside the cave, near the elevators that carry visitors back to the surface at the end of the tour, the restaurant serves box lunches containing fried chicken or ham sandwiches. ~ 505-785-2281. BUDGET.

Cortez has been a popular place with locals for more than 50 years with its affordably priced Mexican dishes. Closed Monday and Tuesday. ~ 506 South Canal Street, Carlsbad; 505-885-4747. BUDGET.

The best budget bargain in town is catfish and homemade pie at **Hazel's Cajun Kitchen**. Closed Saturday and Sunday. ~ 5800 South Main Street, Roswell; 505-623-7441. BUDGET.

Mario's has a reputation for filet mignon, *flautas de pollo* and salmon fillet, and the loyal following to prove it. Pine-paneled booths, Southwestern landscape paintings and Tiffany-style lamps distinguish the contemporary dining room. Closed Sunday. ~ 200 East 2nd Street, Roswell; 505-623-1740. BUDGET.

Ruidoso has an abundance of fine dining establishments. Of the three restaurants at the exclusive Inn of the Mountain Gods, the finest is **Dan Li Ka**, the main dining room, with a wide-ranging menu that offers everything from wild game to shrimp diablo. The lake and mountain view is incomparable. Guests are served on peach linen and seated in metal captain's chairs painted blue-green. Dan Li Ka's decor features American Indian weavings, baskets and modern paintings. ~ Carrizo Canyon Road, Mescalero Apache Indian Reservation; 505-257-5141. DELUXE.

An even more elegant possibility is the **La Lorraine**. Located in an adobe building with green canopies, the chandeliered dining room has upholstered chairs, fine silver, white linen and a good collection of regional art. Entrées include rack of lamb, châteaubriand and roast duck. Closed Sunday. ~ 2523 Sudderth Drive, Ruidoso; 505-257-2954. DELUXE.

At the other end of the dining spectrum, the low-priced **Texas Café** serves grilled marinated chicken and charred burgers. ~ Corner of Mechem and Sudderth drives, Ruidoso; 505-257-3506. BUDGET.

Follow the locals at lunchtime and you're likely to wind up at **The Deck House Restaurant,** one of the best affordably priced restaurants in southeastern New Mexico. Dine out on the deck or indoors among the Southwestern antiques and adobe-style painted walls. The New Mexican menu features corn bread made with whole corn, green chiles and cheese and "squawbread" (the house specialty), a sweet and chewy concoction served with homemade strawberry preserves. We're also partial to the chicken *compuestas* with green chile and sour-cream sauces. Sandwiches and burgers are all served on fresh-baked bread. Closed Wednesday. ~ 202 Mechem Drive, Ruidoso; no phone. BUDGET TO MODERATE.

For the ultimate view of Sierra Blanca reserve a table at **Ahna-Michelle's Restaurant**. Romantic landscape paintings, bells and music add a festive note to this Swiss/Italian restaurant. Knackwurst and bratwurst fans will love the German sausage platter,

---

✔ CHECK THESE OUT—UNIQUE DINING

- *Budget:* Consort with the locals at **Aspen Restaurant** over a hearty breakfast or palate-pleasing lunch or dinner. *page 442*
- *Budget to moderate:* Feast on generous portions of New Mexican cuisine at **Grandma T's,** a friendly place adorned with farmstead antiques and squash blossom jewelry. *page 451*
- *Moderate:* Tour the world when you dine at **Ahna-Michelle's Restaurant,** where knackwurst or St. Moritz manicotti star on the menu. *page 434*
- *Deluxe:* Dine on wild game or shrimp diablo while gazing at the lake or mountain view at **Dan Li Ka.** *page 433*

Budget: under $8 Moderate: $8–$16 Deluxe: $16–$24 Ultra-deluxe: over $24

while those partial to pasta can opt for the St. Moritz manicotti. *Carne asada*, steak and shrimp scampi round out the menu. Open for breakfast and dinner only. ~ 1451 Mechem Drive, Ruidoso; 505-258-3333. MODERATE.

Ruidoso has the **Flying J Ranch** featuring the summer evening combination of barbecue beef and singing cowboys. Reservations are highly recommended. Open nightly from Memorial Day to Labor Day except Sunday. ~ Route 48; 505-336-4330. MODERATE.

In Carlsbad, the gift shop at **Living Desert State Park** sells an assortment of cacti that make good souvenirs. ~ 505-887-5516.

SHOPPING

Collectors of American Indian arts and crafts will be tempted by the Apache cradleboards, Navajo vases, mandelas and turquoise jewelry at **J and K Kountry Kraft.** ~ 110 North Main Street, Roswell; 505-622-1070.

Ruidoso has a number of art galleries that seem to keep a lot of racetrack winnings from leaving town. More than a dozen of them can be found along Mechem and Sudderth drives.

Purchase your very own hand-painted Western shirt or cowboy hat at **The Attic.** In addition to designer items and limited editions, you'll find turquoise, semiprecious stones and sterling silver to accessorize your new duds. ~ 1031 Mechem Drive, Ruidoso; 505-258-5338.

If you have had a hard time finding a pole bed with saguaro cactus–style ribs, you haven't been to **Rio Mercado Furniture,** a showcase for Southwestern design, rustic pieces and collectibles. ~ 2814 Sudderth Drive, Ruidoso; 505-257-3276.

Ceremonial weapons of war along with peace pipes share the shelves at **White Dove.** However, the shop's specialty is authentic American Indian crafts and jewelry, especially Hopi, Navajo and sterling silver designs. ~ 2318 Sudderth Drive, Ruidoso; 505-257-6609.

"We Cheat You Right" is the whimsical slogan at **Rio Trading Company.** It's a barnlike store, well-stocked with everything from donkey carts to miniature windmills and American Indian dream catchers. ~ 2200 Sudderth Drive, Ruidoso; 505-257-9274.

The museum shop located at the **Lincoln County Heritage Trust** sells a remarkable array of Billy the Kid books, comics, posters and motion picture videos. How the outlaw's legend has endured! ~ Lincoln; 505-653-4025.

For evening entertainment, nothing can compete with the sunset flight of almost half a million Mexican freetail bats from the entrance of **Carlsbad Caverns.** The bats put on their show nightly from April through October. They migrate to the tropics for the winter. Call ahead for information. ~ 505-785-2232.

NIGHTLIFE

Near the front gate of Carlsbad Caverns National Park, melodrama is presented at **Granny's Opera House.** Shows run Thursday, Friday and Saturday nights in summer. Closed in winter. ~ White's City; 505-785-2291.

The **Flying J Ranch** near Ruidoso represents a traditional Western genre of tourist entertainment. After a barbecue-beef dinner served "chuckwagon style" (that is, in a chow line), singing cowboys take the stage to perform classics like "Red River Valley" and "Git Along, Little Dogie." Corny but lots of fun. Open nightly from Memorial Day to Labor Day except Sunday. Reservations are highly recommended. ~ Route 48; 505-336-4330.

Ruidoso is the liveliest town after dark in this part of the state. You'll find live music, Texas style, at **Win Place & Show Lounge.** ~ 2516 Sudderth Drive, Ruidoso; 505-257-9982. Live music can also be found occasionally at **Farley's Bar and Restaurant.** ~ Mechem Street at White Mountain Drive, Ruidoso; 505-258-5676.

PARKS

CARLSBAD MUNICIPAL PARK This large park runs through town for more than a mile along the west bank of Lake Carlsbad, a portion of the Pecos River that has been dammed to make it wider and deeper. It is used for waterskiing, swimming, fishing and sailing. A playground, a golf course and tennis and handball courts are also located in the park. On the shore, the park has broad lawns and shade trees. There are restrooms and a picnic area. ~ Take Greene Street east several blocks from Route 285 to the river.

SITTING BULL FALLS Although it is a long drive through uninhabited backcountry, Sitting Bull Falls is a locally popular spot, likely to be crowded on summer weekends. It's one of the largest falls in New Mexico—130 feet high—and practically the only running water in the arid foothills northwest of Carlsbad. Swimming is permitted in the pool at the bottom of the falls. There are hiking trails, a picnic area and restrooms. ~ From Route 285 about 12 miles north of Carlsbad, take Route 137 southwest for 25 miles and watch for a sign to Sitting Bull Falls. The falls are at the end of the eight-mile paved road; 505-885-4181.

BRANTLEY LAKE STATE PARK This irrigation reservoir on the Pecos River north of Carlsbad offers several opportunities for water recreation from boating and fishing to scuba diving and waterskiing. The park features a picnic area, restrooms, showers, volleyball, horseshoe pits, a nature trail and a children's playground; day-use fee, $3. ~ It's 12 miles north of Carlsbad, just off Route 285; 505-457-2384.

▲ There are 51 sites with RV hookups; $11 per night. Primitive camping is allowed; $7 per night.

BOTTOMLESS LAKES STATE PARK 🏃 🚣 ⛵ 🚤 🛶 New Mexico's oldest state park consists of seven natural lakes, small in surface area but as much as 90 feet deep, formed by collapsed underground salt caves. The largest, Lea Lake, is the only one where swimming is allowed. It also has a public beach and rowboat and paddleboard rentals and is a popular site for scuba diving. There's a visitors center near Cottonwood Lake. Trails lead to beautiful Mirror Lake, surrounded by red cliffs. Ducks, geese and other waterfowl abound on the lakes during spring and fall migration seasons. The park has a picnic area, restrooms and showers; day-use fee, $3. ~ From Roswell, take Route 380 for 12 miles east, then turn south on Route 409 for two miles to the park entrance; 505-624-6058.

▲ There are 52 sites (32 with RV hookups); $7 per night for standard sites, $11 for hookups.

BITTER LAKE NATIONAL WILDLIFE REFUGE 🏃 Small wetlands along the Pecos River attracts a lot of migrating waterfowl as they cross this arid region, though few winter here. As many as 30,000 snow geese, 15,000 sandhill cranes and 12,000 ducks stop at Bitter Lake each year. Wilderness area is open for hiking. There's also an auto-tour route. ~ From Route 285 go east on Pine Lodge Road and follow the signs to the refuge headquarters. There is also a road to the refuge from Route 380, midway out to Bottomless Lakes State Park; 505-622-6755.

▼▼▼▼▼▼▼▼▼▼▼▼▼▼▼▼▼▼

South Central New Mexico

Birthplace of the atomic age, a favorite resting place of Apache rebel Geronimo and a bonanza for petroglyph buffs, south central New Mexico is famous for its gypsum dunes and lava fields. Juxtaposing desert and mountains, this Rio Grande region offers a number of popular dammed lakes ideal for outdoor enthusiasts. It is also home to the only city in America renamed for a game show, and a must for ghost town buffs.

SIGHTS

The northern part of the Tularosa Basin, which begins north of Carrizozo and extends 80 miles to the south, is a jagged wasteland of black lava. At **Valley of Fires Recreation Area**, a self-guided nature trail leads across a portion of the 10,000-year-old lava field for a closeup look at this strange and forbidding landscape. Admission. ~ Located off Route 380 just east of Carrizozo; 505-648-2241.

From Carrizozo to Alamogordo, Route 54 runs along the eastern edge of **White Sands Missile Range**, a vast area used by the military to test weapons. It has been off-limits to the public since World War II, when it was the site of the first atomic bomb test. A tour of the Trinity Site where the original bomb was exploded is conducted twice a year in October and April. ~ Route 54; 505-678-1134.

HIDDEN ▶ Halfway between Carrizozo and Alamogordo, the **Three Rivers Petroglyph Site** contains thousands of pictures chipped into the dark patina of boulders by artists of the Mimbres people, an American Indian culture centuries older than the Anasazi of the Four Corners area. A three-quarter-mile often steep trail follows the crest of a high hill to let you see the mysterious pictures of animals, humans and magical beings as well as abstract symbols whose meanings can only be guessed at. A pleasant picnic area lies at the foot of the trail. Admission. ~ Three miles off Route 54.

In Alamogordo, the **International Space Hall of Fame** houses one of the world's largest collections of space exploration artifacts. The gleaming five-story gold cube on the hillside contains antique rockets, space suits, Apollo and Gemini capsules, moon rocks, satellites and lots more. An outdoor park displays larger rockets and the Sonic Wind Rocket Sled, which was used to test the effects of rocket acceleration on humans. Adjoining the museum is the **Clyde W. Tombaugh Space Theater**, a planetarium that presents laser light shows and OMNIMAX movies as well as educational astronomy programs. It is named after the man who discovered the planet Pluto. Admission. ~ Indian Wells Road at Scenic Drive; 505-437-2840, 800-545-4021.

To learn more about the exploration of space, drive up to the National Solar Observatory–Sacramento Peak on the crest of the mountains to the east. First, take the 16-mile drive on Route 82 from Alamogordo to the village of **Cloudcroft**. Nestled in the pines near the crest of the Sacramento Mountains, Cloudcroft has seen little of the rampant resort development evident at Ruidoso on the other side of the Mescalero Apache Indian Reservation, and it retains the weathered charm of a little Rocky Mountain logging town.

Explore a pioneer barn, granary and hand-hewn log house chinked with mud at the **Sacramento Mountains Historical Museum**. Of special interest is an exhibit about the Cloudcroft Baby Sanatorium, a high-country facility that saved the lives of hundreds of children suffering from summer heat sickness in the nearby lowlands between 1912 and 1932. The collection of artifacts includes an Edison cylinder talking machine and a rifle once owned by explorer Zebulon Pike. Closed Sunday and Monday. Admission. ~ Route 82, Cloudcroft; 505-682-2932.

From the museum, take Scenic Byway 6563 for 16 miles, following the signs to "Sunspot." Maintained by the National Science Foundation for the use of various universities, the **National Solar Observatory–Sacramento Peak** has several solar telescopes. The main one extends from 20 stories below ground level to 13 stories above. Visitors on self-guided tours of the facility can view solar flares on a video screen in the small lobby and often watch scientists studying the sun on similar screens. The panoramic view of the Tularosa Basin, White Sands and the Valley of Fires from the observatory's lookout point is worth the drive by itself. ~ Scenic Byway 6563; 505-434-7000.

White Sands National Monument is the world's largest gypsum dune-field, encompassing 300 square miles of sand.

A trip to this area would not be complete without a stop at **White Sands National Monument**. The monument protects the southernmost part of White Sands for public use. A 16-mile round-trip scenic drive takes you into the heart of the white-as-snow gypsum dunes, where you can park and step out into this strange landscape. The juxtaposition of pristine white sand and bright blue sky can make you feel like you're walking on clouds. Admission. ~ Located off Route 70 between Alamogordo and Las Cruces; 505-479-6124.

As beautiful as it is unusual, the landscape is ever-changing: Desert winds constantly reshape the dunes, creating pure white sculptures that disappear with each fresh gust. Surrounded by a spectacular wasteland, with an occasional yucca plant the only sign of life, it's difficult to decide whether this is heaven, hell or simply the end of the earth. Hiking is allowed without limitation, but camping is only permitted at a single backcountry tent site available first come, first serve. Rangers conduct morning and evening nature walks during the summer months.

Las Cruces (population 70,000) is the largest city in south central New Mexico. In addition to being the county seat, Las Cruces is noteworthy for the Organ Mountains that loom east of the city. Vaulting 5000 feet above the valley, they derive their name from the spires and minarets that are like a pipe organ cast in stone.

At the handsome adobe-walled **Branigan Cultural Center** artists exhibit a variety of paintings, sculpture and arts and crafts. Permanent exhibits of turn-of-the-century artifacts and textiles tell the story of this community's formative days. ~ 500 North Water Street, Las Cruces; 505-524-1422.

A short distance southwest of Las Cruces on Route 10, the village of **Mesilla** is one of the state's prettiest and best-preserved historic districts, dating back to 1598. Mesilla achieved further historical significance as the Confederate capital of the Arizona Territory for a short period during the Civil War. The downtown plaza and some of its surrounding Territorial-style buildings have been designated as **La Mesilla State Monument**. Points of interest around the plaza include the **San Albino Church**, the oldest in the area, built in 1853. Also here is the **Gadsden Museum**, with folk art and artifact collections representing the Anglo, Spanish and Indian cultures of the region. Admission. ~ Boutz Road; 505-526-6293.

Fifteen miles north of Las Cruces, **Fort Selden State Monument** includes the ruins of an adobe fort used by the Army from 1865 to 1891. It was a base for troops guarding the Mesilla Valley and providing protection for wagon trains and later the railroad. A small museum recalls life at the fort during the Territorial era. Admission. ~ Route 25; 505-526-8911.

Farther north along Route 25, the main point of interest in **Truth or Consequences**, a sprawling retirement community just south of Elephant Butte Lake, is the **Geronimo Springs Museum**. It is a fairly large museum with 12 exhibit rooms full of Mimbres pottery, ranch antiques, fossils and petrified wood, works by local artists, awards for wool production and other curiosities from all over Sierra County. The highlight of the museum is the Ralph Edwards Room, commemorating the television show that inspired Hot Springs, New Mexico, to change its name to Truth or Consequences in 1950. Open Sunday, 1 to 4 p.m. Admission. ~ 211 Main Street; 505-894-6600.

HIDDEN ► The most interesting of the several ghost towns in the Truth or Consequences vicinity is **Chloride**, 29 miles off the interstate on Route 52 and then just more than two miles on a marked, unpaved forest road. This is one of the few New Mexico ghost towns that looks the way you expect a Western ghost town to look, with about a dozen falsefront buildings still standing along a deserted main street. In its heyday during the late 19th century, Chloride was a center for silver mining and had a population of about 500.

LODGING   Virtually all Alamogordo accommodations are standard highway motels and with few exceptions their rates are in the budget range. Representative of the type is the **Satellite Inn**, which has phones, cable TV and an outdoor heated pool. ~ 2224 North White Sands Boulevard, Alamogordo; 505-437-8454, 800-221-7690, fax 505-434-6015. BUDGET.

A more interesting option is to spend the night in Cloudcroft, high in the mountains and just 16 miles from Alamogordo. The most elegant hotel in town is the **Lodge at Cloudcroft**, with mod-

GETTING INTO HOT WATER

Truth or Consequences' popularity as a spa resort has long since faded, but the hot springs themselves remain intact. Next to the Geronimo Springs Museum is a 115° natural spring where Apache leader Geronimo himself is said to have relaxed. One spring open to the public for bathing is **Sierra Grande Lodge and Health Spa**. Admission. ~ 501 McAdoo Street; 505-894-6976.

erately priced rooms as well as suites in the deluxe range. The three-story lodge has been in operation since the turn of the century and has been completely refurbished and modernized. Rooms have high ceilings and some antique furnishings. ~ Corona Place, Cloudcroft; 505-682-2566, 800-395-6343, fax 505-682-2715. MODERATE TO DELUXE.

The lodge also operates the **Lodge Pavilion Bed & Breakfast,** offering accommodations in the town's oldest building. Both the Lodge and the Pavilion are listed on the National Register of Historic Places. ~ 199 Curlew Street at Chipmunk Avenue, Cloudcroft; 505-682-2566, 800-395-6343, fax 505-682-2715. MODERATE.

For more modest, quiet and cozy lodgings, Cloudcroft has numerous cabins for rent. For example, **Buckhorn Cabins,** located in the center of town, has rustic-style cabins ranging from budget-priced rooms with kitchenettes to moderate-priced two-bedroom cabins with living rooms and fireplaces. ~ Route 82, Cloudcroft; 505-682-2421. BUDGET TO MODERATE.

Equipped with woodburning stoves and tucked amid the pines, **Tall Timbers** is a prime choice for a family holiday. All nine cottage and duplex units offer picnic tables and grills that allow guests to take advantage of the setting—a quiet residential area—as well as kitchenettes. After a day behind the wheel, you'll be happy to fall into the comfy king-size beds. ~ 1102 Chatauqua Canyon Boulevard, Cloudcroft; 505-682-2301. MODERATE.

In Las Cruces, the most luxurious hotel is the **Las Cruces Hilton,** situated in the foothills on the east edge of town off Route 25 and across the street from Mesilla Valley Mall. The modern seven-story hotel features bright, attractive guest rooms with refrigerators, and the swimming pool is surrounded by palm trees. ~ 705 South Telshor Boulevard, Las Cruces; 505-522-4300, 800-445-8667, fax 505-522-7657. DELUXE.

Budget motels cluster along West Picacho Avenue. Try the **Economy Inn,** which offers all standard amenities including outdoor pool, phones and cable television. ~ 2160 West Picacho Avenue, Las Cruces; 505-524-8627. BUDGET.

More unusual lodging can be found at the **Inn of the Arts Bed & Breakfast,** where each of the 20 units are named after well-known New Mexican and American Indian artists. A kiva fireplace is featured in the R. C. Gorman Room while photographs and books of Tony Hillerman fill the author's namesake *casita*. If the weather's good, the innkeepers may fire up the outdoor *horno*, or Indian oven, to bake Indian bread (served later in the adobe gazebo). ~ 618 South Alameda Boulevard, Las Cruces; 505-526-3327, fax 505-647-1334. MODERATE.

Nearby in historic Mesilla is the **Meson de Mesilla,** an elegant bed and breakfast. All 13 rooms in this modern adobe inn have private baths and are appointed in Victorian-period decor. Guests may stroll the flagstone pathway through a courtyard filled with yuccas, cacti and desert blooms or enjoy the sweeping views of the Organ Mountains from the inn's lawn. ~ 1803 Avenida de Mesilla, Mesilla; 505-525-9212, 800-732-6025. MODERATE.

In Truth or Consequences, all accommodations are priced in the budget-to-moderate range, from quality contemporary motor inns to a scattering of very low-priced older independent motels.

In the former category is the **Elephant Butte Resort Inn**. ~ Route 195, off of Route 25 Exit 83, Truth or Consequences; 505-744-5431, fax 505-744-5431. MODERATE.

In the latter group is the **Charles Motel and Bath House**, with simple rooms with kitchenettes, as well as mineral baths, sauna and massage at an extra charge. ~ 601 Broadway, Truth or Consequences; 505-894-7154. BUDGET.

DINING

In Alamogordo, fast-food places are the norm, with the exception of few family-style restaurants such as **Angelina's**, serving pizzas and pastas. Closed Sunday. ~ 415 South White Sands Boulevard, Alamogordo; 505-434-1166. BUDGET TO MODERATE.

Cloudcroft has a number of good restaurants, many featuring Texas-style cuisine. In the middle of town is the cafeteria-style **Texas Pit Barbecue**, a real find for mesquite-smoked beef and *chile con carne*. Open daily in summer; closed Tuesday and Wednesday in winter. ~ Route 82, Cloudcroft; 505-682-2307. BUDGET.

For fine dining, consider **Rebecca's**, the dining room at the Lodge at Cloudcroft, where Continental selections are served in an atmosphere of Victorian elegance with a view of the pine forest. White linen, wicker furniture, historic portraits and a pianist make this a romantic spot, with picture windows overlooking White Sands. ~ Corona Place, Cloudcroft; 505-682-2566. DELUXE TO ULTRA-DELUXE.

Some mornings it seems as though the entire town of Cloudcroft is hunkered over a steaming bowl of oatmeal at the **Aspen Restaurant**. If you prefer to start your day off with more of a bang, try the Cottage Scramble (tomatoes, mushrooms, onions and cheese scrambled with eggs). Lunch and dinner specialties range from tamales smothered in green chiles to the more forgiving (read less spicy) steak and salad. ~ 1315 Route 82, Cloudcroft; 505-682-2526. BUDGET.

In Las Cruces, **Nellie's Café** is a long-time local favorite serving New Mexican and Old Mexican dishes like *carne adovada* and menudo. Closed Sunday. ~ 1226 West Hadley Avenue, Las Cruces; 505-524-9982. BUDGET.

Fine restaurants surround the plaza in Mesilla. The most elegant of them is the **Double Eagle**, with a Continental menu and museum-quality period decor in a restored Territorial adobe listed on the National Register of Historic Places. ~ 308 Calle Guadalupe, East Plaza, Mesilla; 505-523-6700. MODERATE TO DELUXE.

Also on the plaza is **El Patio**, serving traditional New Mexican cuisine. Closed Sunday. ~ Calle de Principal, South Plaza, Mesilla; 505-524-0982. BUDGET.

La Posta de Mesilla is another restaurant on the plaza that serves New Mexican food in a historic building. Closed Monday. ~ South Plaza, Mesilla; 505-524-3524. BUDGET.

Break for caffeine at **Kokopelli**, where lattes and mochas are the order of the day. Smoothies, lemonade and ice cream treats will satisfy the non-caffeine addicts. ~ Calle de Parian west of the Plaza, Mesilla; 505-524-1929. BUDGET.

Most Truth or Consequences restaurants present standard interstate highway exit fare. One exception is the **Damsite Restaurant**, located six miles north of town on the dam road. In an old adobe overlooking Elephant Butte Lake, the restaurant serves American and Mexican food. Closed Tuesday and Wednesday in winter. ~ Englestar Route, Truth or Consequences; 505-894-2073. MODERATE.

SHOPPING

Moore's Trading Post is one of the few places we know that sells live rattlesnakes by the pound. But if you'd just as soon not drive home with a fanged pet, Moore's carries plenty of reptilian "accessories," everything from the egg to the antivenin. If slinky critters give you nothing but the jitters, choose instead from the thousands of secondhand items: furniture, combat boots, military fatigues, guns—you name it. Looking for a fire hydrant? Moore's has them. ~ 215 Route 82 East, Alamogordo; 505-437-7116.

If you need souvenirs, try **Bear in the Woods**, an eclectic shop that carries one-of-a-kind quilted jackets, hand-painted shirts and—best of all—a wide array of toys for the young and those who wish they still were. Handmade dolls, American Indian baskets and dried flowers are also available. ~ 62 Curlew Place, Cloudcroft; 505-682-2094.

Eight miles northeast of Alamogordo via Route 70 and Route 545, local artists and craftsmen show their works at galleries around the small plaza in the old Spanish village of **La Luz**.

Pick up a thriller for the trip home at **Coas: My Bookstore**. This is one of the largest bookstores in southern New Mexico, with more than 100,000 titles—new, used and rare. (Coas also carries games and comics.) ~ 317 North Main Street, Las Cruces; 505-524-8471.

Every Wednesday and Saturday morning more than 350 exhibitors head for the **Las Cruces Farmers and Crafts Market** on the downtown mall. These vendors generally offer the top pick in local produce, nuts, and flowers, though they plug everything from honey and salsa to Southwestern furniture. The toys and dolls make first-class gifts. ~ Between Water and Church streets, Las Cruces; 505-526-0383.

A must for any visitor to the region, **Pebble Pups Gems and Minerals** qualifies as a small museum. Several of the display cases show off the owners' impressive personal collection (of gems and minerals, naturally). And if you can't bear to walk away empty-handed, they'll be happy to sell you a rose quartz, a mastodon tooth or perhaps a pair of agate nodule bookends. There are quality malachite, tourmaline, amethyst and black opals here as well. The shop also carries an array of geology books. ~ Route 28 at Route 10, Las Cruces; 505-526-5773.

Hatch, located midway between Las Cruces and Truth or Consequences off Route 25, has a reputation for producing the best-tasting chile in New Mexico, and most of the stores in the little town are **chile shops**. In September, they sell fresh-roasted green chiles. The rest of the year, they stock it dried, canned, powdered, shaped as Christmas tree lights and as a T-shirt motif.

NIGHTLIFE In Alamogordo, the best bet for fun after dark is the laser light show presented by the **Clyde W. Tombaugh Space Theater** at the International Space Hall of Fame. Open weekends only in winter. Admission. ~ Indian Wells Road at Scenic Drive, Alamogordo; 505-437-2840.

Up in the mountains, the **Lodge at Cloudcroft** has a mellow piano bar. ~ Corona Place, Cloudcroft; 505-682-2566.

Las Cruces, a lively college town, has night spots such as **Cowboys**, which has live country music. Cover Thursday through Saturday. ~ 2205 South Main Street, Las Cruces; 505-526-1610.

New Mexico State University provides a steady flow of cultural activities, notably the continuing **New Mexico State University Film Series**. Screenings are held in the auditorium of Corbett Center Student Union. ~ Breland Drive, Las Cruces; 505-646-3235.

PARKS Several dams on the lower Rio Grande form lakes used for recreation, ranging from little Leasburg Lake—hardly more than a wide spot in the river—to huge Elephant Butte Lake, one of New Mexico's largest bodies of water. From south to north, these lakes are:

LEASBURG DAM STATE PARK This park is located near a small dam on the Rio Grande, set in a desert of creosote bushes and cholla cacti near Fort Selden State Monument. It is a popular area for swimming and boating (canoes and rafts). Fishing is also permitted. The park also features a nature trail, picnic areas, restrooms, showers and a playground; day-use fee, $3. ~ Located 15 miles north of Las Cruces, off Route 25 at Radium Springs; 505-524-4068

▲ There are 50 sites (18 with RV hookups); primitive camping is allowed. Fees are $6 for primitive sites, $7 for standard sites and $11 for hookups.

PERCHA DAM STATE PARK 🕴 ⛰ 🚤 🛶 Another small dam widens the river at this park, which is primarily a campground and riverbank fishing area with sandy beaches. Unlike Leasburg Lake, Percha Dam has tall old cottonwoods to provide shade on hot summer afternoons. Fishing is permitted. Facilities at the park include picnic area, restrooms, showers, a playground and trails; day-use fee, $5. ~ Located off Route 25 near the village of Arrey, 53 miles north of Las Cruces (21 miles south of Truth or Consequences); 505-743-3942.

▲ There are 106 sites (six with RV hookups); $7 per night for standard sites, $11 for hookups. The camping area features green lawns—a rarity in southern New Mexico.

CABALLO LAKE STATE PARK 🕴 ⛴ 🎣 🚤 🛥 🛶 The name, Spanish for "horse," comes from the days when wild horses used to live in Caballo Canyon before it was dammed in the 1930s to form Caballo Lake. The lake is more than a mile wide and 12 miles long, with more than 70 miles of shoreline. It is popular, especially in the spring, with fishermen angling for channel catfish, bass and walleye pike. The visitors center and main campground, picnic area and marina (with boat rentals) are on the west side of the lake (one mile north from Exit 59 off Route 25). From there, Route 187 follows the shore all the way to the upper end of the lake. Below the dam is a river fishing area with drinking water and campsites shaded by cottonwood trees. The park has restrooms and showers; day-use fee, $3. ~ Located off Route 25, 60 miles north of Las Cruces (14 miles south of Truth or Consequences); 505-743-3942.

▲ There are 348 sites (64 with RV hookups) and primitive camping along the shoreline. Fees are $6 for primitive sites (located on the east side of the lake), $7 for standard sites and $11 for hookups.

ELEPHANT BUTTE LAKE STATE PARK 🕴 🐟 ⛴ 🎣 ⛰ 🚤 🛥 🛶 The dam creating this 40-mile-long reservoir, the second-largest lake in New Mexico, was originally built in 1916 to impound irrigation water for the whole Rio Grande Valley downriver. Today, it is New Mexico's most popular state park. Recreational activities include fishing, boating (there are marinas and boat rentals), water-skiing, windsurfing, sailing and even houseboating. The lake also has miles of sand beaches and several protected swimming areas. On display at the visitors center are dinosaur and early mammal fossils found in the area, including a tyrannosaurus rex jawbone. A network of unpaved roads provides access to a series of remote points along the lake's west shore, but all of the east shore can only be reached by boat. In addition to nature trails and a playground, there are picnic areas, restrooms and showers; day-use fee, $3. ~ The dam is due west of Truth or Consequences about six miles on Route 51. From there, Route 195 goes north to Elephant Butte Estates, and smaller roads, unpaved but suitable for passenger cars, follow the shore north for about 15 miles; 505-744-5421.

▲ There are 234 sites (103 with RV hookups) and an area for primitive camping. Fees are $6 for primitive sites, $7 for developed sites and $11 for hookups.

Southwestern New Mexico

Geronimo's base, southwestern New Mexico is home to Mogollon, one of the state's finest ghost towns, as well as the Gila Wilderness, cliff dwellings and the frontier boomtown of Silver City. If you like to pack in to high-country lakes, cycle through national forests or explore cliff dwellings, this remote area is your kind of place. While here you can learn about the legend of Pancho Villa, who made the mistake of invading this area in 1916.

SIGHTS

Gila Cliff Dwellings National Monument, 44 slow miles north of Silver City, preserves five natural caves that were inhabited by people of the Mogollon culture about 700 years ago. Visitors who have seen the Southwest's great Indian ruins, such as those at Chaco Canyon, Mesa Verde or the Jemez Mountains, sometimes find Gila Cliff Dwellings a disappointment because they consist of only 40 rooms, which housed a total of 10 to 15 families. But the small scale of these ruins and nearby pit houses, representative of the many communities scattered throughout the Gila country, is marvelous in the context of the vast surrounding canyonlands. ~ Route 15; 505-536-9344.

The real reason a national monument exists at Gila Cliff Dwellings is to administer the central trailhead for one of the nation's most important wilderness areas. Encompassing much of the 3.3 million-acre Gila National Forest, the rugged mountain and canyon country of the **Gila Wilderness** and adjoining **Aldo Leopold Wilderness** comprise the largest roadless area in the United States outside of Alaska. The Gila was the nation's first designated wilderness area, established by an act of congress in 1924.

An **overlook** on Route 15 just before the descent to Gila Cliff Dwellings gives a good idea of the Gila's extent and complexity. Three forks of the Gila River join near the cliff dwellings. One of the three main hiking and horse trails into the Gila Wilderness follows each fork through a river and high mesa canyon that meanders between mountains for many miles. A treacherous tangle of side canyons off the main ones defied all pioneer efforts at settlement and provided a stronghold for renegade Apache leaders, including Geronimo.

Today mounted rangers take a full week to cross the wilderness as they patrol, and hiking from boundary to boundary is practically impossible without a horse, mule or llama to carry your food supply. The rugged mountains visible from the overlook—the Black, Diablo, Mogollon, San Francisco and Tularoso—are also part of the wilderness area. Of the many natural hot springs in the vicinity, the most popular is a series located a short hike up the Middle Fork from the forest service visitors center.

While the main roads are paved, visitors should not underestimate the trip to Gila Cliff Dwellings. The 44-mile drive from Silver City on Route 15 will take at least two hours; for the 99-mile trip via Routes 152 and 35 from Exit 63 on Route 25 south of Truth or Consequences, allow half a day. There are no gas stations or

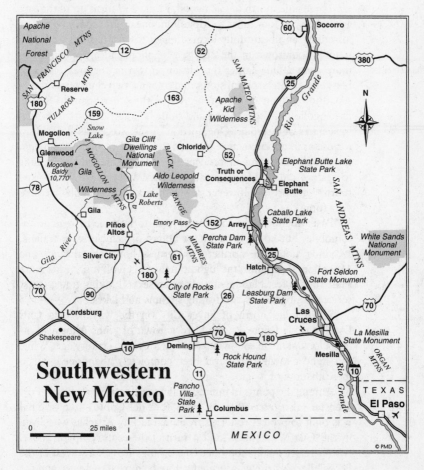

Southwestern
New Mexico

0   25 miles

other travelers' services along the way, with the exception of a small store with a gasoline pump less than four miles from the cliff dwellings on Route 15. Even if you're not planning to hike into the wilderness, it is wise to allow a full day for any trip to the Gila.

Also rewarding is a drive around the **western perimeter** of the Gila Wilderness, taking Route 180 west from Silver City, 63 miles to the little town of Glenwood. Just outside of Glenwood, to divert water for a small hydroelectric generator in the 1890s, a mining company suspended a water pipeline from the sheer rock walls of Whitewater Canyon. To maintain the pipeline, workers had to balance on it 20 feet above the river. Today the mining company and its pipeline are gone, but the forest service has installed a steel mesh walkway, known as **The Catwalk**, along the old pipeline route, affording visitors a unique look at this wild canyon. The upper end of **Whitewater Canyon** is a wilderness trailhead.

HIDDEN ▶

Three miles north of Glenwood, Route 159 turns off to the east and takes you four miles to **Mogollon**, one of New Mexico's most intriguing and beautifully located ghost towns. A silver and gold mining boomtown in the 1890s, Mogollon had a population of more than 2000—larger than in any town in the area today. It boasted a theater, several stores and saloons, two churches and two separate red light districts (one Anglo, the other Spanish). Many of Mogollon's historic wood and stone buildings still stand in various states of disrepair. One portion of the street was spruced up for use as a motion picture location in the 1970s, and since then a few people have taken up residence here during the summer months to restore old buildings, create artwork and engage in low-key tourist enterprises. However, fewer than a dozen people live here year-round.

Past Mogollon, the road turns to dirt, passable by regular automobiles but not by long motor homes or vehicles with trailers. It winds along the northern wilderness boundary through the **Mogollon Mountains**, the highest in the Gila with four peaks more than 10,000 feet high, giving access to several hiking trails, forest service campgrounds and fishing streams and lakes.

Seven miles north of Silver City on the way to Gila Cliff Dwellings via Route 15, the historic town of **Piños Altos** also offers a look at life in southwestern New Mexico a century ago. While this "ghost town" has never been completely abandoned, it is a mere shadow of its glory days.

Among the points of interest in Piños Altos are a replica of **Fort Webster** (also referred to as Santa Rita del Cobre)—the original was built to protect residents from marauding Apaches who lived in the Gila Wilderness—and a turn-of-the-century opera house. Also here are a gift shop built where Judge Roy "Law West of the Pecos" Bean's store was located before he moved to Texas, and the

Hearst Art Gallery, dedicated to the memory of William Randolph Hearst's father, who struck it rich mining in Piños Altos. Admission. ~ Main Street, Piños Altos.

Silver City is a pretty hillside town of 12,000 people, a quarter of them college students. Located in the Piños Altos foothills, the city's Victorian commercial district turns back the clock to frontier days. Bisected by a steep canyon, this town could easily be a set for a Hollywood Western. It's also the jump-off point for one of the state's most picturesque mountain ranges, the Mogollon.

The best sightseeing highlight in Silver City is the **Western New Mexico University Museum**. The museum has the world's largest collection of 700- to 1000-year-old Mimbres pottery, painted with the distinctive animal designs that have been revived as a popular decorative motif throughout southern New Mexico in recent years. One exhibit shows how symbols in some pottery pieces reveal that the Mimbres had advanced knowledge of astronomy. Not easy for visitors to find, the museum is in a three-story white building with peach-colored trim in the center of campus, which is on the hillside on the west side of town. ~ Top of 10th Street; 505-538-6386.

Silver City also has an interesting downtown historic district. While quite a few of the old buildings stand vacant, others provide space for art galleries and student-oriented stores. **Big Ditch Park,** a tree-lined 50-foot-deep arroyo with a small promenade, runs right through the center of town. In fact, it was originally Silver City's main street, but floods washed it away to its present depth, which explains why some of the original storefronts face the ditch instead of the street.

In the downtown area, the **Silver City Museum** displays Victorian-era frontier artifacts collected from ghost towns and ranches throughout the county. Closed Monday. ~ 312 West Broadway Street; 505-538-5921.

Silver City was home for a time to young **Billy the Kid**, as several minor historical sites attest. Downtown are the Antrim cabin, where Billy lived with his mother and stepfather, as well as the first

PANCHO VILLA STATE PARK

Cooperation between the United States and Mexico is commemorated by a monument at **Pancho Villa State Park,** a desert botanical garden where cholla, ocotillo, large prickly pears, century plants, tall yuccas and other plants of the Chihuahuan Desert grow in profusion on the slopes of the only hill around. Visitors may wish to drive the three miles to the border and walk across to the Mexican village of Palomas. Admission. ~ Corner of Routes 9 and 11, Columbus; 505-531-2711.

jail Billy ever escaped from—at the age of 15, while under arrest for robbing a Chinese laundry. His mother's grave is located on the east side of town. For information and tour maps contact the **Silver City/Grant County Chamber of Commerce.** ~ 1103 North Hudson Street; 505-538-3785.

One of the west's premiere ghost towns, **Shakespeare** flourished in an 1870s silver boom, when some 3000 miners came here seeking their fortunes. After a second boom played out in 1932, the town was purchased by the Hill family, which has done its best to preserve local history, going so far as to stage dramatic re-enactments of 19th-century Shakespeare murders and hangings. Guided tours take you to the old Butterfield stagecoach stop, a saloon, the Stratford Hotel and a gunpowder magazine. (Be sure to call ahead for a schedule of the two-hour tours conducted four times a year from February to September.) ~ Take Exit 22 off Route 10 at Lordsburg and follow the signs south two-and-a-half miles; 505-542-9034.

The sleepy little town of **Columbus** lies 32 miles south of Deming on Route 11. Its main claim to fame is that in 1916, Mexican revolutionary leader Pancho Villa invaded the United States with 1000 soldiers, intent on robbing a train carrying a gold shipment. His information was bad, and the train turned out to be carrying coal. After a battle in which 18 Americans and more than 100 Mexicans died, Villa and his men retreated into Mexico with General Pershing and 6000 United States soldiers with motor cars and airplanes in hot pursuit.

The story is recalled at the **Columbus Historical Society Museum** in the restored train station at the crossroads in the center of town and in the smaller state park museum in the old customs house building across the street. ~ Corner of Routes 9 and 11, Columbus; 505-531-2620.

LODGING

On the west side of the Gila Wilderness are a few accommodations in the little town of Glenwood. **Los Olmos Guest Ranch** has stone cabins scattered across several acres of lawn with shade trees. The rates include breakfast. The 13 stone and wood cabins are furnished Western-style, with woodframe beds, upholstered couches and chairs and original Western paintings. The larger cabins offer sitting areas. There are a swimming pool and hot tub on the premises, and bicycles are available for those who want to explore the village. This ranch also has horseshoe pits, a volleyball court and gameroom. Open from March through November. ~ 1 Los Olmos Road, Glenwood; phone/fax 505-539-2311. MODERATE.

Besides conventional motels, Silver City has a couple of special, surprisingly affordable places to stay. **The Palace Hotel** is a bed and breakfast in a former bank building (circa 1882) on the main street of the downtown historic district. The guest accommodations, which range from bath-down-the-hall bedrooms to three-room suites (with full bath), feature Territorial period furnishings and open onto a central sitting room where Continental breakfast is served each morning. ~ 106 West Broadway Street, Silver City; phone/fax 505-388-1811. BUDGET.

A lively ambience characterizes the **Carter House Bed and Breakfast Inn/AYH Hostel,** which features dormitory-style rooms with shared baths. Hostel guests are welcome to use the fully equipped kitchen. There are also five private "bed-and-breakfast" rooms—a full breakfast is included in the moderate prices—each with its own bath. Close to both the downtown area and the Gila Wilderness, this establishment is the ideal locale for the young and adventurous. ~ 101 North Cooper Street, Silver City; 505-388-5485. BUDGET TO MODERATE.

Deming, an agricultural and mining community on an interstate highway, holds no surprises where lodging is concerned. Every motel in town is budget-priced. The town's top-of-the-line hotel is **Grand Motor Inn.** ~ 1721 East Spruce Street, Deming; 505-546-2631, fax 505-546-4446. An older independent motel with rock-bottom rates is the **Mirador Motel.** ~ 501 East Pine Street, Deming; 505-546-2795, fax 505-546-2795. BUDGET.

Columbus, a little town about as far off in the middle of nowhere as any place that can be reached by highway, has a few unexpected touches of sophistication. One is **Martha's Place,** a bed and breakfast. The five elegant second-floor guest rooms have four-poster beds, cable TV and balconies overlooking the rooftops of this one-story town. ~ Main and Lima streets, Columbus; 505-531-2467, fax 505-531-2376. MODERATE.

◄ HIDDEN

DINING

From green enchilada plates to *huevos rancheros,* **Grandma T's** offers generous portions of New Mexican cuisine. This Territorial-style restaurant is a friendly place, planked with hardwood floors and cooled by Casablanca-style fans. Farmstead antiques and squash blossom jewelry complete the decor. ~ Main Street, Reserve; 505-533-6230. BUDGET TO MODERATE.

Silver City being a college town, most restaurants are budget priced. One irresistible breakfast spot is **Schadel's Bakery,** which serves a tasty assortment of baked goods café-style or to go. Closed Sunday mornings. ~ 212 North Bullard Street, Silver City; 505-538-3031. BUDGET.

The fanciest dining in the area is at the **Buckhorn Saloon** in the historic town of Piños Altos, seven miles north of Silver City on Route 15. The restaurant and saloon are in a beautifully restored adobe building from the 1860s with big stone fireplaces and elegant place settings. Steaks are the specialty. Closed Sunday. ~ 62 Main Street, Piños Altos; 505-538-9911. MODERATE TO DELUXE.

In between the chain fast-food places, Deming has a number of local restaurants that feature Mexican food. **La Fonda Restaurant** serves fajitas and has a good salad bar. ~ 601 East Pine Street, Deming; 505-546-0465. BUDGET TO MODERATE.

Sí Señor has stuffed *sopapillas* and red or green *huevos rancheros*. ~ Pine and Silver streets, Deming; 505-546-3938. BUDGET.

The **Grand Restaurant** features a comprehensive menu of steak, seafood and Mexican food. ~ 1721 East Spruce Street, Deming; 505-546-2632. MODERATE.

Even more authentic is the Mexican food at any of the nameless hole-in-the-wall taquerias across the border in Palomas—nothing fancy, but certainly foreign.

SHOPPING   The gift shop at the **Western New Mexico State University Museum** has a good selection of T-shirts, sweatshirts, coffee cups, tote bags, stationery and anything else they determined could brandish the unique Mimbres animal motifs from ancient pottery. ~ On campus, Silver City; 505-538-6386.

A number of local artists have studios in Silver City's downtown historic district. Many of them are well-hidden in the residential blocks north of Broadway. More than a dozen artists participate in monthly Saturday afternoon open studio tours organized by the **San Vicente Group.** ~ 505-388-2007.

NIGHTLIFE   Near Silver City, the historic **Buckhorn Saloon** in Piños Altos is as authentic as Old West saloons come, complete with a collection of paintings of nude women, a buffalo head on the wall and a potbelly stove to warm the saloon in winter. Closed Sunday. ~ 62 Main Street, Silver City; 505-538-9911.

Down in the town of Columbus, the favorite nighttime entertainment is to cross the border to Palomas, where **mariachi bands** perform on the plaza on weekend evenings.

PARKS   **LAKE ROBERTS** 🎣🚤🛶 Gila National Forest has a number of pretty little mountain lakes, of which Lake Roberts is the best known and most accessible. Boating and rainbow trout fishing (seasonally good) are popular on the 65-acre lake. The southeast shoreline is only accessible by foot trail or by boat (electric motors only). One of the two campgrounds is on a mesa overlooking the lake and the other is at the upper end of the lake. About a quarter-mile from the shoreline are some summer cabins. The park features a picnic area, restrooms and boat rentals. ~ Located just off Route 35 about three miles east of the intersection with Route 15 (a narrow mountain road), which is 25 miles north of Silver City on the way to Gila Cliff Dwellings; 505-536-2250.

▲ Mesa Campground has 24 sites; $7 per night. There are 12 additional sites at the upper end of the lake; $7 per night.

SNOW LAKE 🏃 🛶 ⛵ 🚤 🎣 This beautiful 100-acre mountain lake is at the north boundary of the Gila Wilderness at the foot of the Mogollon Mountains. Anglers consider it a great trout lake, especially in the springtime. Some people also catch, boil and eat the abundant crawfish. Use is limited to canoes, rowboats and other small boats without gas motors. There is a picnic area and restrooms. ~ Follow unpaved Route 78 from Mogollon for 30 miles. This is a slow, sometimes narrow, winding and quite scenic unpaved mountain road. It is passable by passenger cars when dry, but tight curves pose problems for long motor homes and towed vehicles. An alternate route is the 40-mile gravel Forest Road 141 from Reserve; 505-533-6231 or 505-533-6232.

▲ Dipping Vat Campground has 40 sites overlooking the lake; $5 per night. No-fee primitive camping is allowed at the north end of the lake outside the recreational boundaries.

CITY OF ROCKS STATE PARK 🏃 South of Silver City on the way to Deming, this park makes an extraordinary spot for a picnic stop. At first sight, it appears to be a no-big-deal rockpile in an otherwise featureless desert marred by open-pit copper mines. As you approach, the strangeness of this little geological park becomes apparent. Picnic sites surround a rock dome that has been fractured and eroded into a fantastic maze of oddly shaped stone monoliths and passages that form a natural playground that children and the young at heart can explore for hours. It is impossible to get lost in the maze, since the park road surrounds it on all sides. The park has a visitors center, restrooms and showers; day-use fee, $3. ~ Located several miles off of Route 180, 20 miles south of Silver City and 24 miles north of Route 10 at Deming; 505-536-2800.

▲ There are 52 sites, six with hookups; $7 per night for tent sites; $11 per night with hookups.

ROCK HOUND STATE PARK 🏃 Mainly of interest to rock collectors in search of the garnets and other semiprecious stones found here, the park has the best public campground in the Deming-Columbus area and offers a close-up look at the arid, rocky slopes of the Florida Mountains. The park features trails, a visitors center, a picnic area, a playground, restrooms and showers; day-use fee, $3. ~ Located 14 miles southeast of Deming off Route 143; 505-546-6182.

▲ There are 33 sites, 27 with hookups; $7 per night for tent sites, $11 per night for hookups.

▼▼▼▼▼▼▼▼▼▼▼▼▼▼▼
Outdoor Adventures

SKIING

Even though you're pretty far south, the high elevations here translate into good skiing. You can swoosh down a 12,000-foot mountain at an Indian-owned resort, or explore the backcountry on skinny skis. So strap the boards on your feet and take to the hills!

SOUTHEASTERN NEW MEXICO Ski Apache, 16 miles northwest of Ruidoso on the slopes of 12,003-foot Sierra Blanca, is one of New Mexico's most popular downhill ski areas. Owned and operated by the Mescalero Apache Indians, Ski Apache has 52 runs and trails. ~ 505-336-4356.

Some trails and primitive roads in **Lincoln National Forest** outside Ruidoso are used for cross-country skiing in the winter. For current trail information and snow conditions, contact the **Smokey Bear Ranger Station.** ~ Ruidoso; 505-257-4095.

Snow Canyon has one chairlift and two surface lifts serving 21 runs. It is at a lower elevation than Ski Apache, and snow conditions can vary despite nightly snow making. Lift tickets cost considerably less than at Ski Apache. ~ 505-682-2333.

SOUTH CENTRAL NEW MEXICO There are well-groomed cross-country tracks at the **Lodge at Cloudcroft Nordic Ski Center,** where ski rentals and lessons are available. ~ 505-682-2566.

RIDING STABLES

Although this region is full of horse-breeding ranches, southern New Mexico offers surprisingly little in the way of public horse rentals or tours.

SOUTHEASTERN NEW MEXICO In Ruidoso, rent horses at the **Inn of the Mountain Gods.** ~ 505-257-5141. Also in the Ruidoso area is **Buddy's Stable.** ~ Gavilan Canyon Road; 505-258-4027. **Cowboy Stables** leads rides. ~ 1764 West Route 70; 505-378-8217.

SOUTH CENTRAL NEW MEXICO In Las Cruces, **Circle S Stables** offers guided part-day and full-day trips into the Organ Mountains from November through April. ~ Baylor Canyon Road; 505-382-7708.

GOLF

Despite the arid climate, golf enthusiasts manage to keep Southern New Mexico green. Grab your caddy and head to one of several private or municipal courses. Fore!

SOUTHEASTERN NEW MEXICO To tee off in southeastern New Mexico head to the **Lake Carlsbad Municipal Golf Course.** ~ 901 Muscatel Avenue, Carlsbad; 505-885-5444. In Roswell, check out **Spring River Golf Course.** ~ 1612 West 8th Street; 505-622-9506. Closed during winter but open the rest of the year is the course at **Inn of the Mountain Gods.** ~ Ruidoso; 505-257-5141. **The Links at Sierra Blanca** is another winning golf course in Ruidoso. ~ 105 Sierra Blanca Drive, Ruidoso; 505-258-5330.

SOUTH CENTRAL NEW MEXICO Play the greens at the **Carrizozo Golf Course**. ~ Route 380, Carrizozo; 505-648-9984. Visitors to the Alamogordo area can work on their swing at the **Alamogordo Municipal Golf Course**. ~ 2351 Hamilton Road, Alamogordo; 505-437-0290. Play a round in Cloudcroft at **The Lodge Golf Course**. ~ 1 Lodge Road; 505-682-2098. Nearby is the **Ponderosa Pines Golf Course**, closed during winter. ~ 878 Cox Canyon Road, Cloudcroft; 505-682-2995.

SOUTHWESTERN NEW MEXICO The New Mexico State University Golf Course is right on campus. ~ Silver City; 505-646-3219. Also in Silver City is the **Scott Park Memorial Municipal Golf Course**. ~ Silver City; 505-538-5041. Hopefully your concentration won't put your game in jeopardy at the **Truth or Consequences Golf Course**. ~ 685 Marie Street, Truth or Consequences; 505-894-2603.

TENNIS

Tennis is pretty scarce in this neck of the woods, but there are some courts to be found.

SOUTHEASTERN NEW MEXICO Courts are available at **Carlsbad Municipal Park**. ~ 505-887-1980. In Roswell, try **Cahoon Park**. ~ West 8th Street. For a fee, nonguests can use the courts at **Inn of the Mountain Gods** near Ruidoso. ~ 505-257-5141.

SOUTH CENTRAL NEW MEXICO In Las Cruces, public courts are at **Apodaca Park** (Madrid Road at Solano Drive), **Lions Park** (Picacho and Melendres streets), **Young Park** (Nevada and Walnut streets) and **Frenger Park** (Park Drive). Call the Las Cruces Parks and Recreation Department for information. ~ 505-526-0519.

BIKING

Low-elevation summers can be sweltering, and high-elevation winters can be frigid, but aside from climatical concerns, cyclists will find good places to pedal in Southern New Mexico. You'll even find a few shops offering rentals, cycling equipment and ride recommendations.

SOUTHEASTERN NEW MEXICO The nine-and-a-half-mile unpaved scenic drive that begins near the visitors center in **Carlsbad Caverns National Park** makes for a good mountain bike ride during the spring or autumn. (In summer months, it's too hot and often has too much car traffic for enjoyable biking.)

In the Roswell area, cyclists ride the back roads in the ranchlands east of town, particularly the paved roads through **Bitter Lakes National Wildlife Refuge** and **Bottomless Lakes State Park**.

Mountain bikers around Ruidoso use the six-mile unpaved forest road from the Ski Apache Road up to Monjeau Campground or any of several jeep roads going into the national forest around Bonito Lake.

SOUTHWESTERN NEW MEXICO Mountain bikes are not allowed within the Gila Wilderness, but several jeep roads in the **Piños Altos** area lead into other parts of the national forest. Ambitious cyclists may wish to tackle unpaved Route 78, which skirts the northern boundary of the wilderness beyond Mogollon.

Bike Rentals Rent bikes in Ruidoso at **Rocky Mountain Sports**. ~ Mechum Drive; 505-258-3224.

In Silver City, the place for mountain-bike rentals is **Gila Hike & Bike**, which offers free information sheets on day hikes, road rides and mountain-bike rides in Gila National Forest. ~ 103 East College Street; 505-388-3222.

HIKING   Whether your interests lean toward history, geology, panoramic views or just plain exercise, you'll find hiking options in this area tempting. Explore a quarter-mile-long cave on your own; scale the steep sides of Sierra Blanca; find the grave of the notorious Apache Kid; or examine ancient petroglyphs and cliff dwellings. Happy trails!

SOUTHEASTERN NEW MEXICO About Three-fourths of **Carlsbad Caverns National Park** is a wilderness area restricted to horse and foot travel, with an extensive trail system. Some of the trails are accessed from the scenic drive that starts near the visitors center, while others start from inconspicuous dirt roads off of Route 62/180.

One of the more interesting hikes is **Yucca Canyon** (2.5 miles), which leads through piñon and oak forest and past old cabins to cool Longview Spring, with a magnificent view of the Carlsbad Caverns Wilderness.

Near the Yucca Canyon trailhead, another trail leads up to **Goat Cave** (3 miles). The cave is only about a quarter of a mile long, but the size of its single room is impressive. Persons wishing to enter the cave must first obtain a special permit (a process that can take a month) from the **Cave Resource Office** (505-785-2232 ext. 63) at the Carlsbad Caverns visitors center, which is also the place to ask for up-to-date information on these and numerous other hikes in the national park.

Lincoln National Forest has a network of more than 50 miles of trails throughout the **White Mountain Wilderness** northwest of Ruidoso.

From the Ski Apache ski area, a five-mile trail leads to the summit of **Sierra Blanca**, the highest mountain in southern New Mexico. This is a strenuous hike with an elevation gain of 2100 feet. In summer and fall, people hike to the summit to enjoy the spectacular view.

Another great hike is up **Argentina Canyon** (2.5 miles) with its lush ancient forest and streams fed by mountain springs. The trail starts at the end of the road past Bonito Lake, which leaves Route 48 exactly 12 miles north of Ruidoso.

SOUTH CENTRAL NEW MEXICO A favorite hiking trail in this part of the state is **Three Rivers Trail** (6 miles), which starts at the national forest campground at the end of the unpaved road beyond Three Rivers Petroglyph Site, midway between Carrizozo and Alamogordo. Eventually the trail climbs up to Elk Point on the north side of Sierra Blanca, where it intersects several other major trails leading to all parts of the wilderness area. Many more hikers enter the wilderness from the other side, near Ruidoso, than from Three Rivers.

The main feature of **Oliver Lee Memorial State Park** (505-437-8284), ten miles south of Alamogordo, is Dog Canyon, a hidden oasis in the barren-looking foothills of the Sacramento Mountains. The easy **Dog Canyon Interpretive Trail** (.5 mile) runs from the visitors center up along a small creek between steep slopes covered with ocatillo and giant prickly pear cacti to a lovely little spring seeping out of the canyon wall.

The steeper, longer **Dog Canyon National Recreation Trail** (14 miles) follows a different route and reaches a higher spring. The trail continues, climbing out of the canyon to a high ridgeline. Note that this trail rises 3000 feet in elevation, making it a very challenging hike.

In the Organ Mountains just east of Las Cruces, the easy **Dripping Springs Trail** (1.5 miles) leads up a steep-walled canyon to Dripping Springs, the former site of a stage stop, a major turn-of-the-century resort and a tuberculosis sanitarium.

The **San Mateo Mountains** west of Truth or Consequences are probably the least-visited mountains in New Mexico. This is a beautiful area characterized by rugged, narrow canyons. It is hot for summer hiking but far enough south to be relatively snow-free in the early spring.

✔ **CHECK THESE OUT—UNIQUE OUTDOOR ADVENTURES**
- Scuba dive (in New Mexico?) at **Bottomless Lakes State Park**, and explore the collapsed underground salt caves. *page 437*
- Drop a line for channel catfish, bass and walleye pike at **Caballo Lake State Park**, with its 70 miles of shoreline. *page 445*
- Search for garnets and other semiprecious stones on the slopes of the Florida Mountains at **Rock Hound State Park**. *page 453*
- Swoosh down one of the 52 runs at **Ski Apache**, a popular downhill ski area owned by the Mescalero Apache Indians. *page 454*

The heart of the San Mateos is the 45,000-acre Apache Kid Wilderness. The main route through the wilderness is the **Apache Kid Trail** (a total of 21.1 miles, 12.9 of which are located within the Apache Kid Wilderness), an ambitious hike that follows Nogal Canyon for about a mile from the trailhead at Cibola National Forest's Springtime Campground and then climbs steeply to the upper ridge of the mountains. Several side trails lead to hidden canyons and midway along the trail is the Apache Kid's gravesite, where he was shot down by local ranchers.

The Apache Kid Wilderness was named for a renegade who hid out here in the late 19th century.

SOUTHWESTERN NEW MEXICO The **Gila Wilderness** is restricted to just foot and horse travel, and more than 400 miles of trails extend to all areas of the wilderness. Several guidebooks devoted to hiking trails in the Gila Wilderness are locally available in Silver City. A few of the top hiking options in the Gila include:

The **West Fork Trail** (33.5 miles) is the longest trail in the Gila Wilderness, and for the first five miles the most used trail. For an adventurous day hike, follow the trail upriver about three miles to a narrow, deep section of canyon where caves containing ancient cliff dwellings can be seen high on the sheer rock faces. The trail fords the cold river 23 times in the six-mile trip.

Those planning longer backpacking trips should note that the trails following the river forks from the Gila Cliff Dwellings area all eventually climb several thousand feet from canyon floors to mountain slopes. A less strenuous approach to the Gila high country is to hike one of the numerous trails that cross the unpaved forest route from Mogollon to Snow Lake on the north boundary of the wilderness. The trails there start at higher altitudes, so less climbing is involved.

Nine major side trails branch off the **Crest Trail** (12 miles), which starts at the marked Sandy Point trailhead, 14 miles up the road from the ghost town of Mogollon. Through lush ancient forest, the main trail climbs to the crest of the mountain range and follows it to the 10,770-foot summit of Mogollon Baldy, where an old fire-lookout station affords a panoramic view of boundless wilderness. It is a moderate two- to three-day backpacking expedition. For a one-day hike, take the first four miles of the trail to Hummingbird Spring.

Another major Gila hiking area, the **Aldo Leopold Wilderness**, is accessible from the top of 8100-foot Emory Pass on Route 152, the most direct way from interstate Route 25 to the Gila Cliff Dwellings. The main trail runs north from the pass through stately ponderosa and Douglas fir forest up 10,011-foot **Hillsboro Peak** (5 miles). On the way up the mountain, it intersects six other major trails that go to all corners of the wilderness.

Carlsbad and Roswell are on **Route 285**, a two-lane
highway that crosses unpopulated plains from Santa Fe
all the way to Del Rio, Texas. The distance from either
Santa Fe or Albuquerque is about 200 miles to Roswell and another 100 miles to Carlsbad Caverns National Park. From El Paso,
it is a 150-mile drive to Carlsbad Caverns via **Route 62/180**.

▼▼▼▼▼▼▼▼▼▼
Transportation

CAR

Ruidoso and Lincoln are both about 65 miles west of Roswell
via **Route 70/380**. The highway forks 47 miles west of Roswell at
Hondo, with Route 70 going to Ruidoso and Route 380 going to
Lincoln.

Two highway corridors run north-and-south through south
central New Mexico: interstate **Route 25** along the Rio Grande
through Truth or Consequences and Las Cruces, and the more interesting and isolated **Route 54** down the Tularosa Valley through
Carrizozo and Alamogordo. Both highways lead to El Paso, Texas.
Four-lane **Route 70/82** links Alamogordo with Las Cruces, making a weekend loop tour of the south central area an enjoyable
possibility.

Southwestern New Mexico is the most remote, undeveloped
part of the state. The most convenient hub for exploring this area
is Silver City, 52 miles north of **Route 10**. An apparent shortcut,
Route 152 from Route 25 south of Truth or Consequences over
the Mimbres Mountains to Silver City, saves mileage but not much
time compared to driving south to Deming and then north again.

Mesa Airlines (800-637-2247) provides passenger service to Carlsbad's **Cavern City Air Terminal** and the **Roswell Industrial Air
Center** from Albuquerque. Mesa Airlines also flies into the **Alamogordo Municipal Airport** as well as the **Las Cruces Municipal Airport** and the **Silver City-Grant County Airport**.

AIR

Many visitors to Carlsbad Caverns fly into the airport at El
Paso, Texas, and rent cars for the trip to the caverns. American
Airlines, America West, Continental Airlines, Delta Airlines and
Southwest Airlines service **El Paso International Airport**. ~ 915-
772-4271.

Silver Stage Lines shuttles passengers from Deming to the international airport in El Paso. ~ 800-522-0162. In Alamogordo,
airport transportation is available from **Alamo–El Paso Shuttle Service**. ~ 505-437-1472. In Las Cruces, call **Las Cruces Shuttle Service**.
~ 505-525-1784.

In the southeastern part of the state, **TNM&O Coaches** has daily
bus service to the terminals in Carlsbad, Roswell, Ruidoso and
Alamogordo. ~ Carlsbad: 1000 South Canyon Street; 505-887-
1108. Roswell: 1100 North Virginia Street; 505-622-2510. Rui-

BUS

doso: 138 Service Road; 505-257-2660. Alamogordo: 601 North White Sands Boulevard; 505-437-3050.

Greyhound Bus Lines serves Las Cruces, Truth or Consequences, Deming and Lordsburg. ~ Reservations: 800-231-2222. Las Cruces: 490 North Valley Drive; 505-524-8518. Truth or Consequences: 507 South Broadway; 505-894-3649. Deming: 300 East Spruce Street; 505-546-3881. Lordsburg: 112 Wabash; 505-542-3412.

CAR RENTALS

In Carlsbad, **McCausland Rent A Car** has its agency at the Cavern City Air Terminal. ~ 800-654-3131. **Independent Auto Rental** offers free airport pickup and delivery. ~ 505-887-1469.

Avis Rent A Car operates from the airport in Alamogordo. ~ 800-331-1212. In Las Cruces, call **Hertz Rent A Car**. ~ Located at the Hilton; 800-654-3131.

Grimes Aviation services the Silver City–Grant County Airport. ~ 505-538-2142, 800-725-2142. **Taylor Car Rental** offers pickup and delivery from the airport. ~ 505-388-1800. Another agency offering the same service is **Ugly Duckling Rent A Car**. ~ 800-528-1584.

At the El Paso airport try **Advantage Rent A Car** (800-777-5500), **Alamo Rent A Car** (800-327-9633), **Avis Rent A Car** (800-331-1212), **Budget Rent A Car** (800-527-0700), **Dollar Rent A Car** (800-800-4000), **Hertz Rent A Car** (800-654-3131) or **National Interrent** (800-328-4567).

TAXIS

Local transportation is provided in the Carlsbad area by **Cavern City Cab Co.** ~ 505-887-0994. In Alamogordo, taxi service is provided by **Radio Cab Company**. ~ 505-437-2292. In Las Cruces, **Yellow Cab/Checker Cab** supplies citywide service. ~ 505-524-1711. **Silver City–Grant County Taxi** also serves Silver City. ~ 505-538-1852.

FOURTEEN

Southwestern Utah

A child's jumbo-size crayon box couldn't contain all the pastels, reds, violets, greens and blues found in the unspoiled lands of southwestern Utah. What's most striking about this country is not only that it has managed to avoid the grasp of developers but also that it's been seemingly skipped by the hands of time. This place puts the letter "p" in pristine.

For starters, consider national parks like Zion, established in 1919, and Bryce, declared a park in 1924. Ever popular, these facilities draw hoards of visitors who go away satisfied without even realizing that the wild beauty of Capitol Reef National Park is close by. Added to this hidden treasure, not more than a few hours away are state parks like Goblin Valley, Kodachrome Basin, Escalante Petrified Forest and the Anasazi Indian Village.

The area we call southwestern Utah is bordered roughly by the Henry Mountains to the east, Vermilion Cliffs and Beaver Dam Mountains to the south and the arid Great Basin to the west. A unique topographic variety is contained within these lands, as high mountain lakes and forests overlook the twisted rock found in Capitol Reef and Goblin Valley. Ever-evolving sculptured rock pinnacles in Bryce coexist adjacent to bristlecone pines, thought to be the oldest living things on earth.

Generally low humidity and rainfall in the lower elevations provide a favorable growing climate for the rare Joshua trees, sagebrush and yucca, while up high the aspen and pine trees, oaks and juniper flourish.

Until recently, the powers in charge appeared to be in no hurry to sell this land. That is really no surprise. Despite being a primary connector, scenic Route 12 between Escalante and Torrey was paved only in the late 1980s. The rugged Henry Mountains, which abut Capitol Reef National Park, were the last range in this country to be charted, and herds of buffalo still roam freely as do bighorn sheep, antelope and bear. The little town of Boulder, hometown to Anasazi State Park, was the very last place in the 45th state to switch over to modern carriers after having its mail delivered by mule team for half a century.

Promotional efforts have begun to expand the possibilities for "Color Country," yet even the construction of skyscrapers couldn't detract from the rainbow-hued rocks, endless forests, lush gardens and those many, many waterways.

Southwestern Utah offers lakes and creeks like Panguitch, Gunlock and Quail brimming with fish not fishermen, hiking trails crying out for someone to traipse over them, ski areas with volumes of snow and biking areas that aren't freeways. Ghost towns have probably stayed that way for a reason.

Working ranches have not yet disappeared, and some towns appear to have more horses than people. The area has managed to remain true to its Western heritage as rodeos are a popular diversion in the summertime. The rugged terrain is well suited to these sturdy beasts. Probably the most famous quote about the area was made by 19th-century pioneer Ebenezer Bryce who said, "It's a hell of a place to lose a cow."

Among the landowners there's still a certain genuine country courtesy that can be traced to their Mormon traditions and culture rooted in a strong work ethic and family values. The accommodations and places to eat reflect this same simplicity in which clean air and water, a good church community and schools are reason enough to celebrate life. But don't be concerned that everything here is rustic. In the resorts and larger cities such as St. George and Cedar City, there are plenty of comfortable places to stay and a range of decent eateries. And while Utah's liquor laws are still a bit confusing and the number of clubs and taverns is limited, the state has made progress in simplifying the process of getting a drink. One unique practice here is the state's "private" nightclubs, which actually are open to the public but require dues (essentially a cover charge) for the evening.

Mind you, in the outlying areas, at times you're better off sleeping under the stars and using the local grocery for main meals. But isn't there a certain beauty in this contrast?

Nor should you fear that this is a cultural wasteland. The Utah Shakespearean Festival, based in Cedar City, draws thousands of theater-lovers to the region each summer. And the internationally acclaimed American Folk Ballet calls Cedar City home as well. Concerts, plays, dance companies and more are booked into large convention complexes and tiny high school auditoriums alike. Both Dixie College in St. George and Cedar City's Southern Utah University are known for their academic excellence.

Still, it's the church that remains the heart of the area. Brigham Young, the Mormon prophet himself, sent 309 families to colonize this corner of Utah in the winter of 1861. While those settlers were less than enthralled by their move to a wilderness, Young envisioned sprawling communities. St. George and Cedar City today are the realization of his dream. And despite some of the misgivings of the settlers, structures such as the towering St. George Temple or more modest Mormon Tabernacle serve as testament to the hard-working and dedicated pioneers who tamed the land with their newfound-irrigation techniques and made the desert bloom.

American Indians once claimed title to this land, beginning with the Desert Gatherers, who were thought to inhabit southwestern Utah about the time of Christ. These American Indians learned gardening skills and built small settlements and

crafted pottery. Another culture, the Anasazi, were agriculturalists who built homes into the rock.

Historians believe the Indians of the desert evolved into the Fremont culture, which disappeared from the area during the 1200s. The more modern-day Paiutes now live in small reservations, having relinquished their territory to early white settlers.

Snow Canyon has served as movie location for several films including *Butch Cassidy and the Sundance Kid.*

Lately, snowbirds and retirees have latched onto Utah's Dixie (so called because the area first served as a cotton mission for the Mormon Church, and the warm, dry, almost subtropical climate reminds many of the South). Their varied backgrounds and interests have infused the region with new life and a desire to grow.

Local city leaders, realizing the region's natural beauty is its greatest resource, work to attract small industry to the area to create jobs that will keep the younger generation here as well. They even *boast* of the "golden arches" along main thoroughfares. Until the 1980s, few national franchises thought enough of southwestern Utah to try their luck. But in less than a decade, cities like St. George have doubled in size.

In this verdant valley among towering cliffs, another modern amenity is taking root: golf courses. Springing up like dandelions, they are taking hold wherever a stretch of land lies vacant. Be it dawn of a June day or high noon in December, you can find someone teeing off the front nine.

But no matter how much growth booms, it only takes a few moments to step back in history. The old courthouses located in Panguitch, Kanab and St. George reflect the best of pioneer architecture. Historic Hurricane Valley Pioneer Park captures the essence of the region's unique history, and hamlets such as Santa Clara, Pine Valley and Leeds are filled with pioneer homes and churches, arranged in traditional grid patterns with the church as the epicenter.

Whether you are looking for the old or the new, want to hit the greens or the greenery, southwestern Utah is waiting. Perhaps for you, too, Utah's Dixie will turn out to be the promised land.

St. George Area

St. George is not only a winter resort for snowbirds and retirees but also a key gateway to Zion National Park, Cedar Breaks National Monument and Snow Canyon State Park. The area is also a historical gold mine, full of restored homes, buildings from the 1800s and fascinating ghost towns.

The city began when Brigham Young sent some 300 families from the lush land of northern Utah to the southern Utah desert. Young envisioned a huge cotton mission that could supplement the West's supply during the Civil War, which had cut off shipments from the South.

Though initially successful, the cotton mission (and one to grow silkworms as well) ultimately failed because of an inability to compete in the marketplace after the end of the Civil War. However, a warm climate and bevy of recreational activities eventually made St. George the fastest-growing city in the state.

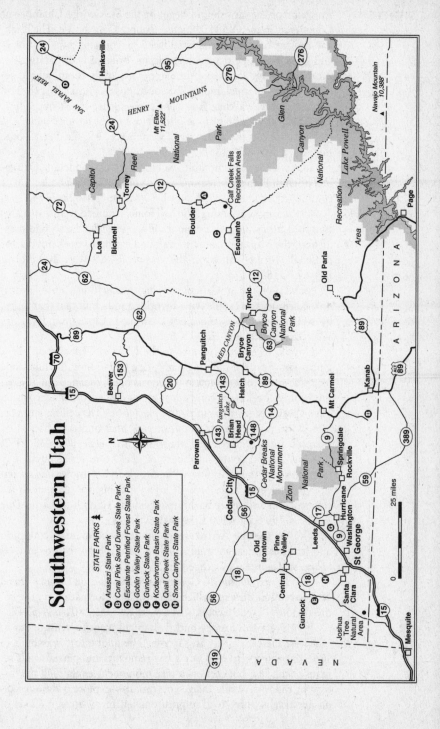

Southwestern Utah

STATE PARKS
A Anasazi State Park
B Coral Pink Sand Dunes State Park
C Escalante Petrified Forest State Park
D Goblin Valley State Park
E Gunlock State Park
F Kodachrome Basin State Park
G Quail Creek State Park
H Snow Canyon State Park

25 miles

0

SIGHTS

Any tour of the city should begin at the **St. George Chamber of Commerce**, in the Old Washington County Courthouse. The brick-and-mortar building, completed in 1876, contains panels of original glass alongside the entrance doors, original wall paintings of Zion and Grand canyons in the upper assembly room, an old security vault and much more. The courthouse serves as first stop on the **St. George Walking Tour**. The three-square-block trek points out 22 sights including some of the city's finest pioneer buildings. Pick up a map at the Chamber of Commerce. ~ 97 East St. George Boulevard; 801-628-1658.

Some of the more notable walking-tour sights include **Daughters of Utah Pioneer Museum**, where you'll see a vast collection of community artifacts. ~ 145 North 100 East; 801-628-7274.

At the **Brigham Young Winter Home**, a guided tour showcases beautiful furnishings and memorabilia owned by the second president of the Mormon Church. Fruit and mulberry trees (fodder for those silkworms) still cover the grounds. ~ 89 West 200 North; 801-673-5181.

Stop 13 on the St. George walking tour is **Judd's Store**, a turn-of-the-century mercantile with a working soda fountain that dishes up welcome treats on those hot Utah days. Closed Sunday. ~ 62 West Tabernacle; 801-628-2596.

It took 13 years to complete the **Mormon Tabernacle**. Tour guides show off the building with pride telling how the limestone for three-foot-thick basement walls was hand quarried and the red sandstone blocks were hand cut stone by stone from a nearby site. Take special note of the intricate, plaster-of-Paris ceiling and cornice work, all shipped to California by boat and then hauled by wagon team to St. George. ~ Main and Tabernacle; 801-628-4072.

Only card-carrying members of the Mormon Church may tread through the sparkling-white **St. George Temple**, but an on-site visitors center does provide a pictorial history of the temple's construction and other background on the Church of Latter Day Saints. ~ 490 South 300 East; 801-673-5181.

The **St. George Art Museum** houses a permanent collection and features rotating exhibits. ~ 175 East 200 North, lower level of the St. George City office building; 801-674-4256.

Also located within St. George is the **Washington County Travel & Convention Bureau**, which can provide information on the entire region. ~ Dixie Center, 425 South 700 East; 801-634-5747.

If you're a real history buff, you might want to venture out to **Old Fort Pierce**, east of St. George. The adobe fort was built in 1866 to protect settlers. Only a few remnants and partial walls remain at the site, but there is a nice monument explaining the history of the fort. While there, you can also explore a series of **dinosaur tracks** (three-toed impressions left in the mud millions of years ago). Getting to Old Fort Pierce and the tracks requires a high-clearance vehicle and dry roads. ~ Follow 700 South to the east until it becomes River Road and take an immediate left on Stake Farm Road. Then follow the signs.

Twenty-five miles north of St. George on Route 18 is the town of Central and the turnoff to **Pine Valley**, a mountain hamlet with a picturesque, satin-white chapel that's believed to be the oldest Mormon chapel still in continuous use. Nestled in the Dixie National Forest, surrounded by 10,000-foot peaks and ponderosa pine, is the Pine Valley campground and reservoir with numerous picnicking areas.

Just north of the Pine Valley turnoff is a stone marker for the **Mountain Meadows Massacre Site and Memorial**. Here, in 1857, a group of emigrants—120 men, women and children—en route to California was slaughtered by Mormons and Indians. The event is considered a dark period in Mormon history and one the church has tried to live down ever since. ~ Route 18.

After visiting Pine Valley, backtrack to Route 18 and travel 22 miles south to the **Snow Canyon State Park** turnoff. Along the way are numerous extinct volcanic cones and lava fields, many beckoning to be explored. A small park, the canyon itself is a white-and-red mix of Navajo sandstone covered with black lava beds. Elevations range from 2600 to 3500 feet atop the cindercones. Grasses, willows, cacti and other shrubbery peer through cracks. Evidence of early man's impressions of Snow Canyon can be seen at several petroglyph sites within the park. ~ Route 18; 801-628-2255.

Leaving the canyon, you'll pass through Ivins and then connect with the rural community of Santa Clara three miles west of St. George. Settled by Swiss immigrants, Santa Clara lays claim to the house built by noted missionary, Indian agent and colonizer Jacob Hamblin. Built in 1862, the rough-hewn, red sandstone **Jacob Hamblin Home** clearly demonstrates the sturdiness of frontier

✔ CHECK THESE OUT—UNIQUE SIGHTS

- Join the tour guides at the **Mormon Tabernacle**, where they proudly tell the story of how the edifice was built from hand-cut stone. *page 466*
- Gaze out over sandstone monuments named for the Biblical figures Abraham, Isaac and Jacob at **Court of the Patriarchs**. *page 473*
- Stand in awe as you take in the gallery of spires, columns and arches awash with varying shades of pastels at **Cedar Breaks National Monument**. *page 482*
- Hike the mile-plus trail to **Bryce Point** for breathtaking views of the monument's nature-hewn amphitheater. *page 488*

construction designed to withstand Indian attack and showcases a number of furnishings and tools from that period. ~ Route 91, Santa Clara; 801-673-2161.

Head south on Route 91 over the summit to the Beaver Dam Slope. As you drive toward the Arizona border you'll pass the 1040-acre, desert-like **Joshua Tree Natural Area**, claimed to be the farthest north these picturesque trees grow. ~ Route 91.

Route 91 connects with Route 15 at Beaver Dam. Head north back toward St. George and drive through the Virgin River Gorge, a giant gash in the rocky earth where the Virgin River heads out of Utah through Arizona and into Nevada. It took 12 years to build this 23-mile stretch of spectacular highway.

Center of the cotton mission, the **Washington Cotton Mill** is a long, rock building constructed in 1865. You can still tour the historic, two-and-a-half-story structure, which is now used for weddings, family reunions and club meetings. The mill is generally open business hours, but call ahead to check. ~ 375 West Telegraph, Washington City; 801-673-0375.

HIDDEN ▶

In search of prehistoric creatures? A short (200-yard) walk takes adventurous souls to more **dinosaur tracks**. Drive to the center of Washington City and turn north on Main until you pass under Route 15. Follow the dirt road north and turn right at the road that goes up the hill to the pink water tank. Park here, then walk up the road to a chained cable gate. Turn right and walk northeast to a deep wash. Go down into the wash and follow it downstream until you find a flat, greenish slab of rock. Here you'll find the foot-long tracks from another age.

Halfway between St. George and Zion National Park on Route 9 lies the town of **Hurricane** (pronounced hur-i-kun), a rural community that often attracts the overflow from Zion into its motels and restaurants. In the center of town lies **Pioneer Heritage Park**. The museum and information center stands amid a grassy lawn filled with pioneer-era wagons and farm machinery. The museum depicts the history of the town and displays pioneer items including an authentic kitchen. ~ 35 West State Street; 801-635-3245.

A relaxing break from the rigors of the road may be found at **Pah Tempe Hot Springs**, a large grouping of five soaking- and swimming-pool areas. Rustic but congenial, Pah Tempe resembles a '60s commune with a tiny bed and breakfast, lodge and campsites. Bathing suits are required. Massage therapy programs, facial packs and other services can be arranged. ~ 825 North 800 East, Hurricane; 801-635-2879.

LODGING

Located at the mid-point between Salt Lake City and Los Angeles, St. George is awash in hotels, motels and bed and breakfasts. Virtually every chain is represented, making it simple to find one that meets your requirements and pocketbook.

No one walks away unsatisfied from the **Seven Wives Inn**, per- ◄ *HIDDEN*
haps some of the nicest accommodations in St. George. Deluxe in
every way except price, the 12-room bed and breakfast is graciously decorated in Victorian antiques. Some rooms boast fireplaces or woodburning stoves, and most have outside doors to
porches or balconies. All have private bath. Rates include a huge
gourmet breakfast in the elegant dining room and use of the swimming pool. ~ 217 North 100 West, St. George; 801-628-3737,
800-600-3737. MODERATE.

There's a lot of bang for the buck at **Ranch Inn**. More than half
the 52 units are classified "kitchenette suites," meaning they house
a microwave oven, refrigerator, conversation-and-dining area, plus
fully tiled bath with mirrored vanity. Indoor jacuzzi, sauna, guest
laundry and heated pool round out the amenities. ~ 1040 South
Main, St. George; 801-628-8000, 800-332-0400. MODERATE.

Situated off the main drag, **Ramada Inn** offers quiet refuge. An
expansive lobby provides portal to 136 rooms, each with desk and
upholstered chairs. The hotel also has one of the prettiest swimming-
pool settings with palm trees surrounding the site. Free continental breakfast is included. ~ 1440 East St. George Boulevard, St.
George; 801-628-2828, 800-713-9435, fax 801-628-0505. MOD-
ERATE TO DELUXE.

The streamlined architecture of **Best Western Coral Hills Motel**
is reminiscent of *The Jetsons*, but the 98 rooms are more down-to-
earth with carpeting, upholstered chairs and dark woods. Indoor
and outdoor swimming pools, spas, putting green and exercise
room are bonuses. ~ 125 East St. George Boulevard, St. George;
801-673-4844, 800-542-7733, fax 801-673-5352. MODERATE.

Holiday Inn at St. George likes to think of itself as a complete
recreational facility. Besides the well-appointed rooms, restaurant
and atrium-style lobby (with mini-waterfall), guests are treated to
a large indoor/outdoor heated swimming pool (you can actually

---

✔ CHECK THESE OUT—UNIQUE LODGING

- *Budget to moderate:* Revel in the warm hospitality, and savor the home-
  cooking at **Zion House Bed and Breakfast**. *page 478*
- *Moderate:* Tuck yourself in at the **Seven Wives Inn**, graciously decorated
  with Victorian antiques. *page 469*
- *Moderate to deluxe:* Slip back in time and stay at **Bryce Canyon Lodge**,
  the only surviving lodge built by the Union Pacific Railroad. *page 490*
- *Deluxe to ultra-deluxe:* Soak in a jacuzzi at **Brian Head Hotel** after
  hours of testing the alpine ski slopes. *page 483*

Budget: under $50 Moderate: $50–$90 Deluxe: $90–$120 Ultra-deluxe: over $120

swim in and out of the hotel), whirlpool, tennis court, putting green, mini-gym, gameroom, video arcade, gift shop and children's play area. ~ 850 South Bluff Street, St. George; 801-628-4235, 800-457-9800, fax 801-628-8157. MODERATE.

The **Bluffs Motel** seems to offer two of everything: double queen suites, two TVs, two phones, even two king suites with private jacuzzi. The 33 rooms are exceptionally well decorated in soft tones and enjoy large bathrooms and a living-room area. There's also an outdoor heated pool and jacuzzi. Complimentary continental breakfast is offered in the sunny lobby. ~ 1140 South Bluff Street, St. George; 801-628-6699, 800-832-5933. BUDGET TO MODERATE.

A collection of pioneer homes makes up **Greene Gate Village**, a unique bed-and-breakfast complex designed to intrigue and delight. Surrounded by a flower-laden courtyard, manicured lawns, swimming pool and garden hot tub, the village boasts elegant decor—wallpapered rooms, duvets, antique furnishings, plump pillows—and a conscientious staff. Four rooms have large whirlpool tubs. A delicious country breakfast completes the picture. ~ 62-78 West Tabernacle, St. George; 801-628-6999, 800-350-6999, fax 801-628-6989. MODERATE TO DELUXE.

The **Best Western Weston's Lamplighter Motel** in Hurricane offers 64 units that are attractively furnished. A pool/ jacuzzi provides respite after a day of touring. ~ 280 West State, Hurricane; 801-635-4647, fax 801-635-0848. MODERATE.

DINING

St. George doesn't lack for choices when it comes to places to eat. Besides the requisite chains (and none are missing), there are plenty that offer a hearty meal at a reasonable cost. At least this side of Utah has heard of the salad bar.

Perched on the third floor of the Tower Building in Ancestor Square, **J. J. Hunan Chinese Restaurant** appears to be the area's choice for Asian cuisine. Seafood, chicken, beef, duck, pork—it's all here presented in a gracious manner. ~ 2 West St. George Boulevard, St. George; 801-628-7219. BUDGET TO MODERATE.

Fajitas are tops at **Pancho & Lefty's**, a busy, fun Mexican restaurant. The menu also features tostadas, burritos and tacos. ~ 1050 South Bluff Street, St. George; 801-628-4772. BUDGET.

Grab a shaded table outside and enjoy a tall glass of iced raspberry tea at **Libby Lorraine's**. The bistro-style café features an array of sandwiches (like the Caribbean—crab and bay shrimp in sour cream and dill dressing on a croissant) and pastas, such as fettuccine alfredo and spaghetti with marinara sauce. Closed Sunday. ~ 1035 Valley View Drive, St. George; 801-673-7190. MODERATE.

Greenery galore and waitresses dressed in early English garb lend a cozy, historic air to **Andelin's Gable House**, unequivocally St. George's finest dining establishment. Patrons here choose from an elegant, deluxe-priced five-course dinner or a moderately priced à la carte menu. Regardless, all are served with pewter mugs and plates and taste delicious. Noteworthy à la carte choices are the roast brisket of beef, orange roughy and chicken pot pie. Save room for dessert. Closed Sunday. ~ 290 East St. George Boulevard, St. George; 801-673-6796. MODERATE TO DELUXE.

Service is erratic, but **The Palms Restaurant** can be a good choice for family dining in a pleasant setting. Besides an extensive salad bar with homemade soups and breads, dinner choices range from roast turkey to mountain trout to chicken teriyaki. Sandwiches, hamburgers and salads comprise the lunch menu, while breakfast includes omelettes and griddle items. ~ Holiday Inn, 850 South Bluff Street, St. George; 801-628-4235. BUDGET TO MODERATE.

SHOPPING

Shopping in this region is pretty much designed with locals in mind. You'll find a few shopping malls and strip centers but little else. One place of note is the **Artist Gallery**, which carries works by more than a dozen regional artists. ~ #5 Ancestor Square, St. George Boulevard and Main, St. George; 801-628-9293.

NIGHTLIFE

World-class entertainers are spotlighted through the **Celebrity Concert Series**. ~ Dixie Center, 425 South 700 East, St. George; 801-628-7003.

The **Southwest Symphony**, a community orchestra, and the **Southwest Symphonic Chorale** perform throughout the year in the M. C. Cox Auditorium. ~ Dixie Center, 425 South 700 East, St. George; 801-628-7003.

Dixie College Theater offers plays and musicals during the school year. ~ 225 South 700 East, St. George; 801-652-7800.

The **Blarney Stone** is a beer bar serving a lively crowd. There's live classic rock music on weekends. ~ 64 North 800 East St. George Boulevard; 801-673-9191.

PARKS

SNOW CANYON STATE PARK Black lava rock crusted over red Navajo sandstone make for a striking visual effect in this colorful canyon. Several volcanic cones welcome visitors to the northern end of the 65,000-acre park, considered a treat for photographers. The park features a covered group-use pavilion, picnic areas, restrooms and hot showers; day-use fee, $4. ~ On Route 18 five miles northwest of St. George; 801-628-2255.

▲ There are 35 sites (including 14 with partial hookups); $10 to $12 per night; reservations recommended in spring and fall. There's a sewage disposal station.

GUNLOCK STATE PARK This 240-acre reservoir is noted for its superb year-round boating, waterskiing and bass fishing. Nestled in the rugged ravine of the Santa Clara River, the reservoir's waters abut redrock hills dotted with green shrubbery. There are restrooms; day-use fee, $3. ~ On old Route 91, 16 miles northwest of St. George; 801-628-2255.

▲ Primitive camping allowed within the camp. Note: You'll have to bring your own drinking water.

QUAIL CREEK STATE PARK Stark rock escarpments surround the 600-acre reservoir with a state park set on its west shore. Quail Creek attracts anglers eager to reel in bass, trout, crappie and bluegill. Besides being an ideal site for camping and picnicking, Quail Creek is noted for its waterskiing, boating and windsurfing. There are picnic areas and restrooms; day-use fee, $3; ~ Located on Route 9, 14 miles north of St. George; 801-879-2378.

▲ There are 23 sites; $8 per night.

RED CLIFFS RECREATION SITE Maintained by the Bureau of Land Management, this camping area is a red-rock paradise at the foot of the Pine Valley Mountains. Desert trees and plants crowd every campsite. Facilities include picnic tables, pit toilets and drinking water. ~ From St. George go north on Route 15 about 17 miles to the Leeds exit. From there, it's four-and-one-half miles south; 801-628-4491.

▲ There are ten sites; $6 per night.

Zion Area

If you've got rocks in your head, you've come to the right place. This is not to question your sanity but rather to underline the spectacular rock formations found here. From canyon walls to monuments to cliffs, the Zion Area has it all. Coupled with this are some neat historic buildings and movie-set towns that have been featured in hundreds of films.

SIGHTS

It's easy to see why the popularity of **Zion National Park** has zoomed in the past few years. Extremely accessible year-round, with a wide variety of hiking trails geared to all abilities, this "heavenly city of God" is a park for all people. Admission. ~ Main entrance: Route 9, Springdale; 801-772-3256.

Grandfather of Utah's national parks, Zion is packed with precipitous canyon walls and massive stone monoliths. Vividly colored cliffs, sheer-rock walls and unique formations make this park one of the state's most popular attractions.

This 127,000-acre park was carved almost singlehandedly by the Virgin River, which flows along the canyon floor. Cottonwoods, willows and velvet ash trees line the river, providing an ever-changing kaleidoscope of colors as one season follows another. To really avoid the crowds and traffic, gear your visit to November through April. Otherwise expect lots of cars, nonexistent parking and lots of other travelers.

Standing guard over the park entrance is **The Watchman**, a 2600-foot monolith of sandstone and shale. Some believe early American Indians may have considered the massive stone formation a symbol of Zion's power.

Be sure to stop at the **Visitors Center** where park rangers are happy to provide maps, brochures and backcountry permits. Specific dates and times for naturalist guided walks, evening programs and patio talks are posted at the center. ~ Located one and a half miles from the entrance.

Youngsters ages six through twelve can get down and dirty with nature at the **Zion Nature Center** through the Junior Ranger Program. From June through Labor Day, park rangers and the Zion Natural History Association conduct a variety of outdoor-adventure and environmental-science programs that acquaint the younger set with everything from the flight pattern of a golden eagle to the difference between a Utah beavertail cactus and a maidenhair fern.

Depending on time and specific interest, you can drive, bicycle or take a guided tram tour through Zion. But don't miss out on the fabulous sights that await just off the roads. Zion is best appreciated close-up, and you'll miss the true majesty of the park if you don't wander around.

Zion Canyon Scenic Drive takes visitors about six-and-a-half miles into the heart of Zion Canyon and its 2000-to-3000-foot-high walls carved inch-by-inch by the Virgin River cutting through the Markagunt Plateau. Just past the entrance you're likely to spot **West Temple**, the highest peak in Zion's southern section. Notice the delineated strata of rock as it rises 4100 feet from base to peak.

One of the first places you might want to pause is **Court of the Patriarchs** viewpoint. From here you can see reverently named monuments like the Streaked Wall, the Sentinel, the Patriarchs (a series of three peaks called Abraham, Isaac and Jacob), Mt. Moroni, the Spearhead and the sheer-walled sandstone monolith Angels Landing, perched 1500 feet above the canyon bed. To the east and above are two other monuments, Mountain of the Sun and the Twin Brothers.

Emerald Pools parking area, two-and-a-half miles up the Scenic Drive, offers access to a trail network serving both the Upper and Lower pools. A creek from Heaps Canyon sends water cascading down waterfalls into pools below. Yucca, cacti and scrub oak line the trail to the upper pool, and the path affords views of shaded, north-facing slopes rich with ponderosa pine and Douglas fir. If you happen to visit Zion between mid-October and late November, this is a prime spot to see the changing colors.

The **Grotto Picnic Area** is the perfect spot to take a break from exploring the park. Here in the cool shade of broadleaf trees and gamble oak you'll find fire grates, picnic tables, water and restrooms.

Pay close attention and you might spot the tiny Zion snail, a creature found in Zion National Park and nowhere else.

Driving the road you'll spot **The Great White Throne** on the east side. Notice how this 2400-foot megalith ranges in color from a deep red at the base to pink to gray to white at the top. The color variations arise because the Navajo sandstone has less iron oxide at the top than the bottom.

A bit farther is a short, paved walk that leads to **Weeping Rock** where continuous springs "weep" across a grotto. Even on a hot day, the spot remains cool. Like other parts of Zion, you should see lush, hanging cliff gardens thick with columbine, shooting-stars and scarlet monkeyflower.

The end of the road, so to speak, comes at **Temple of Sina-wava**, perhaps the easiest area in the park to access. This huge natural amphitheater swarms with visitors enthralled by the sheer, red cliffs that soar to the sky and two stone pillars—the Altar and the Pulpit—in the center. There's a large parking area at the temple, but it fills quickly, so you may be forced to park up to a mile away alongside the Canyon Drive and hoof it in.

Route 9 branches off of Zion Canyon Drive and heads east from Zion National Park on what is called the **Zion–Mount Carmel Highway**. Considered an engineering marvel for its day (1930), the road snakes up high precipices and around sharp, narrow turns before reaching the high, arid plateaus of the east. And, if you've ever ridden Disneyland's Matterhorn, you'll love the mile-long, narrow, unlit tunnel. Rangers control traffic through the darkened tube, stopping drivers when an oversized truck or recreational vehicle is passing through. Even with some delays, the tunnel is a treat with huge, window-like openings allowing sunlight to stream in every so often, affording unparalleled views of the vermilion cliffsides. And was that the Abominable Snowman behind that rock?

On the east side of the tunnel lies the park's "slickrock" territory. It's almost like a time warp from one country to another.

Canyon Overlook is a moderately easy, half-mile self-guided walk on the Zion–Mt. Carmel Highway just east of the long tunnel. Unlike the lush Zion Canyon floor, this area showcases plants and animals that make rock and sand their home. The overlook itself provides views of lower Zion Canyon including the Streaked Wall with its long, black marks sharply contrasting with the red canyon walls; West and East Temples, giant stone monoliths with temple-like edifices perched on top; and the massive, multicolored cliff called Towers of the Virgin.

Don't miss **Checkerboard Mesa**, a prime example of sandstone etched over time with horizontal lines and vertical fractures to resemble a mountainous playing board. You stay on Route 9 out of Zion National Park to connect with Route 89 and head south toward the Arizona border.

All that's missing is the surf at **Coral Pink Sand Dunes State Park**. This is Mother Nature's sandbox just aching to be frolicked in by young and old alike. Some of the dunes reach a couple hundred feet in height. A resident park ranger is on hand to answer questions about this unusual area, and there are a few interpretive signs as well. But those who prefer sand to water will revel in the inviting dunes. ~ Located 12 miles off Route 89 between Mt. Carmel Junction and Kanab; 801-874-2408.

Continuing on Route 89, you'll pass what looks like a giant dinosaur jutting out of a mountainside. That's **Moqui Cave**, which claims the largest collection of dinosaur tracks in the Kanab area. Other displays include Indian artifacts, foreign money and fluorescent minerals. Open only from March through November. Admission. ~ Route 89.

Farther south, Route 89 heads toward the base of the colorful Vermillion Cliffs and **Kanab**, a town known as "Little Hollywood" for the more than 200 movies, most of them B-grade Westerns, filmed in the area. Today, Kanab is a crossroads for travelers headed to Lake Powell, the Grand Canyon or Bryce and has numerous motels and restaurants.

Some movie-set towns are still evident throughout the area. Because most sit on private property, it's safest to check with the **Kane County Travel Information Center** for the latest information on which are open to the public. ~ 78 South 100 East, Kanab; 801-644-5033.

In Kanab, a bit like the Universal Studios tour is **Frontier Movie Town**, a replica of a Wild West movie set that caters to groups but lets individuals tag along. Here, marshals in white hats battle black-hatted villains during mock gunfights. You can walk along the boardwalk and peer into the false store fronts. Shops, a snack bar and historic exhibits are also on-site. The town is only open from March through October. ~ 297 West Center; 801-644-5337.

Heritage House, located at 100 South Main, is an 1886 restored pioneer mansion built of brick and red rock and one of 13 homes making up the Kanab walking tour. You can find brochures at the house or at Kanab's city offices. ~ 76 North Main; 801-644-2534.

Thirty miles east along Route 89 takes you to the **Old Paria** turnoff. Here, fans will find the West of their imaginations come alive on a falsefront movie-set town that's open to the public and was once used for the *Gunsmoke* television series. Some also use

Text continued on page 478.

Ghost Towns of Color Country

While much of Utah's history is neatly preserved in museums and restored homes, a more fascinating (and sometimes poignant) look can be found in the ruins of towns eroded by time, nature and man. Golf courses and condominiums cover most of the region's early settlements, but a few sites remain where you can let your imagination run wild.

Two of the most popular and representative ghost towns of southwestern Utah are Silver Reef and Grafton, as diverse as two cities can be while both paying homage to the pioneers who forged a wilderness state.

"Silver!" was the cry that brought more than 1000 fortune-hunters to the town of **Silver Reef**. According to newspaper accounts, Silver Reef was the only spot in the United States where silver was discovered in a sandstone reef. John Kemple is credited with the 1866 find, and the town boomed into a notorious camp of 1500 (non-Mormon) miners. Citizens of nearby Mormon communities were warned not to mix with the rowdy populace rumored to participate in brawls, shootings and lynchings. With 29 mines scattered over two square miles, Silver Reef proved bountiful, yielding $8 million in silver before shutting down in 1910.

Today little remains, although area historians are slowly working to restore the community. Fittingly, the **Wells Fargo & Co. Express Building**, constructed in 1877 of sandstone blocks and metal doors, survived the ravages of time. It now houses the **Silver Reef Museum**. Authentic mining tools, maps, clothing and other historic paraphernalia fill shelves and glass cases. Old newspapers recount Silver Reef's heyday, and town plats show how vast the boomtown spread. Visitors can even walk into the original Wells Fargo bank vault. Closed Sunday. ~ 801-879-2254.

Half the Wells Fargo building is used by Western bronze sculptor Jerry Anderson as a **studio and gallery**. Both his work and that of other prominent local artists are displayed and sold, along with a good assortment of books recounting Utah's ghost towns. Closed Sunday. ~ 801-879-2254.

Nearby is a small structure that once served as Powder House (for a fun exercise, have your traveling companions guess what this was). Today, Powder House functions as the Silver Reef information center with models of the original township and more original plats. The bank building is home to the **Silver Reef Gallery and Gifts**, a gift store with antiques, collectibles and the like. Closed Sunday. ~ 801-879-2750.

It only takes a few minutes to drive around and look at the nearby stone ruins scattered among a new neighborhood development. At the site of the Barbee and Walker Mill, which began operating in 1887, all that remains are rock walls; likewise the drugstore and Chinese laundry.

While most Utah ghost towns lie in a stark desert environment, **Grafton** is an exception. Amid vast fields, mulberry trees and rambling cattle, the abandoned settlement sits beside the Virgin River near the redrock cliffs of Zion National Park.

Five Mormon families settled Grafton in 1859, naming the town after a Massachusetts community. Assisted by then-friendly Paiute Indians, the families dammed the Virgin River for irrigation hoping to plant cotton. In 1862, a flood ravaged the entire area and swept away homes, barns and fields. Survivors moved their settlement to higher and safer ground, digging a system of canals and ditches. Besides cotton, they planted corn, wheat and tobacco. By 1865, 200 acres were cultivated.

Later, Indian attacks disrupted community life. Settlers were killed in alarming numbers, and Grafton residents were forced to work the fields in armed bands. Occasionally, the entire town was evacuated. After the Indian threat eased in the 1870s, the settlers obtained Brigham Young's permission to plant mulberry trees and grow silkworms.

Grafton headed toward ghost town status after 1907, as persistent problems became too much for the settlers to face. But the quaint village charmed Hollywood, and since 1950 many films, including scenes from *Butch Cassidy and the Sundance Kid*, have been filmed here. Several of the buildings still stand, including a few woodframe homes and the one-room, brick schoolhouse with small belltower. All are open for exploring.

Victims of Indian attacks and other Grafton settlers are buried in the well-maintained Mormon cemetery that lies on the road southeast of town. The cemetery is also open to the public.

To get to Silver Reef, go north on Route 15 about 17 miles to the Leeds exit. Head east one mile through town to a sign marked "Silver Reef." Turn north under the freeway and drive about two miles.

For Grafton, take Route 9 (the road to Zion National Park) to the town of Rockville. Turn south on Bridge Lane, which crosses the Virgin River. After crossing the bridge, head west and backtrack along a rutted, dirt-and-gravel road several miles. Note that in some sections you are crossing or bordering private land so don't abuse the privilege.

Route 89 as a backdoor entrance to Lake Powell, with the highway continuing into Page, Arizona.

LODGING Massive vermilion cliffs surround **Zion National Park Lodge**, located in the heart of the park. A huge, manicured lawn and shade trees welcome guests to the property, which includes motel-style rooms, suites and cabins. While standard furnishings are the norm, location is everything. Cabins afford more privacy and feature fireplaces and private porches. Dining room, snack bar and gift shop are on-site. ~ Zion National Park; 303-297-2757, fax 303-297-3175. MODERATE TO DELUXE.

Rooms at **Flanigan's Inn** range from okay to very nice indeed. Those on a budget might opt for the smaller, somewhat plain rooms. If you place a value on spaciousness, splurge on the larger, suite-like spaces done in oak furnishings with tile baths, bentwillow wall hangings and ceiling fans. Regardless of room, hotel guests can partake of the swimming pool and continental breakfast. ~ 428 Zion Park Boulevard, Springdale; 801-772-3244, 800-765-7787, fax 801-772-3396. MODERATE.

American and English antique furniture fills **O'Toole's Under the Eaves Guest House**. Constructed of sandstone blocks from nearby canyon walls, the home resembles a cheery English cottage. Four rooms have private baths, another two share. Full breakfast is served each morning, and guests can sip a cup of tea in the outdoor gazebo that fairly bursts with flowers. ~ 980 Zion Park Boulevard, Springdale; 801-772-3457. MODERATE TO DELUXE.

HIDDEN ► Located in a quiet neighborhood, **Harvest House Bed and Breakfast** is sure to please even the most demanding. All four rooms are exquisitely decorated in what the owners term "urban eclectic." Expect bright, airy spaces full of wicker furniture, private baths, plush carpeting and balconies with an unparalleled view of Zion National Park. Beverages are available anytime from the dining room wet bar, and there's an extensive library of art and cookbooks. Stargazing from the backyard hot tub is a great way to end the day. A gourmet breakfast is included in the price. ~ 29 Canyon View Drive, Springdale; 801-772-3880, fax 801-772-3833. MODERATE.

Tree-shaded lawns and gardens mark the **Best Western Driftwood Lodge**. Forty-seven oversized rooms bring the outdoors inside with oak furniture and Southwestern artwork, some of it by local artists. A gift shop, outdoor swimming pool and complimentary continental breakfast are nice pluses. ~ 1515 Zion Park Boulevard, Springdale; 801-772-3262, fax 801-772-3702. MODERATE.

Nothing fancy, but good home cooking and warm hospitality are hallmarks of **Zion House Bed and Breakfast**. Two guest rooms offer private baths, two others share. All of the rooms have terrific views. Guests can swap tales of park adventures in the comfortable communal sitting room. A family-style breakfast is served. ~ 801 Zion Park Boulevard, Springdale; 801-772-3281. BUDGET TO MODERATE.

If you must overnight in Kanab, plan to stay at the **Shilo Inn**. The 119 mini-suites are nicely decorated in soft blues and pinks; all include microwaves and refrigerators. Extra amenities including free continental breakfast and fresh fruit raise the complex well above the motel crowd. Plus, there's a swimming pool and spa, gift shop and guest laundry. ~ 296 West 100 North, Kanab; 801-644-2562, 800-222-2244, fax 503-641-1326. MODERATE.

DINING

Located right in the heart of Zion National Park, **Zion Lodge Restaurant** satisfies every appetite with bountiful breakfasts, hearty lunches and gourmet dinners. Hamburgers, salads, seafood and steak are pleasantly presented amid the beauty of Zion. Reservations are required for dinner. ~ Zion National Park; 801-772-3213. MODERATE.

◄ HIDDEN

The rustic appearance of **Bit and Spur Saloon and Mexican Restaurant** belies what many consider Utah's best Mexican restaurant. The menu focuses on traditional cuisine such as flautas and tostadas. Dinner only. Closed Tuesday and Wednesday November through March. ~ 1212 Zion Park Boulevard, Springdale; 801-772-3498. MODERATE.

You can't miss at **Flanigan's Inn Restaurant**. The bright, airy establishment serves up healthy portions of everything from Road Creek Ranch trout to pasta, chicken and beef dishes. The menu also features a wild-game dish. Reservations are recommended for dinner. ~ 428 Zion Park Boulevard, Springdale; 801-772-3244. MODERATE.

✔ CHECK THESE OUT—UNIQUE DINING

- *Budget:* Hankering for a pizza? Make your way to **Pizza Place** for *the* best pizza pie this side of Chicago. *page 491*
- *Budget to moderate:* Don't be afraid to stroll into the livestock market (livestock market?) for a fine taste of the West at **Market Grill**. *page 484*
- *Moderate:* You don't have to go far for a hearty meal in Zion National Park—pop into the **Zion Lodge Restaurant**, located in the heart of the park. *page 479*
- *Moderate to deluxe:* Journey back to merry olde England at **Andelin's Gable House**, where the food is stylishly served on pewter and the cuisine is delicious. *page 470*

Budget: under $8 Moderate: $8–$16 Deluxe: $16–$24 Ultra-deluxe: over $24

NIGHTLIFE   The Grand Circle: National Park Odyssey is a treat for the senses at the O. C. Tanner Amphitheater, May through September. The production takes viewers through Zion National Park and other nearby national treasures. The amphitheater also provides other top entertainment. Admission. ~ Springdale; 801-652-7994.

There are dances every Saturday night at the **Kanab Movie Theater**. ~ 29 West Center Street, Kanab; 801-644-2334.

PARKS   **ZION NATIONAL PARK** 🚶 🚲 🏇 A true gem. Sheer, towering cliffs surround the verdant floor of Zion Canyon as lush hanging gardens and waterfalls stand in marked contrast to the desertlike terrain of stark rock formations and etched redrock walls. There are guided walks and a hiker shuttle service can be arranged through the on-site visitors center. Facilities here include picnic areas, a restaurant, a snack bar, a gift shop and restrooms. The $5 vehicle fee is good for seven days. ~ Main entrance is one mile north of Springdale via Route 9. The east entrance is 25 miles west of Mt. Carmel Junction along Route 9. A one-mile tunnel connects Zion Canyon with plateaus on the east. Buses and many recreational vehicles are too large to navigate the tunnel in two-way traffic, so traffic may be temporarily halted. (The tunnel fee for oversized vehicles is $10); 801-772-3256.

▲ There are about 400 sites in two campgrounds; $8 per night. Primitive camping allowed with permit.

CORAL PINK SAND DUNES STATE PARK 🚶 The beach comes to Utah at this expansive site of coral-pink sand dunes. Visitors here are encouraged to play in the six square miles of sand, ride off-road vehicles or build a sand castle or two. There are restrooms and showers; day-use fee, $3. ~ Located on Route 89 about 25 miles northwest of Kanab; 801-648-2800.

▲ There are 22 sites; $10 per night.

▼▼▼▼▼▼▼▼▼▼▼▼
Cedar City Area   Though now called "Festival City" because of its ties to the Utah Shakespearean Festival, it was iron that initially brought Mormon pioneers to Cedar City. Early Utah settlers worried about the lack of iron ore, and when deposits were discovered in the mountain 15 miles west of what is now Cedar City, an iron mission was established in 1851. Despite initial success, the foundry closed a mere seven years later, but Cedar City managed to survive and today hosts numerous cultural and sporting events.

SIGHTS   One of the best ways to fully explore Cedar City is via the **Historical Tour**. Fourteen sites spread throughout the city are featured, giving visitors a true sense of the entire community. Grab a tour map at the **Cedar City Chamber of Commerce**, which also supplies brochures and helpful advice on what to do in the area. ~ 286 North Main; 801-586-4022.

Iron Mission State Park gives a comprehensive look at early Cedar City and the original foundry. But the park's real show-stopper is the Gronway Parry Horse-Drawn Vehicle Collection. Spanning the late 1800s and early 1900s, there are buggies, surreys, mail carts, sleighs, a bullet-scarred stagecoach, a white hearse and a water-sprinkling wagon. All are in tip-top shape and a real kick to explore. Admission. ~ 585 North Main, Cedar City; 801-586-9290.

Rock Church was built by Cedar City residents during the Depression with native materials and donated labor. Red cedar adorns the interior and benches of the chapel, while the colorful stones (including iron, copper and gold ore) on the exterior were carefully matched. ~ Center and 100 East, Cedar City; 801-586-8475.

Located on the Southern Utah University campus is the **Braithwaite Fine Arts Gallery**, which hosts art exhibits of all types throughout the year. ~ 801-586-5432.

Sixteen miles north of Cedar City on Route 15, the small community of **Parowan** (southern Utah's oldest town) evokes a Western atmosphere with a strong heritage. Gateway to Brian Head Ski Area and Cedar Breaks, Parowan has a few motels and restaurants among many examples of original pioneer architecture.

Old Irontown, 21 miles west of Cedar City on Route 56, still displays remnants of open-pit mining operations of the 1800s. A coke oven, foundry and blast furnace are on-site.

In sharp contrast to the manic crowds at the main section of Zion National Park, the **Kolob Canyons** entrance is virtually deserted. Arches, cliffs and mountains point like fingers to the sky in this part of the park, which claims one of the world's largest free-standing arches. A small visitors center offers backcountry permits and information including an invaluable interpretive auto-drive pamphlet that guides you to 14 stops along the five-and-a-half-mile road into the Finger Canyons of the Kolob. Deeply colored cliffs of vermilion and goldenrod mark Kolob Canyon, a markedly

A MIDSUMMER'S NIGHT . . . PERFORMANCE

Those visiting Cedar City between late June and late August should take in a performance at the renowned **Utah Shakespearean Festival**. Six plays rotate afternoons and evenings at two theaters on the campus of **Southern Utah University**. Even if you can't attend a performance, an authentic re-creation of the Tiring House Theater of Shakespeare's era shows Shakespearean displays and costumes during the festival season in the foyer of the Southern Utah University Auditorium. ~ 351 West Center, Cedar City; 801-586-7700.

different section of Zion. A huge rock scar just left of Shuntavi Butte is the result of a cataclysmic break of the cliff from the rock face in 1983. ~ Just off Route 15 at Exit 40, 17 miles south of Cedar City; 801-586-9548.

Kolob Canyons Viewpoint provides the ideal spot from which to view the canyon walls of massive Navajo sandstone laid down as windblown dunes 150 million years ago that now extend as fingers into the edge of the high terrace. ~ Located at the end of Kolob Canyons Road.

Though a product of the same natural forces that shaped Zion and Bryce, **Cedar Breaks National Monument** clearly holds its own. You head east from Cedar City along Route 14 then turn north on Route 148. The drive through huge glades of evergreen forest doesn't adequately prepare the viewer for the grandeur of the brilliant rock amphitheater. The jaded may surmise they've driven to 10,350 feet for nothing until they look out the huge glass windows of the visitors center. Admission. ~ Route 148; 801-586-9451.

Like the coliseum of ancient Rome, Cedar Breaks is expansive and wide. Only here, visitors gaze upon a natural gallery of stone spires, columns and arches instead of warring gladiators. The sheer cliffs reveal a candy store of colors—lavenders, saffrons and crimsons—all melted together and washed across the rocks.

In marked contrast to the flowers are the bristlecone pines, called the "Methuselah" of trees. Small stands grow on the relatively poor limestone soil that is within and along the rim of the amphitheater. One gnarled and weatherbeaten pine that can be seen from the Wasatch Ramparts Trail near Spectra Point on the breaks' rim is estimated to be more than 1600 years old.

A five-mile road accesses the park's main attractions. Four scenic overlooks, trailheads and all visitor services are on or near the road. Heavy snows close the road during the winter, but the park is open for cross-country skiing and snowmobiling via Brian Head Resort.

Continuing east on Route 14 past the Cedar Breaks entrance, you'll come to **Navajo Lake** and **Duck Creek Reservoir**, splendid spots both known for their trout fishing. Formed by lava flows that left no drainages, Navajo Lake drains through sinkholes that sit beneath the surface and feed water into Duck Creek.

HISTORICAL GRAFFITI

Just over ten miles northwest of Parowan are the **Parowan Gap Petroglyphs**, a bountiful example of ancient Indian rock art etched on a canyon wall. The crude drawings of animals and men date back more than 2000 years to a time when the canyon was a major passageway for the Indians. ~ Head north on Main and then take Route 130 for 19 miles to get there.

The grassy meadows and groves of aspen also surround **Duck Creek Village**, a hamlet best known as the film location for *My Friend Flicka* and *How the West Was Won*. Duck Creek is often frequented by cross-country skiers eager to lay tracks on the extensive trails.

Worth a visit is **Mammoth Cave**, a network of lava tubes that include a two-tiered section of tunnel. Be sure to bring flashlights to explore the cave. To get there from Duck Creek Village, take Route 14 one mile east to Mammoth Creek Road. Follow Mammoth Creek Road north about five miles. A sign to the caves will mark a dirt road on the right, which will take you three miles to the caves. The Duck Creek visitors center has information on the caves. ~ Visitors center: Route 14, one and a half miles east of Duck Creek Village.

◄ *HIDDEN*

LODGING

Paxman Bed and Breakfast House is a turn-of-the-century, two-story, brick farmhouse with three porches. Tastefully decorated with antiques, the upper floor has a small sitting room surrounded by three bedrooms, each with private bath. A main-floor master bedroom is available in the summer. There are homemade baked goods every morning. ~ 170 North 400 West, Cedar City; 801-586-3755. MODERATE.

The **Quality Inn**, a three-story, brick building, has 50 guest rooms furnished in typical hotel fashion—one king or two queen beds, small sitting area, dark-wood dresser and headboards. A large swimming pool (open during the summer) and complimentary continental breakfast are nice touches, and the staff is extremely cordial. ~ 18 South Main, Cedar City; 801-586-2433, 800-228-5151, fax 801-586-4425. BUDGET TO MODERATE.

Holiday Inn Cedar City is one of the area's prettier properties with amenities including restaurant and lounge, pool, sauna, whirlpool and exercise room. As Cedar City has no taxi service, the van shuttle service to the airport is especially handy. ~ 1575 West 200 North, Cedar City; 801-586-8888, 800-432-8828, fax 801-586-1010. MODERATE.

Cedar City's largest hotel is the **Best Western Town & Country Inn**. The hotel is split into two parts, the main motor inn and a newer annex across the street. Rooms are outfitted with typical Best Western aplomb, and guests can use either of the two swimming pools (one enclosed during the winter), spa and gameroom. ~ 200 North Main, Cedar City; 801-586-9900, 800-528-1234, fax 801-586-1664. MODERATE.

French provincial meets nouveau Southwest at the **Brian Head Hotel**, Brian Head ski resort's premier property. Well-appointed, large rooms decorated in warm desert colors give skiers plenty of places to hang their hat . . . and their goggles and gloves and other accouterments. Jacuzzi baths help work out the après-ski kinks. Or visit the on-site exercise room. ~ Route 143, Brian Head; 801-677-3000, 800-272-7426, fax 801-677-3883. DELUXE TO ULTRA-DELUXE.

Brian Head, like all ski resorts, has many, many condominiums of all shapes and sizes for rent. Contact **Brian Head Condominium Reservations** for information. ~ P.O. Box 190217, Brian Head, UT 84719; 801-677-2045, 800-722-4742, fax 801-677-3881.

DINING

Adriana's is one of the busiest restaurants in Cedar City. In keeping with the town's Shakespearean bent, Adriana's features dining in an Old World atmosphere. Châteaubriand is featured nightly along with chicken cordon bleu, fresh jumbo shrimp, filet mignon and pork chops. Reservations recommended. Closed Sunday. ~ 164 South 100 West, Cedar City; 801-865-1234. DELUXE.

You wouldn't expect quality grub inside a livestock market, but the **Market Grill** delivers just that. From hearty country breakfasts to ribeye steaks and chicken fried steak, the grill is a taste of the West. Closed Sunday. ~ 2290 West 400 North, Cedar City; 801-586-9325. BUDGET TO MODERATE.

An extensive menu geared to family dining makes **Sullivan's Café** a popular choice. Sandwiches, soups, salads, steaks, egg dishes and pancakes are among the bountiful selections. The upscale La Tajada Room offers steak, seafood and Italian dishes in a more intimate atmosphere. ~ 86 South Main, Cedar City; 801-586-6761. BUDGET TO MODERATE.

Like its St. George counterpart, **Pancho & Lefty's** serves tasty Mexican fare. ~ 2107 North Main, Cedar City; 801-586-7501. BUDGET TO MODERATE.

HIDDEN ►

A real find is **Yogurt Junction**. Diners snuggle in booths, while a model train encircles the room from above. Besides the requisite yogurt treats, the café serves up hearty soups in a bread bowl, sandwiches and yummy, fresh-baked rolls. Closed Sunday. ~ Cedar South Mall, 911 South Main, Cedar City; 801-586-2345. BUDGET.

At the Brian Head ski area, Brian Head Hotel's **Summit Grill** offers plenty of pasta dishes, fish and fowl of the day and an impressive wine list. Dinner only. Closed for one month before and one month after ski season. ~ Route 143, Brian Head; 801-677-3000. MODERATE.

Also at the Brian Head Hotel, the **Columbine Cafe** serves breakfast and lunch. Closed for one month before and one month after ski season. ~ Route 143, Brian Head; 801-677-3000. BUDGET.

Innovative chicken dishes find their place amid steaks and beef brochettes at the **Edge Restaurant**, which features hearty meals and a nice après-ski ambience. Opens and closes with the ski season. ~ Route 143, Brian Head; 801-677-3343. MODERATE.

Catch ski fever just by walking into **George's Ski Shop**, where you've probably never seen so much merchandise crammed into a single chalet. Past season's gear is discounted for those who really don't care about this year's colors. A variety of skis plus knowledgeable advice make this the ski shop of choice at Brian Head. ~ Reached by chairlift 1, Brian Head; 801-677-2013.

For nordic gear and maps in the wintertime, try **Brian Head Cross Country**. It becomes biking central during the rest of the year, with excellent service, books and technical support. ~ Brian Head Hotel, Route 143; 801-677-2012.

SHOPPING

The renowned **Utah Shakespearean Festival** stages six plays on the Southern Utah University campus from late June through the end of August. Plays are performed both in the Adams Theater, an authentic open-air re-creation of a Shakespearean stage, and the modern indoor Randall L. Jones Theater. Those wishing to really get in the spirit of the evening may dine in the tradition of the Old English great halls at the King's Pavilion located across the street north from the Festival Box Office. The **Renaissance Feaste** offers entertainment, fanfares, lively humor and winsome serving wenches. Reservations required; tickets available at the box office. ~ 351 West Center, Cedar City; 801-586-7878, 800-752-9849.

Southern Utah University plays host to a variety of cultural attractions year-round. The **University Theater Arts Department** (801-586-7880) schedules plays in the fall and spring. **American Folk Ballet** (801-586-7880), a dance troupe that combines ballet with folk dancing, annually performs at the SUU Centrum. Plus, SUU books national and international talent spanning dance, opera, classical music, country and more. The **Summer Evening Concert Series** (801-586-5483), held at the Randall L. Jones Theater, features jazz, classical, country and more. ~ Southern Utah University: 351 West Center, Cedar City; 801-586-7700.

A college crowd likes to hang out at **Sportsmen's Lounge**, where Thursday is karaoke night and there is live music on weekends. Cover Wednesday through Saturday. ~ 900 South Main, Cedar City; 801-586-6552.

The country-music set two-steps at **The Playhouse**, which features live music on the weekends. Cover on weekends. ~ 1027 North Main, Cedar City; 801-586-9010.

Quality bands come from near and far to play at the **Pinnacles Breaks Club** during summer and ski seasons. ~ Route 143, Brian Head; 801-677-3000.

NIGHTLIFE

ZION NATIONAL PARK-KOLOB CANYONS 🏃🏇 Less widely
known than Zion Canyon, Kolob remains relatively untrodden yet provides as much colorful scenery as its more famous counterpart.

PARKS

You will find a visitors center, a picnic area and restrooms. ~ Located off Route 15 at Exit 40, 17 miles south of Cedar City; 801-586-9548.

▲ Backpack camping only with permit.

CEDAR BREAKS NATIONAL MONUMENT 🏃 🏠 Millennia of erosion and uplift have carved one of the world's greatest natural amphitheaters filled with stone pinnacles, columns, arches and canyons of soft limestone three miles from rim to rim and 2500 feet deep. Some call it a Bryce Canyon in miniature. Surrounding Cedar Breaks is a sub-alpine environment with evergreen forest of bristlecone pine, spruce and fir trees, flower-laden meadows and tall grasses. Sorry, no cedars. The Mormon settlers confused them with the gnarled juniper trees found throughout. The monument features a visitors center, a picnic area and restrooms. Services and roads are usually closed from mid-October through mid-May due to heavy snows, though snowshoeing, cross-country skiing and snowmobiling are allowed. ~ Located 21 miles east of Cedar City via Route 14 or take Route 143 south two miles from Brian Head; 801-586-9451.

▲ There are 30 sites; $10 fee.

▼▼▼▼▼▼▼▼▼▼
Bryce Area

A couple of wonderful parks (surprise) await you here along with historic towns and one of the prettiest byways in the West. And for a bonus you can see the log cabin of Ebenezer Bryce, namesake of the region's stunning national park.

SIGHTS

The handsome architecture in the historic town of **Panguitch**, settled in 1864, is evidence of its early pioneering spirit. Around the turn of the century, a communal brick factory was supervised by an English potter who was sent here by Brigham Young to be the company's craftsman. Part of the workers' weekly salaries were paid in bricks!

That accounts for the great number of stately, brick homes still found in Panguitch. English and Dutch influences are also evident in the buildings' Dixie dormers, delicate filigree and Queen Anne windows.

A short walking tour through the center of town gives you a chance to see the best of what's left. Begin the tour at the **Garfield County Courthouse**, built for just over $11,000 in 1907. ~ 55 South Main.

Cross to the **Houston home**, which was constructed of extra-large brick fired in a Panguitch kiln. The home's lumber and shingles also came from a local sawmill. ~ 72 South Main.

The building on the corner of 1st North and Main is a classic bit of architecture called the **Southern Utah Equitable**. It has housed just about every kind of business you can think of, from general merchandise to furniture, groceries and now a gift shop and restaurant.

Prominent on Center (none of this region's main thoroughfares, like Center, Main and Tabernacle, go by the name Street. Why? Ask the locals—you may just make a friend in the process) is the **Panguitch Social Hall Corporation**, which was first built in 1908 but burned shortly thereafter. On the same spot, using some original materials, another social hall was built. Now it houses the Panguitch Playhouse. Next door is a library that was built in 1908 thanks to a generous donation from Andrew Carnegie. ~ 35 East Center.

Finally, the city's **Daughters of the Utah Pioneer Museum**, is a lovely, brick monolith on the site of the old bishop's storehouse. Back in the mid-19th century, members of the Mormon Church paid their tithes with cattle and produce that were kept on this lot. Now, visitors trace the region's history here. Closed November through April. Closed Sunday. Call for hours. ~ Center and 1st East.

Before you leave Panguitch be sure to stop by the recently opened **Paunsagaunte Wildlife Museum**, which is housed in the historic old high-school building. The museum features more than 200 animals from North America in their natural habitats. Other displays include exotic game from Africa, India and Europe, rare birds of prey and American Indian artifacts, tools, pottery and weapons. There are also a number of gift shops in the building. Admission. ~ 250 East Center; 801-670-2500.

Sculptured rock forms come in countless profiles, which have been named "hoodoos." These are ever-changing because of rain and snow seeping into the cracks of the rock, freezing and thawing to wear away the layers.

Driving south from Panguitch on Route 89 takes you to the start of one of the most scenic byways in the West. After passing a few souvenir shops and cafés, Route 12 starts to wind through rock tunnels. That's when you know you're in **Red Canyon**. A visitors center on the road's north side offers information about the small park that's usually bypassed by people hurrying toward Bryce Canyon. Pink and red rocks stand amid huge pines in this compact and user-friendly park.

It's another ten miles on Route 89 to the **Bryce Canyon National Park** turnoff. Bryce is a national park on the jagged edge of the Paunsagaunte Plateau that really does defy superlatives. Even the gigantic summertime crowds can't distract from the natural amphitheaters carved into the Pink Cliffs of Southern Utah. Who'd have ever thought there were this many shades of red or shapes of rock? The limestones and sandstones of Bryce, some softer than others, have been sculpted by eons of erosional forces. Admission. ~ Route 89; 801-834-5322.

Bryce offers 12 huge bowls of spires and pinnacles. Located between 7500 and 9100 feet above sea level, the 35,000-plus acres of Bryce receive more than their fair share of snow during the wintertime. Some say that the rocks covered with dollops of snow are at their most beautiful in winter.

Fifty to sixty million years ago Bryce was covered by an inland lake. Rivers and streams carried silt and sediments from throughout the region to the lake, and the sediments settled to the bottom. With climatic changes, the lake disappeared and the sediments left behind slowly turned to rock. As the different levels of earth emerged they took shape and turned colors as the result of erosion. Red and yellow hues are due to iron oxides. The purples come from manganese. White reveals an absence of minerals in that part of the rock.

At sections of the park like Silent City and other natural amphitheaters, the rock figures resemble chess pieces, a preacher, a woman playing the organ or faces that belong on Easter Island.

Bryce Canyon's nooks and crannies are best explored on foot. If time is a factor, it's wise to drive to the overlooks on the 21-mile park road for a sweeping look at the big picture. Start at the **Fairyland Point** lookout about two miles north of the visitors center to see the imaginary creatures, the looming **Boat Mesa** and mysterious **Sinking Ship** in Fairyland Canyon. The rather strenuous Fairyland Loop Trail also begins here.

For a concentrated collection of formations, travel to the park's nucleus and either the **Sunrise** or **Sunset Point** lookouts to view the chess set–like people in **Queen's Garden**.

Walking along the Rim Trail, which skirts the canyon edge for a round-trip distance of 11 miles, takes you to **Inspiration Point** and the eerie army of stone "people" called the **Silent City**. From the Rim Trail at this point it's possible to see the **Wall of Windows** and the majestic **Cathedral**.

The Rim Trail continues south for another one and a half miles to **Bryce Point**, which allows breathtaking views of the whole Bryce Amphitheater. Three hiking trails, the Rim, Under-the-Rim and Peekaboo Loop, may be accessed from here. Horses share the Peekaboo Loop and take riders past profiles such as the **Alligator** and **Fairy Castle**.

From the main park road continue south for seven miles to **Farview Point** to gaze at the natural wonders stretching hundreds of miles outside Bryce. The flat-topped landform to the east is the **Aquarius Plateau**. Southeast of the park are the distinctive **White Cliffs**.

Natural Bridge, with a huge opening in a rock, stands distinctly about two miles south of the Farview lookout. It's another four miles to **Ponderosa View Point**, where you can pick up the Agua Canyon connecting foot trail while seeing the lovely pink cliffs.

Drive the final two miles to **Rainbow Point** and **Yovimpa Point**, and end up at the park's highest points, towering at over 9000 feet above sea level. A little more barren and rugged than other sections of Bryce, these two overlooks serve as trailheads for several hiking paths. It's worth the short jaunt on the **Bristlecone Loop Trail** to see the rare, gnarled trees up close and personal.

To fully explore the multimillion-year-old wonders of Bryce, begin the at-times arduous 22-mile **Under-the-Rim Trail** from here and travel north on a two- or three-day backpacking excursion. Camping in the park's backcountry is especially rewarding, as the stars tend to put on quite a show in this rarefied, high altitude air.

The closest real town to the park is **Tropic**— hometown to Ebenezer Bryce. Bryce was a Mormon pioneer who helped settle the valley below the park. Neighbors called the beautiful canyon west of his ranch "Bryce's Canyon." There is a back route to Bryce from Tropic for foot travelers only. This trail connects with the Peekaboo Loop and Navajo Loop trails of the main Bryce Amphitheater. The easier way to go is by returning to Route 12 and traversing the ten miles or so through lovely **Tropic Canyon**. You need a sharp eye to spot the recently discovered natural bridge on the east side of the highway about three-tenths mile north of the Water Canyon Bridge.

Utah's most recently discovered arch, a 90-footer named **Shakespeare**, can be seen by taking a ten-minute hike on Chimney Rock Trail, one of six in Kodachrome.

Once in Tropic, stop for a snack or to stretch your legs in this special village that remains true to its name. Flowers seem to dance in the gardens, and old trees stretch their limbs languorously. At the south end of town is **Ebenezer Bryce's old log cabin**, which houses American Indian artifacts.

Another few miles east on Route 12 is **Cannonville**, a town about half the size of Tropic that offers travelers basic services. Best known as the gateway to Kodachrome Basin, Cannonville is also the jumping-off point for little side trips to a handful of caves and the narrow Bull Valley Gorge. Look for signs on the gravel and dirt road south of Cannonville.

Heading south on the only road out of Cannonville, you'll travel seven miles to **Kodachrome Basin State Park**, another wonderful Utah park with red-rock figures and slender chimneys. Stop at the Trail Head station, a little store, for maps and advice. Kodachrome is chock full of petrified geyser holes, 65 at last official count, believed to be freaks of nature and unique to this area. Spires, or "sand pipes," jut toward the sky, and natural arches beckon. Is it a surprise that Kodak is the park's official film? Quiet beauty and serenity are abundant in this out-of-the-way gem. Admission. ~ 801-679-8562.

An amazing feat of nature about ten miles south of the park boundary via a rough, unnamed road is the **Grosvenor double arch**. The delicate colors of the monolith, coupled with a bluebird sky, must be seen to be believed. Petrified wood may be found in the arch's vicinity.

Those with sturdy vehicles can continue south on the road to Cottonwood Canyon past two manmade circles of alabaster stones named **Gilgal**. Vaguely reminiscent of Stonehenge, the concept for Gilgal is biblically rooted and meant to symbolize the modern-day pilgrims who make an annual trek to this area in celebration of the summer solstice.

The entire stretch of road south of Cannonville to Route 89 crosses the Kanab fault several times and offers unusual scenery and fossils plus opportunities for exploring on foot. The road then continues a few miles to the western boundary of Lake Powell. Or return to Route 12 and drive west toward Escalante.

LODGING   Cheap, clean and very basic describes the **Color Country Motel** with its flowered bedspreads and scenic vistas on the walls. ~ 526 North Main, Panguitch; 801-676-2386, 800-225-6518, fax 801-676-8484. BUDGET.

A step up in quality—and price—is the **New Western Best Western**, natty and decorated in paisley patterns and scalloped carpeting in mauves and teals. The housekeeping is spotless and there is a cool pool for those toasty summer days. ~ 180 East Center, Panguitch; 801-676-8876, 800-528-1234, fax 801-676-8876 ext. 165. MODERATE.

The only survivor of the original lodges built by the Union Pacific Railroad at Bryce, Zion, and the North Rim of the Grand Canyon, the **Bryce Canyon Lodge** is listed on the National Register of Historic Places. The four types of rooms—suites, cabins, doubles and studios—fit most budgets and tastes. Splurging on a suite is a treat. These rooms ooze romance, from the white-wicker decor to Cleopatra chairs to the makeup mirror. Quaint log cabins have gas fireplaces, porches and dressing areas. Regular rooms are furnished in Southwest style. Open only from spring until late fall, the lodge tends to book well in advance. ~ Bryce Canyon National Park; 303-297-2757, fax 303-297-3175. MODERATE TO DELUXE.

There's nothing like a full-service resort when you really feel like getting away from it all. **Best Western Ruby's Inn** operates as a world of its own, with a general store, liquor store, campground, helicopter pad, riding stables, even its own post office on site! An international clientele can be found anytime. Rooms are decorated in Southwestern decor, and the staff remains friendly even after a long tourist season. ~ Route 63, Bryce Canyon; 801-834-5341, 800-528-1234, fax 801-834-5265. MODERATE.

A kitchen and fireplace is what the **Bryce Canyon Pines** can offer its guests within cozy, knotty-pine rooms. The 50 rooms are open for groups as well as individuals. ~ Route 12, six miles northwest of the Bryce Canyon entrance; 801-834-5441, fax 801-834-5330. MODERATE.

Another very comfortable residence is the **Bryce Point Bed and Breakfast,** found about eight miles east of Bryce in the perpetually flowering little town of Tropic. Guests enjoy a private entrance and private baths. Each of the five rooms features handmade oak cabinets and picture windows to the garden. ~ 61 North 400 West, Tropic; 801-679-8629. MODERATE.

DINING

You expect country cooking at a place named **Foy's Country Corner,** and that's just what you get. Good juicy hamburgers, chicken-fried steaks and halibut highlight the menu. Closed Sunday. ~ 80 North Main, Panguitch; 801-676-8851. BUDGET TO MODERATE.

When it comes time to settle down and have a semifancy meal, there's little doubt that the top choice in this area is the beautiful old log restaurant in the **Bryce Canyon Lodge.** Service is quick and attentive though hardly fussy, the cuisine Continental but not generic. Homemade breads and Levi-busting desserts complement the generously portioned entrées. ~ Bryce Canyon National Park; 801-834-5361. MODERATE.

Equipped to serve and satisfy large groups, the **Cowboy Steakhouse and Buffet** presents satisfying meals, though surely not imaginative fare, in its spacious dining room. A menu of Continental cuisine features steaks and chops for dinner. The dining room can be a little noisy when large groups converge. ~ Best Western Ruby's Inn, Route 63, Bryce Canyon; 801-834-5341. BUDGET TO MODERATE.

During the busy summer months, the **Canyon Diner,** adjacent to the Cowboy Steakhouse and Buffet, is a convenient spot for quick and tasty on-the-go meals. ~ Best Western Ruby's Inn, Route 63, Bryce Canyon; 801-834-5341. BUDGET.

The booths are inviting, the coffee steaming and the pies and soups fresh and delicious at **Bryce Canyon Pines,** which also offers specials every evening. Closed periodically in winter. ~ Route 12, six miles northwest of Bryce Canyon entrance; 801-834-5441. BUDGET TO MODERATE.

Had a local not made the recommendation, we'd have never stumbled onto the very modest **Pizza Place.** A wise-cracking chef kept the starving wolves at bay, appeasing our ravenous hunger with an order of wonderfully gooey and stringy mozzarella cheese sticks, before the main event—a hefty, generously topped, sweet-crusted pizza that could be the tastiest pie this side of Chicago. Closed Sunday. ~ 21 North Main, Tropic; 801-679-8888. BUDGET.

◄ HIDDEN

SHOPPING

An enticing smell of potpourri tickles the nose upon entering **Favorite Pastimes.** Quilts, wreaths, bookends and knickknacks are carefully selected, if not handmade themselves. ~ 415 East Center, Panguitch; 801-676-2608.

It may seem corny, but you gotta love the **Old Bryce Town**, filled with shops and services. Among them, the **Canyon Rock Shop** has a huge selection of polished stones, fossils and petrified wood, plus a place to pan for gold! Stop in the **Christmas Store** to stock up on ornaments and decorations. The **Western Store** has a great selection of pseudo-Stetsons so you can set out on the range and not feel like a total city slicker. Old Bryce Town is open from the middle of May to the end of September. ~ Route 63, across from Ruby's Inn; 801-834-5337.

Wind chimes and chile *ristras* line the front porch, while Navajo rugs and baskets are omnipresent inside the **Bryce Canyon Trading Post**, a good place to pick up the requisite postcard, T-shirt or turquoise. ~ Routes 12 and 89; 801-676-2688.

NIGHTLIFE   The **Panguitch Playhouse** hosts summer musicals and special events. ~ 50 East Center, Panguitch; 801-676-8573.

Don't be surprised if angry Indians come a'chasing when you're riding in the covered chuck wagon train en route to a hoedown and sing-along. The **B-Bar-D Covered Wagon Company** operates out of the Ruby's Inn complex during the summer season. Expect a huge country supper served on a dutch oven amid the pines before kicking up your heels in the foot stompin' hoedown. It's a hoot. ~ Route 12, Bryce Canyon; 801-834-5202.

Rodeos featuring local talent are held nightly except Sunday throughout the summer at the **Rodeo Grounds** across from Ruby's Inn in Bryce Canyon. Barrel racing, bull wrasslin', roping and riding make for a full evening. ~ Route 63; 801-834-5341.

PARKS   **PANGUITCH LAKE** 🚶 🚵 🛶 🚤 🏊 🎣 One of the top fishing areas in the region, Panguitch Lake offers fishing along its ten-mile shoreline and in boats for rainbow, cutthroat and brown trout. There are boat rentals as well as tourist cabins, a general store and a snack shop; day-use fee, $4.50 per car. ~ On Route 143 about 17 miles south of Panguitch; 801-865-3200.

▲ Panguitch Lake North has 49 sites ($9 per night) and two group sites ($50 per night); across the street, Panguitch Lake South has 17 primitive sites ($7 per night); Whitebridge campground on the south side offer 29 sites; ($9 per night). There are also several privately owned campgrounds in the area.

TROPIC RESERVOIR AND KING'S CREEK CAMPGROUND 🚶 🎣 This recreation site is a nice place for a picnic, a walk past sawmill remains or just a place to fish and relax. The only facilities here are restrooms and drinking water. ~ On an unmarked road off Route 12, about ten miles west of Bryce Canyon junction; 801-676-8815.

▲ There are 34 sites; $7 per night.

RED CANYON 🚶 A lovely collection of sculptured pink, red and scarlet rocks sit in the shadow of Bryce Canyon. Because its neighbor is so well known, Red Canyon tends to be overlooked by visitors. Take advantage and explore the trails of this scenic but compact park. You'll find a visitors center and restrooms. ~ On Route 12 about four miles east of Route 89; 801-676-8815.

▲ There are 36 sites; $8 per night.

BRYCE CANYON NATIONAL PARK 🚶 🐎 🏕 Famous for its stupendous rock formations that seem to change color within the blink of an eye, Bryce contains a maze of trails that wind in and around its many wonders. The park features its own lodge, a restaurant, a visitors center, nature walks, campfire programs, a general store, laundry, restrooms and showers. (Facilities are mainly seasonal; the visitors center is open year-round.) The $5 vehicle fee is good for five days. ~ Located two miles south of Route 12 on Route 63, eight miles northeast of Tropic; 801-834-5322.

▲ Permitted at North Campground and Sunset Campground. More than 200 campsites are open during the summer; $6 per night. There are also several backpacking campsites (permit required).

KODACHROME BASIN STATE PARK 🚶 Vividly colored sandstone chimneys, towering rock spires and arches fill this untouched, 2240-acre park that the National Geographic Society named for its photographic value. Facilities include picnic area, a general store, restrooms and hot showers. ~ Located seven miles south of Cannonville on the only road out of town; 801-679-8562.

▲ There are 27 sites; $10 per night.

▼▼▼▼▼▼▼▼▼▼
Escalante Area

Nature's beauty, wildlife, prehistoric reminders and a region rich in the Indian and Mormon heritage await you in this region along scenic Route 12. Here you'll find a petrified forest, intriguing rock formations, orchards, dinosaur fossils and, for a wonderful surprise, buffalo.

SIGHTS

Route 12 climbs from red rock to lush forest and back again to a semiarid setting. Begin just south of the town of Escalante, which was settled in 1876 by Mormon ranchers, in the **Escalante Petrified Forest State Park**. It's a showcase for petrified wood, fossilized dinosaur bones and remnants from the Fremont Indian Village thought to be 1000 years old. You don't have to be an athlete or even reasonably fit to find and appreciate the petrified wood in this small park, which has trails to suit everyone. Admission. ~ 801-826-4466.

Huge petrified logs in a spectrum of colors, dinosaur bones and nature trails help to explain the evolution of the 160 million-year-old wood turned to stone that became rainbow colored by the earth's minerals. It is thought that ancient trees were buried in the sand, causing the logs to become petrified. Millions of years later the natural weathering process exposed the wood from its rough outer shell. One word of warning: Don't nick any pieces as souvenirs because legend has it that bad things come to those who do. Instead, buy a piece of wood at one of the rock shops located in Escalante.

Hole in the Rock Road, a Mormon pioneer passage, zigs and zags its way to Lake Powell from its starting point just north of Escalante. Along the historic, 62-mile road you'll see landmarks such as Chimney Rock, Dancehall Rock and the Broken Bow Arch. An annual pilgrimage retraces the steps of the first settlers.

It's only been during the past few years that Route 12 has been paved between Boulder and Torrey. The high-altitude road linking Bryce to Capitol Reef has been called one of the most **scenic drives** in America. There are several campgrounds and dirt roads leading to mountain lakes along the way, plus opportunities to view vistas of the Henry Mountains, San Rafael Reef and distant shale deserts.

In tiny Boulder, the last town in the United States to receive its mail by mule team, is **Anasazi State Park**. It's located on the site of a former Anasazi community said to have been nearby between 1050 A.D. and 1200 A.D. before mysteriously disappearing. Here you'll find excavated village Indian artifacts, a self-guided trail through the site and a museum showing informative movies and filmstrips. Admission. ~ Route 12; 801-335-7308.

When Route 12 meets Route 24, it's less than a dozen miles east to the entrance of **Capitol Reef National Park**. Domed cliffs reminiscent of the rotunda in Washington, D.C., prompted early explorers to give Capitol Reef its unusual name. Another explanation for the moniker's origin is that maritime men were reminded of barrier reefs. Long before white men arrived, American Indians were said to have grown corn, beans and squash along the Fremont River. Admission. ~ Route 24; 801-425-3791.

Wrinkled earth that was formed by the forces of nature, Capitol Reef is a mélange of domes and cliffs, spires and other amazing rock formations tossed together in a beautiful jumble. The cliffs of Waterpocket Fold, a 100-mile bulge in the earth's crust, slice through the park's epicenter. The **visitors center** offers a slide show exploring the formation of Capitol Reef. ~ Located on Scenic Drive, right off of Route 24.

Elevations range from 5300 feet to 7000 feet, and summers can be quite warm. Seven miles east of the visitors center are the famous Fremont River and its waterfalls. Swimming is inadvisable due to the river's deceiving undertow.

Capitol Reef has several aspects. To the south, white sand upfolds. Near the center is lush Fruita, with its gardens and orchards.

At Capitol Reef's north end is the grandeur and peacefulness of Cathedral Valley.

When the Mormons came a century ago they planted beautiful orchards on the banks of the Fremont and Sulphur Creek in a settlement first called Junction, later renamed the more fragrant Fruita. Apples, pears, peaches, cherries and apricots are still harvested in **Fruita** orchards, which are administered by the National Park Service. Fruita is also home to a historic reminder of the past, a one-room log schoolhouse built in 1896.

Capitol Reef was established as a national monument in 1937 and became a national park in 1971.

Step back in time at **Behunin Cabin**, a sandstone structure with a dirt floor that was built in 1882. ~ Route 24, six miles east of the visitors center.

Exploration of Capitol Reef's wild beauty continues along the park's 25-mile round-trip scenic drive south of the visitors center where there are numerous opportunities for excursions in the rock. Branch off onto either the dry Grand Wash or Cassidy Arch hiking trails, located east of the road. Stay on the route until its conclusion and access **Capitol Gorge**, a sinuous canyon, and the yellow sandstone monoliths of the Golden Throne Trail.

Petroglyph panels have never been so easy to find as at a pullout on Route 24 about a mile east of the visitors center along the Fremont River.

Backtrack at day's end to a few miles west of the visitors center and cruise by Sunset Point where the light is kind to the mummylike formations and landmark Castle Rock.

Not far from here you can walk up the short **Goosenecks Trail** (.1 mile) overlooking the gurgling Sulpher Creek below or sit on the bench and gaze at Boulder Mountain and the Aquarius Plateau. At day's end, a tiny trek from the car to **Sunset Point** (.2 mile) yields a view of the amazing Waterpocket Fold that reaches southward toward Lake Powell. With the Henry Mountains to the east, this is when Capitol's wild beauty bursts in all its splendor.

It's a rather bleak landscape between Capitol Reef and Hanksville, but before turning north on Route 24 to Goblin Valley, stop at the historic **Wolverton Mill** in Hanksville, a log structure once used to cut wood and crush ore. ~ 406 South 100 West; 801-542-3461.

Looking south from Hanksville, the lush Henry Mountains come into view. Home to the only free-roaming buffalo herd in the country, towering **Mt. Ellen** rises from the barren rock.

Heading north on Route 24 toward Route 70 and Green River, there are few roads and diversions. But on the western part of the road halfway between Hanksville and Green River is the entrance to **Goblin Valley State Park**. On the rough road leading to the park, you'll be stunned by the rock sculptures of Wild Horse Butte and Molley's Castle before entering the park itself. It's an enchanted land of countless standing rocks and troll-like figures. Gravel roads lead to beautiful Little Wild Horse Canyon, where there are two and a half miles of narrows to explore. Admission. ~ Route 24; 801-564-3633.

The effects of wind, rain and sand on rock play tricks on the imagination to where it appears there are goblin-like faces staring from every corner of this small—just two miles by three miles—wonderland. Remote, yet not inaccessible, Goblin Valley would make a great setting for an episode of the *Twilight Zone*. Photographers find many models in the Valley of Goblins.

LODGING   A sign sporting a fishing priest marks the **Padre Motel**. Most rooms feature a wall mural of regional landscape, linoleum-floored bathrooms and a desk. Small but tidy. ~ 20 East Main, Escalante; 801-826-4276. BUDGET.

New and very clean is the **Wonderland Inn,** which sits atop a hill on the edge of town. Cheerful local art dresses up 50 rooms (all with views). Fake-wood furniture is the only detractor. Guests can enjoy an indoor/outdoor pool and jacuzzi. ~ Routes 12 and 24, Torrey; 801-425-3775, 800-458-0216, fax 801-425-3212. BUDGET TO MODERATE.

Capitol Reef Inn & Café provides more than its simple facade would suggest. Spacious guest rooms with two double beds and working area are welcome to those toting a lot of high-country gear. But the walls can seem a little thin, depending on who your neighbors are. Closed November through May. ~ 360 West Main, Torrey; 801-425-3271. BUDGET.

The **Rim Rock Rustic Inn** is a woody sort of Western place that continues the theme with its on-site restaurant. Simple rooms have pine walls and small bathrooms. Rim Rock is the closest hotel to Capitol Reef. ~ 2523 East Route 24, Torrey; 801-425-3843, 800-243-0786, fax 801-425-3855. BUDGET TO MODERATE.

DINING   Fancy meals you won't find, but hearty American food is in abundance at the **Circle D.** ~ 475 West Main; 801-826-4297. BUDGET. A similar menu and price is found nearby at the **Golden Loop Café.** ~ 39 West Main; 801-826-4433. For decent sandwiches, try the seasonal **Mary's Frosty Shop.** Closed October through March. ~ Route 12, Escalante; 801-826-4488. BUDGET.

Torrey, the gateway to Capitol Reef, has one very good restaurant. Specializing in locally raised foods, the **Capitol Reef Café** surprises with its fresh approach to cooking in a land where expectations rarely exceed deep-fried, breaded concoctions. Utah rainbow trout, vegetarian dishes, homemade soups and heaping gardens of salad are the order of the day, along with hearty breakfasts. Espresso and café au lait are nice added touches. The café is often busy so be prepared to wait for a table. Closed November through May. ~ 360 West Main, Torrey; 801-425-3271. MODERATE.

For a quick snack, try **Brink's Burgers**. Closed November through February. ~ 165 East Main, Torrey; 801-425-3710. BUDGET.

Prime rib, steaks and local trout highlight the dinner menu at the **Wonderland Inn Restaurant**. Breakfast features fluffy hotcakes and the usual egg dishes. ~ Routes 12 and 24, Torrey; 801-425-3775. BUDGET TO MODERATE.

You will want to try the pizzas, but pies are the specialty of the house at the **Sunglow Pizza and Creamery**. Pinto-bean pie, fruit pies and a renowned pickle pie outclass the other standard diner fare at this friendly eatery. ~ 91 East Main, Bicknell; 801-425-3701. BUDGET.

SHOPPING

For jeans and T-shirts, but more important, to stock up on backpacking and camping supplies and maps before meeting the wilderness, stop at **Escalante Outfitters**. ~ 310 West Main, Escalante; 801-826-4266.

The store at the **Capitol Reef Inn** has plenty of good guidebooks, maps and trinkets of the area. Closed November through May. ~ 360 West Main, Torrey; 801-425-3271.

PARKS

ESCALANTE PETRIFIED FOREST STATE PARK Trails in this well-known park lead to outcroppings of petrified wood that date back 140 million years. Wide Hollow Reservoir, which is included within the park boundaries, is a good fishing and picnicking spot. There's also an interpretive trail here as well as a visitors center and restrooms. ~ Located one mile west of Escalante on Route 12; 801-826-4466.

▲ There are 22 sites; $10 per night.

CALF CREEK FALLS RECREATION AREA Gorgeous gorges and a waterfall that rushes down 126 feet over sandstone cliffs are reached after a moderate walk. The lush setting of cottonwood trees makes Calf Creek a cool place to dine outdoors. There are restrooms and volleyball courts. ~ On Route 12 about 15 miles east of Escalante; 801-826-5499.

▲ There are 11 sites; $6 per night.

CAPITOL REEF NATIONAL PARK Covering almost a quarter-million acres, this national treasure is veined by roads and hiking trails. They lead past the region's sculptured rock layers to vista points, deep canyons and remote waterfalls. The park features a visitors center, campfire programs, a paved scenic road, developed and undeveloped hiking trails and restrooms. ~ Located on Route 24, 37 miles west of Hanksville; 801-425-3791.

▲ There are 72 sites; $7 per night.

HIDDEN ► **GOBLIN VALLEY STATE PARK** 🏃 This unusual locale features thousands of eerie rock formations. Several trails lead into the heart of the park to canyons, arches and balanced rocks. Helpful rangers can be found roaming the park during the daytime hours. The park has restrooms, solar-heated showers and the only fresh water for 30 miles; day-use fee, $3. ~ Head west on road off Route 24 halfway between Hanksville and Green River until the Goblin Valley turnoff (about four and a half miles). The park is located approximately seven miles south; for information contact Green River State Park (P.O. Box 637, Green River, UT 84525; 801-564-3633).

▲ Goblin Valley has 21 sites, Green River offers 40 sites; $10 per night.

▼▼▼▼▼▼▼▼▼▼▼▼▼▼
Outdoor Adventures

FISHING

Rainbow, German brown and brook trout are plentiful throughout southwestern Utah. More than a dozen reservoirs plus natural lakes, creeks and rivers are stocked for fishing.

ST. GEORGE AREA Try your luck luring bass in **Gunlock and Quail Creek reservoirs.** For more specific locations of prime fishing spots and information on fishing licenses, try **Hurst Store** in St. George. ~ 60 North 500 West; 801-673-6141.

CEDAR CITY AREA **Ron's Sporting Goods** in Cedar City has info on where to catch fish and get a license. ~ 138 South Main; 801-586-9901.

BRYCE AREA **Panguitch Lake** is nearly as popular in the winter for ice fishing as it is as a summer resort. Boats, bait, tackle and licenses can be secured on Panguitch Lake through the **Beaver Dam Lodge.** ~ Lake Shore Road; 801-676-8339. Also offering rentals on the lake is **Deer Trail Lodge.** ~ Clear Creek Canyon Road; 801-676-2211.

ESCALANTE AREA Mackinaw and trout are the catch of the day at **Fish Lake,** 28 miles northwest of Torrey off of Route 24.

WINTER SPORTS

While primarily a summer destination, more and more people are discovering how beautiful southwestern Utah is once the snow flies.

ZION AREA Sledding and tubing are popular at **Coral Pink Sand Dunes** near Kanab.

CEDAR CITY AREA **Brian Head Ski Resort,** 12 miles southeast of Parowan, is renowned for the volumes of light, dry snow it receives. Catering to both alpine and nordic skiers, Brian Head's six chairlifts serve mostly intermediate terrain. Cross-country skiers like to glide to colorful Cedar Breaks and beyond. ~ 329 South Route 143; 801-677-2035.

Elk Meadows Ski Resort in the Tushar Mountains 19 miles east of Beaver on Route 153 is the region's other full-service ski area with three chairs and 18 miles of marked and groomed cross-country ski trails. ~ 801-438-5433.

BRYCE AREA Cross-country trails also are groomed on the rim of **Bryce Canyon.** But within the park skiers can break trail and wander through literally thousands of acres of wilderness, beyond the red-tipped fantasyland of rock spires and figures. Rentals and maps may be secured through **Ruby's Inn.** ~ Route 12, Bryce Canyon; 801-834-5341.

Fish Lake on Route 25 attracts snowmobilers, while sledding and tubing fans head toward **Red Canyon** on Route 12 along with neighboring **Bryce Canyon.**

Since many of Utah's most beautiful roads are unpaved, venturing out on a jeep tour is an excellent idea. Geological wonders, stunning scenery and historical points of interest await.

JEEP TOURS

ZION AREA If you'd like to venture out on a solo backcountry adventure, you might tour **Kolob Terrace Road,** a two-lane, paved path along the fringes of Zion National Park's west side which turns to dirt beyond the park's border. The route provides overviews of the Left and Right Forks of North Creek, climbing through dense evergreen forests past Tabernacle Dome and Firepit Knoll. North Creek canyons, Pine Valley Peak and the Guardian Angels are just a few of the other scenic sights. Kolob Terrace Road starts at the town of Virgin, 14 miles from Zion's main entrance on Route 9.

ESCALANTE AREA **Hondoo Rivers & Trails** offers guided tours of the area, including the trips described below. ~ 90 East Main, Torrey; 801-425-3519.

Burr Trail from Boulder to the Circle Cliffs of Capitol Reef is a gorgeous, 30-mile scenic drive on a chip-and-seal road across Deer Creek, Steep Creek and into the breathtaking Long Canyon. At the junction of Notom Road in Capitol Reef, travelers have the option of driving another 25 miles southeast to Bullfrog Marina at Lake Powell or going north to Route 24 into the heart of Capitol Reef National Park.

Hole in the Rock Road from Escalante to Lake Powell is not to be missed. First forged by Mormon pioneers looking for a "shortcut" to southeast Utah to establish new settlements, the famous and now vastly improved dirt road (54 miles) skirts along the Straight Cliffs and sandstone markers to landmark Dance Hall Rock, a natural amphitheater where the pioneers were said to have held a party and dance. Just past this point are the Sooner Tanks, potholes that often fill with water. Beyond the holes is a set of natural bridges. But this is where the route really deteriorates; just imagine how tough the trail would have been 100 years ago when you were riding in a covered wagon! From the end of the road there is a steep foot trail down to the lake.

Hell's Backbone Road from Boulder to Loa straddles the mountain ridge with the daunting drop of Death Hollow keeping drivers alert. The road winds around Slickrock Saddle Bench, Sand Creek canyons, creeks, hills and vistas.

The 9200-foot Boulder Mountain, located south of Route 24, has excellent four-wheel-drive roads. North of Route 24, over the back of **Thousand Lake Mountain** from Loa is the scenic, 25-mile ride to Capitol Reef's Cathedral Valley. Travelers can either backtrack 25 miles to Loa or complete the 125-mile trip to Route 24.

GOLF

Leave the masses behind and play the golf courses of Southwestern Utah; scenic and uncrowded best describe the greens out here. Most golfing activity centers around St. George, but you can also find courses farther afield.

ST. GEORGE AREA Temperate weather, even in winter, means year-round play. In fact, many believe it's golf that has put St. George on the map. A case in point is the **St. George Golf Club.** ~ 2190 South 1400 East; 801-634-5854. You can also play the links at **Sunbrook.** ~ 2240 Sunbrook Drive; 801-634-5866. **Twin Lakes Golf Course** is another of the area's sterling courses. ~ 660 North Twin Lakes Drive; 801-673-4441. Duffers may also want to try **Green Spring Golf Course.** ~ 588 North Green Spring Drive; 801-673-7888. You can also tee off at **Dixie Red Hills.** ~ 645 West 1250 North; 801-634-5852. **Southgate Golf Course** also offers a nice place to play a round in the sun. ~ 1975 South Tonaquint Drive; 801-628-0000.

ZION AREA **Coral Cliff Golf Course** is the best course near Zion National Park. ~ 755 East Fairway Drive, Kanab; 801-644-5005.

CEDAR CITY AREA **Cedar Ridge** is the place to play in Cedar City. ~ 200 East 900 North, Cedar City; 801-586-2970.

TENNIS

Where there's golf, there's usually tennis. Though southwestern Utah isn't packed with tennis courts, there are a few spots for lobbing the ball.

ST. GEORGE AREA St. George holds court at **Vernon Worthen Park.** ~ 400 East 200 South; 801-634-5869. **Dixie High School** also has public courts for St. George residents and visitors alike. ~ 350 East 700 South; 801-673-4682. Extensive courts for guests can be found at **Green Valley Spa and Tennis Resort.** ~ 1871 West Canyon View Drive; 801-628-8060.

CEDAR CITY AREA Tennis courts at **Southern Utah University** are open to the public. ~ 351 West Center, Cedar City; 801-586-

1937. And there's plenty of tennis action at **Cedar City's municipal tennis courts.** ~ Cedar Canyon Park, Route 14 three blocks east of Main; 801-586-2950.

BRYCE AREA **Panguitch City Park** has courts open to the public. ~ Route 89.

RIDING STABLES

Riding through the sometimes rugged Color Country on leisurely horseback trips is one of the best ways to explore steep canyons. The horses are likely to be as sure-footed as mules at the Bryce and Zion National Park concessions, the only horse rides allowed into the park—the others are relegated to its periphery.

ST. GEORGE AREA For trail rides contact **Snow Canyon Stables.** ~ At Snow Canyon State Park, Route 18; 801-628-6677.

BRYCE AND ZION AREAS The main place to hitch up with a riding stables is **Bryce-Zion Trail Rides.** ~ 801-679-8665. In Bryce Canyon you can also try **Best Western Ruby's Inn.** ~ Route 12, Bryce Canyon; 801-834-5341.

ESCALANTE AREA **Hondoo Rivers & Trails** offers trips with a minimum of two nights and three days. ~ 90 East Main, Torrey; 801-425-3519.

BIKING

Cyclists are starting to discover this region for its sights, interesting topography and varied terrain. While mountain bikers overrun Moab at certain times of the year, these trails are just being discovered.

ST. GEORGE AREA An intermediate loop ride is **Pine Valley Pinto**, a 35-mile trek across dirt road and pavement. Best ridden between April and October, the route is mostly gentle, although hills sneak in on occasion. Give yourself three to five hours. Take Route 18 north from St. George 25 miles to the town of Central. Turn right (east) toward Pine Valley recreation area. The loop begins on Forest Road 011, six miles from the Route 18 junction.

Snow Canyon Loop takes riders about 24 miles, passing through the towns of Santa Clara and Ivins before climbing through Snow Canyon State Park. Start the loop at the northwest end of St. George along Bluff Street. Go west at the Bluff Street and Sunset Boulevard intersection. Route 91 takes you to Santa Clara, veer north to Ivins, then climb six miles to the park. After one climb, Route 18 is downhill all the way home.

ZION AREA An easy ride is Route 9 from **Springdale through Zion National Park** (11 miles), but there is a one mile tunnel through which bicycles are not permitted to pass. You should arrange for a car to transport you and your bicycle through the tunnel. A bicycle is one of the best ways to tour Zion Canyon Scenic Drive from the south visitors center to the Temple of Sinawava, a massive rock canyon. Another good bike route in Zion is the two-mile **Pa'rus Trail** which follows the Virgin River from the South entrance of the park to Scenic Drive.

CEDAR CITY AREA Both beginners and advanced riders will enjoy **New Harmony Trail**, one of southern Utah's finest singletrack rides. The 3.6-mile trail offers a view point of Kolob Canyons, then a gradual uphill climb to Commanche Springs. Take Route 15 to the town of New Harmony and park your car at the far outskirts of town.

Mt. Carmel Junction to Coral Pink Sand Dunes is another favored road ride. Take Route 89 toward Kanab, and after three uphill miles you'll spot a turnoff sign to the park ten miles away.

Fir and aspen forests enshroud Route 14, a scenic byway from **Cedar City to Cedar Breaks National Monument**. While the paved road is a delight, you'll need stamina and good lung capacity to make the more than 4000-foot climb (25 miles).

When the snow melts, bike lovers hold forth on the trails around Brian Head. Experts enjoy the single-track rides, while those less inclined to tight spaces go for the dirt roads and double-track trails. A moderately easy ten-mile loop in the Brian Head vicinity is the **Scout Camp Loop Trail**. Begin from the Brian Head Hotel, turn south on Route 143 and ride to Bear Flat Road and Steam Engine Meadow. There's a cabin and, you guessed it, an engine on the trail. The trail continues toward Hendrickson Lake and the namesake scout camp.

Another popular ride that's relatively easy is **Pioneer Cabin**, about a six-mile journey on a wide, dirt road and single track that begins from Burt's Road. The 1800s-era cabin has aspen trees growing out of its roof!

BRYCE AREA Dave's Hollow Trail (4 miles) near Bryce Canyon National Park is a pleasant ride through meadows and pine forests that's recommended for all abilities. At the boundary line to the park, about one mile south of Ruby's Inn, is a dirt road that heads west. Follow the road about one-half mile, then turn right about three-fourths mile along the trail. This begins a ride along a mellow, double-track trail that ends at the Forest Service station.

ESCALANTE AREA Atop the Aquarius Plateau, highest plateau in the United States, via the true-to-its name Hell's Backbone Road from Escalante, mountain bikers have a party on the spur roads near **Posy Lake** and the **Blue Spruce Campground**.

Bike Rentals For rentals and knowledgeable advice in St. George, try **Swem's Cyclery**. ~ 1060 Tabernacle, St. George; 801-673-0878. Close to Snow Canyon State Park is **The Second Mile**. ~ 202 North Snow Canyon Road, Ivins; 801-628-9558. You can rent bikes near Zion National Park from **Bike Zion**. ~ 445 Zion Park Boulevard, Springdale; 801-772-3929. You can rent gear and equipment in Cedar City from **Bike Route**. ~ 70 West Center; 801-586-4242. Despite its name, you can get bikes from the **Brian Head Cross Country Ski Center**. ~ 223 Hunter Ridge Drive, Brian Head; 801-677-2012.

Some of the most spectacluar hiking in the country can be found in this corner of Utah. Take your pick of national parks and monuments, fill your water bottle and head for the trails.

HIKING

ST. GEORGE AREA   Short on time and even shorter on endurance? We have just the place for you. Drive north on Main until it dead-ends, take a hard right and wind to the top of Red Hill. Park at the base of **Sugar Loaf**, the red sandstone slab with the white DIXIE letters and start walking for a few yards. The view of St. George is nothing short of spectacular.

Snow Canyon offers several excellent hikes. One of the most popular is **Hidden Pinyon** (.75 mile) which takes you by a wide variety of plant life and geological formations. See if you can find the Hidden Pinyon Pinetree at the end of the trail.

Another popular Snow Canyon hike is to the **Lava Caves** (.75 mile) near the north end of the canyon. If you plan on exploring the rugged caves, believed to have once sheltered Indians, take along a flashlight and good judgment. Watch for the sign along the road north of the campgrounds.

ZION AREA   **Zion National Park** is considered one of the best hiking parks in the nation with a variety of well-known trails. A comprehensive list is included in the Zion National Park brochure. Regardless of which trail you choose, expect the unexpected—a swamp, waterfall, petrified forest or bouquets of wildflowers.

Expect company, and lots of it, on **Riverside Walk** (1 mile), which traces the Virgin River upstream to Zion Canyon Narrows, just one of the tight stretches where 20-foot-wide canyons loom 2000 feet overhead. The concrete path winds among high cliffs

✔ **CHECK THESE OUT—UNIQUE OUTDOOR ADVENTURES**
- Spend a cold winter's day testing your ice-fishing skills on **Panguitch Lake**. *page 498*
- Saddle up one of the sure-footed horses at **Bryce** or **Zion** national parks and explore the steep, color-filled canyons. *page 501*
- Hop on your mountain bike and head for the **New Harmony Trail** near Cedar City, one of southern Utah's finest single-track rides. *page 502*
- Hike the **Lower Calf Creek Falls** in mysterious Escalante Canyons and be rewarded with a cascading waterfall. *page 506*

and cool pools of water where many visitors stop to soak their tootsies. This easy trail begins at the Temple of Sinawava parking area.

For a more moderate hike, continue past the end of the paved path and along the **Orderville Canyon Trail** (2.8 miles). Much of the trip involves wading through the Virgin River, at times four feet deep! But, if you don't mind the wet, the narrows is an amazing contrast of Navajo sandstone arches, grottoes and fluted walls looming high over tight chasms. Because of the rapidly changing conditions of the river, the park posts a Zion Narrows Danger Level each day. Be aware of that level and also check with rangers for specific tips on fording the river safely.

Angels Landing (2.4 mile) is a strenuous hike that begins at the Grotto picnic area and offers incredible views over the sheer drops of Zion Canyon. Believe it or not, the trail is built into solid rock, including 21 short switchbacks called "Walters Wiggles." The last half-mile follows a steep, narrow ridge with a 1500-foot dropoff. While a support-chain railing is of some help, the trail isn't recommended for the faint of heart or anyone with "high" anxiety.

Another heavily visited trail system is at **Emerald Pools**. The easy, paved trail (.3 mile) to Lower Emerald Pool is shaded by cottonwood, box elder and Gambel oak. Trail's end finds a waterfall with pool below. The more stout-of-heart can venture to the Upper Pool (1.3 miles), a rough and rocky trail. The trailhead is at the Emerald Pools parking area.

Views of the West Temple, Towers of the Virgin and the town of Springdale are the reward at the end of **The Watchman** (1 mile), a large, red-brown, 2600-foot crag that overlooks the southern portion of Zion Canyon. Considered moderately difficult, the trailhead is located near the entrance to Watchman campground.

Considered one of the most strenuous hikes within Zion, **West Rim Trail** (13.3 miles) takes two days, culminating at Lava Point. Hikers are blessed with scenic vistas including Horse Pasture Plateau, a "peninsula" extending south from Lava Point, surrounded by thousand-foot cliffs. Lightning strikes are frequent on the plateau, and uncontrolled wildfires have left some areas robbed of vegetation. Other views along the way include Wildcat Canyon, the Left and Right Forks of North Creek and Mt. Majestic. The trailhead starts at the Grotto picnic area.

CEDAR CITY AREA   There are two developed trails within Kolob Canyons. **Taylor Creek Trail** (2.7 miles) follows a small creek in the shadow of Tucupit and Paria Points, two giant redrock cliffs. The creek forks in three directions, but the path straight down the middle goes past two of the three homesteading cabins that still exist in Kolob Canyons and ends at Double Arch Alcove, a large, colorful grotto with a high arch above. The trail starts from the Taylor Creek parking area two miles into Kolob Canyons Road.

The only way to see one of the world's largest freestanding arch involves a two-day trek along **Kolob Arch Trail** (7 miles), a strenuous descent following Timber and La Verkin creeks. After reaching the magnificent arch, which spans 310 feet from end to end, you might continue on to Beartrap Canyon, a narrow, lush side canyon with a small waterfall.

Two highcountry trails are within **Cedar Breaks National Monument**. Both explore the rim but don't descend into the breaks itself. **Alpine Pond Trail** (2 miles) is a loop that passes through a picturesque forest glade and alpine pond fed by melting snow and small springs. The trailhead begins at the Chessmen Meadow parking area.

Ramparts Trail (2 miles) starts just outside the visitors center and ends at a 9952-foot overlook of the Cedar Breaks amphitheater. Along the way, pause at Spectra Point, a 10,285-foot viewpoint.

BRYCE AREA   Two hours worth of hiking time in Red Canyon can bring big rewards. The **Buckhorn Trail** (1 mile) begins at the campground and ascends high above the canyon past handsome rocks. **Pink Ledges Trail** (.5 mile) is a simple, short jaunt through brilliant-red formations. The trailhead starts near the visitors center. If you don't mind sharing your turf with a horse, try the **Cassidy Trail** (8.7 miles), named for that famous outlaw, which traverses ponderosa pine and more of those ragged rocks.

Bryce Canyon is hiking central because it's so darn beautiful. Uneasy around hordes of people? Either set out extra early or later in the day—the light shines deliciously on the rocks at both sunrise and sunset—or plan on spending a few days in the backcountry to wander into castles and cathedrals, animal farms, temples, palaces and bridges. There are more than 60 miles worth of trails on which to wander.

The outstanding **Under-the-Rim Trail** (23 miles) connecting Bryce Point with Rainbow Point could be turned into a multiday trip if side canyons, springs and buttes are explored to their full potential.

Riggs Spring Loop Trail (8.8 miles) starts at Yovimpa Point and takes best advantage of the Pink Cliffs. More moderate is the **Bristlecone Loop Trail** (1 mile) that begins atop the plateau and leads to sweeping views of spruce forests, cliffs and bristlecone pines.

One of the most famous, and rightly so, trails within the Bryce boundaries is **Queen's Garden** (1.5 miles). Start from Sunrise Point and dive right into this amazing amphitheater. Taking a spur to the **Navajo Loop Trail** (an additional mile) brings you within view of the Silent City, a hauntingly peaceful yet ominous army of hoodoos. The trail ends at Sunset Point.

In the park's northern section is the **Fairyland Loop Trail** (8 miles). Moderately strenuous, the loop provides views of Boat Mesa and the fantasy features of the fairy area. Near the splitting point for the horse trail is the monolith known as Gulliver's Castle. An easier route is **Rim Trail** (up to 11 miles) along the edge of the Bryce Amphitheater that can be taken in small or large doses.

At **Kodachrome Basin State Park** the trails are short and sweet, offering plenty of satisfaction with little effort. From the **Panorama Trail** (3 miles) you get to see the Ballerina Slipper formation. At **Arch Trail** (.2 mile) there is—surprise, surprise—a natural arch. The most arduous of Kodachrome's trails is **Eagle View Overlook** (.5 mile), but the valley views make it all worthwhile.

Driving or hiking south of Kodachrome on the dirt road for about 15 miles brings you to **Cottonwood** and **Hackberry Canyons** that merit exploration for their fossils, springs and hidden wonders. Because this is such virgin country, a good topographic map is imperative before setting out.

ESCALANTE AREA There are several access points to the awesome and somewhat mysterious **Escalante Canyons**. A main point of departure is east of town one mile on Route 12. Turn left on the dirt road near the cemetery and left again after the cattle guard. Follow to the fence line and begin at the hiker maze. The trail leads into the upper Escalante Canyon portion of Death Hollow, an outstanding recreation area. For an overnight or three-night trip continue on to where the trails come out 15 miles down the river.

Quite popular here is the **Lower Calf Creek Falls Trail** (2.8 miles), about a mile up the highway from the lower Escalante Canyon entrance. The sandy trail passes towering cliffs on a gradual incline. You are rewarded with a beautiful waterfall.

Plenty of terrain awaits your exploration in **Capitol Reef National Park**, twice the size of nearby Bryce. Trails range from easy to steep, offering enough unexplored back country that you might not see people for days. Rock cairns mark some trails, while other routes are found with careful study of topographic maps.

Near Route 24 is **Hickman Bridge** (1 mile), a self-guided nature hike to a 133-foot rock rainbow with a gentle enough elevation gain (400 feet) to make it do-able for the whole family. Skirt past the Capitol Dome with its white domes of Navajo sandstone capping the rock. Keep going up the rim, past triple-decker ice cream cone-colored rocks to the overlook (2.3 miles).

From the **Chimney Rock** (1.75 miles) trailhead, three miles west of the visitors center on a trail with petrified wood, the path winds past the sandstone up switchbacks. Remember, no collecting of any kind is permitted in national parks.

The **Lower Spring Canyon Route** (9 miles), which skirts through chocolate-brown canyons, begins at the Chimney Rock Trail and requires negotiating two ten-foot dry falls and a river crossing. Some of the path is on a river bed so don't set out in threatening weather. Arrange for a car at the river's end or return the same way.

South of Route 24, on Scenic Drive, the splendid Waterpocket Fold ridge seems to go on forever. A logical first stop is the flat **Grand Wash** (2.3 miles), which cuts through towering thrones en route through the fold. The trail takes you into narrow canyons and past pockmarked rocks.

A short, steep detour off the Grand Wash to **Cassidy Arch** (1.8 miles) goes from canyon depths to cliffs. The 19th-century outlaw Butch Cassidy is said to have hidden out in these honeycombs.

From Burr Trail, a rugged road shaves over two miles off the **Upper Muley Twist** (5.5 miles) hike, which offers drama in the form of Saddle Arch and narrows within the Waterpocket Fold. Access is one mile west of the Burr Trail switchbacks.

Lower Muley Twist (12 miles) boasts areas that are steep and narrow enough to "twist a mule pulling a wagon." The colorful route traverses Waterpocket Fold. Start from Burr Trail, off Notom-Bullfrog Road.

Much easier but still spectacular hiking amid sheer walls and similar scenery is **Surprise Canyon** (1 mile), north of The Post turn-off. The Navajo people called this the "Land of the Sleeping Rainbows." They were right.

There are only two "trails" in Goblin Valley but plenty of room to wander. **Carmel Canyon** (1.5 miles) is an erosion trail to the Molly's Castle formation. It's located on the edge of the Valley of Goblins, a land of funny, little shapes, forms and hideaways in the rock.

Across the park's only road is a trail to the **Curtis Formation** (1 mile). In this parched soil, wild daisies and mule ear seem to miraculously bloom in the spring as does greencantian, an unusual plant that changes shape depending on the season.

▼▼▼▼▼▼▼▼▼▼▼
Transportation

CAR

Route 70 almost slices Utah in two as it runs east-west from the Colorado border. It ends at **Route 15**, Utah's main north-south artery that passes through Cedar City and St. George.

Route 14 branches east off Route 15 at Cedar City toward Cedar Breaks, while **Route 9** heads east from Route 15 to Springdale and the entrance of Zion National Park.

Route 89, a scenic byway, heads south from Route 70 through parts of Dixie National Forest before crossing Kanab. **Route 12** provides a pretty path to Bryce Canyon National Park and Escalante Canyons before bisecting **Route 24**, the only access to Capitol Reef National Park.

AIR

SkyWest/Delta Connection serves **St. George Municipal Airport** and **Cedar City Municipal Airport**. For taxi service in St. George call **Pete's Taxi**. ~ 801-673-5467.

BUS
Greyhound Bus Lines can bring you to southwestern Utah from around the country. There are stations in St. George and Cedar City. ~ Reservations: 800-231-2222. St. George: 1233 South Bluff Street in the McDonald's; 801-673-2933. Cedar City: 1355 South Main; 801-586-9465.

CAR RENTALS
Rental agencies at St. George Municipal Airport are **Avis Rent A Car** (800-331-1212) and **National Interrent** (800-227-7368). Other agencies in town include **Budget Rent A Car** (800-527-0700) and **Dollar Rent A Car** (800-800-4000).

At the Cedar City Municipal Airport, cars can be rented from **Avis Rent A Car** (800-331-1212) and **National Interrent** (801-586-7059). **Speedy Rental** (800-328-4567) serves Cedar City as well.

FIFTEEN

Southeastern Utah

How best to describe southeastern Utah? For starters, Teddy Roosevelt, America's quintessential outdoorsman, once traveled here. Then consider the fact that amusement-park thrills and man-made attractions have nothing on this place. Forget the Coney Island roller coaster. Plummet down a 30-degree incline at Moki Dugway or the Moab Slickrock Bike Trail. The rickety bridge to Tom Sawyer Island in Disneyland? You can sway and swing across a genuine suspension bridge over the San Juan River outside Bluff. And Gateway Arch in St. Louis becomes a mere modern toy after you see Mother Nature's natural design at Arches National Park.

This truly is a magic kingdom for the outdoors enthusiast, the naturalist, the archaeologist. Leave those luxury resorts, white-sand beaches and gleaming steel museums behind. In this region, the land reigns.

What's really amazing is that Mormon exiles thought they were entering America's wasteland when they fled to Utah in 1847. For this land is anything but barren. Take all the earth's geologic wonders, toss them into a blender and you have southeastern Utah. An array of mesas abuts dense forests adjacent to broad deserts with red-rock canyons and slender spires thrusting out of semiarid valleys. In this portion of the Colorado Plateau lie the spectacular Arches and Canyonlands national parks, Glen Canyon National Recreation Area (Lake Powell), two national monuments and a host of state parks.

Because southeastern Utah is so vast and diverse we have divided it into three geographic areas—Lake Powell, San Juan County and Moab. At the heart of the entire region sits Canyonlands National Park. Canyonlands also divides into three sections, which though contiguous are not directly connected by roads. Therefore you will find The Maze section of the park described in the Lake Powell section, the Needles district in the San Juan County listings and the park's Island in the Sky section within the Moab area listings.

Erosion is the architect of southeastern Utah. Over the millennia, land masses pushed through the earth's crust, rivers and streams carved deep canyons, wind and water etched mountainsides. On some of the rock walls are pictures and stories left behind by early man that seem to transcend the ages.

The first known people in southeastern Utah were here long before the Europeans even knew about America. They were the ancestors of today's Pueblo Indians. Evidence of these early builders and farmers is still abundant in the sites of their homes found among the cliffs, on the mesa tops and in the canyons.

When the tribes disappeared from southeastern Utah and the Four Corners region around the 13th century, they left dwellings, tools and plenty of personal possessions behind. Theories abound as to what prompted their hasty departure. Some look to about 1276 A.D. when a long drought ruined the harvest and depleted the food supply. There were dangers from marauding bands of fierce nomadic tribes. Others theorize that inexplicable fears caused by religious beliefs may have contributed. Regardless of influences, the Pueblo peoples abandoned the region, and examination of their living spaces and remnants continues to fascinate generations of archaeologists and amateur sleuths.

By the 14th century, the Navajo had become part of the landscape. Today, their reservation sprawls across 16 million acres of Utah, Arizona and New Mexico.

The first known contact by Europeans came in 1765 when Juan Maria de Rivera led a trading expedition north from New Mexico hoping to establish a new supply route with California. That route, which became known as the Old Spanish Trail, opened portions of southeastern Utah near what is now Moab.

In July 1776, a small band led by Franciscan friars, Fathers Francisco Dominguez and Silvestre Velez de Escalante, ventured from Santa Fe, New Mexico, to Monterey, California. They never made it, but their adventurous journey took them in a great loop through unexplored portions of the region including what is known today as Wahweap Marina at Lake Powell.

When traders finally realized that the crossing of the Colorado River near Moab bypassed more hazardous terrain in Colorado, the 1200-mile Old Spanish Trail opened great portions of Utah to commercial wagon trains. By 1830 the trail began to serve as a major trade route for European expansion into the West.

Nearly a century after the adventurous Spanish priests, a one-armed veteran of the Civil War, John Wesley Powell, led an expedition party on a thrilling and sometimes dangerous 1400-mile row boat trip from Green River in Wyoming to the lower Grand Canyon, charting the Colorado River and the lake that would later bear his name.

To extend its boundaries and promote its principles throughout Utah, the Mormon Church decided to settle the area. Brigham Young sent 42 men down the Old Spanish Trail to Moab. But after an attack by Ute Indians, the settlers departed. Twenty-two years later, however, another group of hearty souls tried again, this time establishing the town of Moab in 1877.

In April 1879, an exploration party scouted the San Juan country and reported that the area could be colonized. A group of 250 pioneers, 83 wagons and a thousand head of cattle left the relative safety of Cedar City in southwestern Utah for a 325-mile journey to what is now Bluff. Originally estimated as a trip of six weeks,

GLENN KIM '92

their arduous journey took six months as they chiseled and chopped their way through sand and rock and at one point lowered wagons down the western wall of Glen Canyon through what is now the legendary Hole-in-the-Rock.

Settlers here discovered that Mother Nature rewarded southeastern Utah with more than scenic beauty. Rich with tremendous natural resources, the land bursts with coal, crude oil, oil shale, natural gas and more. Uranium mining formed the heart of this area until the boom turned bust, but beds of potash and magnesium salts found deep within the soil continue to be mined.

Whether a pioneer Mormon or a modern-day adventurer, people have always found the weather to be a blessing. It gets hot here (summers average in the 90s), but during the other seasons the climate by and large is mild. Winter ranges in the 30s to low 40s, and precipitation is extremely low except in October, when there might be all of an inch of rainfall. Yet within the La Sal and Abajo mountains, skiers, snowmobilers and snowshoers find abundant powder in wintertime.

To this day, southeastern Utah remains sparsely populated. Towns here are small (the largest, Moab, boasts just over 4000 residents) and exude a "pioneer" atmosphere. Tightly clustered buildings set up in traditional Mormon pattern along wide streets, these are sensible towns with a strong backbone. Youngsters still ride their bicycles at sunset or walk hand-in-hand to Sunday services. Going out for a drink is more likely to mean a soda pop than a beer.

Moab now supports a diverse and growing population based on tourism, mining, agriculture and retirement. It is considered one of the most cosmopolitan small communities in Utah and is one of its fastest growing.

Present-day San Juan County has a population of more than 12,000 scattered among farms, hamlets and communities like Monticello, Blanding and Bluff. Most growth can be attributed to natural resource-based industries. The Navajo and Ute indian reservations comprise a large portion of the southern end of the county, with American Indians making up about 47 percent of the San Juan population.

In southeastern Utah, history and geology combine to draw the curious and the hearty. Though man has always explored the region by foot or automobile, the advent of mountain bikes opened up entirely new portals into the back country areas. John Wesley Powell's historic trip down the Green and Colorado rivers can now be easily run by whitewater enthusiasts. And onetime rugged cattle-drive routes are covered up with asphalt for the less-intrepid explorers.

Prized nooks and crannies are being "discovered" every day. This glorious land remains ever changing, continually revealing surprises long after any new wonders were thought to remain.

▼▼▼▼▼▼▼▼▼▼▼▼▼ Lake Powell Area

Like life, Lake Powell is grand, awesome and filled with contradictions. Conservationists considered it a disaster when Glen Canyon Dam was built in Page, Arizona, flooding beautiful Glen Canyon and creating a 186-mile-long reservoir that extended deep into the heart of Utah.

Today the environmental "tragedy" is Utah's second-most popular tourist destination. Part of the Glen Canyon National Recreation Area that covers one-and-a-quarter *million* acres, the lake boasts 2500 miles of meandering shoreline. Not only is that more shoreline than along the entire west coast of the United States, much of it is in the form of spires, domes, minarets and multi-hued mesas.

The depth of Lake Powell's turquoise waters varies from year to year depending on mountain runoff and releases from Glen Canyon Dam. An interesting cave discovered on one trip may well be under water the next season. The same holds true for favorite sandy beaches, coves and waterfalls. But part of the fun of exploring this multi-armed body of water is finding new hidden treasures and hideaways around the next curve.

SIGHTS

The lake can be entered from four marinas accessible by car. **Hite** is the most northern facility. ~ Route 95; 801-684-2278. **Bullfrog** (801-684-2233) and **Hall's Crossing** (801-684-2261), are neighboring marinas providing convenient car and passenger ferry service. The 20-minute ferry crossing eliminates 130 road miles. ~

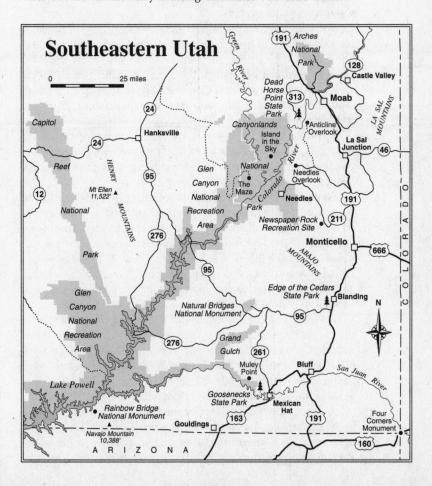

Southeastern Utah

Route 276. **Wahweap Marina** offers the most services to boaters, sightseers and overnight visitors. ~ Route 89 near the Glen Canyon Dam; 520-645-2433, 800-528-6154.

Dangling Rope Marina in mid-lake about seven miles southwest of the entrance to Rainbow Bridge Canyon is a floating refueling stop and supply store accessed only by boat. Enjoy a softserve ice cream cone while pumping gas. ~ 520-645-2969.

Lake Powell's waters usually warm to a comfortable temperature for swimming by May or early June. During the summer months, when the majority of the three million-plus annual visitors come, the surrounding temperatures can exceed a sizzling 100 degrees. Vacationers seek cool relief and a relaxing getaway in this stark desert ocean. Even at peak periods like July 4th and Labor Day weekends, when all the rental boats are checked out and hotel rooms booked, Lake Powell still manages to provide ample shoreline for docking and camping and, as always, clear, blue-green water for aquatic pursuits.

You can become acquainted with Powell from atop its sky-high buttes and adjacent byways, but those truly interested in getting to know the complex personality, curves and quirks must travel by vessel to the quiet box canyons and deep, gleaming pools for an experience akin to spiritual cleansing. Aficionados claim the best season to visit is early fall when rates and temperatures drop to a comfortable level.

Speed boats and houseboats are most popular for exploring, but a smaller water vehicle like a skiff or canoe will give access to outlying areas where you can just pitch a tent or throw down a sleeping bag on the shore.

Groups of friends and family typically rent a fuel-inefficient houseboat, fully equipped with bunks, bathroom and kitchen, as their mobile base and pull along a smaller boat for exploring nooks not easily charted with the lumbering mother ship. Sole concessionaire for Lake Powell is **Lake Powell Resort & Marinas**, which rents boats at all marinas except Dangling Rope. Hall's Crossing and Wahweap Marina have houseboats equipped for travelers with disabilities. ~ 800-528-6154.

Before setting out, the logical place to become acquainted with the second-largest manmade lake in the country is the **Carl Hayden Visitors Center**. The visitors center has a relief map, changing exhibits and the story of Major John Wesley Powell and his nine companions' charting of the waters by rowboat in 1869 and then again in 1871. ~ Route 89, Page, AZ; 520-608-6404.

Tours of the adjacent **Glen Canyon Dam**, which was completed in 26 separate vertical blocks by the Army Corps of Engineers in September 1963, are offered at no charge. The dam, a Bureau of Reclamation project, traps the river to provide water storage and hydroelectric power generation for many areas in the West. Tours are offered April through October.

Once out on the water, a must-see is, of course, the world's largest stone arch, **Rainbow Bridge National Monument**. Located about 50 water miles from either Wahweap, Bullfrog or Hall's Crossing marinas, "Nonnezoshi"—or rainbow turned to stone, as it's called by the Navajos—spans 275 feet. Declared a national monument in 1910, it wasn't until Glen Canyon Dam was completed 53 years later, and the lake started to fill, that the site became a favorite destination. Well touristed and commercialized on countless posters and cards, the stone arch with its awesome girth and prisms of color never ceases to amaze. Rainbow Bridge is reached only by boat, foot or horseback.

South of the awesome bridge, between Warm Creek and Wahweap bays, is **Antelope Island**, site of the first known expedition of whites to the area. Franciscan priests Francisco Dominguez and Silvestre Velez de Escalante trekked across a low point in the river (before it became a lake) and established camp on the island. Nearby **Padre Bay** was also named for the priests. Within these waters is the rock fortress called **Cookie Jar Butte**.

A landmark visible from the Wahweap section of the lake is the hump-backed, 10,388-foot **Navajo Mountain** and the striking **Tower Butte**, both located on the Navajo Indian Reservation. They are good landmarks to keep in mind when your directional sense gets churned in the water.

A primitive Indian "art gallery" is located approximately ten miles east of the Rainbow Bridge Canyon up the San Juan River arm in **Cha Canyon**. You must motor past what are termed the Bob Hope Rock (check out the profile) and Music Temple Canyon to reach Cha.

✔ **CHECK THESE OUT—UNIQUE SIGHTS**

- Boat out to **Rainbow Bridge National Monument**, the world's largest stone arch spanning 275 feet. *page 515*
- Be sure to read **Newspaper Rock**, a sandstone panel etched with petroglyphs spanning three distinct periods. *page 520*
- Cross the rickety swinging footbridge to view **Fourteen Window Ruin**, a honeycomb cliff dwelling also known as Apartment House Ruin. *page 525*
- Venture up the Colorado River at sunset with **Canyonlands by Night**, a voyage that gives you a unique look at river landmarks. *page 539*

When the heat is on, you'll be spending a lot of time in the refreshing, crystal-clear water. Five miles upstream (while some landmarks and obstacles are marked with buoys, a map is still essential) from Dangling Rope Marina is a water cave in Cascade Canyon that invites exploring. If you're more interested in things that swim than swimming, throw in a line and wait for the bass, crappies, pike and trout to bite.

Highly recommended for fishing is the **Escalante River Arm**, located about 25 miles north and east of Dangling Rope. Bridges and arches and ravines also abound in the Escalante's coves. Keep an eye peeled for prehistoric dwellings and drawings on a ledge above the mouth to **Willow Creek**, nine-and-a-half miles from the confluence with the main channel.

From Moki Canyon upstream about five miles are the odd and eerie **Moki steps,** thought to be hand and foot holds of this same tribe of ancient climbers.

Continuing farther into the Escalante arm, at approximately the 20-mile mark, you'll come to **Coyote Gulch** and its natural bridge and pair of arches.

From the main channel, the steep sandstone ridges of the Straight Cliffs and the 100-mile-long rock uplift called the **Waterpocket Fold** loom to the north. Respect must be given to those who were unintimidated by these fortresses. Just imagine being among the 230 or so Mormons who reached the towering canyons above the river in 1880 en route to establishing a new settlement—and not turning back.

Men blasted in solid rock for more than a month to create the **Hole-in-the-Rock**, permitting passage through the earth's mantle. The steep slope and landmark near the mouth of the Escalante River is still worth scaling, although erosion has partially closed the original notch.

North and east of the Hole-in-the-Rock is a little ol' swimming hole called **Annie's Canyon** about 12 miles from Bullfrog Marina. Boaters may notice more traffic and wake when nearing Halls Creek Bay, Bullfrog Bay and the busy marinas. Those on multiday excursions may want to stock up on ice and other necessary items at this point.

About five miles north of Hall's Crossing is **Moki Canyon**. With its archaeological sites and petroglyphs, the area holds many secrets of the Pueblo peoples. Supposedly the canyon was a miniature city back in prehistoric times.

Turn right and follow the next water pocket to Forgotten Canyon. At the end is the **Defiance House Site**, believed to have been occupied during the Pueblo's peak years from 1050 A.D. to 1250 A.D. Defiance House represents the lake's finest restored sites and petroglyphs and includes unusual animal/man anthropomorphs.

You'll pass by Tapestry Wall on the left side of the channel before coming to the long stretch of water in handsome **Good Hope**

Bay, below the mesa of the same name, that's usually a haven for flatwater—a waterskier's dream. The lake twists and turns past a handful of other canyons in the remaining 15 miles to Hite Marina, the start, or end, depending on how you look at it, of Lake Powell.

For more extensive history and sightseeing tips on Lake Powell, Stan Jones' *Boating and Exploring Map* is essential to your enjoyment and is available at any Lake Powell shop.

CANYONLANDS NATIONAL PARK—THE MAZE   Natural boundaries of rock and water divide Canyonlands National Park into three distinct districts—Island in the Sky, Needles and the Maze—and make travel between the sections almost impossible. Island could be considered the park's overlook, Needles leads visitors into the heart of rock country, while the remote Maze fulfills the promise of solitude and renewal that some seek.

Henry David Thoreau would have liked the uncharted territory of Canyonlands' Maze District because it demands self-reliance. Services to this section, considered by some to be a "mini-Grand Canyon," are almost nonexistent save for the emergency water available at the **Hans Flat Ranger Station.** The ranger will probably want to check your vehicle for road-worthiness before allowing you to proceed. Extra gas, and of course plenty of water, must be on hand before proceeding because you may not see another car for days. The Maze remains some of the wildest land in the West and is accessible only by foot or high-clearance four-wheel drive vehicle. ~ Ranger Station: 46 miles from the Route 24 turnoff via rough dirt road; 801-259-6513.

Puzzle-like chasms twist and turn through no-man's land where the junipers, piñon pine, sagebrush, yucca and spring wildflowers seem surprising given the desert dryness. From Hans Flat it's 34 miles to the Maze Overlook, a good starting point for hikes or for a bird's-eye view of the rock **Chocolate Drops,** which resemble candy bars left too long in the sun.

Hikers who drop into the steep canyon below the lookout are rewarded with eight-foot-tall pictographs at **Harvest Scene.** As with any remnants of ancient art, it is important not to touch these stunning works because human body oils can cause damage over time.

Traversing from one section to another in the Maze can be difficult and confusing because of the puzzle of canyons. Using Hans Flat as your starting point again, drive 45 miles past Bagpipe Butte Overlook and Orange Cliffs to the Land of Standing Rocks. There you'll have the option for further foot exploration of the **Doll House'**s redrock spires and massive fins in Ernie's Country. You may actually see more people here than in other sections of the Maze because some backcountry outfitters and rafting companies access the canyons from the edge of the Colorado River. Still, it's far from a thoroughfare.

Horseshoe Canyon, on the northwestern edge of the Maze about 32 miles from the Route 24 turnoff, contains the prehistoric rock-art collection of the **Great Gallery**. Considered some of this country's best-preserved pictographs and painted art, the gallery is full of haunting, life-size drawings of people and animals. There is evidence that a prehistoric Indian culture, as well as the later Anasazi and Fremont tribes, dabbled on these walls.

LODGING   At the **Defiance House Lodge**, cool desert room colors mimic the canyon hues outside. Marble basins, tile floors and fluffy towels are standard fare in all 48 rooms. Many rooms have lakeside views. ~ Bullfrog Marina; 801-684-2233. DELUXE.

Set on a cliff overlooking Lake Powell's westernmost bay is **Wahweap Lodge**. Featuring airy rooms with decor similar to its sister property (the Defiance House Lodge), Wahweap gets bonus points for its large swimming pool and manicured grounds. ~ Wahweap Marina; 520-645-2433, 800-528-6154. MODERATE.

Three-bedroom housekeeping cottages with linens, kitchens and utensils are a viable option for families. Cottages are available at **Bullfrog** (801-684-2233), **Hall's Crossing** (801-684-2261) and **Hite** (801-684-2278, 800-528-6154) marinas. MODERATE.

Even those who don't enjoy roughing it in a tent and sleeping bag will take to the great outdoors experience on a **houseboat**. Under Lake Powell's silent, starry skies, waves gently rock the boat, providing the perfect tonic for deep sleep. During the day, is there a more relaxing pastime than reclining on the boat's flat-topped roof with book or drink in hand? The mobile floating homes come equipped with all-weather cabins, bunk beds, showers, toilets and kitchens. Three sizes of boats sleep up to 12 people. **Lake Powell Resort & Marinas** (800-528-6154) rents houseboats at the Wahweap (520-645-2433), Bullfrog (801-684-2233), Hall's Crossing

---

✔ CHECK THESE OUT—UNIQUE LODGING

- *Budget to moderate:* Shelter yourself from the hot Utah sun under of one **Recapture Lodge's** shade trees while lounging on a lawn chair. *page 527*
- *Moderate to deluxe:* Experience the outdoors in the comfort of a floating mobile home on one of Lake Powell's **houseboats**. *page 518*
- *Moderate:* Save money and make your own breakfast at **Cedar Breaks Condos**, where collages of Indian petroglyphs adorn the rooms. *page 536*
- *Deluxe to ultra-deluxe:* Soak in an outdoor hot tub while taking in the views of red-rock monoliths at **Castle Valley Inn**. *page 537*

Budget: under $50 Moderate: $50–$90 Deluxe: $90–$120 Ultra-deluxe: over $120

(801-684-2261) and Hite (801-684-2278, 800-528-6154) marinas. To make reservations more than a week ahead of time, contact Lake Powell Resort & Marinas. Otherwise, call the marina directly. Prices vary depending on the season and the number in the party. MODERATE TO DELUXE.

Restaurants are few around Lake Powell as most visitors opt to eat on their houseboats or at their campsites. But realizing that people need a break, Lake Powell Resort & Marinas, which operates as the sole concessionaire for the National Park Service in Lake Powell, has two better-than-average restaurants in its on-shore hotels.

DINING

At the Bullfrog end of the lake is the **Anasazi Restaurant**. The restaurant sits perched above the marina and serves Continental cuisine. Steaks, burgers, fish and chips and Southwestern specialties please most palates, especially those who've eaten houseboat food for a week. ~ Defiance House Lodge, Bullfrog Marina; 801-684-2233. MODERATE.

Cornish game hens, slabs of prime rib, American Indian specialties and plenty of chicken dishes are well prepared and served with salads and generous side orders at the **Rainbow Room**. Considering the volume of traffic handled, the food is surprisingly good. Save room for one of the homemade desserts. ~ Wahweap Lodge and Marina; 520-645-2433. MODERATE.

At Lake Powell, enjoy a sunset cruise with dinner on the **Canyon King Paddlewheeler** from Wahweap. This is a favorite time of day to be on the lake because natural-rock amphitheaters appear to change colors before your very eyes as the late afternoon sun makes its curtain call. If you prefer not to dine on the water, sunset cruises are also available on other boats. ~ 520-645-2433.

NIGHTLIFE

GLEN CANYON NATIONAL RECREATION AREA

PARKS

Glen Canyon Dam confines the waters of the Colorado River forming Lake Powell, the second-largest manmade reservoir in the world. The 1869-square-mile area harbors countless inlets, caves and coves sheltering Pueblo Indian sites that are ever-changing because of the water level. Marinas are found at five separate locations on the lake: Hite, Bullfrog, Hall's Crossing, Dangling Rope and Wahweap. All kinds of water sports, from skiing to windsurfing, kayaking to inner tubing, have their place at Powell. You'll also find hotels, restaurants, groceries, visitors centers, picnic areas and restrooms. ~ Both Routes 95 and 89 lead to Lake Powell; 520-645-2471.

▲ There are 400 sites at five campgrounds: Bullfrog, Hall's Crossing, Lee's Ferry and Wahweap; $8.50 per night. Primitive campsites are available at Bullfrog and Hite; free. RV hookups are available ($21) through a private concessionaire (520-645-2433) at Wahweap, Bullfrog and Hall's Crossing only. There is free back-country camping with a permit. Camping is not allowed within one mile of marinas and at Rainbow Bridge National Monument.

RAINBOW BRIDGE NATIONAL MONUMENT 🏃🏇🚤 Greatest of the world's known natural bridges, this symmetrical, salmon-pink sandstone span rises 290 feet above the floor of Bridge Canyon. Rainbow Bridge sits on 160 acres within Glen Canyon National Recreation Area. Tours of the monument leave regularly in the summer season from Wahweap and Bullfrog marinas; during the rest of the year there is sporadic service out of Wahweap. Facilities are limited to restrooms. ~ Accessible by boat, on foot or by your own horse. To go the land route means traversing mostly unmarked trails through Navajo Indian Reservation land and requires a permit (520-871-6647); the number at the monument is 520-645-2471.

CANYONLANDS NATIONAL PARK—THE MAZE 🏃🚴 The Colorado and Green rivers naturally divide this 337,570-acre, unspoiled park into three distinct and separate districts: Island in the Sky, Needles and the Maze. Uncharted and untamed, wild formations of the Maze are enjoyed only after charting a labyrinth of canyons and jumbled rock. Another option for reaching the Maze is from the Colorado River's edge. The seemingly other-worldly formations and Indian artifacts in this 30-mile-wide jigsaw puzzle are found west of the Colorado and Green rivers. There are no facilities here. ~ Located via Route 24 south 46 miles to the dirt road turnoff to the east; 801-259-6513 or National Park Office (Moab), 801-259-7164.

▲ Primitive camping is allowed at Land of Standing Rocks and Maze Overlook with a permit ($25); no water available. Reservations are highly recommended for camping and may be made by calling 801-259-4351. People planning to camp with a vehicle must provide their own portable toilet system, which can be rented or purchased at Moab.

▼▼▼▼▼▼▼▼▼▼▼▼▼▼
San Juan County Area Most people come to San Juan County to visit either Canyonlands National Park Needles District or to drive the Trail of the Ancients. Time permitting, the two combined reveal more about the geology and history of southeastern Utah than almost any other tour.

Route 211 to the Needles sidles along Indian Creek, named for the area's first settlers. As you approach the steep canyon curves leading to Newspaper Rock, sparse desert landscape turns lush and green—is it any wonder Indian tribes settled here?

SIGHTS Blink and you might miss the turnoff to **Newspaper Rock Recreation Site**. The monument's sign is small, the right turn quick. This tiny park is usually on the "hit and run" list of most visitors. Though somewhat tarnished by graffiti, the huge sandstone panel is etched with fascinating Indian petroglyphs. This "rock that tells a story" is a compendium of American Indian history over a 2000-year span. The petroglyphs span three distinct periods, making this giant mural an archaeological find.

Some of the figures, such as the horseman with a bow and arrow, were not made by the Pueblo peoples but were done by later Indians (probably the Ute and Navajo), indicating that the sacred nature of the shrine was abandoned. A quarter-mile interpretive loop around the monument offers a chance to check out native flora and fauna, and some opt to set up camp here rather than amid the starker Canyonlands. ~ Route 211; 801-587-2141.

CANYONLANDS NATIONAL PARK—NEEDLES   In the Needles section of Canyonlands National Park you tend to feel a part of the scenery rather than a casual and detached observer. With its myriad of roads and trails, Needles is the most user-friendly of the Canyonlands sections. It also features the finest collection of petroglyphs and prehistoric sites in the park and is positively packed with natural stone sculptures in the form of arches and monoliths. Admission. ~ Route 211; 801-259-4711.

The adobe-style **Needles Visitors Center** can provide maps and advice to adventurers. From here a paved road leads six and a half miles into the park. Just past the visitors center a quarter-mile loop trail passes **Roadside Ruin**, an ancient Pueblo granary. Down the road, **Cave Spring Trail** loops three-fifths of a mile past a cave and former cowboy camp.

Needles Outpost Store is a necessary stop before heading into the back country. Ice, food, propane, firewood and guidebooks are sold at non-ripoff prices. Camping and four-wheel-drive rentals also available. ~ Route 211, outside Canyonlands Needles District; 801-979-4007.

Farther along, **Squaw Flat Rest Area** is a fine place to get your bearings and absorb the magic of the orange, rust and white-striped stone fortresses ("the needles") ahead. Then follow the main road to **Pothole Point Nature Trail** (.6 mile), another short loop that passes a series of potholes formed in the eroding sandstone. The vistas along the way of distant mesas are spectacular. At the end of the road you'll find **Big Spring Canyon Overlook**, gateway to a view of the Colorado and Green rivers' meeting place.

The Pueblo peoples left their mark throughout the Needles with Canyonlands sites dating from 900 A.D. to 1200 A.D. A four-wheel-drive vehicle or well-equipped mountain bike and good pair of legs are key to exploring the **jeep roads** leading to backcountry arches, canyons and the Pueblos' ancient drawings. A dirt road around the park's circumference is a fine way to view the Needles' unique topographic features. But beware, this route is not for the unsophisticated driver.

For a grand view of the Needles section of Canyonlands, be sure to take in the **Needles Overlook**. Getting there means driving back on Route 211, heading north a few miles on Route 191, then turning west on a dead end road. You'll be rewarded with a mesa-top vista that scans the Abajo and Henry Mountains, Colorado River and extends all the way to the park's Maze district.

Fifteen miles south of the Needles turnoff on Route 191, civilization reappears. Named for Thomas Jefferson's Virginia home, **Monticello** is the San Juan County seat. Complete information on the nearby national parks and monuments, state parks and local attractions can be obtained at the **Multi-Agency Visitors Center**. ~ Located in the County Courthouse, 117 South Main, Monticello; 801-587-3235.

Early area history is revealed at the **Monticello Museum** in the County Library. Besides Pueblo artifacts, the museum contains articles from pioneer life—an old stove, wagon keg, sewing machine, vanity case, picture albums and flat irons. ~ 80 North Main; 801-587-2281.

Another 20 miles south on Route 191 is **Blanding**, once a trading center for nearby ranches. The log building a few miles farther along is home to **Huck's Museum & Trading Post**. Owner Huck Acton has assembled a stellar display of pottery and American Indian artifacts dating back to ancient times. The private collection of arrowheads, beads, pendants, effigy bowls, cooking pots and tools is sure to impress. Admission. ~ Route 191; 801-678-2329.

HIDDEN ► A gem of the Utah state park system is **Edge of the Cedars Museum and Indian Ruin**. Site of an Anasazi Indian ruin, Edge of the Cedars allows visitors to explore the small village inhabited from 750 A.D. to 1200 A.D., even climbing down a wooden ladder into a large underground room. The modern museum details the many cultures—Anasazi, Navajo, Ute and Anglo—that have played a role in regional development. The exhibits include clothing, artifacts, ceremonial objects and tools as well as video presentations. The museum walls showcase reproductions of ancient Indian pictographs. Admission. ~ 660 West 400 North, Blanding; 801-678-2238.

TRAIL OF THE ANCIENTS A scenic, historical and archaeological tour of southern San Juan County begins at Edge of Cedars, just south of Blanding, and follows a counterclockwise, 125-mile loop that includes more than a dozen sites of interest such as Natural Bridges National Monument and the cities of Mexican Hat and Bluff. The trail derives its name from Anasazi, "the ancient ones," and much of the tour passes ancient sites of this now-extinct people. Detailed maps are available at the Edge of the Cedars Museum and Indian Ruin.

Just west of Blanding a paved access road from Route 191 leads across a swinging natural bridge to the **Westwater** cliff dwellings, which include five kivas (circular, underground structures used for gathering of kin groups) and open work areas. The dwelling was occupied from around 1150 A.D. to 1275 A.D. Unfortunately, much of the site has been destroyed by vandals searching for ancient relics.

From Route 191, the trail turns west onto Route 95, passing Cottonwood Falls, Butler Wash and Comb Ridge. Only a large depression, almost 80 feet in diameter, marks the great kiva at **Cottonwood Falls**. Looking south from the eastern end of the hole, a prehistoric road may be spotted. **Butler Wash** houses the highly developed stonework remains of a 20-room dwelling area plus several smaller Anasazi structures. The cliff houses can be viewed from an observation area at the end of a mile-long hiking trail. **Comb Ridge** is an eroded monocline, or bending of the earth's crust in a single direction, and extends some 80 miles south into Arizona.

Before man's ability to blast solid rock, Comb Ridge was a natural barrier to east/west travel.

The highway continues to cut through the red walls of **Arch Canyon** where centuries of erosion have chiseled and sculpted massive sandstone formations. Seven ancient towers, thought to have been built more than 900 years ago, are clustered high atop the rim of **Mule Canyon**. Three of the seven are visible at the site and considered a rare find because only a few such tower-like ruins are still standing.

At the actual **Mule Canyon Ruin and Rest Stop** are an excavated, 12-room pueblo with a pair of kivas and a tower, all extremely well preserved and stabilized. The Bureau of Land Management has even constructed a sheltering ramada over the kiva, affording extra protection and interpretive signs offering clues to its history.

Later explorers of the region included an 1879 scouting party that lost its way while looking for the Hole-in-the-Rock Trail. The scouts climbed to the top of **Salvation Knoll**, from where they were able to regain their bearings and continue their search for a passable route to the east.

What the scouting party didn't spot was **Natural Bridges National Monument**. Records show it wasn't discovered by white men until 1883. Home to three of the largest known natural bridges in the world, the park maintains a visitors center, hiking trails, campground and paved, nine-mile loop road. Each mammoth stone bridge can be viewed by walking a short distance to an overlook. Archaeological sites can be seen from perches along the rim. Admission charged March through October, free in winter. ~ Route 95; 801-692-1234.

The monument area is mostly desert-like with a smattering of piñon-juniper trees, shrubs and grasses among the white sandstone. While ancient Indian tribes lived in the area, the canyons were apparently too small to sustain the farming activities of many families. Nonetheless, Horsecollar Site, the cliff dwelling remains of one community, can be viewed.

The three bridges, which resemble arches but are formed solely by flowing water, are known as Sipapu, Kachina and Owachomo. **Sipapu**, a fat-topped spur of rimrock, is the largest bridge in both height (220 feet) and span (268 feet). Its name means "the place of emergence." The "younger" **Kachina Bridge** was found to have prehistoric pictographs resembling kachinas (dancers). White Canyon floodwaters, frosts and thaws are still enlarging Kachina Bridge. Taken from the Hopi language, **Owachomo** or "rock mounds" is so named for the large, rounded rock mass found nearby and is the oldest of the three bridges with only a narrow strip of nine-foot-thick rock remaining in the center of the bridge.

Owachomo is tall enough to fit Washington's Capitol building underneath.

Backtrack from Natural Bridges and turn south on Route 261 to continue the Trail of the Ancients tour. Still primitive, by today's standards, is **Grand Gulch** where Anasazi habitation was omnipresent. Found within the 50-mile-long canyon system (managed as an outdoor museum) are six representative sites from both Basketmaker and Pueblo periods. Extensive remains of Anasazi dwellings, tools and artwork may be seen. Travel is limited to horseback riders and hikers.

Like stepping into a new world, **Muley Point Overlook** abruptly jolts travelers from cedar forests to austere desert scenes. In the distance, keen observers can spot the monolith-filled Monument Valley. Be warned: Route 261 leading to Muley Point travels over the Moki Dugway, a graveled, three-mile series of tight (and we mean tight!) switchbacks ascending to the lookout.

Descending from the overlook, the road leads into the **Valley of the Gods** which, with its unique rock formations jutting hundreds of feet into the air, is considered a mini-Monument Valley.

An interesting offshoot is **Goosenecks State Park**. From the canyon rim of the park, you can view the San Juan River 1000 feet below forming a series of "gooseneck" switchbacks as it winds its way toward Lake Powell. ~ Route 261; 801-678-2238.

Continuing on the Trail of the Ancients, **Mexican Hat** is a tiny community separated from the Navajo Indian Reservation by the San Juan River. Its name comes from a stone formation resembling an upside-down sombrero just outside town. There are a few trading posts, motels, cafés, service stations and an RV park. ~ Two miles west of the Route 163 intersection with Route 261.

The Trail next heads east on Route 163 passing to **Sand Island**, primary boat launch for the San Juan River. Petroglyph panels here showcase five Kokopelli flute players—mythological Indian figures.

At the intersection of Routes 163 and 191 is the tiny town of **Bluff**. While the Mormons first settled Bluff in 1880, some archaeologists believe Paleo Indian hunters may have stalked bison herds through the area 11,000 years ago. Kiva and cliff dwellings confirm the presence of ancient Pueblo tribes. Visitors to the town (the oldest community in San Juan County) may view sandstone Victorian-style homes left by early settlers, some of whom are buried in the historic **Pioneer Cemetery** overlooking the town. The cemetery is easy to get to: Follow the Bluff Historic Loop past Rim Rock Drive to the end of the road.

On your way to Pioneer Cemetery you will pass the **Old County Jail**, a hand-hewn sandstone structure in the center of town that was originally erected as an elementary school in 1896. ~ Bluff Historic Loop.

St. Christopher's Episcopal Mission, two miles east of Bluff, is a house of worship built of native sandstone. The Navajo Madonna and Child stand on the site of the original church, which was destroyed by fire. ~ Route 163.

About three miles east of Bluff, across a swinging footbridge that spans the San Juan River, is the **Fourteen Window Ruin** cliff dwelling (also known as the Apartment House Ruin). Take the dirt road on the south side of the highway to the bottom of the hill. After crossing the rickety bridge and coming to the clearing, the site can be spotted straight ahead in the rock. For closer inspection of these honeycombed dwellings, walk the additional mile on the dusty trail. Please be respectful—this site is on Navajo tribal land, and access can be denied at any time.

Those with ample time may want to stay on the Trail of the Ancients into Hovenweep National Monument located in both Colorado and Utah. If not, Route 191 goes north from Bluff through the Ute Indian Reservation back to Blanding.

LODGING

As tourism generates most of this area's summer economy, hotels are numerous. Yet with few exceptions, most are of the motel variety designed to provide a clean bed and bath but little else.

Top of the line in every way, **Days Inn Monticello** won't disappoint. The two-story complex is decorated in soft blues, gray and mauve. Rooms are large with ample drawer space. Adding to the hotel's popularity are complimentary "heavy duty" continental breakfasts, a huge indoor swimming pool, with a whirlpool spa and an outdoor lawn area with lawn chairs. ~ 549 North Main, Monticello; 801-587-2458, 800-329-7466. MODERATE.

Without question the **Grist Mill Inn Bed and Breakfast** is an exquisite property. Originally an old flour mill, the meticulously restored inn maintains many original features like hand-hewn rough timber beams and loft ceilings. Six rooms, each with private

◀ *HIDDEN*

bath, are scattered among three stories for ultimate privacy. In addition, there are three similarly decorated guest rooms in the recently converted granary and a separate room in a restored caboose. Antiques, lace curtains, overhead fans and clawfoot tubs add to the luxury. Guests awake to a full country breakfast. Other amenities include indoor whirlpool, television room, library and on-site country store featuring local handcrafted gifts. ~ 64 South 300 East, Monticello; 801-587-2597, 800-645-3762. MODERATE.

Though nothing to write home about, the **Best Western Wayside Inn** is nevertheless a good place to hang your hat for a night or two. Rooms are large, with dark green carpets, oak furniture and computer jacks. The on-site swimming pool and hot tub are pluses, as are the tastefully landscaped grounds. ~ 197 East Central, Monticello; 801-587-2261. BUDGET TO MODERATE.

Budget-minded travelers will appreciate **Navajo Trail National 9 Inn**. Immaculate rooms have typical hotel decor but offer large, yellow-and-blue-tile showers. For a few extra dollars, a kitchen can be yours complete with stove, refrigerator and microwave. ~ 248 North Main, Monticello; 801-587-2251, 800-524-9999. BUDGET.

The **Grayson Country Inn** should be called "Grandma's House." Even when every other area hotel is full, they manage to find an empty sofa for a stranded traveler. Seven bright and spacious rooms all have private baths and are filled with country knick-knacks—antiques, patchwork quilts, throw pillows and tiny framed prints. A generous breakfast is served on the sun-filled, enclosed porch. ~ 118 East 300 South, Blanding; 801-678-2388. BUDGET.

One of the better properties in the area, the **Best Western Gateway Motel** boasts nicely appointed rooms and a congenial staff. Contemporary appointments in blues and earth-tones are used in both the large lobby area and 60 spacious units. The swimming pool and free continental breakfast are nice extras. ~ 88 East Center, Blanding; 801-678-2278. BUDGET.

Rooms at the **Prospector Motor Lodge** range from good to so-so. Many have knotty-pine walls, floral-pattern bedspreads and tile baths. Others are more plastic with laminate furniture. Still, the single-story, red-brick motel is immaculate. Just ask to view a room first. ~ 591 South Main, Blanding; 801-678-3231. BUDGET.

Designed by a student of architect Frank Lloyd Wright, the **Cliff Palace Motel** has many unusual features, including floor-to-ceiling windows, indirect lighting in bathrooms and dressing areas, tiled seats in showers and built-in luggage racks. Fifteen rooms are decorated in a Southwest style, although some retain the blue shag carpeting from the previous decor. ~ 132 South Main, Blanding; 801-678-2264, 800-553-8093. BUDGET.

Claustrophobics will find the **Kokopelli Inn** somewhat confining, but the 26 rooms are spotless. Surprisingly, baths are oversized, and there are walk-in closets. ~ Route 191, Bluff; 801-672-2322, 800-672-2325. BUDGET.

There's something very inviting about the **Recapture Lodge**. An oasis of shade trees populates the site, shielding guests from the hot Utah sun. There are 32 homey rooms, nothing fancy, but quiet and comfortable. Lawn chairs, ideal for lounging, line the upper deck. A nice-sized swimming pool provides another way to beat the heat. Adventuresome souls can arrange geologist-guided tours of the nearby canyons, cliff dwellings and American Indian sites—or even multiday llama treks—through the lodge. ~ Route 191, Bluff; 801-672-2281. BUDGET.

DINING

Don't expect to watch your cholesterol in San Juan County. Basic country cooking is standard fare, with a real salad bar about as rare as a rosebush in the desert. Hearty, homemade dishes make **Juniper Tree** a popular dinner choice. Steaks, prime rib, fish and spaghetti are served with huge chunks of homemade bread and a trip to the soup/salad bar. The only question is, "What is that fluffy, purple concoction at the salad bar?" ~ 133 East Central, Route 666, Monticello; 801-587-2929. MODERATE.

An adobe exterior replete with vigas houses **La Casita**. The menu offers burritos, chimichangas, enchiladas and hamburgers. Family friendly, La Casita also caters to extra-hungry hombres with the "wild burrito." Closed Sunday. ~ Route 666, Monticello; 801-587-2959. BUDGET TO MODERATE.

A quick pizza fix may be had at **Wagon Wheel Pizza**. Fresh deli sandwiches, calzones and pizzas are prepared in a flash. Take out or hunker down in a red-leather booth under mock Pepsi-Cola Tiffany lamps. ~ 164 South Main, Monticello; 801-587-2766. BUDGET.

A safe bet for breakfast and lunch is **Houston's of Monticello**. The breakfast menu features blue-corn pancakes and fruit waffles

---

✔ **CHECK THESE OUT—UNIQUE DINING**

- *Budget:* Head to **Honest Ozzie's Café & Desert Oasis** to satisfy your vegetarian and dessert cravings. *page 538*
- *Budget to moderate:* Go out of your way to dine on scrumptious cuisine in an old log-and-stone trading post at **Cow Canyon Restaurant**. *page 528*
- *Moderate:* Save room for the homemade desserts at the **Rainbow Room**, where the menu is varied and the selections are tasty. *page 519*
- *Deluxe:* Sidle up to the extensive salad bar and feast on mesquite-broiled steaks and seafood at the oil-lamp illuminated **Pack Creek Ranch Restaurant**. *page 538*

Budget: under $8 Moderate: $8–$16 Deluxe: $16–$24 Ultra-deluxe: over $24

while for lunch you can choose from healthy, fresh sandwiches and vegetarian dishes. Vegetables come from local organic farms in summer. Closed Tuesday. ~ 296 North Main, Monticello; 801-587-2531. BUDGET.

Sit-down restaurants are in short supply in Blanding, but the **Elk Ridge** offers typical country cooking—chicken-fried steak, hamburgers, chicken—and hearty breakfasts. Locals enjoy Elk Ridge because it has a small salad bar, and the homemade cherry pie is scrumptious. Closed Sunday. ~ North Route 191, Blanding; 801-678-3390. BUDGET.

HIDDEN ▶

Surprisingly, it's in the tiny town of Bluff where you'll discover some of the best dining. **Cow Canyon Restaurant** changes its entrées weekly. They feature traditional Navajo dishes, vegetarian and sometimes even French cuisine. One week the choices might be spinach lasagna, Greek salad or stuffed butternut squash. Desserts range from an apple dumpling to ice cream splashed with Kahlua and baked almonds. Housed in an old log-and-stone trading post, Cow Canyon's ambience more than matches the food. Dinner only. Closed Tuesday and Wednesday. ~ Route 191, Bluff; 801-672-2208. BUDGET TO MODERATE.

The Navajo Taco—fry bread topped with pinto beans, lettuce, tomato, cheese, onion and red or green chiles—supposedly originated at **Sunbonnet Café**. Log-cabin walls and high tongue-and-groove ceilings provide an authentic Western touch. Breakfast, sandwiches, hamburgers, steaks and chicken are served, along with the pinkest pink lemonade you'll ever see. Closed Sunday. ~ Historic Loop, Bluff; 801-672-2201. BUDGET.

SHOPPING

As gateway to Navajo tribal lands, San Juan County is blanketed with trading posts. Best of the lot is **Cow Canyon Trading Post**, a log-and-stone structure dating from the 1940s. Jewelry, pottery, rugs and ethnographic artifacts of the Navajo and Ute are well displayed and honestly priced. ~ Route 191, Bluff; 801-672-2208.

Other trading posts selling sandstone folk art, pottery, baskets, silver jewelry, pipes, papooses and rugs are **Thin Bear Indian Arts** (1944 South Route 191, Blanding; 801-678-2940), **Blue Mountain Trading Post** (South Route 191, Blanding; 801-678-2570), **Hunt's Trading Post** (146 East Center, Blanding; 801-678-2314), **Burches Trading Post** (Route 163, Mexican Hat; 801-683-2221), **San Juan Inn Trading Post** (Route 163, Mexican Hat; 801-683-2220) and **Twin Rocks Trading Post** (Historic Loop, Bluff; 801-672-2341).

After perusing the wares for sale at **Cedar Mesa Pottery** take a behind-the-scenes tour of the pottery factory. Here, you can watch American Indian artisans create and decorate their hand-painted pottery. Closed weekends in winter. ~ 333 South Main, Blanding; 801-678-2241.

The Olde Bridge Bar and Grille is open Monday through Sunday for over-the-bar beer sales, while the grill offers dinner nightly. Occasional live music in the bar. ~ San Juan Inn, Route 163 and the San Juan River, Mexican Hat; 801-683-2220.

NEWSPAPER ROCK RECREATION SITE 🚶 Hiking and camping within this 50-acre park are encouraged, and the lush, evergreen area provides sharp a contrast to nearby Canyonlands. The only facilities available here are toilets. ~ From Monticello take Route 211 northwest 15 miles, then Route 191 southwest for 11 miles; 801-587-2141.

▲ There are eight sites; free.

CANYONLANDS NATIONAL PARK—NEEDLES DISTRICT 🚶🚲 Sculptured rock spires, arches, canyons and potholes dominate the landscape. Grassy meadows like Chesler Park offer striking contrasts to the mostly bare rock. Traces of the Pueblo Indians can be found throughout the area in well-preserved pictographs and petroglyphs. The meeting place of the Colorado and Green rivers, before they join forces and rumble down to Lake Powell, can be seen from Confluence Overlook. If Island in the Sky is the observation deck for Canyonlands, then the Needles could be considered the main stage—you start out right at ground level and become immediately immersed in its unfolding tale. The park has a visitors center, picnic areas and restrooms. ~ Proceed south from Moab on Route 191 for 40 miles, then 35 miles southwest on Route 211; 801-259-4711 or National Park Office (Moab), 801-259-7164.

▲ There are 26 primitive sites; $6 per night. Water is not available in winter. Nearby, there is also camping at Needles Outpost Store from March to October (801-979-4007).

NATURAL BRIDGES NATIONAL MONUMENT 🚶 Three natural bridges, including the world's second and third largest, are within this 7500-acre, canyon-like park first discovered by white pioneers in 1883. You'll find an exhibit hall and restrooms. ~ Located on Route 95 about 40 miles west of Blanding; 801-692-1234.

▲ Permitted at 13 primitive sites; $5 per night. Water is available at the visitors center.

GOOSENECKS STATE PARK 🚶 An impressive example of "entrenched meander," Goosenecks is a 1000-foot-deep chasm carved by the San Juan River as it winds and turns back on itself for more than six miles while advancing only one and a half miles west toward Lake Powell. A picnic area and restrooms are the park's only facilities. ~ Located nine miles northwest of Mexican Hat off Route 261; 801-678-2238.

▲ Primitive camping is allowed within the park; free. Note: No water is available.

▼▼▼▼▼▼▼▼▼
Moab Area

Movies made Moab famous, but the area has a lot more going for it than this. Used as a home base for many who explore southeastern Utah, the city has a well-preserved, colorful history. Add to this two wonderful national parks in the region, a neat loop drive, even a winery. What more could you want?

Moab truly is an oasis in the wilderness. Red-rock cliffs really do meet verdant valleys, all in the shadow of the towering La Sal Mountains. First settled in 1855 by missionaries, Moab is laid out in typical Mormon fashion with large, square blocks, wide streets and huge poplar trees. And as in southwestern Utah, the word "Street" is simply not used in the names of thoroughfares. What you might call Main Street back home is simply known as Main here. The city takes its name from a remote biblical kingdom east of the River Jordan. Present-day Moab is "sporting central" for the lean-and-mean lycra-wearing crowd. Spring is high season in Moab, as thousands of ski bums and heat-seekers flock here for desert warmth.

SIGHTS

Moab serves as gateway to both Arches National Park and Canyonlands National Park—Island in the Sky. For area information, stop at the **Moab Visitors Center.** ~ Center and Main; 801-259-8825.

Moab's rich history is preserved in the **Dan O'Laurie Museum.** Though the collection is small, it is comprehensive, examining the geology and paleontology of Moab's beginnings. Dozens of photographs recount the development of mining, ranching, early transportation and the Old Spanish Trail. There's even the old switchboard that served all of Moab until 1951. Closed Sunday. ~ 118 East Center; 801-259-7985.

Star Hall, just northeast of the museum, is the start of the **Moab Historic Walking Tour** of 23 homes and commercial structures. Pick up a map at the visitors center.

It was young geologist Charles Steen who first discovered uranium deposits in the region, touching off the rush of miners. The "uranium king" built a **million-dollar home** overlooking the Moab Valley and rivers. The house is now Mi Vida Restaurant. ~ 900 North Route 191; 801-259-7146.

Director John Ford put the area on the map when he filmed the 1949 classic *Wagonmaster* here. Ford returned to film *Rio Grande* the following year, and Hollywood has favored it ever since. A detailed guide to area movie locations—including *The Greatest Story Ever Told*, *Cheyenne Autumn*, *Indiana Jones and the Last Crusade* and *Thelma and Louise*—is available at the visitors center.

Utah's only commercial winery now has a tasting room in Moab. **Arches Vineyard** uses 50 acres of premium grapes in and around the Moab area. The winery went into production during the late 1980s, and now everyone can taste the fruit of its labors. Besides sampling the various whites and reds, you can walk through the winery itself. Closed Sunday. ~ 420 Kane Creek Boulevard; 801-259-5397.

ARCHES NATIONAL PARK Traversing the width and breadth of Arches National Park on the paved road that author Edward Abbey deplored in his book *Desert Solitaire* (a must-read for any visitor) is easy—maybe too easy. To truly experience the greatest number of natural arches in the country, get out of your car and wander. You won't want to miss the sensation of sandstone beneath shoe, the delicious scent of juniper and sage, even the hauntingly lonely sound of whistling desert wind on the short hiking trails. Admission. ~ Route 191, five miles north of Moab; 801-259-8161.

The world's largest concentration of natural stone arches, extraordinary products of erosion, makes this 73,378-acre park one of the most spectacular in red-rock country. Sandstone panoramas formed by weathering, movement of the earth's crust and erosion range in size from three to 306 feet. Natural monoliths in this semiarid land resemble everything from city skyscrapers to a whale's orb: The interpretation is all in the eye of the beholder.

Make your first stop the **Visitors Center** for a bevy of maps and other publications as well as a slide show orientation, geology museum and history exhibit. Rangers can point out many of the best attractions. ~ Route 191 at the entrance to the park; 801-259-8161.

From the visitors center the main park road climbs into the heart of the arches region. **Moab Canyon,** a multi-hued example of geological slippage, opens to view about a mile from the center. About six million years ago activity along the Moab fault caused one section of the canyon to shift resulting in rock formations on the bottom of one side that are identical in age with those on the far side of the canyon.

Farther along at the **South Park Avenue Overlook** you'll see giant sandstone rockfaces that rise sheer on either side of a dry creek bed.

Appearing to defy gravity is **Balanced Rock,** a formation that looks like it might fall from its pedestal at any moment. A short but strenuous trail (.3 mile) can be taken to examine all the boulder's vantage points.

One of the easiest areas to visit is **Windows.** Four large arches that provide natural picture frames for distant panoramas can be effortlessly viewed. The North and South Windows are a short walk in one direction from the parking lot. Take a jaunt the other way and see the Turret Arch. Splendid Double Arch is just across the road. Preludes to the panoramic windows via the Windows road are Garden of Eden viewpoint, providing sweeping views to the north, and Elephant Butte. ~ About 12 miles from the visitors center via the main park road and Windows turnoff.

Balanced Rock marks the start of a rough, four-wheel-drive road into the more secluded Willow Flats and **Herdina Park** sections. Herdina Park's claim to fame is that it's the home to five mini-canyons and the unusual **Eye of the Whale Arch**. With a little imagination, you can see the beast's orb.

Those with heavy-duty vehicles may want to venture another ten miles to the vast and scenic Klondike Bluffs, home to the **Tower Arch**, a hole in a wall of solid rock, and minarets that form the **Marching Men**. Check with the ranger for conditions before traveling this road.

The park's northern section, where the main park road ends, has the largest grouping of spires and openings-in-the-rock. No less than seven arches can be viewed in **Devil's Garden**, the park's longest maintained trail. The most distant of these arches is the Double O, which is about a two-mile trek from the trailhead that feels longer under the hot desert sun. If stamina allows, hike an extra quarter-mile on a more primitive trail to the ominous **Dark Angel** formation. Halfway to the trail end is **Landscape Arch**. At 306 feet long (and at one spot only six feet thick) it's one of the world's longest natural stone spans. **Navajo Arch**—did it protect Indians at some juncture?—is one and a half miles from the trailhead. Piñon plants, junipers—the most common tree in the park— the Mormon tea plant, the obnoxious prickly pear and evening primrose and Indian paintbrush flowers dot the area. Pick up an interpretive brochure at the visitors center before setting out to enhance your understanding of the desert garden.

> Some early explorers interpreted Delicate Arch as being a bowlegged cowboy!

From Devil's Garden it's about one mile south on the main road to the fins (yes, they do look like fish fins) of up to 100 feet high in **Fiery Furnace**, which does not live up to its threatening name on hot days. Indeed, the pinnacles provide a degree of relief when temperatures scorch. The ranger-guided tour of the Furnace is recommended, since winter erosion and labyrinthine trails make this an easy place to get injured or lost.

HIDDEN ▶ Traveling back toward the park entrance, take the first turnoff to the left and drive two miles to the **Delicate Arch** trailhead. Set aside several hours to really enjoy this graceful monument that stands 65 feet high, with a 35-foot opening. Arguably Utah's most beautiful natural wonder, the sensuous bit of slickrock stands boldly against the desert and distant La Sal Mountains. The one-and-a-half-mile trail skirts the historic **Wolfe Ranch**, sole remains of a 19th-century cattle operation that somehow survived more than a generation in this harsh land. Those unable or uninterested in hiking to Delicate Arch can drive an additional mile from the trailhead to the **Delicate Arch Viewpoint** and gaze from there.

CANYONLANDS NATIONAL PARK—ISLAND IN THE SKY On your way to Island in the Sky, be sure and stop at **Dead Horse Point State Park**. An isolated, 5400-acre island mesa, 6000 feet above sea level and surrounded by steep cliffs, Dead Horse Point State Park showcases 150 million years of canyon erosion, buttes, pinnacles, bluffs and towering spires plus the Colorado River 2000 feet below. Views from the park overlook 5000 square miles of the Colorado Plateau including the La Sal and Abajo mountain ranges. Admission. ~ Route 313; 801-259-2614.

◄ *HIDDEN*

If ever you doubted Utah scenery could steal your breath away, this promontory will change your mind. Depending on weather and time of day, the Colorado River Gorge below is an artist's palate of ever-changing hues. For a spectacular view of the park, you can't beat the back deck of the **Visitors Center**. Nearby paths also offer an interpretive guide to regional flora. But don't make the center your only stop. From there drive another mile and a half to the park's majestic overlook. It won't disappoint. Admission. ~ Visitors Center: Route 313; 801-259-6577.

Wilder and less trodden than the Arches is its neighbor, Canyonlands National Park—Island in the Sky district. It's a broad, level mesa serving as observation deck for the park's 527 square miles of canyons, mesas, arches and cliffs. From this vantage point the visitor can enjoy views of the two powerful rivers that constitute the park's boundaries, the Colorado and Green, and three mountain ranges, the La Sals, Abajos and Henrys.

Just past the Island in the Sky Visitors Center on the left side is the **Shafer Canyon Overlook** and the winding Shafer Trail Road, which swoops down the canyon to connect to the **White Rim Trail**, so named for the layer of white sandstone that forms its line of demarcation. The White Rim parallels the Colorado and later the Green River forming a belt around the Island in the Sky's circumference. Permits are required for campsites along the relatively level trail (reservations recommended; there is a $25 charge), which can be comfortably covered by bike or sturdy four-wheel-drive vehicle in two to four days.

Back on top of the mesa that is the Island, enjoy a bird's-eye view of **Lathrop Canyon** and the Colorado River via the Mesa Arch path. Short and sweet, this trail provides a vantage point for distant arches like Washer Woman, menacing Monster Tower and Airport Tower.

Just one-quarter mile west, near the intersection of the park's only two roads, are the Willow Flat campground and the true-to-its-name **Green River Overlook**, a fine contrast to the muddy Colorado. On the road's north side is the short trail to **Aztec Butte** where you'll find Indian archaeological sites.

At the end of this side road, see the bulbous **Whale Rock** jutting out of its parched home near the geologic paradox of **Upheaval Dome**, a 1500-foot-deep crater with a questionable origin. Theories are divided whether this was a natural occurrence or meteor-created. Weird, moonlike craters with peaks spring from its center.

At the most southerly end of the main road is the **Grand View Point Overlook**. From this vantage point at 6000 feet above sea level, Utah's geologic contrasts become crystal clear. There are totem pole-like spires and the rounded La Sal and Abajo mountains in the distance. The Colorado River cuts so deeply in the canyon below that it's invisible from the overview. Columns and fins and other contorted rocks comprise a gang of soft sandstone structures called **Monument Basin**. By traversing the White Rim trail it's possible to get a closer look at these monuments.

HIDDEN ▶

SOUTH FROM MOAB   Mountains meet red rock along the **La Sal Mountain Loop Drive**. The round-trip ride from Moab is about 60 miles from start to finish and can be driven in either direction. Plan on a minimum of three to four hours to fully enjoy the views and side trips in the evergreen-laden forests that rise 4000 feet above the red rock. Look for the road marker about eight miles south of Moab off Route 191. Turn left and head into the hills.

The land seems to change almost immediately as sandstone gives way to forests and foothills. A popular fishing hole and wind-surfing spot, **Ken's Lake**, is off to the left, via a dirt road. Another few miles farther and you're at the Pack Creek Ranch, which operates riding trips in the summer and backcountry skiing excursions during the winter. Continuing on the La Sal Mountain Loop Drive brings you to a turnoff on the right called Geyser Pass. This road accesses a popular area for cross-country skiing.

Back on the loop road another few miles are turnoffs on the right to scenic lakes Oowah and Warner and a U.S. Forest Service campground. At this point the scenery may make it difficult to remain focused on driving.

Viewing the different stratified layers of the Upheaval Dome provides a glimpse into its millions of years of geologic history.

Three miles farther on the left is the back entrance to Moab via Sand Flats Road. It's a 20-mile bumpy ride back into town. If you choose to continue on the loop road to the summit, you'll be rewarded with sweeping views of the Castle Valley below.

Nearby on the left side is a turnoff to the **Pinhook Battlefield Monument** and burial grounds. Here, eight members of a posse were laid to rest after battling Indians.

Across the loop on the right is the rough road to the site of an 1890s gold camp called **Miner's Basin**. This ghost town is reported to have produced gold ore in excess of $1000 per ton. Note: A four-wheel-drive vehicle is often needed to get to the 10,000-foot-elevation spot.

Beginning your descent into the Castle Valley brings you to Gateway Road on the right side—it's the rear entrance to Gateway, Colorado—and the abandoned mining town of **Castleton**, which boomed in the early 1900s with a hotel, two grocery stores, a school and two saloons.

The desert returns past Castleton as you ease into the truly stunning **Castle Valley**. At left is the volcanic remnant **Round Mountain**. There are the **Priest and Nuns** rock formations (yes, they do resemble a padre and his faithful sisters) jutting heavenward to your right, as well as the landmark **Castle Rock** that's been featured in more commercials than Joe DiMaggio.

In another four miles the loop road merges with Route 128 and the scenic river route back to Moab. A worthwhile stop before returning to the city is at the Big Bend picnic area for swimming, camping and picnicking.

Fifteen miles south of Moab is **Hole 'n the Rock**. You can't miss the gargantuan white letters painted onto the cliffside announcing the place. Attractions like this you either love or hate, and those intrigued by a 5000-square-foot home and gift shop inside solid sandstone will love it. Check out the sculpture of Franklin D. Roosevelt on the rock face above the entrance. Admission. ~ Route 191; 801-686-2250.

LODGING

Don't be put off by the plastic and neon located along the Route 191 strip through Moab. While generic, two-story motels dominate, a few blocks off the main drag are some charming inns that welcome weary travelers with a personal touch.

◄ *HIDDEN*

Proving once again that a book shouldn't be judged by its cover, the **Westwood Guest House** is a gem set in a bland, brick, apartment-house facade. A country motif fills the seven three-room condominium apartments. Antique iron bedsteads covered with handmade patchwork quilts are complemented by overstuffed easy chairs and wooden rockers. Each unit has a predominant color scheme—pink, blue, apricot, yellow—that pervades down to the washcloths and potpourri. Fully equipped kitchen with do-it-yourself breakfast included. Hot tub in the back. ~ 81 East 100 South, Moab; 801-259-7283, 800-526-5690, fax 801-259-7780. BUDGET TO MODERATE.

Southwestern decor dominates the **Canyon Country Bed & Breakfast**, a favorite among mountain bikers and whitewater rafters. Fresh flowers enliven the five nicely appointed bedrooms (four with private baths), and an inviting living room is filled with a mini-library of books. A large backyard with a patio, hot tub, barbecue, volleyball court and horseshoes adds to the homey feel of this inn. There are mountain bike and kayak rentals. ~ 590 North 500 West, Moab; 801-259-5262. MODERATE TO DELUXE.

The pink-adobe exterior with hanging dried chiles makes the **Kokopelli Lodge** easy to spot. Though small, the eight rooms are clean, and the service is friendly. Cyclists appreciate a secured area set aside for bikes, and breakfast is served on a garden patio each morning from March through October. ~ 72 South 100 East, Moab; 801-259-7615, 800-505-5343. BUDGET.

Best of the "strip" motels is the **Best Western Greenwell**. Seventy-two rooms are conventionally furnished in pinks, mauves and blues with queen-size beds and sitting areas. Bonuses include the on-site restaurant, a rarity in Moab, and outdoor swimming pool. ~ 105 South Main, Moab; 801-259-6151. MODERATE.

A Colonial-style brick exterior houses **The Landmark Motel**. Thirty-five units feature tile baths, individual air-conditioning and hand-painted panoramic murals above the beds. Offering a pool, hot tub and guest laundry, the motel is popular among families, especially large ones who appreciate the rooms with three queen beds and extra-thick walls. ~ 168 North Main, Moab; 801-259-6147, 800-441-6147. MODERATE.

Slick Rock Inn blends the charm of an old house with modern amenities. Lace curtains, antique mirrors and soft quilts sit aside Southwest-style tables and rugs. Guests make extensive use of the inn's resource library and curl up on the plush mauve sofa or one of two high-back chairs in front of a cozy fire. The whole house rents for $225 per night for up to ten people; lower rates may be available for smaller groups. ~ 286 South 400 East, Moab; 801-259-2266. MODERATE.

A complete make-your-own breakfast is the best reason to try **Cedar Breaks Condos**. The half dozen one- and two-bedroom condominiums have full bath, kitchen and living room decorated with plants and collages of Indian petroglyphs. Upstairs units feature private balconies, and a complimentary full breakfast (March through mid-November only) is stocked daily for guests to prepare at their leisure. ~ Center and 4th East, Moab; 801-259-7830. MODERATE.

Certainly off the beaten track, hidden behind a storage center, is the **Lazy Lizard International Hostel**. You can't go wrong at the cheapest sleep in Moab. Both the dormitory and the private rooms are clean, and bedding is provided. New log cabins are available

LOOK OVER FROM AN OVERLOOK

Southwest of Moab at the end of Route 279 is the **Anticline overlook**, a 2000-foot-high mesa overlooking archlike rocks, the mighty Colorado Dead Horse Point and Arches National Park to the north. Here Canyonlands travelers can see where they've been and where they're going.

for a few dollars more than the private rooms. Popular with a European clientele. Hot tub. ~ 1213 South Route 191, Moab; 801-259-6057. BUDGET.

Nestled in the foothills of the La Sal Mountains just 15 miles southeast of Moab, **Pack Creek Ranch** is a slice of the Wild West complete with red-roofed log cabins and bunkhouse. Fourteen cabins have been refurbished in a Southwest style, including woven rugs and bent-willow furniture. All have full kitchens—and most feature stone fireplaces with a plentiful wood supply. Hollyhocks and day lilies line walkways between the cabins and paths to the main lodge/dining room. Lithe aspen trees surround the outdoor swimming pool. Pack Creek is an ideal winter basecamp for cross-country skiers. Rates include meals. ~ La Sal Mountain Loop Road; 801-259-5505. DELUXE TO ULTRA-DELUXE.

Art and archaeologic finds predominate at **Castle Valley Inn**, 17 miles northeast of Moab right off scenic Route 128. The bed and breakfast is decorated with original Navajo art and signed prints by noted photographers such as Ansel Adams. The eight units all have private baths, and an outdoor hot tub offers spectacular views of both the red-rock monoliths and mountains. A hearty, healthy breakfast is served. ~ 424 Amber Lane, Castle Valley; 801-259-6012. DELUXE TO ULTRA-DELUXE.

Locals say Moab restaurants have improved greatly of late to meet demands of a more sophisticated, traveling public. As the town is a center for so many outdoor activities, burning calories have created a demand for decent fueling spots.

DINING

Pizza reigns supreme at **Eddie McStiff's**, Moab's oldest legal brewery. Pastas, salads, sandwiches and steaks are offered, but the best bets are the special combination pizzas such as the Dosie Doe topped with roasted garlic, sundried tomatoes, parsley, scallions, and gorgonzola and parmesan cheeses. Beverages, including a selection of twelve house-microbrewed beers and homemade root beer, are served in mini-pitchers, a nice touch for parched desert thirsts. ~ 57 South Main, Moab; 801-259-2337. BUDGET TO MODERATE.

It's back to the '50s at **Westerner Grill**, a slice of Americana where red-leather booths, original chrome counter and red carpet drive the nostalgia home. Fare hot off the grill includes breakfast standards (anytime), hamburgers, liver and onions, pork chops, chicken-fried steaks, buffalo wings and homemade chili. ~ 331 North Main, Moab; 801-259-2395. BUDGET.

It's no secret Utahans love their ice cream (they consume more per capita than any other state in the nation), and parlors in the desert seem as prolific as jack rabbits. **The Soda Fountain** at the **T-Shirt Shop** won't disappoint any ice cream connoisseur. Thick, frosty shakes, malts, sodas, floats and sundaes are popular items.

The menu also features cherry phosphates—remember those? ~ 38 North Main, Moab; 801-259-5271. BUDGET.

Ciao or chow: Italian cuisine is **Catarina's** claim to fame. The menu is typical Italian entrées with spaghetti, calzones, lasagna, shrimp and chicken dishes. Dinner only. Closed Sunday and Monday during the winter. ~ 51 North Main, Moab; 801-259-6070. MODERATE.

What looks like a log fort from the outside is actually a haven for American cuisine. **Buck's Grill House** boasts grilled steaks, fresh fish and game and luscious homemade desserts. Dinner only. ~ North Route 191, Moab; 801-259-5201. MODERATE.

Vegetarians flock to **Honest Ozzie's Café & Desert Oasis** closely followed by anyone with a sweet tooth. Though tables are a tight squeeze, linen tablecloths and the soft songs of a guitarist add to the peaceful nature. Menu selections run the gamut from Mexican to Asian to vegetarian. And homemade desserts like Amaretto cheesecake and honest carrot cake more than make up for the under-salted main courses. There's even an extensive tea list. Healthy breakfasts are also a specialty; lunch consists of deli sandwiches. Closed mid-November through January. ~ 60 North 100 West, Moab; 801-259-8442. BUDGET.

Pack Creek Ranch Restaurant is the closest you'll find to a gourmet establishment. Oil lamps softly illuminate tables, as do the wagon-wheel chandeliers. The menu reflects ranch-house life with mesquite-broiled steaks and seafood, fresh fish, prime rib, barbecue chicken and roast duckling. Dinner includes an extensive salad bar, fresh vegetables, rice or potato and homemade dill rolls. Reservations are a must. Closed November through April. ~ La Sal Mountain Loop Road, 15 miles southeast of Moab; 801-259-5505. DELUXE.

SHOPPING   Admittedly, Moab is not a mecca for shoppers. Souvenir and T-shirt shops are primarily what you can expect to find here. Still, there are a few noteworthy exceptions.

Moab Mercantile & Gallery of Fine Art also showcases several local artists with an emphasis on prints, photos and pottery. ~ 78 North Main, Moab; 801-259-2985.

Across the hall from Moab Mercantile, **Hogan Trading Co.** carries an impressive variety of Indian art such as kachina dolls, pottery and alabaster sculptures. ~ 5 North Main, Moab; 801-259-8118.

What must be one of the most comprehensive collections of books on the Southwest can be found at **Back of Beyond Bookstore**. Edward Abbey, Tony Hillerman and others with local ties take up the most shelf space, and there is a plethora of works on the outdoors, natural and Western history, American Indian studies and the environment. Popular novels are stocked, too. ~ 83 North Main, Moab; 801-259-5154.

The hub for sports of all sorts, **Rim Cyclery** sells practical outdoor gear, footgear, regional guides and, of course, tools of the trade. Wise-cracking mechanics proffer knowing advice about destinations if you seem credible. "Cool central" for serious sporting athletes, or at least those who look the part. ~ 94 West 100 North, Moab; 801-259-5333.

Utah's strict liquor laws mean an abbreviated bar scene. Moab fares better than most with a few nightspots.

Live music and dancing on weekends keep **Rio Colorado Restaurant and Bar** hopping. Cover on weekends. ~ 2 South 100 West, Moab; 801-259-6666.

The **Sportsman's Lounge** has a huge dancefloor and live country music for two-steppin' every weekend. Occasional cover. ~ 1991 South Route 191, Moab; 801-259-9972.

One of the oldest nightly entertainments in the Moab area is **Canyonlands By Night**, a boat trip at sunset up the Colorado River. Complete with light and sound show, the voyage offers a unique perspective on river landmarks. Canyonlands also offers a nightly Dutch-oven dinner, cooked and eaten on the banks of the Colorado. May to October only. ~ 1861 North Route 191, Moab; 801-259-5261, fax 801-259-2788.

ARCHES NATIONAL PARK 🚶🚲 Popular with plenty of easily accessible geologic wonders, Arches National Park is a magnet for the recreational-vehicle crowd and backcountry enthusiasts alike. Guided walks are offered March through October and may be arranged through the visitors center. The park features picnic areas, a visitors center and restrooms. ~ Located on Route 191, five miles north of Moab; 801-259-8161.

▲ There are 52 sites located at **Devil's Garden**; $8 per night.

DEAD HORSE POINT STATE PARK 🚶 This 5400-acre mesa has been preserved as a popular park that offers innumerable possibilities for hikers, campers and other outdoor enthusiasts. Park facilities include a visitors center, picnic areas and restrooms. ~ From Moab go north on Route 191 nine miles, then Route 313 for 22 miles; 801-259-2614.

▲ There are 21 sites with electric hookups (no water hookups for RVs); $7 per night. Reservations are recommended and can be made by calling 800-322-3770 (there is a $5 reservation fee).

CANYONLANDS NATIONAL PARK—ISLAND IN THE SKY DISTRICT 🚶 This "island" mesa, 6000 feet in elevation, features rugged and beautiful terrain veined with hiking trails. The sparse vegetation and rain on the Island does not keep wildlife like foxes, coyotes and bighorn sheep from calling this land their home. The park has picnic areas, a visitors center and vault toilets. ~ From Moab go north on Route 191 nine miles, then Route 313 for 26 miles; 801-259-6577 or National Park Office (Moab), 801-259-7164.

▲ There are 12 primitive sites; no water available.

▼▼▼▼▼▼▼▼▼▼▼▼▼

Outdoor Adventures

The mighty Colorado River weaves its way through the desert rock of southeastern Utah en route to its final destination in the Gulf of Mexico. Burnt sienna–colored water rushes boldly in some sections, slowing to a near crawl in others. Kayaking, canoeing, whitewater rafting and jetboat tours are abundant throughout the region.

RIVER RUNNING & BOAT TOURS

LAKE POWELL AREA At Lake Powell, you can "see Rainbow Bridge and leave the driving to someone else." Guided full-day and half-day tours of the monument are available from **Bullfrog Marina**, which also leads an early-evening cruise past archaeological sites. ~ 801-684-2233. **Wahweap Marina** also leads tours of Rainbow Bridge and has shorter sightseeing tours to Antelope and Navajo canyons. ~ 520-645-2433.

MOAB AREA To explore canyons such as Westwater (northeast of Moab via Route 70) by kayak or whitewater raft contact **Tag-A-Long River Expeditions**. ~ 452 North Main, Moab; 801-259-8946, 800-453-3292. **Western River Expeditions** leads kayak and rafting tours as well. ~ 1371 North Main, Moab; 801-259-7019, 800-453-7450.

Like ducks in a shooting gallery, you can't miss finding a professional river-running company along the Moab highway. All enjoy good reputations and can verse travelers in the water's idiosyncracies. Alphabetically first is **Adrift Adventures**. ~ 378 North Main; 801-259-8594. **Canyonlands by Night** is another reliable operator. ~ 1861 North Route 191; 801-259-5261, 800-394-9978. **North American River Expeditions** runs the river regularly. ~ 543 North Main; 801-259-5865, 800-342-5938, fax 801-259-2296. Or take to the whitewater with **Sheri Griffith River Expeditions**. ~ 2231 South Route 191; 801-259-8229, 800-332-2439.

SWIMMING

Desert summers heat up like a microwave oven. When temperatures soar into the 90s and above, any body of water looks good. Many people opt for a dip in the Colorado or Green rivers and, of course, in Lake Powell.

SAN JUAN COUNTY AREA For swimming, fishing, picnicking and nonmotorized boating in the Monticello area try **Lloyd's Lake**, on the road to Abajo Peak, about three miles west of town. Another good swimming hole is the multipurpose **Recapture Reservoir** about five miles north of Blanding. Turn west off Route 191 and follow the signs.

MOAB AREA One of the most popular spots for swimming around here is at **Big Bend Recreation Area,** 12 miles north of Moab. Don't stray too far from shore, however, as strong currents are likely.

CLIMBING

Experienced climbers can test their mettle on the precipices near Fisher Towers, Arches National Park and in the Potash region near Moab and Indian Creek east of the Canyonlands Needles entrance. Sunbaked walls make summer climbing a drag, but temperatures are generally pleasant during the rest of the year. Deep, sunless canyons are also prime ice-climbing spots in the winter. For gear, a partner or climbing advice, check in with **Moab Adventure Outfitters.** ~ 600 North Main, Moab; 801-259-2725.

WINTER SPORTS

The only commercial ski area in the region, Blue Mountain in the Abajo range near Monticello, is now defunct. But nordic aficionados still criss-cross the slopes, ski the trees and camp out in snow caves.

MOAB AREA The La Sal Mountains are the second-highest range in the state, so adequate white stuff is rarely a problem. Snow-filled meadows beckon cross-country skiers. **Rim Cyclery** rents cross-country ski equipment in Moab. ~ 94 West 100 North; 801-259-5333.

JEEP TOURS

Much of Southeastern Utah's rugged, undeveloped wilderness remains inaccessible to regular vehicles. For that reason, many visitors opt for a jeep tour.

LAKE POWELL HOUSEBOATING AND WATER SPORTS

The best way to see Lake Powell is from the stern of a boat with the breeze passing through your hair and water sprays cooling the temperature. **Lake Powell Resorts & Marinas** offers plenty for rent at the Wahweap, Bullfrog, Hall's Crossing and Hite marinas, including flat-topped houseboats (they only average two miles a gallon, so many groups also rent a powerboat or jet skis for exploring the shoreline). Waterskis, tubes, bobsleds, kneeboards and water weenie-like "wavecutters" are also available. A word to the wise: Don't be in a hurry to check out boats. Lake employees seem to operate on a "desert clock" and the time-conscious visitor only adds stress to a vacation by trying to hurry the process. ~ Wahweap: 520-645-2433. Bullfrog: 801-684-2233. Hall's Crossing: 801-684-2261. Hite: 801-684-2278.

MOAB AREA   With **Adrift Adventures** discover the stunning beauty of the natural Gemini Bridges located northwest of Moab; from an overlook here, you'll see La Sal Mountain and the surrounding layers of red sculpted rock. ~ 378 North Main, Moab; 801-259-8594.

Canyonlands 4x4 Rentals and Guided Tours will take you to the spectacular Onion Creek. You'll pass fluted red cliffs and drive through the creek with water splashing at your wheels. ~ 600 Mill Creek Drive, Moab; 801-259-4567.

Lin Ottinger Tours explores the multicolored hues and eroded spires along **Hurrah Pass Trail**. You'll pass numerous vista points with sweeping views of the surrounding area. ~ 600 North Main, Moab; 801-259-7312.

North American River Expeditions offers full-day tours of nearby national parks. One tour delves into the spectacular scenery of Canyonlands National Park's **Shafer Trail** where you'll see the mighty Colorado River roaring by. ~ 543 North Main, Moab; 801-259-5865, 800-342-5938, fax 801-259-2296.

To explore historical American Indian sites, contact **Tag-A-Long Expeditions**. Tag-A-Long offers packages ranging from half-day tours to week-long customized trips. A six-day adventure tour begins in Moab and travels to Navajo National Monument and Canyon de Chelly in northern Arizona. ~ 452 North Main, Moab; 801-259-8946, 800-453-3292.

GOLF   The desert heat seems to keep golf courses from springing up in southeastern Utah, but the few available ones are well maintained, albeit not championship in caliber.

SAN JUAN COUNTY AREA   Monticello offers the nine-hole **Blue Mountain Meadows County Golf Course**. ~ 549 South Main; 801-587-2468. Or you can bring your clubs to the **Blanding Golf Course**. ~ North Reservoir Road; for information, call the chamber of commerce at 801-678-2539.

MOAB AREA   In Moab, there's the eighteen-hole **Moab Golf Course**. ~ 2705 Southeast Bench Road; 801-259-6488.

RIDING STABLES   Clippity-clopping leisurely on horseback is one of the best ways to explore the La Sal Mountains or any of the nearby national parks.

MOAB AREA   Trail rides and pack trips can be arranged through **Pack Creek Ranch**. ~ La Sal Mountain Loop Road, Moab; 801-259-5505. **Old West Trail Rides** will also get you out on the range. ~ South Route 191, Moab; 801-259-7410.

BIKING   The Moab area has become mountain-biking central for gearheads throughout the West. Miles and miles of dirt, sandstone and paved trails within a 40-mile radius offer options for fat-tire enthusiasts of all abilities.

Up the River With (or Without) a Paddle

Running the rivers in Utah allows a pure view of the land from deep within the canyons. It's a different world, thousands of feet away from manmade distractions. Sometimes the only sounds are the whoop of a crane, the river's gurgle or a paddle dipping into the water. Novices shouldn't be deterred by the challenging Class 5 rapids of sections in Cataract Canyon; tours are offered in all degrees of difficulty. Those seeking rushing rapids must be willing to put up with frigid mountain runoff in early spring. By mid-summer, the rivers are warmer and more mellow. Because of the rivers' idiosyncracies, it's wise to verse yourself in their courses before taking the plunge.

Along the Colorado River northeast of Moab via Route 70 is **Westwater**, which packs a real punch in a relatively short jaunt. Pre-Cambrian, black-granite walls line the deep canyons and stand in contrast to the red-sandstone spires above. Westwater, with 11 telling sections sporting names like Skull Rapid, is a favorite destination for whitewater junkies.

The most heavily used section of the Colorado River is below **Dewey Bridge** off Route 128. When runoff peaks, there are a few mild rapids between here and Moab. But for most of the year expect to kick back and enjoy a scenic float. **Fisher Towers**, **The Priest and Nuns** rock formations and **Castle Valley**—backdrop of many favorite Westerns—can be lazily viewed from a raft, kayak or canoe, or in low water on an air mattress or inner tube.

Floating along the sinuous Green River and in the rapidless **Labyrinth and Stillwater canyons** is a first choice for families and river neophytes more interested in drifting past prehistoric rocks than paddling through a wild ride.

When the Colorado meets the Green River in the heart of Canyonlands National Park, crazy things happen. Below the confluence is the infamous **Cataract Canyon**, where no fewer than 26 rapids await river runners. During the period of highwater (usually May and June), Cataract can serve up some of the country's toughest rapids, aptly named Little Niagara and Satan's Gut. When the river finally spills into Lake Powell at Hite Crossing, 112 miles downriver from Moab, boaters breathe a sigh of relief.

Unique to the **San Juan River**, another tributary of Lake Powell, are sand waves. These rollercoaster-like dips and drops are caused by shifting sands on the river bottom. Below the town of Mexican Hat, the San Juan meanders among deep goosenecks through the scenic Cedar Mesa Anticline and charges through reasonable rapids before spilling into Lake Powell.

Moab's main highway is lined with competitive outfitters. A business ready to help get your feet wet is **Tag-A-Long River Expeditions**. ~ 452 North Main, Moab; 801-259-8946. Also in Moab is **Adrift Adventures**. ~ 378 North Main; 801-259-8594. In the San Juan area, try **Wild Rivers Expeditions**. ~ 101 Main, Bluff; 801-672-2244.

LAKE POWELL AREA Outfitters are an absolute necessity if you are planning to tour the remote **Canyonlands Maze District**. You can zigzag on the slickrock trails in Teapot Canyon en route to the rock fins of the Doll House. The inaccessibility of the Maze ensures that few others will traverse your cycling tracks.

Canyonlands is spectacular from any vantage point, but to really enjoy its splendor from the ground up, take the 100-mile round-trip **White Rim Trail**. The trip typically takes about four days and meanders through rainbow-colored canyons and basins, skirting the Colorado and Green rivers. Since it's almost impossible to carry enough water and supplies in your panniers, a supported trip from an outfitter is recommended. The trail starts 40 miles from Moab via Routes 191, 313 and Shafer Trail Road.

SAN JUAN COUNTY AREA **Gold Queen Basin** in the Abajo range near Monticello winds through nine miles of fragrant aspen and pine stands to the Blue Mountain skiing area. Mountain greens provide stark contrast to the redrock country in the north. Take the ski area road due west of Monticello and follow the signs.

MOAB AREA By far the most popular ride is **Slickrock**, a technically demanding grunt located a couple miles east of downtown Moab on Sand Flats Road. Slickrock has become so well known that in spring cyclists line up wheel-to-wheel at the trailhead. Super steep to the point of being nearly vertical in some sections, Slickrock's 10.3-mile trail can take up to six hours to complete. But canyon, river and rock views, coupled with thrilling descents are dividends to those willing to work. Not for the faint of heart, leg or lung.

Kane Creek Road begins as a flat, paved, two-lane road that hugs the Colorado River. It's the gateway to numerous biking trails. Access Kane Creek from Route 191, just south of downtown Moab.

The **Moab Rim Trail**, about 2.5 miles from the intersection, is a short route for experienced cyclists that climbs steadily from the trailhead. Views of the La Sal Mountains and Arches vie for your attention; don't forget to look for ancient petroglyphs on rock walls.

Several miles down Kane Creek Road the pavement turns to dirt as it climbs through the canyon. You can head toward the **Hurrah Pass Trail** (17 miles) at this point. Another fun ride, **Behind the Rocks** (25 miles), ends on Kane Creek Road. Pick up the trailhead 13 miles south of town via Route 191. The trailhead will be on the right side of the road marked Pritchett Arch. As its name suggests, ride behind the rocks and through Pritchett Canyon. Consult a detailed topographic or bike map before embarking on these journeys, as it is easy to get lost amid the sandstone.

There may be other traffic on the famous **Kokopelli's Trail**, but you're as likely to share space with animals as humans. American Indians considered the humpbacked Kokopelli to be a magic being, and the trail more than lives up to its namesake. Single-track trails, four-wheel-drive roads, dirt-and-sand paths for traversing mesas, peaks and meadows, you'll find them all along the 128 miles. Detailed maps showing access points are available at bike shops and the Moab Visitors Center.

Follow your nose to **Onion Creek** four-wheel-drive trail. The colorful, easy-to-moderate, 19-mile trail, with views of rock, river and mountains, saves its toughest hill until the end. Take Route 128 north 20 miles from Moab; watch for the turnoff between mileposts 20 and 21, near the road to Fisher Towers.

Hidden Canyon Rim is also called "The Gymnasium." The eight-mile trip can be completed in three hours by almost anyone. About 25 minutes from Moab via Route 191 to Blue Hills Road. Trailhead is approximately three-and-a-half miles from the road.

When the desert turns furnace hot, cyclists pedal for the hills. In the La Sal Mountains near Moab, try **Fisher Mesa Trail**. The 18-mile round-trip passage appeals to less-experienced riders. Drive 15 miles north of Moab on Route 128 to the Castle Valley turnoff. Take the road about 13 miles to where the pavement ends. Look for Castleton/Gateway Road. The trail begins on the left side off this road about four miles from the turnoff.

Bike Rentals   For friendly advice, bike rentals or to arrange private guides or fully supported tours try **Kaibab Mountain Bike Tours**. ~ 391 South Main Street, Moab; 801-259-7423. **Western Spirit Cycling** also does the White Rim, as well as longer Telluride-to-Moab and Bryce-to-Zion trips. ~ 478 Mill Creek Drive, Moab; 801-259-8732. **Slickrock Adventures Inc.** specializes in excursions to the White Rim. ~ 76 South Main, Moab; 801-259-6996. Also

✔ **CHECK THESE OUT—UNIQUE OUTDOOR ADVENTURES**

- Camp among the wild formations of the Maze in **Canyonlands National Park**. *page 520*
- Explore the waters of **Westwater Canyon** by kayak or whitewater raft. *page 543*
- Ride your bike on **Hidden Canyon Rim**, also called "the Gymnasium," an eight-mile trip that even the beginner can complete. *page 545*
- Put up your windsurfing sail and glide across **Ken's Lake**, also a popular fishing hole. *page 534*

try **Rim Cyclery** for bikes and equipment. ~ 94 West 1st North, Moab; 801-259-5223. Rim Cyclery's outfitter component is called **Rim Tours**. ~ 1233 South Route 191; 800-626-7335. **Poison Spider Bicycles** also has bikes for rent. ~ 497 North Main, Moab; 801-259-7882.

Coyote Shuttle Service offers drop-offs for cyclists who want to do one-way rides. They also arrange trips through local bike shops. ~ 801-259-8656.

HIKING

Expect the unexpected when hiking in the Utah desert. For around the next bend there could be Indian petroglyphs, a stunning rock bridge or, be prepared—a rattlesnake.

LAKE POWELL AREA If you can tear yourself away from the water, Lake Powell has plenty of petroglyphs, arches and archaeological sites waiting to be explored.

Up the Escalante River arm, about 25 miles from Hall's Crossing marina is **Davis Gulch Trail** (1.5 miles). Climb through the lovely "cathedral in the desert" and the Bement Natural Arch to what some consider one of the lake's prettiest sections.

John Wayne, Zane Grey and Teddy Roosevelt all visited the Rainbow Lodge. It's now the **Rainbow Lodge Ruins**. The trail (7 miles) begins about a mile past Rainbow Natural Bridge National Monument and skirts painted rocks, cliffs and Horse Canyon en route to its destination in the shadow of Navajo Mountain.

Take the left-hand spur from the monument and head toward Elephant Rock and Owl Arch via the **North Rainbow Trail** (6 miles).

From the Glen Canyon Dam, there is a short hike to a lovely arch in a recently charted area called **Wiregrass Canyon** (1.5 miles). Drive about eight miles north of the dam on Route 89 to Big Water. Turn east on Route 277 to Route 12 and continue four-and-one-half miles south on Warm Creek Road to the start of Wiregrass Canyon.

SAN JUAN COUNTY AREA Like spires reaching for the sky, the striped rock formations of **Canyonlands Needles district** beckon visitors to explore their secrets. A trail starting at Elephant Hill trailhead meanders through Elephant Canyon with optional side trips to Devil's Pocket, Cyclone Canyon and Druid Arch. Depending on your chosen route, the trip can be as long or as short as you choose.

Chesler Park (3 miles), one of the park's most popular routes, is a desert meadow amid the rock needles. Accessible from the Elephant Hill trailhead.

Lower Red Lake Canyon Trail (8.5 miles) leads to the gnarly Cataract Canyon section of the Colorado River. Start this steep and demanding multiday hike at Elephant Hill trailhead.

A spur of the Trail of the Ancients, the **Butler Wash** (.5 mile) interpretive trail is exceedingly well marked with cairns and trail symbols. After crossing slickrock, cacti, juniper and piñon, the hiker is rewarded with an Anasazi cliff-dwelling overlook. Take Route 95 east from Blanding. Turn right between mile markers 111 and 112.

Several scenic hikes are found within **Natural Bridges National Monument.** Paths to each bridge are moderate to strenuous in difficulty, and you may encounter some steep slickrock. But the National Park Service has installed handrails and stairs at the most difficult sections.

Owachomo Bridge Trail (.2 mile) is the shortest of three hikes at Natural Bridges National Monument; it provides an up-close and personal view of the bridges.

MOAB AREA   **Arches National Park** teems with miles of trails among the monoliths, arches, spires and sandstone walls.

Delicate Arch Trail (1.5 miles) sports a 480-foot elevation change over sand and sandstone to Delicate Arch. Along the way, you'll cross a swinging bridge and climb over slickrock. The most photographed of all the famous arches, Delicate Arch invites long, luxurious looks and several snaps of the Instamatic.

◄ HIDDEN

Another Arches favorite, **Windows** (.5 mile or less) culminates with an opportunity to peer through the rounded North and South Windows, truly one of nature's greater performances. This easy and accessible trail starts just past Balanced Rock at the Windows turnoff.

Canyonlands National Park provides both short walks and long hikes for exploring some of its most outstanding features. **Upheaval Dome Crater View Trail** (.5 mile) is a short hike to the overlook of dramatic Upheaval Dome in the Island in the Sky section of Canyonlands.

You can also opt to traverse the entire dome via the **Syncline Loop Trail** (8 miles), an arduous route with a 1300-foot elevation change.

Neck Spring Trail (5 miles) leads through the diverse landscape of the Canyonlands—Island in the Sky district. From the trail, hikers can view seasonal wildflowers and the sandstone cliffs of the Navajo Formation. The trail follows paths that were originally established by animals using the springs, so don't be surprised if a mule deer or chipmunk crosses your path.

A stream will be at your side for the length of the **Negro Bill Canyon Trail** (2 miles), a favorite Moab stomping ground. Negro Bill ends up at Morning Glory Bridge, the sixth-longest rock span in the U.S. At canyon's end is a spring and small pool. From Moab, take Route 128 three miles east of the junction with Route 191.

▼▼▼▼▼▼▼▼▼▼

Transportation

CAR

From the Colorado border, **Route 70** heads due west forming the northern boundary of the region. **Route 191** travels north-south, passing through Moab, Monticello and Blanding as well as the entrances to Arches and Canyonlands National Parks. Those traveling west from the Colorado border should opt for **Route 128**, a scenic byway that connects with Route 191.

Route 95 branches off Route 191 west toward Natural Bridges, while both Route 95 and **Route 276** lead to Glen Canyon National Recreation Area and Lake Powell.

AIR

Few visitors to southeastern Utah choose to come by commercial air. Those who do use Alpine Air, which services **Moab's Canyonland Field.** Shuttle service into Moab is provided by either **Coyote Shuttle** (801-259-8656) or **Thrifty Car Rental** (800-367-2277).

Visitors to Lake Powell fly into Page, Arizona's **Lake Powell Airport.** Page is served daily by SkyWest Airlines. In Utah, airstrips help connect vast desert distances divided by mountains, canyons and rivers. There are public landing fields near the Bullfrog and Hall's Crossing marinas.

TRAIN

The nearest **Amtrak** station servicing the Moab and San Juan County areas is a whistle stop in Thompson, about 35 miles north of Moab. You will take one of three trains—the "Zephyr," "Desert Wind" or "Pioneer"—depending on your destination. ~ Reservations: 800-872-7245.

CAR RENTALS

Rental companies in Moab are **Canyonlands 4x4 Rentals** (801-259-4567) and **Thrifty Car Rental** (800-367-2277). Both also offer four-wheel-drive vehicles, a must for exploring the backcountry roads and byways.

Other rental agencies strictly renting four-wheel-drive vehicles in Moab include **Farabee Adventures** (801-259-7494, 800-806-5337) and **Slickrock 4x4 Rentals** (800-792-0165).

NATURE WALKS

The **Canyonlands Field Institute** sponsors seminars, workshops, field trips and naturalist hiking for groups of eight or more. Contact them for the schedule. ~ 1320 South Route 191, Moab; 801-259-7750.

SIXTEEN

Southwestern Colorado

From the Anasazi, who built their remarkable cliff dwellings here 700 years ago and then mysteriously disappeared, to the 19th-century miners who made millions in the silver and gold fields, southwestern Colorado has always been synonymous with adventure. Today, myth and dreams surround this region that is home to American Indians, cowboys who work cattle in the high country and tourists who flock to its mountain meadows and peaks. Arguably the most picturesque mountain range in the Americas, the local San Juans compare favorably with the Swiss Alps.

Three hundred yearly days of sunshine and reliable water supplies cascading out of snow-capped mountains were probably two big reasons the Anasazi became the first known settlers of the area—the same reason for today's thousands of yearly visitors. Originally nomadic, the Anasazi eventually settled the fertile mesas, raising beans, corn and squash in the lush river valleys flowing out of the San Juan Mountains.

They first lived in caves or pit houses dug out of the ground, weaving baskets of yucca and hemp that earned their nickname—Basketmakers. They had no written language—historical records consist of paintings and carvings on cave walls that can still be seen today. Combined with other archaeological artifacts, including the architecturally unique dwellings made of rock dating back to 550 A.D., visitors now find only mute evidence of these early inhabitants.

The later Cliff Dwellers built the multistory cliff-side and mesa-top dwellings that are best preserved in Mesa Verde National Park's 52,000 acres, the first national park to be dedicated to preserving manmade artifacts. Other Anasazi sites are more remote and less well known, such as the Sand Canyon Pueblo—possibly the largest ruin in the Southwest. The Ute Mountain Tribal Park surrounds Mesa Verde on three sides and contains stabilized but unrestored cliff dwellings.

These ancient Indians dispersed around 1200 A.D., gradually drifting away from Mesa Verde and nearby locations, losing any traceable cultural identity. They left behind intact buildings as well as the mystery surrounding their departure. Was it brought on by drought, famine, warfare? To this day, no one knows for certain.

Later tribes—the Ute, Pawnee and Navajo—passed through, claiming the land by the 1600s. Around the same time, Spanish explorers stopped long enough to leave their mark.

The town of Silverton was founded in 1874, Cortez, now a small ranching community and access point to ancient and modern Indian lands, was first settled in 1889. Dolores, favored today by anglers, hikers and river runners, sprang to life when the railroad came to town in 1891, prospering for 60 years until the trains pulled out for good in the mid-20th century.

The railroad company built bridges over raging rivers and blasted through vertical rock cliffs to provide lucrative service to the mines, which were churning out millions of dollars in gold and silver ore. As the boom continued and money flowed out of the mountains, the region grew to include gunfighters, prostitution, gambling and rowdy saloons. Today, many of the towns created by the mining and agriculture boom have found a new life catering to tourists eager to explore this rugged corner of the world.

The physical geography of southwestern Colorado cuts through two distinct landscapes. The jagged peaks of the San Juan Mountains attain heights above 14,000 feet near Silverton. Then the western edge of the Rockies drops off and the peaks merge with the Colorado plateau—characterized by dramatic mesas, buttes and graceful sandstone configurations carved over eons by wind and water.

Today's visitor to the southwestern corner of Colorado can experience the best of the region's scenic beauty and history. The largest city in this mountain region is Durango, population 13,000. Second is Cortez, with 8000, trailed by the smaller communities of Dolores, Mancos, Hesperus and Silverton. Far from interstate highways, each of these communities showcases the region's rich and varied history.

The towns are separated by vast reaches of trails to hike or ski, rivers to run or fish, forests to camp in or hunt, deserts spotted with ruins and canyons to ride in or explore. An outdoor-lover's mecca, Durango hosts several mountain-biking competitions—there are hundreds of miles of world-class bike trails on and off the roads of the entire region. Equestrians, hikers and backpackers trek the hundreds of pristine wilderness trails preserved from development. River rafters, canoeists and kayakers ply the waters of the Animas and Dolores rivers, claiming some of the most challenging whitewater in the world. Controlled hunting for deer and elk still attracts aficionados from far and wide, and the fishing is good. Add top-class skiing, world-class archaeological digs and warm hospitality served up with a historic Western flare and you have an idea of how the heirs of cowboys and Indians are doing things today in this holy place known to the Utes as "the rim of the little world."

Durango–Silverton Area

Steam trains sending up billowing clouds as they wind along river canyons. Brick office blocks, saloons with mirrored back bars, newspapers with handset type and grand hotels where the furniture is museum quality. Remote trails leading up through alpine forests to remote mountain lakes. Resorts accessible only by rail or helicopter. Chuckwagons and American Indian galleries. Is there any reason not to visit Durango and Silverton?

SIGHTS   Each of these mountain towns has a distinctive spirit that will immediately transport you back in time. The largest community in these parts, **Durango** is a shady Animas River town with historic boulevards, one of the West's most popular tourist railroads and classic Victorian architecture. More placid, Silverton comes to life in the summer when the frontier-style hotels, restaurants and shops cater to the tourist trade. A well-preserved mining town, this community is an ideal base for jeep and fishing trips, hiking, mountain biking and tracking down ghost towns. Unspoiled and well preserved, here's your chance to slip back into the 19th century.

First laid out in 1882 to haul an estimated $300 million in gold and silver out of what is now the San Juan National Forest, the **Durango & Silverton Narrow Gauge Railroad**—a National Historic Landmark and a National Civil Engineering Landmark—is the biggest attraction in these two towns. Admission. ~ 479 Main Avenue, Durango; 970-247-2733.

This train out of yesteryear belches black, billowing gusts of smoke and cinders, exactly as it did in 1891. It still carries more than 200,000 passengers each year over the 45 miles of track between Durango and Silverton, one of the most stunning rail trips anywhere. In keeping with the historic responsibility of one of the longest remaining narrow-gauge routes, authentic orange-and-black 1880s Victorian-style coaches and open gondola cars are pulled by coal-fired, steam-powered locomotives originally made for the Denver & Rio Grande Railroad between 1902 and 1925. All equipment is kept in top condition at the station roundhouse in Durango. The roundhouse is open for **Yard Tours** of the locomotive service area, turntable, machine shop and car shop where impossible-to-find parts are fashioned from scratch and the train cars are restored and serviced. Admission. ~ 479 Main Avenue.

The train chugs through remote areas of the national forest, crossing the Animas River several times, running parallel to the river for much of the route. These areas are accessible only by the train, on horseback or on foot. There are no roads through these steep-sided narrow gorges, pine forests and undisturbed lands that look much the same as they did in the 1880s.

The trip takes three-and-a-half hours each way, with a two-hour layover in Silverton, covering an elevation gain of nearly 3000 feet from Durango. The train currently makes the run to Silverton from early May to mid-October; during the winter months, it only travels halfway to Silverton and back. Starting in September, fall color is an exceptional time on the tracks when the forest colors envelop the swaying train cars. Hop aboard anytime for the lonesome train whistle, clattering metals and clouds of coal smoke that harken back to times when fortunes and accompanying romance rode the rails.

A small collection reveals the manmade and natural history of the region at the **Animas Museum**. Exhibits featured in the turn-of-the-century schoolhouse include local history displays, Anasazi, Navajo and Ute artifacts, and the pioneer "Joy Cabin." Closed Sunday and November through April. Admission. ~ 31st Street and West 2nd Avenue, Durango; 970-259-2402.

The **Center of Southwest Studies** is part of the Fort Lewis College Museum and Archive. Displays include Southwestern and American Indian artifacts, as well as books, photographs, documents and maps pertaining to the historic background of the entire Four Corners region. ~ Fort Lewis College, College Heights, Durango; 970-247-7456.

For a soothing dose of history updated in a modern context, **Trimble Hot Springs** offers refreshing access to an ancient mineral hot springs favored by Chief Ouray and his Ute warriors. Now it's listed as a National Historic Site. The property includes an Olympic-

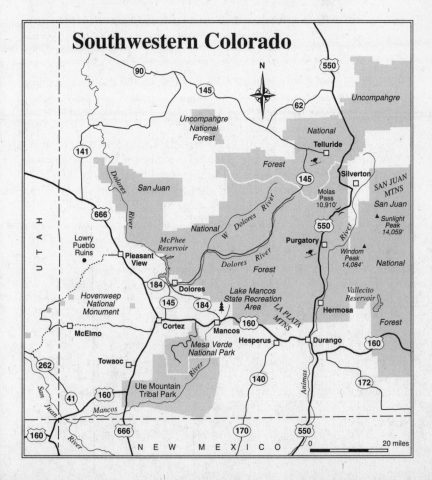

Southwestern Colorado

size lap pool and two therapy pools. Massages available. This spot is a particular favorite with weary bike riders, hikers and skiers. Admission. ~ 6475 County Road 203, Durango; 970-247-0111.

Molas Pass, 40 miles north of Durango on Route 550 at 10,910 feet, is the highest point on the road between Durango and Silverton. The views make you feel as if the world is at your feet. Maybe it is.

Silverton, "the mining town that never quit," is a historic testament to the boom years of the mining industry, with virtually every building on Greene Street dating to the turn of the century. The entire town is a registered National Historic Landmark. Among the most informative of these Victorian-era structures is the County Jail, built in 1902 and now home to the **San Juan County Historical Museum**. Exhibits detail early-day Silverton life and mining history. The museum is open from Memorial Day through mid-October, but the new archive and research facility, in an adjacent building, is open year-round. Admission. ~ 1567 Greene Street; 970-387-5838.

Next door to the old jail, the **San Juan County Court House** is capped by an ornate gold-painted dome and clocktower. It was built in 1907 and is still in use today. ~ 1512 Greene Street; 970-387-5790.

The Silverton Standard and Miner is the oldest continuous newspaper and business in western Colorado. The frame building it occupies housed a general store when it was constructed in 1875. ~ 1257 Greene Street; 970-387-5477.

Completed in 1901, the **American Legion Hall** was the original home of the Western Federation of Miners. The brick structure contains a large dance hall on the second floor, now used for local theatrical productions. Legionnaires use the downstairs for a bar and meeting rooms. ~ 1069 Greene Street; 970-387-5560.

◆◆◆

✔ CHECK THESE OUT—UNIQUE SIGHTS

- All aboard! Hop on the **Durango & Silverton Narrow Gauge Railroad** for a round trip through remote gorges and pine forests unspoiled by civilization. *page 552*
- Strike it rich at **Animas Forks**, a ghost town where gold and silver ore were mined in the 1880s. *page 555*
- Step back in time at the **Anasazi Heritage Center**, where one of the world's largest collections of ancient Indian artifacts waits to be perused. *page 562*
- Explore deserted canyons, cliff dwellings and mesa-top sites at **Mesa Verde National Park**, southwestern Colorado's number one tourist attraction. *page 566*

The **United Church of Silverton** was constructed in 1880 to house Silverton's Congregational Church at a time when the first call to worship was achieved by pounding on a saw blade. Constructed of stone, it is the oldest Congregational Church structure in the state still offering services, though the denomination has changed. ~ 1060 Reese Street; 970-387-5715.

The town's public library, **Silverton Public Library** was erected in 1906. The interior furnishings are largely original period antiques, and the lower level has been restored through a mammoth local effort to provide library services. The library replaced a series of free reading rooms that had been scattered throughout the community since the 1880s. Closed Sunday and Monday. ~ 1111 Reese Street; 970-387-5770.

Thirteen miles northeast of Silverton, accessed by following Greene Street East, is **Animas Forks**, a ghost town where gold and silver ore were mined in the 1880s. Abandoned structures include houses, foundations and basic mine structures. A four-wheel-drive vehicle is recommended for the ride that passes through several shallow river beds as it follows the Animas River to its headwaters.

LODGING

The best-known historic hotel among many in the region is the **Strater Hotel**. Built in 1887, it is a repository of the largest collection of antique Victorian walnut furniture west of the Mississippi and has been certified as a museum. Each of its 93 rooms is different; comfortable and impeccably cared for, they are furnished with antiques, and all have modern tiled bathrooms. A restaurant and a jacuzzi are added amenities. The building is a Durango landmark, located two blocks from the Durango–Silverton Narrow Gauge Train Station. Reservations may be scarce at times during the summer. ~ 699 Main Avenue, Durango; 970-247-4431, 800-247-4431, fax 970-259-2208. DELUXE TO ULTRA-DELUXE.

Located a block closer to the train station, the **General Palmer Hotel** is another Victorian-era structure, although this one is furnished mainly with reproductions. The 38 guest rooms are individually decorated with four-poster beds, pewter and brass lamps, etched glass and hand-crocheted bedspreads. Most are on the small side and some "inside rooms " have no windows, though all are well maintained. Continental breakfast included. ~ 567 Main Avenue, Durango; 970-247-4747, 800-523-3358, fax 970-247-1332. DELUXE.

The **Leland House Bed and Breakfast** offers ten creatively decorated rooms in a restored brick building. Each room is named after a historic figure associated with the home. Breakfast is served directly across the street at the Rochester Hotel. ~ 721 East 2nd Avenue, Durango; 970-385-1920, 800-664-1920, fax 970-385-1967. DELUXE.

For great train-watching, the restaurant at the **Iron Horse Inn** is located next to the train tracks. Guests can watch the train chug by, and enjoy the spectacular views of Animas Valley, from the deck. The guest rooms are spacious bi-level suites, and all come with fireplaces. Amenities include an indoor pool, a spa and a sauna. ~ 5800 North Main Street, Durango; 970-259-1010. MODERATE TO DELUXE.

Jarvis Suite Hotel features studios and one- and two-bedroom suites decorated in a Southwest style. Rooms are small but compensated by cozy living rooms and full kitchens. Rates represent an especially good deal for families who use the sleeper sofa in the living room. ~ 125 West 10th Avenue, Durango; phone/fax 970-259-6190, 800-824-1024. MODERATE TO DELUXE.

On the bare-bones end of the spectrum is the **Durango Hostel**. Less expensive than some camp sites, with men's and women's dorms, as well as two private rooms decorated in Salvation Army–style decor, there is a kitchen where you can fix your own meals. The cheap rates do provide you with a roof over your head. ~ 543 East 2nd Avenue, Durango; 970-247-9905. BUDGET.

At the north end of town, the 20-room **Edelweiss Motel** has ordinary wood-paneled guest rooms with tiny kitchenettes. It is not fancy, though clean and quiet. There is a fruit orchard on the grounds, views of the Animas River and the narrow gauge train tracks are across the street. The motel's restaurant is one of the best in Durango. ~ 689 Animas View Drive, Durango; 970-247-5685. MODERATE.

Located 18 miles north of Durango, **Tamarron Hilton Resort** offers 350 spacious units with kitchens, exposed-timber beams and contemporary Western furnishings. All deliver expansive views of the beautiful high country north of Durango. The resort has a huge

✔ CHECK THESE OUT—UNIQUE LODGING

- *Budget:* Climb the several flights of zigzag stairs for a unique night in the **fire lookout tower** that has been converted into a wilderness version of an efficiency apartment. *page 567*
- *Moderate:* Excavate the Indian ruins on the 100-acre property of **Kelly Place**, a get-away-from-it-all bed and breakfast. *page 563*
- *Deluxe to ultra-deluxe:* Relax amid the largest collection of antique Victorian walnut furniture west of the Mississippi at the **Strater Hotel**. *page 555*
- *Ultra-deluxe:* Take a train or helicopter to **Tall Timber**—that's the only way to get to this plush resort in the heart of a national forest. *page 557*

Budget: under $50 Moderate: $50–$90 Deluxe: $90–$120 Ultra-deluxe: over $120

indoor-outdoor pool, saunas, whirlpool, children's program, golf, tennis, cross-country ski trails, horseback riding, ski shuttle to nearby Purgatory, two dining rooms and a deli. ~ 40292 Route 550 North, Durango; 970-259-2000, 800-678-1000, fax 800-950-1022. ULTRA-DELUXE.

Tall Timber is among the most highly regarded properties in ◄ *HIDDEN* the United States. Accessible by the narrow gauge train or heli-copter only, it is situated in the heart of the San Juan National Forest in a pristine and peaceful valley, five miles from the nearest road. For privacy seekers who relish comforts, there are ten luxu-rious modern units with fireplaces and decks. Guests may use an indoor-outdoor pool, sauna, whirlpool, nine-hole golf course, ten-nis court, ski and hiking trails and an exercise room. Horseback riding and fishing are also available. Rates include meals and trans-portation to the resort. Four-day minimum stay. ~ SSR Box 90A, Durango, CO 81301; 970-259-4813. ULTRA-DELUXE.

Located 20 miles northeast of Durango, **Lake Haven Resort** is situated right on Vallecito Reservoir. With over 25 cabins to choose from, there's one to fit everyone's budget. Smaller cabins sleep two people and are priced in the budget to moderate range, while larger cabins can sleep up to 17 people and carry a deluxe tab. Fishing, boating and horseback riding are some of the activities of-fered. Open from Memorial Day to Labor Day. ~ 14452 County Road 501, Bayfield; 970-884-2517. BUDGET TO DELUXE.

Silverton's **Alma House Bed and Breakfast** was built in 1898 and has been restored in keeping with that era. The small rooms are simply appointed with modern amenities, including queen-size beds, as well as antique dressers, brass lamps and period wallpa-per. Some rooms share a bath. ~ 220 East 10th Street, Silverton; 970-387-5336, 800-267-5336, fax 970-387-5974. MODERATE.

The Grand Imperial Hotel offers 40 rooms with private baths, some with oak pull-chain toilets. Rooms feature antique decor such as brass beds, brocade settees and crystal chandeliers con-verted from candles to electricity. There are a restaurant and a sa-loon, complete with bullet holes in the back bar. The hotel is open year-round, with lower rates in winter. ~ 1219 Greene Street, Silverton; 970-387-5527. MODERATE.

The nicest bed and breakfast in the entire region is **Blue Lake Ranch**, about 15 miles west of Durango. The 100-acre property includes a main house with four antique and flower-bedecked suites, two suites in the old barn, a three-story log cabin set in the woods, as well as a homestead set on the river. There are flower and herb gardens and a European breakfast including wheels of cheese, fruits, meats, cereal and juice every morning. Deer are fre-quent visitors. Breakfast included. ~ 16919 Route 140, Hesperus; 970-385-4537, fax 970-385-4088. DELUXE.

DINING

For a touch of the continent in the heart of the Rockies, the **Edelweiss Restaurant** offers German, Italian and American cuisine prepared expertly in a casual and friendly atmosphere. The menu includes weinerschnitzel, bratwurst, cannelloni Florentine and prime rib, as well as vegetarian entrées and imported draft beers. ~ 689 Animas View Drive, Durango; 970-247-5685. MODERATE.

Although far from any ocean, the **Red Snapper** nevertheless manages to offer remarkably fresh seafood. Cajun shrimp and Colorado trout are among selections that vary daily. All this is served in a stylish contemporary setting highlighted by 200 gallons of aquariums filled with tropical fish. The 40-item salad bar is the best in town, and for dessert, Death by Chocolate should not be missed. ~ 144 East 9th Street, Durango; 970-259-3417. MODERATE.

The Palace Grill wins recognition year after year as one of Durango's most popular restaurants in local opinion polls. A location adjacent to the narrow gauge train station and its 200,000 yearly visitors does not hurt business. The Victorian decor is attractive and the service verges on stiff formality, a rarity in these casual parts. Specialties include honey duck and goulash; vegetarian dishes can be made to order. Outdoor patio dining. Closed Sunday in winter. ~ 3 Depot Place, Durango; 970-247-2018. DELUXE.

One probably thinks of Mexican food in the Southwest, and the best in town can be found in a small drive-in on a side street. **Griego's Taco House** offers smothered burritos and tacos, as well as burgers and shakes. Eat in your car or at a picnic table. Griego's North, on Main Avenue, has a dining room, but the food is not as good. ~ 1400 East 2nd Avenue, Durango; 970-247-3127. BUDGET.

Another local favorite in the budget range is the **Durango Diner**. Nothing fancy here, just plain formica counters and tables, fast service and huge servings of standard breakfast and lunch selections such as bacon and eggs, pancakes, homemade hash browns, green chile sandwiches and homemade pies—all spiced with local gossip, making this a good place to find out what is going on around town. ~ 957 Main Avenue, Durango; 970-247-9889. BUDGET.

At **Carver's Bakery and Brew Pub** you can dine casually on fresh salads, eggs Benedict, sandwiches and locally brewed beer. Bread and pastries are baked in-house. ~ 1022 Main Avenue, Durango; 970-259-2545. BUDGET.

Chip's Place is worth the 12-mile drive from Durango. Again, nothing fancy—plastic chairs, cinder-block walls—but Chip's has been inducted into the Cheeseburger Hall of Fame. The super-chili cheeseburger is spectacular, the corned-beef sandwiches may be the best west of the Hudson River, and steaks are more tender and tasty than you will find locally at any price. The low-priced menu will make you think you have gone back in time. Closed Monday in winter. ~ 4 County Road 124, Hesperus; 970-259-6277. BUDGET.

The best Italian food in the area is found at another affordably priced restaurant, **Mama's Boy**. Ambience is zilch, with small, crowded tables overlooking gas pumps at a service station, but the pizza is primo. Also check out the antipasto, eggplant parmesan, ravioli and calzones. Closed Monday. ~ 32225 Route 550 North, Hermosa; 970-247-9053. BUDGET.

Silverton is justifiably un-renowned for dining. Most restaurants cater to the narrow-gauge train passengers who have an hour or two layover at lunch time. Open year-round, however, is the **French Bakery**, located on the ground floor of the Teller House Hotel. Victorian decor cannot mask the standard fare of burgers, soups, salads, pizzas and a somewhat more imaginative assortment of pastries. No one would mistake this place for a Parisian café. Open May through October. ~ 1250 Greene Street, Silverton, 970-387-5423. BUDGET TO MODERATE.

SHOPPING

Durango's Main Avenue and side streets are chock-a-block with gift shops and galleries. The best one in town, featuring fine art, jewelry and contemporary Western and American Indian crafts, is **Toh-Ahtin Gallery**. ~ 145 West 9th Street, Durango; 970-247-8277.

Another location offers prints, posters, artwear, jewelry and original art, **Art on Main**. ~ 865 Main Avenue, Durango; 970-247-4540.

For an interesting assortment of antiques, collectibles, railroad memorabilia, used and rare books, try **Southwest Book Trader**. ~ 175 East 5th Street, Durango; 970-247-8479.

Unusual gifts collected from travels around the world and local crafts are available at **Jodie's Haircuts and Boutique**. ~ 102 East 8th Street, Suite 213, Durango; 970-247-0300.

If your head is simply aching for a custom-fitted cowboy hat, try **O'Farrell of Durango**. They make hats by hand, the old fashioned way, and have produced customized models for Ronald Reagan and George Bush. ~ 563 Main Avenue, Durango; 970-259-2517.

✔ **CHECK THESE OUT—UNIQUE DINING**

- *Budget:* Drive the 12 miles from Durango for the best cheeseburgers you'll ever consume at **Chip's Place**, nothing fancy, but oh so good! *page 558*
- *Budget to moderate:* Line up at the seafood buffet table on Friday night at **Millwood Junction**; save room for the homemade desserts. *page 567*
- *Moderate:* Feast on the food and views at **Stromsted's**, a fashionable restaurant built into a hillside overlooking Mesa Verde. *page 564*
- *Deluxe:* Join the locals for a special night out at **The Palace Grill**, with its Victorian decor and formal service. *page 558*

Budget: under $8 Moderate: $8–$16 Deluxe: $16–$24 Ultra-deluxe: over $24

An influx of **factory outlets** to Durango has brought Ralph Lauren, Benetton, Levis, London Fog and other name-brand discounters to the small downtown area.

Silverton contains a plethora of take-your-pick gift shops clustered mainly along Greene Street between 11th and 14th streets. None stand out. All seem to offer souvenir rocks, T-shirts, jewelry, cowboy hats, leather goods, train whistles, as well as practical area guidebooks, maps and camping gear.

NIGHTLIFE   Many of the area's evening offerings are seasonal. The **Bar D Chuckwagon** has a chuckwagon supper and Western show, May through October. ~ 8080 County Road 250, Durango; 970-247-5753.

The **Diamond Circle Theatre** features musicals and turn-of-the-century melodramas. ~ 699 Main Avenue, Durango; 970-247-4431.

The **Durango Pro Rodeo** presents professional rodeo events on Tuesday and Wednesday evenings from June through August. ~ La Plata County Fairgrounds, 25th Street and Main Avenue, Durango; 970-247-2308.

Aside from these activities, nightlife is pretty much limited to restaurants, bars and a few movie theaters. The **Diamond Belle Saloon** features an antique gold-leaf filigree back bar, a honky-tonk piano player, waitresses dressed in 1880s saloon-girl finery and bartenders with garters on their sleeves. ~ 699 Main Avenue, Durango; 970-247-4431.

Farquahrt's is an antique-filled rock-and-roll bar with live music nightly. Cover on weekends. ~ 725 Main Avenue, Durango; 970-247-5440.

Silverton's nightlife makes Durango seems like Manhattan by comparison. Try the **Gold King**, a Victorian-appointed bar located in the Grand Imperial Hotel. ~ 1219 Greene Street, Silverton; 970-387-5527.

PARKS   **SAN JUAN NATIONAL FOREST**   The site is huge. The national forest covers four million acres of southwestern Colorado, offering hundreds of miles of trails and the San Juan Skyway, a scenic byway connecting Durango, Silverton, Telluride and Cortez. Vallecito Reservoir and Lemon Reservoir among other sites, satisfy anglers with trout, kokanee salmon, bluegill and crappie. Windsurfers are made happy by the wind and water. Also here are rivers for swimming and boating, hunting grounds and some of the most spectacular scenery of alpine lakes, cataracts and waterfalls you'll ever see. Unusual geologic formations and historic mines add to the splendor. Deer, elk and eagles live in the pine and aspen forests that are a special treat during fall when bright colors are abundant. With the towering elevations found here (peaking at 14,000 feet), snow is usually on the ground in the high country until July and may fall again as early as September. There are picnic areas and restrooms; restaurants and groceries are in towns within or adjacent to the forest. ~ The national forest extends from Telluride to the New Mexico border, from McPhee Reservoir to Pagosa Springs, 47 miles east of Durango. The main access is via Routes 160 and 550; 970-247-4874.

▲ There are 41 campgrounds; less-developed sites are free while standard ones are $5 to $10 per night; for reservations, call 800-280-2267.

WEMINUCHE WILDERNESS 🏃 🐎 🛶 One of the nation's largest wilderness areas, Weminuche consists of 490,000 acres set aside by the federal government to retain its primeval character. The average elevation of the area is 10,000 feet and there are 400 miles of hiking trails. Hiking and horseback riding are allowed through this very rugged slice of the scenic West. Fishing is permitted while bicycles and motorized vehicles are not. There are no facilities here. Restaurants and groceries are available in communities outside the wilderness area. ~ Located 26 miles northeast of Durango, main access is via hiking trails at Vallecito Reservoir, from trails outside of Silverton or Purgatory ski area, or via the Durango–Silverton Narrow Gauge Railroad; 970-247-4874.

▲ Backpack camping is allowed, but permits are required for ten or more people.

▼▼▼▼▼▼▼▼▼▼▼▼▼▼
Cortez–Dolores Area

Many of southwestern Colorado's most fascinating destinations are a short drive from popular Mesa Verde. One of the finest Indian preserves in the Americas, the Ute Mountain Tribal Park offers a American Indian–led look at Anasazi country. You can also see another side of this region's special heritage at Lowry Ruins and Hovenweep National Monument, straddling the Colorado-Utah border. Because each is slightly off the beaten track you'll be able to enjoy a leisurely uncrowded visit to this magical region.

SIGHTS

The scrubland desert north of the San Juan River is broken by mesas and isolated canyons where pre-Columbian Pueblo Indians lived until around 1300. Established on the Colorado-Utah border in 1923, **Hovenweep National Monument** contains 784 acres and six groups of ruins. These ruins are most noted for the substantial size of the community they once housed, as well as their square, oval, circular and D-shaped towers, indicating sophisticated masonry skills. Some of the walls stand 20 feet high despite the total deterioration of ancient mortar over the centuries. ~ 40 miles west of Cortez off Route 666; 970-529-4461.

Square Tower Ruins are the best preserved. All sites are essentially accessible by car, although hikes of varying lengths are necessary for close examination of the ruins. Noteworthy ruins include the two pueblos of Cajon Ruins, located in Utah, which are the least well preserved, having been heavily vandalized before the monument was established, and Holly, Hackberry Canyon, Cutthroat Castle and Goodman Point Ruins, located in Colorado.

Sixteen miles north of Hovenweep lies a smaller National Historic Landmark, Lowry Pueblo Ruins. The site, believed to have housed 100 farmers who raised corn, beans and squash for fifty to a hundred years until at least 1140 A.D., contains one of the largest circular communal gathering spots, known as kivas, yet discovered in the Southwest. The site also contains 40 rooms, some of which were three stories tall, and eight smaller kivas. It is here you will find the painted kiva with its five layers of ancient plaster paintings, covered by a modern roof to help preserve it. Although the site is open year-round, the road is not maintained in winter. ~ Marked gravel road off Route 666, eight miles west of Pleasant View; 970-247-4082.

Considered one of the world's largest collections of ancient Indian artifacts, the Anasazi Heritage Center is adjacent to the 12th-century Dominguez and Escalante pueblos. Materials from the excavations of these ruins are displayed in the very fine museum operated by the Bureau of Land Management. There are hands-on displays involving computers and microscopes, as well as *metate* stones for grinding corn, a loom and a partially reconstructed full-size pit house. ~ 27501 Route 184, Dolores; 970-882-4811.

Many of the museum items at the Anasazi Heritage Center were rescued prior to the flooding of a local valley—retrieved from an area now under water at Dolores's McPhee Dam and Reservoir.

The Crow Canyon Archaeological Center is a school and research center developed to create a greater understanding of the prehistoric Anasazi who populated the Four Corners area. Visitors who have made advance reservations may take day tours of the laboratory research facilities and a working archaeological site, or sign up for cultural education programs led by Pueblo scholars. A tiny museum off Main Street in downtown Cortez, the Cortez Center (25 North Market Street; 303-565-1151) offers displays on the Basketmaker and Pueblo periods of Anasazi culture, as well as informative videos on various aspects of Anasazi life. Admission. ~ 23390 County Road K, Cortez; 970-565-8975.

South of Cortez and surrounding nearby Mesa Verde on three sides, the Ute Mountain Tribal Park has long been considered sacred ground by the Ute Mountain tribe whose reservation encompasses the park. Following the Mancos River valley, the site contains hundreds of surface ruins, cliff dwellings, petroglyphs and paintings. Maintained as a primitive area and administered by American Indians, this is one of the most evocative Anasazi sites in all of southwestern Colorado.

Visitors must make reservations for a daily guided tour with a tribe member. The tours cover nearly 100 miles in six hours (half-day tours are also available)—stopping numerous times to walk through fields littered with thousands of distinctive pottery shards, to stand beside pit houses and burial mounds, to hike to petroglyphs, rock paintings and sentinel posts, or to scale ladders as high as thirty feet to reach excavated but unrestored Anasazi ruins, left intact much the way they were 800 years ago. Bring water, food and a full tank of gas. A day here can be physically exerting and there are no facilities available. Admission. ~ Towaoc; 970-565-9653, 800-847-5485.

Sleeping Ute Mountain west of the tribal park is a landmark you cannot and should not miss. From its head to the north, to its feet to the south, this mountain with an elevation of more than 9800 feet appears to be an Indian lying on his back with his arms folded across his chest.

LODGING

Strip motels and chains predominate, but there are a few unusual choices.

An original railroad hotel has been in operation for 95 years in Dolores. The **Rio Grande Southern** is the oldest building in town. It has six small rooms decorated with reproduction antiques and local artwork. There is also a restaurant. Full breakfast included. ~ 101 5th Street, Dolores; 970-882-7527, 800-258-0434. BUDGET.

◄ HIDDEN

A real get-away-from-it-all bed and breakfast is located between Cortez and Hovenweep National Monument. **Kelly Place** is situated on a secluded dirt road, miles from anywhere. Set in the midst of a piñon-juniper forest and sandstone canyons, the eight rooms are large and comfortably furnished in contemporary Western style. There are Indian ruins on the 100-acre property which guests can help excavate. Pottery and weaving instruction in the Anasazi style, as well as classes in canning, quilting, tanning, botany or farming with draft horses are added features. ~ 14663 County Road G, Cortez; 970-565-3125. MODERATE.

DINING

Here we truly begin to stretch in seeking the best restaurants. Chains are well-represented along with a number of small cafés serving undistinguished food. However . . .

Ponderosa Restaurant and Lounge serves hamburgers, sandwiches, Mexican dishes, home-baked pies, cinnamon rolls, cookies, muffins and sourdough Danish in a setting of nouveau K-Mart decor. This restaurant and lounge is convenient to McPhee Reservoir. ~ Route 145 and 8th Street, Dolores; 970-882-7910. BUDGET.

Old Germany Restaurant, which looks like a Bavarian cottage, serves dumplings, shrimp, German-style sausage and Bavarian specialties, imported beers and German wines. Closed Sunday and Monday, and November through mid-January. ~ Route 145 and 8th Street, Dolores; 970-882-7549. BUDGET TO MODERATE.

Stromsted's is on the south end of town, built into a hillside, with interesting woodwork in the dining room and a deck affording views of Mesa Verde and Sleeping Ute Mountain. The steaks, seafood and barbecued ribs are the best in town. ~ 1020 South Broadway, Cortez; 970-565-1257. MODERATE.

Genuine Mexican food is served at plant-bedecked **Francisca's.** Entrées include *chile rellenos*, chimichangas, stacked enchiladas and vegetarian dishes. Also popular are the Blue Curaçao margaritas. Closed Sunday and Monday. ~ 125 East Main Street, Cortez; 970-565-4093. BUDGET TO MODERATE.

For a relaxing afternoon, stop by **Earthsong Haven and Quality Bookstore.** A combination bookstore-café, they serve sandwiches, soups, quiches and delicious carrot cake. ~ 34 West Main Street, Cortez; 970-565-9125. BUDGET.

Western hospitality with no frills might help describe the **M&M Truckstop and Restaurant.** Open 24 hours, this is the locals' choice for breakfast anytime. Eggs with refried beans, Navajo tacos, pancakes served in multiples of five, fries made from real potatoes, steaks, sandwiches and everything else on the menu are bargain-priced. ~ 7006 Route 160, Cortez; 970-565-6511. BUDGET.

SHOPPING The gift shop at the **Anasazi Heritage Center** offers books on the Southwest, anthropology, archaeology and children's topics, plus a small selection of replica pottery. ~ 27501 Route 184, Dolores; 970-882-4811.

In Cortez, the gift shop at **Cortez Center** has some of the best prices in the region on a small selection of contemporary American Indian pottery, weavings and other crafts. ~ 25 North Market Street, Cortez; 970-565-1151.

Mesa Verde Pottery/Gallery Southwest has a selection of American Indian pottery crafted on the premises, as well as drums, sandpaintings, collectible Pueblo pottery, kachina dolls, weavings, jewelry and sculptures. ~ 27601 East Route 160, Cortez; 970-565-4492.

NIGHTLIFE In Cortez, limited to summer months only, there are American Indian storytellers weeknights at the **Cortez Center,** and from June to September, American Indian dances are performed at the Center. ~ 25 North Market Street, Cortez; 970-565-1151.

During the rest of the year try the **M&M Truckstop and Restaurant.** It is open 24 hours and likely to be the liveliest place in town after dark. ~ 7006 Route 160, Cortez; 970-565-6511.

The **Ponderosa Restaurant & Lounge** may offer a semblance of nightlife at times. ~ Route 145 and 8th Street, Dolores; 970-882-7910.

HOVENWEEP NATIONAL MONUMENT 🚶🚲 This 784-acre park straddles the Colorado-Utah border. Here you will find six major sites of American Indian ruins in nearly mythic Colorado plateau country. Camping, hiking and bike riding are allowed in the slickrock canyon country characterized by sweeping unobstructed vistas of the pastel high desert. The monument's facilities are limited to picnic sites and pit toilets; restaurants, food, gas and supplies are available in Cortez, at Hatch Trading Post (16 miles west) or Ismay Trading Post (14 miles southeast). ~ Located 49 miles west of Cortez, access is via McElmo Canyon Road, three miles south of Cortez or by the Pleasant View Road, 20 miles north of Cortez; 970-529-4461.

▲ There are 30 tent sites. From April to October water is available and sites are $6 per night. From November to March, there is no water available and sites are free.

MCPHEE RESERVOIR 🚶♨️⛴️🚣🏊🚤🛥️🎣 This 4500-acre manmade lake is located northwest of Dolores and offers a full range of recreational opportunities, including swimming, fishing and boating. Most activities are centered around the developed areas at Lone Dome, House Creek, the Great Cut Dike and the McPhee Recreation Area. Open since the late 1980s, the lake is snuggled in between mountains to the west and the desert to the east. There are groceries, water, picnic sites, hiking trails, a marina, restrooms and showers. ~ Located northwest of Dolores, main access is via Route 145; 970-882-7296.

▲ McPhee Campground has 73 sites (eight with hookups); $8 to $10 per night. House Creek Camp has 43 sites (12 with hookups); $10 per night.

UTE MOUNTAIN TRIBAL PARK 🚶🚲🐎 This is a primitive area surrounding Mesa Verde on three sides. There are limited facilities, and access is restricted to group tours or those who reserve an Indian guide for backpacking, biking or horseback trips through the 125,000 acres of rugged canyon country and prehistoric Indian ruins. Surrounding the once-lush Mancos River Valley, the arid parklands sprawl through cactus and sage-studded habitats for elk, deer and mountain lions. The only facilities are picnic tables and restrooms; restaurants and food are available in Cortez. ~ Located 18 miles south of Cortez in Towaoc, access is via Route 666; 970-565-9653 ext. 282 or 800-847-5485.

▲ Camping is allowed here in a designated area; $10 per night per car.

PARKS

▼▼▼▼▼▼▼▼▼▼▼
Mesa Verde Area

Travel east from Cortez on Route 160 to reach the turnoff to Mesa Verde National Park. Ascending the highway to this legendary plateau, you'll enjoy panoramic views of the Four Corners region. The turnoff will take you south into the park; if you continue on Route 160, you'll head into Mancos, the town closest to Mesa Verde. The park has some food and lodging facilities in the high season; Mancos handles the overflow and off-season travelers. As you travel through this magical region, keep an eye out for the great Kachinas, the gods of the tribal lands. If you don't spot a real one, you'll have plenty of opportunity to purchase carved renditions of them in the Mesa Verde gift shop.

SIGHTS

Mesa Verde National Park is the number-one tourist attraction in southwestern Colorado, drawing 700,000 visitors yearly to its deserted canyons, outstanding views and preserved archaeological sites. Easily reached by a convenient loop drive, each of the cliff dwellings, pit houses and other Pueblo sites is an authentic Southwestern treasure. Tucked inside sandstone cliffs, many of these dwellings are inaccessible today. Those you can visit, thanks to guided tours, make it clear that these American Indians were among the leading architects of their day. Admission. ~ Route 160; 970-529-4465.

Although major cliff dwellings and mesa-top sites may be seen from overlooks on roadways, visits to other sites are strenuous, requiring hikes varying in altitude from 6040 feet to 8572 feet, aided by steps and ladders.

Traveling up the steep entrance road for four miles, **Morefield Village** is the site of the park's only campground and the starting point for three hiking trails most popular for panoramic views. The shortest trail (1 mile) leads to **Point Lookout** at the tip of the mesa.

Nine miles farther along the road is the **Far View Visitors Center**, the commercial hub of the park and location of most visitor services. The visitors center displays contemporary American Indian arts and crafts.

In summer only, **Wetherill Mesa** may be accessed from a turnoff at Far View. It is a rugged 21-mile ride to the **Step House** and **Long House Sites**, containing 1400-year-old subterranean pit houses from the Basketmaker period and 800-year-old structures from the Classic Pueblo period around 1200 A.D.

The main park sites and a fascinating archaeological museum are clustered around Chapin Mesa, 21 miles from the park entrance, a minimum 45-minute drive. The museum contains exhibits and artifacts detailing the history of the Pueblo peoples as well as the development of the national park. From here you can take a short hike to **Spruce Tree House**, one of the major park sites (which can also be viewed from an overlook).

Other significant sites and isolated cliff dwellings, carved improbably out of sheer rock faces, are accessible via two loops on the Ruins Road. The westerly loop, a paved road well marked with signs, leads over its two-mile length past several interesting sites, including **Square Tower House**, pit houses and Pueblo ruins, **Sun Point** overlook at the edge of **Fewkes Canyon** and **Cliff Canyon** and the **Sun Temple**. The easterly loop is approximately the same length, also paved. It leads through similar pine, scrub brush and sage hillsides along the mesa top to numerous view sites as well as the **Cliff Palace** and **Balcony House**.

Guided interpretive tours led by rangers are conducted at all major cliff dwellings in the summer. In winter, guided tours are offered to Spruce Tree House only, weather permitting. A minimal fee is charged for the tours. Although the park is open year-round, roads may be closed due to weather conditions in winter months. Winter is the least crowded and most haunting time to visit the park.

LODGING

The only motel within the national park is the **Far View Lodge**. It is actually a fairly modest place in a spectacular setting. Each of 150 rooms is standard motel style, with American Indian print bedspreads and a balcony offering 100-mile views across the mesa country. There's a restaurant on the premises. Open May to October. ~ P.O. Box 277, Mancos, CO 81328; 970-529-4421. MODERATE.

For a truly *hidden* lodging experience deep in the San Juan National Forest, travel 14 miles north of Mancos along Forest Road 561, a gravel road. Prices are budget rate at "Jersey Jim," and you won't be troubled by noisy neighbors. However, you'll have to climb several flights of zigzag stairs en route to your room, a glass-lined facility measuring 15 feet square. But once you arrive the views are extraordinary. Jersey Jim, it seems, is a **fire lookout tower** that has been converted into a wilderness version of an efficiency apartment. Sleeping up to four people (bring your own sleeping bags), it contains a stove, refrigerator and lanterns. Water is available at a campground four miles away, and can be hauled up to the tower by a pulley system. Reservations are required. ~ Call the Jersey Jim Foundation at 970-533-7060. BUDGET.

◄ *HIDDEN*

For dudes and dudettes, **Lake Mancos Ranch** offers 17 units accommodating 55 guests in private cabins or ranch house rooms. Decor is plain—Western wood-paneled rooms with wooden furniture—but guests do not come here to stay inside. They come to enjoy horseback riding, fishing, jeeping, mountain biking and the great outdoors. There are a pool and supervised children's programs. Meals and activities are included in the rates. Riding is extra. Minimum stay is one week. ~ 42688 County Road N, Mancos; 970-533-7900, 800-325-9462. DELUXE.

DINING

The best restaurant in this area is seven miles east of the national park entrance. **Millwood Junction** serves budget-priced specials nightly, moderately priced dinners and a memorable Friday night seafood buffet in a comfortable rough-hewn, wood-paneled dining room. Regular menu items include châteaubriand and baby back ribs, as well as oregano chicken, steak and lobster, and blackened catfish. The salad bar is a meal in itself, but save room for home-made ice cream, cheesecake, black-bottom pie or a raspberry torte. ~ Route 160 West, Mancos; 970-533-7338. BUDGET TO MODERATE.

Within the national park you will find three restaurants oper-ated by the concessionaire. The **Far View Terrace Café** and **Spruce Tree Terrace** are budget-priced cafeterias offering Navajo tacos, burgers, sandwiches and salads. The moderately priced **Metate Room**, at Far View Lodge, serves New York strip steak, a beef and vegetable Mexican sauté, fried shrimp and other Mexican and American dishes. ~ 970-529-4421. BUDGET TO MODERATE.

SHOPPING   **Mesa Verde National Park** has a gift shop (970-529-4421) and bookstore (970-529-4445) located at the park headquarters on Chapin Mesa, as well as a gift shop at the Far View Visitors Center. The bookstore is well stocked with research relating to the entire southwestern Colorado region.

NIGHTLIFE   Nightlife in this neck of the woods consists largely of looking at expanses of stars in a clear sky. **Millwood Junction** has occasional live music. ~ Route 160 West, Mancos; 970-533-7338.

PARKS   **MESA VERDE NATIONAL PARK**   In the high-canyon country between Cortez and Mancos, the park offers scenic roads leading to short trails to American Indian ruins and stunning mesa-top views of the desert and the mountains. Maintained by the Na-tional Park Service, the area contains the most accessible concen-tration of prehistoric cliff dwellings in the U.S. Biking is limited to specified roads. Restrooms, groceries, gas, showers, laundromat; motel and restaurants in the park; the ranger station, visitors cen-ters and services operate mid-April to October only, though the park and museum are open year-round. ~ The park entrance is on Route 160, seven miles east of Cortez; 970-529-4543.

▲ Morefield Campground has 450 sites including 15 with hookups; $9 to $16.50 per night. ~ 970-529-4421.

LAKE MANCOS STATE RECREATION AREA   Lake Mancos is situated at 7800 feet and surrounded by 338 acres of mature ponderosa pine forest laced with hiking and horseback trails. Nonmotorized boats are permitted. The park has picnic sites, restrooms and showers; groceries and restaurants five miles away in Mancos. ~ Located ten miles northeast of Mesa Verde, the park is north on Route 184 in Mancos to County Road 42, then four miles farther to County Road N; 970-833-2208.

▲ There are 24 tent sites; $9 per night.

Anyone with a license can hunt big game, such as deer and elk, and fish for rainbow, cutthroat and brown trout. A number of outfitters make their livings by knowing where these babies may be found.

FISHING & HUNTING

DURANGO–SILVERTON AREA   In Durango, try **Buck's Livery**. ~ Route 550 North; 970-259-5675. **Ron-D-View Ranch** also has the lowdown. ~ Durango; 970-563-9270. **San Juan Outfitting** arranges high-country pack trips to hunt elk, deer, bears or bighorn sheep, using bow and arrow, muzzleloading rifles and regular rifles. ~ 186 County Road 228, Durango; 970-259-6259.

The best fishing is found north of Durango at Haviland Lake, Lemon Lake or Vallecito Reservoir. For fishing trips call **Duranglers** or check with other outfitters. ~ 801-B Main Avenue, Durango; 970-385-4081.

CORTEZ–DOLORES AREA   Fly fishing is good on the Dolores River. McPhee Reservoir is stocked with trout, kokanee salmon, large- and smallmouth bass, perch, bluegill and catfish. **Circle K Ranch** arranges guided, outfitted trips for hunting, and fishing is also available. ~ 27758 Route 145, Dolores; 970-562-3808.

BOATING & CANOEING

Anyone ever told you to paddle your own canoe? Now's the time to take them up on the challenge! View the beauty of Southwestern Colorado's reservoirs from the floating vantage point of your own canoe or rowboat. And don't forget to take a picture of yourself to prove you can paddle with the best of them.

DURANGO–SILVERTON AREA   Gentler than whitewater, the lakes and reservoirs are fine for small boats and canoes. For canoes and boats of various sizes at Vallecito Reservoir contact **Shorty's**. ~ Vallecito Reservoir, Bayfield; 970-884-2768. You can also rent from **Mountain Marina**. ~ 14810-A County Road 501, Bayfield; 970-884-9450.

RIVER RUNNING

Whether the rivers are raging during spring runoff, or relatively calm, waterborne sports are always a good way to explore desert canyons or mountain streams. The upper stretch of the Animas River from Silverton to Rockwood offers the only two-day Class V whitewater trip in the West and is suitable for expert kayakers or experienced rafters only. The lower reaches may be rafted by one and all. The Dolores River is considered tops for whitewater in late May.

DURANGO–SILVERTON AREA   You can take a trip downriver with **Southwest Adventures**. ~ 780 Main Avenue, Durango; 970-259-0370. **Four Corners River Sports** is another of the area's leading outfitters. ~ 360 South Camino del Rio, Durango; 970-259-3893. **Durango Rivertrippers** is a whitewater specialist. ~ 720 Main

Text continued on page 572.

Skiing the Best— The Southwestern Rockies

Many experts think some the best skiing in the world is found in the southwestern Rockies of Colorado. The snow is deep, averaging more than 300 inches a year of feather-soft powder; temperatures average ten degrees higher than more northerly resorts. Telluride and Purgatory offer unparalleled vertical terrain amid crowning mountain beauty. It's only because the areas are harder to reach than better-known ski resorts that they tend to stay less crowded.

Telluride Ski Area—It's the mountain! Top elevation is an ethereal 11,890 feet, with a vertical drop of 3522 feet, offering distinct ski terrain for all levels of skiers. Experts enjoy controlled, out-of-bounds skiing, but must be willing to hike half an hour or more to reach the sites.

The growing popularity and powerful reputation of Telluride has been helped by scheduled airline service into Telluride Regional Airport—the highest commercial airport in the United States at elevation 9086 feet.

Telluride opens in late November. Some special programs offered include, "Ski week," emphasizing a daily two-hour class focusing on physical, mental and social aspects of skiing. ~ Route 145, Telluride; 970-728-4424.

The entire old mining town of Telluride is a National Historic Landmark. Victorian structures predominate. The **New Sheridan Hotel**, where William Jennings Bryan delivered his famous "Cross of Gold" speech in 1904, is a gem. ~ 231 West Colorado Avenue; 970-728-4351, 800-200-1891.

Need a place to hang your ski boots? You can stay in the New Sheridan Hotel—in the opulent historic style of antique Victorian, or at a condominium which rents by the night or week, such as the **Dahl House Condominium**. ~ 127 South Oak Street; 970-728-4158.

One of the most beautifully located guest ranches in the West is **Skyline Ranch**, open year-round. They have cross-country ski trails and horseback riding for guests. ~ P.O. Box 67, Telluride, CO 81435; 970-728-3757. Ski-in, ski-out lodging, lift-ticket sales, equipment rentals, ski school, restaurant and nursery services are located at **Telluride Ski and Golf**. ~ 565 Mountain Village Boulevard; 970-728-3856, 800-525-3455. The **Peaks of Telluride** offers ski-in, ski-out access, as well winter activities including snowmobiling, ice skating and dinner sleigh rides. ~ Country Club Drive; 970-728-6800, 800-789-2220.

Purgatory-Durango Ski Resort is north of Durango and around 100 road miles from Telluride, though actually just over the hill—the hill being ridges of the San Juan Mountains, roughly 14,000 feet high.

The area covers 630 acres with good snow and mild weather, all adding up to record-breaking ski days year after year. The difference here, for some, is in the vertical terrain. Purgatory has long been considered an intermediate skier's nirvana. Now, however, an area called The Legends has boosted the overall ski field by 25 percent and added nine advanced trails with a vertical drop of 2000 feet. Nevertheless, a good portion of the resort's business comes from a low-key, fun-loving trade, compared with Telluride's trendier skiers.

Half of Purgatory is considered mid-level terrain, and there is a separate Columbine Station area for beginners. It is serviced by its own triple chairlift, providing novices with a private, pristine spot for learning the basics. A justified claim to fame here is that there is rarely a lift line, even during peak season. Purgatory serves 300,000 skiers yearly, the most of any southwestern Colorado area. Five triple chairs and four doubles help.

Purgatory-Durango opens in late November. Every adult beginner at Purgatory can get a free half-day lesson with the purchase of a lift ticket, and the excellent instructional programs also include group lessons, as well as individualized classes. They also have cross-country ski trails. ~ Route 550 North, Durango; 970-247-9000.

Condominiums line the base of Purgatory's slopes. Ten miles south is highly rated **Tamarron Resort** (see "Lodging" in the Durango–Silverton Area section) with free ski buses. Durango is 25 miles south, offering various lodging-ski-transportation packages through hotels such as the **Strater Hotel** (see "Lodging" in the Durango–Silverton Area section). The **Durango Lift** (970-259-5438) offers inexpensive bus transportation between Purgatory and Durango.

Southwestern Colorado also boasts some fantastic cross-country skiing. **Hesperus Ski Area** offers cross-country skiing and downhill skiing, as well as snowboarding and night-skiing. ~ 9848 Route 160, Hesperus; 970-259-3711. Cross-country skiing is very good at **Hillcrest Golf Course**. ~ 2300 Rim Drive, Durango; 970-247-1499. **San Juan National Forest** also has some great cross-country spots. ~ 701 Camino del Rio, Durango; 970-247-4874. **Mesa Verde National Park** has cross-country trails among the archaeological ruins. ~ 970-529-4465.

See you on the slopes!

Avenue, Durango; 970-259-0289. **Peregrine River Outfitters** is another adventure company based in Durango. ~ 64 Ptarmigan Lane; 970-385-7600.

JEEP TOURS Traveling the four-wheel-drive roads between Silverton and Lake City is the best way to get close to the stunning Fourteeners, the group of mountains in this area that top 14,000 feet. These roads are among the highest in the country; careful on the curves as you cruise past Handies, Sunshine and Redcloud peaks. For guided jeep tours in this area, call 800-494-8687.

If you want to drive on your own, you can rent jeeps at **Silverton Lakes Campground.** ~ 2100 Kendall Street; 970-387-5721. Also renting jeeps is the **Triangle Service Station.** ~ 864 Greene Street; 970-387-9990.

GOLF Out here, golf usually takes a back seat to the rugged high desert and mountain terrain, but if you're bent on being a duffer, there are a few places to swing and putt.

DURANGO–SILVERTON AREA To tee off, visit the **Hillcrest Golf Club.** ~ 2300 Rim Drive, Durango; 970-247-1499. Located nearby in Durango is the **Tamarron Resort.** ~ 40292 Route 550 North; 970-259-2000.

CORTEZ–DOLORES AREA **Conquistador Golf Course** is the main course in this area. ~ 2018 North Dolores Road, Cortez; 970-565-9208.

TENNIS The courts around here are all public, pardner, so don't worry about donning fancy duds; throw on your old sweats, grab your racquet and head to one of these school or park tennis courts.

DURANGO–SILVERTON AREA In Durango there are courts at the **Durango High School.** ~ 2390 Main Avenue; 970-259-1630. You'll also find public courts in Durango at **Fort Lewis College.** ~ College Heights; 970-247-7010. In Silverton there are courts in **Memorial Park** at the northeast end of town.

CORTEZ–DOLORES AREA Cortez has tennis courts in **City Park.** ~ 830 East Montezuma Avenue; 970-565-3402.

RIDING STABLES & PACK TRIPS There are still plenty of horses in this part of the West, and you can ride gentle or spirited steeds for an hour, a day or as long as you can take it, pal. In addition, you can hike with a llama that carries your gear over terrain ranging from high desert to forested alpine trails.

DURANGO–SILVERTON AREA To arrange a trip, call **Over the Hill Outfitters.** ~ 3624 County Road 203, Durango, 970-247-9289 and 13391 County Road 250, 970-259-2834. Another place to saddle up in Durango is **Southfork Stables**. ~ 28481 Route 160 East, Durango; 970-259-4871. If you're in Bayfield, check out **Wit's End/Meadowlark Ranch**. ~ 254 County Road 500, Bayfield; 970-884-4113. **Silverado Outfitters** leads tours from Silverton. ~ 1155 Mineral Street; 970-387-5747. You can also mount a steed at **Silver Trails**. ~ 600 Cement Street, Silverton; 970-387-5815.

Day hikes with llamas are available from Durango's **Buckhorn Llama Co., Inc.** Advance reservations are required. ~ P.O. Box 64, Masonville, CO 80541; 970-667-7411.

MESA VERDE AREA In Mancos you can take a trail ride from **Echo Basin Ranch**. ~ 43747 County Road M, Mancos; 970-533-7000.

BIKING

Fast becoming one of the most popular sports in the region, mountain biking has taken off in a big way, due in part to the popularity of two events. The Iron Horse Bicycle Classic, held yearly over Memorial Day weekend, pits riders against the narrow-gauge train in a 50-mile race over two 10,000-foot mountain passes from Durango to Silverton. The best bike riders always beat the train. And the first unified World Mountain Biking Championship was held in Durango in 1990. The championship course at Purgatory is open to riders in the summer. The terrain for biking is challenging and scenic. The variety of roads and trails on public lands is immense.

DURANGO–SILVERTON AREA The Animas Valley Loop is considered easy by locals who always ride at 6500 feet; it is mostly flat, rising only 280 feet, and can be ridden in 15- or 30-mile versions. The long route follows County Road 250 north out of Durango and up the east side of the Animas Valley, crossing the main Route 550 at Baker's Bridge and heading back to Durango via County Road 203, on the west side of the valley.

One-hour, half-day, full-day or overnight dog-sled trips of national forests north of Mancos are arranged by **Sunset Kennels**. ~ 25 Sunset Acres, Hesperus, CO 81326; 970-588-3641.

A beautiful intermediate ride is **Old Lime Creek Road**, between Silverton and Cascade Creek, north of Purgatory. It starts 11 miles south of Silverton, off Route 550, and follows the old highway for 12 miles past beaver ponds and a brick retaining span called the "Chinese Wall, " which once separated stage coaches from a sheer drop down the steep mountainside.

The **Animas City Mountain Loop** follows an advanced, five-and-a-half-mile trail that gains 1250 feet in elevation. The trail starts off of 4th Avenue, north of 32nd Street, in Durango, and offers stunning views of Falls Creek, the Animas Valley and the West Needle Mountains from the top of a tilted mesa.

CORTEZ-DOLORES AREA   The **Horseshoe Ruins Trail** starts 23 miles south of Pleasant View off the road to Hovenweep. It is an easy ten-mile loop through the rolling mesa country that predominates in this area. It takes you to Horseshoe, Holly and Hackberry Ruins within the national monument. The **Cutthroat Castle Trail** starts in the same place, circling north over similar terrain into Hovenweep Canyon and past the Cutthroat Castle ruin. The 17-mile loop is for intermediate riders.

MESA VERDE AREA   Several easy-to-intermediate rides may be found on roads through **Mesa Verde National Park**, particularly in the spring and fall when the air is cooler and there are fewer cars on the roads. ~ 970-529-4465.

Bike Rentals   **Mountain Bike Specialists** rents bikes. ~ 949 Main Avenue, Durango; 970-247-4066. Also renting bikes in Durango is **Hassle Free Sports**. ~ 2615 Main Avenue, Durango; 970-259-3874, 800-835-3800.

HIKING

Looking for that Rocky Mountain High? Southwestern Colorado may not be the heart of the Rockies that John Denver was crooning about, but the scenery and altitudes make it pretty darn close. Trails in this region will lead you up to the Continental Divide, or over 12,000 feet on the Colorado Trail. If you're bent on bagging Fourteeners, you can ride a narrow-gauge railroad to a high-country trailhead and take your choice of three peaks over 14,000 feet. Or, opt for the desert terrain, and explore ancient settlements at Hovenweep and Mesa Verde.

DURANGO-SILVERTON AREA   Numerous hiking trails are found in the San Juan National Forest and Weminuche Wilderness Area. Backpacking trips of several hours to several days are possible. Forest service maps and information are available from the Columbine Ranger District, 303-247-4874.

The southwest portion of the 469-mile **Colorado Trail**, connecting Durango and Denver, begins in the La Plata Mountains, west of Durango atop Kennebec Pass. Access is at the end of County Road 124, in Hesperus or via Junction Creek from downtown Durango. This trail offers rugged hiking through alpine wilderness ranging from 7000 to 12,680 feet in altitude.

Perins Peak Trail (5 miles) is a difficult loop trail starting at the end of 22nd Street in Durango. It takes you through pine forests and includes a ten-foot cliff that must be scaled to afford scenic views of Durango and the La Plata Mountains to the west.

Needle Creek Trail (14 miles) is accessed via the narrow-gauge railroad that will drop off passengers in Needleton for rugged hiking in the Weminuche Wilderness. Hikers then flag the train down for the return trip to Durango or Silverton. The trail leads to Chicago Basin, Mount Eolus (14,084 feet), Sunlight Peak (14,059 feet) and Windom Peak (14,084 feet).

Elk Creek Trail (8 miles), also accessed via the train at Elk Park, leads hikers to the Continental Divide above Elk Creek Valley.

Cascade Creek Trail (4 miles) begins 26 miles north of Durango on the east side of Route 550. It leads to the Animas River. Seven miles farther on the **Animas River Trail** you will end up in Needleton and the Weminuche.

CORTEZ–DOLORES AREA The big attraction to hikers in this part of Colorado is the numerous Anasazi Indian sites in the slickrock and canyon country. Hikes along mesa tops afford 100-mile views on clear days.

Navajo Lake Trail (5 miles) begins at Burro Bridge campground off West Fork Road, 12.5 miles east of Dolores and then 24 miles up Forest Road 535. The trail leads to Navajo Lake, at 11,154 feet, which sits at the foot of 14,000-foot El Diente Peak.

Hovenweep Trails are accessed via short marked trails within the national monument leading to the Cajon Ruins in Utah, or in Colorado, to Holly Ruins, Hackberry Canyon Ruins, Cutthroat Castle Ruins and Goodman Point Ruins. The trails wind through arid mesa country, mostly treeless scrublands that see few visitors. Since there are no roads for vehicles, hiking is the only way to see these sites.

Ute Mountain Tribal Park contains numerous hiking trails leading to excavated and unexcavated Pueblo sites along a 25-mile stretch of the Mancos River. You must have an Indian guide with you at all times. The most popular hiking trail covers 13 miles from the park entrance following the river and affording views of wildlife as well as sites of archaeological interest.

MESA VERDE AREA Hikes in this region of Indian country pass through piñon and juniper forests, canyons, mesas and archaeological sites, including cliff dwellings. Hiking within the national

---

✔ CHECK THESE OUT—UNIQUE OUTDOOR ADVENTURES

- Cast your fly and pretend you're on the set of *A River Runs Through It* as you fly fish on the **Dolores River**. *page 569*
- Cross-country ski among the **Mesa Verde Ruins** in winter, the most haunting (and least crowded) time to visit the park. *page 571*
- Pack your llama for a day hike in terrain that ranges from high desert to forested alpine trails in the **Silverton–Durango** area. *page 573*
- Roll through mesa country on the **Horseshoe Ruins Trail**, an easy ten-mile bike loop in the Cortez–Dolores area. *page 574*

park is limited to five well-marked trails, and hikers must register at the ranger's office. It is very hot in the summer. Bring water.

Petroglyph Point Trail (3 miles) begins on the Spruce Tree House Trail adjacent to the park office and museum. It travels along the mesa top leading to ancient rock art at Petroglyph Point.

Spruce Canyon Trail (2 miles) also begins on the Spruce Tree House Trail and leads into forested Spruce Tree Canyon at the base of the mesa.

▼▼▼▼▼▼▼▼▼▼▼
Transportation

CAR

Southwestern Colorado is a large, sparsely populated area with few major roads along the vast stretches of desert and forest lands and dispersed communities. The main north-south highway connecting Durango and Silverton is **Route 550.** From Durango to Cortez the main road is **Route 160,** which is also the access road to Mesa Verde National Park. It veers south in Cortez and shares a designation with **Route 666** for 20 miles. At that point Route 160 heads west to the Four Corners Monument and Arizona, while Route 666 continues south into New Mexico.

Cortez and Dolores are connected by **Route 145.** Dolores and Mancos are connected by **Route 184,** which meets Route 160 in Mancos.

To reach Hovenweep National Monument the main access is south of Cortez on Route 160 to **McElmo Canyon Road,** only partially paved, or north of Cortez, via Route 666 to the **Colorado turnoff** at Pleasant View, which also passes Lowry Ruins.

AIR

The main airport with scheduled service for the entire region is the **Durango–La Plata County Airport.** Much smaller, and with far fewer flights daily, is the **Cortez–Montezuma County Airport.** For ski buffs, there's **Telluride Regional Airport.**

Durango is served by America West Airlines and United Express. Cortez and Telluride are served by United Express.

BUS

Greyhound Bus Lines (800-231-2222) and **TNM&O Coaches** offer scheduled service through Durango and Silverton. ~ Durango: 275 East 8th Avenue; 970-259-2755. Silverton: Silverton Drive-In, 12th and Greene streets; 970-387-5658.

CAR RENTALS

In Durango, contact **Avis Rent A Car** (800-331-1212), **Budget Rent A Car** (800-527-0700), **Dollar Rent A Car** (800-800-4000), **Hertz Rent A Car** (800-654-3131) or **National Interrent** (800-227-7368).

PUBLIC TRANSIT

The only scheduled public transportation in southwestern Colorado is the **Durango Lift** which operates within the city limits year-round and offers winter service between Durango and Purgatory-Durango Ski Area. ~ 970-259-5438.

Service in Durango is offered by **Durango Transportation**. ~ 970-259-4818, 800-626-2066.   **TAXIS**

A true bird's-eye view of Durango, the Animas Valley and the majestic San Juans from the plexiglass cockpit of a quiet glider is offered by **Val-Air Soaring**. ~ 27290 Route 550 North; 970-247-9037. For airplane charters or scenic flights contact **Gregg Flying Service**. ~ Animas Air Park, Durango; 970-247-4632.   **AERIAL TOURS**

Lodging Index

Dining Index

Index

Area chapters are **Arizona:** *Eastern Arizona, Grand Canyon, North central Arizona, Northeastern Arizona, South central Arizona, Southern Arizona and Western Arizona;* **Colorado:** *Southwestern Colorado;* **New Mexico:** *Albuquerque and central New Mexico, Northwestern New Mexico, Santa Fe area, Southern New Mexico and Taos and the Enchanted Circle area;* **Utah:** *Southeastern Utah and Southwestern Utah.*

Notes

Notes

Notes

Notes

Notes

Notes

Notes

Notes

HIDDEN GUIDES

Adventure travel or a relaxing vacation?—"Hidden" guidebooks are the only travel books in the business to provide detailed information on both. Aimed at environmentally aware travelers, our motto is "Adventure Travel Plus." These books combine details on unique hotels, restaurants and sightseeing with information on camping, sports and hiking for the outdoor enthusiast.

THE NEW KEY GUIDES

Based on the concept of ecotourism, The New Key Guides are dedicated to the preservation of Central America's rare and endangered species, architecture and archaeology. Filled with helpful tips, they give travelers everything they need to know about these exotic destinations.

ULTIMATE FAMILY GUIDES

These innovative guides present the best and most unique features of a family destination. Quality is the keynote. In addition to thoroughly covering each destination, they feature short articles and one-line "teasers" that are both fun and informative.

Order Form

Ulysses Press books are available at bookstores everywhere. If any of the following titles are unavailable at your local bookstore, ask the bookseller to order them. Or you can order them directly from Ulysses Press (P.O. Box 3440, Berkeley, CA 94703; 510-601-8301, 800-377-2542).

HIDDEN GUIDEBOOKS

____ Hidden Boston and Cape Cod, $9.95
____ Hidden Carolinas, $15.95
____ Hidden Coast of California, $15.95
____ Hidden Colorado, $12.95
____ Hidden Florida, $14.95
____ Hidden Florida Keys and
     Everglades, $9.95
____ Hidden Hawaii, $15.95
____ Hidden Idaho, $13.95
____ Hidden Maui, $12.95
____ Hidden Montana, $12.95

____ Hidden New England, $16.95
____ Hidden Oregon, $12.95
____ Hidden Pacific Northwest, $16.95
____ Hidden Rockies, $16.95
____ Hidden San Francisco and
     Northern California, $15.95
____ Hidden Southern California,
     $15.95
____ Hidden Southwest, $16.95
____ Hidden Tahiti $15.95
____ Hidden Wyoming $12.95

THE NEW KEY GUIDEBOOKS

____ The New Key to Belize, $14.95
____ The New Key to Cancún and
     the Yucatán, $13.95
____ The New Key to Costa Rica, $15.95

____ The New Key to Ecuador and
     the Galápagos, $15.95
____ The New Key to Guatemala, $14.95

ULTIMATE FAMILY GUIDEBOOKS

____ Disneyland and Beyond, $11.95

____ Disney World and Beyond, $12.95

Mark the book(s) you're ordering and enter the total cost here ➡

California residents add 8% sales tax here ➡

Shipping, check box for your preferred method and enter cost here ➡

❑ BOOK RATE   FREE! FREE! FREE!
❑ PRIORITY MAIL $3.00 First book, $1.00/each additional book
❑ UPS 2-DAY AIR $7.00 First book, $1.00/each additional book

Billing, enter total amount due here and check method of payment ➡

❑ CHECK   ❑ MONEY ORDER
❑ VISA/MASTERCARD_____EXP. DATE _____

NAME _____PHONE _____

ADDRESS_____

_____

CITY_____ STATE _____ ZIP_____

MONEY-BACK GUARANTEE ON DIRECT ORDERS PLACED THROUGH ULYSSES PRESS.

ABOUT THE AUTHORS & ILLUSTRATOR

RICHARD HARRIS, author of the introductory, Northwestern Arizona, Central New Mexico and Southern New Mexico chapters, has written or co-written eight other guidebooks including *Hidden Rockies* and *Hidden Colorado*. He has also served as contributing editor on guides for John Muir Publications, Fodor's, Birnbaum and Access guides. He is president of PEN New Mexico.

LAURA DAILY is an award-winning freelance journalist living in Snowmass Village, Colorado. A member of the Society of American Travel Writers, she regularly contributes travel features to national magazines, including *National Geographic World* and *Active Time*. Together with Madeleine Osberger she co-authored the Utah and Northern New Mexico chapters.

MADELEINE OSBERGER has written for a variety of newspapers and magazines, including the *Denver Post, Aspen Times*, the *Chicago Tribune, Newsweek* and *Snow Country*. She is also the Aspen correspondent for the Associated Press and a columnist for the *Snowmass Sun*.

CAROLYN SCARBOROUGH, who penned the Southern Arizona chapter, is an award-winning freelance writer living in Phoenix. A former travel editor of *Southern Living* magazine, her writing credits include more than 300 published articles in magazines and newspapers across the country.

MARY ANN REESE, author of the Northeastern Arizona chapter, was associate travel editor at *Sunset* magazine for 17 years, covering Arizona and New Mexico. She also wrote wilderness and urban stories about the West and foreign countries. Earlier, she was London Bureau Chief for the *Stars and Stripes* newspaper. She is currently putting travel material online.

RON BUTLER, author of the Central Arizona chapter, is based in Tucson, Arizona. He has held editorial staff positions at *True* and *Penthouse* magazines. He is the author of *The Best of the Old West* (Texas Monthly Press) and *Fodor's Guide to New Mexico*. His work has appeared in *Travel & Leisure, Travel Holiday* and *Ladies Home Journal*.

STEVE COHEN lives in Hesperus, Colorado and writes extensively about the Southwest. Author of the Southwestern Colorado chapter, he has also written for the *Los Angeles Times, Travel Holiday, Denver Post* and *Miami Herald*. He is a member of the Society of American Travel Writers and has written several guidebooks including *The Adventure Guide to the High Southwest*.

GLENN KIM is a freelance illustrator residing in San Francisco. His work appears in many Ulysses Press titles, including *Ultimate Washington* and *The New Key to Belize*. He has also done illustrations for the National Forest Service and Sega Genesis, as well as a variety of magazines, book covers and greeting cards. He is now working with computer graphics and having lots of fun.